The SAGE

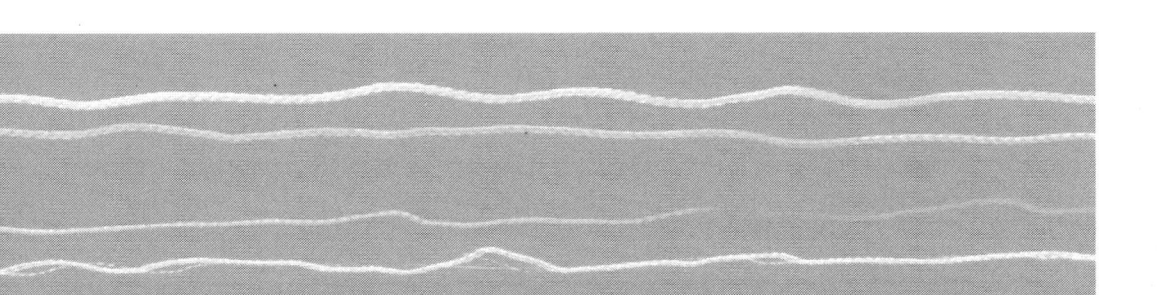

Power

The SAGE Handbook of
Power

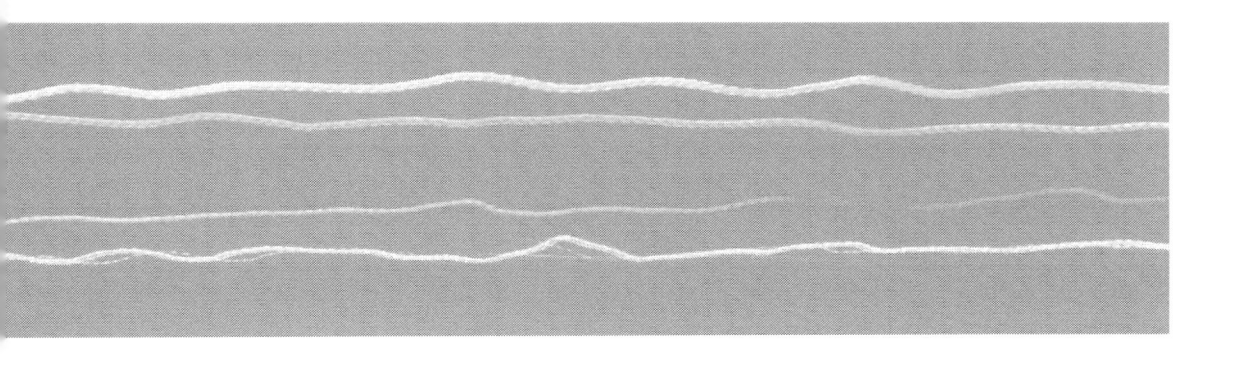

Edited by
Stewart R. Clegg
and Mark Haugaard

Introduction © Mark Haugaard and Stewart R. Clegg 2009
Chapter 1 © Gerhard Göhler 2009
Chapter 2 © Keith Dowding 2009
Chapter 3 © Peter Morriss 2009
Chapter 4 © Charles Tilly 2009
Chapter 5 © Rob Stones 2009
Chapter 6 © Jacob Torfing 2009
Chapter 7 © Rolland Munro 2009
Chapter 8 © Richard Jenkins 2009
Chapter 9 © John Allen 2009
Chapter 10 © Mitchell Dean 2009
Chapter 11 © Nigel Rapport 2009
Chapter 12 © Fredrik Engelstad 2009
Chapter 13 © Mark Haugaard 2009
Chapter 14 © Ray Gordon 2009
Chapter 15 © Siniša Malešević 2009
Chapter 16 © Amy Allen 2009
Chapter 17 © Stewart R. Clegg 2009
Chapter 18 © David Courpasson and Françoise Dany 2009
Chapter 19 © Kevin Ryan 2009
Chapter 20 © Bob Jessop 2009
Chapter 21 © Philip G. Cerny 2009
Chapter 22 © Stewart R. Clegg and Mark Haugaard

First published 2009

Apart from any fair dealing for the purposes of research or private study, or criticism or review, as permitted under the Copyright, Designs and Patents Act, 1988, this publication may be reproduced, stored or transmitted in any form, or by any means, only with the prior permission in writing of the publishers, or in the case of reprographic reproduction, in accordance with the terms of licences issued by the Copyright Licensing Agency. Enquiries concerning reproduction outside those terms should be sent to the publishers.

SAGE Publications Ltd
1 Oliver's Yard
55 City Road
London EC1Y 1SP

SAGE Publications Inc.
2455 Teller Road
Thousand Oaks, California 91320

SAGE Publications India Pvt Ltd
B 1/I 1 Mohan Cooperative Industrial Area
Mathura Road, Post Bag 7
New Delhi 110 044

SAGE Publications Asia-Pacific Pte Ltd
33 Pekin Street #02-01
Far East Square
Singapore 048763

Library of Congress Control Number: 2008926494

British Library Cataloguing in Publication data

A catalogue record for this book is available from the British Library

ISBN 978-1-4462-7045-5

Typeset by CEPHA Imaging Pvt. Ltd., Bangalore, India
Printed in Great Britain by The Cromwell Press, Trowbridge, Witshire
Printed on paper from sustainable resources

Contents

List of Contributors		vii
INTRODUCTION: Why Power is the Central Concept of the Social Sciences *Mark Haugaard and Stewart R. Clegg*		1
PART I	**FRAMING THE FIELD**	**25**
1	'Power to' and 'Power over' *Gerhard Göhler*	27
2	Rational Choice Approaches *Keith Dowding*	40
3	Power and Liberalism *Peter Morriss*	54
4	Power and Democracy *Charles Tilly*	70
5	Power and Structuration Theory *Rob Stones*	89
6	Power and Discourse: Towards an Anti-Foundationalist Concept of Power *Jacob Torfing*	108
7	Actor-Network Theory *Rolland Munro*	125
8	The Ways and Means of Power: Efficacy and Resources *Richard Jenkins*	140
9	Powerful Geographies: Spatial Shifts in the Architecture of Globalization *John Allen*	157

PART II   POWER AND RELATED ANALYTIC CONCEPTS   175

10 Three Conceptions of the Relationship between Power and Liberty   177
    Mitchell Dean

11 Power and Identity   194
    Nigel Rapport

12 Culture and Power   210
    Fredrik Engelstad

13 Power and Hegemony   239
    Mark Haugaard

14 Power and Legitimacy: From Weber to Contemporary Theory   256
    Ray Gordon

15 Collective Violence and Power   274
    Siniša Malešević

PART III   POWER AND SUBSTANTIVE ISSUES   291

16 Gender and Power   293
    Amy Allen

17 Managing Power in Organizations: The Hidden History of Its Constitution   310
    Stewart R. Clegg

18 Cultures of Resistance in the Workplace   332
    David Courpasson and Françoise Dany

19 Power and Exclusion   348
    Kevin Ryan

20 The State and Power   367
    Bob Jessop

21 Reconfiguring Power in a Globalizing World   383
    Philip G. Cerny

22 Discourse of Power   400
    Stewart R. Clegg and Mark Haugaard

Index   466

List of Contributors

Amy Allen is an Associate Professor of Philosophy and Women's and Gender Studies at Dartmouth College. Her research focuses on the concepts of power, subjectivity, agency and autonomy in the work of Arendt, Foucault, Butler and Habermas. Her articles on these topics have appeared in journals such as *Constellations*, *Philosophy and Social Criticism*, *Hypatia*, *Philosophical Forum* and *Continental Philosophy Review*. She is the author of two books: *The Power of Feminist Theory: Domination, Resistance, Solidarity* (Westview Press, 1999), and *The Politics of Our Selves: Power, Autonomy, and Gender in Contemporary Critical Theory* (Columbia University Press, 2008).

John Allen is a Professor of Economic Geography in the Faculty of Social Sciences at The Open University. His research interests include power and spatiality, with particular reference to topology and scale and issues of urban and social theory. Recently he has engaged with issues of pragmatism and geography, together with the privatization of authority and the geography of state power. He has authored or edited over twelve books, the most recent of which is *Lost Geographies of Power* (Blackwell Publishing, 2003), which forms part of the Royal Geographical Society/Institute of British Geographers Book Series.

Philip G. Cerny is a Professor of Global Political Economy at Rutgers University–Newark (New Jersey, USA). He is the author of *The Politics of Grandeur: Ideological Aspects of de Gaulle's Foreign Policy* (Cambridge University Press, 1980; French edition, Flammarion, 1986) and *The Changing Architecture of Politics: Structure, Agency and the Future of the State* (Sage, 1990). He is co-editor of *Power in Contemporary Politics: Theories, Practices, Globalizations* (with Henri Goverde, Mark Haugaard and Howard H. Lentner, Sage, 2000) and *Internalizing Globalization: The Rise of Neoliberalism and the Erosion of National Varieties of Capitalism* (with Susanne Soederberg and Georg Menz, Palgrave, 2005). In addition to the articles and chapters cited in this book, he is recently the author of 'The Governmentalization of World Politics', in Kofman and Youngs (eds), *Globalization: Theory and Practice* (London: Continuum, 3rd edition, 2008), 'Restructuring the State in a Globalizing World: Capital Accumulation, Tangled Hierarchies and the Search for a New Spatio-temporal Fix', *Review of International Political Economy* (October, 2006), and 'Terrorism and the New Security Dilemma', *US Naval War College Review* (Winter, 2005).

Stewart R. Clegg is a Professor at the University of Technology, Sydney and Research Director of the Centre for Management and Organization Studies; a Visiting Professor of Organizational Change Management, Maastricht University, Faculty of Business; a Visiting

Professor to the EM-Lyon Doctoral Program, and Visiting Professor and International Fellow in Discourse and Management Theory, Centre of Comparative Social Studies, Vrije Universiteit, Amsterdam, and also at Copenhagen Business School. He is a prolific publisher in leading academic journals in management and organization theory who has published a large number of papers and chapters and is the author and editor of over forty monographs, textbooks, encyclopedia and handbooks. He is a Fellow of the Academy of the Social Sciences in Australia and a Distinguished Fellow of the Australian and New Zealand Academy of Management. He is also an International Fellow of the Advanced Institute of Management Research. To his surprise he has been researched as one of the top 200 business gurus in the world (*What's the Big Idea? Creating and Capitalizing on the Best New Management Thinking* by Thomas H. Davenport, Lawrence Prusak and H. James Wilson, 2003).

David Courpasson is a Professor of Sociology at EM Lyon Business School, France and researcher at OCE-EM Lyon Research Center. He is also Research Dean and PhD Director at EM Lyon, and Visiting Professor at Lancaster University, UK. His research interests include new forms of power and resistance in organizations, the dynamics of bureaucratic regimes of power and of structures of domination. He has published extensively on these topics in recognized journals like *Journal of Management Studies*, *Organization Studies* and *Organization*. He co-authored the *Power and Organizations* (Sage, 2006) with S. Clegg and N. Phillips, and authored the book *Soft Constraint*, which was published in 2006 by Liber/Copenhagen Business School Press. He is the forthcoming editor-in-chief of *Organization Studies*.

Françoise Dany is a Professor of HRM at EM Lyon Business School, France. She is the Head of the research center OCE (Organisations, Careers New Elites). Her research interests include HRM, and the evolution of the employment relationship. She has done a lot of comparative research as well as critical research in order to put forward new insights regarding changes within modern organizations. She has published in academic journals such as *Organization Studies* and the *International Journal of Human Resource Management*. She is also author of several books in French.

Mitchell Dean is a Professor of Sociology at Macquarie University, Sydney, and Dean of the Division of Society, Culture, Media and Philosophy, and is a founding member of the Centre for Research on Social Inclusion. His publications include *Governmentality: Power and Rule in Modern Society* (Sage, 2nd edition, 2009) and *Governing Societies* (Open University Press, 2007). His interests include the analysis of different forms and contexts of power including sovereignty, biopolitics and liberalism, and various aspects of domestic and international rule.

Keith Dowding is the Head of Political Science Program in the Research School of Social Sciences at the Australian National University in Canberra and was formerly a Professor of Political Science at the London School of Economics. He has published two books and many articles on political power and is editing a two volume *Encyclopedia of Power* for Sage. He has also published widely in political science, public administration, urban studies, social and rational choice theory and political philosophy in journals such as *American*

Political Science Review, American Journal of Political Science, British Journal of Political Science, European Journal of Political Research, Public Choice, Public Administration, Rationality and Society and *Urban Studies Quarterly*. He has been co-editor of the *Journal of Theoretical Politics* since 1996.

Fredrik Engelstad is affiliated to the Department of Sociology and Human Geography at the University of Oslo. He also holds a part-time position at the Institute for Social Research, where he was director for two decades. In addition to general sociological theory his research interests include power as reflected in social elite structures, in industrial relations, in culture, and in images of power in fiction literature. Trained as a sociologist of working life, his research is based on survey methods as well as intensive interviews and historical approaches. He was member of the core group of the Norwegian Power and Democracy Study 1998-2003, where he co-authored several books, on working life, business, and social elites. He is series editor of the yearbook series *Comparative Social Research*, and for many years member of the board of European Consortium for Sociological Research.

Gerhard Göhler is a Professor Emeritus and taught political theory and the history of political ideas at the Free University Berlin until 2006. He is currently coordinating a research project on power and soft control at the Berlin research centre 'Governance in Areas of Limited Statehood'. His research interests include the theory of political institutions, theories of power and control, the history of political ideas in modernity and the history and theory of political science. He is co-editor of the collected works of Ernst Fraenkel, one of the founding fathers of German political science after 1945 (6 volumes, 1999–2008). He wrote on the early Hegel, Marx's dialectic, liberalism and conservatism in the 19th century, and institutional theory (*Institution Power Representation. What Institutions Stand For and How They Work*, 1997).

Ray Gordon is the Head of the School of Business and the Associate Dean of Research for the Faculty of Business, Technology and Sustainable Development at Bond University. His research interests include power in organizations, leadership, ethics and social control systems. He is an ethnographer and employs discourse analysis, narrative and story-telling methods. He has published extensively in internationally recognized academic journals such as the *Leadership Quarterly, Organization Studies*, the *Journal of Public Administration* and the *Organization Management Journal*. He authored the book entitled *Power, Knowledge and Domination*, which was published in 2007 by Liber/Copenhagen Business School Press as part of its *Advances in Organizations Studies* series.

Mark Haugaard is Senior Lecturer in social theory in the Department of Political Science and Sociology, National University of Ireland, Galway, and was Jean Monnet Fellow at the European University Institute, Florence. He is founding Editor of the *Journal of Power* (Routledge). He has published over thirty articles and books on power and related subjects, including the following: Siniša Malešević (co-eds.) *Ernest Gellner and Contemporary Social Thought* (Cambridge University Press, 2007); Haugaard and Howard Lentner (co-eds.) *Hegemony and Power* (Lexington Books, 2006); Haugaard 'Reflections on Seven Forms of Power' *European Journal of Social Theory*, (Sage, 2003); Haugaard and Siniša Malešević (co-eds.) *Making Sense of Collectivity: Ethnicity, Nationalism and Globalization*

(Pluto Press, 2002); Haugaard (ed.) *Power: A Reader* (Manchester University Press, 2002); Haugaard, Henri Goverde, Philip Cerny and Howard Lentner (co-eds.) *Power in the Contemporary Politics: Theories, Practices, Globalizations* (Sage, 2002); and Haugaard *The Constitution of Power* (Manchester University Press, 1997). Currently he is working on the relationship between power and legitimacy.

Richard Jenkins is a Professor of Sociology at the University of Sheffield, England. Trained as an anthropologist, his research and theoretical interests focus on identity and processes of identification, the nature of human collectivity and modern (re)enchantments; substantively, his long-standing research fields are Ireland and Denmark. Among his recent books are *Foundations of Sociology* (2002), *Pierre Bourdieu* (2nd edition, 2002), *Flag, Nation and Symbolism in Europe and America*, (edited, with Thomas Hylland Eriksen, 2007), *Rethinking Ethnicity* (2nd edition, 2008) and *Social Identity* (3rd edition, 2008).

Bob Jessop is a Distinguished Professor of Sociology and was the Founding Director of the Institute for Advanced Study at Lancaster University. He has previously taught in the Universities of Cambridge, Chicago, Essex and Frankfurt am Main and been a visiting researcher in Bielefeld, the European University Institute and Roskilde. He describes his work as pre-disciplinary in inspiration, trans-disciplinary in practice and post-disciplinary in aspiration. His main fields of research comprise state theory, critical political economy, post-war political economy, welfare state restructuring, governance and governance failure, critical geography, critical realism and the philosophy of social science. His most important publications include *The Capitalist State* (1982), *Nicos Poulantzas* (1985), *Thatcherism: A Tale of Two Nations* (1988), *State Theory: Putting the Capitalist State in Its Place* (1990), *The Future of the Capitalist State* (2002), *Beyond the Regulation Approach: Putting Capitalist Economies in Their Place* (2006, co-authored with Ngai-Ling Sum) and *State Power: A Strategic-Relational Approach* (2007). He also published some 90 journal articles and 140 book chapters on these and related topics. He is currently researching the contradictions of the knowledge-based economy and writing, with Ngai-Ling Sum, a major contribution to the emerging field of cultural political economy.

Siniša Malešević is a political sociologist who lectures at the School of Political Science and Sociology, National University of Ireland, Galway. Previously he was a Research Fellow in the Institute for International Relations (Zagreb) and the Centre for the Study of Nationalism (Prague). He also held visiting research fellowships in the Institute for Human Sciences (Vienna) and the London School of Economics. He has published extensively on ethnicity and nationalism, theories of ideology, war and violence and sociological theory in journals such as *Ethnic and Racial Studies, Nations and Nationalism, Government and Opposition, Nationalism and Ethnic Politics, International Political Sociology, Journal of Language and Politics, East European Quarterly, Journal of Power, Development in Practice* and *Europa Ethnica*. His recent books include *Identity as Ideology: Understanding Ethnicity and Nationalism,* (Palgrave/Macmillan, 2006), *The Sociology of Ethnicity* (Sage, 2004), *Ideology, Legitimacy and the New State* (Frank Cass, 2002), and co-edited volume *Ernest Gellner and Contemporary Social Thought* (Cambridge University Press, 2007). He is currently completing a book *The Sociology of War and Violence* for the Cambridge University Press.

Peter Morriss teaches in the Department of Political Science and Sociology at the National University of Ireland, Galway. He is the author of *Power: A Philosophical Analysis* (Second edition; Manchester University Press, 2002; originally 1987). He has written a number of articles on the concept of power and mathematical power indices. He has also written articles in academic journals applying normative political philosophy to various issues (such as marriage), and has written empirical articles on the politics of South Korea.

Rolland Munro is a Managing Editor of *The Sociological Review* and Professor of Organisation Theory at Keele University. He has published widely on culture, power and identity and is internationally regarded for bringing new theoretical insight to the study of organization with his ethnographies of management practice. Writings on accountability, affect, bodies, cars, class, ethics, knowledge, landscape, language, money, polyphony, reason, time, wit and zero, among other topics, have kept him at the cutting edge of interdisciplinary collaborations and have culminated in two forthcoming books, *The Demanding Relation,* which explores our entanglement with technology and *Dividing Cultures,* which illuminates the everyday divisions through which culture works us.

Nigel Rapport, holds the Chair of Anthropological and Philosophical Studies at the University of St. Andrews, Scotland, and directs the Centre for Cosmopolitan Studies. He has also held the Canada Research Chair in Globalization, Citizenship and Justice at Concordia University of Montreal. He has undertaken four pieces of participant-observation fieldwork: among farmers and tourists in a rural English village (1980–1); among the transient population of a Newfoundland city and suburb (1984–5); among new immigrants in an Israeli development town (1988–9); and among healthcare professionals and patients in a Scottish hospital (2000–1). His research interests include social theory, phenomenology, identity and individuality, conversation analysis and links between anthropology and literature and philosophy. His books include *Transcendent Individual: Towards a Literal and Liberal Anthropology* (Routledge, 1997), *The Trouble with Community: Anthropological Reflections on Movement, Identity and Collectivity* (with Vered Amit, Pluto, 2002), *'I Am Dynamite': An Alternative Anthropology of Power* (Routledge, 2003) and, as editor, *British Subjects: An Anthropology of Britain* (Berg, 2002).

Kevin Ryan is a lecturer in the School of Political Science and Sociology at the National University of Ireland Galway, and is author of *Social exclusion and the politics of order*, (Manchester University Press, 2007). Other recent publications include 'Truth, reason and the spectre of contigency', in *Ernest Gellner and contemporary social thought* (edited by S. Maleševic and M. Haugaard, 2007, CUP), and 'Environmental conflict and democracy: between reason and hegemony', in *Environmental arguing as intercultural arguing* (edited by R. Edmondson and H. Rau, 2008, Peter Lang). He is currently researching the history of the playground and its connection to citizenship, with a focus on how the organization and supervision of children's play configures the relationship between discipline and freedom.

Rob Stones is a Professor in Sociology at the University of Essex, and was the Head of Department from 2004 to 2007. His research interests lie in the development of structuration theory; the bridge between social theory and empirical case studies; documentary and feature films' representations of modernity and post-modernity; and the deepening of links between moral and political philosophy and sociological theory. His books include *Sociological Reasoning* (1996), *Structuration Theory* (2005), the 2nd edition of the edited volume *Key Sociological Thinkers* (2008) and the edited volume (with Sandra Moog) *Nature, Social Relations and Human Needs: Essays in Honour of Ted Benton* (2008). Recent articles include 'Theories of Social Action', in Bryan Turner (ed.), *The Blackwell Companion to Social Theory* (3rd edition, 2008); (with Sung Kyung Kim) 'Film, Postmodernism and the Sociological Imagination' in Jason Powell and Tim Owen (eds.), *Reconstructing Postmodernism* (2007); and 'Rights, Social Theory and Political Philosophy: A Framework for Case Study Research', in Lydia Morris (ed.), *Rights: Sociological Perspectives* (2006). He is the editor of two book series for Palgrave Macmillan, *Traditions in Social Theory*, and the forthcoming *Themes in Social Theory*.

Charles Tilly[†] is Joseph L. Buttenwieser Professor of Social Science at Columbia University. He studies political and interpersonal processes in comparative-historical perspective. His most recent books are *Why?* (2006), *The Oxford Handbook of Contextual Political Analysis* (co-edited with Robert Goodin, 2006), *Contentious Politics* (with Sidney Tarrow, 2006), *Regimes and Repertoires* (2006), *Democracy* (2007), *Explaining Social Processes* (2008) *Credit and Blame* (2008) and *Contentious Performances* (2008).

Jacob Torfing is a Professor in Politics and Institutions at Roskilde University, Denmark. He is a political scientist and his research interests include discourse theory, employment policy, democratic participation and governance networks. He has published widely on discourse theory and democratic network governance. His books include *Theories of Democratic Network Governance* (2007) – co-edited with Eva Sørensen, *Discourse Theory in European Politics* (2005) – co-edited with David Howarth, *New Theories of Discourse* (1999) and *Politics, Regulation and the Modern Welfare State* (1995). He is director of Centre for Democratic Network Governance and a former member of the Danish Social Science Research Council.

[†] Deceased

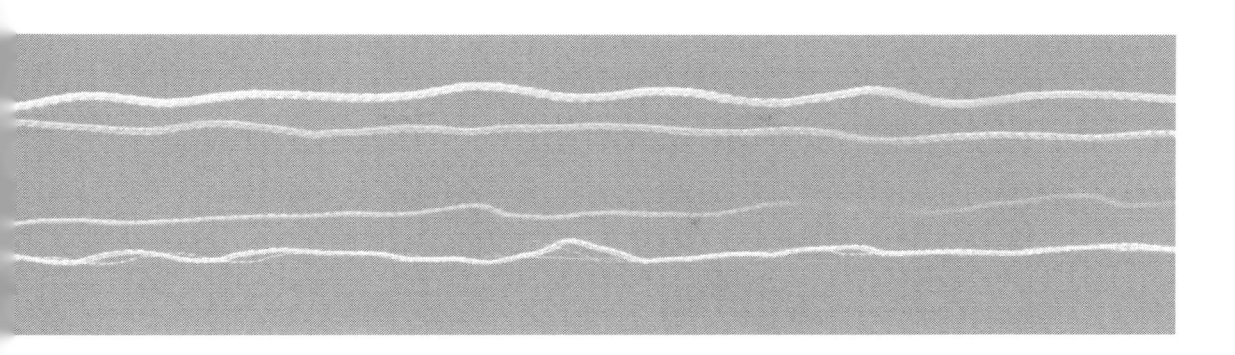

Introduction: Why Power is the Central Concept of the Social Sciences

Mark Haugaard and Stewart R. Clegg

The concept of power is absolutely central to any understanding of society. The ubiquity of the concept can be seen by a comparative Google search. The score for 'social power' is 376 million hits, for 'political power' 194 million which compares with 334 million for 'society', 253 million for 'politics', 52 million for 'sociology', 'social class' at 280 million and 'political class' at 111 million. Of course, such measures are crude but the fact that the combined 470 million social and political power hits outstrip any of the other categories, including the combined hits for 'social' and 'political class', indicates the absolute centrality of the concept. However, despite this ubiquity it is arguably one of the most difficult concepts to make sense of within the social sciences. Nonetheless, it has been a core concept for as long as there has been speculation about the nature of social order (Wolin 1960).

The Ancient Athenians distinguished between legitimate and illegitimate power in terms of a contrast between power that accorded to the dictates of law (*nomos*) and power which exalted the glorification of a specific individual (*hubris*). In the work of Aristotle, arguably the world's first empirical political scientist, this became refined in terms of a sixfold classification of governments according to whose interests are served. Monarchy is the government of the many in the interests of all, Aristocracy by the few in the interests of all, constitutional government is by the majority in the interests of all, while the corrupt illegitimate versions of this are Tyranny, Oligarchy and Democracy, in which the one, the few or the majority each govern in their own interests, disregarding the interests of the whole.

In Machiavelli's *The Prince* (1981) we find images of power as domination and control, which work in subtle ways; the successful Prince manages society through the manipulation of flows and movements of power. The distinction between legitimate and illegitimate power becomes subsumed under the dominant discourse of practical success and failure. Power is exercised *over* others and society constituted through the domination of the weak by the strong. If Niccolò Machiavelli offers one influential modern template for thinking about power, Thomas Hobbes offers another.

In Hobbes (1968), power flows from society to the individual. The political actor creates society as an architectonic product, which gives individuals a capacity for action. The ultimate backing for power is violence and coercion over which the Sovereign holds a monopoly. As represented in the frontispiece of the *Leviathan*, society is the sum of individuals who carry and constitute power. If Hobbes' discourse was closely tied to the legitimacy of sovereign power as a presupposition of a commonwealth, by the late nineteenth century the terms of power's address were changing radically.

For Nietzsche (1968), power is a capacity to define reality. If you can define the real and the moral, you create the conditions of legitimacy. The terms of trade of legitimacy have changed markedly: what is at issue now, of course, is not normative legitimacy, as in Aristotle, but legitimacy as a sociological fact of domination and, as it had been in Machiavelli, the fate of mankind. What sometimes may appear as an escape from power and domination is really the replacement of cruder forms of domination by more sophisticated and thus less visible forms. In Weber (1978), the English term 'power' covers both *Herrschaft* and *Macht*, which correspond to authority and coercion respectively; thus, power can either be legitimate or based upon the threat of violence.

The intricacies of legitimate versus illegitimate power; of coercion versus authority; of collective systemic versus individual agent specific power; of constitutive power versus power from which there is escape, and of power as autonomy versus constraint, are all aspects of power's many faces which have shaped contemporary perceptions of power in the social sciences. Tangled up with these central perceptions of power's empirical character are a great many normative issues, often encoded in different forms of address of the same topic. For instance, political philosophy or political theory were both more inclined to engage with power in normative terms, with what should be done, while political science and political sociology were more inclined to engage with power in empirical terms, looking at what is done rather than what should be done. Yet, for all this institutional separation, there has been a tendency for normative issues to intrude, except for the most self-consciously ascetically empiricist of practitioners. This is especially the case in more recent debates in which the threads of genealogy, that we have briefly sketched, have tended to wend their way into empirical analysis.

After World War II, the consensual view of power, as a capacity for action, as 'power to', came to the fore through the work of Hannah Arendt (1970), Talcott Parsons (1964) and Barry Barnes (1988). For these thinkers, power constitutes the opposite of coercion and violence, and is thus a prerequisite for agency. The Hobbesian view of power, as domination exercised by individuals, is reformulated by many including by Robert Dahl (1957, 1961, 2006), Peter Bachrach and Morton Baratz (1962, 1963, 1970) and Steven Lukes (1974, 1977, 1986, 2005). Foucault (1977) emerges as the prime rejuvenator of the Machiavellian and Nietzschean view of power as a systemic phenomenon which is constitutive of social reality. Following this, Stewart R. Clegg (1989), Ernesto Laclau and Chantal Mouffe (1985), and Mitchell Dean (1999) constitute contemporary refiners of these positions. The attempt to distinguish legitimate from illegitimate power has been central for many political theorists both in continental theory, such as Habermas (1984) and in the analytic traditions associated with British theorists such as Peter Morriss (1987, 2002) and Brian Barry (1989). The link between power and interests as a criterion distinguishing legitimate from illegitimate power, as in Aristotle, remains central for Lukes' analysis (1974, 2005). In addition, there are a number of attempts at synthesis such as rational choice theory, where Keith Dowding (1996) has merged the idea of power as agency-based and systemic phenomenon, as have Giddens (1984) and Haugaard (1997, 2002) in their respective accounts.

While the plethora of accounts of power is complex the complexity is one of requisite variety. What emerges is that 'power' is not a single entity. It represents a cluster of concepts. Power as domination, which is linked to (the capacity for) violent agency, is the dominant perception of power in everyday speech and, quite likely, would represent the majority of the combined 470 million Google hits for 'social' and 'political power', if we were to examine them. However, if we look to the academic social science literature, increasingly the conception of power as essentially grounded in coercion represents a minority view. One of the characteristics of the development of the literature over the last thirty years has been a move away from this 'common sense' view to more systemic, less agent specific, perceptions of power that see it as more generally constitutive of reality. Such a move is coupled with a more inclusive perception of the concept, whereby the idea that there is a single thing-in-the-world corresponding to power, as some kind of essence, has fallen out of favour.

The fact that few claim that *their* view of power constitutes 'The Concept of Power' is a healthy development, which heralds the abandonment of the search for the holy grail of the essence of power. At the height of the seventies power debate, when a singular perception of power was *de rigueur*, Lukes (1974) shifted the debate by arguing that power is an 'essentially contested' concept. Essential contestation refers to matters that cannot be settled empirically. In Lukes, for instance, liberal, reformist and radical accounts of power are differentiated. Each differs precisely in what their value-commitments will admit as evidence and data, as a result of definitional inclusion and exclusion. Concepts become essentially contested because normative evaluations are smuggled into what appear to be empirical statements. For instance, if we term a set of political institutions as 'legitimate', the latter is 'an essentially contested' concept because this is not simply an empirical statement. It is an implicitly normatively evaluative statement, endorsing certain political arrangements. Thus, while the concept of legitimacy is doing ostensibly empirical work – identifying institutions acceded to be legitimate – it is simultaneously endorsing evaluative presuppositions. With regard to power, this works in reverse, whereby power constitutes 'domination', which we normatively condemn. Thus, from this perspective, whether or not any interaction is deemed as entailing power implies a tacit negative normative evaluation. However, as our brief account of power's genealogy implies, not all evaluations of power are implicitly normatively negative in this way. Thus, while the idea of power as 'an essentially contested' concept captures some aspects of the power debate, it does not describe them all.

While to speak of power as essentially contested captures a part of the debate, where different theorists seem to be wilfully not grasping the points that other theorists make, because of their more or less implicit normative assumptions, perhaps a more accurate model would come from the application of Wittgenstein's description of 'family resemblance' concepts (Wittgenstein 1967). Family resemblance concepts do *not* share a single essence. Rather, they embody a cluster of concepts with overlapping characteristics. Just as in an extended family, there may be similarities which make each member recognizable as a member, yet there is not a single set of characteristics which all the family have in common – John resembles his father through his complexion and his mother by his posture, while Mary resembles great Aunt Beth, etc. Wittgenstein used as an example of family resemblance concepts the word 'game'. If we examine cards, football and chess, it might appear that the essence of the word 'game' lies in winning and losing. However, if we observe a solitary child playing a game of ball, there is no winning or losing (Wittgenstein 1967: 32). Solitaire is a game but there are no competitors. Thus, applying these views, when we examine power in the writings of Lukes and Dahl, it may appear that domination defines the essence of power, while if we read Arendt and Parsons, it would appear to be legitimacy, and so on.

For Wittgenstein, concepts premised on family resemblances are not considered particularly problematic with regard to usage; they are not so much muddled concepts as much as they simply defy singular essentialist definitions. As a family resemblance concept, 'power' covers a cluster of social phenomena central to the constitution of social order. As with most family resemblance concepts meaning is defined by localized language games, which are a set of relations between different concepts. These family relations will be exhibited in the practice of both lay and professional theorists. In lay terms, in certain empirical settings, certain actors will think of and do power in ways that are more or less coherent. What is considered as coherent, will of course, already be an effect of the domination of certain empirically modulated ways of doing things. Think of the US policy of *extraordinary rendition*, which allows the exercise of certain powers of violence and torture on the body of 'suspects' that would not be normatively appropriate in other countries. The policy trades off the different ways of thinking about and doing power in countries such as Poland and Egypt from the US. Theoretically, the same differentiation in practices also occurs. Some language games that have developed around power as a theoretical practice will cohere around certain dominant ordering conceptions. For instance, if a given theorist, such as Arendt (1958, 1970), is primarily interested in clusters of concepts, such as 'authority', 'legitimacy' and 'citizenship', which she defines in opposition to 'totalitarianism' and 'violence', then her concept of 'power' is defined relative to these other concepts. Just as within large-scale languages, such as English and Spanish, words are defined relative to each other through difference and similarity. Just as there can never be exact translation between languages, so too, a local language game creates differences of usage which are not exact equivalents of each other. Thus, the concept of 'power' in the anthropological/sociological literature on the different types of capital outlined by Jenkins in Chapter 8 is different from Cerny's international relations usage in Chapter 21 or Dean's genealogical account in Chapter 10. Some usages will be closer than others, for instance Dean and Clegg, are relatively close, while both are far from that used by Dowding in his rational choice language game.

No one of these usages is right or wrong. These concepts are conceptual tools, each of which enables the author in question to make sense of certain aspects of social life, presumably those aspects that most interest them and which they think most important, most powerful. If their usage brings clarity to the perspective the 'conceptual tool' is being used well; if the contrary, then their usage is poorly developed. Of course, it can be argued that when local usage is so singular as to make a specific usage appear 'forced', relative to everyday usage, this is less than desirable. That point accepted it is still better to think of power as plural, as shaped by local context, as a tool which enables us to make sense of the social world rather than embodying a singular essence; and it is always a translational tool – not only between different academic language games but between these and the world of mundane practices. Different concepts will articulate different practices; some will reveal more of some practices; others more or less of these and, perhaps, other practices.

The articles in this Handbook represent paradigmatic perceptions of power within theoretically conceived 'local language games'. The articles are not intended as summaries of particular debates, rather they provide exemplars of 'cutting edge', 'state of the art' work, drawing on various social science perspectives. Power is not the property of any one social science discipline. Political Science, Sociology, Anthropology, Political Theory, Organization Studies, Geography and different perspectives within and transcending each of these, such as Feminism, all make a contribution. All use the concept of power as a central and defining concept. Within each of these broad disciplinary divisions, there are local power debates, each of which encapsulates a vision of its own, defined by a perspective.

In commissioning for the Handbook, the editors have sought to provide exemplars of best practice within fields. In explaining the nature of paradigms, Thomas Kuhn argued that when one has understood an exemplar of a piece of work within a paradigm one should, within that paradigm, be able extrapolate from that work to problem-solving in general. If, as a competent member of a scientific community, one properly understands Newton's account of the gravitational forces acting upon falling objects, one should be able to apply this to pendulums without ever having been shown how to do so (Kuhn 1962). The social sciences do not have the predictive consistency of the natural sciences, nor, in terms of their being sciences of culture rather than of nature, should they necessarily ascribe to this as a holy grail. Nonetheless, it is still the case that specific well chosen exemplars of a debate or perspective within sub-disciplines, should give the less initiated reader, or the power specialist reading outside their paradigm, a way into the terrain of core power debates. Simultaneously, to the specialist, each of these contributions is intended as an original contribution which pushes a particular paradigm further.

FRAMING THE FIELD

In the first chapter Gerhard Göhler introduces the distinction between 'power to' and 'power over', a debate that has its roots in Aristotle's distinction between legitimate and illegitimate power. The point of departure for the chapter is the theorization of power as it appeared after Lukes' (1974) summary of the field. In that summary, power, it was argued, was a concept with an essence that was highly contested; liberal, reformist and radical approaches to the concept had been identified. The 1980s complicated the picture; the idea that there might be a single essence at the back of diverse conceptions became harder to hold. For Göhler, as for a number of other scholars, the distinctions of ordinary language are a possible way out of conceptual confusion. The salient difference between 'power over' and 'power to' is a distinction that Göhler finds inconsistent with ordinary language usage therefore he seeks to replace it with the concepts of 'transitive' and 'intransitive' power. Using this opposition he develops a fourfold typology of power that is used to explore a rapprochement between the theory of two of power's major contributors: Max Weber and Hannah Arendt.

In Chapter 2, Keith Dowding integrates agency and situational advantage as a systemic quality, within rational choice theory, thus using the concept of power to overcome the accusation that rational choice theory is a purely agent-centred perspective. He starts from the auspices of neo-classical economic theory where, as he notes, power has little or no purchase as a concept. Power has been implicitly analysed away by contrasting preferences held by an actor at different times without taking account of different contextual circumstances. Retaining the rationality of the active choosing agent, choices occur in what sociologists are wont to call differential 'situated actions'. Where there are multiple actors involved in these choice situations, Dowding suggests, rational choice methods allow us to analyse power in the relative bargaining strengths of different actors, represented by the sets of resources they command. A paradigmatically clear case for his argument is provided in the literature on voting, from which discussions the idea of constructing a power index has emerged. The discussion of voting is coupled with the distinction that Morriss (2002) makes between 'ability' and 'ableness' Ability makes actors more or less capable of doing something given the resources that they have at their disposal. Ableness refers to the position in which someone finds themselves; for instance, in the voting case, the preferences of all voters would need to be addressed. Developing this essentially agent-centred distinction, Dowding moves the analysis forward by examining the power structure of societies, which shape the types of power available to actors.

In Chapter 3, the analytic tradition in political theory that Dowding draws on is developed further by its prime representative, Peter Morriss, who demonstrates how an analytically clear understanding of power is central to making sense of legitimacy within the liberal tradition. Traditionally liberal theorists have placed exclusive emphasis upon freedom without taking account of power, which is an imbalance that Morriss seeks to address. A society can fail to live up to the normative criteria of liberal legitimacy in two ways: it can prevent its members from having the freedom to choose the way that want to live and/or it can be unsupportive, doing nothing to foster the prospects of its inhabitants, so that they have nothing to choose between. A society can either be tyranny in which power is exercised *over* people so that they have no freedom or because its members have limited *power to* do any of things that they might wish to.

If one accepts the inevitable fact that all societies, including liberal ones, have to limit freedom to some extent and that they cannot be expected to give its members infinite powers, this raises the obvious question determining criteria of acceptability. What kinds of limits of freedom and absence of capacity for action should liberal concern themselves with? In answer to this Morriss examines a number of liberal perspectives, including the currently dominant view, which holds that human agency is a crucial criterion determining relevance. Rejecting these, Morriss argues that the one of the defining criteria of a liberal society has to be that its institutions do not insult or humiliate its members. Thus, constraint upon freedom and deprivation of power which either insults or humiliates is normatively unacceptable.

It is interesting to reflect that in instances when societies deliberately insult the status of some of their members one can see the complex interrelationship between freedom and power. In those societies that discriminate what their citizens are free to do, who they can have sexual relations with, and where they can live, be educated or work, on the basis of ethnic classifications (for instance, the Apartheid regime of South Africa, the Bhumiputra regime of Malaysia, the caste system of India (or Japan), or the Aboriginal Protectorate Agencies of Australia) lack of freedom to do something which one cannot currently do may be sufficient to dissuade one from acquiring the required ability.

In Chapter 4, using the methods of comparative political sociology, Charles Tilly shows us how power indices can be used to make sense of levels of democraticness and political stability. (As he notes at the outset, female suffrage is often taken as an index of democracy and cites Finland as the first to admit female suffrage. This is not strictly true, as Finland's advent in 1906 was preceded by Australia's in 1902 and New Zealand's in 1893.) The number of democracies advanced from zero in 1900, on the criteria he adopts from Freedom House, to 192 by the end of the twentieth century. Of course, it is not a Whiggish history of progress so much as one of set-backs and stalling as much as a forward march. Democracy depends on a specific type of power relations. A distinctive and historically unusual form of power is involved. Its essence is the subordination of authority to collective power expressed in voting in elections. Central to democracy are power relations between central authorities and the populations nominally subordinate to them. Once again, we find Tilly using the 'power to' and 'power over' distinction to advance his argument. All definitions of democracy hinge on different methodologies for the exercise of democratic power which ensure that citizens exercise collective control over some central executive. At the core of this measure must be a focus on practices rather than principles; it is not so much what actors are constitutionally represented as doing so much as what they actually do that is significant. The key practices, suggests Tilly, are how wide are the range of citizens' actually expressed demands; how demands are translated into state behaviour; the extent to which expressed demands receive state political protection, and the extent to which the process of their translation into practice commits both citizens and state. On this basis, regime democracy entails political relations between state and citizenry that feature broad, equal, protected, mutually binding consultation; but there is one other thing: states must have a capacity to enforce their political decisions and, as Tilly explains, these capacities can vary greatly. What explains the variance, he proposes, is the extent and character of trust networks or ramified interpersonal connections, the extent of inequality between citizens construed in terms of various membership categories, such as race, ethnicity and gender, which, typically, tend to be intersectional, and the extent and detachment of autonomous power centres from formal public politics, especially where they control autonomous coercive means. A large plurality of trust networks well integrated into the polity, a low degree of discriminatory membership categorization devices, and a high number of politically participating autonomous power centres with relatively equal access to political resources and with little or no recourse to autonomous power resources favours democratization. Hence, power relations are at the core of democracy in ways that are far more elaborated than the merely ceremonial aspects of democratic participation in acts of voting.

Rob Stones, in Chapter 5, both introduces and develops further our understanding of power within structuration theory, as a paradigm concerned to link power to agency and structure. Structuration theory, developed and popularized by Anthony Giddens, has been a major contributor to power debates in the past (see Clegg 1989; Haugaard 1997). Giddens developed structuration theory in the 1970s and early 1980s, and it has undergone a subsequent process of conjecture and refutation, largely, but not entirely, conducted in terms of social theory rather than applied research. (Interestingly, in Giddens' own more policy-oriented writings on modernity and Third Way politics it is sometimes difficult to see the writing as an exemplification of structuration theory. Stone notes that the later work seems underpinned by a 'non-reductionist pluralism' geared to macro analysis rather than by structuration theory.) The version of structuration theory that Stone deploys shares Giddens' emphasis on hermeneutics, situated practices and the 'duality of structure' at its core but is more empirically oriented. Stone analyzes the strengths and core principles of structuration theory and the role of power within the theory. To do this he engages with the debates that have centred on Steven Lukes' (1974, 2005) substantial contributions to the analysis of power, especially the third 'dimension' of power, centring on different ways of conceiving what the 'interests' of subjects might be, such that we can maintain that the actors' conceptions of their interests prevent the manifest emergence of 'real' grievances. At issue is the analytical sense one should make of the proposition that one might 'have' an interest that is externally imputed to one, on the basis of a structural analysis of the situations one might be in, even if one is ignorant of, or resists, that imputation? As Stone notes, most of what is significant in recent debates about power hinge on how one addresses these issues, relating power, structure and agency. For instance, how one resolves issues centred on gender and ethnic relations, for instance, hinge on how one construes 'real interests' in the face of professions to the contrary by knowledgeable social subjects. Ultimately, of course, theoretical debates and arguments about ontological principles only go so far, intriguing as they may be for the theorist; how the theoretical positions elaborated can contribute to empirical studies of power is what is significant, as Stone concludes.

In Chapter 6, Jacob Torfing explains how power functions in discourse theory through the constitution of meaning and reality (Machiavelli and Nietzsche). The debates that he draws on, from post-structuralist discourse theory, provide an increasingly fashionable approach to the study of social identity and political power. Abandoned are the prime movers of historical materialism or the rational calculating homunculus of neo-classical and analytical theory. Instead, he sees power as those constitutive acts that shape and reshape structures and agencies constituting the conditions for how we make sense of the world, the categorical inclusions and exclusions made, and the action that flows from these differently embedded ways of seeing. The empirical field on which he projects his analysis of power is that of the welfare state. What is constituted as welfare reform depends on the relative influence of social and political actors as well as on path-dependencies produced by political and institutional legacies in different countries. Increasingly, however, political agendas and vocabularies are being shaped by a discourse of globalization that forms a relatively coherent whole. Power is a crisscrossing field of forces and strategies that constructs particular subjectivities and particular institutional structures. Post-structuralist theories demonstrate how discourses are constructed through political conflicts and power struggles, and how they structure the identity, perceptions and actions of the social and political actors thus constituted.

With clear Machiavellian antecedents, in Chapter 7, Rolland Munro shows how networks constitute fabrics of power, which provide conditions of possibility for social action which actors use, more or less effectively. These networks comprise agents of various kinds: there is no privileging of the human subject in actor-network theory. Agency is restored to things other than people. One consequence of this way of seeing agency is to lessen the centrality of intention: if agents can be non-intentional and still have effects how can they be held to be responsible actors? Lukes (1974) established that questions of responsibility were inseparable from those of power but, in a technology-saturated world, where stock markets behave erratically because of decisions triggered by computer chips, and where databases profile people as intentionally typified, irrespective of their real intentions, it seems somewhat arcane to preserve matters of agency for human beings or overly reductionist to insist on the human ghost in the machine. Hence, actor network theorists prefer to focus not on intentions, will or consciousness, but focus instead on *effects*.

Using an anthropological backdrop, Richard Jenkins explores the complex ways in which agents create power resources for themselves through networks of capital in Chapter 8. The chapter adopts Max Weber's discussion of legitimacy and domination (1978: 53–4, 212–54) as one point of departure. The other embarkation point is a significant and influential debate that flourished in anthropology during the 1960s between formalists and substantivists (Firth 1967; Sahlins 1974). Formalists argued that the models and assumptions of conventional economics – most specifically, maximising 'economic man', 'the market', and 'scarcity' – can, and should, be applied to all human groups and ways of life. Thus, they aligned themselves with those for whom context is immaterial except in so far as essential and universal actions unfold differently in differently resourced contexts. Substantivists opposed this view: for them, taking terms that were deeply embedded within the emergence of neo-classical economic orthodoxy and assuming that had a universal applicability demonstrated a deep cultural imperialism – assuming that the master narratives of a master discourse of the most dominant societies had universal applicability, separate from the times and places in which they were coined. That is one should be doubly blind: blind to the specificities of the societies under study and equally as blind to the specificities of the tools with which one studies them. The priority of local meanings (encoded as 'culture') and relevancies was the crucial thing – not the imposition of essentially alien categories. Hence, when we come to apply categories such as authority to explain how power operates in specific contexts we need to acknowledge the limitations of general categories and should be sure to ground them in local 'folk' models. We cannot understand the sense of a situated action unless we grasp how the constitutive sense of the phenomenon is embedded in concrete members' practices. To achieve this intensive fieldwork is required.

Certain doubts about the usefulness of grand narrative categories, such as power, are raised by the line of argument that Jenkins follows. Concepts such as 'power' may not be very useful analytical categories because they abstract too far from everyday life. It may be better, suggests Jenkins, to focus on those resources – such as beer, money, women or pigs – that are valued in specific contexts and focus on the relations that surround their deployment, use and exchange – what he terms their 'efficacy'. Such things may represent local capital – in the sense of the term that stresses it as a process and social relation on which value and values are pivoted, around which value can be maximized, husbanded, invested, increased or decreased. To do all these things requires some socially organized social networks that offer access to resources and, as such, can be considered a resource in their own right. It is in these networks of social capital that, anthropologically speaking, Jenkins wishes to locate power. People, whether as hunter-gatherers or trans-national masters of business, adopt problem-solving approaches to their lives, and draw on resources, such as a hunting party or an organization, that are often institutionalized 'power containers' as and when appropriate to do so.

Coming from Economic Geography as a disciplinary approach, but appropriating a considerable element of post-Foucauldian theory, John Allen considers 'Powerful Geographies: Spatial Shifts in the Architecture of Globalization' in Chapter 9. In this chapter he contributes a notion of a *topological* world which disrupts our sense of what is near and what is far and loosens defined times and distances, calling into question the idea that power may be simply distributed or extended over a given territory, or that it can be regarded as something which flows through extensive networks. It is a landscape in which settled administrative entities that have territorial definition and location fuse with more fluid, networked activities of economic corporations and social movements. The risk with this approach is in assuming a *given* global backdrop largely composed of territorial fixity and networked flows. Against this idea Allen proposes that power is more spatially ambiguous than is often recognized. A new geography of power is emerging in which the global is both instantiated in the national and the national in the global which moves beyond simply mapping global distributions of domination and authority in a 'cartography of power'. The two authors who do most to overcome this way of thinking, Allen suggests, are Ulrich Beck (2002) and Saskia Sassen (2002), whose work he goes on to consider.

Beck introduces the notion of a meta-power game whose rules of engagement between national and international system of states are being radically changed and rewritten. Globally networked, digitally connected corporations use the leverage of being able, in principle, to exit and invest elsewhere against states that do not provide what they want. However, it must be said that this leverage is perhaps more remarked on than engaged in practice. Many organizations are so deeply embedded in the life of specific places that they root there. Moreover, they often have to engage with equally global and digitally connected social movements and NGOs. States, NGOs, social movements and corporations can ally on occasions as potential forces for integration and enablement at the global scale rather than being merely antagonistic.

Saskia Sassen alerts us to an overlapping mix of spaces and times as the hallmark of the global. National spaces and times are increasingly interpenetrated with global conceptions. Elements of older public management, institutional authority, legal rights and territorial infrastructure are recomposing into private and public/private social relations that are neither national nor global and represent an unstable power formation in the making. Global banks, media and construction – one channelling capital, one representing power to the people while the other channels state power into infrastructure and mega-projects – are exemplary cases of these newly emergent relations. They lace together the boardrooms and state rooms of global cities across the planet. Allen concentrates on the role of private equity arrangements – although these might be seen as a symptom of their times rather than a constitutive characteristic. Nonetheless, as Allen puts it, states are both confronted by and are part of a new geography of power that does *not* have territorial exclusivity as its defining characteristic. Global cities are the containers of power for the new ordering of inter/national affairs. In these cities financial and corporate business tangle stretched with proximate social relations and circuitous with more immediate styles of power; in turn tangled up with these are civil society, NGO, and social movement relations that often latch on to emblematic sites or representations as icons to oppose, such as Nike or McDonald's.

POWER AND RELATED ANALYTIC CONCEPTS

In Chapter 10, using Sir Isaiah Berlin's (2003) distinction between positive and negative liberty as a backdrop, Mitchell Dean considers them within the competing traditions of liberal and Foucauldian social thought. The chapter begins by taking a concrete and controversial policy innovation: the direct intervention by the Australian state into the conduct of people in remote aboriginal communities which severely circumscribed the liberties of these people. Such interventions are seen as a denial of the politics of neo-liberalism, based on consumer sovereignty and free choice, to select groups of citizens. Instead, a new paternalism can be seen to be in play. Liberalism, in its variants, makes a normative claim that power should best operate by the shaping of liberty and through the exercise of choice. In the new paternalism, however, these assumptions are dropped in favour of a view of the exercise of power that seeks to shape a specific form of freedom by means of close supervision and detailed administration of the individual. The connection with classical debates on power is evident: new paternalists claim to know the interests of subjects better than these subjects do themselves. Indeed, it is the inability of certain classes of subjects – the feckless, indigenous, poor etc. – to know what their real interests should be that necessitates the state having to intervene in order that they might better realize them rather than the deviant interests which have so undermined their capacity for personal responsibility such people cannot make appropriate choices for themselves even if they know what such a choice would be.

The discussion then shifts to classical and central conceptions of liberty: for Berlin, as much as for Mill or Hobbes, one is free to the extent that one is not prevented in realising one's will, i.e., there is no interference in the area in which one wishes to act. When one agency has a causal effect on another in a significant manner by interfering in the area in which the other would act, then there is an exercise of power which entails the subtraction of liberty from the party or agency so constrained. Hence, in this classical conception, power and liberty are mutually opposed. As Dean (p. 181), puts it, 'To be free is to be free from power. To exercise power is to limit the area of freedom of others; thus, there is a quantitative and inverse conception of the relation between power and liberty'. Dean observes that the legitimacy of sovereignty rests on the members of a political community voluntarily acceding to being ruled. If this is the case, then the forms of intervention with which he began the chapter are deeply problematic in liberal terms, as is the assumption that there is an inverse, quantitative relationship between power and liberty.

In contrast to the classically liberal accounts of liberty Dean considers Foucault's notion of governmentality. At the core of this, rather than an inverse relation between power and liberty, there is an assumption that, in principle, all subjects of power are at liberty to act in one way or another; hence power relations become a series of strategic games between liberties and the rationalities – the more or less systematic ways of thinking about problems to be addressed, the means by which they can be solved, the actors and identities involved, and the goals sought in so doing – that support them. From this perspective, neo-liberal programs try to shape the conditions under which these liberties are expressed as choices while neo-paternalism seeks to rectify what is defined as previously irresponsible use of liberty by close surveillance and supervision of future actions. While they share similar vocabularies their means of shaping the conduct of conduct clearly differ markedly.

In the classical liberal tradition the subject is posited as either conforming or resisting acts of power, which are conceptualized as something that is external to the will of the subject whose choices are preformed – they either want to do something or they do not. In governmental approaches practices try to shape the conditions under which choice is made by seeking to produce different kinds of identity and freedom among specified individuals and populations. Dean argues that these governmental practices are not merely a respecification of Lukes' third dimension of power; for one thing, they do not seek to shape consciousness but rationally thought out conduct; they are not insidious and subtle mechanism but overt and explicit analytics of governance.

Dean's conception of the self on whom practices work is clearly 'thin'; it is a tabula rasa written on by diverse governmental practices. Drawing on the anthropological cannon, in Chapter 11 Nigel Rapport reaches the conclusion that the central questions in power relations relate to how we constitute the meaning of the self: What is the relationship between a humanism that stresses the generic human rationality and the biological unity of mankind and evident structural variation in languages, cultures and social arrangements in which this humanism is constituted? The enduring nature of power relations is that they are inscribed on human beings who, in principle are free in consciousness and individuality, but for whom this freedom can only ever be expressed socially, which means that the freedom will always be culturally and collectively structured: no agency without structure and no structure without agency, in other words, with power relations inscribing their articulation substantively around different conceptions of what constitutes the available identities that actual men and women may readily assume or resist. Hence, discourses that privilege humanism or other claims, though widespread in some versions of modernity, are by no means guaranteed, because they are historically contingent. Nonetheless, we should not simply say that all discourses are relative: some make claims whose substantive commitments are more laudable than others, and humanism, despite its evident blindness and shortcomings, offers a better basis for a rights and equity project of humanity than the competition. It enables us to escape the essentialism of structural and given identity determination. For Rapport, power is important because understanding it enables us to address the politics of identity. Identity emerges from a sociocultural realm that is not conceived so much as a distinct ontological domain but rather as a phenomenological space that is, as he says, continuously affected and effected by the diversity of individual interpretation and intention. Identity is not just something formed by the great structural prime movers of history and sociology; it is something that is formed both politically or institutionally *and* existentially or personally as a manifestation of power. Thus, power relations shape and are articulated in the everyday sensemaking that people engage in, using the discursive and other resources that are available to them. For Rapport, we must begin analysis with the individual situation, albeit with an emphasis on the relational nature of identity. He conceives of social science as the study of the effects, intended and unintended, direct and tangential, which human beings have upon one another as energetic things-in-the-world. These effects are clearly power-effects. The most primitive, or first power-effect, is that of the subject over self, matters realized in the working out of issues of identity as an answer to the question 'who am I?' As he puts it, 'Only as a self, active in the world towards an ongoing accruing of meaning and identity, does an individual construe otherness and relate, consciously and intentionally, to other things-in-the-world'. Power is first of all exercised over the self before it is exercised over others.

In the world at large power is closely coupled with identity; it occurs through a capacity to create *our selves* as the kinds of being that can and do exist in the very different systems of symbolic classifications of identity which we continue creating – and resisting. It is in the interplay of collective cultures and individual identities that we create and recreate the worlds in which we live, through the classification devices we find contingently conventional to use – or which we resist using. Finally, while Mitchell Dean began the previous chapter with Sir Isaiah Berlin's famous distinction between negative and positive freedoms, Rapport concludes with discussion of this distinction, in order to state, once again, what he sees as the primacy of existential power over and against structural power and of an extensive conception of identity over and against a conception of it as essential.

Fredrick Engelstad shows, in Chapter 12, how an actor's interpretative horizons shape and influence relations of power and domination, taking his cue from Michael Mann's influential work, especially his concept of ideological power, which is here rendered in terms of a concept of 'culture' conceived in terms of generalized patterns of communication and interpretation. Within this cultural frame Engelstad follows Foucault in seeing power in terms of actions that work upon other actions; within a cultural perspective power in seen to operate by acting on social actors' interpretational modes and thereby influencing their social behaviour. Thus, power is seen to work on, in and through actors' beliefs about the worlds they imagine and in which they operate. Hence it works on the ways in which they conceive of their self, relationally.

Various mechanisms are envisaged that collect and focus power: aggregation, networks, organization and institutionalization. These are not to be confused with the more usual rational mechanisms of the mainstream accounts of power that dominated most of twentieth century analysis until the 1970s, in which culture played little or no role. One way in which the role of culture is most evident is in the ways that legitimacy is constituted, often through origin myths, or through appeals to procedural legitimacy, or through the delineation of specific spaces in which specific rights are recognized and others not.

All culture is based on the communication of meanings that entail mechanisms of selection, framing, valorization and ascriptions of causality. These are used to try to connect, in various ways, with those who positioned in, by and through relation to these meanings. Sometimes the clarity of a meaning will be its chief feature; other times its ambiguity may be the key feature. One effective way in which power and culture interconnect is through the institutionalization of ritual that participants see as mirroring values that they hold to, or which they defer to or resist. Often, the accoutrements of ritual – the spectacle, the sense of occasion, the costumes, music and dance – in a word the 'ritual' – are what one responds to: the hymns that move the spirit; the vows that one defers to; the music that stirs the heart.

At the core of all culture and all acts of power is the self that presents itself as the self it is signified to be, and seeks to be signified as, to others as it seeks to shape their and its social appearance. The ways that power adorns the self seeking to exhibit its will always be contextually contingent, and a great deal of the skill in wielding power will be choosing the appropriate and contextually attuned significations. One recalls, for instance, the put down of Michael Heseltine when he sought to lead the conservative party in the UK in the 1990s, by party grandees, that he was a man who had bought his own furniture – rather than inherited it.

Power does not always occur in the public sphere – indeed, one of the most successful elements in political life is to maintain certain issues and agendas as outside the pubic sphere. However, insofar as it does, then the forms of its representation in various media may be decisive for how the politics of situations or events are interpreted. Institutionally, the Western public sphere has always been framed by the construction of spaces, by the state, religion and commerce, designed to awe, control and subdue. From the nineteenth century, the public space was increasingly filled by more centralized media that also discursively framed a shifting range of normalcy's and deviancies as major instruments of cultural power, along with the various disciplines that emerged to organize civic, public and academic life.

These public spaces, on the whole, are not characterized by the hegemonic projects that many Marxists imagine. On the contrary, large-scale modern societies are more characterized by continuous struggles over values and norms, which, in the Weberian sense, often have unintended effects. Some of these unintended effects are the result of what Engelstad refers to as aggregation. For instance, individual advertisers seek to sell the commodities they are promoting as effectively as possible. In doing so they will use whatever means are legitimate and available to persuade the public to consume. Sometimes this involves appealing to instances of irrationality in the public, thus, perhaps inadvertently, creating a commercial culture with strong elements of irrationality in it.

All communication may be thought of as a system of distinctions that form members' categorization devices for constructing and interpreting the worlds in which they live and relate to. These distinctions and categories will be riven through by the cleavages and fissures that mark the social in all its complexity of gender, age, ethnicity, status groups, classes and so. Many of these fissiparous deployments will be occasions for struggles over values and norms in which the battle for ascendancy may be thought of in terms of a struggle for cultural hegemony, whereby the categories become fixed and immutable, with the their implicit interests attached.

At the heart of Engelstad's formulations, just as with Rapport, is the self. Various subject positions – the alienated, conformist, protesting, empowered, reflective, condescending and aggrandized self – are rehearsed. Who knows what new and enticing senses of the self will emerge from the Internet generation, with Facebook and YouTube, ruminations with which Engelstad concludes.

Mark Haugaard explores how the Gramscian perception of power, as based upon the creation of consent, recurs in much of the contemporary sociological and political science literature in Chapter 13. Thus, there are evident continuities with the previous chapter by Engelstad. At the core of such conceptions of power is a view that power is less about the coercive imposition of will on others and more to do with producing qualified levels of consent to the will of the relatively powerful on the part of the relatively powerless. Gramsci's work on hegemony began to shape research thinking on power from the 1970s, when it first appeared in English. Prior to this time, the debates about power had largely been about pluralism versus elitism, an argument about both methodologies and ideologies and about issues and non-issues, a debate largely about epistemologies. By the time that Lukes (1974) entered debate in the mid-1970s, the matters at issue were both epistemological and ideological, and he sought to demonstrate alliances between explicit methodologies, epistemologies and ideologies, usually dubbed, for shorthand, the liberal, reformist and radical views of power. At the same time, these were not just relativist and equivalent constructions: Lukes wanted to be able to say that there was greater explanatory purchase in the radical view of power, where power was seen, in terms framed by hegemony, as acting against an agent's 'real interests'. The key to identifying 'real interests' is not simply some objective truth but the existence in the agents of an alternative world-view, which typically manifests itself in moments of radical rupture. When the veil of normalcy is ripped apart a deeper and more appropriate understanding of the situation may occur, suggests Lukes. Lukes (2005) maintained these views, at greater length, in the second edition of his book. He argues that radical, or three-dimensional, power entails domination, which renders social agents less free *'to live as their nature and judgment dictate'* (Lukes 2005: 114 – italics orig.).

The crucial problematic for Lukes' radical view of power, as for Gramsci's (1971) account of hegemony, is why subordinated agents frequently appear to *consent* to their own domination? Indeed, if any question may be said to have been the central issue in power over the past thirty years or so, it is this question. Theorists have typically addressed the issue by claiming that in some way they can better know the interest of the subordinate agents than the subordinate agents can themselves, largely because the conditions of existence of their subordination do not allow these agents to know their real interests. Feminists and Marxists have been adept at deploying these arguments.

While Lukes' account is certainly representative of a central tradition in power analysis, with roots that delve as deep as Hobbes (Clegg 1989), Haugaard reminds us that there is a tradition exemplified in modern times by Hannah Arendt, which stresses that power is the 'capacity to act in concert' (1970: 44). Such a view, with its stress on positive power and undistorted communication, is precisely the opposite of what Lukes dubs the deepest form of power. Power in Arendt becomes a civic virtue, an essential element in phronesis, rather than its antithesis. There are resonances with Parsons' conceptions of power. Parsons sees power as a system attribute of the polity in which the unequal distribution of power may be the key to its effective creation, as a non-zero sum and positive phenomena. He imagines that power is derived from consensus on system goals. The assumption of consensus hardly begins to describe many contemporary organizational and societal situations which are far more likely to be characterized by value conflicts than value consensus.

There is a dualism in the conceptualization of power that Haugaard finds also reflected in theories of hegemony, where it is conceived as both a source of domination (bourgeois hegemony) and as founded on consent, where it constitutes a form of collective will (subordinated proletarian consciousness). The special enemy of dualism in recent times has been Anthony Giddens' (1984) structuration theory, which, as Haugaard observes, provides a conceptual bridge between the consensual and conflictual power traditions.

Giddens views power both as 'power to' and as 'power over' (Giddens 1976: 111–2, 1981: 50). Agents derive the power to do things, in Giddens' formulation, from what social structures enable them to do. For some agents, social structures enable them to exercise power over some other agents. When routinized and regularized this equates with domination; thus, 'power over' is a subset of 'power to'. Domination is not a total and asymmetrical zero-sum phenomenon but implies a social relation. Giddens sees the consensual basis of conformance with power to reside in general, tacit, social knowledge lodged in practical consciousness. Under given circumstances and situations agents are smart enough to know that while it may not be in their ideal interests to go along with things as they are there is little point is putting themselves on the line only to endure defeat. In more sophisticated conceptions of practical consciousness, which Haugaard associates with Bourdieu's (1977) concept of *habitus*, practical consciousness is itself an effect of power – what Foucault called power/knowledge. Foucault's advantage is that he does not constitute the dynamics of these power/knowledge relations in terms of classical figures, such as labour and capital, as do Gramsci and Bourdieu. Hence, Foucault never gets hung up on the differentiation of true from false consciousness – which is why he opposed the notion of ideology, because as a notion signifying falsehood, it demanded that its other be 'truth'. For Foucault, truth was historically contingent rather than a transcendent category and plays a key role in the dynamics of power, by reifying regimes of power/knowledge, fixing them, one might say, as hegemonic. Certain regimes are more likely to be more effective under certain conjunctures than other regimes. Centralized, coercive sovereign power, where the masses were unimportant and only occasionally dealt with, has lost its efficacy in modern neo-liberal orders, where the masses must be trained to be docile in all the institutional areas for the expression of their selfhood, such as sexuality, schooling, work, family life etc., areas in which power will be far more constitutive, producing subjects with desires to become certain sorts of agents, agents that are simultaneously free subjects as they are objects of domination. Subject to surveillance, socialization and systemic pressures, the spaces for resistance are whittled down, if never entirely eliminated. What they are not is preordained by the prime movers of history: the sources of resistance may be classes or genders but not necessarily so. In this respect, theorists such as Foucault, suggests Haugaard, provide a more profound knowledge of the modern system of domination than was available to Gramsci and his Marxian analysis. Theorists who have built on these post-Fouauldian foundations include Clegg (1989; Clegg et al. 2006) and Haugaard (1997, 2003, 2006), as well as Flyvbjerg (1998, 2001). For Flyvbjerg, to conceptualize truth as something divorced from power is the characteristic deception legitimating modern forms of domination, which allows the rationalization of power to flourish as reason, a theme taken up by Gordon in the next chapter.

Gordon (Chapter 14) fuses Foucauldian and organizational perspectives to re-examine the classic Weberian account of the relationship between power and authority. The point of departure is Weber's account of rationalization. Within this account, Weber sketches a role for power that is as well known as any in the literature. There is some continuity with the Marxist stress on power flowing from the control of the means of production which is supplemented by the importance of differential skills in the means of production, with class being cross-cut by status ascriptions of various kinds. Gordon situates power in Weber's frame of bureaucracy in the context of the modern conception of organizations. All organizational members have access to varying degrees of power, which they may use to further either conformance or resistance to authoritative structures of dominancy. Interestingly, the influence of Parsons' functionalist translation of Weber meant that it was the legitimate, authoritative rather than the resistant use of power that was stressed. Weber did not see that the legitimacy of rationality is always to be taken for granted; it has a contextual, historical and value laden dimension. Substantively, power should always be seen within the context of structures of dominancy. In mainstream accounts of organizations this has rarely been the case because such structures have invariably been seen, *a priori*, as legitimate. Hence, analysis becomes morally skewed: right always resides with the legitimate and opposition to it, resistance, can only ever be illegitimate. Authority, because of its taken for granted legitimacy, is viewed as something different to power; power is reserved for action that is not sanctioned by authority, hence resistance is always an act of power while authority is not.

In accounts of power, Gordon suggests, more critical accounts of power emerged out of the Community Power Debate, when Bachrach and Baratz (1962, 1970) began to look at the ways in which legitimate agendas were framed to exclude what became non-issues for the elites and how it was the resistance of the excluded that reframed these non-issues as legitimate matters for exclusion, and transformed the politics of decision making in the process. On the back of these interventions Lukes (1974) was to develop his celebrated radical view of power, hinging on the extent to which subjects were capable of comprehending what their 'real interests' were and the extent to which analysts were able to formulate what these interests were when the subjects did not know themselves. The thorniness of these issues was best spelled out by Benton (1981) in his discussion of 'the paradox of emancipation': if people were deluded about their real interests, then having these specified for them by some external agency could never be emancipatory: it could ever be another imposition on their consciousness. Contrasted with the functionalist and moral agendas hitherto discussed, Gordon turns his focus to a pragmatic account of power, originating with Machiavelli and Nietzsche and shaped by Foucault in his various approaches of the archaeology of knowledge, the genealogical perspective and the concern with care for the self.

Finally, Gordon reviews current work on power and legitimacy, including contributions by Clegg (1989; Clegg et al. 2006), Haugaard (1997), Flyvbjerg (1998), Courpasson (2006), and Gordon et al. (2008). Much of this work points to the importance of the 'legitimisation of legitimacy' – the process by which members of a social system legitimize certain forms of legitimacy and exclude others. Gordon clearly favours the pragmatic approach to analysis of power.

Weber was one of a number of theorists at pains to differentiate power from violence; violence, however, especially as it is lodged in state capacities, has rarely been separate from the practice of many states, as Siniša Maleševiæ explores in Chapter 15, seeing the intrinsic structural relation between power and violence, almost exclusively monopolized by the state apparatuses, as characterizing modernity. In fact, in his account, modernity is covered in the gore of violence in a way that the Enlightenment thinkers failed to anticipate. Indeed, it was only the German militaristic tradition of social thought that emerged with the German nation-building project in the nineteenth century, which saw systematic violence as a necessary step towards modernity. For reasons that are all too apparent, after the Second World War, this bellicose and specifically German tradition of social thought was discredited. Moreover, in the immediate post-war era, the stress was on a consensus mode of thinking that stressed shared central values, normative order and regulation with the threat of violence removed to the margins of mutually assured destruction in the case of this order being threatened in its heartland in Western Europe and the United States by other states. In the margins, in Latin America or Asia, then the absence of shared values acted as a prompt for violent intervention.

From the 1980s onwards, historical and comparative sociologists increasingly began to focus on both actual violence and the possibilities of it occurring between states. Almost all did so within a more or less explicitly Weberian frame of analysis; the exception may be Michael Mann (1986, 1993), who places social power and state expansion at the centre of societal change. Social change occurs as a result of four networks of power organized politically, economically, militarily and ideologically. Military power, as the 'social organization of concentrated lethal violence' (Mann 2006: 351), is clearly the basis of state power but, in most instances, not its limit. Other recent writers, such as Poggi (2004) and Collins (1975, 1986, 1999), also draw on the militaristic tradition of thought.

For Malešević there is one key question: 'Why modern self-reflexive beings, socialized in the environment that abhors the sacrifice of human life, nonetheless tolerate and often tacitly support murder on a massive scale?' To answer this question properly, he suggests, one needs to take ideological power much more seriously than contemporary historical sociologists have done. Violence as state power always has ideological underpinnings, he suggests. Religions have had a key role to play in providing these in the past, and still do, as events in the Balkans, Middle East, Africa and Chechnya demonstrate; however, modern ideologies are also often underpinned by the authority of science, humanist and other secular ethics. Nonetheless, even modern states can be deeply theological as well as scientific, humanist etc.: although Israel may be the best example there are arguments that would suggest that under the sway of the 'evangelicals' in the Republican party in the US, this would not be an entirely inappropriate characterization. Perhaps the power of religious ideologies is too diminished by Malešević and the reason of contemporary ideologies too emphasized?

POWER AND SUBSTANTIVE ISSUES

One of the chief battlegrounds in both theory and practice has been the arena of gender relations. With few exceptions, Amy Allen suggests, in Chapter 16, that power has rarely been explicitly theorized by feminists in their discussions of the intersection of gender, race, class and sexuality. With respect to these exceptions, a wide variety of often incompatible theoretical strategies and conceptions of power have been deployed, with little agreement about the meaning of power, the key term. Allen uses feminist perspectives to explore the relationship between 'power to', 'power over' and 'power with', which allows her to fuse power as 'domination' with power as 'emancipation', as she tries to clarify what she refers to as a 'muddy terrain'.

In surveying the field she observes that while poststructuralist approaches integrate 'power over' and 'power to', they neglect 'power with'. She begins with Beauvoir, and her account of the 'othering' of women. Women are self-conscious human beings and capable of transcendence but compelled into immanence by patriarchal cultural, social and political conditions that deny them that transcendence. Although one of her main points of reference is Marxism, it is the phenomenological elements in her thought that proved more productive. Marxist thinking did have an impact on late twentieth century feminism, through dual systems theory and segmented labour market analysis, but there was always a clash of essentialisms at work in its frame in Marxist-feminist analyses. Other approaches that flourished at this time were psychoanalytic accounts, in which the psychological impact of a social ordering arranged as a system of gender-based subordination was explored. What all these approaches had in common was the equation of power with domination. Other approaches produced different conceptions through a fusion of analysis of power with biology: out of the womb may spring not only life but a care for the other that is uniquely nurturing and empowering rather than dominating. From such perspectives then power conceived principally as power over others is far too restricted and masculinist, although Allen thinks that restricting power to this nurturing conception may be mistaken: how useful is it, she asks, to redefine power in such a way that gender, race, class and sexual subordination can no longer be seen as relations of power at all?

Judith Butler (1990) is the most recognized post-structuralist contributor to feminism and follows Foucault in seeing power as subjecting, as forming the subject. She recognizes that from this perspective, therefore, none of us can be outside of power relations as we are all subjects. Consequently, any attempts to maintain that there are pure analytical starting points unaffected by power relations can only be a mistake made from within a particular analytic of power, her take on Foucault's power/knowledge relations. There are affinities, Allen suggests, between poststructuralism and ethnomethodology in their accounting of gender.

The key text for ethnomethodology is Candace West and Don Zimmerman (2002), which analyses the social accomplishment of gendered performance as an engagement engage in everyday behaviour which will always be the subject of close scrutiny as to how it is being accomplished. From this perspective, it is the everyday categories through which gender is accomplished that are important; how ordinary people do gender in everyday life. Both post-structuralist and ethnomethodological approaches emphasize neither women as victims nor the possessors of a unique empowerment but as agents who play an active and creative role the maintenance, reproduction and questioning of subordinating social norms. Allen clearly favours the micro-focus of approaches such as ethnomethodology, which seek to find the structuring of social order in the grain of everyday life, while being alert to the criticism that they have been neglectful of relations of dominance and subordination embedded in macrostructural and institutional dimensions of power, as well as collective power, and the intersectional cross-cutting of gender, race, class and sexual relations.

Themes of agency and structure and their calibration form a backdrop to a number of the contributions that we have discussed thus far, as well for Stewart R. Clegg's Chapter 17, which explores how organization theory can build upon Machiavellian, Nietzscheian and Foucauldian perspectives to give us an account of power. The central focus is on managing as an action, considered historically, in terms of the emergence of the categories of the manager and the employee, the one specialist in authority and the other a specialist in obedience. The worker is constituted as a basic labour power (energy to work) while the manager is defined by knowledge, which grants the authority to conduct (others') behaviours. Together, they comprise the essential unity between power-knowledge as the base of modernity.

The first definitive codification of this power-knowledge occurred when Frederick Winslow Taylor produced the first modern technology of power, one oriented to constituting a utilitarian political economy of the body. Management emerges as a pragmatic science that works in a positive ways by shaping the dispositions that define what employees take, normally, to be true. Management seeks to constitute central aspects of identity through relations of power over both ones' self, qua manager, and other people and things. Managing means making things happen through the exercise of initiative and agency, which entails power. Modern managers, after Taylor, confront modern employees who do not exist merely as creatures of habit, tradition or craft but become *objects* of scientific knowledge and *subjects* produced by the application of that knowledge; they become utilitarian subjects in an elaborately reformist and timed ethnography of work. However, increasingly the project of reform could not be contained within work itself; it spilled out into the broader social ordering with the Ford Sociological Department, as Clegg demonstrates, before shifting into the management of abstractions such as social capital and knowledge. Taken in their totality these forms of managing are attempts to manage power/knowledge, as Foucault suggests. Finally, there is an irony in the ways that management and organization theory have theorized power; largely, the way in which the chapter has treated the concept is not how the discourse normally attends to it. In Clegg's theorization power is embedded in practices that, very largely, do not theorize it as such.

Closely related, but dwelling on relations of resistance, David Courpasson and Françoise Dany, in Chapter 18, discuss the processes through which a taken-for-granted phenomenon (for instance, managerial hegemony) is more or less suddenly unveiled by certain social actors and made questionable and thinkable by the same social actors, using changes in the form of power to open up its relations. The chapter demonstrates, as did Gordon, that power and resistance are not necessarily illegitimate activities; indeed the thrust of the chapter is to demonstrate the ways in which power organized as resistance, rather than being merely antithetical and illegitimate, can also transform the nature of legitimate power relations by being the trigger that generates new organizational forms. The focus is on the emergence of processes by which power structures and relationships are modified, altered and relations of power changed.

Courpasson and Dany write against the grain of many recent studies of resistance. Rather than focusing on resistance through subjective distanciation and escape attempts they see resistance through the creative capacities it entails and enhances. What is striking and interesting about resistance is its creative power. Contemporary managerial 'soft domination' (Courpasson 2006) facilitates the emergence of productive and creative forms of resistance that are capable of changing managerial imperatives and directives through a 'culture of empowerment'.

In Chapter 19, Kevin Ryan explores how power relations are constituted not only through the positioning of the powerful but also through constitution of a social world in which certain categories of person become synonymous with powerlessness, with exclusion. He begins the chapter with a discussion of two types of power – biopower and disciplinary power that we know well from Foucault, using examples of eugenics and psychology to demonstrate how power, knowledge and empire were bundled up together. What connected them were issues of government; indeed, Ryan suggests that to be governed is to be free to articulate a certain type of discourse by thinking, speaking and acting within a distinct order of possibilities and limitations represented in what he terms, after Foucault, a regime of truth.

The chapter begins, in a classical manner, with regimes of truth that predate modernity: those that constituted the 'three estates' in pre-revolutionary France and the disciplinary society that held these estates together, largely in terms of functions that policed the society for the state. There were two ways of doing this, which combined disciplinary and pastoral powers, seeking to ensure the strength and security of the state and secure the happiness and prosperity of the population. In other words, to pattern the combination of negative interventionary and positive organizational power in such a way as to govern, as relatively easily and economically as possible, the relation between what Ryan terms 'each and all'. For Ryan, the various adumbrations of the Poor Law and its attempted reform through the nineteenth century were the space in which these dynamics can be seen in their workings. At the heart of these laws and their reform were shifting categorizations of what constituted indigence, citizenship and responsibility centred on notions of the vagabond and the indigent, defining illiberal subjects who had to be regulated. Positive power, defining the liberal subject, and exclusionary power, reforming the illiberal subject, operates not only through law but also through norms, especially those established in terms of the distribution of characteristics in a population. Increasingly, in the prison, the workhouse, the factory, the asylum, the hospital, the school and the family a new normative order of the normal and its deviancies began to be established. Thus was modernity defined and constructed.

In the final part of the chapter, Ryan turns his attention to the order of advanced liberal modernity that characterizes our times. He dwells on the panoply of devices used for delineating degrees of social inclusion and exclusion, such as various mechanisms of social audit, regulation and, in short, governmentality. Together the actuarial logic of performance, the organizational power of partnership, and the regulatory power of auditing and accounting prove to be techniques of control that secure order.

Chapter 20 constitutes a strategic-relational perspective on the state-power nexus in which Bob Jessop explains that the state should not be conceived as a unitary subject or as a thing that is capable of acting but should instead be conceptualized as a set of relations constituted through power. What is at issue is how it is possible for a state to act *as if* it were a unified subject and what could constitute its unity as a 'thing' and how is it that social actors come to act *as if* the state were a real subject or a simple instrument? In short, how is it possible that such everyday reification is possible?

Approaches are considered and discarded. The state cannot be defined by those institutions it constitutes and governs, for instance, as Weber remarked, there is no activity that states always perform and none that they have never performed (1948: 77–78). Nor can we determine the limits of the state through its top management team when so much state activity is contracted out or conducted at arms length by agencies such as national media, employers associations or trades unions. The legitimate monopoly of the means of violence may be necessary but it is hardly sufficient as a defining feature for it is too minimalist and hardly addresses the normal everyday body of state business which does not entail the troops, police or riot squad. Nor does territorial definition help greatly when we have states that are members of super-state entiries such as the EU and simultaneously, such as France and Italy, have elected representatives from overseas territories over which they may, or may not, have sovereignty. (One of the editors lives in a neighbourhood in Sydney, Australia, that elects a deputy to the Italian parliament.) As such examples suggests states are embedded in wider political systems, articulate their relations with other institutional orders, and are linked, in different ways, to different forms of civil society.

The state is both one institution amongst many but also that which polices all aspects of the functioning of the society in which it is embedded. It is continually called upon to resolve society's problems just as much as it is held responsible for having created many of these problems in the first place. Against this background Jessop has defined the state, minimally, as a distinct ensemble of institutions and organizations whose socially accepted function is to define and enforce collectively binding decisions on a given population in the name of their 'common interest' or 'general will'. It is a minimalist definition, however, and Jessop quickly moves to qualify it in a number of ways. Bundled up in the definitional a question is the matter of state power; again, ever the minimalist, Jessop defines it as the capacity of a given force (the state) to produce an event that would not otherwise occur. Essentially, he sees the state as a system of political domination, variations in the capacities of which, their organization, and exercise, has effects on states' capacities to project their power into social realms well beyond whatever institutional boundaries may be taken to define the state in question. How these are constituted are themselves subject to evolutionary processes of selection, retention and variation. On the basis of the discussion that we have just summarized, Jessop arrives at a definition of the state as an effect of those strategies that traverse it, which are contested and constituted within its arenas; thus state power is an institutionally mediated condensation of the changing balance of political forces. And these forces are expressed in changing strategies that will be more or less explicitly formalized as such, to which the analyst can attend; to wit, Thatcherism, neo-liberalism and so on. Such strategies may emerge as techniques for governing the economy, the labour-capital relation and so on, but they are also equally likely to be emergent with respect to the intersection of an infinite number of possible identities that do not necessarily privilege those of relations of production.

In Chapter 21 Phil Cerny begins by noting that, from a neo-realist perspective, in order to explain what happens in world politics in politics between states it is necessary to focus on the power-seeking actions of states as well as 'state actors' in terms of the structured, ongoing relations of power that occur between and among states. Such relations at their most basic are between those who are members and those who are not, those who are insiders and those who are outsiders, or between us and them, where they are 'foreigners'.

In the contemporary conditions of a globalizing world the relations among global states have become far more complicated, with cross-cutting forms of power evident from the emergence of new institutions and actors within the changing structure of the global economy and social relations among states and other global actors and institutions. Power in international relations is typically defined power in terms of the *relative* power of states *vis-à-vis* each other, where states are seen as relatively homogenous actors capable of collective and unitary action. Typically, states acted on states. Today, however, economic, political and social relationships that cut across state borders undercut these clear categories. Revived, emerging and hegemonic cross-cutting linkages and loyalties are increasingly seen as intruding on state politics. Modes of 'transnational' action create webs of collective action far more subtle and sophisticated than power politics. The chapter discusses some of these new forms in detail, forms such as international institutions, regimes and 'global governance', non-state and transgovernmental actors, the changing structure of the global economy, evolving transnational social and cultural bonds, the loosening of frontiers and borders, the emergence of transnational pluralism, the restructuring of the state and the growing 'civilianization' of power in a world of complex interdependence. The overarching and global window on power that is provided by Cerny seems to be an appropriate ending to this journey through the family of power.

CONCLUSION

In the conclusion the editors reflect, in conversation, on the diversity of power perspectives and their relevance to power research. Overall, they acknowledge that the Handbook is premised upon the idea that there is no single correct interpretation of power; thus, they do not seek to impose one. Power is a conceptual tool not a single essence that is eternally contested. A screwdriver can double as a chisel but it is not as fit for the purpose as a specifically designed and appropriate tool. So it is with power. Just as both a screwdriver and a chisel may generically belong to a category of metal-bladed hand tools, so power may collect different devices under its category. Just as a specific tool may be fit for one purpose but not so good at another, so it is with different conceptual tools of power. Different tools arise from overlapping perceptions of power each of which is shaped by particular local language games, which function much as if they were paradigms, shaping certain problems and questions surrounding the concept. In bringing together this Handbook we have brought together exemplars of each tradition, which can serve either as a point of entry for those who are new to or exploring power fields while, for the expert, the chapters constitute exciting new developments within specialist areas of research.

REFERENCES

Arendt, H. (1958) *The Human Condition*. Chicago: University of Chicago Press.
Arendt, H. (1970) *On Violence*. New York: Harcourt Brace and Company.
Bachrach, P. and Baratz, M. S. (1962) 'Two faces of power', *American Political Science Review*, 56: 947–952.
Bachrach, P. and. Baratz, M. S. (1963) 'Decisions and non-decisions: An analytical framework', *American Political Science Review*, 57: 641–651.
Bachrach, P. and Baratz, M. S. (1970) *Power and Poverty: Theory and Practice*. Oxford: Oxford University Press.
Barnes, B. (1988) *The Nature of Power*. Cambridge: Polity.
Barry, B. (1989) *Democracy, Power, and Justice: Essays in Political Theory*. Oxford: Oxford University Press.
Beck, U. (2002) *Risk Society: Towards a New Modernity*. London: Sage.
Benton, T. (1981) '"Objective" interests and the sociology of power', *Sociology*. 15(2): 161–184.
Berlin, I. (2003) *The Proper Study of Mankind: An Anthology of Essays*. London: Chatto and Windus.
Bourdieu, P. (1977) *Outline of a Theory of Practice*. Cambridge: Cambridge University Press.
Butler, J. (1990) *Gender Trouble: Feminism and the Subversion of Identity*. New York: Routledge.
Clegg, S. R. (1989) *Frameworks of Power*. London: Sage.
Clegg, S. R., Courpasson, D. and Phillips, N. (2006) *Power and Organizations*. Thousand Oaks, CA: Sage.
Collins, R. (1975) *Conflict Sociology*. New York: Academic Press.
Collins, R. (1986) *Weberian Sociological Theory*. Cambridge: Cambridge University Press.
Collins, R. (1999) *Macro History: Essays in Sociology of the Long Run*. Stanford: Stanford University Press.
Courpasson, D. (2006), *Soft Constraint: Liberal Organizations and Domination*. Liber: Copenhagen Business School Press.
Dahl, R. A. (1957) 'The concept of power', *Behavioral Science*. 20, 201–15.
Dahl, R. A. (1961) *Who Governs*. New Haven: Yale University Press.
Dahl, R. A. (2006) *A Preface to Democratic Theory, Expanded Edition*. Chicago: University of Chicago Press.
Dean, M. (1999) *Governmentality: Power and Rule in Modern Society*. London: Sage.
Dowding, K. (1996) *Power (Concepts in Social Thought)*. Minneapolis, MN: University of Minnesota Press.
Firth, R. (ed.) (1967) *Themes in Economic Anthropology*, London: Tavistock.
Flyvbjerg, B. (1998) *Rationality and Power: Democracy in Practice*, Chicago: University of Chicago Press.
Flyvbjerg, B. (2001) *Making Social Science Matter*. Cambridge: University of Cambridge Press.
Foucault, M. (1977) *Discipline and Punish: The Birth of the Prison*. London: Allen & Lane.
Giddens, A. (1976) *New Rules of Sociological Method*. London: Hutchinson.
Giddens, A. (1981) *A Contemporary Critique of Historical Materialism*. London: Macmillan.
Giddens, A. (1984) *The Constitution of Society*. Berkeley: University of California Press.
Gordon, R. D., Kornberger, M. and Clegg, S. R. (2008) 'Power, rationality and legitimacy'. *Organisation Studies*, forthcoming.
Gramsci, A. (1971) *From the Prison Notebooks*. London: Lawrence and Wishart.

Habermas, J. (1984) *The Theory of Communicative Action*. Cambridge: Polity.
Haugaard, M. (1997) *The Constitution of Power*. Manchester: Manchester University Press.
Haugaard, M. (ed.) (2002) *Power: A Reader*. Manchester : Manchester University Press.
Haugaard, M. (2003) 'Reflections on seven ways of creating power', *European Journal of Social Theory*, 61(1): 87–113.
Haugaard, M. (2006) 'Power and hegemony in social theory'. In Haugaard, M. and Lentner, H. (eds). *Hegemony and Power*. New York: Lexington Books, 45–67.
Hobbes, T. (1968) *Leviathan*. Harmondsworth: Penguin.
Kuhn, T. S. (1962) *The Structure of Scientific Revolutions*, Chicago: University of Chicago Press.
Laclau, E. and Mouffe, C. (1985) *Ideology and Socialist Strategy*. London: Verso.
Lukes, S. (1974) *Power: A Radical View*. London: Macmillan.
Lukes, S. (1977) *Essays in Social Theory*. London: Macmillan.
Lukes, S. (1986) *Power*. Oxford: Blackwell.
Lukes, S. (2005) *Power: A Radical View* (second edn). London: Palgrave.
Machiavelli, N. (1981) *The Prince*. Harmondsworth: Penguin Books.
Mann, M. (1986) *The Sources of Social Power Volume I: A History of Power from the Beginning to AD 1760*. Cambridge: Cambridge University Press.
Mann, M. (1993) *The Sources of Social Power Volume II: the Rise of Classes and Nation States from 1760–1914*. Cambridge: Cambridge University Press.
Mann, M. (2006) 'The sources of social power revisited: A response to criticism'. In: Hall, J. A. and Schroeder, R. (eds). *An Anatomy of Power: The Social Theory of Michael Mann*. Cambridge: Cambridge University Press.
Morriss, P. (1987) *Power: A Philosophical Analysis*. Manchester: Manchester University Press.
Morriss, P. (2002) *Power: A Philosophical Analysis* (second edn). Manchester: Manchester University Press.
Nietzsche, F. W. (1968) *The Will to Power*. London: Weidenfeld & Nicolson.
Parsons, T. (1964) *Essays in Sociological Theory*. New York: Free Press of Glencoe.
Poggi, G. (2004) 'Theories of state formation'. In: Nash, K. and Scott, A. (eds). *The Blackwell Companion to Political Sociology*. Oxford: Blackwell.
Sahlins, M. (1974) *Stone Age Economics*. London: Tavistock.
Sassen, S. (2002) *Global Networks, Linked Cities*. New York: Routledge.
Weber, M. (1978) *Economy and Society*. Berkeley: University of California Press.
West, C. and Zimmerman, D. H. (2002) 'Doing gender'. In: Fenstermaker, S. and West, C. (eds). *Doing Gender, Doing Difference: Inequality, Power, and Institutional Change*. New York: Routledge.
Wittgenstein, L. (1967) *Philosophical Investigations*. Oxford: Blackwell.

PART I
Framing the Field

1

'Power to' and 'Power over'

Gerhard Göhler

The distinction of *power to* and *power over* has featured prominently in the discussion of power in the last few decades. This may seem surprising, since both *power to* and *power over* appear to be simple phrases, the term 'power' merely extended by two prepositions. After all, Hanna Pitkin coined both terms almost by chance in 1972, but it soon became clear that they express a fundamental distinction in our understanding of power, with the result that the distinction between *power over* and *power to* has been no less than groundbreaking in the years since. Power, then, is either a property or actually exercised. Why has this distinction proved to be so successful? There appear to be two reasons.

The first is that experiences of power are particularly complex. Among the concepts that describe fundamental social phenomena, the concept of power seems to be one of the most unclear and controversial. There have been countless endeavors to define power more precisely and conclusively, all of their results remain as unsatisfactory as ever (Morriss 1987: 1). Initially this sounds surprising, since we think of power as distinctly experienceable and identifiable in everyday life. However, the academic discussion of power can demonstrate that this impression is misleading, since a more penetrating analysis is consistently able to discover new characteristics of power. The work since the 1980s has contributed greatly to this, which is the second reason for the increasing use of *power to* and *power over*.

The complexity of power, which has, in any case, long been acknowledged in the discussion of power, became a main focus of social science's discussion of power in the 1980s. In the 1960s and 70s the concern was still to broaden empirical research on dimensions of *power over* that had hitherto escaped immediate perception. Thus, "new faces" of power were discovered (Bachrach/Baratz 1977, Lukes 1974 and 2005) as part of an endeavor to tighten the elements of critique against an affirmative understanding of power. Since the 1980s things have become less straightforward. The discussion about power has widened and become even more complex. Manifold, formerly unconsidered aspects have been introduced, new perspectives opened. More often than stemming from professional empirical analysis, these were by-products of broader social theories: Talcott Parson's structural functionalism, Hannah Arendt's description of the *conditio humana*, Michel Foucault's discourse analysis, Pierre Bourdieu's exposition of the concepts of capital and hegemony as put forward by Western Marxism, Niklas Luhmann's subtle system theoretical modeling. All in all, it seems, the new elements in the discussion of power in the 1980s and 90s have brought about a muddled situation that is hard to disentangle. It becomes increasingly difficult to incorporate the different approaches of analysis into a comprehensive concept or a common definition of power.[1] Consequently, it becomes more difficult to give a systematic overview of the current ideas of power.[2]

In this situation, it proves to be extraordinarily helpful to distinguish *power to* and *power over* as the two fundamental dimensions of power. This differentiation – having become prominent in the last 20 years – allows to better place different approaches to the current discussion of power, and to grasp the coherence of the concept despite its multifold aspects. Therefore, I will take the distinction between *power to* and *power over* as a starting point for structuring the newer concepts of power, and I will explore this direction as far as possible.[3] It has to be acknowledged, however, that in some respects even the distinction between *power to* and *power over* is not unproblematic and needs further clarification. As will be seen, the *power to* and *power over* framework does not always bring clarity to the multiple ramifications of contemporary understanding of power and recent discussions often progress beyond the initially illuminating distinction between *power to* and *power over*. Therefore, in my final analysis, I will argue in favor of restructuring the concept of power in a way that goes beyond *power to* and *power over*. I propose to use the distinction between transitive and intransitive power for further differentiations. The analytic value of this elaboration can be illustrated using the classic opposition of Max Weber's and Hannah Arendt's concepts of power. Seen as transitive and intransitive power, they turn out to be complementary to each other and refer to an integrative concept of power.

THE 'POWER TO' AND 'POWER OVER' DISTINCTION AND ITS LIMITS

The distinction of the two concepts was introduced by Hanna Pitkin, who formulated it for political science in a study on Wittgenstein and justice:[4]

> One may have *power over* another or others, and that sort of power is indeed relational (...) But he may have *power to* do or accomplish something all by himself, and that power is not relational at all; it may involve other people if what he has power *to* do is a social or political action, but it need not. (Pitkin 1972: 277)

Power over means power over other people, enforcement of one's own intentions over those of others, and is thus only conceivable in a social relation. *Power to*, on the other hand, is not related to other people. It is an ability to do or achieve something independent of others. It is not a social relation. This distinction corresponds to a different normative judgment of power. Exercising *power over* within a social relation always produces a negative result for those subjected to it, because it narrows their field of action. This is the case regardless of the possibly noble intentions or positive outcomes of the exercise of power. A's autonomy within a power relationship necessarily means correspondingly less power for B. *Power to*, on the other hand, is generally considered favorably. The reason for this is that *power to* is not directed at others, but at the individual or the group as actors themselves. The focus is not on the effects of power on others, those subjected to it, but on power as the ability to act autonomously. In this sense, power is constitutive for society.

Pitkin's conceptual distinction is the starting point for further differentiation which has become definitive for the contemporary discussion of power. Even when *power over* and *power to* are not explicitly mentioned as terms, contemporary accounts of power typically no longer define it merely as a social relation which one may or may not view critically. It is also seen as a precondition for communal life, in which individuals may then be constituted as such. A common expression of this point of view is the idea of the 'productivity' of power. *Power to* produces the social relations through which power acts and in which the individual is thus also 'produced'. For those concerned, the results of this are contradictory. On the one hand, *power to* creates autonomy while, on the other, *power over* limits the field of action. Modern concepts of power can be placed on either one side or the other, but there are cases in which both aspects can be united. Then ambiguities emerge which are hard to reconcile in everyday speech. Foucault demonstrates this using the word 'sujet' (subject): 'There are two meanings of the word 'subject': subject to someone else by control or dependence, and tied to his own identity by a conscience or self-knowledge' (Foucault 1982: 212). Hence, power operates as *power over* and *power to*; it is repressive and productive at the same time. In the following, we will see how far the contemporary discussion of power can be structured according to the terms *power over* and *power to*, and where the distinction is not adequate.

'POWER OVER'

Power over covers all concepts of power which – in keeping with the everyday use of the term – define having power as prevailing over others. *Power over* is subjective when imposing one's will, interests or preferences, or objective when carrying out inherent necessities or given norms. Here, the self-referential definition of *power to* is either silently implied or explicitly excluded (Wartenberg 1990). A classic *power over* analysis is the debate on 'faces' or 'dimensions' of power, which took place in the 1960s and 1970s. Its starting point is Robert A. Dahl's empirical study on actually exercised power. He aims to show that American society is not ruled by elites but that it is pluralist despite the criticism suggesting otherwise (Dahl 1961, 1968). This point of view is questioned by Peter Bachrach and Morton Baratz on the basis that Dahl only addresses the openly exposed face of power. Bachrach and Baratz present an additional, second dimension of power, the dimension of 'non-decisions' which can have tremendous consequences just because they are not apparent. Non-decisions are provisions which ensure that some issues do not even make it onto the agenda. In this respect, American society is indeed ruled by elites and not at all pluralist (Bachrach and Baratz 1970). Steven Lukes adds a third dimension: power is not only the suppression of subjective, but also of objective interests – interests that those subjected to power are not aware of, but would pursue if they knew that they corresponded with their objective situation (Lukes 1974, 2005).

The debate can by now be considered to have ended (Ball 1988; Clegg 1989). It developed mainly in the context of 'left-wing', essentially Marxist social critique, which could not be continued without strain in the 1990s in the face of increased awareness of the oppressive practices of Eastern bureaucracies in the name of socialism. (Phillips 1991: 12)

Still unconcluded is the question of who exercises *power over*: agency or structure? Also, what is the status of *power to* and *power over* in the feminist discussion of power? *Agency or structure:* From the actor's perspective, power relationships are mainly oriented toward acting persons or collective actors (agency). From the perspective of the system, they are mainly impersonal mechanisms (structure). Both perspectives address very different aspects, and it would make little sense to reduce them to the same thing. Thus, both perspectives will continue to exist alongside each other. This remains certain, despite mediations. Since Gidden's theory of structuration at the latest, it can be argued that *agency* and *structure* must be seen as complementary. 'Structuration' means that society is the product of a reciprocal process: 'Human agency produces structures which simultaneously serve as the conditions for reproduction of human agency in a continuing process' (Clegg 1989). For instance, the feminist discussion of power sees *agency* and *structure* together from the beginning. The power women are submitted to – the 'subjection of women as the conditions for reproduction of human agency in a continuing process.' (Clegg 1989: 139) Power is exercised in two ways. Actors limit the field of action of others. If they are continually successful in doing this, existing structures are either reinforced or changed. At the same time, these structures purport all personal exercise of power within one field of action.

Therefore, the feminist discussion of power sees *agency* and *structure* together from the beginning. The power women are submitted to – the "subjection of women" (John Stuart Mill) relates to actions as well as to structures: it is both the direct suppression of women by men and the overpowering of women by the structural asymmetry of the sexes which results from patriarchy and is often also internalized by women themselves. Undoubtedly power affects women through discrimination on the basis of sex, which must be abolished – either by establishing equality between the sexes (equality feminism) or by acknowledging the intrinsic value of womanhood (difference feminism).

The starting point of these analyses is power as *power over*, but the feminist discussion of power does not stop there. It includes power as *power to* (see below) or destroys – sometimes in connection with *power to* – the basis of the simple idea of *power over* in relations between the sexes. This inevitably leads to difficulties. Anyone who wants to measure the exercise of power must establish who exercises it and who endures it. From the feminist perspective, this signifies a clear identification of sexes; but this premise has been questioned by postmodern, post-structuralist approaches since the 1980s. Sexes are mostly culturally conditioned and socially constructed. Sex consists of (biological) sex and (social) gender, and even this differentiation is questionable (Butler 1993). Nothing solid, substantial remains. Because of this, power can no longer simply be seen as *power over*, no matter whether it results from male actions or structures. It is no longer enough to insist on a fundamental and universal difference between those exercising power and those submitted to it, as does 'point-of-view feminism' (Dunker 1996).

Critics of this development fear that the feminist concept of power may lose its bite, with violence and dominance becoming diffuse (Holland-Cunz 1998) and the previously well-defined subject disappearing rather than resisting (Benhabib 1996). Nancy Hartsock (1990), analyzing this from a Marxist position, argues similarly: within the manifold relations of power, one loses sight of the real suppression of the acting subject. Emphasizing the social construction of gender differences, searching for new feminist strategies which draw less on the common experience of oppression than on a diversity of coalitions (Mouffe 1998, 2000) – all this has made locating *power over* in gender relations increasingly difficult (Butler 1993).

'POWER TO'

The analysis of power relations described as *power over* presupposes that at least one of the parties is able to execute more power than the others. Here, power is a precondition: it first has to exist before it can be exercised; but it is really power if it is not exercised over others? Obviously, power is not only the realization of options to act; it is these options. Therefore, it is useful to not only analyze the effects of power on others but also as a property or ability. This is the aspect of *power to*. In analyses that relate to *power to*, *power to* either precedes *power over* and defines the preconditions for power relations (Dowding 1996; Morriss 1987), or it is not considered simply as a precondition but as a form of power in itself, a fundamental aspect of social relations.

As far as the preconditions for exercising power are concerned, power is primarily a disposition: it is a capacity as opposed to exercised power; while it remains unexercised it is latent, still invisible, and only potential, not actual (Wrong 1979; Morriss 1987; Dowding 1996). In essence, all these descriptions of *power to* are similar, even though they appear with different connotations within the discussion. When power is considered as a disposition, it is also latent and only potential.

Concepts that deal primarily with *power to* reject a hasty analysis of power relations along the lines of *power over* (Morriss 1987). There is indeed a problem in so far as a simple examination of the effects of power remains too superficial to recognize the real underlying social and political connections. On the other hand it is argued that empirical research on power can only be conducted by examining its effects, and that the analysis of *power to* therefore has a merely heuristic value (Wartenberg 1990; Dowding 1996). One wonders whether the discussion could not be ended by the simple suggestion that both aspects of power belong together. *Power over* can only be effective if it also exists as a potential – on the other hand, the mere potential of power remains undefined and therefore nonexistent unless it is realized and becomes visible in social relations. In this context, *power to* is generally analyzed in terms of the resources needed to make power relations effective, and *power over* is analyzed in terms of the effects of power capacities on social relations. It makes sense, nevertheless, not to approach power analysis via this symmetrical question, but first to pursue the aspect of *power to* alone.

The starting point is the observation that power is not always a zero-sum game as supposed in all concepts of *power over*. In a zero-sum game, the purpose of exercising power is to strengthen one's own position and to diminish the power of the addressee. However, this idea is not adequate for analyzing power processes in which both sides may gain. The transition from a concept of power as a zero-sum game to a concept of power as productive for all participants is most clearly demonstrated by *Talcott Parsons* and *Niklas Luhmann*: in relationships of reciprocal interaction, power engages with counterpower in such a way that the power of A is strengthened by the power of B and vice-versa. The increases in power on both sides of the relationship are mutually dependent on one another (see Göhler 2000: 45). For Parsons (1963), power, like money, is a circulating medium by which obligations are exchanged within the political system. It is in this way that the possibility of common action is created and increased: power is 'the generalized medium of mobilizing resources for effective collective action' (Parsons 1963: 108, cf. Clegg et al. 2006: 191–7).[5] For Luhmann, power is a symbolically generalized medium of communication. Via the medium of power, credit is given and performance is expected: the high performance expected of leaders by those being governed demands an 'investment' in the form of increased support. The result is a joint increase in power. (Luhmann 1975, 2000; cf. Clegg et al. 2006: 201–3).

Finally, the transition to productive power is given a radically normative twist by Hannah Arendt. She defines power exclusively as people speaking and acting 'in concert' (Arendt 1970: 44) – meaning fundamentally that the public and political sphere exists and people are constituted as individuals only by speaking and acting in human society (Arendt 1958, 1970). Thus, Arendt takes an extreme position by explicitly limiting her definition to *power to* and rejecting *power over* as violence, that is to say the opposite. Power is a purely self-referential relation, not referring to one individual, but to a group and therefore to a community of individuals. Since human cohabitation and politics are produced by power, it is not only a potential but exactly the opposite: realized power through communication. Power is not only a capacity but also empowerment, people gaining the ability of autonomous action. Here, making a difference between potential and actual power is meaningless. The normative approach is the decisive antipole to our basic understanding of *power over* in the everyday sense of the words. At the same time, it radically questions the common differentiation of the two terms. If it is even the slightest bit convincing, the seemingly helpful concept of *power over* and *power to* becomes obsolete.

'POWER TO' AND 'POWER OVER'

At this stage it seems that only two alternatives remain. The first alternative is to combine *power over* and *power to*.[6] Indeed, there are concepts of power where the differentiation of *power over* and *power to* does not hold water, because they cover both aspects or at least it is not conclusive which side they are on. The second alternative is more far-reaching. In light of all the difficulties in distinguishing *power over* and *power to*, might it not be necessary to replace the *power over/power to* concept with something new to avoid these difficulties? In the following section we will look at the first alternative. Concepts of power in which the differentiation of *power over* and *power to* does not work have an ambiguous understanding of *power to* – either as a capacity (1) or as empowerment (2).

(1) The theories of international relations usually distinguish four approaches: realism, institutionalism, liberalism, and constructivism (e.g. Schimmelfennig 1998). Realist approaches focus on states as the main actors within the international system; institutionalist approaches on international centers of power in the form of organizations (the UN, the World Bank) or regimes (GATT, WTO); liberal approaches point to the domestic system as determining the behavior of a state within the international arena; and constructivist approaches to the structuring of the international system through ideas and norms. What does this mean for a theory of power? Realist, institutionalist and liberal approaches discuss whether power should be viewed as a capacity or a social relation (Baldwin 2002). Any capacity

obviously becomes effective only in a relation between actors at the point where resources are unevenly distributed, so that threats suffice (see Morgenthau 1948). Here, institutionalist and liberal approaches look not only at actors, but are also interested in structures. For constructivist approaches the connection between *agency* and *structure* is central because ideas and norms are structural factors influencing actors' behavior. At the same time, actors are able to change guiding ideas and regulating norms within the international system – it is not a one-sided dependency (Guzzini 1993, Wendt 1999).[7] In this co-dependent relation, *power to* would be attributed to the structures, *power over* to the actors – structures set the framework within which actors actually exercise power. But if this relation is generally open and interchangeable, it seems to make very little sense to preserve the differentiation of *power over* and *power to*. On the contrary, it almost seems consistent that the theories of international relations should take very little notice of the differentiation at all.

(2) But power can be defined not only as a capacity but also as empowerment, as gaining and retaining autonomous *power to* act. Theories that use *power to* in the sense of empowerment occasionally distinguish *power over* and *power to* but they see the two concepts as complementary to each other. Constructivist approaches within the theories of international relations already contain the idea of power as empowerment because ideas and norms not only structure actions, but also give them their initial *power to* act (Barnett and Duvall 2005). In the contemporary discussion of power in the social sciences, this aspect has gained in importance, especially in the theories of Foucault and Bourdieu, who call it "productive power". Individuals are constituted as autonomous individuals only in the sense that they are subjects, i.e. subjected to social power relationships. In this case, then, *power over* and *power to* must be distinguished and preserved at the same time. Foucault and Bourdieu both view power critically as a means of domination, as *power over*. Foucault considers power a 'multiplicity of force relations' (Foucault 1990: 92), in which the individual is entrapped not so much by repression as by the structures of discourse and social practices, which pervade him or her to the innermost. Bourdieu discusses structures of capital and emphasizes symbolic capital. Prevailing symbol systems are the dominating form of expression in every society. Accordingly, individuals are located within the social system of power by their form of expression, their 'habitus'. This is also the individuals' own perspective of perception, so they accept the symbolically cemented power relations as legitimate, even if they are disadvantageously positioned within the social system by them (Bourdieu 1977, 1987). Power relations of this sort are constitutive for both societies and individuals. Foucault considers the fact that power pervades the body of the individual as a precondition for the constituting of subjects as individuals. They internalize the norms of social discourse and practice, but because of the tensions emerging in the process, they are also able to realize their individuality and develop potential for resistance against ruling social force relations. Bourdieu is more cautious in this respect; all the same, the individual can enhance his or her status and – enlightened by intellectuals – penetrate relations of dominance and fight them in symbolic struggles.

Feminist concepts of power often refer to Foucault – and Hannah Arendt – with the aim of connecting *power over* and *power to*. Thus, Judith Butler interprets Foucault's concept of power in such a way as to allow norms of mutual acceptance between individuals to develop within force relations. All-pervading power affects the body in its self-preservation and its desires. Under these conditions, how can a form of individuality develop which depends on mutual acceptance? Power is the medium. It 'orchestrates [...] the way in which we affectively reassure ourselves of our identity or give it up' (Butler 1993: 66). Amy Allen – referring to Foucault, Arendt and Butler – explicitly takes up the problem of the distinction of *power over* and *power to* for the feminist discussion of power and attempts to resolve it by introducing a third dimension: *power with* (Allen 1999). She takes *power over* as the ability to limit other people's opportunities for choice; *power to* as the individual ability to achieve a goal or resist; *power with* as the ability to act jointly and in solidarity. In this way, she attempts to link Foucault and Arendt from a feminist perspective. In comparison with *power over* and *power to*, however, *power with* is a far more normative category, since joint actions of solidarity may well be urgently desired, but cannot be empirically presupposed to exist. Hence, the difficulties in distinguishing *power over* and *power to* remain, while *power with* begins at a whole different level. Amy Allen has worked through the contemporary discussion of power intensively and moved it on with impressive consistency. Nonetheless, simply adding another dimension leaves too many questions unanswered to restructure the concept of power in a useful way. A more fundamental approach is necessary.

RESTRUCTURING THE CONCEPT OF POWER: TRANSITIVE AND INTRANSITIVE POWER

In relation to Hanna Pitkin's distinction of *power over* and *power to*, how can the ability of an individual or a collective actor be considered effective at all without referring to the realization of power in a social relation? It seems clear that *power over* and *power to* cannot easily be separated. Nevertheless, there is evidence that – in a very different way – *power over* and *power to* must not necessarily be connected. Military strength is a form of power that must not necessarily be exercised in order to influence others' behavior and reach one's goals. Here, power is – in the sense of *power to* – the ability to accomplish something, but power is not only about its effect on others. As Hannah Arendt has shown, a group's power *to* act can only be won through its power *over* itself, and here, *power to* as a group's self-reference exists before its influence on the outside. So in addition to the difficulty in distinguishing *power over* and *power to,* the latter is ambiguous in itself. As we have seen already in the previous section, *power to* means

- on the one hand: the capacity to achieve something,
- on the other hand: generating – i.e. gaining and keeping – the autonomous empowerment of an individual or a group.

In the first case, *power to* is potential. The possible effects of *capacity* can, of course, only be assessed when it is actualized, but when there is adequate experience, it does not need to be actualized to be effective (see military strength again); the threat suffices – and appears even more intense (Luhmann 1975). Power, then, is latent; it creates its effects without acting. The threat has to be visible to its addressee – possibly through earlier experiences – but is not actualized again to further influence actions (compare Bachrach and Baratz's 'non-decisions').

In the second case, *power to* is actual. When speaking of *empowerment*, the power of an individual or a group is either existent or not. If existing, it is always actual; if potential, it is not. Autonomous power *to* act always has to be actualized to exist: through renewed integration of citizens (Smend 1928) or through the continuous communication of everyone concerned (Arendt 1958, 1970). It does not exist without being permanently actualized. But, *power over*, too, is ambiguous in this sense: Firstly, *power over* signifies a social relation in which one actor prevails over another. This relation is a manifest influence, i.e. an observable social event; actual and related to an addressee with a relationship of wills. But *power over* can also be self-referential and potential. This is the case when a society binds itself by obligating itself in a constitution not to substantially change certain inalienable rights of the individual or fundamental norms of the social system (how ever disputed they might be in a given case), and to tie important decisions to the consent of a substantial majority. The effect is potential, because it is only questioned in case of violation; at the same time, it influences the behavior of everyone within that society. They orient themselves in a certain way out of conviction or to avoid sanctions (Elster 1983).

Both *power over* and *power to* mean different things, depending on their potentiality or actuality and on whether their point of reference is inside the group (self-reference) or outside:

Table 1.1 'Power to' – 'power over'

	Potential	Actual
Reference to the outside	*power to* capacity	*power over* influence
Self-reference	*power over* self-binding	*power to* empowerment

So one can explain why the two dimensions of *power over* and *power to* are so hard to distinguish, even though they are intuitively illuminating. What they mean is in both cases ambiguous and mutually entwined.

In view of these results, I propose structuring the concept of power differently (Göhler 1997, 2000). Power referring to the outside is *transitive power*, i.e. power which translates the will of an actor into another actor's will and thereby exercises influence. Power referring to the inside, i.e. power as self-reference, is *intransitive power*, i.e. power that is produced and preserved by itself, by society. Both – transitive and intransitive power – can be actual and potential:

Table 1.2 Transitive – intransitive power

	Potential	Actual
Transitive power: reference to the outside	capacity	influence
Intransitive power: self-reference	self-binding	empowerment

Both tables do not differ concerning the contents, but using the differentiation of transitive and intransitive power, the two basic aspects of power – potential and actual – can be clearly distinguished. The intuition of the differentiation between *power to* and *power over* is maintained but its ambiguity banned. If the categories *power over* and *power to* are transferred to the categories transitive and intransitive power, all characteristics of power introduced by the distinction of *power over* and *power to* can be upheld. At the same time despite the similarities, distinguishing transitive and intransitive power solves some of the analytical difficulties the discussion of power has been faced with since the introduction of *power to* and *power over*.

CONCLUSION: MAX WEBER, HANNAH ARENDT AND THE IDEA OF AN INTEGRATIVE CONCEPT OF POWER

The starting points of the distinction of transitive and intransitive power are the two classic theories of Max Weber and Hannah Arendt, which seem almost incompatible. Max Weber sees power as being transitive, while Hannah Arendt understands it to be intransitive. Max Weber understands power as enforcing one's own will within a social relation, which can also be done by using violence: 'Power is the probability that one actor within a social relationship will be in a position to carry out his own will despite resistance, regardless of the basis on which this probability rests'. (Weber 1978: 53) Exerting an influence over others is a widespread understanding of power within the social sciences. But Weber only speaks of a probability or a chance. Power for Weber is potential, a capacity, which has to be translated into actual influence. Hannah Arendt on the other hand understands power as communicating with one another and acting 'in concert' (Arendt 1970: 44). Power for her is the opposite of violence. Here, power is a relation people produce by acting and communicating together; it is not primarily directed on others. Were it only potential, it would not matter. The relation is only power when it is public; power is empowerment when realized. Both with Max Weber and with Hannah Arendt it would be too short sighted to only speak of *power over* (Max Weber) or of *power to* (Hannah Arendt). With Max Weber, power is capacity as well as influence, with Hannah Arendt power is self-binding as well as empowerment. Thus, Max Weber's concept of power is not only *power over* but it is transitive, while Hannah Arendt's concept is not only *power to* but it is intransitive. At the same time, both concepts are complementary.

In this way, they are both starting points for an integrative concept of power covering both its transitive and intransitive dimensions. Power is the medium in social relations to structure fields of action. When power emerges or is exercised, certain options to act are opened up or closed off to the parties involved. More precisely: there are significant disadvantages to be expected when disregarding opened up options to act or pursuing closed off options, or there are significant advantages to be expected when pursuing opened up options to act or disregarding closed off options. Even though it appears that other media, like money or love, might also structure the involved parties' options to act in other ways, at a closer look, the structuring medium is always power. If money is not only about earning and love not only about affection, but when they structure the participant's fields of action, it is the power of money or the power of love affecting this.[8] Power can structure fields of action in a dual way, transitively or intransitively. In the transitive sense, power means that actor A influences actor B with the intention to open up or close off specific options to act to him or her. This can be done potentially by capacity or actually by influence. More difficult to understand is that intransitive power can also structure the fields of action of actors involved, especially and not least according to the understanding of power of Hannah Arendt. While transitive power interlocks the fields of action of the parties involved in social relations by executing influence, intransitive power creates a common field of action in the first place by 'speaking and acting in concert' (further Göhler 2000: 48–9). By way of communication, a community is not only created, but structured because it opens up certain options to act and closes off others. It is the trademark of common action or a common basis for individual action that the options to act are not arbitrary but oriented toward a community or at least framed by common values. Who complies with them is included into the community, who does not is excluded.

There are certainly other approaches than the normative concept of power by Hannah Arendt, which help to understand the intransitive dimension of power. Foucault can also help us comprehend how common power as a medium can generate structure (Göhler 2000: 46). But the opposition of Hannah Arendt and Max Weber illustrates especially well how transitive and intransitive power work, how they do not exclude each other, but how they are complementary. Altogether, they thereby open up the perspective on an integrative concept of power, even if each concept taken by itself may not suffice to incorporate all the differentiations of the contemporary discussion of power.

NOTES

1 As Haugaard notes, 'There is no single essence that defines the concept but there are a number of overlapping characteristics, as in a large family, which define membership. Each theory has local usage which makes sense for that theory but is not entirely applicable in a different context'. (Haugaard and Lentner 2006: 9).

2 Recent overviews of the different concepts of power are given by Lukes (1986), Clegg (1989), Imbusch and Leutner (1998), Haugaard (1999, 2002, 2003), Scott (2001) and Clegg et al. (2006, see footnote 3).

3 Similarly, Clegg et al. (2006: 190–227) present *power to* and *power over* as 'two major theoretical auspices for the social theory' (190). They facilitate new insights in the understanding of power even if in the last analysis they cannot be separated. 'Power will always consist in a complex contingent tension between a capacity to extend freedom of some to achieve something and an ability to restrict the freedoms of others in doing something or other'. (191)

4 Pitkin hereby refers to the late Wittgenstein, to use the ordinary-language philosophy for the understanding of power: 'A Wittgensteinian approach will suggest that we begin by asking not what power is, but how the word "power" is used'. (Pitkin 1972: 276)

5 In this context, Barnes, with Parsons, develops a concept of social power connected to the cognitive order of a society: 'Social power is the added capacity of action that accrues to individuals through their constituting a distribution of knowledge and thereby a society.' (Barnes 1988: 57)

6 Here, Haugaard (Haugaard and Lentner 2006: 10) position Giddens, Morris, Foucault and himself. Presupposing that the understanding of *power to* is consensual, while that of *power over* is conflictual (Haugaard 2002: 4), he understands social reality as a system of meanings always constructed from 'confirming-structuration' where *power to* capacitates action, and from 'destructuration' where *power over* creates new hierarchies (Haugaard and Lentner 2006: 50–4, cf. Haugaard 1997, 2002). Gramsci's, Laclau's and Mouffe's concept of hegemony fulfils exactly these premises (Haugaard and Lentner 2006; with emphasis on autonomy: Lentner 2005).

7 This differs from structural theories in international relations. Dependency theories and modernization theories assume that the existing power gap between the First and the Third World cannot be explained by the actions of politicians. Rather, it is founded on structural conditions, namely the differing degrees of development, which lead to unequal conditions of exchange (Galtung 1971, Strange 1989).

8 Thus, power is not only the specific code of politics (Luhmann 1986, ch. XIII), it appears in all social relationships as a structuring medium (Foucault 1976).

REFERENCES

Allen, Amy (1999) *The Power of Feminist Theory. Domination, Resistance, Solidarity*. Boulder: Westview Press.
Arendt, Hannah (1958) *The Human Condition*. Chicago: University of Chicago Press.
Arendt, Hannah (1970) *On Violence*. London: Allen Lane, Penguin. New York: Harcourt, Brace and World.

Bachrach, Peter and Baratz, Morton S. (1970) *Power and Poverty. Theory and Practice*. New York, London, Toronto: Oxford University Press.
Baldwin, David A. (2002) 'Power and international relations'. In: Carlsnaes, Walter, Risse, Thomas and Simmons, Beth A. (eds), *Handbook of International Relations*. London: Sage, 177–191.
Ball, Terence (1988) 'The changing face of power'. In: *Transforming Political Discourse*. Oxford, New York: Blackwell, 80–105.
Barnes, Barry (1988) *The Nature of Power*. Cambridge: Polity Press.
Barnett, Michael and Duvall, Raymond (2005) 'Power in international politics'. *International Organization*, 59: 39–75.
Benhabib, Seyla (1996) 'From identity politics to social feminism: A plea for the nineties'. In: Trend, David (ed.), *Radical Democracy: Identity, Citizenship, and the State*. New York: Routledge. 27–41.
Bourdieu, Pierre (1977) 'Sur le pouvoir symbolique'. *Annales*, 32: 405–411.
Bourdieu, Pierre (1987) 'Espace social et pouvoir symbolique'. In: *Choses dites*. Paris: Les Éditions de Minuit, 147–166.
Butler, Judith (1997) *The Psychic Life of Power: Theories of Subjection*. Stanford: Stanford University Press.
Butler, Judith (2003) Noch einmal: Körper und Macht. In: Honneth, Axel, Saar, Martin (eds), *Michel Foucault. Zwischenbilanz einer Rezeption*. Frankfurt: Suhrkamp, 52–67.
Butler, Judith (1993) *Bodies that Matter: On the Discursive Limits of 'Sex'*. New York, London: Routledge.
Clegg, Stewart R. (1989) *Frameworks of Power*. London: Sage.
Clegg, Stewart R., Courpasson, David and Phillips, Nelson (2006) *Power and Organizations*. London: Sage.
Dahl, Robert A. (1961) *Who Governs? Democracy and Power in an American City*. New Haven: Yale University Press.
Dahl, Robert A. (1968) 'Power'. In Shills, D. L. (ed.), *International Encyclopedia of the Social Sciences*. Vol. 12. New York: Macmillan, 405–415.
Dowding, Keith (1996) *Power*. Buckingham: Open University Press.
Dunker, Angela (1996) Macht- und Geschlechterverhältnisse. 25 Jahre feministische Machttheorie aus heutiger Sicht. In: Penrose, Virginia and Rudolph, Clarissa (eds), *Zwischen Machtkritik und Machtgewinn*. Frankfurt, New York: Campus, 17–33.
Elster, Jon (1983) *Sour Grapes: Studies in the Subversion of Rationality*. Cambridge: Cambridge University Press.
Foucault, Michel (1976) *La Volonté de savoir. Histoire de la Sexualité 1*. Paris: Gallimard.
Foucault, Michel (1982) 'The subject and power'. In Dreyfus, Hubert L. and Rabinow, Paul (eds), *Michel Foucault. Beyond Structuralism and Hermeneutics*. New York: Harvester Wheatsheaf, 208–226.
Foucault, Michel (1990) *The History of Sexuality. An Introduction*: Vol 1. New York: Vintage Books.
Galtung, Johan (1971) 'A structural theory of imperialism'. *Journal of Peace Research*, 8: 81–117.
Giddens, Anthony (1984) *The Constitution of Society*. Cambridge: Polity Press.
Göhler, Gerhard (2000) 'Constitution and use of power'. In Goverde, Henri et al. (eds.), *Power in Contemporary Politics*. London: Sage, 41–58.
Göhler, Gerhard (ed) (1997) *Institution – Macht – Repräsentation. Wofür politische Institutionen stehen und wie sie wirken*. Baden-Baden: Nomos.
Guzzini, Stefano (1993) 'Structural power. The limits of neorealist power analysis'. *International Organization*, 47: 443–478.
Hartsock, Nancy (1990) 'Foucault on power: A theory for women?' In Nicholson, Linda J. (ed.), *Feminism/Postmodernism*. New York, London: Routledge, 157–175.
Haugaard, Mark (1997) *The Constitution of Power. A Theoretical Analysis of Power, Knowledge and Structure*. Manchester University Press.
Haugaard, Mark (1999) 'Power, social and political theories of'. In Kurtz, Lester (ed.), *Encyclopedia of Violence, Peace, and Conflict*. San Diego: Academic Press, 1710–1724.
Haugaard, Mark (2002) *Power. A Reader*. Manchester: University Press.
Haugaard, Mark (2003) 'Reflections on seven ways of creating power'. *European Journal of Social Theory*, 6: 87–113.
Haugaard, Mark and Lentner, Howard H. (eds.) (2006) *Hegemony and Power. Consensus and Coercion in Contemporary Politics*. Oxford: Lexington Books.
Holland-Cunz, Barbara (1998) 'Die Wiederentdeckung der Herrschaft'. In: Kreisky, Eva and Sauer, Birgit (eds), *Geschlechterverhältnisse im Kontext politischer Transformation. Politische Vierteljahresschrift. Sonderheft 28*. Opladen, Wiesbaden: Westdeutscher Verlag, 83–97.
Imbusch, Peter (ed.) (1998) *Macht und Herrschaft*. Opladen: Leske & Budrich.

Lentner, Howard H. (2005) 'Hegemony and autonomy'. *Political Studies*, 53: 735–752.
Luhmann, Niklas (1975) *Macht*. 2nd edn. Stuttgart: Enke 1988.
Luhmann, Niklas (1986) *Ökologische Kommunikation*. Opladen: Westdeutscher Verlag.
Luhmann, Niklas (2000) *Die Politik der Gesellschaft*. Frankfurt: Suhrkamp.
Lukes, Steven (1974) *Power: A Radical View*. London: Macmillan.
Lukes, Steven (ed.) (1986) *Power*. New York: University Press.
Lukes, Steven (2005) *Power. A Radical View*. (The Original Text with Two Major New Chapters.) Basingstoke: Palgrave Macmillan.
Morgenthau, Hans J. (1948) *Politics Among Nations. The Struggle for Power and Peace*. New York: Knopf. (5th edn 1972).
Morriss, Peter (1987) *Power: A Philosophical Analysis*. Manchester: University Press. (2nd edition 2002).
Mouffe, Chantal (1998) 'Für eine anti-essentialistische Konzeption feministischer Politik'. *Deutsche Zeitschrift für Philosophie*, 46: 841–848.
Mouffe, Chantal (2000) *The Democratic Paradox*. London: Verso.
Parsons, Talcott (1963) 'On the concept of political power'. In: Lukes, Steven (ed.), *Power*. New York: University Press (1986); 94–143.
Phillips, Anne (1991) *Engendering Democracy*. Cambridge: Polity Press.
Pitkin, Hanna F. (1972) *Wittgenstein and Justice*. Berkeley: University of California Press.
Schimmelfennig, Frank (1998) 'Macht und Herrschaft in Theorien der Internationalen Beziehungen'. In Imbusch, Peter (ed.), *Macht und Herrschaft*. Opladen: Leske & Budrich, 317–331.
Scott, John (2001) *Power*. Cambridge: Polity Press.
Smend, Rudolf (1928) Verfassung und Verfassungsrecht. In *Staatsrechtliche Abhandlungen*. (2nd edn). Berlin: Duncker & Humblot (1968).
Strange, Susan (1989) 'Toward a theory of transnational empire'. In Czempiel, Ernst-Otto and Rosenau, James N. (eds), *Global Changes and Theoretical Challenges*. Lexington, MA: Heath, 161–176.
Wartenberg, Thomas E. (1990) *The Forms of Power. From Domination to Transformation*. Philadelphia: Temple University Press.
Weber, Max (1978) *Economy and Society (1922)*. In G. Roth and C. Wittich (eds), . Berkeley, Los Angeles, London: University of California Press.
Wendt, Alexander (1999) *Social Theory of International Politics*. Cambridge: University Press.
Wrong, Dennis H. (1979) *Power*. Oxford: Blackwell.

Rational Choice Approaches

Keith Dowding

The concept of power has had hardly any role to play in neo-classical economics. The term was rarely used except in the sense of 'monopoly power' demonstrating the bargaining strength of the monopolist and signalling some welfare sub-optimality as the monopolist would under-produce goods compared to a competitive market. Perhaps the main reason that economists have not utilized power in their work is that economics has traditionally seen the economy as a process of voluntary exchange between individuals. However, that is not an excuse for economics not considering power as a key concept. Modern economics, particularly since the game-theory revolution, extensively examines the problems that emerge in voluntary exchange for optimal outcomes: problems of credible commitments, agency problems, asymmetric information, moral hazard, collective action or public good problems and so on. Moreover, power is not absent from classical economic situations, such as the position of traders in situations of voluntary exchange. I might volunteer to trade my good X for your good Y; but why I 'voluntarily' do so depends on many other conditions. When the rains have not arrived the poor farmer might trade his goat for a week's supply of food when ordinarily he would not trade it for month's supply. His situation has dramatically changed his bargaining power. It is then a small step to seeing voluntary exchange in different types of coercive or exploitative relationships (Roemer 1982, 1986, 1996)

One reason, perhaps, that economics has tended to ignore the concept of power is that it has implicitly been analysed away. We can represent the changed bargaining situation of our poor farmer precisely in terms of what he would have accepted when the rains come; and what he accepts when they do not. That monetary difference measures the change in his bargaining power. Essentially, that is the line that I take in this chapter. Rational choice methods allow us to analyse power, not simply in terms of monetary exchange, but in the relative bargaining strengths of different actors. However, 'bargaining' here takes on a much broader meaning than it ordinarily does, also covering situations of complete coercion. And the relative strength of the actor might be thought to be represented by the sets of resources they command.

I begin by reviewing some discussions in mainstream rational choice political science to try to demonstrate that these analyses hold important lessons for those interested in political and social power, even though these arguments do not address the power question explicitly. In this review I follow Terry Moe's (2005) recent review showing rational choice has sidelined power in its analyses. I then turn to where rational choice has addressed the power question explicitly, and try to tease out from controversies in that analysis why mainstream rational choice has ignored power.

THE INSTITUTIONAL TURN

Social choice forms the heart of rational choice in political science. Social choice theory has demonstrated that collective voting decisions are subject to instability (McKelvey 1976, Schofield 1983). These findings set the parameters for political science inquiry. With large numbers of voters and several issue-dimensions, if preferences are not homogenous then any winning coalition could be beaten by another, simply by varying the points on each issue-dimension to provide a new bundle of policies preferred to the first bundle by a majority of voters. We note from the outset that these social results rely upon heterogeneous preferences and a common culture can overcome that instability (see Regenwetter et al. 2006). In other words, the so-called 'chaos models' are 'preference free', that is voters can have any preference that is logically possible. By the late 1970s rational choice scholars were asking why politics seemed so stable given the instability predictions that flow from the social choice results. The dominant answer was that institutions exist to freeze policies and reduce instability. For example, by moving decisions into single-dimension committees of the US Congress it becomes more difficult to bundle sets of policies across dimensions to form new winning coalitions (Shepsle 1979; Shepsle and Weingast 1981). Or the development of political parties, with hierarchical control and the discipline to enforce decisions on members encourages policy stability, as do bargains within cabinets (Cox 1987). These arguments should be of interest to power scholars since they formalize the idea that institutions – rules, conventions, laws – institute certain winning policies and ensure those policies remain winning for longer than they ordinarily would. To the extent that rules are initially designed by individuals who would take into account their own preferences when designing those institutions, the rules, conventions and so on are likely to privilege certain types of policies or outcomes over others. Once those rules are in place they institute that privilege. Even if rules are not designed to privilege one group over another, we know that the same individual preferences within a collective might give different results dependent upon the aggregation rule used to count them (Arrow 1952). Thus, once a rule is adopted it might privilege certain types of outcomes over others, and thereby increase the probability that some people get what they want (at the expense of others), relative to a different decision rule. Whether or not that means the decision rule adopted increases the power of the winners (and decreases the power of the losers) is an issue in power conceptualization, but it certainly tells us something about how important institutions are when we are concerned with people getting what they want.

Further inquiry demonstrates that it follows from Arrow's theorem that all decision mechanisms, such as voting can be manipulated (Gibbard 1973; Satterthwaite 1975); that is, voters need not reveal their true preferences when voting and agenda-setters such as committee chairmen (or governments) can manipulate the issues to increase the probability of getting the result they want. From these instability and manipulability results Riker (1982, 1986) suggests that the possibility of combining different interests into different bundles of policies crossing issue-dimensions allow what he calls 'heresthetic' politicians to transform politics and even polities.[1] The importance of these manipulability results for politics has been challenged (Mackie 2003; cf. Dowding 2006), whilst others have suggested they simply form a part of the game of politics, and that power inequality is really contained in asymmetric information and the resources that allow some to manipulate at the expense of others (Dowding and van Hees 2008). However, no matter how important manipulation is, or its precise form, it can hardly be denied that its possibility is relevant to power analyses: both the power to take more for oneself, and, maybe, the power to institute changes that affect the fortunes of all others.

THE STATE

Given the importance of institutions their historical development is of great interest when considering the structure of present-day society. Over the past twenty years rational choice scholars have closely examined the development of institutions. The Nobel laureate Douglass North (1981, 1990, 2005) has been very important in this regard. He has argued that countries that developed better institutions were able to grow faster and thus come to dominate internationally. One of the most important aspects of development is the idea of credible commitment.

Perhaps the result in rational theory most known to those outside is the collective action or free-rider problem (Olson 1971; Sandler 1992). Where individuals can gain the benefits of some public good without having to contribute to its provision they have incentives to free ride. If too many people free ride then the good is under-provided and everyone – contributors and free-riders alike – is worse off. Dowding (1991, 1996) directly applies this result to power studies arguing that it shows that people might be powerless even if there is no other powerful agent acting against their interests. Few other studies directly show the relationship between collective action and power questions. However, the issue of how collective action is possible is one example of a commitment problem. If one can get everyone to agree that a given public good is in everyone's interest, and can get them credibly to agree to contribute; then the problem is solved; but getting people to credibly commit is itself a (collective action) problem. One solution, of course, is to force commitment through some outside body. So, for example, the state forcibly collects taxes to pay for public goods. The problem with outside coercion, however, is that the external force might also use power for predation; for instance, it might take too much of the taxes for itself. I consider the predation problem below, but how did some nations create institutions for credible commitment and others not?

An important article by North and Weingast (1989) shows how the English Glorious Revolution solved the commitment problem by setting up institutions independent of the Crown and so not subject to the King's arbitrary will. Both a more independent judiciary to preside over property rights disputes and the institution of the Bank of England enabled the Crown to raise money for war and facilitated the rise of capitalism in Britain faster than in many other European states. Parliament developed greater powers at this time as part of this settlement.[2] The development of independent banks enabled an increase of trade, not only in the UK but across northern Europe, which enabled higher rates of growth and the beginnings of capitalist dominance, first in Europe and then as similar trust-developing institutions in other parts of the world. Thus no matter what the initial reasons for setting up an institution, they can have massive later effects on the structure of power.

As well as allowing rulers to exploit others, power can enable them to deliberately create rules to the advantage all. In an important book Robert Bates (1989) shows how Kenya's rulers used their power to shape property rights with long-term beneficial results for the nation. In this and later work Bates (2001) he has shown how the use of the legitimate monopoly of violence can be socially beneficial and that cooperation and power are inextricably intertwined.

Collective action problems generally led to the demand for a state strong enough to ensure that commitments made are kept; to police stable property rights that are also necessary for trade, and latterly (the last hundred and fifty years or so), to provide public goods. There is a large rational choice literature on the predatory side of the state, however. To begin we might consider Mancur Olson's (2000) account of the development of modern states, given that he was also the modern popularizer of the collective action or free-rider problem. Against contractualist accounts of the state (Hobbes 1651; Rawls 1971; Nozick 1974) Olson develops the idea that the state can be seen as the outcome of predators realizing that rather than simply plundering, giving something back would be in their own interest. Peaceful farmers might be preyed upon by teams of roving bandits but as the numbers of bandit teams increase, the amount they can steal from the farmers goes down. So bandits realize they might be better off remaining stationary and protecting and husbanding their farmers against other roving bandits. Whilst this story is as much a fantasy as contractors making deals behind a veil of ignorance, it is no less a model for state and puts predation, rather than mutual advantage, at the heart of state processes. By putting predation at the centre, the explanatory focus switches to suggest that what the state provides for people is a by-product of the exploitation they endure at the hands of the state, rather than predation being a by-product of setting up a sovereign to provide public goods.

Other rational choice scholars provide mixed models of state-citizen relations where predation is kept in order whilst the public gain their goods. Margaret Levi (1988, 1997; see also Knight 1992) argues that the institutions of the state are shaped by power considerations. Whilst the state is predatory, it can extract more when it works with citizens, providing them with goods, and citizens provide quasi-voluntary compliance. Rulers can only encourage such quasi-voluntary compliance if they create institutions that are seen as legitimate; and that means they must provide people with a measure of what they want. Furthermore, it is in competing elites' interests to accept the institutions; they are established to ensure elite legitimacy and ensure the continued streams of benefits that these elites can extract from the populace.

Perhaps it does not really matter when examining power structures in the modern state which of these fantasies (contractualism or bandit predation) we utilize. What matters for practical concerns is to manage predation whilst ensuring that public goods are provided. Through many of the examples I have given, the major rational choice contribution to political science might be seen as analysing problems of trust and control in different areas of the state. Wherever one looks in rational choice – models of the bureaucracy; models of bureaucracy-legislative relations; models of citizen-candidates; models of party competition; relationships within federations and so on – the issues centre on the nature of the bargaining relationships and how the principal can control the agent from shirking or predatory behaviour whilst the agent provides the services the principal demands.

PRINCIPAL-AGENT MODELS

The basic ideas underlying principal-agent models are increasingly being utilized in political science and public administration. The relationship between elected politicians (the government) and unelected administrators is seen in terms of politicians as principals and administrators as their agents. In principal-agent models the principal (or uninformed player) signs a contract with the agent (or informed player) for the latter to carry out the wishes of the former. The principal-agent (or agency) problem arises due to the asymmetric information and non-convergent interests of the two players. How well the agent carries out the wishes of the principal depends upon the degree of asymmetry of information and divergence of interest between the two players. Much of the theoretical economics literature is devoted to explaining how the problem might be solved by writing incentive-compatible contracts: that is, contracts which reward the agent to the degree that he carries out the principal's wishes.[3] In contrast, the theoretical literature in political science and public administration is devoted to the more specific problems encountered in the politician-bureaucracy relationship or the citizen-politician relationship. Most interest here has focussed upon the incentives that principal-agent relationships provide for the degree of discretion that politicians should want to give to bureaucrats – based on how much they can trust them – and what types of monitoring procedures should be adopted given the amount of discretion allowed.

The formal economics literature has identified several different types of principal-agent problem. Simplifying from Rasmusen (1989), there are at least four different types of principal-agent problem: (1) Moral hazard with hidden action. Here the contractors begin with symmetric information, but once the contract is signed the agent can act in ways unobserved by the principal. (2) Moral hazard with hidden information. Here the principal and agent begin with symmetric information, but once the contract is signed nature acts in a way observed by the agent but not by the principal. (3) Adverse selection. Here the nature of the agent is known to the agent but not the principal. (4) Signalling games. The agent signals his type (that is, whether he is a shirker or efficient, qualified or not qualified etc.) to the principal prior to the contract being made, but the signal is noisy: that is, the agent may not act as his signal suggests once the contract is signed.

Principal-agent models have been applied most extensively to bureaucratic relations. The most famous model outside of rational choice is Niskanen's (1994) budget-maximizing model where bureaucrats' monopoly of information allows them to extract far more than politicians and the public would wish and keep the excess for themselves. More general models examine the relationship between the bureaucrats and oversight procedures put in place to ensure they behave as their political master's wish. So according to

McCubbins et al. (1987, 1989) the ruling coalition of legislatures and public pressure put in place rules, decision and reporting procedures to try ensure bureaucracies do what legislatures and publics want. According to another set of models, bureaucratic agencies can become captured by the very agents they are supposed to be regulating (Stigler 1971; Peltzman 1976). Civil servants suggest legislation in favour of their clients and not the public. For instance, who really gains from ever tighter legislation governing gas appliances in homes: the public or the gas suppliers whose market is continually expanded by the regulated obsolescence of their products?

Other models of legislative-bureaucratic relations examine what politicians really want from the civil service. In many rational choice models of politician-elector relationships the politicians do not themselves have any policy preferences. They will simply promise what will get them elected and then enact whatever will get them re-elected. Their only concern over the oversight of civil servants is to do enough to ensure that the public is kept happy. Simply allowing the public to oversee civil servants might not be enough (McCubbins and Schwartz 1984) and politicians may want to give greater discretion to civil servants the more likely it is that there will be policy disasters. By giving greater discretion politicians can shift the blame. Furthermore, politicians will give less discretion where they have policy preferences oriented to trying to control future politicians who may have different preferences. The amount of discretion given to the civil service therefore is based upon the degree to which politicians have policy preferences, the risk involved, and so the amount of blame they might want to shift away from themselves (as those who pass the legislation) onto the bureaucrats who interpret it (Huber and Shipan 2002).

These sorts of bargaining models can also be applied to the law. It is argued that judges ought to take into account the preferences of lawmakers when interpreting the law, for if judges depart too far from what the lawmakers want, they will encourage further legislation (Rogers 2001; Rogers and Vanberg 2002). The message here, which I take up below, is that we have to interpret actions carefully. The rule of anticipated reactions is an important aspect of the power structure.

This brief run-through mainstream rational choice writing has demonstrated, I hope, that rational choice theory provides analyses central to discussion of political and social power. Rarely however, is the relationship between the explanations offered and power analysis made explicit. Why might this be? Some might suggest an ideological bias – either because rational choice writers do not want to make links between their 'positive' analyses and power due to the normative connotations of the latter; or simply because the bias of mainstream political science is to avoid power issues altogether; but there might be another reason. In addition, the remainder of the chapter will explore an issue which is at the heart of recent disputes in those parts of rational choice analysis which have explicitly discussed power. Should the preferences of the actors involved in any coalitional or conflictual situation be included in the analysis of those actors?

POWER INDEX APPROACH

In rational choice, power only takes central place in the analysis and use of power indices. These are concerned with measuring the power of different actors in voting situations – though some have tried to generalize their use to broader social power questions (Harsanyi 1969a, 1969b; Dowding 1991, 1996; Morriss 2002). Examining voting power has been stimulated by weighted voting problems. Luther Martin, the Maryland delegate to the 1787 Constitutional Convention, considered the issue as he was concerned that large states would have disproportionate power to small states in the US House of Representatives and argued that voting power could not be equated with voting weight (that is it cannot be equated with the number (or value) of votes a voter, in this case a state, has) (Riker 1986). Penrose (1946) was interested in the voting power of the United Nations, especially given its permanent Security Council, Banzhaf (1965) was exercised by the interpretation of 'one person one vote' in the Fourteenth Amendment to the US Constitution and what this meant in terms of unequal size and heterogeneity of voting districts. In more recent years, power indices have been studied (and created) largely by European scholars under the stimulus of the European Union's Council of Ministers, which has weighted voting for different sized countries. The exception to this generalization about the relationship between specific institutions and measures of voting power is Lloyd Shapley who has been interested in power more broadly, in terms of cooperative game theory, where the power of player is given by his Shapley value (Shapley 1953; Roth 1988). The use of the Shapley-Shubik power index to measure voting power is an outgrowth largely taken over by others (though see Shapley and Shubik 1954).

There are numerous and largely rival voting power indices (though as Dan Felsenthal and Moshé Machover have shown in various writings they are not always as rival as the proponents think – see Felsenthal and Machover 2005). I am not going to define their differences in this paper – interested readers should consult Felsenthal and Machover (1998, 2005). Approaches to voting power measurement can be seen in terms of those who measure the probability of a voter being on the winning side – Penrose (1946) is the first – and those who normalize the measure to make power zero sum such that a gain in one voter's power entails a loss in at least one other voter's power – here Shapley and Shubik (1954) are the first.

The differences in approaches to voting power indices are best explained by a distinction introduced by Felsenthal and Machover (1998) between *I-Power* and *P-Power*. I-Power can be thought of as being the influence a voter might wield over an outcome. P-Power is the voter's relative share in some fixed prize available to the winning coalition in any voting game. It is quite clear that these two broad approaches to voting power have completely different consequences and that the type of measure that one might adopt should depend upon the precise questions being posed. One complication is that the I-Power measures – in Penrose (1946), but more particularly in Banzhaf (1965) and Coleman (1971) – have often been normalized to give measures more akin to the Shapley-Shubik index but without the same theoretical justification. Defenders of these normalized measures have fought over almost meaningless differences in power scores for no obvious reason. As Felsenthal and Machover (1998) point out, normalizing the I-Power measures in this fashion means they lose a lot of information and there seems little reason for not using Shapley-Shubik if a zero-sum or P-Power measure is what the analysis requires.

What is the interest in these measures? Well if you are designing a constitution for, say, the European Union, and want to specify how many votes each member of the Council of Ministers should have, or how many seats each country should be allocated in the European parliament, one might be interested in the relative voting power of different weighting systems. If one is interested in the probability that a given country, say Germany, will be on the winning side in any vote, then I-Power is what one is interested in. However, if there is a fixed prize (perhaps a fixed number of cabinet positions in a government) then P-Power might be the more appropriate measure. The Shapley-Shubik measure was brought to the attention of political scientists by Riker's (1962) application to coalition formation. Riker argued that the government rewards in multi-party systems were largely composed of cabinet seats, and so the coalition should be a minimum-winning one. Coalition partners would not want excess parties in the coalition, or they would have to give them cabinet seats, and so lose some of those positions themselves.

Growing out of the power index approach has been a long-running debate about whether the measurement of power should include agent's preferences. If what we want is the probability of a given voter being on the winning side, then any information about the likely line-up of voters on one side of a division or the other, (including abstentions), should be factored in. However, if one is designing a constitution, then perhaps, though not necessarily, preferences should be ignored and voting weight assigned by some reasonable fairness criterion. For example, the population of a given country might be the only criterion for assigning voting weights, rather than whether that country is likely to vote with another country. However, even here, we might think preferences matter. Assigning votes purely on population size might not make a good constitution if the relevant populations are ethnically and religiously divided for example. Some other equality or constitutional provisions might be thought desirable.

Those who argue for including preferences in power indices or propose moving beyond power indices into game theory (see below) give examples where preference-free models seem to provide the wrong answer. Think of a simple voting situation with five voters $N = (a, b, c, d, e)$, requiring an absolute majority of three voters for an issue to be passed. In a Shapley-Shubik analysis the power of each voter is given by the number of times a voter is pivotal or provides the vote necessary for majority in all ordered sequences. The answer, not surprisingly in this example, given that all voters are equal, is that each has the power 1/5. However, this assumes that all sequences of votes are possible. What if some voters would never vote with each other? Imagine the five voters line up on an ideological dimension as in Figure 2.1. The placement of each voter is their ideal or bliss point for the issue to be voted on. The current policy, the status quo is marked as SQ. All voters would prefer a rightward shift in policy. Voter b, might propose point b, preferred by b, c and d to SQ. Voter d might propose d, preferred by c, d and e. But voter c is in a powerful position. She can propose point c, which b, c, d and e all prefer to the status quo, and she can veto any proposal to her right (as a and b both prefer to the status quo to points to the right of c, and can stop b by proposing c which both

Figure 2.1 Power of median voter

d and e prefer to b. On this analysis then, c gets precisely what she wants and so seems all powerful.[4]

Or consider the situation in a voter-game $N = (a, b, c)$ where b and c are sworn enemies and would never vote together. Here there are two viable coalitions, (a, b) and (a, c). Shapley-Shubik gives a's power as ½ and b's power as ¼ and c's as ¼; but if any coalition is worse than no coalition, then surely a can use the fact that someone has to vote with her so as to offer very little to the other actors. As long as she offers enough then her power seems almost absolute.[5] For these reasons, many argue that measures of power in power indices that do not take account of preferences simply mis-specify the real power of actors.

The acute conceptual analysis of Peter Morriss (1987, 2002) can be brought to bear on this issue. Morriss makes a distinction between power as ableness and power as ability. Ability is the quality in an agent that makes them capable of doing something. Thus, it can be reduced to the resources they have at their disposal. Ableness is the position in which someone finds themselves and thus, in the voting case, should include the preferences of all the voters. One might simply make a conceptual distinction and suggest that using power indices preference-free leads to an account of 'power-as-ability' while using them whilst taking into account preferences leads to an account of 'power-as-ableness'. However, this apparently arcane dispute demonstrates a problem at the heart of power analysis, and also explains why power has had so little resonance in mainstream rational choice analysis.

ABLENESS AND ABILITY

In the example above if b and c really never vote together, then a can determine policy. This does seem to make a all-powerful; but, we should note, the source of a's power is the *fact* that b and c do not vote together. The differential in power between a and each of b and c's power resides in the latter's dispute. All three voters have the same voting resource. In that sense, it is within the power of b and c to reduce a's power. All they need to do is to form a coalition and they can together exclude a. It is their preferences – their all-abiding hatred of each other – that ensures that this does not occur. Brian Barry (1991) considers that voter a is lucky rather than all-powerful in this example. It is a's luck to be in a voting game with two other voters who, by their dispute, allow a to determine the result.[6] In terms of the ability-ableness distinction a's ability to determine the outcome does not proceed from anything in a. Why should we prefer to call a lucky rather than powerful? If one farmer prospers because the rain falls and the sunshine occurs at the right time, while another farmer's crops failed because the rain fell and sun shone at the wrong times, we would surely think the first lucky and the second unlucky. We would consider the second as having no power to determine whether his crops succeed (partly by the fact they failed) but surely the fact that the first farmer's crops succeeded does not make us think that he can determine their success. Rather we would decide the power each farmer has over success or failure to be given by the causal effects each could have on her crops. If, given climatic conditions, one succeeded because she planted at the right time, and one failed because he planted at the wrong time, then we might think one had more power than the other (due to knowledge perhaps) over the success and failure of their respective crops. Analogously then, we should not impute more power to a median voter simply because they determine the result, unless they have some power over the distribution of preferences. Hence we attribute luck.

Morriss equates luck with ableness power and further argues that power-as-ableness is more important than power-as-ability (Morriss 2002, p. xxxvii and p. 83). The reason is that he thinks that what we are interested in are what people can do, given the position they are in (including the preferences they or others have). In that claim he is surely right, though it does not follow that because what we are most interested in examining is the structure of society (or 'power structures') that we should call 'luck' a kind of power.

In my own work I have suggested that luck is 'systematic' when it non-contingently attaches to certain social locations (Dowding 1991, 1996). Thus, the median voter is lucky to be the median voter, but some people might be at the median non-contingently. If that is so through their own actions – voter a develops and ensures that both voter b and c continue their feud – then they have caused themselves to be median and it is through that cause that they are powerful. In this example, the power of voter a consists in the ability to ensure that b and c continue to feud. However, if the continued median position of voter a is non-contingent, but the cause lies outside of a's power, then a remains lucky, but systematically so. We can examine the structures that lead to this systematic luck. It is these structures that Morriss thinks we should be interested in.

Typically, when analyzing power structures we are interested in the resources that people do not have, since we are explicitly or implicitly comparing the powers of *classes* or *types* of people. Because of this it can be misleading to consider examples of token people; George, or Martha and so on. Typically the sorts of questions we ask in the social science are: what is the US President able to do when another party controls the legislature? How does his power differ from that of the French President under those same circumstances? Or, can institutions be designed to counteract the power of developers in local politics? Is the march of globalization inevitable? Many more factors enter into these considerations than whether someone will do their best or not to try to help the CIA (which is one of Morriss's examples 2002, pp. 77–79); and many of these factors involve the mechanisms that may (or may not) exist within the structures of the legislatures and the political systems of the respective countries (in the example of the Presidents), as well as considering the actions and reactions of the multitude of actors involved (in all the examples).

Morriss's arguments are directed almost exclusively to looking at a token individual's power. However, my focus is almost exclusively on examining the power structure of societies and thus on the power of types of actors. Thus part of what is an actor's ableness – their skill – 'is, of course, itself a dispositional term …' (Morriss 2002, p. 138). From the type-perspective however, we can assume that the unobservable elements such as 'skill' within a *type* are normally distributed across the set of actors within the type, and therefore we need not worry too much about this aspect of their resources. We may assume their luck is also normally distributed. It is only when we come to compare across types, that we become interested in relative resources and luck. Morriss has a very inductivist approach to understanding and truth. Time and again he suggests that we can only discover actors' true powers (and the dispositions of objects such as sugar) by experiment. Theoretically however, once we understand why salt dissolves in water we should be able to predict that substances with similar 'sub-visible' structures such as sugar will also dissolve in water. Demonstration in science and the social sciences is not always through experiment or empirical observation.[7] Morriss's inductivist and suppositionist approach leads him to discount realism and underlies his approach to the ability-ableness distinction.

REALISM AND RATIONAL CHOICE

Realism in the social sciences generally maintains that there are structures or mechanisms that underlie many social phenomena and in order to understand the processes that lead to the types of outcomes that emerge we need to understand those structures and mechanisms. Realism is often juxtaposed to quantitative methods in the social sciences, though it should only really be seen as critical for inductive quantitative methods. For that reason, rational choice theories and realism should make comfortable bedfellows as rational choice models institutions that structurally suggest courses of action to agents (Grafstein 1983, 1992; Dowding 1991, 1994). Institutions structurally suggest such courses of action to token individuals who are members of classes or types of people and we need to model those structures in terms of those types. If some types of people are advantaged by their social position – an advantage that may lead to gains even if they take no actions themselves (or even could take actions themselves) to bring about those gains, then those people gain advantages through systematic luck. If they use those positions to get further gains, then those positions are part of their agential power. They use their privileged position to gain further advantages. People can, of course, be systematically lucky and powerful (Dowding 2003). Nevertheless, systematic luck is designed to demonstrate the advantages that accrue to people through no active process on their part. Even the weak can be systematically lucky with regard to some of their wishes, if they non-contingently share preferences with others who act to bring about certain types of outcomes. Morriss calls this systematic luck 'passive power', and perhaps there is not much in a name. However, the fact that outcomes can be structured to the advantage of some, even if they do little to bring those outcomes about, might explain why, as the review in the early part of this chapter demonstrates, power plays only a small role in much of the rational choice literature.

If power is seen as power-as-ability then the power of an agent is given by what he could achieve no matter what others do. What he can achieve is, of course, structured by what others could do too. In that sense agents' power is then measured by the set of winning coalitions of which they are a member (Braham 2006) and is not measured by the set of coalitions that are most likely to form. When we examine existing societies we are generally interested in the coalitions that are most likely to form (or historically have formed) and thus are interested in questions that go beyond individual agential power. These questions can rightly be described as being about the power structure: but the power structure is also concerned with the distribution of luck, specifically systematic luck, as well as agential power. In game-theoretic terms, individual powers are modelled in game-forms; the actual struggles are modelled by game-theory. Since most of the rational choice accounts of political processes and institutions reviewed in the first part of the chapter model those struggles directly, they rarely find room for explicit accounts of power. The resources of the model agents are specified along with their preferences in order to solve games and provide predictions and explanation of social and political processes and social and political institutions. Rational choice is directly concerned with the power structure in many guises, though the literature rarely mentions the term 'power'.

NOTES

1 'Heresthetic' is a made-up term to contrast with rhetoric. The latter persuades people to change their minds, the former does not change preferences rather it puts together issue-dimensions to create new political cleavages.

2 More recently of course, central banks have been given more independence by democratic governments in order to underpin a credible response to inflationary pressures even when anti-inflationary policies are unpopular with the electorate.

3 I follow the common practice in agency models of referring to the principal as 'she' and the agent as 'he'.

4 Of course, this is an application of Black's (1948) median-voter theorem.

5 In fact ultimatum games played in the laboratory show that people rarely accept tiny amounts, but would sooner punish the powerful even if they make themselves worse off. Even if a was forced to offer $\frac{6}{10}$'s of the pie to b or c to get either to vote for her, then her power in terms of the fixed prize would be $\frac{6}{10}$ with probability 1, and b and c's would each be $\frac{4}{10}$ with probability ½ so equivalent to $\frac{2}{10}$. The preference-free analysis seems to get the wrong answer.

6 More carefully, the difference between a's power as a voting resource (1/3) and the fact she can determine the result with probability 1 constitutes her luck. So her luck is $1 - 1/3 = 2/3$.

7 Of course, in the sugar example, empirical demonstration may well be easier than theoretical demonstration! However, this is not so for all cases in the sciences or social sciences.

REFERENCES

Arrow, Kenneth J. (1952) *Social Choice and Individual Values*. New Haven: Yale University Press.

Banzhaf, J. E. (1965) 'Weighted voting doesn't work: A mathematical analysis', *Rutgers Law Review*, 19: 317–343.

Barry, Brian (1991) 'Is it better to be powerful or lucky?', in *Democracy and Power: Essays in Political Theory 1*. Oxford: Clarendon Press, 270–302.

Bates, Robert H. (1989) *Beyond the Miracle of the Market: The Political Economy of Agrarian Development in Kenya*. Cambridge: Cambridge University Press.

Bates, Robert H. (2001) *Prosperity and Violence: The Political Economy of Violence*. New York: W. W. Norton.

Black, Duncan (1948) 'On the rationale of group decision-making', *Journal of Political Economy*, 56: 23–34.

Braham, Matthew (2006) 'Measuring specific freedom', *Economics and Philosophy*, 22: 317–333.

Coleman, James S. (1971) 'Control of collectivities and the power of a collectivity to act', in B. Lieberman (ed), *Social Choice*. New York: Gordon and Breach.

Cox, Gary W. (1987) *The Efficient Secret*. Cambridge: Cambridge University Press.

Dowding, Keith (1991) *Rational Choice and Political Power*. Aldershot: Edward Elgar.

Dowding, Keith (1994) 'The compatibility of behaviouralism, rational choice and the "New Institutionalism"', *Journal of Theoretical Politics*, 6: 105–117.

Dowding, Keith (1996) *Power*. Milton Keynes: Open University Press.

Dowding, Keith (2003) 'Resources, power and systematic luck: A response to Barry', *Politics, Philosophy and Economics*, 2: 305–322.

Dowding, Keith (2006) 'Can populism be defended? William Riker, Gerry Mackie and the interpretation of democracy', *Government and Opposition*, 41 (3): 327–346.

Dowding, Keith and Martin van Hees (2008) 'In praise of manipulation', *British Journal of Political Science*, 38: 1–15.

Felsenthal Dan S. and Moshé Machover (1998) *The Measurement of Voting Power: Theory and Practice, Problems and Paradoxes*. Aldershot: Edward Elgar.

Felsenthal Dan S. and Moshé Machover (2005) 'Voting power measurement: A story of misreinvention', *Social Choice and Welfare*, 25 (2–3): 485–506.

Gibbard, Allan (1973) 'Manipulation of voting schemes: A general result', *Econometrica*, 41: 587–602.

Grafstein, Robert (1983) 'The social scientific interpretation of game theory', *Erkenntnis*, 20: 27–247.
Grafstein, Robert (1992) *Institutional Realism*. New Haven: Yale University Press.
Harsanyi, John C. (1969a) 'Measurement of social power, opportunity costs and the theory of two-person bargaining games', in R. Bell, D. V. Edwards and R. H. Wagner (eds), *Political Power: A Reader*. London: Collier-Macmillan.
Harsanyi, John C. (1969b) 'Measurement of social power in n-person reciprocal power situations', in R. Bell, D. V. Edwards, and R. H. Wagner (eds), *Political Power: A Reader*. London: Collier-Macmillan.
Hobbes, Thomas (1651) *Leviathan*. Harmondsworth: Penguin, (1968).
Huber, John D. and Charles R. Shipan (2002) *Deliberate Discretion? The Institutional Foundation of Bureaucratic Autonomy*. Cambridge: Cambridge University Press.
Knight, Jack (1992) *Institutions and Social Conflict*. Cambridge: Cambridge University Press.
Levi, Margaret (1988) *Of Rule and Revenue*. Berkeley: University of California Press.
Levi, Margaret (1997) *Consent, Dissent and Patriotism*. Cambridge: Cambridge University Press.
Mackie, Gerry (2003) *Democracy Defended*. Cambridge: Cambridge University Press.
McCubbins, Mathew D., Roger G. Noll and Barry R. Weingast (1987) 'Administrative procedures as instruments of political control', *Journal of Law Economics and Organization*, 3: 243–277.
McCubbins, Mathew D., Roger G. Noll and Barry R. Weingast (1989) 'Structure and process, politics and policy', *Virginia Law Review*, 75: 431–482.
McCubbins, Mathew D. and Thomas Schwartz (1984) 'Congressional oversight overlooked: Police patrols versus fire alarms', *American Journal of Political Science*, 28: 165–179.
McKelvey, Richard D. (1976) 'Intransitivities in multidimensional voting models and some implications for agenda control', *Journal of Economic Theory*, 12: 442–82.
Moe, Terry (2005) 'Power and political institutions', *Perspectives on Politics*, 3: 215–234.
Morriss, Peter (1987) *Power: A Philosophical Analysis*. Manchester: Manchester University Press.
Morriss, Peter (2002) *Power: A Philosophical Analysis*, 2nd edn. Manchester: Manchester University Press.
Niskanen, William A. (1994) *Bureaucracy and Public Economics*. Aldershot: Edward Elgar.
North Douglass C. (1981) *Structure and Change in Economic History*. New York: W. W. Norton.
North Douglass C. (1990) *Institutions, Institutional Change and Economic Performance*. Cambridge: Cambridge University Press.
North Douglass C. (2005) *Understanding the Process of Economic Change*. Princeton: Princeton University Press.
North Douglass C. and Barry R. Weingast (1989) 'Constitutions and commitment: The evolution of institutions governing public choice in seventeenth-century England', *Journal of Economic History*, 49 (4): 803–832.
Nozick, Robert (1974) *Anarchy, State and Utopia*. Oxford: Basil Blackwell.
Olson, Mancur (1971) *The Logic of Collective Action*. Harvard: Harvard University Press.
Olson, Mancur (2000) *Power and Prosperity: Outgrowing Communist and Capitalist Dictatorships*. New York: Basic Books.
Peltzman, Sam (1976) 'Towards a more general theory of regulation', *Journal of Law and Economics*, 19: 211–240.
Penrose, L. S. (1946) 'The elementary statistics of majority voting', *Journal of the Royal Statistical Society*, 109: 53–57.
Rasmusen, Eric (1989) *Games and Information: An Introduction to Game Theory*. Oxford: Basil Blackwell.
Rawls, John (1971) *A Theory of Justice*. Oxford: Oxford University Press.
Regenwetter, Michel, Bernard Grofman, A. A. J. Marley and Illa M. Tsetlin (2006) *Behavioral Social Choice: Probabilistic Models, Statistical Inference and Applications*. Cambridge: Cambridge University Press.
Riker, William H. (1962) *The Theory of Political Coalitions*. New Haven: Yale University Press.
Riker, William H. (1982) *Liberalism Against Populism: A Confrontation Between the Theory of Democracy and the Theory of Social Choice*. San Francisco: W. H. Freeman and Co.
Riker, William H. (1986) 'The first power index', *Social Choice and Welfare*, 3: 293–295.
Roemer, John E. (1982) *A General Theory of Exploitation and Class*. Cambridge: Cambridge University Press.
Roemer, John E. (1986) 'The mismarriage of bargaining theory and distributive justice', *Ethics*, 97: 88–110.
Roemer, John E. (1996) *Theories of Distributive Justice*, Boston, MA: Harvard University Press.
Rogers, James R. (2001) 'Information and judicial review: A signaling game of legislative-judicial interaction', *American Journal of Political Science*, 45 (1): 84–99.
Rogers, James R. and Georg Vanberg (2002) 'Judicial advisory opinions and legislative outcomes in comparative perspective', *American Journal of Political Science*, 46 (2): 379–397.

Roth, Alvin E. (ed) (1988) *The Shapley Value: Essays in Honor of Lloyd S. Shapley*. Cambridge: Cambridge University Press.
Sandler, Todd (1992) *Collective Action: Theory and Applications*. Ann Arbor: Michigan University Press.
Satterthwaite, Mark. (1975) 'Strategy proofness and Arrow's conditions', *Journal of Economic Theory*, 10:187–217.
Schofield, Norman (1983) 'Generic instability of majority rule', *Review of Economic Studies*, 50: 695–705.
Shapley, Lloyd S. (1953) 'A value for *n*-person games', in H. W. Kuhn and A. W. Tucker (eds), *Contributions to the Theory of Games II (Annals of Mathematics Studies 28)*: Princeton: Princeton University Press.
Shapley, Lloyd S. and Martin Shubik (1954) 'A method for evaluating the distribution of power in a committee system', *American Political Science Review*, 48: 787–792.
Shepsle, Kenneth A. (1979) 'Institutional arrangements and equilibrium in multidimensional voting models', *American Journal of Political Science*, 23: 27–59.
Shepsle, Kenneth A. (1981) 'Structure-induced equilibrium and legislative choice', *Public Choice*, 37 (3): 503–519.
Stigler, George C. (1971) 'The theory of economic regulation', *Bell Journal of Economics and Management Science*, 2: 160–167.

3

Power and Liberalism

Peter Morriss

INTRODUCTION

Power is a concept that has recently been used primarily by political scientists and political sociologists, not political philosophers. I will argue that that is unfortunate; political philosophers should pay more attention to the concept of power, as it plays an important role in liberal political theory.

Liberalism can be characterized by three core elements: individualism, equality and rationalism.[1] Individualism has many elements, but the one most significant here is that individuals are seen as the most *important* beings in society. This, when combined with the belief in the equal moral worth of individuals, produces an 'ultimate moral principle of the supreme and intrinsic value, or dignity, of the individual human being'.[2] Morality is, then, concerned principally with the well-being and right treatment of individuals; and – crucially for political philosophy – societies are to be judged by how (ordinary) individuals fare. In pre-liberal times, a society was judged (at least in secular terms) by its richness or its populousness or its extent, with the most praised societies being the great empires of history; now we look not at the qualities of the society itself, or of the state, but at how it treats its populace. Morality is defined, as it were, from the individual outwards.

There is a further important consequence of combining these three core ideas. When we combine a belief in human equality and in rationality, we come to the conclusion that we *all* have reason; and so we *all* can use it to solve our problems. We think that each and every one of us has sufficient reason to understand at least his or her own life. This belief has descriptive and normative components. The descriptive aspect is that, since you have reason, you must be considered to be in control of your own life – to be able to determine (more or less) how it goes. What each of us makes of their life, then, is up to him or her; for we are rational actors, not puppets on strings or playthings of the gods.[3] As a consequence, each person can be held responsible for his or her actions.[4] The normative version of this view gives us a picture of the ideal human life: in it, an individual takes control of his or her own life, choosing what sort of life they are going to lead – what sort of person, indeed, they are going to be. Constraints that stop you living *your* life should be minimized.

There are two aspects of this that I wish to stress. The first is the familiar emphasis on liberty.[5] That this is important to the liberal is clear from the etymology of the words: as one liberal put it, a liberal believes in liberty, just as a nudist believes in nudity.[6] It is important to the liberal both that no person is forced to be a sort of person that she does not want to be (for instance, forced into a role that she would not choose), and that every person should be as free as possible to do or be whatever they should choose.

The second is perhaps less familiar. It is the view that we should maximize what we are able to do (or be). However free we may be, we are not flourishing human beings if we are starving to death. Since it is individuals that matter, it matters what those individuals can do. The more that they can do, the better.

A society, then, can fail in one (or both) of two ways. It can be a tyranny, and allow its subjects no freedom to live their lives the way that they choose. Or it can be unsupportive, and do nothing to foster the prospects of its inhabitants, so that they have nothing to choose *between*. Liberals condemn societies that fail in either of these ways.[7]

In the last thirty years or so, analytic political philosophers have done much excellent work on the concept of freedom. I will look here at two of the best recent books on freedom: those by Ian Carter and Matthew Kramer.[8] But, careful and thorough as these authors are, I will suggest that their accounts of freedom can be improved by paying more attention to the similarities and differences between freedom and power.

Two preliminary points on what I will here understand by power.[9] We must distinguish between 'power over' (another person), and 'power to' (bring something about). 'Power to' is the more general concept; the core one. What we have the power to do *may* be to kick others around (or harm their interests, or get them to do something they didn't want to do), and then we might say that we have power *over* them. But we also have the power to do things that do *not* involve harming others. Hence 'power to' is the more basic notion.

Further, if you have the power to do something, then you are able to do it: a power is, then, a sort of ability.[10] My concern in this article will be how the claim that you are able to do something (or unable to do it) relates conceptually to the claim that you are free (unfree) to do it.[11] I shall do this by first discussing (aspects of) the accounts of freedom offered by Carter and Kramer.

IAN CARTER'S ACCOUNT OF FREEDOM

Carter does not discuss the relationship between freedom and power; nor does he offer a definition of freedom. However, it seems to me that by 'freedom' he means almost exactly what I mean by 'power'. This seems, on the face of it, odd: we normally think that 'freedom' and 'power' are distinct concepts, even if related ones. We would not expect a revolutionary movement to inscribe 'Power, Equality, Fraternity' on their banners; nor would anyone have written a book called *The Freedom Elite*.[12] Exactly *what* the differences are between freedom and power will be explored later. Here, I will (first) briefly show how Carter is really discussing power, and then show how that creates some problems for his account of freedom.

Carter mentions the relationship between freedom and power only in a couple of asides.[13] When setting out the plan of the book, Carter says that his account of freedom will be 'compatible...with the idea of freedom as ability',[14] and later (albeit in a specific context) he claims that a distinction between unfreedom and inability is 'not necessary' for his purposes.[15]

More compelling is the account of freedom that Carter develops. His thesis is that 'the extent of my freedom is a function of the extent of action available to me'[16] – that is, what I can do, or have the power to do (or bring about). Further, whilst many writers have considered that one is only unfree if rendered unable to do something by some specific sort of constraint, Carter adopts an agnostic position on which constraints matter.

Much of Carter's analysis of freedom employs concepts and distinctions with which I would agree.[17] But there is an important difference. One of the main aims of Carter's book is to argue against (what he calls) the *specific freedom thesis*. This thesis has three parts, one of which (the only one I will here be concerned with) is the *normative* specific freedom thesis. This thesis seems to me probably to involve several distinct claims, but undoubtedly one of them (and a central one) is the claim that the value of our freedom is determined by 'the value we attach to the specific things [we are] free to do'.[18] Carter denies this claim. Carter thinks that there is 'an interest people have in freedom itself':[19] that at least part of the value of freedom is separate from the value of the things we are free to do. Put somewhat rhetorically: 'the love of liberty can be something more than just the love of being free to do certain specific things'.[20] Therefore Carter supports the *non*specific freedom thesis. (From now on I will call this the 'nonspecific value thesis', which better captures its content.)

This perhaps sounds plausible, at least initially. By contrast, I hold to what might be called the *specific power thesis*: that the value of your power is indeed determined by the value we attach to the specific things you have the power to do. I think that this also sounds plausible. Valuing power somehow *for its own sake* seems like a character defect (as is a miser's valuing money for its own sake); also, we would not tend to talk approvingly in an analogous way of 'the love of power...'. This would seem to suggest that maybe there is a larger difference between power and freedom than Carter has realized. I will return to that suggestion later; but here I want to analyse in more detail Carter's own argument for the nonspecific value thesis, and suggest that it is weaker than Carter thinks.

Carter usefully distinguishes four ways in which freedom might have *nonspecific* value (that is, value over and above the specific things that can be brought about). One of these – that freedom has unconditional value – is a claim that Carter thinks that liberals should not make, and so I will not consider it here. Another – that freedom has intrinsic value – Carter seems unsure about: his conclusion is the weak one that whilst it is 'difficult to argue for [it], it is no less difficult to argue against'.[21] Part of the problem here, as Carter points out, is that it is difficult to *argue*, as opposed to just *asserting*, that something has *intrinsic* value – and assertions should have little philosophical validity. Hence Carter's discussion of intrinsic value is brief.[22]

What Carter does argue for, at some length, is that freedom has *nonspecific instrumental* value: that is to say, it 'is a means to some other valuable phenomenon', 'without regard to the nature of its specific value'.[23] (This is in addition to freedom's undoubted *specific* instrumental value.) Freedom is *non*specifically instrumentally valuable because, thanks to our ignorance and fallibility, 'we are not *sure* about the value of the various options'.[24]

To illustrate this, Carter offers an analogy with money, which is valuable not (only) because it allows us to buy certain, specified, things, 'but also as a means to satisfying *whatever* our future desires may turn out to be'.[25]

But this claim, whilst true, seems too weak to support the nonspecific value thesis. For if this was the only reason we valued freedom, it would *not* be true to say that the value of freedom is separate from the value of the things we are free to do. Instrumental value is *precisely* value of this sort. Suppose that you are free to have ice-cream or yogurt, but not both; and that at present you prefer, and would choose, ice-cream. Having the freedom to get yogurt might then seem worthless, as you wouldn't choose it and therefore will never get it: you are no better off *with* the option for yogurt than without it. But, Carter's argument goes, you *are* better off having the yogurt-option because (and in so far as) you might come to change your mind (or discover some facts that lead you to re-evaluate the comparative worth of ice-cream and yogurt). Since you know that that always *might* happen (for any two alternatives), you are always better off having as wide a range of options as possible. In *that* sense, freedom is valuable, and so is power. But it is, to repeat, *only* valuable because of some value that the unchosen option might (come to) have; if it is (somehow) intrinsically valueless (or certain to be valueless), the freedom/power to get it is itself valueless. (I shall qualify this statement later.[26])

Perhaps another way of looking at this is to realize that Carter's statement, quoted earlier, that 'we are not sure about the value of the various options',[27] is ambiguous: as Carter wrote it, there are two ways of reading 'we'. The first reading (which I think is Carter's) is that the 'we' refers to the actor(s) whose freedom/power we are considering.[28] As Carter realizes, this produces a well-known problem in evaluating freedom, or power – a problem that has particularly exercised economists. If the actor prefers some X to Y, she will always choose X; she will never choose Y; therefore she will never get any value from Y; therefore she will be no worse off if that choice is removed. Indeed, we can generalize over *all* outcomes, and say that actors will never be any worse off if all unchosen outcomes are not part of their choice-set: we only get value from what we do (or get), not what we don't do (or get). Unused options are then always valueless.

There are two standard ways out of this problem. One is to suggest (as Carter does) that your unchosen options are still valuable because you might change your mind. The second is to claim that we may not be interested (exclusively) in the *actor*'s evaluation of the outcomes; the 'we' in Carter's sentence might refer, not to the actor(s), but to the observers or analysts. *Political philosophers* might, for instance, think that it is very important that you can get yogurt, even if you never choose it; it is important because it makes a big difference to how we evaluate your society whether you have an unhealthy diet because you choose it, or because it is the only one available to you. It matters because *political philosophers* think it matters, even if you don't. If we are willing to allow that sometimes our valuation of the outcomes can (legitimately) not follow the actors' evaluations, then we can certainly put a value on unchosen outcomes. If we do, the instrumental value of freedom/power is real, but it is always *specific* instrumental value.

The final argument that Carter offers for the nonspecific freedom thesis is that freedom can have (nonspecific) *constitutive* value. An example of this is a famous one of Sen's: a religious (or political) believer might want to go on a fast (or hunger-strike), but it is a logical truth that he could only fast if the possibility of eating is open to him, and is rejected: to fast is not to starve involuntarily. Therefore a rejected alternative can be valuable because it changes the nature of the outcome that is chosen: changes it to a *chosen* outcome, rather than one that would have occurred anyway. However, this particular example will not do for Carter, as he acknowledges, because it is an example of *specific* constitutive value (specific to this outcome), and Carter requires *non*specific constitutive value. As Carter puts it, he requires that 'freedom is valuable because human agency is valuable'.[29] Carter endorses this rather weakly.[30] However, Carter here seems to overlook the distinction that he holds to elsewhere, between 'freedom to act' and 'free action':

> When we talk of 'free action' [or 'acting freely'] we refer to freedom as a property of actions, whereas when we talk of 'freedom to act' we refer to freedom as a property of agents.[31]

Carter's book is concerned with freedom to act, not free action; yet the value being endorsed here would seem to be that of free action.

One might think that there is another argument that Carter could use to support the nonspecific value thesis: freedom is nonspecifically valuable because choice is valuable in itself. That is, you might care more that it is *your* choice whether you get ice-cream or yogurt than you care about which dessert you actually get. Carter (to my surprise) does not discuss this view. He does, however, have a brief discussion[32] of a somewhat similar claim by L. Crocker, who associated freedom with the 'autonomy complex'.[33] Crocker's argument was that it is important that we should be able to engage in 'behaviour which we value', even when the consequences are 'unfortunate'; such valuable behaviour includes 'risk-taking, holding to principle [and] sacrificing'.[34] Carter thinks that this won't quite do for his purposes, since these 'are all *specific* kinds of behaviour'.[35] But that surely misunderstands his own thesis (or, at least, the version of it which I am here discussing). The thesis is not about nonspecific kinds of *behaviour* (or actions); it is to separate the value of freedom from the value of *outcomes*. If risk-taking (etc.) is valuable, then it is completely nonspecific as to the outcomes for which the risks are being taken (or, indeed, the unwelcome outcomes that will eventuate if the risky actions go wrong). It seems to me that this argument is an important one that Carter underplays.[36]

MATTHEW KRAMER'S ACCOUNT OF FREEDOM

Unlike Carter, Kramer is crystal clear about the relationship between freedom and ability (power). Kramer's argument is based on two 'postulates', the first of which is

F postulate: A person is free to Φ if and only if he is able to Φ. [37]

Nevertheless, Kramer wants to distinguish between freedom and ability, or rather between *un*freedom and mere *in*ability. (Almost every time Kramer writes 'inability' he feels the need to append the adjective 'mere'.) For Kramer, only *some* constraints that render you unable to do something also render you unfree to do it. I will first discuss Kramer's reasons for distinguishing at all between unfreedom and inability; I will then turn to *how* he distinguishes between them.

Despite the title of his book, Kramer is concerned at least as much with *un*freedom as with freedom. (Much the same could also be said of Carter.) And he wants your unfreedom to be narrower than your inabilities, because (he thinks) the latter are infinite, and therefore we cannot meaningfully compare the extent of two people's inabilities.[38] Consequently, Kramer wants to be able to say, of many (most) of the things that you are unable to do, that you are nevertheless not unfree to do them. Of course, you are not *free* to do them either (refer back to the F Postulate). There is then, for freedom, a threefold classification: there are things you are free to do, things you are unfree to do, and things that you are not free to do but not unfree to do either. For power (ability) there is only a twofold classification: you either can do them or you cannot.

This three-fold classification is required because Kramer does not want your unfreedoms to be infinite. But why not? The answer to that is perhaps the least satisfactory part of Kramer's book. Kramer seems to assume that any assessment of what he calls your overall freedom must involve a ratio: the numerator is a measure of those things you are free to do, and the denominator should include those things you are unfree to do. We cannot allow the denominator of the ratio to be necessarily infinite, as then the ratio itself will be necessarily zero.[39] Kramer thinks that it would not be helpful to have to say that everybody's overall freedom was necessarily zero. Hence, for this approach to work, and if our inabilities are indeed infinite, we require our unfreedoms to consist of some (finite) subset of our inabilities.

I want to make three quick comments on this line of argument. The first is that Kramer doesn't consider what we might mean by overall *power* (ability). If overall *freedom* is such a ratio, why isn't overall *power*? If overall power is defined analogously to overall freedom, then we have exactly the problem that Kramer wants to avoid: the unhelpful conclusion that everybody's overall power is necessarily zero. So we will have to adopt some different approach to 'overall power'. Why, then, should we not adopt the same approach, whatever it is, to the closely related concept of overall freedom?

Secondly, there is something paradoxical in the claim that freedom is a ratio of this sort. What I will here call the 'ratio approach' to freedom is adopted by both Carter and Kramer, and originated with Hillel Steiner, who represented 'freedom' as the ratio $F/(F+U)$, where F and U stand for a measure of the actions that the actor is free and unfree to perform, respectively.[40] The paradox arises because $(F+U)$ is not fixed: technological advances can increase the range of actions open to us (that is, $F+U$). Now suppose that, at present, your F is 10 and U is 90, so that your 'overall freedom' is 0.1. And suppose that a possible technological advance increases by 1 the value of the actions which you are free to do (whilst having no detrimental affect on the ones you were free to do previously); but this advance increases by 20 the measure of those actions you are *unfree* to do. Then your freedom has increased but your 'overall' freedom has simultaneously *de*creased.[41] It is not at all clear to me why the ratio should matter more than the absolute value of F. (After all, the reason that F has been chosen as the appropriate letter for use in the formula is that it represents your freedom.) If we *really* valued your freedom (and nothing else) would we not welcome this technological 'advance', which increases the things you are free to do?

Steiner responds to this objection (which he himself produced) as follows:

> The problem with this objection is that it confuses liberty with ability. If this is a proper conception of liberty at all, it is certainly not the one which concerns us as political philosophers. Liberty is a social relation, a relation between persons. The restraints imposed upon us by nature, and our struggles and successes in overcoming them, are subjects deserving of our closest attention. But it is not to physicists, doctors or engineers whom we turn in seeking answers to the question of 'How free?' For while it is undoubtedly true that the average member of an advanced society is able to do, and unrestrained from doing, many more actions than his counterparts in less advanced societies, it is equally true that he is able to do, but

> restrained from doing, many more actions than they. That is, there are many more actions which he is *unfree* to do. Simply to ignore them in estimating the extent of a person's liberty, is to misconstrue the object of such an exercise.[42]

But there are many ways of 'not ignoring' unfreedom, other than by constructing a ratio. I will suggest one such later. Given this, the 'ratio approach' requires far more supporting argument than it has hitherto received.[43]

Thirdly, Kramer adopts here a quite misguided approach to the analysis of concepts. His argument is that we want to measure freedom by a ratio of the sort described, and therefore we construct the concept so that we *can* produce such a measure. Now we can certainly create *a* concept like this, but we will have no idea whether the concept is one that covers what we want to cover by 'freedom'. If we call it 'Concept X', we have no problem. But if we want to call our new concept 'freedom' (as Kramer does), then we have to pay more attention to whether it works *as* a concept of freedom. To do this, we have to start from the other end. We have to work out what we want the concept of freedom to do: *why* it is an important part of our vocabulary. Exploring this will allow us to start creating a concept that we can be fairly sure is indeed a concept of freedom. When we have elaborated this concept, we can work out how to measure it. It may be that we can measure it by using a ratio; or it may be that we cannot produce a measure of freedom at all, but at least we will know that we have a concept of *freedom*, and not a mysterious Concept X.

It is now time to look at *how* Kramer distinguishes unfreedom from (mere) inabilities. He does this in his second postulate:

> U postulate: A person is unfree to Φ if and only if both of the following conditions obtain: (1) he would be able to Φ in the absence of the second of these conditions; and (2) irrespective of whether he actually endeavours to Φ, he is directly or indirectly prevented from Φ-ing by some action(s) or some disposition(s)-to-perform-some-action(s) on the part of some other person(s).[44]

Now there is much going on in this Postulate that I cannot discuss here, but what Kramer is basically arguing for is the familiar view that for you to be unfree, you must be rendered unable *by some other person* (rather than by a natural occurrence or by your own choice). As we will see, Kramer considers that the required human intervention does not have to be a *deliberate* interference with your ability: an inadvertent one will do.

However, Kramer does have a problem to cope with. His distinction between an unfreedom and a (mere) inability is a dichotomous one: you are either unfree (to do some action, at some time, etc.), or you are merely unable. Yet the intervention that renders you unable/unfree may be a mixture of human and natural forces, and that fact may tempt us to consider that you are therefore a *bit* unfree and a *bit* unable. Kramer thinks that we should resist this temptation: such hybrid interventions must either produce cases of fully fledged unfreedoms or not produce unfreedoms at all. Kramer plumps for the alternative that hybrid interventions *do* create unfreedoms, so that 'even a tiny contribution by the actions of some person P to an inability of some other person Q is enough to warrant our designating that inability as an unfreedom'.[45]

Let us consider Kramer's discussion of variants of an example which is familiar in the literature.

Scenario 1
You are in a cave, and your enemy, seizing his opportunity, rolls a large boulder over the only entrance, trapping you inside so that you are unable to leave. This action, standardly, makes you *unfree* as well as unable. Kramer agrees: your 'countless new inabilities are unfreedoms rather than mere inabilities'.[46]

Scenario 2
You are in the same cave, and are trapped inside by the same boulder. But this time the boulder was pushed there by a falling tree, which itself was blown over by a strong gust of wind. As this does not involve any human intervention, it renders you 'merely' unable to leave, and not unfree to leave. (But see Scenario 5, below, for some difficulties that Kramer has with falling trees.)

Scenario 3
This is like Scenario 2, except that the reason that the tree fell – pushing the boulder and thus causing you to be trapped – was that it was cut down by a local woodman (or even knocked over inadvertently by a passing hiker) who was quite unaware that you were in the cave (and, indeed, quite unaware of your very existence). Your resulting inabilities are, for Kramer, unfreedoms, since a human intervention is causally responsible for them. The responsibility at issue here, Kramer thinks, is causal and not moral: he thinks that we are not interested in whether the human intervener should be *blamed* for your incarceration, merely whether he did cause it.[47]

Scenario 4
As Scenario 2, except that, as the boulder rolls down the hill (given impetus by the tree blown down by the wind, with no person within miles), it hits an obelisk, erected some centuries ago. Bouncing off the obelisk, the boulder comes to rest at the mouth of the cave, trapping you inside. If the obelisk had never been erected, the boulder would not have hit it, and would therefore have taken a different path, not ending up at the mouth of the cave, and so you would not have been trapped. The existence of this obelisk is, then, causally necessary to your being trapped. 'Therefore, because the presence of [the obelisk] was a product of someone else's actions, the incapacitation amounts to an array of unfreedoms rather than to an array of mere inabilities'.[48]

Now this seems to me as close as one could get to a *reductio ad absurdum* of Kramer's position. Why on earth should it matter if the boulder bounced off an obelisk, rather than off an identically-shaped piece of rock (naturally produced)? But Kramer does not see this argument as a *reductio*; he is perfectly happy with it. Thus he claims, immediately before introducing this example, 'that the trammels in question derive from human interrelationships and that they are therefore [*sic*] of special interest to political philosophers'.[49] Unfortunately, Kramer gives not a hint why a political philosopher (or, indeed, anybody else) should be concerned in the slightest as to whether the object that the boulder bounced off was, or was not, put there, centuries earlier, by somebody. Our concepts should be designed to capture distinctions that are of some importance to us; I am quite at a loss to understand what of any importance is being distinguished here.

Scenario 5
To indicate that this is not an isolated aberration, here is another of Kramer's examples.[50]

A large tree is blown down in a gale, blocking a nearby road, so that motorists can no longer drive along the road. Are these motorists unfree? Well, says Kramer,

> A tree growing on a parcel of land adjacent to a road has very likely been planted by some human being(s) in the past.... . If so, then the curtailment of the freedom of motorists by the toppling of the tree into the highway is an increase in the unfreedom of each motorist affected. Each motorist is unfree, rather than merely not free [i.e., unable], to drive past the point at which the tree is blocking the road. The planting of the tree, which was a human action, was a but-for cause of the tree's subsequent tumble onto the highway, even if those two events were separated by many decades.[51]

On the other hand – presumably – if the seed that grew into the tree was excreted in that spot by some passing bird, then the falling tree would *not* affect the motorists' freedom. So, on Kramer's account, we cannot tell whether the motorists (and you, in your cave) are or are not unfree, until we know whether the tree that was blown over happened to grow from a seed dropped a century ago by a bird or a person. It is difficult to think of a clearer counter-example to a philosophical thesis.

FREEDOM AND POWER

So how *do* freedom and power differ? I think that Steiner, Carter and Kramer are right to stress the importance, in any analysis, of *un*freedom. But, having correctly realized its importance, they mistake what that importance *is*. For it is *not* that the more things we are unfree to do, the less overall freedom we have. The relationship is, I think, a quite different one.

Let us start by considering Kramer's (important) claims that your *freedoms* are co-extensive with your *powers*, and, secondly, that your *un*freedoms are only a subset of those outcomes you lack the power to bring about.[52] I have criticized the reasons Kramer offered for this second claim; but let us suppose (as most writers do) that the claim is correct. Then *why* should we be concerned to draw a distinction between two different sorts of things we lack the power to do? Why should we have a concept in our vocabulary that does this? We create our concepts for a *reason* (or reasons), and it is always legitimate – and usually instructive – to enquire what these reasons are.[53]

One familiar reason (discussed and rejected by the writers I've been considering) is that our unfreedoms are those things that we could otherwise do, but are *wrongly* prevented from doing, whilst things that we are *justifiably* prevented from doing shouldn't be considered as unfreedoms. This has been called, following Jerry Cohen, a 'moralized' definition of freedom.[54] This term has stuck, although, as we shall see, I think that it is unhelpful. Carter, amongst many others (including Cohen), rejects the moralized definition of freedom. 'Does the justly imprisoned thief in a high-security prison not lack the freedom to leave?' he asks, rhetorically.[55] And he is, of course, right. The simple claim that rightful interferences do not limit freedom is incorrect. At least, it is incorrect as a matter of linguistic fact about what (most of us) think are core instances of unfreedom.

Yet there would seem to be a sense in which Carter must think that freedom *is* a moralized concept. Carter, after all, claims that freedom has a nonspecific *value*: it is valuable, over and above the value of the things which we are free to do. Freedom, then, for Carter is not morally neutral:[56] although there can be justified restrictions to your freedom, such restrictions, at the very least *require* justification. Absent justification, they are unjustified. There is, then, an underlying moral component in the liberal conception of freedom,[57] which there is not in the liberal conception of power.

What might that be? I think that Kramer is right that 'freedom' implies taking a view on the *constraints* that prevent us from doing things.[58] After all, when we talk about freedom, we often talk about what we are free or unfree *from*.[59] This is reflected in MacCallum's rightly influential 'triadic' conception of freedom.[60] The reason that we make a distinction between things we are free to do and things we are able to do (and conversely, and more importantly, between things we are unfree to do and things we are unable to do) is that certain constraints *matter* more than other constraints. (Why *else* would we make this distinction?) 'Freedom' is a concept that concerns itself with the constraints that matter, as opposed to those that don't matter. The reason that Kramer's examples fail (those of the boulder bouncing off the obelisk [rather than a rock] and the blown-down tree having been planted by a person [rather than a bird]) is that the distinctions he draws do not matter.[61]

So what constraints do matter? Some (including Kramer) have thought that it matters whether the constraint has been introduced by a person or by nature. The reason it matters, presumably, is that we can rail against people in a way that we cannot rail against nature. As Stanley Benn has pointed out,

> because the concept of personal freedom is most at home in the context of complaints, grievances, claims, and justifications, th[e] distinction [between being unfree and being unable] clarifies when someone's inability to Φ will sustain at most a *regret* that he cannot do it, and when it can properly be the subject of a *complaint* that he is unfree to do it.[62]

If this is right, it reinforces my earlier thought that Kramer has drawn his distinctions in the wrong places: I suppose you might, when trapped in the cave by the bouncing boulder, mutter something like 'bloody stupid place to leave an obelisk' – but I doubt if you would mean it as a serious *complaint*. Rather, you would rue your ill fate.

Avichai Margalit has written a book that starts from the interesting idea that '[a] decent society is one whose institutions do not humiliate people'.[63]

> Humiliation is any sort of behavior or condition that constitutes a sound reason for a person to consider his or her self-respect injured.
> This is a normative rather than a psychological sense of humiliation.
> ...
> Only humans can produce humiliation, although they need not actually have any humiliating intent. There can be no humiliation without humans to bring it about, but there can be humiliation without humiliators, in the sense that the people causing the humiliation did not intend to do so.[64]

The constraints that we focus on when considering freedoms are those that humiliate.[65]

A similar emphasis has also been suggested by Cohen. In considering an argument by Jo Wolff,[66] Cohen argues that restrictions on liberty matter, even when they have no effect on what you can and cannot do, because 'it is an *insult to the status of persons* when certain acts are forbidden to them'.[67] I think that that is correct: it points to *why* freedom matters. It also points to why freedom might have nonspecific value, whilst power has not: freedom has this value because it includes (only) constraints that humiliate or insult our status.[68] Note that this is *not* a moralized conception of freedom, in Cohen's sense: certain instances of these constraints may well be justified, so the prisoner is still unfree when justly imprisoned.

I want finally to make four quick points that follow from this analysis, although I do not have the space here to develop them as they should be developed.

(I) To some extent, we all disagree about what constraints *do* humiliate or insult; that is to say, we disagree about moral philosophy. The Stoics claimed that being confined to a cell was of no consequence, as one could still think; if we agree that imprisonment is not humiliating or insulting or a cause for a grievance, then we would (presumably) not regard your being locked in a jail cell as a diminution of your freedom. But note that the *actor's* beliefs (or victim's beliefs, in this case) are *not* the relevant ones, because, as many have argued, you are just as unfree (or free) to do something even if you have no desire whatsoever to do it. The relevant values are *ours* – the people who make (and deny) claims *about* freedom: it is the people who *use* the concept who draw the boundaries, and they draw them where *they* want to draw them. Hence you and I could disagree as to whether Freda was unfree or 'merely' unable to do something, even though we agree on all the facts about Freda (including subjunctive ones); we disagree because we disagree on which constraints (should) matter.

I think this explains Cohen's puzzlement that some writers (usually, but not always, on the Right) have not seen lack of money as a relevant constraint when considering freedom.[69] It is undoubtedly the case that, in a capitalist society, you cannot board an airplane to (say) Rome if you haven't bought a ticket; and some people are too poor to be able to afford such a ticket.[70] Such people are unable to fly to Rome; but are they unfree to do so? Well, it may be that, living in a capitalist society, capitalist values are so engrained in us that we do *not* find it insulting or humiliating when ticketless poor people are denied access to airplanes. That you need to buy a ticket for an airplane seems, to many, as much a fact of the world as that to get on the plane you need to get through the door (and therefore someone who weighs 60 stone, and cannot physically squeeze on to the airplane, is unable but not unfree to fly). Now to see this as a *fact* is, of course, to take an ideological view (in the Marxist sense) of the 'naturalness' of a capitalist economy; an ideological view that Cohen certainly does not share. Yet, for those who *do* accept the ideology – for whom it is part of their background assumptions of appropriate behaviour – to be denied a service for which one hasn't paid is not humiliating or insulting.

In short, there is no *objective* truth about where one should draw the line between constraints that matter and constraints that don't matter. Those in thrall to capitalist assumptions can legitimately believe that lack of money is not, by itself, an unfreedom-creating constraint; Cohen can legitimately believe the opposite.

(II) Constraints matter, I have argued, in so far as they insult or humiliate. Constraints also matter because they *constrain*: but that is adequately captured by saying that they render you *unable* to do the thing in question. Yet constraints can insult even when they *don't* constrain: for instance, when you were unable to do the thing in any case. Hence, the first part of Kramer's U Postulate is mistaken: you can be unfree even when you are in any case unable. Thus suppose that you are able to speak Irish, but the (imperialist British) government ruling Ireland prevents you from doing so; this, uncontentiously, makes you unfree to speak Irish. Now suppose that you are actually *un*able to speak Irish, but, if you could, the tyrannical government would prevent it. You are now living under a constraint that is *exactly* as humiliating as before. (That now the edict does *not* stop you doing something you could do has precisely no relevance.) Since we are not here considering what you can and cannot do, but we are considering which of the constraints under which you live are humiliating ones, we can easily have a humiliating constraint that hurts even when it has no limiting effects. So unfreedom is not a subset of inability; it is a different concept altogether.[71]

For what it's worth, this seems readily to fit ordinary usage: even when we are unable to do something, we can still be described as either free[72] or unfree[73] to do it. Indeed, your lack of freedom to do something which you cannot currently do, may well dissuade you from acquiring the required ability: when women were not free to practise medicine, that constraint provided a strong disincentive to their trying to gain the required competence.

(III) Constraints matter, I have argued, in so far as they insult or humiliate. But that may mean that it matters who or what is doing the constraining. Cohen suggests this in his rebuttal of Wolff:

> So why is it worse for the state to forbid me access to, say, Glasgow, than for the railway company to do so? Because the former involves a judgment on my status, and the latter doesn't.[74]

If this is right (and I think it is), then looking solely at the extent of an actor's freedom and unfreedom, and ignoring altogether by *whom* she is made unfree, misses something very important.

(IV) There is a final, and very different, reason why the current focus by political philosophers on freedom rather than power is unfortunate, particularly when freedom is analysed along Carter/Kramer lines. This is that it ignores altogether what I am *unable*, but not unfree, to do. This is not defensible. To return for the last time to the cave example, it is quite inappropriate to describe your inability to escape from the cave as *merely* an inability: it is probably of crucial and immediate importance. We should rescue you. If we can rescue you, but don't bother,[75] we are doing serious wrong.[76] And it makes no difference whether your inability to leave the cave is or is not also an unfreedom: the inability may be a *far* more important consideration.[77]

The same is true of societies. Society A may imprison a few dissidents, whilst also striving hard, and successfully, to ensure that the rest of the population flourishes. Society B may imprison nobody, whilst also doing nothing to look after the citizens' welfare, with the result that many starve.[78] The liberal should criticize both, even though only Society A is infringing freedoms.[79] Freedom is not all that matters. Liberals should be vehement in condemning a society that does nothing to enable people to flourish, but instead lets them die. (On a global scale, this censure can, of course, currently be addressed to *all* rich societies.)[80] It is not difficult to argue that a concern about people's inabilities (or lack of power) is far more important than a concern about their unfreedoms. Political philosophers should pay the concept more attention.

ACKNOWLEDGEMENT

I am grateful to Ian Carter, Jerry Cohen and Hillel Steiner for sending me unpublished work, and discussing their ideas with me; between them, they have saved me from many mistakes and, alas, I am sure they have not saved me from many more. I seem to be both able and free to make mistakes.

NOTES

1 For a defence of this claim, and a more extended account of it, see P. Morriss, *Contemporary Political Philosophy* (unpublished) Chap. 1: Liberalism – available from me on request. See also A. Arblaster, *The Rise and Decline of Western Liberalism* (Oxford: Blackwell, 1984).

2 S. Lukes, *Individualism* (Oxford: Blackwell, 1973) p. 45. Lukes's book remains the best account of individualism.

3 The discipline of sociology, which tends to focus on how much we are subject to the constraints of social forces, is then in considerable tension with liberal assumptions.

4 Apart from special cases, such as children or the insane – but these *are* special cases.

5 Like most recent writers (but not all: see, for instance, J. Wolff, 'Freedom, Liberty and Property', *Critical Review* 11 [1997] pp. 345–357), I will treat the words 'liberty' and 'freedom' as synonyms.

6 M. Cranston, *Freedom* (Third edition; London: Longmans, Green, 1967) p. 47.

7 Doubtless these two demands may sometimes be in tension, so that one has to be sacrificed for the other. I will not explore that complication here.

8 I. Carter, *A Measure of Freedom* (Oxford: Oxford University Press, 1999), hereafter Carter, *Freedom*; M.H. Kramer, *The Quality of Freedom* (Oxford: Oxford University Press, 2003), hereafter Kramer, *Freedom*.

9 For my full account of power, see P. Morriss, *Power: A Philosophical Analysis* (Second edition; Manchester: Manchester University Press, 2002; originally 1987), hereafter Morriss, *Power*.

10 The full story is, of course, far more complicated. See Morriss, *Power*, particularly Parts I and II.

11 By 'to do something' I include 'to be something or get something or bring about some end' – but it will not be important in this article exactly what the *content* of the power/freedom claim should be.

12 A Google check on this phrase reveals that 'Freedom Elite' is a type of speedboat, a fuel (a petrol/ethanol mix), and a life insurance brand, amongst other things – none of which are remotely near what C. Wright Mills had in mind!

13 More recently, Carter has written on the relationship between freedom and power (I. Carter, 'How are Power and Unfreedom Related?', in C. Laborde and J. Maynor [eds], *Republicanism and Political Theory* [Oxford: Blackwell, 2008] and I. Carter, 'Social Power and Negative Freedom', *Homo Oeconomicus* 24 [2007] pp. 187–229), but, unfortunately, the power he considers is power *over*.

14 Carter, *Freedom* p. 6.

15 Carter, *Freedom* p. 235; see also a similar claim on p. 222. Another hint at the closeness between power and Carter's freedom is provided by his use of Alvin Goldman's analysis of *power* in elaborating points about *freedom* (Carter, *Freedom* pp. 97, 250).

16 Carter, *Freedom* p. 170.

17 Some of which were also developed in my *Power*.

18 Carter, *Freedom* p. 33.

19 Carter, *Freedom* p. 33.

20 Carter, *Freedom* p. 32.

21 Carter, *Freedom* p. 66.

22 Carter, *Freedom* pp. 41–3.

23 Carter, *Freedom* p. 44.

24 Carter, *Freedom* p. 45.

25 Carter, *Freedom* p. 36; my emphasis. See also p. 51. It might be noteworthy that money is more often used as an analogy of *power* than of freedom.

26 See n. 71.

27 Carter, *Freedom* p. 45.

28 I think it is unfortunate that Carter tends to discuss the meaning of the phrase 'our freedom'; I prefer to think of it in the form 'your freedom/power', which I think is less likely to create inadvertent ambiguities.

29 Carter, *Freedom* p. 58.

30 'There is no decisive argument here, but the idea surely has some plausibility' (Carter, *Freedom* p. 59).

31 Carter, *Freedom* p. 217.

32 Carter, *Freedom* pp. 59–60.

33 L. Crocker, *Positive Liberty* (London: Nijhoff, 1980) p. 115.

34 Carter, *Freedom* p. 59.

35 Carter, *Freedom* p. 59.

36 I suspect that he downplays it because it would conflict with other positions he holds, but I will not explore that here.

37 Kramer, *Freedom* pp. 3 or 15.

38 See, for instance, Kramer, *Freedom* p. 44.

39 Unless the numerator is also infinite. Kramer seems unaware that sometimes a ratio of two infinite numbers is determinate: the set of all positive integers is infinite, and the set of all integers is also infinite, and the ratio between them is (exactly) half.

Incidentally, there is a parallel problem – which has gone unnoticed in the literature – in using such ratios: the problem is that we cannot say that dying reduces your overall freedom. This is because those who are dead are presumably able to do nothing, and, therefore, both free and unfree to do nothing. The ratio determining their overall freedom is, therefore, zero divided by zero, which (mathematically) is undefined. Thus the ratio approach does not allow us to say anything about their freedom (or lack thereof); specifically, we cannot say that when you are dead you have less freedom than when you are alive. This would seem to me to be a drawback.

40 H. Steiner, 'How Free? Computing Personal Liberty', in A. Phillips Griffiths, ed., *Of Liberty* (Cambridge: Cambridge University Press, 1983) p. 74; I have dropped Steiner's subscripts. Carter accepts this definition: Carter, *Freedom* pp. 171–3. Kramer prefers the formula $F^2/(F+U)$, for reasons that need not detain us here: see Kramer, *Freedom* p. 369. Note that Steiner has had some second thoughts about his article (see H. Steiner, *An Essay on Rights* [Oxford: Blackwell, 1994] p. 42n), but he still adheres to the ratio approach (personal communication: 14 January 2008).

41 From 0.1 to 0.09 on Steiner's measure, and from 1.11 to 1 on Kramer's version.

42 Steiner, 'How Free' pp. 74–5. Of course, I certainly do not agree that ability and inability do not concern us as political philosophers.

See also Steiner, *Essay on Rights,* p. 43, where he says that it is 'common sense' 'that we take into account not only what [an actor] is free to do but also what he is *unfree* to do'; since this is (allegedly) common sense, it does not get any supporting argument.

43 I cannot find any serious argument in Kramer's book for his decision to adopt the ratio approach, although perhaps I have missed it. (See, perhaps, Kramer, *Freedom* pp. 272–3 and 368–9.) Carter is equally quick to accept it (see Carter, *Freedom* pp. 171–3). Further, it is not at all clear to me that Carter's advocacy of the nonspecific value thesis is compatible with his acceptance of this formula (which, after all, measures freedom solely in terms of the outcomes that one is free and unfree to bring about).

44 Kramer, *Freedom* pp. 3 or 15.

45 Kramer, *Freedom* p. 318.

46 Kramer, *Freedom* p. 305. Strictly, of course, these new unfreedoms are not 'countless', as Kramer's earlier argument requires precisely that we *can* count them.

47 Kramer's notion of causal responsibility is the 'but-for' test: event X is causally responsible for event Y if it were the case that, but for the occurrence of X, Y would not have occurred. His thesis is that, where there is more than one such cause, the resulting inabilities are unfreedoms if (and only if) at least one of the 'but-for' causes involved human intervention. Note that Kramer avoids a standard problem for the 'but-for' test: that of over-determination. Thus consider that someone is shot dead by two people firing fatal shots simultaneously. It is true of neither shooter that, but for his shot, the victim would have lived; therefore neither is causally responsible for his death. Yet the victim is indeed dead, and only because he was shot; if neither of the shooters killed him, who did? This problem is avoided by Kramer, because he thinks that, however one interprets this case, the consequences were a result of human actions, and therefore any resultant inabilities are also unfreedoms. But Kramer can only avoid the problem in this way because he is completely uninterested in *who* is the cause of your unfreedom, as opposed to *that* you are unfree. (Carter shows the same disinterest.) I shall suggest later that this disinterest is a mistake.

48 Kramer, *Freedom* p. 314.

49 Kramer, *Freedom* p. 313.

50 Based on one introduced by David Miller: D. Miller, 'Reply to Oppenheim', *Ethics* 95 (1985) pp. 311–12, or D. Miller, *Market, State and Community* (Oxford: Oxford University Press, 1989) pp. 33–4. Miller – like me – regards this example as a refutation of the position adopted by Kramer.

51 Kramer, *Freedom* p. 336.

52 It is significant that the word 'unpower' does not exist; as I shall suggest, that reflects a difference between freedom and power.

53 For support of this claim, see Morriss, *Power* chaps 6 and 25 (and, indeed, *passim*).

54 Cohen has used the term in a series of writings; see, for instance, G.A. Cohen, 'Freedom, Justice and Capitalism', in G.A. Cohen, *History, Labour, and Freedom: Themes from Marx* (Oxford: Oxford University Press, 1988) p. 295: 'On that definition, which I shall call the *moralized* definition, I am unfree only when someone does or would *unjustifiably* interfere with me, when what he does or would do prevents me from doing what I have a right to do'.

55 Carter, *Freedom* p. 71 (see pp. 69–71 for his discussion of the moralized definition).

56 This idea shines through Carter's book, and many of his subsequent writings.

57 Miller agrees: 'Freedom...is a morally loaded term' (*Market, State and Community* p. 36) and, more forcefully, 'The view that the idea of freedom has no built-in evaluative force seems to me incredible' ('Reply to Oppenheim' p. 313). For a discussion of this idea, see P. Westen, ' "Freedom" and "Coercion" – Virtue Words and Vice Words', *Duke Law Journal* (1985) pp. 541–58, 589–93, and the sources discussed therein.

58 Although he draws the line in quite the wrong place and for the wrong reasons.

59 Consider perhaps the most famous advocacy of freedom in the twentieth-century: Roosevelt's 'four freedoms' speech; two of these freedoms were of the form 'freedom from' – freedom from want, and freedom from fear. (F.D. Roosevelt, 'Address to Congress', 6 January 1941, available on the website of the Franklin and Eleanor Roosevelt Institute.) On the other hand, we never talk about '*power* from'.

60 '[F]reedom is...always...*from* something'. G.C.MacCallum, 'Negative and Positive Freedom', *The Philosophical Review* 76 (1967) pp. 312–34; as reprinted in D. Miller, ed., *Liberty* (Oxford: Oxford University Press, 1991); the quotation is from p. 102.

61 At least, they don't matter to me, or to others whom I have asked; and Kramer gives no *reasons* why they should, beyond those discussed and rejected in the last section.

62 S. Benn, *A Theory of Freedom* (Cambridge: Cambridge University Press, 1988) p. 126; my emphases. I would like to put on record here that I very much regret that Benn never wrote the book on power that he started working on; judging by the articles he did write, it would have been invaluable.

63 A. Margalit, *The Decent Society* (Cambridge, MA: Harvard University Press, 1996) p. 1.

64 Margalit, *The Decent Society* pp. 9, 10.

65 Of course, not all humiliations restrict your freedom; only *constraints* restrict your freedom, and there are many and varied humiliations of other kinds.

66 Wolff, 'Freedom, Liberty and Property'.

67 G.A. Cohen,'Freedom and Money', *Revista Argentina de Teoría Jurídica* 2 (2001) p. 31.

68 For a slightly more extended justification of this line of argument, see Morriss, *Power* chap. 15. A somewhat similar approach is that adopted by David Miller, in his 'Constraints on Freedom', *Ethics* 94 (1983) pp. 66–86 and *Market, State, and Community* chap. 1.

69 Cohen, 'Freedom and Money' *passim*, but particularly nn 33 and 43.

70 Or, at least, they were in pre-Ryanair days.

71 It follows from this that Kramer's three-way distinction – between free, unfree, and neither free nor unfree – does not hold.

The argument here gives some support to the so-called republican concept of freedom, as developed by Philip Pettit and Quentin Skinner. One of their claims is that you can be unfree if dominated; that is, if someone *could* stop you doing something, but does not. Unfortunately, I do not have space to discuss this interesting idea here. If it is true, then it follows that all four possible combinations formed by freedom/unfreedom and ability/inability are possible. Note also that a constraint that stops you from doing something *valueless* might still insult; this is the qualification promised in the text to n. 26.

72 For instance, 'I am free to play the sonatas of Beethoven but, never having learned to play the piano and being naturally inept, I am quite unable to' (Miller, *Market, State, and Community* p. 31).

73 We have (I think) no problem in saying that I am unfree to harangue passers-by in Galway by reciting the Koran at them at the top of my voice (I am unfree because I would be arrested for disturbing the peace long before I reached the end of the work), even though I am in any case unable to do it (as I don't know the Koran).

74 Cohen, 'Freedom and Money' p. 32. Cohen also considers that he 'would...consider it an insult if [he] were forbidden by a state to travel to Australia (whether it be by Canada or by Australia – though the insults might be of different significance and/or weight in the two cases)' (p. 31). For those who do not know, Cohen is Canadian, though he has lived in England for decades; it is not clear to me from this passage whether he would *not* find it an insult if it was the UK that forbade him from travelling. Whether true or not, it is presumably a possibility, and that possibility must affect the way we interpret freedom.

75 Whether through maliciousness or laziness.

76 Kramer thinks that *omissions* cannot render people unfree; so if you are trapped in the cave by a naturally occurring landslide, but then not rescued when you could be rescued, you are not thereby made unfree. Other writers (e.g. Miller) disagree.

77 When I was 17, I was trapped in quicksand whilst walking on a beach on a cold February morning. I was eventually rescued at dusk, by a combination of an alert passer-by, the fire brigade, and a local Air Sea Rescue helicopter (a service, I understand, that no longer exists). If I had not been rescued, I would undoubtedly have died of hypothermia. As far as I am aware, the presence of the quicksand was the result of a cliff fall that could not in any way be traced to human intervention. For Kramer, my being trapped would have solely reduced my abilities and not my freedoms. Yet I resent the suggestion that it would therefore be unimportant – or 'mere'.

78 Or die of hypothermia, for want of rescue services.
79 This might seem like a Marxist, or perhaps communist, move; but I think that liberals should also be able to recognize the importance of ensuring that people do not preventably die.
80 Consider Peter Singer's requirement that we rescue a drowning child from a pond (which is structurally identical to rescuing a person trapped in a cave), and his use of this example to argue that we should show a similar concern to aid those starving in the Third World: P. Singer, 'Famine, Affluence and Morality,' *Philosophy and Public Affairs* 1 (1972) pp. 229–43.

4

Power and Democracy

Charles Tilly

The democracy-monitoring organization Freedom House considers a regime to be an electoral democracy if it maintains established competitive parties, more or less universal adult suffrage, contested elections, and free access of parties to the voting public. By these criteria, no electoral democracies existed in 1900; no country anywhere had yet enacted female suffrage, although Finland would do so in 1906. As of mid-century, Freedom House retroactively counts 22 of the world's 80 then independent regimes as electoral democracies: 28 percent of all regimes, accounting for 31 percent of the world's population. By century's end (1999), decolonization and the shattering of socialist federations had expanded the total number of independent states to 192. Of them, Freedom House rated 120 (63 percent) as democratic; they included 58 percent of the world's population (Karatnycky 2000: 7–8).

Of course a number of reversals occurred after 1900; just think of how European regimes Austria, Finland, France, Germany, Greece, Hungary, Italy, Portugal, Romania, Spain, and Russia de-democratized between 1900 and 1950, or how military regimes took over previously more or less democratic Argentina, Brazil, Chile, Venezuela, plus numerous other Latin American states, at various points between 1950 and 2000. Yet Freedom House tallies indicate, on the average, a net increase of 1.6 new democratic regimes per year between 1900 and 1950, a net increase of 0.8 new democratic regimes per year between 1950 and 2000. The figures project a vision of vigorous, if unevenly distributed, democratization throughout the century.

Since 1972, Freedom House has performed a great service by evaluating the democratic credentials of every independent regime each year. It has gone further, using detailed checklists to rate each regime separately from 1 (high) to 7 (low) on political rights and civil liberties year by year. Qualified by the difficulties that raters based in the United States face in arriving at equally informed judgments about the undemocratic or democratic functioning of, say, Canada and Myanmar, of France and Vanuatu, Freedom House evaluations thus document a zigzag but upward advance of political rights, civil liberties, and electoral democracy across much of the world for decades. Looked at more closely, furthermore, they display the concentration of democratization in bursts such as the movement of many former European colonies into democratic independence during the 1970s and the transformation of multiple former state socialist regimes into democracies after 1989.

Nevertheless, analysts of democracy, democratization, de-democratization, and power cannot settle simply for quantitative indicators, much less for the quick conclusion that democracy may take a while, but eventually becomes irresistible. Too much is at stake. Neither classifications of electoral democracy nor ratings of political rights and civil liberties tell us much about the processes that produce democratization and de-democratization, the general relationship between democracy and power, or the conditions under which the exercise of power undermines democracy.

This chapter brings some order and connection into those three issues. More precisely, it addresses these questions:

1. How can we arrive at theoretically, politically, and substantively satisfactory models of power, democracy and democratization?
2. How do democratization and de-democratization actually occur?
3. What parts do changing forms and exercises of power play in democratization and de-democratization?

By the end, it should at least be clear that static yes/no criteria for democracy – this regime is democratic, that one isn't – will only carry us a short distance toward satisfactory understanding of how democracies wax and wane, and what their waxing and waning has to do with the exercise of power. We are asking questions about unceasing dynamic changes, not about static conditions.

POWER

To answer those questions, we must know about power. Whatever else it involves, democracy entails a distinctive and historically unusual form of power, one in which the bulk of the population living under the jurisdiction of some authority exercise substantial collective control over how that authority behaves. As a definition of democracy, that simple statement will not do, but it highlights the centrality to democracy of power relations between central authorities and the populations nominally subordinate to them.

Let us work with an elementary and familiar conception of power: a relation of outputs to inputs. Begin with a pair, A and B. For simplicity, we can think of A as an actor that exerts an effort on B. B can be another actor, but B can also be a situation from which some output could emerge. A has power over B to the extent that A's input of effort – resources, coercion, persuasion, what have you – elicits a compliant response from B. (We can gauge compliance either in terms of correspondence to demands A makes or by conformity to our evaluation of A's interests.) The greater B's response for a given unit of effort, the greater A's power. This means, of course, that the power relation between A and B describes not a point but a curve. It also means that any power curve abstracts

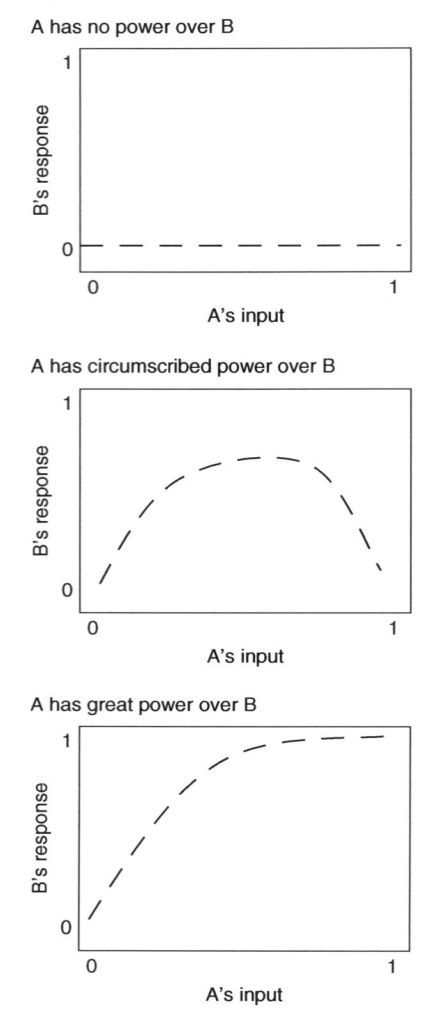

Figure 4.1 Three power configurations. Excerpts from Held, David, *Models of Democracy*, 3rd edition, Copyright © 1987, 1996, 2006 David Held. Used with the permission of Polity Press and Stanford University Press, www.sup.org

from multiple observed interactions over time; it offers a dynamic, not static, image of power.

Figure 4.1 sketches three alternate situations: A has no power over B, A has circumscribed power over B, and A has great power over B. The ranges 0 to 1 describe minima and maxima: if, for example, B offers no response whatsoever to A's overture, we set the response at 0; if B yields every resource under his control, we set B's response at 1. If A has no power over B, then, no matter how much effort A puts in B fails to respond. If A has circumscribed power over B, up to a limit B yields or conforms increasingly to A's augmented inputs, but beyond that point B's response falls off. That happens, for example, when B has a limit of tolerance, and starts resisting A's demands or overtures beyond that limit. Finally, A has great power if B's response increases rapidly with A's increased input, and that response never declines until B's resources run out.

This simple scheme accommodates the conventional distinction between 'power over' and 'power to'. In power over, both A and B are actors, either individual or collective. In power to, B is a situation that A can hope – or, if A is powerless, cannot hope – to alter. It will accommodate Michael Mann's distinctions among ideological, economic, military, and political sources and organizations of power (Mann 1986: 22–27). These sorts of power differ fundamentally in the means by which A (now conceived of as a network of relations among persons and groups) produces responses from B (now conceived of as many, many people within the same society).

Mann's equally famous distinction between despotic and infrastructural forms of power rests on the contrast between directly coercive means and elicitation of cooperation. On the whole, Mann portrays despotic control as forcing reluctant cooperation, hence no significant increase in a population's collective capacity. In contrast, the cooperation associated with infrastructural power adds to a population's collective capacity. As Mann sums up:

> Power is most fruitfully seen as *means*, as *organization*, as *infrastrucure*, as *logistics*, In the pursuit of their myriad, fluctuating goals, human beings set up networks of social cooperation that imply both collective and distributive power. Of these networks, the most powerful in the logistical sense of being able to bring forth cooperation, both *intensively* and *extensively*, over definite social and geographical space, are ideological, economic, military, and political power organizations. Sometimes these organizations appear in societies as relatively specialized and separate, sometimes as relatively merged into each other. Each attains its prominence by virtue of the distinct organizational means it offers to achieve human goals (Mann 1986: 518).

In these terms, democracy brings together ideological, economic, and military power organizations in configurations that affect *political* power organizations in a distinctive way: through cooperation, they subordinate those political power organizations to popular will. So doing, they increase the whole population's collective capacity. How can we identify the conditions and processes that produce such a distinctive – and historically exceptional – historical outcome?

MODELS OF DEMOCRACY AND DEMOCRATIZATION

We can start by recognizing that democracy has meant very different forms of politics to different thinkers and peoples. What Athenians sometimes called *demokratia* differed deeply from the democratic political arrangements Karl Marx imagined for true communism. We are looking for analyses of democracy that accomplish four things: (1) allow us to decide whether existing regimes do or don't match the representation at hand; (2) permit us to array regimes with regard to their degree of democracy; (3) facilitate examination of the same regime at different points in time to determine whether it is becoming more or less democratic; (4) specify what features and changes of regime valid accounts of democratization and de-democratization must explain. In these pursuits, observers of democracy and democratization generally choose, implicitly or explicitly, among five main types of definition: ideal, constitutional, procedural, substantive, and process-oriented (Andrews and Chapman 1995; Collier and Levitsky 1997; Engelstad, and Østerud 2004;

Inkeles 1991; Lafargue 1996; Markoff 2005; Morlino 2003; O'Donnell 1999; Ortega Ortiz 2001; Schmitter and Karl 1991; Tilly 2004).

Ideal definitions combine prescriptions and descriptions that match ideas of the institutions that would produce democratic outcomes, specifications of those outcomes, and indications of existing instances (if any) the models are supposed to match. David Held has heroically disciplined the entire ideal history of democracy into a very limited number of types: classical democracy in the Athenian form, two varieties of republicanism, two varieties of liberal democracy, two varieties of socialist democracy, plus six twentieth-century variants:

- competitive elitist democracy
- pluralism (with classic and neo-pluralist variants)
- legal democracy
- participatory democracy
- democratic autonomy
- cosmopolitan (internationally oriented) democracy

To give the flavor of Held's distinctions, Box 4.1 summarizes the key features Held attaches to what he calls the 'classic' models.

Box 4.1 Key Features in David Held's Alternative Classic Models of Democracy

Classical Democracy: direct participation of citizens in legislative and judicial functions; assembly of citizens has sovereign power; scope of sovereign power to include all the common affairs of the city; multiple methods of selection of candidates for public office (direct election, lot, rotation); no distinctions of privilege to differentiate ordinary citizens and public officials; with the exception of positions connected to warfare, the same office not to be held more than twice by the same individual; short terms of office for all; payment for public services.

Protective Republicanism: balance of power between 'the people', aristocracy and the monarchy linked to a mixed constitution of missed government, with provision for all leading political forces to play an active role in public life; citizen participation achieved via different possible mechanisms, including election of consuls, or representatives to serve on ruling councils; competing social groups promoting and defending their interests; liberties of speech, expression and association; rule of law.

Developmental Republicanism: division of legislative and executive functions; direct participation of citizens in public meetings to constitute the legislature; unanimity on public issues desirable, but voting provision with majority rule in the event of disagreement; executive positions in the hands of 'magistrates' or 'administrators'; executive appointed either by direct election or by lot.

Protective Democracy: sovereignty ultimately lies in the people, but is vested in representatives who can legitimately exercise state functions; regular elections, the secret ballot, competition between factions, potential leaders or parties and majority rule are the institutional bases for establishing accountability of those who govern; state powers must be impersonal, i.e. legally circumscribed, and divided among the executive, the legislature and the judiciary; centrality of constitutionalism to guarantee freedom from arbitrary treatment and equality before the law in the form of political and civil rights or liberties, above all those connected to free speech, expression, association, voting and belief; separation of state from civil society, i.e. the scope of state action is, in general, to be tightly restricted to the creation of a framework which allows citizens to pursue their private lives free from risks of violence, unacceptable social behavior and unwanted political interference; competing power centres and interest groups.

> *Developmental Democracy*: popular sovereignty with a universal franchise along with a 'proportional' system of vote allocation; representative government (elected leadership, regular elections, secret ballot, etc.); constitutional checks to secure limitations on, and divisions in, state power and to ensure the promotion of individual rights, above all those connected with freedom of thought, feeling, taste, discussion, publication, combination and the pursuit of individually chosen 'life plans'; clear demarcation of parliamentary assembly from public bureaucracy, i.e. separation of the functions of the elected from those of the specialist (expert) administrator; citizen involvement in the different branches of government through the vote, extensive participation in local government, public debates and jury service.
>
> *Direct Democracy (Socialist Version)*: public affairs regulated by Commune(s) or council(s) organized in a pyramid structure; government personnel, law officers, administrators subject to frequent elections, mandates from their community and recall; public officers to be paid no more than workers' wages; people's militia to sustain the new political order subject to community control.
>
> *Direct Democracy (Communist Version)*: 'government' and 'politics' in all forms give way to self-regulation; all public affairs governed collectively; consensus as decision principle on all public questions; distribution of remaining administrative tasks by rotation or election; replacement of all armed and coercive forces by self-monitoring.
>
> Excerpts from Held, David, *Models of Democracy*, 3rd edition. Copyright © 1987, 1996, 2006 David Held. Used with the permission of Polity Press and Stanford University Press, www.sup.org

The types do not exhaust all possibilities. As Held says, for example, they neglect anarchist visions of democracy and a number of other utopias. They do, however, cover the range of possibilities that compete for the attention of today's power holders when they attempt to shape democracies. They differ significantly with respect to the division of labor between officials and ordinary citizens as well as with respect to the organizational mechanisms governing relations between officials and ordinary citizens; but they all pivot on methods for ensuring that a body of citizens exercises collective control over some central executive. In that sense, they all describe forms of power. To that extent, they imply a very broad definition of democracy: any system that does, indeed, ensure collective citizen control over a national executive. The trouble, obviously, starts there: how will we know that effective control exists? Recognizing that difficulty, most analysts of democracy settle for narrower definitions.

When it comes to democratization and de-democratization, ideal definitions provide hardly any descriptive or explanatory leverage. We might imagine that one of Held's ideal types comes into being – hence democratization occurs – when an elite or a people decides that a given model appeals to them. Similarly, we might reason that de-democratization occurs when a model democratic regime collapses from popular disillusion, internal contradictions, or external conquest. However, such sketches provide no way of arraying regimes according to their degree of democracy, tracking changes in a given regime's democratic performance, or explaining how change and variation occur.

A narrower *constitutional* approach concentrates on laws concerning political activity a regime enacts. Thus we can look across history and recognize differences among oligarchies, monarchies, republics, and a number of other types by means of contrasting legal arrangements. Within democracies, furthermore, we can distinguish between constitutional monarchies, presidential systems, and parliament-centered arrangements, not to mention such variations as federal vs. unitary structures. For large historical comparisons, constitutional criteria have many advantages, especially the relative visibility of constitutional forms. Alas, almost all the world's contemporary constitutions declare their regimes to be democracies, including the vast majority of the 72 regimes that Freedom House declared undemocratic in 1999. Large discrepancies between announced principles and daily practices often make constitutions misleading.

Constitutional definitions of democracy, to be sure, greatly simplify the description of democratization and de-democratization: we watch for the moments when regimes adopt or suspend formally democratic sets of laws. In addition to the difficulty of knowing whether laws on the books actually give power to the people, however, such criteria beg the questions of how, when, and why moves toward more fully or less fully democratic legal systems occur. They will not serve our purposes well.

Advocates of *procedural* definitions single out a narrow range of governmental practices to determine whether a regime qualifies as democratic. Most procedural observers center their attention on elections, asking whether genuinely competitive elections engaging large numbers of citizens regularly produce changes in governmental personnel and policy. If elections remain a non-competitive sham and an occasion for smashing governmental opponents, procedural analysts reject them as criteria for democracy, but if they actually cause significant governmental changes, they signal the procedural presence of democracy. (In principle one could add or substitute other consultative procedures such as referenda, recall, petition, and even opinion polls, but in practice procedural analysts focus overwhelmingly on elections.)

Freedom House evaluations incorporate some substantive judgments about the extent to which a given country's citizens actually enjoy political rights and civil liberties, but when it comes to judging whether a country is an 'electoral democracy', Freedom House looks for mainly procedural elements:

1. A competitive, multiparty political system
2. Universal adult suffrage for all citizens (with exceptions for restrictions that states may legitimately place on citizens for criminal offenses)
3. Regularly contested elections conducted in conditions of ballot secrecy, reasonable ballot security, and in the absence of massive voter fraud that yields results that are unrepresentative of the public will.
4. Significant public access of major political parties to the electorate through the media and through generally open political campaigning (Piano and Puddington 2004: 716).

When Freedom House raters looked more closely at political rights and civil liberties in 2003, however, they decided that 29 of their 117 electoral democracies failed to qualify as 'free'. In those 29 regimes, significant deficits existed in rights and liberties (Piano and Puddington 2004: 5). Here, then, is the trouble with procedural definitions of democracy, democratization, and de-democratization: despite their crisp convenience, they work with an extremely thin conception of the political processes involved.

Substantive approaches focus on the conditions of life and politics a given regime promotes: does this regime promote human welfare, individual freedom, security, equity, social equality, public deliberation, and peaceful conflict resolution? If so, we might be inclined to call it democratic regardless of how its constitution reads. Two troubles follow immediately, however, from any such definitional strategy. First, how do we handle tradeoffs among these admirable principles? If a given regime is desperately poor but its citizens enjoy rough equality, should we think of it as more democratic than a fairly prosperous but fiercely unequal regime?

Second, focusing on these possible outcomes of politics undercuts any effort to learn whether some political arrangements – including democracy – promote more desirable substantive outcomes than other political arrangements. What if we actually want to know under what conditions and how regimes promote human welfare, individual freedom, security, equity, social equality, public deliberation, and peaceful conflict resolution?

In principle, nevertheless, substantive definitions of democracy could yield valuable approaches to describing and explaining democratization and de-democratization. One could imagine setting out a set of performance criteria on the model of the United Nations' Human Development Index (UNDP 2005), going beyond Freedom House by directly measuring a wide variety of rights, freedoms, and resolutions of conflict. Existing comparisons of performance among different sorts of welfare systems (e.g. Goodin et al. 1999) suggest that it might be possible. Coupled with adequate theories of how such rights, freedoms, and resolutions of conflict wax and wane, substantive approaches could thus contribute powerfully to our understanding of democratization and de-democratization. Alas, no investigator so far has come close.

Process-oriented approaches to democracy differ significantly from ideal, constitutional, procedural, and substantive accounts. They identify some minimum set of processes that must be continuously in motion for a situation to qualify as democratic. In a classic statement, Robert Dahl stipulates six distinctive institutions: elected officials; free, fair, and frequent elections; freedom of expression; alternative sources of information; associational autonomy; and inclusive citizenship (Dahl 1998: 85; Dahl 2005: 188–189). The final standard – inclusive citizenship – ironically rules out many cases that political philosophers including David Held have regularly taken as great historical models for democracy: not only Greek and Roman polities but also Viking crews, village assemblies, and some city-states. All of them built their political deliberations by means of massive exclusion, most notably of women, slaves, and paupers. Inclusion of all (or almost all) adults basically restricts political democracy to the last few centuries.

Notice how Dahl's criteria differ from ideal, constitutional, procedural, and substantive standards for democracy. Dahl abstains from describing the structure of consent and control. He specifies no constitutional forms or provisions. Dahl's criteria do include the procedure of free, fair, and frequent elections, but the list as a whole describes how a regime works, not what techniques it adopts to accomplish its goals. He carefully avoids building social prerequisites or consequences into the definition. His scheme of 'polyarchal democracy' describes an interlocking set of political processes.

Yet there is a catch. Basically, Dahl provides us with a static yes-no checklist: if a regime operates all six institutions, it counts as a democracy. If it lacks any of them, or some of them aren't really working, it doesn't count as a democracy. For an annual count of which regimes are in or out, such an approach can do the job even if critics raise questions about whether elections in such places as Jamaica are free and fair. Suppose, however, that we want to use process-oriented standards more ambitiously. We do not merely want to count the democratic house at a single point in time. Instead, we want to do two more demanding things: first, to compare regimes with regard to how democratic they are; second, to follow individual regimes through time, noticing when and how they become more or less democratic.

Like Freedom House raters of relative political rights and civil liberties, we can reasonably ask whether some regimes rank higher or lower than others, if only to see whether those rankings correlate with other factors such as national wealth, population size, recency of independence, or geographic location. If we want insight into causes and effects of democratization or de-democratization, we have no choice but to recognize them as continuous processes rather than simple steps across a threshold in one direction or the other. In short, for purposes of comparison and explanation we must move from a yes-no checklist to one or more crucial variables.

Most of Dahl's standard democratic institutions – elected officials; free, fair, and frequent elections; freedom of expression; alternative sources of information; associational autonomy; and inclusive citizenship – lend themselves awkwardly to comparison and explanation. We might, of course, ask *how* free, fair, and frequent elections are, and so on down the list; but the more we do so, the more we will recognize two drawbacks of Dahl's criteria when it comes to the work at hand:

1. Together, they describe a minimum package of democratic institutions, not a set of continuous variables; they do not help much if we are asking whether Canada is more democratic than the US, or whether the US became less democratic last year.
2. Each of them operates within significant limits, beyond which some of them conflict with each other; working democracies often have to adjudicate deep conflicts, for example, between freedom of expression and associational autonomy. Should a democracy muzzle animal rights organizations because they advocate attacks on associations that hold dog shows or support animal experimentation?

Again, the autonomy of powerful elitist, racist, sexist, or hate-mongering associations regularly undermines the inclusiveness of citizenship. Should a democracy let well-financed pressure groups drive punitive anti-immigrant legislation through the legislature? To enter fully into comparison and explanation, we will have to improve on Dahl's criteria while remaining faithful to their process-oriented spirit.

ELEMENTS OF DEMOCRACY, DEMOCRATIZATION, AND DE-DEMOCRATIZATION

How can we move ahead? Before identifying process-oriented criteria for democracy, democratization, and de-democratization, let us clarify what we have to explain. In order to do so, it will help to simplify radically. Let us adopt three simple ideas.

First, we start with a state, an organization that controls the major concentration of coercive means within a substantial territory, exercises priority in some regards over all other organizations operating within the same territory, and receives acknowledgement of that priority from other organizations, including states, outside the territory. You begin to see the complications: what about federal systems, civil wars, warlord-dominated enclaves, and rival factions within the state? For the time being, nevertheless, we can pose the problem of democracy more clearly by assuming a single, fairly unitary state.

Second, we lump everyone who lives under that state's jurisdiction into a catch-all category: citizens. Again complications immediately come to mind: what about tourists, transnational corporations, members of the underground economy, and expatriates? Most historical regimes have lacked full-fledged citizenship, which plays a crucial part in democracy, but for a start, calling everyone who lives under a given state's jurisdiction a citizen of that state will clarify what we have to explain. Democracy will then turn out to be a certain class of relations between states and citizens, democratization and de-democratization to consist of changes in those sorts of relations.

Dahl's principles already imply such a step; even associational autonomy, for example, depends on state backing of associations' right to exist rather than the sheer presence of many, many associations. Let us call a set of relations between states and citizens a *regime*, with the understanding that we will eventually have to complicate that idea by including relations among major political actors (parties, corporations, labor unions, organized ethnic groups, patron-client networks, warlords, and more) in regimes as well.

In the meantime, notice that the second step breaks sharply with a common (and at first glance appealing) notion. It rejects the widespread idea that if only existing holders of power agree on how they want a regime to operate they can decide on democracy as a more attractive – or less disagreeable – alternative to existing political arrangements. In this view, workers, peasants, minorities, and other citizens may cause enough trouble to make some concessions to representation and inclusion less costly to elites than continuing repression, but the citizenry at large plays only a marginal role in the actual fashioning of democratic politics. Such a view underlies the policy of exporting democracy from the US or the European Union by making attractive deals with national leaders – or, for that matter, by coercing leaders to adopt democratic institutions. On the contrary, this analysis of democratization (and of de-democratization as well) centers on state-citizen struggle. Even a conquering military power such as the western Allies in Japan and Germany after World War II must bargain extensively with citizens to create a new democratic regime where authoritarians previously ruled.

Third, let us narrow our analytic range to public politics: not all transactions, however personal or impersonal, between states and citizens but those that visibly engage state power and performance. Public politics includes elections, voter registration, legislative activity, patenting, tax collection, military conscription, group application for pensions, and many other transactions to which states are parties. It also includes collective contention in the form of coups d'état, revolution, social movements, and civil war. It excludes, however, most personal interactions among citizens, among state officials, or between state officials and citizens.

Some of public politics consists of *consulting* citizens about their opinions, needs, and demands. Consultation includes any public means by which citizens voice their collective preferences concerning state personnel and policies. In relatively democratic regimes, competitive elections certainly give citizens voice, but so do lobbying, petitioning, referenda, social movements, and opinion polling. This time the missing complications are obvious: bribes, patron-client chains, favors to constituents and followers, kinship connections among officials, and similar phenomena blur the boundary between public and private politics. What is more, any close student of democracy soon discovers that she can't make sense of public politics by focusing on citizen-state interactions alone, but must examine coalitions, rivalries, and confrontations among major political actors outside of the state as well. For the moment, we scrutinize public political interactions between states and citizens for signs of democracy, democratization, and de-democratization.

What do we look for in those interactions? One more simplification can guide us. Judging degree of democracy, we return to the core conception of democratic power: we assess the extent to which the state behaves in conformity to the expressed demands of its citizens. Gauging democratization and de-democratization, we assess the extent to which that conformity is increasing or decreasing. So doing, we set aside venerable alternatives in democratic theory. We do not ask whether the state is enhancing its citizens' welfare, whether it behaves in accordance with its own laws, or even whether ordinary people control the levers of political power. (Nothing bars us from asking later or elsewhere whether democratization thus understood enhances popular welfare, entails the rule of law, or depends on citizens' direct empowerment.)

Judging conformity of a state's behavior to its citizens' expressed demands necessarily involves four further judgments: how wide a range of citizens' expressed demands come into play; how equally different groups of citizens experience a translation of their demands into state behavior; to what extent the expression of demands itself receives the state's political protection; and how much the process of translation commits both sides, citizens and state. Call those elements breadth, equality, protection, and mutual binding.

In this simplified perspective, *a regime is democratic to the degree that political relations between the state and its citizens feature broad, equal, protected, mutually binding consultation.* Democratization means net movement toward broader, more equal, more protected, and more binding consultation. De-democratization, obviously, then means net movement toward narrower, more unequal, less protected, and less binding consultation. In Germany, we can reasonably say that the formation of the Weimar Republic in the German Empire's ruins after World War I introduced a measure of democratization, while Hitler's seizure of power in 1933 pushed the country brutally back into de-democratization. In Japan, we can reasonably treat the buildup of militarized state power during the 1930s as a time of de-democratization while treating the period of Allied conquest, occupation, and reconstruction as a start of democratization.

The terms broad, equal, protected, and mutually binding identify four partly independent dimensions of variation among regimes. Here are rough descriptions of the four dimensions:

1. *Breadth*: from only a small segment of the population enjoying extensive rights, the rest being largely excluded from public politics, to very wide political inclusion of people falling under the state's jurisdiction (at one extreme, every household has its own distinctive relation to the state, but only a few households have full rights of citizenship; at the other, all adult citizens belong to the same homogeneous category of citizenship)
2. *Equality*: from great inequality among and within categories of citizens to extensive equality in both regards (at one extreme, ethnic categories fall into a well defined rank order with very unequal rights and obligations; at the other, ethnicity has no significant connection with political rights or obligations and largely equal rights prevail between native-born and naturalized citizens)

Together, high levels of breadth and equality comprise the crucial aspects of citizenship: instead of a mosaic of variable relations to the state depending on particular group memberships, all citizens fall into a limited number of categories – at the limit, just one – whose members maintain similar rights and obligations in their interactions with the state. By themselves, breadth and equality do not constitute democracy. Authoritarian regimes have often imposed undemocratic forms of citizenship from the top down, but in the company of protection and mutually binding consultation, breadth and equality qualify as essential components of democracy.

3. *Protection*: from little to much protection against the state's arbitrary action (at one extreme, state agents constantly use their power to punish personal enemies and reward their friends; at the other, all citizens enjoy publicly visible due process)

4. *Mutual binding*: from non-binding and/or extremely asymmetrical to mutually binding (at one extreme, seekers of state benefits must bribe, cajole, threaten, or use third-party influence to get anything at all; at the other, state agents have clear, enforceable obligations to deliver benefits by category of recipient)

Net movement of a regime toward the higher ends of the four dimensions qualifies as democratization. Net movement toward the lower ends qualifies as de-democratization. When, for example, Freedom House put downward arrows on Jamaica's political rights and civil liberties ratings for 2004, it was warning that Jamaica ran the risk of de-democratizing (Freedom House Jamaica 2005: 2). In terms of our four dimensions, it called special attention to Jamaica's increases of inequality and decreases of protection.

STATE CAPACITY AND REGIME VARIATION

So far I have omitted an important feature of regimes, whether democratic or undemocratic: the state's capacity to enforce its political decisions. Power figures crucially in this regime feature. No democracy can work if the state lacks the power to supervize democratic decision-making and put its results into practice. That is most obvious for protection, where a very weak state may proclaim the principle of shielding citizens from harassment by state agents, but can do little about harassment when it occurs. Very high capacity states run the opposite risk: that decision-making by state agents acquires enough weight to overwhelm mutually binding consultation between government and citizens.

State capacity has already entered our discussion indirectly. Some of the Freedom House political rights and civil liberties, for example, would mean nothing without substantial state backing. Note these detailed questions that Freedom House raters are supposed to answer for each regime (Karatnycky 2000: 524–525):

PR # 3: Are there fair electoral laws, equal campaigning opportunities, fair polling, and honest tabulations of ballots?
PR # 4: Are the voters able to endow their freely elected representatives with real power?
CL # 5: Does the rule of law prevail in civil and criminal matters? Is the population treated equally under the law? Are police under direct civilian control?
CL # 10: Are property rights secure? Do citizens have the right to establish private businesses? Is private business activity unduly influenced by government officials, the security forces, or organized crime?

We see Freedom House evaluators trying to find a middle ground between too little and too much state capacity, on the implicit assumption that either one hinders political rights and civil liberties. That assumption generalizes: extremely high and extremely low state capacity both inhibit democracy.

State capacity means the extent to which interventions of state agents in existing non-state resources, activities, and interpersonal connections alter existing distributions of those resources, activities, and interpersonal connections as well as relations among those distributions. (State-directed redistribution of wealth, for example, almost inevitably involves not only a redistribution of resources across the population but also a change in the connection between the geographic distributions of wealth and population.) In a high-capacity regime, by this standard, whenever state agents act their actions affect

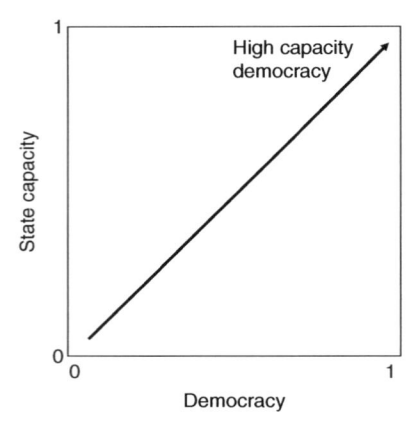

Figure 4.2 Variation in regimes

citizens' resources, activities, and interpersonal connections significantly. In a low-capacity regime, state agents have much narrower impacts no matter how hard they try to change things.

We begin to see the value of distinguishing capacity from democracy before relating them analytically. Clearly capacity can range from extremely low to extremely high independently of how democratic a regime is, and democracy can appear in regimes that vary markedly with regard to state capacity. Figure 4.2 schematizes the field of variation. It identifies some distinctly different zones of political life marked by varying combinations of capacity and democracy.

On the vertical axis, state capacity varies from 0 (minimum) to 1 (maximum). Although we could think of capacity in absolute terms, for comparative purposes it helps more to scale it against the histories of all states that have actually existed within a given era. Over the period since 1900, for example, the dimension might run from Somalia or Congo-Kinshasa in 2006 (minimum) to colossal Nazi Germany on the eve of World War II (maximum). On the horizontal axis, we find the familiar range from minimum democracy at 0 (for which the authoritarian rule of Stalin's Russia might be a candidate) to maximum democracy at 1 (where today's Norway would certainly be in the running).

For many purposes, another radical simplification will aid our attempt to describe and explain variation in regimes. Figure 4.2 identifies the four crude regime types implied by our more general map of regimes. It reduces the space to four crude types of regime: low-capacity undemocratic, high-capacity undemocratic, high-capacity democratic, and low-capacity democratic. Examples of each type in the diagram include:

High-capacity Undemocratic: Kazakhstan, Iran
Low-capacity Undemocratic: Somalia, Congo (Kinshasa)
High-capacity Democratic: Norway, Japan
Low-capacity Democratic: Jamaica, Belgium

Over human history regimes have distributed very unevenly across the types. The great bulk of historical regimes have fallen into the low-capacity undemocratic sector. Many of the biggest and most powerful, however, have dwelt in the high-capacity undemocratic sector. High-capacity democratic regimes have been rare and mostly recent. Low-capacity democratic regimes have remained few and far between.

Over the long run of human history, then, the vast majority of regimes have been undemocratic; democratic regimes are rare, contingent, recent creations. Partial democracies have, it is true, formed intermittently at a local scale, for example in villages ruled by councils incorporating most heads of household. At the scale of a city-state, a warlord's domain, or a regional federation, forms of government have run from dynastic hegemony to oligarchy, with narrow, unequal citizenship or none at all, little or no binding consultation, and uncertain protection from arbitrary governmental action.

Before the nineteenth century, furthermore, large states and empires generally managed by means of indirect rule: systems in which the central power received tribute, cooperation, and guarantees of compliance on the part of subject populations from regional power-holders who enjoyed great autonomy within their own domains. Even in supposedly absolutist France, for example, great nobles only started to lose their regional power during the later seventeenth century, when Louis XIV undertook a sustained (and ultimately successful) effort to replace them with government-appointed and removable regional administrators. Before then, great lords ran their domains like princes, and often took up arms against the French crown itself.

Seen from the bottom, such systems often imposed tyranny on ordinary people. Seen from the top, however, they lacked capacity; the intermediaries supplied soldiers, goods, and money to rulers, but their autonomous privileges also set stringent limits to rulers' ability to govern or transform the world within their presumed jurisdictions.

Only the nineteenth century brought widespread adoption of direct rule: creation of structures extending governmental communication and control continuously from central institutions to individual localities or even to households, and back again. Creation of direct rule commonly included such measures as uniform tax codes, large-scale postal services, professional civil services, and national military conscription. Even then, direct rule ranged from the unitary hierarchies of centralized monarchy to the segmentation of federalism. On a large scale, direct rule made substantial citizenship, and therefore democracy, possible. Possible, but not likely, much less inevitable: instruments of direct rule have sustained many oligarchies, some autocracies, a number of party- and army-controlled states, and a few fascist tyrannies. Even in the era of direct rule most regimes have remained far from democratic.

Location in one or another of the four quadrants makes a powerful difference to the character of a regime's public politics (Tilly 2006). Here are preliminary descriptions of the kinds of politics that prevail in each quadrant:

High-capacity Undemocratic: little public voice except as elicited by the state; extensive involvement of state security forces in any public politics; regime change either through struggle at the top or mass rebellion from the bottom
Low-capacity Undemocratic: warlords, ethnic blocs, and religious mobilization; frequent violent struggle including civil wars; many political actors including criminals deploying lethal force
High-capacity Democratic: frequent social movements, interest group activity, and political party mobilizations; formal consultations (including competitive elections) as high points of political activity; widespread state monitoring of public politics combined with relatively low levels of political violence
Low-capacity Democratic: as in high capacity democratic regimes, frequent social movements, interest group activity, and political party mobilizations plus formal consultations (including competitive elections) as high points of political activity, but less effective state monitoring, higher involvement of semi-legal

and illegal actors in public politics, and substantially higher levels of lethal violence in public politics

These are, of course, 'on the average' descriptions. Within the high capacity undemocratic quadrant, for example, we find some regimes whose states' monitoring and intervention extend throughout the whole territory and population; Iran fits the description; but we also notice others in which the state has nearly the same control over its central territory but has edges or enclaves that largely escape control; Morocco, with authoritarian rule in its main territory but a long-running civil war with independence-minded Polisario forces in the former Spanish Sahara, belongs to this subset of regimes.

PROCESSES THAT CAUSE DEMOCRATIZATION AND DE-DEMOCRATIZATION

Can we specify any necessary conditions for movement into the high-capacity democratic quadrant of Figure 4.3 from the other three quadrants? What about exits from the high-capacity democratic quadrant? Once you rule out conditions that belong to democratization and de-democratization by definition, I do not believe that any necessary, much less sufficient, conditions for either one exist. Comparison of otherwise similar cases in some of which democratization or de-democratization occurs and in others doesn't can clarify what we have to explain, but it will not identify universal conditions. At least no one has identified such conditions so far.

I do think, however, that some necessary *processes* promote democratization, and that reversals of those processes promote de-democratization. For the moment, let us neglect de-democratization, and concentrate on democratization, to make this line of argument clear. For democratization to develop in any regime, changes must occur in three areas: trust networks, categorical inequality, and autonomous power centers.

'Trust networks' are ramified interpersonal connections, consisting mainly of strong ties, within which people set valued, consequential, long-term resources and enterprises at risk to the malfeasance, mistakes, or failures of others. Trading diasporas, kinship groups, religious sects, revolutionary conspiracies, and credit circles often comprise trust networks. Over most

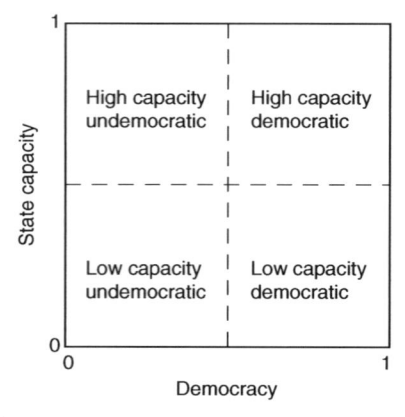

Figure 4.3 Crude regime types

of history, participants in trust networks have carefully shielded them from involvement in political regimes, for justified fear that rulers would either seize their precious resources or subordinate them to the state's own programs.

So long as they remain entirely segregated from regimes, however, trust networks constitute obstacles to democratization; their segregation blocks members' commitment to democratic collective enterprises. Democratization becomes possible when trust networks integrate sufficiently into regimes that they provide the means of mutual binding – the contingent consent of citizens to programs proposed or enacted by the state (Tilly 2005). Two large processes affecting trust networks therefore underlie democratization: (1) dissolution or integration of segregated trust networks and (2) creation of politically connected trust networks.

Within the two processes appear a series of recurrent mechanisms, for example:

- disintegration of existing segregated trust networks e.g. decay of patrons' ability to provide their clients with goods and protection promotes withdrawal of clients from patron-client ties
- expansion of population categories lacking access to effective trust networks for their major long-term risky enterprises e.g. growth of landless wage-workers in agrarian regions increases population without effective patronage and/or relations of mutual aid
- appearance of new long term risky opportunities and threats that existing trust networks cannot handle e.g. substantial increases in war, famine, disease and/or banditry visibly overwhelm protective capacity of patrons, diasporas, and local solidarities

Each of the three mechanisms just listed promotes the dissolution of segregated trust networks and the creation of politically connected trust networks (Tilly 2005).

What of categorical inequality? The term means organization of social life around boundaries separating whole sets of people who differ collectively in their life chances, as is commonly the case with categories of gender, race, caste, ethnicity, nationality and religion, and is sometimes the case with categories of social class. To the extent that such inequalities translate directly into categorical differences in political rights and obligations, democratization remains impossible. Any democratization process depends not necessarily on diminution of categorical inequality but on insulation of public politics from categorical inequality. Two main processes contribute to that insulation: equalization of the categories themselves in some regards, and buffering of politics from the operation of those categories.

Here are the sorts of mechanisms that operate within the broader processes of equalization and buffering:

- equalization of assets and/or welfare across categories within the population at large e.g. booming demand for the products of peasant agriculture expands middle peasants
- reduction or governmental containment of privately controlled armed force e.g disbanding of magnates' personal armies weakens noble control over commoners, thereby diminishing nobles' capacity to translate noble-commoner differences directly into public politics
- adoption of devices that insulate public politics from categorical inequalities e.g. secret ballots, payment of officeholders, and free, equal access of candidates to media forward formation of cross-category coalitions

All three of these mechanisms operated widely, for example, in the waves of democratization that Europe experienced during the nineteenth century (Tilly 2004).

Autonomous power centers operate outside the control of public politics, of regular citizen-state interactions. They can include all those interpersonal connections that provide political actors – both individuals and segments of the citizenry – with the means of altering (or, for that matter, defending) existing distributions of resources, population, and activities within the regime. Sometimes they exist within the state itself, most obviously when the military run the state or operate independently of civilian authorities. The configuration of lineages, religious congregations, economic organizations, organized communities, and military forces in a given regime strongly affects the possibility that the regime's public politics will move toward broad, equal, protected, and mutually binding consultation. It does so both because that configuration shapes what sorts of political actors are readily available, and because it affects which segments of the citizenry are directly available for participation in public politics. To the extent that power centers, especially those controlling autonomous coercive means, remain detached from public politics, democratization remains difficult or impossible.

Democracy-promoting processes involving autonomous power centers include (1) broadening of political participation, (2) equalization of access to political resources and opportunities outside the state, and (3) inhibition of autonomous and/or arbitrary coercive power both within and outside the state. Although their weights and timing vary from one case of democratization to another, to some degree all three must occur for democratization to happen.

Mechanisms within these processes include:

- coalition formation between segments of ruling classes and constituted political actors that are currently excluded from power e.g. dissident bourgeois recruit backing from disfranchised workers, thus promoting political participation of those workers
- central co-optation or elimination of previously autonomous political intermediaries e.g. regional strongmen join governing coalitions, thus becoming committed to state programs
- brokerage of coalitions across unequal categories and/or distinct trust networks e.g. regional alliances form against state seizure of local assets, thus promoting employment of those alliances in other political struggles

All these mechanisms reduce the autonomy of coercive power centers. They thereby increase popular control over the whole of public politics, and the influence of public politics over state performance. In all these regards, they promote democracy.

Obviously larger changes in social life lie behind these crucial alterations of trust networks, categorical inequality, and non-state power. Eventually we will have to pay attention to transformations of economic organization, mass communications, population mobility, and education. The three democracy-promoting processes nevertheless remain crucial to the effects of economic organization, mass communications, population mobility, and education. By themselves, all of them may equally promote democracy or autocracy. The intervening transformations of trust networks, categorical inequality, and non-state power fundamentally affect the possibility of democratization.

Democratization and de-democratization do not occur in perfect symmetry. Disaffected elites, for example, play significant parts in de-democratization, which often occurs rapidly when elites defect. In contrast, democratization generally moves more slowly, and depends more heavily on organized popular support (Bermeo 2000, 2003; Karatnycky and Ackerman 2005; Schock 2005). Nevertheless, the three major democracy-promoting processes have negative counterparts. Withdrawal of integrated trust networks from public politics, insertion of categorical inequalities directly into public politics, and acquisition of new autonomy by coercive power centers all promote de-democratization powerfully when they occur.

At least this brief survey underlines the value of adopting a process approach to democracy, democratization, and de-democratization. It establishes the necessity of giving full attention to processes involving the exercise of power.

REFERENCES

Andrews, George Reid and Herrick Chapman (eds), (1995) *The Social Construction of Democracy, 1870–1990*. New York: New York University Press.

Bermeo, Nancy (2000) 'Civil society after democracy: Some conclusions', in Nancy Bermeo and Philip Nord (eds), *Civil Society before Democracy. Lessons from Nineteenth-Century Europe*. Lanham, Maryland: Rowman & Littlefield.

Bermeo, Nancy (2003) *Ordinary People in Extraordinary Times. The Citizenry and the Breakdown of Democracy*. Princeton: Princeton University Press.

Collier, David and Steven Levitsky (1997) 'Democracy with adjectives: Conceptual innovation in comparative research', *World Politics* 49: 430–451.

Dahl, Robert A. (1998) *On Democracy*. New Haven: Yale University Press.

Dahl, Robert A. (2005) 'What political institutions does large-scale democracy require?' *Political Science Quarterly*, 120: 187–197.

Engelstad, Fredrik and Øyvind Østerud (eds), (2004) *Power and Democracy. Critical Interventions*. Aldershot: Ashgate.

Freedom House Jamaica (2005) 'Freedom in the world – Jamaica', http://www.freedomhouse.org/template.cfm?page=22&country=2956&year=2004&view=mof, viewed 27 February 2006.

Goodin, Robert E., Bruce Headey, Ruud Muffels and Henk-Jan Dirven (1999) *The Real Worlds of Welfare Capitalism*. Cambridge: Cambridge University Press.

Held, David (1996) *Models of Democracy* (2nd edn). Stanford: Stanford University Press.

Inkeles, Alex (ed.) (1991) *On Measuring Democracy* (2nd edn). *Its Consequences and Concomitants*. New Brunswick, NJ: Transaction.

Karatnycky, Adrian (ed.) (2000) *Freedom in the World. The Annual Survey of Political Rights and Civil Liberties 1999–2000*. New York: Freedom House.

Karatnycky, Adrian and Peter Ackerman (2005) 'How freedom is won. From civic resistance to durable democracy', www.freedomhouse.org/65.110.85.181/uploads/special_report/29.pdf, viewed 12 March 2006.

Lafargue, Jérôme (1996) *Contestations Démocratiques en Afrique*. Paris: Karthala & IFRA.

Mann, Michael (1986) *The Sources of Social Power. Volume I: A History of Power from the Beginning to A.D. 1760*. Cambridge: Cambridge University Press.

Markoff, John (2005) 'Transitions to Democracy', in Thomas Janoski, Robert R. Alford, Alexander M. Hicks and Mildred A. Schwartz (eds), *Handbook of Political Sociology. States, Civil Societies, and Globalization*. Cambridge: Cambridge University Press.

Morlino, Leonardo (2003) *Democrazie e Democratizzazioni*. Bologna: Il Mulino.

O'Donnell, Guillermo (1999) *Counterpoints. Selected Essays on Authoritarianism and Democratization*. Notre Dame, IN: University of Notre Dame Press.

Ortega Ortiz, Reynaldo Yunuen (ed.) (2001) *Caminos a la Democracia*. Mexico City: El Colegio de México.

Piano, Aili and Arch Puddington (2004) *Freedom in the World 2004. The Annual Survey of Political Rights and Civil Liberties*. New York and Washington: Freedom House.

Schmitter, Philippe C. and Terry Lynn Karl (1991) 'What democracy is ... and is not', *Journal of Democracy* 2: 77–88.

Schock, Kurt (2005) *Unarmed Insurrections. People Power Movements in Nondemocracies*. Minneapolis: University of Minnesota Press.

Tilly, Charles (2004) *Contention and Democracy in Europe, 1650–2000.* Cambridge: Cambridge University Press.
Tilly, Charles (2005) *Trust and Rule.* Cambridge: Cambridge University Press.
Tilly, Charles (2006) *Regimes and Repertoires.* Chicago: University of Chicago Press.
UNDP (2005) United Nations Development Programme, *Human Development Report 2005. International Cooperation at a Crossroads: Aid, Trade and Security in an Unequal World.* New York: UNDP.

5

Power and Structuration Theory

Rob Stones

This chapter will look at the distinctive insights which structuration theory can offer to the analysis of power. Whilst it will necessarily draw heavily from the more general account of the history and recent developments of the approach in my book *Structuration Theory* (2005), it will be distinctive in placing the focus much more squarely on power. I will organise the chapter around two central distinctions, and whilst I will spend much more time on the first this does not lessen the importance of the second.

The first distinction is one between Anthony Giddens's formulation of structuration theory in the 1970s and early 1980s, and the present state of structuration theory which has resulted from developments, debates, counter-debates, and syntheses over the last twenty years or so. This distinction will form the basis for an analysis of the implications of the more refined, stronger, version of structuration theory for Giddens's original observations about power. The more developed version retains Giddens's emphasis on hermeneutics, situated practices, and the 'duality of structure' at its core but is in a position to draw on a more adequately specified and refined set of concepts within this province, and to be much more attuned to the implications of these ontological concepts for the research and analysis of in situ empirical cases.

I regard the distinctive contribution of structuration theory as being in the analysis of the meeting points and processes of interaction between structure and agency. It follows that its distinctive contribution to an analysis of power will be on the insights it can offer on the detailed analysis of the roles played by power in the constitution of these meeting points. In the first section I will present the strengths and core principles of structuration theory in Giddens's version of the approach; the significant refinements and developments in the tradition over the last two decades; and the role of power within all of this. I will conclude the section by engaging with Steven Lukes's recent defence of the conception of 'real interests' in the 2005 revised and enlarged edition of his classic work, *Power: A Radical View*. Dealing here with one limited but important aspect of power – the insidious third face of power which prevents the manifest emergence of 'real' grievances by shaping 'perceptions, cognitions and preferences' (Lukes, 2005 [1974] p. 28) – I try to illustrate the force of the revised version of structuration theory by showing that it allows us to problematise, refine and deepen Lukes' discussion of what is involved in attempting to ascribe real interests to those who don't immediately share that view.

The emphasis on meeting points and junctions between structure and agency leads to the second distinction mentioned at the outset, that between Giddens's structuration theory *per se* and other non-structuration aspects of his social theory. These are typically insufficiently distinguished from one another, not least by Giddens himself. It is argued that his approaches to historical sociology, modernity and Third Way politics are best understood as being underpinned by a 'non-reductionist pluralism' geared to macro analysis rather than by structuration theory. It is argued that an appreciation of this latter distinction is an indispensable precondition for being able to properly understand what structuration theory *per se* can bring to analyses of different aspects of power. It is implicit here that whilst structuration theory is a powerful approach, it also has its limits. An appreciation of these limits is a precondition for understanding how case studies of power based on structuration theory can often be fruitfully framed and mediated by other approaches to power, particularly, but not only, at the macro level of analysis.

STRUCTURATION THEORY AND POWER: EXPOSITION, DEVELOPMENTS AND ANALYSIS

A characteristic feature of structuration theory is that it goes beyond just looking at structures or just looking at agents, or of giving an *a priori* primacy to one or the other. Thus, it emphasises both social structures and agents as one of its characterising features, but this is not, by itself, what makes structuration distinctive. Its distinctiveness lies in the particular way that it *conceptualises* structures and agents. First, it places phenomenology, hermeneutics and practices at the heart of the interrelationships and interdependencies between the two. It conceives of these aspects – phenomenology, hermeneutics and practices – as highly significant components of the hinge between structures and agents. Second, it is not only the conception of the hinge that is affected by the emphasis on these aspects. That is, the reason why the hinge – the links and connections – between structures and agents is affected in large part by phenomenology, hermeneutics and practices is because the latter aspects are always at the heart of the very nature of *both* structures and agents, at the heart of what they are. The social structures that we live within, and which can confront us as both external constraints and as facilitating conditions almost always either have agents within them and/or are the product of the past practices of agents; and agents, for their part, have social structures within them, not least in the form of particular forms of phenomenological and hermeneutic inheritance. Social structures are not reified entities denuded of human beings, just as the views and experiences that prompt the thoughts and actions of social agents are not those of beings who are islands unto themselves, separated from social currents.

Giddens sets out to build a social theory, to build an approach to the causes, processes and movements of history and society that avoids two pernicious misconceptions prevalent in social thought. The two traps, from which social theorising needs to free itself, are objectivism and subjectivism. The first, objectivism, places all the emphasis on impersonal forces and subject-less structures, in which agents, if they are considered at all, are no more than the playthings or puppets of reified social systems. The second, subjectivism, reduces the whole of social life to the actions of individual agents or groups, their actions, interactions, their goals, desires, interpretations and practices. Subjectivism uproots agents from their socio-structural context, treating them as deracinated, free-floating, individuals, whereas objectivism treats them so derisively that they sink without trace, conceptualised as if they lack the autonomy to cause even the slightest ripple of disturbance on a social surface determined wholly by powerful and impersonal systemic tides. Giddens wants to find a way of avoiding the reification involved in objectivism and the voluntarism involved in subjectivism. He sees conventional uses of structure as most often falling prey to the sins of objectivism, for example in self-consciously structuralist or structural-functionalist forms of thought, and many of the various schools of interpretative sociology, from phenomenology through existentialism and symbolic interactionism to ethnomethodology, as most often falling prey to the sins of subjectivism. The strategy he pursues in order to overcome the misconceptions in each is to attempt to produce a social theory which conceptualises structures without reification and agents without voluntarism. To do so he draws from what he considers to be the best from the insights of both objectivist and subjectivist social theories.

It is for these reasons that the notion of the duality of structure is the most fundamental conceptual building block for the theory of structuration (Giddens, 1979, p. 5; 1984, p. 25; and see, e.g., McLennan, 1984, p. 126; Sewell Jnr., 1992, pp. 12–13; Sydow and Windeler, 1997, p. 462). Essential to this conception is a 'structural-hermeneutic' core in the way structuration theory characterises and understands social processes, practices and relations.[1] Giddens defines this in terms of:

> ...the essential recursiveness of social life, as constituted in social practices: structure is *both medium and outcome* of the reproduction of practices. Structure enters simultaneously into the constitution of the agent and social practices, and 'exists' in the generating moments of this constitution (Giddens, 1979: 5, my emphasis).

There is a complex and mediated connection between what is out-there in the social world and what enters in-here into the phenomenology of the mind and body of the agent. Structures serve as the 'medium' of action as they provide, through memory, the bases upon which agents draw when they engage in social practices. Giddens often refers in this context to structures having a 'virtual' existence, meaning simply that much of structure exists as a set of capabilities ready to be drawn on by agents engaged in particular activities. They are and remain virtual as the part played by, say, the memory of a norm or a fact, or an internalised sense of an external balance of power, in informing the production of a subsequent practice remains in large part a virtual one, invaluable and necessary to the production of the action but not manifest within it.

As Gregor McLennan has observed, it would perhaps be more appropriate to speak of this moment in the structuration process as a 'duality of structure and agency' as both are involved when agents draw on structures as a 'medium' in their practices (McLennan, 1984, p. 126). Meaningful and ordered social action would be impossible without this 'medium'. Structures, are also, however, the *outcome* of these practices of agents. This is true whether one is talking about the knowledge produced by reading books, the reproduction of a living language through speech, the building of a house, the defeat of an opponent in an individual trial of physical strength or as a general on the field of battle, the convening of a regional parliament, or the institution of a national tax system. Giddens doesn't make the distinction but there are two dimensions to such outcomes. The first is that the patterns of social practices in various areas of social life – and also the effects of these on later patterns through both intended and unintended consequences – are the outcome of agents drawing on structures in order to produce these practices. The second is that these interactional sequences, in which agents participate and thus experience, also have consequences – phenomenologically mediated – for the structures *within* agents at the beginning of the next cycle of structuration.

To overcome subjectivism and objectivism Giddens thus combines the subjective and the objective within his basic conceptualisation of structure, and within his conception of the agent. Giddens sees agents not only as always rooted in a structural context, but also as always and inevitably drawing upon their knowledge of that structural context when they engage in any sort of purposeful action. In its most general sense power refers to the transformative capacity of human action, and will derive in the main from this ability of agents to harness structures to their projects (1979, pp. 88–94). The very notion of action, Giddens argues, is *'logically tied to that of power*....Action intrinsically involves the application of 'means' to achieve outcomes, brought about through the direct intervention of an actor in a course of events........power represents the capacity of the agent to mobilise resources to constitute those 'means' (Giddens, 1993 [1976], p. 116, original emphasis). The possibility of agents actually being able to mobilise or draw on such potential capabilities will rest, at least in part, on the agent's perception and understanding of their availability and inherent potential. Giddens analytically divides these structures-within-knowledgeability into three different types: the structures of domination [power], signification [meaning], and legitimation [norms] (e.g. Giddens, 1979, p. 82). The three are, in reality, closely intertwined and so assessments of the balance of power in any one situation will inevitably also involve interlinked judgements about meanings and norms. Hence, structures-within-knowledgeability involve phenomenologically inflected 'stocks of knowledge' about the external context and conditions of action. This is knowledgeability about the distributions and configurations of power, meaning and norms within the terrain of action. The analytical distinction between the three types of structure allows one to focus on any one of the structures independently, and also, in principle, to examine the particular ways in which they are combined.

When focusing in more detail on power Giddens uses the term 'resources' to refer to what he calls the 'structure of domination', within which he includes both control over economic, or allocative, power resources *and* control over people or authoritative resources. He uses another term, that of 'rules', as shorthand to refer to the structures of both signification (meaning) and legitimation (norms). Thus, he often refers to agents drawing upon rules and resources. Giddens's inclusion of the three types of structures is meant to avoid the unintentional or unacceptable neglect of any one of them in instances when this would lead to distorted accounts of the social. It also provides him with a set of categories with which to focus in detail on the precise ways in which other theorists treat any one of these factors in their work. Giddens's criticism of Talcott Parsons' work on power can be seen in this frame. The criticism is not simply restricted to what might be expected, given the widespread contemporary conception of Parsons as simply putting far too much emphasis on the role of norms and values at the expense of other factors. Giddens does ultimately think that the relative weight given to norms as opposed to power in Parsons is disproportionate. However, he acknowledges that Parsons' writings on power, specifically a series of journal articles from the early 60s,[2] contain a typology of compliant behaviour that explicitly recognises 'the role of non-normative factors in social action' (Giddens, 1977, p. 341, also see pp. 336–7; *originally published 1968,* see below), although he notes that there is no 'systematic discussion of the interplay between them and values' (p. 343). Rather, Giddens's primary criticism is about Parsons' handling of power *per se* and it revolves around the latter's concern to show the productive, systemic, aspects of power which emerge once the ruled place their trust in a legitimate leader who pursues collective goals from which everybody gains (p. 335). Because of this focus, Parsons is 'concerned to emphasise that power does not necessarily entail the coercive imposition of one individual or group over another' (Giddens, 1977, p. 341), and the result, Giddens argues, is that the notion of power being exercised over someone[3] 'slips away from sight almost completely.' Giddens also argues that Parsons 'virtually ignores, quite consciously and deliberately, the necessarily hierarchical character of power, and the divisions of interest which are frequently consequent upon it' (Giddens, 1977, p. 341).

Stewart R. Clegg has taken Giddens to task for reading these writings of Parsons on power in abstraction from his overall analytic schema (Clegg, 1989, p. 137; also see Turner, 1986: 179–206) in which, Clegg argues, neither conflict nor hierarchy are disregarded. He also chides him for rhetorically erasing what he has already acknowledged, the fact that Parsons' explicit and specific purpose and focus in these writings was to develop a broader, facilitative conception of power against the overly narrow conception of power he'd found in C. Wright Mills's *The Power Elite*. Clegg writes that: 'It is not so much that 'power over' slips away from Parsons' conceptualisation but that he focuses on the more economical, subtle and productive aspects of power rather than on those that automatically produce conflict' (Clegg, 1989, p. 136). Perhaps Giddens would have been more sensitive to this focus had the original publication of this article (1968) not been before his elaboration of structuration theory with its clear recognition of productive – enabling – power, power as transformative capacity, as the most fundamental conception of power, with 'power over' being just one of its sub-classes (see 1976, p. 118; 1979, pp. 88–94). Parsons' approach is entirely in line with this later recognition by Giddens that power in it most generic sense can be equated with transformative capacity, and the writings of both thus have interesting and intriguing parallels with Foucault's emphasis on productive power. Giddens' critique of Parsons' emphasis seems to forget the basic epistemological point that the specific problem being addressed by a theorist needs to be taken into account in any meaningful critique of the resulting work. A related point we will return to is that even within a given focus, say the subtle and productive aspects of power focused on by Parsons, the relative balance between consensus and conflict, and the interplay between them, will ultimately be an empirical question, albeit one whose analysis will be more or less adequately guided by relevant theoretical concepts.

In developing the precise positioning of power within the framework of structuration theory, Giddens makes a distinction between, on the one hand, the structures of domination, legitimation and signification existing as knowledgeability in memory traces, and, on the other hand, what he calls 'modalities', the ways in which agents in particular circumstances can draw on or employ these structures as rules and resources in interaction.

Thus, he distinguishes, for example, between the overall structure of *domination* that is potentially available within the memory traces of individuals and then the more limited and task-specific *facilities* that these agents subsequently, and actually, draw on, on the basis of the prior availability, when they engage in a definite interaction. The agent's use of facilities within a social practice or interaction is said to be an exercise of *power*. The three levels of conceptualisation used by Giddens in explaining what is involved when agents draw on structures are useful in that there is often good reason to distinguish between these different moments. However, the terminology is unduly cumbersome and restrictive and it can make sense to use the notion of power for any of the levels depending on the context. Thus, whilst it is extremely useful to keep the different levels in mind it makes a lot of sense still to speak of power structures (instead of structures of domination), or of drawing on power (instead of drawing on facilities).

There is a certain lack of analytical clarity here with respect to two issues central to Giddens's conceptualisation of power. The first regards the relation between 'structures as memory traces' and 'structure as resources'. Giddens seems to be unsure himself about what he wants to say on this point.[4] On the one hand, he sometimes appears to include certain material elements of context and capability in the notion of structure as resources. Thus, in *Central Problems in Social Theory* he writes of resources as the 'material levers' of all transformations of empirical contents (1979, p. 104). But at other times, as in the definition he gives to structure in *The Constitution of Society*, he sees structure as resources as existing only as memory traces and as instantiated in action (1984, p. 377). The latter definition logically rules out structures as resources having any material content, a conclusion that Giddens would be hard put to defend as consistent with many of the points he makes about power and transformative capacity. Coherence would demand a careful combining of elements from both definitions, and specific empirical instances of either allocative or authoritative power would involve various combinations of material levers and memory traces in the instantiation of actions. Strong structuration consequently works with the assumption that 'structure as resources', the structural basis of power, has both phenomenological and material dimensions.

The second, related, issue concerning a lack of clarity regards the boundaries of the agent and of the structures that are available to be drawn upon by the agent.[5] If these structures are to be seen as being in one way or another *within* the agent, either as memory traces or capability then one needs to be clear, for example, whether or not any particular resources beyond the human body itself should be said to be either 'part of' or 'belonging to' a particular agent. Should, for example, material objects employed by an agent in the performance of an action – from tokens of exchange through clothes and weapons to technologically sophisticated means of transportation or communication – be thought of as part of the agent's embodied capability informed by the hermeneutic structures within that 'body', or should they be thought of as material things external to the agent?[6] This would need clarification before we could ascertain in any empirical instance which material resources should be seen as internal to the agent and which as external to the agent but available to be drawn upon as part of the external structure of domination. The difference is highly significant as it is the difference between power being in the hands of one's own agency and it being dependent upon the compliance of others.

It seems to me that this issue is harder to deal with at a high level of abstraction than it would be with respect to a particular empirical case. It should not be particularly difficult, in principle, in a given case, to determine those boundaries of an agent which are relevant to the particular question or problem at hand. This is the kind of issue that Giddens has never been particularly good at addressing. For all their intrinsic attraction and promise his categories seem schematic, underdeveloped and relatively empty once on begins to ask more precise and detailed questions of them. His version of structuration theory possessed a number of characteristics which, collected together, left it with a distinct tendency towards what I will call *methodological voluntarism*.

The characteristics of ontological voluntarism are (1) an excessive concern with abstract ontological concepts (ontology-in-general) at the expense of thinking about how they might be employed at the empirical level (ontology-in-situ, or the ontic); (2) the absence of a conceptualisation of the institutionalised meso-level of social relations and their networks, captured in different ways by Robert K. Merton's notion of role relationships (e.g. Merton, 1957a, 1957b), Norbert Elias's elaboration of figurations (e.g. Elias, 1978), Pierre Bourdieu's conception of differentiated fields (e.g. Bourdieu, 1993) , or Ira J. Cohen's concept of position-practice relations developed from within the problematic of structuration theory (Cohen, 1989, pp. 207–13), within which given individual and collective agents interact at the empirical level (the meso-level of ontological scale); and (3) as a consequence, I believe, of not being exposed to the exigencies and challenges that would have been posed by a greater engagement with one and two, Giddens' version of structuration inadequately developed and insufficiently specified an appropriate range of empirically sensitive ontological concepts around the central notion of the 'duality of structure'; and (4) again as a consequence of one and two, there was a failure to pay sufficient attention to questions of epistemology and methodology, particularly with respect to issues within theoretically informed empirical research. These characteristics left Giddens' structuration theory insufficiently equipped, with deficits on each count, to deal with grounded substantive issues. A fatal consequence for substantive judgements was a methodological freedom which allowed Giddens to move far too easily between accounts that conveyed conflicting extremes of agency voluntarism and structural determinism. The agency voluntarism here is perhaps best captured by Giddens' repeated insistence that agents can 'always choose to do otherwise' (e.g. Giddens, 1984, p. 14), a claim which is so abstract that it leaves aside all the most interesting sociological questions about when, where and to what extent, in what ways, and at what cost, this is in fact the case.

The stronger version of structuration theory that has emerged from debate, counter-debate, empirical applications and ensuing theoretical synthesis over the last two decades has addressed the deficits in each of these areas. A core dimension of this is a more refined conceptualisation of the duality of structure which distinguishes between four different aspects involved in any structuration cycle, each of which is attuned to the variability of content at the empirical, in-situ, level. The first dimension singles out **external structures** as conditions of action in a clear statement that there is much more to structuration theory than the phenomenology and memory traces of the current agent-in-focus. Nicos Mouzelis has written lucidly on the variable levels of intractability or malleability of these external structures, and this is necessarily related to the specific positioning and power resources available to the agent who confronts them (see Mouzelis, 1991, pp. 37–9; 1995, p. 156; see also Archer, 1995). The external structures can be thought of as the agent-in-focus's context of action, and will involve her methodologically in an *agent's context analysis* of relevant position-practice relations; this form of analysis can also be engaged in by an external theorist who may be more or less well informed than the agent-in-focus.[7] The second aspect of the structuration cycle involves **internal structures** within the agent, which are the embodied phenomenological conditions which allow agents to mediate between external structures and their own orientation towards future actions. These internal structures can be divided into: (1) *general dispositions*, akin to Bourdieu's notion of habitus, which refers to the specific and variable dispositions, cultural and discursive schemas, conventional understandings and typifications, 'stocks' of transposable knowledge, principles of action, emotional investments and value-commitments,[8] skills, aesthetic tastes, and habits of speech and gesture within the agent-in-focus. These will typically be pluralistic and internally differentiated in character;[9] and (2) *conjuncturally-specific knowledge*, which refers to the variable knowledge and understanding any agent-in-focus has of the external context of action within a specific conjuncture. Included will be knowledge related to the different analytical, but empirically intertwined, domains of power relations, norms and meaning, and also of the combination of material and non-material factors relevant to action and its probable consequences. Again, such knowledge will typically be linked to a plurality of differentiated sets of position-practice relations and their incumbents relevant to the conjuncture and to particular goals and interests. The third aspect is that of **active agency**, including a range of factors potentially implicated when agents draw upon internal structures in producing practical action. Important amongst these for the discussion of Lukes' approach to real interests is the agent's tendency to order or sort their concerns and value commitments into a hierarchy of priorities or purposes. More or less critical reflection may be involved, and the various orderings may be more or less clear-cut or blurred and indeterminate. The final dimension of the structuration cycle is that of the intended and unintended **outcomes or consequences of actions** (which have an impact upon external and internal structures, as well as on events and the general well being of actors).

The quadripartite cycle of structuration is trained on the point at which an agent-in-focus is involved in institutionalised practices, within unfolding time and relational space, and at the junction with other individual and collective actors in a field of socially relational and cross-cutting position-practices. All these relational practices are horizontally and/or hierarchically organised, a point made cogently and at length by both Cohen and Mouzelis in their contributions to the structuration synthesis (Cohen, 1989, pp. 207–213; and Mouzelis, 1991, 1995), and this clearly has important implications for the conceptualisation of power. Power relations are always embedded within these fields of position practices, with actors involved in a whole series of projects, each involving their own relevant sets of position-practice relationships. Power will be a dimension of each one of these relationships, and, to adopt the clear and precise conceptual discriminations detailed in Dennis H. Wrong's account of the forms, bases and uses of *Power* (1988 [1979]), it may primarily take the consensual form of legitimate authority in which both parties experience the power relations simply as productive (to echo the earlier discussion of Parsons) and without oppression or domination, or it may take the form of coercive authority, which at the extreme manifests itself in direct force, or, alternatively, it may take the form of manipulation or persuasion. We may add, following Bourdieu (e.g. 1977 [1972]), that it can also take a form, beyond intentional manipulation or persuasion, of largely unintentional but socially structured processes of socialisation which shape and mould the dispositions, skills, discursive categories and perceptions of relationally situated individuals in unequal and socially patterned ways. Any concrete empirical configuration of power relations could potentially combine all these forms of power within it. This is Dennis Wrong's essential point in chapters devoted to 'The Forms of Power' whose subtitles are, respectively, 'Combinations and Interrelations' and 'The Interaction of Coercion and Legitimation'. Within the summary of the latter chapter he writes:

> The familiar dichotomy between consensus and constraint theories of society, and between legitimate and coercive authority, is usually drawn much too sharply, for both are present and interact to form different 'mixes' or compounds in virtually all power relations. The motivation for compliance even of single individuals combines constraint and duty – 'fear' and 'love' – and the relative predominance of one or the other of these varies widely in a population subject to extensive authority (Wrong, 1988, p. 122)

It is a central tenet of strong structuration approaches that a truly satisfactory analysis of any one configuration of power is a task that requires careful, systematic and judicious discrimination on the basis of guidance from a combination of:

- Refined ontological concepts, adequate to the task at hand, including a conceptualisation of the meso-level of social relations and their networks
- Epistemological and methodological sensitivity to the relationship between the abstract (ontology-in-general), and the concrete, empirical (ontology-in-situ)

The ontological concepts within the structuration approach would, of course, be those which focus on the conceptual field demarcated by the duality of structure and agency, and it is on the basis of such that I will analyse Lukes' defence and discussion of real interests. Lukes characteristically wants to avoid any dogmatic or crude ascription of interests to others, whether these be class interests, gender interests or whatever (Lukes, 2005, pp. 145–6). However, he does want to defend the legitimacy of more considered attempts to take a view of people's interests that is external to their own view. He bases his defence on the resolute belief that an agent's 'compliance to domination can be secured by the shaping of beliefs and desires'. Lukes argues that this compliance can, counter-factually, be said to be against person B's interests if one could say that without the existence and interference in B's life of A's power then B, now acting under conditions of relative autonomy, would not choose compliance (p. 146). In a situation of resigned pragmatic acquiescence towards existing conditions which B had never in any case felt were in her interests then the favourable change in the power relations would change behaviour but not her beliefs and desires. However, if B was someone who had never questioned traditional ways but was now exposed to alternative possibilities which she found attractive then she could well change her beliefs and desires as well as her behaviour. In the former case one could say that B knew her own 'real interests' all along, but the conditions of power prevented her from pursuing them, but in the latter case it required a change in the conditions of power for B to even see her 'real interests'. Lukes believes that this kind of claim about the shaping of beliefs and desires by previous power structures can have an empirical basis. In support of this he cites: the women's development groups in Andhra Pradesh in India referred to by Martha Nussbaum, among whose members '[t]raditions of deference that once seemed good have quickly ceased to seem so'. For, as Nussbaum writes, if

> someone who has no property rights under the law, who has no formal education, who has no legal right of divorce, who will very likely be beaten if she seeks employment outside the home, says that she

endorses traditions of modesty, purity and self-abnegation, it is not clear that we should consider this the last word on the matter.

We should, in short, 'reflect before we conclude that women without options really endorse the lives they lead' (Nussbaum, 2000: 43); but nor should we just assume that people *with* options do so, if those options are loaded and internal constraints work against their interests (Lukes, 2005, p. 146).

Immediately after this section Lukes responds to Ted Benton's powerful criticisms of the first edition of the book with respect to:

1 the problematic nature of any vantage point from which 'real interests' could be attributed; and to
2 the problems in identifying empirically what counts as the relative autonomy required for the expression of 'real interests', especially given the problem of specifying 'which of the indefinitely large class of counter-factual conditions are to be the privileged ones for purposes of interest-ascription' (Benton, 1981, pp. 289–91; cited in Lukes (2005), p. 148).

Lukes makes a significant but cogent concession on the first point, accepting that what counts as 'real interests' are a function of one's explanatory purpose, framework and methods, which in turn have to be justified. I think this is right and it opens up many interesting further issues and questions which require the resources both of normative theory and the kind of epistemological and methodological issues addressed by strong structuration.[10] It is on the second point, however, that I want to focus here. Benton simply asks how we know when just the right amount and kind of power has been withdrawn from the context of action by A, or C, or someone else, for us to be able to say that B's expressed interests at a given point of time are now her 'real interests'? We have already noted that an agent's hermeneutic constitution, and hence interests, are always situated in a nexus of cross-cutting position-practice relations. Agents are never free of all influences, pressures, potential sanctions, inducements, implicit threats of force, discourses and so on. They will never be agents floating free from all social constraints and able to choose the social relations within which they can follow their 'real interests'. They will always exist and engage in practices within a constraining as well as facilitating nexus of power relations. We have noted Lukes' view that we shouldn't just assume that people *with* options necessarily 'endorse the lives they lead, if those options are loaded and internal constraints work against their interests' (Lukes, 2005, p. 146, original emphasis), but given what we have just said about agents never floating free from all social constraints this raises more problems than he acknowledges about the empirical and normative status of real interests. If options are always loaded with internal constraints then a failure to endorse one's own life because it is loaded with internal constraints does not necessarily mean that this life is not in one's own real interests. I will return to this below in introducing the idea of 'conjunctural real interests'.

In defence of Lukes, the example from Andhra Pradesh illustrates graphically the important possibility that actors who become free from a definable threat from one or other significant power holder/set of social forces in given circumstances will become patently happier, more fulfilled, and/or more capable, than previously. The point is not contradicted by any of the objections raised so far which, in one way or another, circumscribe the scope and status of the conception of real interests. His example convinces us that there are instances in which people don't know what they want, or would want, until conditions preventing them from seeing this are removed. These conditions are enough to justify further exploration of the idea of 'real interests' and the conditions under which they may be recognised and realised. Having said this, the choice of the example from the Indian women's collectives is an overly simple case to adopt as a model with which to test out the existence of real interests in the majority of circumstances. Other cases will typically involve many more complicating factors. To expand on these points I will, firstly, draw on strong structuration theory to sketch out just some of the additional complicating factors and, secondly, I will say more, by way of contrast, about the relatively simple character of the example from the women's collectives.

To begin with, it is important to note that Lukes, even in this example from Andhra Pradesh, does recognise that if there was a further factor, a third force, which could sufficiently interfere with the relative autonomy of the women, this would undermine the claim that they are now following their real interests (Lukes, 2005, p. 148). Explicitly, this acknowledges the embeddedness of all expressions of interests and as a logical consequence it also accepts a distinction between what we can call *real conjunctural interests* and *real ideal interests*. The former, which are the only 'real interests' that count in practice, are those which, within specifiable social conditions and within a given, albeit variable, time frame, refer to:

1 *interests* which the actor may have (whether subjectively felt and externally imputed; or just externally imputed) in attempting to change the power relations which define her existing circumstances; which are combined with a
2 *judgement* that the interests in pursuing change are not entirely voluntaristic – that it is not a potentially dangerous indulgence in rash idealism to expect those circumstances to change; and which are
3 *not being manipulated or the result of being misled* by other power sources which have not been taken into account.

Any in situ application of Lukes' idea of 'real interests' thus requires complex and refined judgements about the configuration of relations of power, structure and agency. Strong structuration theory has developed many guiding concepts specific to this domain which would be invaluable in any attempt to develop and employ the idea in empirical research and political endeavour. There may, for example, be many alternative real conjunctural interests potentially available to actors – knowledge of which will require what we've called *agent's context analysis* – that they don't think about or covet simply because it has never occurred to them that there might be such possibilities. The crucial questions are thus those of strategic possibilities and constraints, to be sure, and they do involve the possibility of rewards, but they also concern the danger of sanctions (sanctions of varying degrees of severity) and what it would really mean in practice for flesh and blood people, with lives, emotions and value-commitments rooted in definable circumstances, to have a truly meaningful choice between the pursuit of competing interests, one of which we might designate as real and another as not so.[11]

When thinking of real interests in this embedded way one needs to acknowledge that people typically possess a number of different emotional and value commitments, and adhere to a number of related and overlapping practical concerns which are ordered more or less reflectively according to a complex hierarchy of priorities. Each of these concerns is linked through a hermeneutic-structural nexus, involving internal perceptions of external structures, which is dependent upon cross-cutting sets of position-practice relationships.

People don't often fully endorse every aspect of their lives. They accept, more or less, that all lives will be loaded with a variety of constraints, and they make compromises according to their situations and values.

Most people will typically endure less than ideal circumstances in one area of these relationships either in order to secure certain conditions in another area of life which figures in their concerns, or so as to attain deferred rewards at a later date from within the same area. To echo Dennis Wrong, not only constraint and duty but also 'fear' and 'love' are involved in a person's overall set of commitments (Wrong, 1988, p. 122). The less than ideal compromises between domains can include, at one end, simply working at a less than ideal job in order to bring in money to live on, or leaving a fulfilling job and receiving welfare benefits in order to care for an ill and loved parent, partner, or friend. Towards the other end of conditions of treatment there are people who put up with less than minimum wages and inhuman working conditions in order to put food on the table for their family, or who refrain from speaking out about a grievous wrong because they fear for their jobs or their safety, or, to return to Nussbaum's example, who don't seek employment outside the home because if they did they would be beaten. A responsible attribution of real conjunctural interests to people caught in these webs of relations would have to show them a credibly feasible way of genuinely improving upon their present predicament.

Things are more complicated still once one brings in genuine psychological and emotional ambivalence towards the value-commitments themselves. Nussbaum herself quotes Indian feminist philosopher Uma Narayan's understanding of her own mother's emotional value commitments as Janus-faced. She taught her daughter subservience, silence and submissiveness and the value of unquestioning obedience to adult male authority, whilst at the same time protesting articulately about 'the misery such confining traditions' had caused (Nussbaum, 2000, p. 42). As an outsider one can feel that there is something wrong here, but one cannot purely and simply discount the ambivalence as a battle between real and false interests. The ambivalence, rather, may express two kinds of value commitments, both of which the mother may care about equally.

Compared with the difficulties posed for the conception of real conjunctural interests by many situations, the case of the Andhra Pradesh women which Lukes invokes is thus relatively simple. Not least, the judgement about it is after the event, when things have worked out well. We now know that the women's fear that 'their husbands would react harshly' was not realised, and that the women's more general apprehension that change would 'make things worse' was misplaced as 'over time they began to see that many advantages could be gained by collective discussion and action: now they get the health visitor to come more regularly, they demand that the teacher show up' (Nussbaum, 2000, p. 43). It is easy, in this case, now, at this point in the unfolding sequence of events, for an outsider, basing her or his explanatory and normative framework on the expansion of women's capabilities, to say with confidence to these women in this place and at this time that their real conjunctural interests were indeed in the construction of women's collectives. No longer do they 'peep out of their houses' and not take any action in the world; their conjunctural real interests seem to be self-evident, but, before the event, one would have wanted to know much more about the relational social conditions in which the government's Mahila Samakhya project was to be implemented in this desert area about ninety minutes from Mahabubnagar, as well as in any other areas in which it was tried out, than either Nussbaum or Lukes provides us with. Taking one of Nussbaum's own examples: if we can agree, as I trust we can,[12] that the attribution of real ideal interests is unproblematic, but of little use, to a woman who will be beaten if she leaves the house, agreement over the attribution of her real conjunctural interests is much more problematic. To consider the question of her real conjunctural interests properly we need to know a lot about the agent's strategic context of action. We need to know what she would do in the actual circumstances of action if, first, aspects of her beliefs and desires had not been shaped as they have, and, second, if she had an adequate knowledge of the conditions of action and of the likely consequences of different courses of action. Knowing these things would require both a close phenomenological knowledge of the woman's general dispositions and conjuncturally specific knowledge, and of the potentially plural forces within the external strategic context of action, including the distribution of power within it and the various normative schemas likely to be involved in its deployment.

If the woman who is beaten if she leaves the house will not be beaten if the idea that she *should* leave the house enters the community from, for example, local or central government, or from a political party or NGO, then it would be better to know something about this in advance. If the contrary is the case then we would want to know. It is the configuration of the situated and phenomenologically inflected power relations within a specific context that makes the attribution of real conjunctural interests problematic. For the conception of real interests to have any practical and strategic import it needs to be combined with the best conceptual and methodological tools available to analyse the phenomenological-structural nexus which inhabits the people with the putative interests, and to analyse the relevant relational nexus of position practices that they inhabit.

DISTINGUISHING NON-REDUCTIONIST PLURALISM FROM STRUCTURATION THEORY PROPER

It should be apparent by this stage that whilst I hold Giddens's version of structuration to be wanting in a number of significant respects, I still wish to reserve an important place for many of his undoubtedly seminal contributions to the approach. Given the important role that his work would continue to play within the renewed conception of structuration I have presented, albeit often amended and refined, it follows that if the distinctive contribution of structuration theory to social theory, and of structuration theory to the analysis of power, is to be established with some precision, then one will need to be clear about which parts of Giddens's entire corpus of writings fall into the category of structuration theory, and which do not. It needs to be recognised, that is, that not all of Giddens's work can properly be labelled as structuration theory. It follows that not all criticism of Giddens's work is criticism of structuration theory (even when it thinks it is) and, conversely, of course, not all criticism of Giddens's structuration theory amounts to criticism of all of Giddens's work. It is possible, moreover, to be sympathetic to much of what I will call Giddens's anti-reductionist work – by which I refer primarily to his substantive work on historical sociology, on the institutions of modernity, and on Third Way politics – but to reject the notion that this work is itself a manifestation of structuration theory. It is important to distinguish the appropriate domain of structuration theory from these other aspects of Giddens's writings as both he and others consistently conflate the two. I want to stress that the non-reductionist or anti-reductionist elements of Giddens' work are informed, at best, only by the abstract conception of structuration, one that remains at the level of philosophical principles, which has little if any impact on the kinds of substantive or empirical claims and insights he makes in this work. Indeed, the corollary of the fact that most of Giddens's explicit writing on structuration remains at the philosophical, meta-theoretical level is that most of his substantive writing is hardly touched by it.

I will first say a little more about what I mean by anti-reductionist pluralism before distinguishing it from the ontology of structuration theory. By anti-reductionism I refer to a general movement in social theory that rejects explanations of social phenomena that reduces them to an overly limited number of causes. A classic case of reductionism would be the economic determinism of some kinds of Marxism whereby the political, legal and ideological superstructures are reduced to the status of epiphenomena of the economic base. This kind of conception has been criticised over time by an array of both Marxists and non-Marxists. For example, Gramsci and neo-Gramscians developed conceptions of relative degrees of autonomy of the cultural and discursive spheres from the economic base (cf. Gramsci, 1971; Hall, 1980); Althusser argued for the relative autonomy of the ideological, legal and political levels from the economic, which was said only to be determinate in 'the last instance' (cf. Althusser, 1969; Benton, 1984). Poulantzas, in similar vein but taking things further, developed first a 'regional' and then a 'relational' account of just one of these levels, the political, that in both cases gave it a developed *sui generis* reality of its own that was irreducible to, albeit deeply influenced by, the economic (cf. Poulantzas, 1973, 1978; Jessop, 1985; cf. McLennan, 1996, pp. 55–61).

Just as Neo-Marxism stretched further and further away from economic determinism, and at its edges gave way to the 'necessary non-correspondence' and the 'discursive autonomy' of Post-Marxism (cf. Hindess and Hirst, 1977; Laclau and Mouffe, 1985), theorists working in adjacent or overlapping theoretical traditions also began to (or continued to) frame their work in terms of an explicit non-reductionism. In this sense there was a convergence of traditions. Michael Mann's *The Sources of Social Power* (1986, 1993) is based on a pluralist non-reductionist approach explicitly focused on power, on four different but overlapping spheres of social power – of Ideology, Economy, Military and Political (the latter divided between centralised-territorial state spheres and geographical-diplomatic state spheres) – each with their own organising means and institutional networks. Non-reductionism *per se* was sometimes accompanied by a more or less serious and concerted attempt to look at the way in which a number of different levels, mechanisms or domains were held to be jointly responsible for the production of events, practices, social phenomena (e.g. Parsons, 1991; Lindblom, 1977; Mann, 1986; Giddens, 1984, 1985; Walby, 1990). The different domains were held to articulate with each other, to interweave and interconnect in ways that combined both necessity and contingency (cf. Jessop, 1990, pp. 11–12). The emphasis of non-reductionism, however, was heavily weighted towards establishing the distinctiveness of spheres or levels rather than towards explicating precisely what was involved in the articulation itself. No doubt this was partly because of the recalcitrant complexity of the challenges involved in undertaking the latter. The consequence was that questions concerning issues of joint or plural causality, of relational interdependencies, and of junctions between structures and agencies, involving the macro, the meso and the micro, were only broached at an imprecise and vague level.

In the more abstract cases there was little attempt to trace through detailed sequences in which non-reductionist spheres were brought back together in interwoven chains of mutual influence. Judgements here were more a function of general philosophical intuition or belief than of a well-developed framework of conjunctural analysis. Giddens's broad ranging substantive writings typically fall into this abstract and under-specified category.

In *Central Problems in Social Theory* (1979) there is a direct transposition of Giddens's ontological account of structures onto an account of the substantive institutional domains of political institutions, economic institutions, law/modes of sanction, and symbolic orders/modes of discourse. Each one of these domains is said to be constituted by a mixture of the universal social constituents (structures) of signification, domination and legitimation, but with one or other of them dominant depending upon the institutional domain. Thus, for example, allocative power is dominant in economic institutions but this doesn't mean that the constituents of signification and social norms are not also required to communicate the negotiations and decisions, and to make sure that those involved can be sufficiently trusted to carry out those allocative policies. The impulse towards non-reductionist pluralism can explain why Giddens here would want to distinguish between different types of institution, and between different constituent elements within institutions. What is not clear is what he thought he had achieved by the unmediated transposition of the ontological categories of signification, domination and legitimation involved in the duality of structure onto the institutional domain. The nature of the relations between the three ontological categories and historically significant institutional categories is extremely under-developed. The most we have is a preliminary sketching out of an area for future development. It is notable, in fact, that the direct transposition disappears in the later, still theoretically informed, books such as *The Nation State and Violence* (1985), and *The Consequences of Modernity* (1990). The latter, for example, simply refers to the more substantive entities of the world capitalist economy, the nation-state system, the international division of labour, and the world military order which are articulated not with the abstract ontological structures of domination, legitimation/norms and signification, but with key explanatory mechanisms said to be specific to the historical period of modernity, and to have intensified within the period of late modernity. These are mechanisms such as the disembedding mechanisms of expert systems and symbolic tokens which reorganise social relations across large time-space distances; the growth of institutional reflexivity; and the specific contours of trust in environments of manufactured risk and uncertainty. The same is true of the more substantive, historically emerging, explanatory categories in other 'large sweep' books, such as the emphasis in *The Nation State and Violence* (1985) on the ability of modern states 'to concentrate and centralise authoritative resources within a national "power container"' (Jessop, 1989, p. 107), and on the three combined sets of power capacities within this: surveillance and supervision, specialisation in intellectual labour, and military and police sanctions (Giddens, 1985). Many aspects of these bases of power can be accumulated and stored as potential resources in other power containers, such as the work-place, courts, and cities (Jessop, 1989, p. 107). These are interesting substantive points, germane to a historically embedded account of developments with wide ranging consequences for social relations, but we are a long way from the fine grained contextualised detail of the structuration processes by which these various explanatory mechanisms and stored power capacities are drawn on as media and emerge as outcomes in specific and identifiable situated practices.

If the institutional categories of *Central Problems* are meant to be at a higher level of abstraction than those in the later books, and there is no doubt in my mind that they are, then an enormous amount of work needs to be done in spelling out both the connection between the different levels of analysis and the explanatory pay-off one might expect from taking the trouble to formulate any such connection. Neither is self-evident. I suspect that the decision not to invest the immense energy required for anything like a meaningful theoretical and conceptual connection helps to explain the gradual but inexorable retreat from any kind of systematic theorisation, as opposed to intelligent empirical synthesis, descriptive taxonomy, and political argument in Giddens's most recent writings such as *The Third Way* (1998) and *Europe in the Global Age* (2007).

The absence of structuration theory at the level of pluralistic non-reductionism was, in effect, acknowledged and consolidated by Giddens's introduction of what he called 'institutional analysis' as a method of approaching the larger picture. He defines institutional analysis as: 'Social analysis which *places in suspension the skills and awareness of actors*, treating institutions as chronically reproduced rules and resources' (Giddens, 1984, p. 375, my emphasis). Giddens himself never explicitly drew the logical conclusion from the use of this form of bracketing, namely that it is impossible to even begin to address the duality of structure from within it; but even according to his definition, institutional analysis is not interested in the interpretative or hermeneutic ways in which actors draw upon their perceptions of the structures of domination, signification and legitimation, as they go about their social interactions. The structural-hermeneutic core of structuration is therefore absent.

In treating the universal social constituents of domination, signification and legitimation (rules and resources) 'as chronically reproduced features of social systems' (Giddens, 1979, p. 80), Giddens brackets out the phenomenology of structurally situated agents, brackets out the way that agents perceive and draw upon their structural context.[13] In consequence he is unable to provide any guidelines by which the insights of his macro sociology could be used, for example, to inform the kinds of analyses of the strategic context of position-practice relations which faced the women of Andhra Pradesh before their decision to participate in the women's collectives' project. The absence is disappointing – although not surprising for the task is a daunting one – and a serious gap as the advisability or otherwise, the likely success or otherwise, of all kinds of civil and political action depends not only upon the immediately apprehensible context of action but also on the ways in which macro historical and social structural forces frame and impinge upon the meso context.

Given the axiom we started out with regarding the centrality of the 'duality of structure' for structuration theory it is clear that one needs more than non-reductionism *per se* to grasp the process of structuration *in situ*. Non-reductionist pluralism, by itself, cannot grasp structure as a 'medium' of agent's practices, it cannot grasp agent's conduct. Neither can it know about the frame of meaning within which an agent perceives external structuration processes, or whether an agent perceives those structures accurately or inaccurately. Neither can it know which structuration 'outcomes' are intended and which are unintended. Even with more developed ontological links *between* structures at the most abstract level *and* more substantive notions of institutions, the methodological bracket of institutional analysis would still place in suspension crucial components of every one of the four parts of the quadripartite process of structuration intrinsic to the duality of structure. Consequently, any writing produced loyally within the confines of this form of bracketing will not fall within the parameters of structuration theory. For institutional analysis simply does not allow for any of the bridging concepts, procedural methodological guidelines, or substantive historical detail that would denote the movement *from* the non-reductionist insistence on the distinctiveness of institutional clusters and practices *to* accounts of the sequential and interlocking articulation or mutual influencing – informed by notions of hermeneutics, phenomenology and duality, and position-practice relations – of different institutional clusters in the production of social outcomes.

NOTES

1 It is this emphasis that is important in the commitment to a duality of structure' and a 'duality of structure and agency' and not some kind of commitment to the word 'duality' as such, or to any insistence that the elements of structure and agency cannot, in principle if not always in fact, be disentangled in order to reveal the relations between them (analytical dualism). Prominent critiques by critical realists (Archer, 1995; Parker, 2006) of both Giddens's version of structuration and my own 'strong' structuration are confused in believing that a commitment to duality in the manner expressed here also involves a rejection of analytical dualism. It is entirely possible, indeed preferable, to adhere to both.

2 The discussion refers to the following of Parsons's writings on power: 'On the Concept of Political Power', *Proceedings of the American Philosophical Society*, vol. 107, 1963, pp. 232–62; 'Some Reflections of the Place of Force in Social Process', in Harry Eckstein, *Internal War*, Glencoe, 1964; 'On the Concept of Influence', *Public Opinion Quarterly* , vol. 27, 1963, pp. 37–62; 'The Political Aspect of Social Structure and Process', in David Easton, *Varieties of Political Theory*, Englewood Cliffs, 1966; and 'Authority, Legitimation and Political Action', pp. 170–98, and 'The Distribution of Power in American Society (A Review of C.Wright Mills' *The Power Elite*), pp. 199–225, both in T. Parsons, *Structure and Process in Industrial Societies*, Glencoe, 1960.

3 Giddens's assertion in the relevant sentence that 'power is always exercised *over* someone!' is at worst simply wrong, and at best a dreadful oversimplification, and is ostensibly at odds with what he has argued in the first part of the article about the use of power not necessarily implying a zero-sum game.

4 Compare, for example, the point made about resources as the 'material levers' of all transformations of empirical contents in 1979, p. 104, with the definition of structure as existing only as memory traces and as instantiated in action in 1984, p. 377. If resources, as defined in the first case, were instantiated in action in the second case then they would also have to have an existence as prior potential in that case. This would make the definition of structure in the second case inadequate and misleading.

5 These are issues that Giddens can be forgiven for ignoring, certainly in his early writings, as the works which have done most to draw attention to their theoretical significance emerged during the 1980s and 1990s. See, for example, Michel Callon. 'Some Elements of a Sociology of Translation', In John Law (ed.), *Power, Action and Belief. A New Sociology of Knowledge*. London, Routledge and Kegan Paul, 1986, pp. 196–232; Michel Callon and Bruno Latour, 'Unscrewing the Big Leviathan: How do Actors Macrostructure Reality? In K. Knorr-Cetina and A.V. Cicourel (eds.), *Advances in Social Theory and Methodology: Toward an Integration of Macro and Micro Sociologies*. London, Routledge, 1981, pp. 277–303; Donna Haraway, 'The Promises of Monsters: A Regenerative Politics for Inappropriate/d Others. In L. Grossberg, C. Nelson and P. Treichler (eds.), *Cultural Studies*. New York: Routledge, 1992, pp. 295–337; and Nigel Thrift, N. *Spatial Formations*. London, Sage, 1996.

6 Things are further complicated, of course, by the consideration of technologically manufactured parts that become part of the human body itself, from prosthetics to microchip implants.

7 For an elaboration of agent's context analysis see Stones, *Structuration Theory*, London, Palgrave Macmillan, 2005, pp. 121–25.

8 For a powerful elaboration of the case for a more systematic inclusion of the emotional investments and moral-commitments of actors into social theory see Andrew Sayer's *The Moral Significance of Class*, 2005, Cambridge, Cambridge University Press.

9 On plurality within the general-dispositional structures see Stones, *Structuration Theory*, pp. 104–7.

10 See Rob Stones, 2006, 'Rights, Social Theory and Political Philosophy: A Framework for Case Study Research', in Lydia Morris (ed.), *Rights: Sociological Perspectives*. London: Routledge, pp. 133–51, for a discussion

of the relationship between structuration theory and normative issues, and *Structuration Theory*, pp. 116–27 for an extended discussion of epistemological and methodological issues in strong structuration.

11 For a more detailed discussion of some of these issues see 'External Structures: Conditions, Outcomes and Irresistible Causal Forces', pp. 109–115, in ch.3, 'Ontology' of *Structuration Theory*.

12 The 'we' here is explicitly circumscribed and based upon a shared normative position.

13 For some limited ways in which Giddens does employ structuration theory, albeit at a relatively abstract and generalising level, in some of his later work see Rob Stones, 'Anthony Giddens' G.Ritzer (ed.), *Encyclopaedia of Social Theory*. Thousand Oaks: California, 2004, and Rob Stones, *Sociological Reasoning*, London, Macmillan, 1996, Chapter 4.

REFERENCES

Althusser, L. (1969 [1965]) *For Marx*. London: Allen Lane, (translation: Ben Brewster).
Archer, M. (1995) *Realist Social Theory: The Morphogenetic Approach*. Cambridge: Cambridge University Press.
Benton, T. (1981) '"Objective" interests and the sociology of power', *Sociology*, 15: 161–84.
Benton, T. (1984) *The Rise and Fall of Structural Marxism: Althusser and his Influence*. London: Macmillan.
Bourdieu, P. (1977 [1972]) *Outline of a Theory of Practice*. Cambridge: Cambridge University Press, (translation: Richard Nice).
Bourdieu, P. (1990 [1980]) *The Logic of Practice*. Cambridge: Polity Press, (translation: Richard Nice).
Bourdieu, P. (1993) *The Field of Cultural Production*. Cambridge: Polity Press.
Callon, M. (1986) 'Some elements of a sociology of translation'. In J. Law (ed.) *Power, Action and Belief. A New Sociology of Knowledge*. London: Routledge and Kegan Paul, 196–232.
Callon, M. and Latour, B. (1981) 'Unscrewing the big leviathan: How do actors macrostructure reality?' In K. Knorr-Cetina and A.V. Cicourel (eds.), *Advances in Social Theory and Methodology: Toward an Integration of Macro and Micro Sociologies*. London: Routledge, pp. 277–303.
Clegg, S.R. (1989) *Frameworks of Power*. London: Sage.
Cohen, I.J. (1989) *Structuration Theory: Anthony Giddens and the Constitution of Social Life*. London: Macmillan.
Elias, N. (1978) *What is Sociology?* London, Hutchinson (original German publication 1970).
Giddens, A. (1976) *New Rules of Sociological Method: A Positive Critique of Interpretative Sociologies*. London: Macmillan (second edition, Cambridge: Polity Press, 1993).
Giddens, A. (1977) *Studies in Social and Political Theory*. London: Hutchinson.
Giddens, A. (1979) *Central Problems in Social Theory: Action, Structure and Contradiction in Social Analysis*. London: Macmillan.
Giddens, A. (1981) *A Contemporary Critique of Historical Materialism: Vol 1: Power, Property and the State*. London: Macmillan.
Giddens, A. (1984) *The Constitution of Society: Outline of the Theory of Structuration*. Cambridge: Polity Press.
Giddens, A. (1985) *The Nation-state and Violence: Volume Two of A Contemporary Critique of Historical Materialism*. Cambridge: Polity Press.
Giddens, A. (1990) *The Consequences of Modernity*. Cambridge: Polity Press.
Giddens, A. (1998) *The Third Way: The Renewal of Social Democracy*. Cambridge: Polity Press.
Giddens, A. (2007) *Europe in the Global Age*. Cambridge: Polity Press.
Gramsci, A. (1971) *Selections from the Prison Notebooks*. London: Lawrence and Wishart.
Hall, S. (1980) 'Popular-democratic vs authoritarian populism'. In A. Hunt (ed.) *Marxism and Democracy*. London: Lawrence and Wishart, pp. 157–185.
Haraway, D.J. (1992) 'The promises of monsters: a regenerative politics for inappropriate/d others'. In L. Grossberg, C. Nelson and P. Treichler (eds) *Cultural Studies*. New York: Routledge, pp. 295–337.
Hindness, B. and Hirst, P. (1977) *Mode of Production and Social Formation*. London: Macmillan.
Jessop, B. (1982) *The Capitalist State: Marxist Theories and Methods*. Oxford: Martin Robertson.
Jessop, B. (1985) *Nicos Poulantzas: Marxist Theory and Political Strategy*. London: Macmillan.
Jessop, B. (1989) 'Capitalism, nation-states and surveillance', in D. Held and J.B.Thompson (eds), *Social Theory and Modern Societies: Anthony Giddens and his Critics*. Cambridge: Polity Press, pp. 103–28.
Jessop, B. (1990) *State Theory: Putting Capitalist States in their Place*. Cambridge: Polity Press.
Laclau, E. and Mouffe, C. (1985) *Hegemony and Socialist Strategy*. London: Verso.

Lukes, S. (2005) *Power: A Radical View* (enlarged second edition). London: Palgrave Macmillan (first edition, 1974).
Mann, M. (1986) *The Sources of Social Power, Volume 1: A History of Power from the Beginning to AD 1760*. Cambridge: Cambridge University Press.
Mann, M. (1993) *The Sources of Social Power, Volume II: The Rise of Classes and Nation-states, 1760–1914*. Cambridge: Cambridge University Press.
McLennan, G. (1984) 'Critical or positive theory? A comment on the status of Anthony Giddens' social theory'. *Theory, Culture and Society*, 2 (2): pp. 123–9.
McLennan, G. (1996) 'Post-Marxism and the "four sins" of modernist theorizing'. *New Left Review* 218: pp. 53–74.
Merton, R.K. (1957) 'The role-set: problems in sociological theory'. *The British Journal of Sociology*, 8: pp. 106–120.
Merton, R.K. (1967) 'On sociological theories of the middle range'. In R. Merton, (ed.), *On Theoretical Sociology: Five Essays, Old and New*. New York: The Free Press, pp. 39–72.
Mouzelis, N. (1991) *Back to Sociological Theory: The Construction of Social Orders*. London: Macmillan.
Mouzelis, N. (1995) *Sociological Theory: What Went Wrong? Diagnosis and Remedies*. London: Routledge.
Nussbaum, M.C. (2000) *Women and Human Development: The Capabilities Approach*. Cambridge and New York: Cambridge University Press.
Parker, J. (2006) 'Structuration's future?: From "all and every" to "who did what, where, when, how and why?"', *Journal of Critical Realism*, 5; 1: 122–138.
Parsons, T. (1963) 'On the concept of political power', *Proceedings of the American Philosophical Society*, 107: 232–262.
Parsons, T. (1964) 'Some reflections of the place of force in social process', In Harry Eckstein (ed) *Internal War*, New York: Free Press of Glencoe.
Parsons, T. (1963) 'On the concept of influence', *Public Opinion Quarterly*, 27: 37–62.
Parsons, T. (1966) 'The political aspect of social structure and process', In David Easton (ed), *Varieties of Political Theory*, Englewood Cliffs, NJ: Prentice-Hall.
Parsons, T. (1960a) 'Authority, legitimation and political action', In *Structure and Process in Industrial Societies*, Glencoe, IL: The Free Press, pp. 170–98.
Parsons, T. (1960b) 'The distribution of power in American society (a review of C.Wright Mills' *The Power Elite*),' In *Structure and Process in Industrial Societies*, Glencoe, IL: The Free Press, pp. 199–225.
Poulantzas, N. (1973) *Political Power and Social Classes*. London: New Left Books.
Poulantzas, N. (1978) *State, Power, Socialism*. London: Verso.
Sayer, A. (2005) *The Moral Significance of Class*. Cambridge: Cambridge University Press.
Sewell, W. (1992) 'A theory of structure: duality, agency and transformations', *American Journal of Sociology*, 98: 1–29.
Stones, R. (1996) *Sociological Reasoning: Towards a Past-modern Sociology*. London: Macmillan.
Stones, R. (2004) 'Anthony Giddens'. In G. Ritzer (ed.), *Encyclopaedia of Social Theory*. Thousand Oaks, CA: Sage.
Stones, R. (2005) *Structuration Theory*. London: Palgrave Macmillan.
Stones, R. (2006) 'Rights, social theory and political philosophy: A framework for case study research', in Lydia Morris (ed.) *Rights: Sociological Perspectives*. London: Routledge, 133–51.
Sydow, J. and Windeler, A. (1997) 'Managing inter-firm networks: A structurationist perspective'. In C. Bryant and D. Jary (eds.), *Anthony Giddens: Critical Assessments*, Volume IV. London: Routledge, 455–95.
Thrift, N. (1996) *Spatial Formations*. London: Sage.
Urry, J. (1991) 'Time and space in Giddens' social theory, In C. G. A. Bryant and D. Jary (eds), *Giddens' Theory of Structuration: A Critical Appreciation*. London: Routledge, pp. 160–175.
Walby, S. (1990) *Theorizing Patriarchy*. Oxford: Blackwell.
Wrong, D. (1988) *Power: Its Forms, Bases and Uses*. Oxford: Blackwell (reissue; first issued 1979).

Power and Discourse: Towards an Anti-Foundationalist Concept of Power

Jacob Torfing

Post-structuralist discourse theory provides an increasingly fashionable approach to the study of social identity and political power. It aims to analyze the more or less sedimented systems of rules, norms and meanings that condition the construction of social, political and cultural identity and action. Moreover, it insists that the discursive context of social action is constituted in and through contingent power struggles that are neither predetermined by rational calculations, objective class interests, nor the inner laws of capitalism. As such, post-structuralist discourse theory claims that power should not be analyzed in terms of the relative influence of utility-maximizing actors or in terms of the generative effects of deep-seated socioeconomic structures. Rather, power should be seen as a constitutive act of inclusion and exclusion that shapes and reshapes structure and agency and, thereby, constructs the conditions for how we make sense of the world and act appropriately.

Today, welfare reforms calling for budget cuts, privatizations and strategic investments in research and innovation are prompted by a hegemonic globalization discourse that constructs nation states as competitors in a global race and the political decision makers as strategic leaders who must struggle to convince the resilient voters that 'there is no alternative to the necessary reforms'. The actual content of the current welfare reforms depends on the relative influence of social and political actors as well as on the lock-in effects produced by the political and institutional legacies in the different countries. However, the political reform agenda, the sense of political urgency, and the whole vocabulary within which the political negotiations take place, are shaped by the globalization discourse that articulates a range of dissimilar concepts, arguments, goals and policy arenas into a relatively co whole. Post-structuralist discourse theory provides a tool for analyzing how such disc are constructed through political conflicts and power struggles, and how they structu.. identity, perceptions and actions of the social and political actors.

The present chapter aims to provide a systematic introduction to the power analytics advanced by post-structuralist discourse theory. It aims to show how the works of leading post-structuralist scholars can help us to develop an *anti-foundationalist conception of power* that takes us beyond the modern notion of power as causation and advances a postmodern understanding of power. Modernity was founded on a devastating critique of the religious foundation of the world by God that was common in Middle Age's Europe. However, the empty space left by demolishing belief in the divine grounding of the world was reoccupied by the modern belief in the unlimited reign of Reason (Blumenberg, 1986). Postmodern thinking challenges the firm belief in Reason and urges us to abandon all ideas about a transcendental grounding of society and to insist on the contingency of language, selfhood and community (Rorty, 1989). Henceforth, an anti-foundationalist conception of power must resist the temptation to view power as a determinable and calculable effect of structure and agency. Indeed, it must give up the very idea of power as causation, which comes from the works of Hobbes.

The chapter will be structured in the following way. The first section will briefly review the causationist notion of power by explicating the agency-based and structure-based notions of power. The second section expounds the Foucauldian power analytics that tends to see structure and agency as products of discursive power strategies that involve 'the conduct of conduct'. The third section further sustains the idea of the constitutive role of power by introducing Jacques Derrida's deconstructive argument about how binary hierarchies are constructed through ethico-political decisions taken in an undecidable terrain of non-totalizable openness. The fourth section elaborates further on the deconstructive argument by linking the anti-foundational concept of power as a constitutive set of inclusions and exclusions to the notions of hegemony, dislocation and social antagonism that have been developed by Ernesto Laclau and Chantal Mouffe. The fifth section draws on central insights from Lacanian psychoanalysis in order to show how social and political identity is constructed through hegemonic articulation of identities that are in turn constructed through acts of identification. The chapter concludes with a brief discussion of how discursive power is sustained by ideology and why resistance must take the form of a deconstructive 'denaturalization' and an attempt to decentre and disperse political passion.

THE CAUSATIONIST NOTION OF POWER

Thomas Hobbes' *Leviathan* (1986) has had an enormous influence on the modern conceptualization of power as a causal effect of either agency or structure. Hobbes saw the hereditary, sovereign monarch as the ultimate solution to the horrifying chaos associated with the state of nature. If left to themselves, self-interested human beings will engage in a violent struggle with each other over the allocation of scarce goods, and the result will be an insecure world of continual fear and permanent danger; but because self-interested humans are reasonable, they will eventually agree to lay down their arms and transfer their right to self-defence to a sovereign power that will create a stable social order by means of laws, sanctions and punishment. As such, civil society is an artificial construction that is made possible by the repressive power of the state. Political power is the cause of the social. Hence, in the words of Hobbes himself: 'Power and Cause are the same thing' (Hobbes, 1839: 72).

The model of causality on which Hobbes built his notion of power was derived from the new science of mechanics pioneered in the seventeenth century (Ball, 1975: 214; Clegg, 1989: 41). In Hume's elaboration of Galileo's early formulation, causality can exist between separated, but contiguously related entities. The liberalist focus on unencumbered, intentional individuals provided a perfect analogy of such entities, since their desires, wants and preferences were individually embodied. Interacting individuals might have causal effects on each other and, with reference to Hobbes, these effects can be conceptualized as power relations. As such, power can be conceived as a causal relation between intentional individuals.

With the behavioralist revolution in political science, the obscure notion of 'intentional' individuals was abandoned in favour of an exclusive focus on individual behaviour. This led to a reformulation of the agency-based notion of power in terms of a causal relation between the actual doings of individuals (Clegg, 1989: 41–44). The limits of the behavioralist concept of power are explored by Steven Lukes in his seminal study *Power: A Radical View* (1974). Lukes critically examines what he defines as the three faces of power, but ends up recommending a three-dimensional notion of power that includes all three faces.

The *first face of power* Lukes finds in the works of Robert A. Dahl who claims that power is exercised when A gets B to do something that B would not otherwise do (Dahl, 1957). The focus is on the behaviour of two actors, A and B, who are engaging in the making of decisions on key issues over which there is an observable conflict of interest, which is expressed in the actions and policy preference of the actors (Lukes, 1974:15). A can be said to exercise power over B in so far as A's preferences prevail in concrete policy decisions.

The problem with Dahl's explicit focus on overt conflicts over key issues is that it blinds him to the less visible forms of power. As pointed out by Peter Bachrach and Morton Baratz, 'power is also exercised when A devotes his energies to creating or reinforcing social and political values and institutional practices that limit the scope of the political process to public consideration of only those issues which are relatively innocuous to A' (Bachrach and Baratz, 1970: 7). This *second face of power* emphasizes A's ability to control the political agenda and to suppress, or delay, decisions on controversial issues. Hence, power is not only about who prevails in actual decisions on issues over which there is an observable conflict, but also about taking decisions and about deferring decisions that might threaten the interests of A. In the latter case, the conflict between A and B cannot be openly observed, although one might be able to detect some sub-political grievances on the part of B. The behavioural paradigm is challenged in the situation where B does not articulate a particular problem, or issue, due to his or her anticipation of A's unwillingness to discuss it. However, as long as A has deliberately given B reasons to anticipate A's reaction, we remain within the confines of the behavioural approach.

According to Lukes (1974), the blind spot of Bachrach and Baratz's two-faced notion of power is that it fails to see that power also involves the attempt of A to prevent conflict (overt or covert) by means of influencing, shaping and determining the wants of B

(Lukes, 1974: 21–23). A might also exercise power by creating a manipulated consensus. If A can make B perceive his or her subjective interests as being closer to A's interests than to B's own objective interests, there might not be any conflict at all, or, at least, there will only be a latent conflict. The *third face of power* emphasizes the suppression of latent conflicts through a combination of action and inaction. As such, A might influence B's subjectively perceived interests either by means of invoking particular forms of collective action and ideas or by relying on the mobilization of particular forms of institutional bias. The emphasis on the role of ideology and the impact of institutional structures brings Lukes into conflict with the behavioralist approach underlying the first two faces of power. Yet his commitment to a Kantian ethics of responsibility prevents him from adopting a structuralist position that emphasizes the determining effects of anonymous structures. Structures cannot be held responsible for their power effects. They cannot be taken to court.

The causal model of power is perfectly compatible with a structure-based notion of power. A structuralist notion of power as causation is to be found in both the liberal theory of Talcott Parsons and the Marxist theory of Nicos Poulantzas. Parsons does not conceive power as a relation between social agencies. Power is, rather, conceived as a property of social systems. The survival of the social system is conditional upon the fulfilment of four basic functions: adaptation, goal attainment, integration and patterns maintenance. The subsystem is responsible for collective goal-attainment through the production of binding obligations, and power is defined as the generalized capacity of the political system to secure binding obligations. Power is a mechanism to acquire control over outputs, or as Parsons puts it: 'a specific mechanism operating to bring about changes in the action of the other units, individual or collective' (Parsons, 1986: 95). Thus, as in Lukes, power is conceived as a causal effect on social agency. However, the origin of this causal effect is not another social agent, but the institutional and organizational capacities of a particular social subsystem.

Poulantzas also conceives power in systemic, or structural, terms. Power is defined as 'the capacity of a social class to realize its specific objective class interests' (Poulantzas, 1987: 104). However, both the objective class interests, and the political capacities of the social classes are determined by the social, economic, political and ideological structures. Hence, according to Poulantzas, 'power is not located in the levels of the structure, but is an effect of the ensemble of these levels' (Poulantzas, 1987: 99–100). This structure-based conception of power is in line with the notion of power found in the transcendental realism of Benton (1977) and Bhaskar (1978). Here power is defined as 'the freedom to act in such a way as to realize the inherent *dispositions* of either the structure of a thing or its place in a structure of relations' (Clegg, 1989: 121).

The agency-based and structure-based notions of power exhaust the logical possibilities of the modern concept of power as causation. Power is a causal effect which is either produced by a clearly identifiable social agency or by some anonymous social, economic or political structure. Agency and structure are both equipped with a generative capacity to affect and constrain social actions, decisions and outcomes.

POWER AS 'THE CONDUCT OF CONDUCT'

The post-structuralist political philosopher Michel Foucault turns this argument upside-down by claiming that power cannot be viewed as a causal effect of either agency or structure since these are themselves constructed in and through power strategies that are operating at the level of discourse. Foucault (1972) introduced his notion of discourse in his *archaeological analysis* of knowledge and science. Discourse is not defined merely as a particular set of spoken or written statements. Foucault develops a quasi-transcendental notion of discourse that focuses on the contingent and historically variable 'rules of formation' that condition the production of utterances within a particular setting. The rules of formation regulate what can be talked about; how to talk about it; who is authorized to talk in such a way; and how utterances can be combined in the strategic elaboration of the discourse. The rules have no independent existence, but are imbedded in the sedimented forms of discourse that they are regulating. Hence, the discursive conditions of possibility are always penetrated by facticity.

The quasi-structuralist search for the underlying rules of formation that govern the production of statements enabled Foucault to identify different historical discourses about madness, punishment, etc. However, the archaeological approach did not help him to analyze the formation and transformation of discourse. Initially, Foucault conceived the historical development of discourse as characterized by radical ruptures whereby one discursive formation is replaced by another. Later, Foucault criticized this idea claiming that discourses are gradually transformed through an endless number of displacements that are produced in and through a myriad of power struggles that dis- and rearticulate meaning (Foucault, 1986a).

It was insight into the contingent and power-ridden character of these displacements that spurred the development of Foucault's *genealogical method*. Whereas the archaeological method aimed to analyze the synchronic layers of discourse, the genealogical method aimed to analyze the diachronic movements through which the present layers of discourse are formed through incessant power struggles that invoke the inclusion and exclusion of meaning, identity and social practices. The juridical notion of sovereign power is found wanting as its emphasis on repression, prohibition and taboo fails to capture the productive aspects of power that aim to constitute, accentuate and disseminate particular forms of identity, knowledge and action. Foucault solves the problem by developing a new concept of discursive power that he defines nominally as 'the name of a complex strategic situation' (Foucault, 1976: 92). Power is neither defined as the power of one actor over another actor (power as a relation of subordination) nor as the power to do certain things (power as a capacity to act). Rather, power is defined as a crisscrossing field of power strategies that form and regulate the relational identities of the social actors, their conception of the world, and their range of appropriate actions. Because of its productive role in shaping meanings and identities, power is intrinsically linked to knowledge, and local forms of power-knowledge are imbedded in institutions, technologies, or what Foucault (1986b) calls 'dispositifs'.

When defined in this way power cannot be confined to the realm of the state and its legitimate forms of government and repression. 'Power', Foucault claims, 'is everywhere; not because it embraces everything, but because it comes from everywhere'. Power is not external to social relations, but immanent to all kinds of economic, organizational, scientific, and sexual relations that are shaped and reshaped through power. Power comes from below in the sense that 'there is no binary and all-encompassing relation between rulers and ruled at the root of power relations' (Foucault, 1976: 94). Power is a decentred network of forces and strategies that multiplies and distributes differences, homogeneities and relations, and if there are crosscutting antagonisms that traverse local oppositions and link them together, then these are results of hegemonic articulations (Foucault, 1976: 94). In sum, power is an ontological category as the social is constructed in and through crisscrossing power strategies. The power strategies are 'intentional and non-subjective' in the sense that they always aim to achieve something, but cannot be mastered and controlled by any individual or collective subject or actor (Foucault, 1976: 95).

Foucault's power analytic is sometimes criticized for eliminating individual freedom. Although Foucault (1976: 95) insists that resistance always exists internal to power, power circumscribes the individual and forms and regulates its subjectivity through the construction of a thick web of institutions and technologies. However, this critique overlooks Foucault's emphatic insistence that power can only be exercised over free subjects and only in so far as they are free (Foucault, 1986c: 221). If individual or collective actors are deprived of any alternative options and are incapable of acting differently, we have a situation of domination rather than power. Power is necessitated by and thrives upon the capacity of the actors to act freely. Power aims to regulate free and autonomous actors who are acting on the basis of different interests, motives and ideologies, but it does not aim to strip the individual or collective actors of their capacity for free action. Rather, it seeks to mobilize the energy, knowledge and resources of the free actors who are placed within a relatively institutionalized discursive framework that aims to ensure conformity with the telos of power, but is incapable of avoiding resistance and non-intended behaviour. The different subjectivities always have the possibility of saying no, or acting in a non-prescribed way. Even a death sentenced prisoner standing in front of his executioners can refuse to ask for pardon and refuse to participate in the rituals that are supposed to take place before the execution.

In the years before his death in 1984, Foucault (1986c, 1991) began to equate power with government, which he defined as the 'conduct of conduct'. Playing on the double meaning of the term 'conduct' in both French and English language, 'the conduct of conduct' refers to the power-ridden practice through which the current and future actions of free and resourceful actors is mobilized and shaped in accordance with some overall goals (Foucault, 1991). As such, Foucault's notion of government as the 'conduct of conduct' clearly transgresses the classical understanding of government as the sovereign power exercised by elected politicians and executive administrators. According to Foucault (1991), government is basically a process of subjectivation, i.e. a process through which man is turned into a subject in the double sense of constituting a particular free subjectivity and of being subjected to a particular conception of normalized behaviour. It is the reformulation of the notion of power in terms of government that prompts Foucault to shift the focus of his genealogical approach from the analysis of particular institutions like the school, the prison or the mad house to an analysis of the shifting historical conditions for government.

The historical conditions of a particular form of government are captured by the notion of 'governmentality' that is defined as the art of governing. The hegemonic governmentality is founded on particular discursive constructions of the subjects, objects, means and telos of government (Dean, 1999). These discursive constructions are invested in a dense network of institutions and technologies that establish and distribute different roles, identities, rules, norms, calculations, conceptions, values and imaginaries. Governmentality is transformed through problematizations of the old governmentality program that tend to open a terrain for political struggles aiming to form a new one.

The liberal governmentality emerged in the eighteenth century. Before that, the state had merely been preoccupied with defending its territory, collecting taxes and building the infrastructure of society. Now, the new social statistics revealed that there were movements, tendencies and effects in the rapidly growing population that could not be governed within the institutional framework of the family. In response to this problematization of the regulatory capacity of the family, the regulation of the population was increasingly seen as a task for the state. Imitating the pastoral power developed by the Christian church, the state should govern the entire population and individuals through a combination of knowledge, support, care and empowerment. The state should aim to strengthen the population as a precondition for strengthening itself.

The governmentalization of the state through the gradual involvement of the state in the government of the population and its welfare resulted in a displacement of the dominant power strategy of the state. The citizens of the feudal state were subjected to a *sovereign power* based on centralized authority, laws, prohibitions and physical punishment. In the administrative state, which emerged in the transition to modern liberal society, power was increasingly exercised by the deployment of *disciplinary techniques* aiming to create docile bodies through institutional regulation of corporeal behaviour in time and space and *normalizing practices* aiming to shape and regulate the soul by means of defining what is normal and what is pathological. Later, with the mounting emphasis on the government of the population, power was increasingly exercised by subtle attempts to *mobilize and shape the freedom* of individual actors and target groups on the basis of institutionalized goals, standards and norms specifying how this freedom should be exercised and what its exercise should accomplish. The liberal governmentality and the governmentalization of the state were the conditions of emergence of the exercise of power through the shaping of freedom (Rose, 1999). The new and subtle power strategy facilitated a flexible adjustment of the boundaries between state and society and ensured that society was regulated by rationalities and techniques that were acceptable to the population.

In sum, the governmentality analytics aims to answer the basic question of 'how to govern and be governed' by analyzing 'the conduct of conduct'. Hence, the historical displacements in the exercise of power are analyzed on the basis of a new understanding of power as a complex network of forces and strategies that shape and reshape agency and structure by including and excluding particular forms of meaning and identity.

POWER AND UNDECIDABILITY

Another post-structuralist thinker, Jacques Derrida, was contemporaneous with Foucault, although not an explicit theorist of power. In fact, Derrida deliberately shied away from referring to power in order to avoid reducing it to a unified substance that suppresses its quantitative and qualitative differences (Derrida, 1988: 149). Nevertheless, Derrida frequently refers to the 'violent inscription' of binary textual hierarchies, which under the spell of the Western metaphysics of presence tend to privilege presence over absence, unity over dispersion, continuity over discontinuity, homogeneity over heterogeneity, etc. The binary hierarchies, which help to render the world intelligible, are constructed through the inclusion and exclusion of meaning and identity. The binary oppositions that privilege a superior inside over an inferior outside can be justified neither by an appeal to nature, reason, nor divine design, but are constructed and upheld by the deployment of force and textual violence. Hence, in line with Foucault, Derrida implicitly perceives power as an ontological category. However, Derrida does not focus on the power strategies that are creating and sustaining particular discourses, but rather aims to show the contingent and precarious character of any binary hierarchy. Through a careful reading of philosophical and literary texts Derrida reveals the undecidable play of meaning that the violent inscription of binary hierarchies must necessarily presuppose.

Derrida (1978) arrives at the notion of discourse through a deconstruction of the notion of structure. Structure is another name for the closure of a topography, a construction, or an architecture, whose internal order is determined by a privileged centre that keeps everything in place. According to Derrida (1978: 279), the notion of structure is contradictorily coherent as it assumes that the centre shapes the entire structure while itself escaping the process of structuration. The centre is supposed to be both within the structure and outside it. Such a paradox expresses the force of the desire to master the anxiety that emanates from being implicated in the process of structuration. Mastery is achieved by suppression of the play of meaning by a privileged centre which is itself beyond play. The always unfulfilled desire for a transcendental centre, origin, or foundation tends to give rise to endless series of displacements and substitutions that undermine the full presence of the centre. As such, it can be shown that the centre is not a fixed locus, but rather a non-locus in which an infinite number of substitutions come into play. This is important since, as Derrida remarks, 'in the absence of a centre or origin, everything becomes discourse' (Derrida 1978: 280). Discourse is here defined as a system of differences within which the play of meaning extends almost infinitely due to the absence of a transcendental signified that can bring the play of meaning to a premature halt.

The absence of a fixed centre prevents a complete totalization, and thus closure, of the discursive field of signification. However, the absence of an ultimate closure does not hinder the structuration of discourse through the establishment of an ambiguous and temporary order that is 'grounded' in a multiplicity of mutually substituting centres. The creation of a relative structural order is conditional upon the exclusion of a constitutive outside, which threatens the relative order of the structure (Staten, 1985). As such, the discourse of Western civilization, which is structured around key signifiers such as 'progress', 'science' and 'democracy', is unified by the exclusion of the evil force of 'barbarism'.

The violent inscription of a binary hierarchy between civilization and barbarism, or more generally between a privileged inside and an inferior outside, presupposes a pre-ontological undecidability. Hence, if the construction of a binary hierarchy is always based on a violent inscription, it is because the world is ultimately characterized by a non-totalizable openness that presents us with an endless oscillation between determinate possibilities that, on the one hand, resists both strategic calculation and a dialectical *Aufhebung* and, on the other hand, calls for a decision (Derrida 1988). The social world might appear to us as decided and unambiguous, but this is merely due to the naturalization of a set of binary hierarchies that are constructed through an impossible decision made in the context of an undecidable terrain in which the choice between determinate possibilities cannot be subjected to any higher-order rule, principle, or logic. For instance, we might believe that the market constitutes a superior mode of governance in a globalized world. However, markets and hierarchies both have particular strengths and weaknesses as modes of governance, and if we privilege markets over hierarchies it is due to a political decision since there is no ultimate reason for choosing markets to hierarchies or vice versa.

According to Rudolpho Gasché (1986), the formation of discursive structures is a result of a violent inscription of binary hierarchies that presupposes a pre-ontological level of undecidable infrastructures such as 'difference', 'supplementarity', 'iterability', etc. We might aspire to transgress the metaphysical hierarchies, but the metaphysical tradition of the West is inescapable. However, we might be able to destabilize the metaphysical hierarchies by accounting for the undecidable infrastructures that are both the condition of possibility and the condition of impossibility of the binary hierarchies that structures the social world. This can be achieved through deconstruction, which is a textual labour that involves a double reading of the text (Derrida 1988: 21). The first reading is a faithful attempt to follow the dominant strategy, or interpretation, of the text, its presuppositions, its concepts and its arguments. The second reading then consists in tracing the excluded, repressed and inferior strategy, or interpretation, which forms the undercurrent of the text. When the textual hierarchy is established, it is shown that the dominant strategy, or interpretation, is dependent on what it excludes and represses. Thus, in the case of supplementarity, it is shown that, if B supplements a primordial lack in A, then the relation between A and B is more important than A itself. The implicit revaluation of the constitutive outside results in an overturning of the textual hierarchy. However, deconstruction is not content with a simple reversal of the textual hierarchies, but aims to account for the undecidable oscillation between the two poles A and B. Thus, continuing the previous example, it can be shown that the market will only function properly when regulated by the state and that effective public governance by the state depends on the extraction of economic resources from a well-functioning market economy.

HEGEMONY, DISLOCATION AND SOCIAL ANTAGONISM

According to Derrida, deconstruction reveals the undecidable infrastructures conditioning the contingent formation of binary hierarchies. The reverse movement from undecidability to decidability hinges on an ethico-political decision (Derrida 1988: 116). The decision is ethical and political precisely because it is taken in an undecidable terrain where the structural context of rules and norms fails to provide a determinate solution to the dilemma, or aporia, at hand. Derrida himself did not develop this notion of an ethico-political decision any further, but Ernesto Laclau (1993) has argued that his neo-Gramscian theory of hegemony is precisely an attempt to understand how a contingent discursive closure is reached through a political decision taken in an undecidable terrain of non-totalizable openness. As such, Laclau claims that deconstruction and hegemony are intrinsically linked in the sense that they constitute the two complementary and reciprocal movements that link decidability with undecidability and vice versa. Whereas hegemony brings us from undecidability to decidability, deconstruction shows the contingent and constitutive character of decidable hegemonic articulations by revealing the undecidability of the decision.

When taking a political decision in an undecidable terrain we never arrive at a situation where the decision is taken by the structure and presented as a fait accompli. We are faced with an endless oscillation between actual and plausible options and the only way to make a decision is by trying to create a consensus for a certain option through persuasion. Persuasion is an attempt to make somebody give up one set of beliefs in favour of another by offering a redescription of the world, which presents the new set of beliefs as more suitable, appropriate or likely (Rorty, 1989). As such, persuasion might provide good reasons and strong motivations for choosing A rather than B, C, or D. It might even use different rhetorical devices in support of a particular quasi-logical argumentation, but persuasion will never succeed in providing an ultimate ground for a decision in the sense of linking, in a rational and apodictive way, the belief in that decision with a cause, reason or motive, which is itself derived from an absolute truth. Hence, in the final analysis, the constitutive choice of A rather than B, C and D will necessarily involve repression and force (Laclau, 1990: 30). In sum, political decisions taken in an undecidable terrain both involve consensus and force.

The notion of hegemony advanced by the Italian Marxist Antonio Gramsci (1971) aims to capture the intrinsic link between consensus and force. Hegemony is conceived as consensus protected by an armour of coercion. Hegemony is the form of politics in modern mass society where organic intellectuals aim to create broad consensus, while succeeding in eliminating oppositional forces. As convincingly demonstrated by Laclau and Mouffe (1985), the notion of hegemony was introduced into the discourse of Marxism in an attempt to supplement the deterministic logic of economic necessity with a political logic of contingency. The early debates in Marxist circles about hegemony arose in the context of the situation in Russia in 1905, which seriously problematized the Marxist idea of a 'normal development' driven by the dialectical development of the forces and relations of production. The Russian bourgeoisie was too weak to organize a bourgeois revolution that could bring about a capitalist and liberal democratic society. Therefore, the proletariat had to lead the revolution against the Tsarist regime and, thereby, realize the class task of another class. It was this contingent political intervention, which interrupted the 'normal development', which was named as hegemony. Hegemony was defined as the political leadership of the proletariat over a broad alliance of classes, which should 'strike together, but march separately'. Hegemony was initially conceived as an exception to the rule, since it was linked to the 'uneven and combined development' in Russia, but Leon Trotsky claimed that an uneven and combined development was found in all countries and this drastically extended the general validity of the notion of hegemony. If Trotsky expanded the scope for the contingent logic of hegemony, it was Gramsci who reformulated its content. For Gramsci (1971) hegemony was not merely the proletariat's tactical-political leadership of a class alliance, where all the classes insisted on the specific class interests. Hegemony could also be exercised by the bourgeoisie and was, first and foremost, a moral-intellectual leadership that aimed to create a 'collective will' with a national-popular character. The struggle for hegemony is a struggle for the hearts and the minds of the people, and the hegemonic class must transgress its narrow class interests in order to win the consent of the masses. The hegemonic force must articulate a variety of interests, demands and beliefs in a political project that provides a particular reading of the socio-political problems and offers a way of solving them in accordance with cherished norms and values.

Gramsci's attempt to transgress the class reductionist scheme of Marxist theory was hampered by his insistence that it is only the fundamental classes, i.e. the proletariat and the bourgeoisie, who are capable of becoming hegemonic. This economistic attempt to anchor the contingent logic of hegemony in the economic structures has been abandoned by Laclau and Mouffe (1985), who insist that the economy is an institutionalized discursive terrain that is crisscrossed by political struggles and power strategies and, therefore, fails to provide a pre-political anchorage point for the hegemonic struggles. The elimination of the economistic residue in Gramsci permits Laclau and Mouffe (1985) to define hegemony as an articulatory practice that partially fixes social meaning and identity around tendentially empty signifiers that function as nodal points. Articulation is defined as the forging of a relationship among dissimilar elements that results in a mutual modification of their identity. Hegemonic articulation presupposes the unfixity of meaning as well as the presence and expansion of political frontiers.

Hegemonic articulations construct a discursive system of differences. Foucault (1972: 21–39) had shown that the limits and unity of a hegemonic discourse cannot be constituted with reference to a common object, theme, vocabulary or style since these features are often shared with other discourses. Nor is it possible to construct the limits and unity of a hegemonic discourse in relation to an external element which is different from the moments within the discourse, since in that case the external element will be reduced to yet another differential identity within the differential space of the discourse. What is needed is the positing of a constitutive outside, which has no common measure with the inside and therefore poses a threat to the discourse in question (Laclau, 1996). In other words, what is needed is the construction of a social antagonism.

According to Laclau and Mouffe (1985), social antagonism is constructed through the exclusion of discursive elements. The excluded elements are articulated in a chain of equivalence that collapses their differential character. The chain of equivalences does not construct an identity among the excluded elements, but merely emphasize their 'sameness'. In the beginning it might be possible to see a certain family resemblance among the elements in the chain of equivalence. However, as the number of excluded elements expands, it becomes clear that the only thing they have in common is that they pose a threat to the discourse from which they are excluded. Hence, the chain of equivalence constructs a constitutive and threatening outside. If the discourse is A the external threat is anti-A. The positing of an external enemy helps to construct the limits and unity of the discourse while, at the same time, preventing its closure. A cannot be fully A because it is negated by anti-A.

The construction of antagonistic political frontiers separating 'friends' from 'enemies' is an irreducible aspect of politics (Mouffe, 1993). Political decisions involve power in terms of constitutive acts of exclusion, and the excluded meanings and identities are caught up in antagonistic chains of equivalence. Social antagonisms pervade the entire fabric of society, but may take different forms. Sometimes, they take the form of popular antagonisms that tend to divide society into two opposed camps. At other times, they take the form of democratic antagonisms that only divide minor social spaces (Laclau and Mouffe, 1985). The production of a major political rupture requires the articulation of democratic antagonisms into a popular antagonism.

Now, if social antagonism is an irreducible aspect of the political, then how is a democratic politics based on mutual respect possible? According to Mouffe (1993, 2005), the answer lies in the development of an agonistic democracy. An agonistic democracy is antithetical to a Habermasian deliberative democracy based on a communicative reason, since it does not aim to eliminate power and social antagonism. A vibrant democracy requires the presence of conflict and strife, but antagonism must be turned into agonism. This requires a widespread consensus about the basic democratic norms and values, while allowing dissent over the precise interpretation of these norms and values and about their implications for our political choice between different policies and different ways of organizing society. Hence, in an agonistic democracy 'enemies' are turned into 'adversaries'. Whereas 'enemies' aim to eliminate each other, 'adversaries' insist on combating each others' politics, while respecting each others' legitimate right to voice their opinion, defend their views and engage in hegemonic struggles.

THE SUBJECTIVATION OF THE SPLIT SUBJECT

As pointed out by the Lacanian psychoanalytical philosopher Slavoj Zizek (1990), Laclau and Mouffe's initial formulation of their theory of hegemony and social antagonism failed to develop an adequate theory of the subject. It still relied on a structuralist notion of the subject as a bundle of structurally determined subject positions, which are stamped on the subject through the process of socioeconomic determination and practices of ideological interpellation. The problem of the structuralist theory of subjectivation is that it ends up reducing the subject to an objective position within the structure and, thus, threatens to eliminate subjectivity altogether. As Zizek (1990) points out, the problem cannot be solved merely by referring to the destabilizing effects of social antagonism. Social antagonism might point out the limits of any social objectivity, but the 'impossibility of society' is not due to the presence of social antagonism. Hence, the identity A, which is negated by the antagonizing force of anti-A, is always-already negated by the disruption of the symbolic order that is caused by the Lacanian real, i.e. the traumatic kernel of social reality which always resists symbolization.

Laclau (1990) responds favourably to Zizek's constructive criticism by making a clear distinction between the role of dislocation and the role of social antagonism. Dislocation refers to the emergence of events that cannot be symbolized, represented, or in other ways domesticated by the discursive structure, and, therefore, leads to a more or less complete disruption, or breakdown, of the discursive system of signification. Social antagonism will, in this situation, emerge as a part of the discursive response to structural dislocation. In order to heal the rift in the dislocated structure, competing hegemonic projects will be formed. The hegemonic projects will struggle to provide credible readings of the crisis and they will seek to externalize the internal failures and disruptions to a constitutive outside of enemy forces that are held responsible for all evil. Hence, economic decline and rising unemployment might be construed as the result of the disruptive force of globalization or as a result of the influx of refugees and immigrants who are accused of 'stealing our jobs and our welfare'. As such, the positing of an external enemy helps to create and maintain a new social order in the wake of dislocation.

The notion of dislocation has profound implications for the theory of the subject. Dislocation is the traumatic event of chaos and crisis that disrupts the symbolic order and ensures the incompleteness of the structure. As such, dislocation is the concept of the impossibility of structural determination, or as Laclau (1990: 41–43) puts it, dislocation is the very form of temporality, possibility and freedom. If this is so, the subject cannot be conceived in terms of a structurally determined location within a fully constituted structure. The subject is internal to the structure, but the structure is dislocated by events that it fails to domesticate, and the dislocation prevents it from fully determining the identity of the subject. The failure of structural determination does not mean that the subject is characterized by a complete lack of structural identity. Rather, the subject has a failed structural identity. The subject aims to represent itself at the level of discourse, but the disruption of the discursive structure means that the subject cannot be what it seeks to be. In order words, the subject is penetrated by the traumatizing force of structural dislocation and thus has an incomplete structural identity. However, what is crucial to see is that the subject's failure of representation is also its positive condition. The incompleteness of its structural identity constitutes the subject as the locus of a decision about how to establish itself as a concrete subjectivity with a fully achieved identity. The subject before its subjectivation is thus partially self-determined in the sense that it constitutes the locus of a decision that is not determined by the structure, which is always-already dislocated (Laclau, 1990: 30).

The subject before its subjectivation is penetrated by a constitutive lack, and the process of subjectivation, the process of becoming somebody, takes the form of an attempt to fill the empty space of the lack through acts of identification (Laclau, 1990: 60; Zizek, 1989: 181). However, these acts of identification, or of decision, take place within an undecidable terrain that is revealed by the dislocation of the discursive structure. Thus, the subject is exactly the distance between the undecidable structure and the decision of how to heal the rift in the dislocated structure by means of identifying with a hegemonic project that promises an illusionary full identity (Laclau, 1990: 30). There are many possible points of identification for the split and divided subject. The female student who is caught cheating and kicked out of the university might identify with being a 'perfect mother', a 'committed environmentalist activist', or 'an elite athlete'. The peasants that are expelled from their land might identify with the nationalist appraisal of traditional rural symbols, the communist struggle against the big landowners, or the religious promise of future redemption. Finally, the faithful state functionary in Eastern Europe, who has lost his job and his status as a consequence of the collapse of Communism, might identify with the reforms of liberal modernizers, the nationalist call for unification, or the forces aiming to secure a return to the safe heaven of Stalinist rule. Of course, there is always the possibility of not identifying with anything at all and indulging in self-blame or defeatism, that will eventually lead to self-destruction and, finally, the annihilation of the subject.

The crucial point of discourse theory is that our political identifications are not determined by our identity. By contrast, it is our lack of identity that forces us to try to construct a fully achieved identity through acts of identification. The struggle for hegemony involves competing attempts to craft and disseminate credible narratives about how the split and traumatized subject can regain his or her lost identity through the articulation of different points of identification. The hegemonic forces must produce myths and social imaginaries that promise to recapture the original loss of identity. However, they must not only show that their hegemonic project is relatively coherent, that it can solve the problems at hand, and that it is in continuation with cherished norms and values. They must also find ways of constructing the hegemonic project as an object of desire. Politics and hegemony hinge on the generation and mobilization of passion and a strong and long-term attachment to a hegemonic project requires the production of enjoyment, or what Lacan refers to as *jouissance* (Zizek, 1989). The solution lies in the development of social fantasy (Stavrakakis, 2005). Fantasy structures our desire, and this enables social fantasy to produce two import effects. On the one hand, fantasy can help showing how the hegemonic project can cover over the lack produced by dislocation and produce a harmonious resolution of social antagonism. On the other hand, fantasy can help to take into account the ultimate failure of our identifications to bring about a full and complete identity. This is done through a fantasmatic construction of the threatening Other (for instance, the Jew, the Axis of Evil, or the Empire) who is accused of either having a secret access to an excessive *jouissance* or of having stolen our original enjoyment. Hence, by focussing on the 'theft of enjoyment' its present lack is explained and by focussing on the 'access to excessive *jouissance*' our faith in its existence and the possibility of recapturing it is ensured.

THE GRIP OF IDEOLOGY

Hegemony can be based on either metonymy or metaphor. A certain contiguity among discursive moments, obtained through a displacement of meaning, is necessary for the expansion of a hegemonic project. Hence, the hegemonic force must be capable of linking different political issues and it must be able to demonstrate that its efforts to deal with social problems relating to unemployment also have relevance for dealing with other and related issues of education, housing, democratic participation, etc. However, the formation of a strong hegemony will often require that the hegemonic force is capable of unifying and condensing a number of political norms, values and aspirations into an overriding metaphor that can function is a surface of a limitless inscription of social demands. Political metaphors such as 'the welfare state', 'modernization', and 'national unification' may help to sustain a political as well as moral-intellectual leadership.

The formation of a metonymical or metaphorical hegemony relies on the construction of ideological closure. However, post-structuralist discourse theory forces us to rethink the very notion of ideology. The classical Marxist conception of ideology as a false and distorted consciousness must be abandoned since it presupposes the idea of an unmediated access to the objective reality that ideology is supposedly misrepresenting and distorting. According to discourse theory, we only have access to reality in and through its discursive construction, which is always more or less ideological. There is no extra-ideological reality against which we can measure and finally unmask the ideological misrepresentations, since the world is always-already ideological. Hence, as Laclau (1996: 201–3) remarks, the death of the Marxist theory of ideology is not a result of the removal of ideological alienation, but rather a result of its imperialistic success.

Ideology is a crucial aspect of hegemonic power, but instead of conceiving ideology as misrecognition of an objective and fully constituted social reality, we should conceive ideology as misrecognition of the contingent, incomplete and ultimately undecidable character of the politically constructed discourses through which social reality is constructed. As such, ideology can be defined as the totalizing gesture of any discourse that aims to conceal the precarious character of any positivity and the impossibility of an ultimate suture (Laclau, 1990: 92). Hence, when neo-liberalism claims that the unfettered rule of the market forces can solve all the urgent problems of our time such as falling standards of public welfare service, rising poverty and inner city decay, and climate chaos caused by global warming, this is a good example of a totalizing ideological closure that seeks to cover over the failure of the market to provide stable, egalitarian and proactive solutions based on negotiation and trust.

Ideology masks the fact that the social is structured around a constitutive impossibility and traversed by social antagonism. However, in our 'post-ideological' society many people no longer trust ideological truths and no longer take ideological propositions seriously (Sloterdijk, 1983). However, even when we keep an ironical distance from totalizing ideological representations, we still act in accordance with these representations. We act as if the totalizing and reductive forms of ideology are true and serious, although we know that they are not. By living out the ideological fantasies we get access to a certain enjoyment. As such, we continue to act 'as if', not because it is rational to do so, but because it produces a certain enjoyment to cover over the impossible and antagonistic character of the social, to conceal our failure to inscribe ourselves with the symbolic order, and to blame the threatening Other for excessive enjoyment of money, sex, brotherhood, or work – all the things we praise ourselves (Zizek, 1990: 53–57). It is this access to a pre-ideological enjoyment through ideological fantasy that ensures the grip of ideological power.

The main political consequence of the workings of ideological fantasy is that the totalizing drive of ideology cannot be combated and exposed merely by means of revealing the undecidable character of the world that ideology aims to conceal, although such a deconstructive move is certainly important. The critique of ideology must necessarily aim to divide and decentre the passion that the political actors have invested in hating the excessive enjoyment of a particular enemy. Such a decentring might involve a hybridization of identity that consists in making people realize that their identity is multiple in the sense of constituting an overdetermined ensemble of identifications (Mouffe, 1994: 110–11). For example, by showing a group of nationalists that they are not only 'Serbs', but also 'women', 'poor', 'Europeans', etc., one might succeed in dividing their loyalties and passions and, thereby, weakening their chauvinistic demonizing of other ethnic groups.

THE POST-STRUCTURALIST CONCEPT OF POWER

The post-structuralist concept of power abandons the search for foundations and claims that power is not a causal effect of pregiven forms of agency and structure. Rather, power is a crisscrossing field of forces and strategies that constructs particular subjectivities and particular institutional structures. According to Foucault, power is an act of inclusion and exclusion that defines what is normal and natural, and thereby manages to efface the traces of exclusion. The world is structured by binary hierarchies privileging the inside over the outside, and according to Derrida, these hierarchies are constituted by ethico-political decisions that are taken in an undecidable terrain where the absence of 'super hard rules' force us to construct identity through acts of exclusion. The binary hierarchies can be destabilized through deconstructive movements that show that the outside is always inside and, hence, that the world is ultimately undecidable. As Laclau demonstrates, the reverse movement that brings us from the pre-ontological level of undecidability to the decidable forms of discourse can be analyzed in terms of hegemonic practices that aims to articulate a social order in the face of dislocation while seeking to stabilize it through the construction of social antagonism. Zizek's version of Lacanian psychoanalysis can further help us to understand the process through which the split and traumatized subject becomes subjectivated through acts of identification and to appreciate the role of ideological fantasy, which helps to maintain the grip of ideology.

The scholars that have here been discussed under the broad label of post-structuralism each provide a crucial insight into the workings of power, and together they offer a relatively coherent understanding of the anti-foundationalist concept of power. Let us conclude the discussion with a few words on the post-structuralist conception of the relation between power and emancipation. If power is a constitutive force, it follows that emancipation cannot be the emancipation from power. Hence, as Laclau puts it, 'if emancipation eliminates power through a contingent act of struggle, it must itself be power' (Laclau, 1993: 293). However, this assertion does not lead to the nihilistic assertion that emancipation is impossible. For 'if all emancipation must constitute itself as power, there will be a plurality of powers, and, as a result, a plurality of contingent and partial emancipations' (Laclau, 1993: 293–94). Emancipation in this sense cannot be thought of as the liberation of an essential human nature that was previously suppressed by power, but can now blossom. Emancipation only exists as a resistance within power, which is itself power, but which aims to advance new ways of governing and being governed that are more acceptable, less oppressive and maybe permit new kinds of social experimentation.

REFERENCES

Ball, T. (1975) 'Models of power: past and present', *Journal of the History of the Behavioural Sciences*, July: 211–222.
Bachrach, P. and M.S. Baratz (1970) *Power and Poverty: Theory and Practice*. Oxford: Oxford University Press.
Benton, T. (1977) *The Philosophical Foundations of the Three Sociologies*. London: Routledge and Kegan Paul.
Bhaskar, R. (1978) *A Realist Theory of Science*. Brighton: Harvester.
Blumenberg, H. (1986) *The Legitimacy of the Modern Age*. London: MIT Press.
Clegg, R. (1989) *Frameworks of Power*. London: Sage.
Dahl, R.A. (1957) 'The concept of power', *Behavioural Science* 2(2): 201–205.
Dean, M. (1999) *Governmentality. Power and Rule in Modern Society*. London: Sage.
Derrida, J. (1978) *Writing and Difference*. London: Routledge & Kegan Paul.
Derrida, J. (1988) *Limited Inc.* Evanston: Northwestern University Press.
Foucault, M. (1972) *The Archaeology of Knowledge*. London: Tavistock.
Foucault, M. (1976) *The History of Sexuality*, Vol. I. Harmondsworth: Penguin.
Foucault, M. (1986a) 'Nietzsche, genealogy, history', in Rabinow (ed.), *The Foucault Reader*. Harmondsworth: Penguin, pp. 76–100.
Foucault, M. (1986b) *Power/Knowledge*. Brighton: Harvester.
Foucault, M. (1986c) 'The subject and power', in Dreyfus and Rabonow (eds), *Michel Foucault: Beyond Structuralism and Hermeneutics*. Brighton: Harvester, pp. 208–226.
Foucault, M. (1991) 'Governmentality', in Burchell, Gordon and Miller (eds), *The Foucault Effect*. Hertfordshire: Harvester Wheatsheaf, pp. 87–104.
Gasché, R. (1986) *The Tain of the Mirror*. London: Harvard University Press.
Gramsci, A. (1971) *Selections from Prison Notebooks*. London: Lawrence and Wishart.
Hobbes, T. (1986) *Leviathan*. Harmondsworth: Penguin.
Hobbes, T. (1839) *The English Works of Thomas Hobbes*. London: J. Bohn.
Laclau, E. (1990) *New Reflections of the Revolution of Our Time*. London: Verso.
Laclau, E. (1993) 'Power and representation', in Foster (ed.), *Politics, Theory and Contemporary Culture*. Oxford: Blackwell, pp. 431–437.
Laclau, E. (1996) 'The death and resurrection of ideology', *Journal of Political Ideologies*, 1(3): 201–220.
Laclau, E. and C. Mouffe (1985) *Hegemony and Socialist Strategy*. London: Verso.
Lukes, S. (1974) *Power: A Radical View*. Basingstoke: Macmillan.

Mouffe. C. (1993) *The Return of the Political*. London: Verso.
Mouffe, C. (1994) 'For a politics of nomic identity', in Robertson et al. (eds), *Travellers' Tale*. London: Routledge, pp. 105–113.
Mouffe, C. (2005) *On The Political*. London: Routledge.
Parsons, T. (1986) 'Power and the social system', in Lukes (ed.), *Power*. Oxford: Basil Blackwell, pp. 94–144.
Poulantzas, N. (1987) *Political Power and Social Classes*. London: Verso.
Rorty, R. (1989) *Contingency, Irony, Solidarity*. Cambridge: Cambridge University Press.
Rose, N. (1999) *Powers of Freedom: Reframing Political Thought*. Cambridge: Cambridge University Press.
Sloterdijk, P. (1983) *Kritik der Zynischen Vernuft*. Frankfurt am Main: Suhrkamp.
Staten, H. (1985) *Wittgenstein and Derrida*. Oxford: Basil Blackwell.
Stavrakakis, Y. (2005) 'Passions of identification: discourse enjoyment and European identity', in Howarth and Torfing (eds), *Discourse Theory in European Politics*. Basingstoke: Palgrave-Macmillan, pp. 68–92.
Zizek, S. (1989) *The Sublime Object of Ideology*. London: Verso.
Zizek, S. (1990) 'Beyond discourse analysis', in Laclau (ed.), *New Reflections of the Revolution of Our Time*. London: Verso, pp. 249–260.

Actor-Network Theory

Rolland Munro

This chapter introduces key ideas about power within the nexus of thought labelled 'actor-network theory' (ANT). Yet this task is not as straightforward as it might seem. For the founders of the movement, Bruno Latour and Michel Callon, have more than a reworking of power in their sights. Ambitiously, their aim is to rethink the nature of society away from its anthropocentric legacy and return locutions of 'the social' to their wider planetary and cultural contexts.

As grand inquisitors of social theory, Latour's and Callon's agenda is to replace humanism with what is called *heterogeneity* (see also Law 1991). Sensing with Foucault (1970) the end of the 'human sciences', they avoid therefore any privileging of minds over materials. Instead of limiting agency to humans – inherent in talk about the 'powers of consciousness' – Latour (1998) talks of a 'summing up'. What he means is that he wants to focus on the circulation of *effects*, and abandon looking for socio-psychological *causes*. Latour wants to stick to what happens; and avoid recourse to pseudo-explanation in the form of motives, interests and intentions. For him, the detail *is* the explanation.

Actor-network theory rejects that solace of humanism, 'man's mastery of technology'. Instead of consciousness being seen as the fulcrum of power, the focus in ANT is on the organising powers of combinations. Or, in their preferred term, *agencement*. *Agencement* refers to effects of an 'association'. It is to stick to whatever is being generated by virtue of an arrangement, rather than speculate on the intrinsic qualities of different constituent parts. For example, in terms of ordinary language, Muniesa et al. (2007: 2) suggest that the notion of display 'fosters a similar intuition'. As we will see, the networks of ANT are those that come into being from prosthetic technologies *combining* with different kinds of cultural mores. For this reason, among others, actor-networks are not to be confused with conventional social groupings, such as elites or old boy networks.

Sites for research extend from the complexities of science laboratories (Law 1994; Latour and Woolgar 1979) and electric vehicles (Callon 1986a) to dance (Cussins 1996) and intellectual property rights (Strathern 1998), while topics range from autism (Hendriks 1997) and blindness (Hetherington 1998; Schillmeier 2007) to markets (Callon 1998), organising (Czarniawska and Hernes 2005), and quality management (Munro 1995). Analysis focuses not only on 'stuff' – the objects and materials that make the semiotic work of interpretation possible. The emphasis is also on intricacies of relations that may, I argue, be more absent than present. As the rest of this chapter explains, the world of actor-networks brings to the surface a temporality to flows of power which most previous theories lack.

AGENCY AND POWER

Actor-network theory begins its re-working of theories of power in two ways. For the moment we discuss how ANT broadens time-honoured conceptions of agency away from human consciousness. Then, later in the chapter, we consider the stress in ANT on a diversity of *forms* of agencies (more recently also called 'modes of existence').

Agency, in Western philosophy, concerns the *medium* by which things are accomplished. Clearly this could entail all manner of things, such as a hydraulic pump for drawing water, or the print on the page for conveying messages. However, the long-standing convention is to accord only to humans the means to act, the ability to do things through the medium of consciousness. The presumption is that behind every action lies an *intention*. Someone, somewhere, 'willed' something and so 'caused' it to happen.

Actor-network theorists want to persuade others to abandon this dualism of action and intentions; but they have not found this easy. Arguably, images of body and mind being in concert sustain conceptions of agency as the sole preserve of humans, but more than this, the very idea of agency being human is itself pivotal to the notion of holding someone to account. So many institutions, such as the law, proceed on this basis. In the case of murder, for example, the body cannot act alone. What has to be proved beyond reasonable doubt in a court of law is the *intent* to kill; for action to be deemed murder rather than manslaughter, acts must involve not only the body but also premeditation.

Yet, today, in a world that mixes gigantism with miniaturisation, huge cranes on the one hand with computer chips on the other, this limit on our understandings of action can seem ludicrous. Consider, for example, all the mountains of the world being quarried into roads and highways; who or what is organising all this? Or a hydro-electric dam on the Rhine; who is really in charge here: the weather, the geology, the engineers or the customers? Or a hole-in-the-wall cash machine; who has actually passed you the cash – the person who filled up the machine, or the one who issued you with the banker's card, or the person whose fingers played out the PIN?

The philosophical trope that only humans can have agency seems long outplayed. As those working in other traditions suggest, people either find themselves dwelling in a world that is 'pre-figured' (Strathern 1992), or they are 'emplaced' (Weber 1995; Heidegger 1993) in ways in which technology 'works us' as much as we work it. Pointedly, the choices we face today appear entirely conditional: if you want this, then you must do that. If the homophony can be forgiven, life has become more a matter of *routes* rather than roots, of repertoires and routines rather than beliefs and belongings.

DECENTRING THE HUMAN IN SOCIETY

The convention of tying agency to humans still holds sway within sociology, principally for grounding power in ways that make its exercise tractable. Yet by the time ANT enters the scene in the last quarter of the twentieth century, sociology and social theory have long arrived at an impasse. On the one hand are normative thinkers like Talcott Parsons, whose grand narratives reified 'structures' into overarching systems that gloss agency and deny change. On the other are symbolic interactionists and ethnomethodologists, whose minute examination of everyday conduct ostensibly leaves them without a theory to explain power.

Yet attempting just to add back agency to structure, as social theorists such as Giddens (1984) suggest, hardly addresses the way in which the lifeworld is colonised by 'system' (Habermas 1987). As Latimer and Munro (2006) argue the matter, systems not only 'self-construct' and take on agency-like powers (Mingers 2002), they are also *engrossing*. Yes, as with Urry's (2006) 'car system', they grow and feed themselves on the action of others, who help bring them into existence; but systems of the ilk of money and science do more. They not only hijack the energies and actions of other actors, they do so in ways that drive out other possibilities for conduct, like those of barter and intuition.

So has ANT found a way round the impasse? Well, as is discussed below, perhaps. First, in using terms like *agencement* (Callon 2007) or 'association' (Latour 1986), actor-network theorists permit system-like effects to be adduced. However since they do not go as far as reifying actor-networks into existence as real (Callon n.d.), they should not be confused with the kind of systems that are treated as 'wholes'. Generally any talk of entities that exert force in their own right, a tendency to be found in the otherwise exemplary work of Tom Hughes (1983), is avoided. In the form of agencements, actor-networks may indeed act as if they were self-organised, when they do so act, but an inherent precariousness in their formation and reformation should prohibit any hasty presupposition of continuity and independence.

Second, as discussed next, associations include *materials* of all kinds. This is primarily the ground that takes ANT past Lukes's (1974) influential analysis of different forms of domination. Important antecedents include Lewis Mumford (1961) along with the recently deified Gabriel Tarde (Latour 2005). Yes, the associations of ANT exclude stuff like intentions, even consciousness, at least when such matters are treated as if they are purely mental phenomena; but, as already indicated, matters like inscriptions can be pivotal, since the forms of knowledge these 'carry' have already been materialised. How material like strategies 'associate' with other materials is discussed next.

ASSOCIATIONS AND THEIR 'EFFECTS'

This emphasis on association, in the form of *agencement*, is the central plank in the actor-network rethinking of the nature of society. Instead of limiting agency to humans, inherent in ideas of human consciousness, the focus in ANT is on the 'powers' of association (Latour 1986). A good way of getting started here is to forget about imagined 'sources' of power, such as intentions, will or consciousness, and focus instead on effects (cf Callon 1998).

Let's consider for example the raised pieces of tarmac dotted around the inner ring road of the university campus where I teach. The effect of these 'sleeping policemen' is to slow down the oncoming traffic. Another effect is for pedestrians, people going to and from lectures, to feel they can cross the road more safely. As they approach the sleeping policeman, the cars slow down, thus making crossing possible, provided one is quick.

The 'effect' generated here is more or less a necessary effect. However, some cars may do more. Since the car has to slow down, some drivers on occasion may even stop, inviting the pedestrian to cross in front of them. In this way a courtesy and consideration effect, however momentary, may also be generated. What is changed, however, need be nothing intended, either in the mind of the driver or the pedestrian.

Specifically, what is altered in this particular case is the 'association' made possible by links between the road surface and the wheels of the car. Raising the gradient of the tarmac has altered the conditions that previously made driving fast possible. Intermittently, points of contact have been shaped away from those that avail speed towards those that imperil any vehicle not being carefully negotiated.

What is crucial to understanding the 'powers' of association here is an ability to set aside any analysis that grounds itself in notions about consciousness, all that stuff about intentions, motives and desires, and focus instead on changes to the *action*. Possibly drivers anticipate their car being damaged by the tarmac ramp – and this may be thought to explain why they slow down? Or perhaps it might be argued that the requests to slow down are simply more visible? But who can settle such questions? Who knows what the drivers are really thinking? Who is to say what is visible and what is not?

The point, notwithstanding these debates, is that the drivers *do* slow down. So the explanations themselves remain spurious. Underlying trajectories for the car drivers, for instance, may not have changed at all. We can add or subtract intentions and motives, as we like without changing the action at all, but add ramps and, suddenly, there are points for crossing the road; students can walk, more or less freely, about the campus. Alternatively, take away the ramps and, almost immediately, the boy racers are back.

Here's the nub. Rather than assume power is 'sourced' solely by humans, stemming from their intentions, or some other mental phenomena, power is traced instead, as already described, to sets of 'effects'. The effects of special interest are those that both derive from associations and in turn add to, or subtract from, these powers of association, but we should nonetheless be careful not to assume that change is being explained, as ever, by recourse to stories of innovation.

CULTURE AND POWER

These changes in effects discussed above draw hardly at all on understandings of 'culture' – at least as these are normally configured. By dint of contrast, it is worth comparing for instance the way in which power has been explained recently as exercised through surveillance. Here the focus is on a transfer from visible forms of power to the invisible, particularly that which accomplishes a transfer in the duties of supervision from hierarchy to self (Rose, 1989). Any deviance to what has become known as social rules can thus be nipped in the bud more efficiently by an occasional and intermittent supervision of bodies.

Little of this line of thinking is in fact that new ideas of power already centre on the more invisible forms of domination (see also Lukes 1974; Clegg 1989). Indeed, conformity in action is, for example, often related to notions of internalisation. Although bodies may be initially brought into line, made docile, by being subjected to 'dressage', the theses of socialisation and subjectification both suggest a habituation through the processes of routines and repetitions. So domination becomes hidden and the exercise of power more latent. As something easily exhausted, power is best conducted 'silently' (Giddens 1968). Force, and its use, thus becomes secondary, something to be deployed only occasionally in a democratic state, a spectacle that others in turn are intended to find instructive and salutary.

At first glance Latour's (1987) early thinking here seems to go in the opposite direction to these psuedo-cultural explanations of power. Certainly his term 'sleeping policemen' emphasises, deliberately or not, a very specific, and time-honoured, path of Western technology: the replacement of human agency by machines. What seems to be happening on the surface is no more than a crude alteration in the conditions of possibility for driving at speed? And the technological advantage of this kind of policemen is not just that they still work when asleep, but also that they can be replicated endlessly. Like the metal and plastic feet designed by surgeons for the 'bladerunner', the man with no legs who not only is currently winning paraplegic races but is even threatening to outpace the very top athletes.

On further analysis, however, it can be seen that what is actually being changed is the path for power to travel along. In this way, the introduction of sleeping policemen does suggest a cultural turn. Specifically, the authorities in charge at Keele University have selected a different *route* for power. The previous mode of choice, the passing of instructions from one human to another, is now diverted into the creation of possibilities for 'happenings', potential events that are intensely localised and distributed. This move signals a shift away from conventional modes of representation, namely the use of roadside instructions and emails about safe driving, towards the Keele authorities adopting more novel modes of intervening, namely a re-engineering in the *relationality* of material objects.

ANT thus challenges analyses that rely on artificial distinctions between culture and technology; and it does so without recourse either to assumptions about hegemonic cultures, or to notions of 'docile' bodies. This suggests that ANT's focus on the effects of power (instead of sourcing it back to its putative causes), helps widen the net of interpretations about what is called power. Where the humanist thinks of the artefacts of culture as at her or his command, ANT aims at more 'symmetrical' understandings. Indeed, since actor-network theorists contest power in the form of agency, as that granted solely to the 'subject', the perennial focus of humanistic thought, it is hardly surprising that their notion of culture extends well beyond that meant by sociologists.

POWERS AND INTERMEDIARIES

So how might a 'non-human' idea of power work? A first way of progressing is to reimagine the world in terms of *intermediaries*. Intermediaries can of course be all manner of things, including – as the very term agency implies – other persons. What has changed, for example in the case of the Keele campus road, is that new intermediaries have been introduced in the form of the tarmac ramps, and, critically for the pedestrians, the new intermediaries are no longer on the side of the drivers. Far from the smoothness of the tarmac being something to be taken for granted, the road now has gradients that oppose the possibility of speed.

This emphasis on material effects is of course far from novel as the work of Gasterlaars (1992), drawing on Mumford (1961) among others, illustrates:

> Buildings, things (and rituals) materialize health morality. They 'make' people move, and, above all, they embody the identification, separation and finally the removal of 'dangerous' dirt; moreover, they 'show' people what is healthy. They even are *intended* to do so, as our case histories show.

Whether buildings can be so coded, a stress on intermediaries risks being conflated with other visions of combinant forms. This is not just to raise questions about the concept of intermediaries (and the need to distinguish carefully between intermediaries and mediators, Latour 2005). Especial care should be taken over parallels with other popular ideas, such as that of the hybrid (Michael 2000) or the cyborg (Haraway 1991).

Let me explain. Just as with a reification of systems, there are pitfalls in the tendency to treat intermediaries as entities-in-themselves. The key issue is surely that of ensuring the relations that establish themselves among the artefacts of technology are accorded as much importance as that given to human interaction? Yes, research on actor-networks highlights the prominence of all sorts of intermediaries, such as ships, maps, light bulbs, vaccines and so on endlessly and, yes, when these come into association they have also come to be known as *assemblages* (see also Cooper 1998). However, it is vital to avoid the classic mistake of thinking of humans *plus* objects as concrete entities.

This granted, followers of ANT need to appreciate that key 'assemblages' are often transient, even temporary. Intermediaries, as is discussed again later, can be understood as also helping *detach* groups of people as well as attaching them. For example, in an early interactionist study, a 'spike' is used in restaurants to mediate between the staff, separating those waiting on the tables from those cooking in the kitchen. So instead of creating asymmetries in power, in which those in one room are given direct authority over those in the other, the waiters stick the orders on the spike. The cooks can then take the orders off in their own time and so manage in the way they best determine.

As already indicated, ANT seems at its best when it sticks to the relationality of material objects, which is why I have stressed the theme of associations ahead of that of intermediaries. In treating humans as intermediaries, more or less like any other 'things', ANT may well hold to its principle of symmetry (cf Bloor 1976), but the effect is seen by others to have created a sociology that is too overtly anti-human. One can doubt, for this reason alone, the wisdom of seeking to attain symmetry by creating a 'parliament of things' as Latour (1993) has notoriously suggested. Highlighting the complexity of 'our' relations with technology is, in my view, more helpfully, seen as expounding visions of the post-human rather than say the 'inhuman' (Lyotard 1991).

What is critical, surely, is an emphasis on humans being *emplaced* within the frame of technology. It is this idea of emplacement that reverses the time-honoured trope of imagining technology as something to master (Heidegger 1993). As is now discussed, this is partly a question of translation. What matters is precisely the moment-to-moment way in which diverse relations might be understood as 'translating' themselves into kinds of action. Interpretation and action, on the ground, fuse together. They do so despite all our efforts to keep them separate analytically; and they do so albeit there may be any number of possible interpretations being generated simultaneously, though not necessarily at the same time and in the same place.

POWER AND TRANSLATION

The crux of the notion of 'translation' is to see how and when any drawing together of relations takes place. A story about European hotelkeepers may help spell out more precisely what it is actor-network theorists are up to with the idea of translation. As told by Latour (1987), the hotelkeeper has a problem. This is that, in Europe, hotel guests have a habit of leaving the hotel with their room keys.

A first strategy adopted by the hotelkeeper might be to instruct the receptionist to request guests to deposit their keys every time they go outside the hotel, no matter for how short a time. This seems simple enough. Yet following these instructions is onerous for the receptionist. For the guests forget. However often the receptionist asks, the key is in their handbag, or pocket, and the guests are out of the door and down the street before they can remember. *Too far to turn back now.*

A second strategy is to inscribe the hotelkeeper's request on a large notice board. When placed in front of the hotel door, the inscription is only mildly intrusive to the guests. So some guests respond in kind. There is, in Latour's language, a partial 'translation' in action. Unfortunately, others fail to read the notice or simply treat the board as an obstacle to get round; and others still may anticipate a queue at the desk when they return, and so feel unwilling to wait in line just to retrieve a key. *No-one will mind if I just take the key with me this time.*

A third strategy involves the hotelkeeper attaching a large metal weight to each key. The effect is to change the nature of the key from being very 'handy' into it becoming a heavy, cumbersome object, a mobile obstacle for the body that the guest is only too ready to put down at the first opportunity. Consequently this materialisation of effects conjures up a more durable translation that leads to action becoming more stable: the guest appears now to be only too happy to leave the key at reception. Should they find themselves outside with the key, it is suddenly a small matter to turn back and return the key, rather than carry this unwelcome presence any further. *I'll just pop back to drop the key off.*

What ANT is 'after', what it is out to challenge and alter, is explanation, either in the form of over-simplistic ideas of authority, on the one hand, or notions of cultural hegemony on the other. As these forms of explanation are usually deployed, they imply power in the ubiquitous form of 'action at a distance', either in terms of rules for conduct in the first case or in the power of tradition in the second. What is thus brought into relief by the detail of this story of Latour's is the fact that bosses do not hold unlimited powers of either force or persuasion over other people. This is true with employees, far less guests. So the specifics of the story help to de-mystify tales of domination and co-operation.

As with the earlier example of the sleeping policemen, what ANT likes to challenge are not just the facts, so much as their explanation. As presented so far, the hotel story suggests several ways in which the actions of the guests are brought into 'alignment' (Munro 1996a). The first strategy, issuing instructions, is sufficient to enrol a few of the guests into the project of returning their keys. The second strategy, barring the exit with a large notice board, collects a few more, but it is not until the third strategy is adopted, the attachment of heavy weights (undesired) to the keys (desired), that things really change with the action of the guests being *translated* into directions that best suit the hotelkeeper. Only at this point can it be said that the translations become durable; only at this point is the action of the guests made stable (Latour, 1987).

POWER AND STABILITIES

Here, for the moment, lies a new direction for sociology. Most theories dwell upon power as something one person 'holds' over another. ANT has a different thesis: it is the relationality of materials that holds things in their place. All that stuff, humans and objects alike, that goes to make up the world at the very moment it is constructed. In sociology's privileging of humans, stuff like keys and heavy weights has previously been made absent. Attention is paid solely to interaction in the form of instructions, conversation or communication; any trace of heterogeneity being played down as mere objects under our command.

So instead of simply assuming that certain aspects of the sociality (the lifeworld or its systems) *are* stable (à la Weber, Marx and Parsons), the question becomes one of asking how they might be stable? And I would add: When? This is to say that it is the so-called 'structures' themselves that need explaining. So instead of concentrating, say, on deviance, as did post-war sociology, it is stability itself, in the form of norms, rules or hegemony, that calls for exploration. If translation is indeed an open process, almost anything could happen. When it does not, when things become fixed and when the world becomes predictable, this should strike us as odd (cf Latimer, 1997). When relations and networks appear durable, when action becomes routine and repetitious, explanation is called for.

In his analysis of science in action, Latour (1987) sums this inversion up pithily in the aphorism that things do not hold because they are true; which is the story spun by science in the classroom. Instead, he argues that things are true *because they hold*. The world is not stable, for example, because routines and repetitions get in the blood. Routines and repetitions get held in place for other reasons. Although the argument differs from the hegemony view of Laclau and Mouffe (2001) – for instance in the ANT refusal of concepts like subjectivity – their findings overlap in suggesting any stability means just one thing: that power is being exercised.

At this point it should not surprise that power today is being theorised in a much more radical way than Lukes (1974), Poulantzas (1973) or even Foucault (1977). Into the picture of power come materials, such as a lock on the door. Or the raised tarmac of the 'sleeping policemen'; or vaccines; or X-rays; or personality profiles; or the balance sheet; or the packaging in the supermarket aisle (Barrey 2007). It is this *incorporation* of materials into social rules that leads from the apparent relativity of ANT's idea of translation to Latour's startling thesis of 'society being made durable'.

ACTION AT A DISTANCE

Exchanges created by the division of labour play through the social; and, as Durkheim argues, change its volume, intensity, and rigidity. In adding materials to the picture of labour, the aim of ANT is not, however, just to see how 'associations', take place *within* institutions (cf Latour 2005). It is to understand how *agencement* – together and its associated processes of translation – takes place *across* a whole variety of institutions, including science, government, the factory and markets.

Where techniques of *abstraction*, such as writing, drawing and cartography develop, representations flow from these processes of abstraction. These *inscriptions* become, in Latour's terms, 'miniaturised', 'mobile' and 'stable'. With the invention of writing, for example, a sealed letter detailing instructions could be sent instead of entrusting the messenger. Or a map can be made of a navigation route and sent back from the Americas to the court of Queen Elizabeth I. So much so that, unlike Caesar or Alexander, those who are building empires never have to leave home (see also Law 1986).

All this sets up the conditions of possibility for what are called 'centres of calculation'. Interventions can now be made from afar. Consequently, some features of modern organisation stem from understanding how 'discipline' can be conducted remotely (Cooper 1992). A home can be bought today on the internet and then resold tomorrow, or a business in Wyoming can be sold, in whole or in part, by someone working in Tokyo or Mumbai; just from a glance at a balance sheet or a computerised spreadsheet.

So, rather than seeing people as having to move about within a relatively 'fixed' social geometry in order to do things, Latour (1987) argues that it is these 'inscriptions' that start, instead, to travel the world. *And change the world as they go* (Callon and Latour 1981) For instance, accounting numbers (see also Miller, 1992) in the form of budgets and other devices transverse the organisation, ranging across its divisions and cutting across its parts in ways that few managers might.

Actor-networks such as these have been portrayed by Latour *as* durable; especially those that incorporate the power play of the more 'monstrous' modes of representation (cf Law 1991); but this assumption can be challenged, especially since ANT associations are not to be confused with those solid links in a chain, like that of a railway network or an electricity grid.

FOLLOWING THE ACTORS

ANT has spread its wings widely from the earliest applications, such as Latour and Woolgar's (1979) ethnography of laboratory practice. Yet ANT continues to think of itself as symmetrical, as refusing to discriminate ahead of events. It thus avoids, it thinks, legislating between different kinds of translation, laws of motion for the movement of physical bodies and laws of inference for the understanding of mental constructs. It defers on these possibilities in favour of following the 'actors' to see which translation actually takes place.

Until proven otherwise, ANT holds onto the position that *any* translation is possible. Few others have been so bold. Ethnomethodology aside (see also Silverman 1993), many sociologists engage in only one form of translation. They insist on thinking of the world as dualistic, in which there is one level of reality – action – where observable things happen and another level of thought – intentions – in which the world is interpreted and understood. Consequently, the question of how we can know (epistemology) is always being cut off from questions about what things really are (ontology).

Strangely, power is typically observed in one world, the realm of action, and understood in another, the realm of intentions! However, a moment's thought should tell us, from Weber onwards, that this splitting of the world makes *verstehen* impossible, not to say also intractable. On the one hand there can be no such thing as action without interpretation. Observation is never mind-independent; it is shot through with surmise and prior understandings. Equally, thought can never be divorced from interpretations of reality. In the vain attempt to get to a 'foundational' level, a pure reality that remains stubbornly closed off to investigation, inquiry can end up in a never-ending process of self-examination, digging deeper into itself as it proliferates ideas on ideas, theories about theories, research on research.

So instead of locking interpretation into the realm of pure thought, or critique, and thus locking it outside, as it were, from the realm of pure reality, those who profess ANT assume that interpretation is entirely *operational* to action. Everything gets interpreted in the self-same moment as a connection is made in the form of action. Here Callon's (1986b) study has been particularly influential. Self-appointed 'spokespersons' enrol others, especially the silent or silenced, who may be as much mineral as animal, and not only 'represent' *their* views, but also draw on technologies that in turn help the spokesperson to *re*-present these in ways that align them to their own.

FUSING IDENTITY AND ACTION

This brings me to the vexed and muddy issue of identities. As already indicated, more is going on in ANT than a return to the systems theory models of the 1960s. This is, in part, why I proposed the idea of people acting as 'centres of discretion' (Munro 1999) in order to help off-set some of the rigidity of the discussion on centres of calculation. In returning ANT to its ethnomethodological roots, I previously argued that deferral and ambiguity lie at the heart of interaction. Today I want to go further and suggest that there may be a vital asymmetry in association that is relatable specifically, if not solely, to humans.

Arguably, people are, wittingly or unwittingly, always displaying their *identity*. If so, what is going on in the hotel story goes beyond what has been discussed so far. Yes, people like hotelkeepers adopt strategies; and, yes, in line with writings on performance and consumption that do not subscribe to ANT, people can be understood as continuously 'attaching' and 'detaching' themselves to materials (Munro 1996b; Strathern 1991). Yet, as Douglas and Isherwood (1980) have shown, people use goods to reveal their 'belongings'.

As discussed earlier in the example of the European hotelkeeper, each form of alignment had its different merits, but it is only with the third form that we might say that identities change. Two effects might be particularly noted. First, that it is when the key is itself made 'unhandy' for the guests – and only then – that the guests become responsive. Only when the key becomes an obstacle for their own projects, do most guests find themselves enrolled in the hotelkeeper's project. Only when the key changes its identity – and becomes an unwelcome object for all times other than the moment of opening their door – are the guests turned into allies.

Second, it is not only the key that is shifting its meanings. Even the identity of the receptionist is altering. Far from his or her surveillance over guests making them a near–enemy, stopping one from nipping quickly in and out, the receptionist has suddenly become a potential ally. Especially welcome is the receptionist who is already at hand to relieve one of the burden of this heavy weight. For the moment, this receptionist might almost be a friend!

Identities are thus subject to constant processes of 'translation'. Instead of attributing action solely to the authority of the hotelkeeper, or entirely to cultural dominance, say in the form of the goodwill of the guests, we can perceive how there is also a *circulation of identities*. The appellation of 'friend' or 'enemy' is always on the move as people shift their focus and alter their projects. Rather than see identities as entirely akin to inscriptions, as stable and mobile, they are better understood, instead, to be transient and transmutable.

INTERPRETATION AS ACTION

In their attachments (and commensurate detachments), people are of course making 'calculations' (see also Barnes 1988) as they shift their lines of strategy, but it is safe to suggest that they are also busy making *readings* of identities. At a minimum, and in line with a decentring of consciousness, people 'read' how the effects that flow from certain relations magnify a particular identity or they may notice instead how alternative alignments could diminish other identities. Allowing for these shifts in identity and performance entail no centring of consciousness, since no assumptions are made about the existence of fixed intentions, or unequivocal meanings.

Yet identity is not to be considered as entirely fluid either. Instead, identity, as I have argued elsewhere, is better understood today as *punctualised* (Munro 2004). Identity not only takes on an intensely local character; it also becomes 'timed'. Timed to arrive, that is, at the very moment when it is most demanded; or perhaps, à la Goffman (1959), performed where it might have most effect. The nod. The sudden smile. The grip in the hand. Even if signification is never to be controlled directly, or absolutely, identities can be worked, and reworked, as people represent (and re-present) the 'interests' of class, gender or ethnicity.

Sociology has yet to understand how it is that power, for its very existence, might still require that vital quality of appearing when needed and yet disappearing when not. When the world is presented one way at one moment, and another way the next, power becomes invisible in ways that even Foucault has not delineated. And where there is motility in form, then power becomes harder – to use the language of Latour – to attack. The power that humans have, which is lacking in machines, is precisely their *motility* (Latimer 2004, 2007; Munro 1996b, 1999, 2004), their ability to configure the world one way and then see it as other the next. Consequently it is possible to deploy humans to make certain key connections in ways, and at specific times, that help make the actor-networks themselves harder to pin down or specify.

In terms of power, any association that is entirely made up of durable translations must be more open to attack, and I do not think that ANT researchers have fully taken the importance of this possibility on board. While I see signs of a broader movement emerging in more recent volumes, such as that on 'market devices' (Callon et al. 2007), actor-network theory tends to pay too much attention to associations that seem 'strong', or even permanent, and overlook links that rely on power in the form of discretion. Whatever bodies its vocabulary of domination, be this heterogeneous materials or elites, research in sociology and ANT has to open up to asymmetries in power that not only nurture the ephemeral, but rely on the intermittency of such links.

SUMMARY

Actor-network theory is one of the most provocative and well-articulated programmes to emerge in recent years. At the time of writing, the main ideas remain controversial with even its leaders taking a somewhat ironic stance to theory and regarding any settled formalisation with suspicion (e.g. Latour 1998). *Agencement* sounds of course rather intractable. Which, as we have seen, it is! Yet understood as arrangements emerging out of an engagement and abutment of diverse sets of materials, the main object is to highlight a relationality among material forms of life that goes beyond the human. This alone implies a decisive abandonment of Kantian ethics.

Most instructive is actor-network's broadening out of sociological understandings, especially in how power works. Yet, relations of domination aside, the notion of power, as conventionally understood, is not really a central preoccupation for ANT. As has been shown, asymmetries and trials of strength are more compatible with its approach. So, too, ANT theorists like Callon (2008) are busy today with understanding differentiation; asking, for example, how issues are transformed into 'political', 'scientific' and 'economic' problems. For the ability to define topics, or prefigure debate is itself always an exhibition of power.

Whatever the perspective, the ideas of ANT have proved useful in extending the analysis of power beyond the more closed versions of interaction and in clarifying some previously misunderstood notions, such as that of 'action at a distance'. What is certainly being contested is a time-honoured reduction of social institutions to interactions in which only humans seem to matter. This granted, however, I have gone on to question the notion of society being made durable. Probably this is how it often feels, but one has to note a simultaneous rise in ideas of the social being 'liquid' (Bauman 2005), a theme espoused also by the major populiser of ANT in the UK, John Law.

This is not the place to resolve the self-contradictions inherent in such debates but, as indicated above, too much in my view is made about mobility and too little attention given to the related issue of motility (Munro 1996b; Latimer and Munro 2006). The way a 'world' is in place at one moment, generating its effects and then, just as quickly, vanishing when ostensibly under focus or attack. Materials, for example, are not always ready to hand; or the prosthetics of their use may cross professional boundaries (Latimer 2004). So, too, their consumption can be impeded by hierarchical devices, such as the denial of access as well as by shifts in accountability (Munro 2001).

While accepting arguments about heterogeneity, I find I cannot abandon humanism altogether. I think we miss the key ways in which power is exercised if we make people entirely symmetrical to materials. In particular, I have long argued that power is affected through a *circulation* of identities as much as by the distribution of materials. Presence, as is more widely understood today, is never just a matter of physical proximity; it is also about how consumption is punctualised. Who can make identities count – and when? Until these aspects of power are made more explicit, ANT continues to run the risk of proselytising an accumulation of force as the only alternative to Weberian notions of authority.

REFERENCES

Barnes, Barry (1988) *The Nature of Power*. Oxford: Polity Press.
Barrey, Sandrine (2007) 'Struggling to be displayed at the point of purchase: The emergence of merchandising in French supermarkets', in M. Callon, Y. Millo and F. Muniesa (eds), *Market Devices*, Sociological Review Monograph. Oxford: Blackwell.
Bauman, Zygmunt (2005) *Liquid Life*. Cambridge: Polity.

Bloor, David (1976) *Knowledge and Social Imagery*. London: Routledge & Kegan Paul.
Callon, Michel (1986a) 'The sociology of an actor-network: The case of the electric vehicle', in M. Callon, J. Law and A. Rip (eds), *Mapping the Dynamics of Science and Technology*. London: Macmillan, pp. 19–34.
Callon, Michel (1986b) Some elements for a sociology of translation: Domestication of the scallops and the fishermen of St-Brieuc Bay, in J. Law (ed.), *Power, Action and Belie: A New Sociology of Knowledge?* Sociological Review Monograph. London: Routledge & Kegan Paul.
Callon, Michel (1998) 'Actor-network theory: The market test', in J. Law and J. Hassard (eds), *Actor Network Theory and After*, Sociological Review Monograph. Oxford: Blackwell.
Callon, Michel (1998) 'Introduction: The embeddedness of economic markets in economics', in M. Callon (ed.), *The Laws of the Markets*, Sociological Review Monograph. Oxford: Blackwells.
Callon, Michel (2007) 'What does it mean to say that economics is performative?' in D. Mackenzie, F. Muneisa and L. Siu (eds), *Do Economists Make Markets: On the Performativity of Markets*. Princeton: Princeton University Press.
Callon, Michel, Millo, Yuval and Muniesa, Fabian (eds) (2007) *Market Devices, Sociological Review Monograph*. Oxford: Blackwell.
Callon, Michel (2008) 'Civilizing markets: Carbon trading between in vitro and in vivo experiments'. *Accounting, Organisations and Society*, forthcoming.
Callon, Michel and Bruno Latour (1981) 'Unscrewing the big leviathan: How actors macrostructure reality and how sociologists help them do so', in K.D. Knorr-Cetina and A. Cicourel (eds), *Advances in Social Theory and Methodology: Towards an Integration of Micro- and Macro-sociologies*. London: Routledge & Kegan Paul, pp. 227–303.
Clegg, Stewart (1989) *Frameworks of Power*. London: Sage.
Cooper, Robert (1992) 'Formal organization as representation: Remote control, displacement and abbreviation', in M. Reed and M. Hughes (eds), *Rethinking Organization: New Directions in Organisation Theory and Analysis*. London: Sage.
Cooper, Robert (1998), 'Assemblage notes', in R. Chia (ed.), *Organized Worlds: Explorations in Technology and Organization with Robert Cooper*. London: Routledge.
Cussins, Charis (1996) 'Ontological choreography: agency for women patients in an infertility clinic', in M. Berg and A. Mol (eds), *Differences in Medicine*. Durham; NC: Duke University Press, pp. 166–201.
Czarniawska, Barbara and Tor Hernes (eds) (2005) *Actor-network Theory and Organizing*. Malmo: Liber & Copenhagen Business School Press.
Douglas, Mary and Baron Isherwood (1980) *The World of Goods*. Harmondsworth: Penguin Education.
Foucault, Michel (1970) *The Order of Things: An Archaeology of the Human Sciences*. London: Tavistock.
Foucault, Michel (1977) *Discipline and Punish*, translated by A. Sheridan. London: Allen Lane.
Gasterlaar, Marja (1992) 'What do buildings do? The health policy system and the materialisation of morality', *Proceedings of Technologies of Representation Conference*, December 16–18, Warwick University: Warwick.
Giddens, Anthony (1968) ' "Power" in the recent writings of Talcott Parsons', *Sociology* 2(2): 257–272.
Giddens, Anthony (1984) *The Constitution of Society*. Cambridge: Cambridge University Press.
Goffman, Erving (1959) *The Presentation of Self in Everyday Life*. Harmondsworth: Penguin.
Habermas, Jurgen (1987) *The Theory of Communicative Action, Volume 2: Lifeworld & System*, Cambridge: Polity Press.
Haraway, Donna (1991) *Simians, Cyborgs and Women: The Re-invention of Nature*. New York: Routledge.
Heidegger, Martin (1962) *Being and Time*, translated by J. McQuarrie and E. Robinson. London: SCM Press.
Heidegger, Martin (1993) 'The question concerning technology', in D.F. Krell (ed.), *Basic Writings*. London: Routledge.
Hendriks, Ruud (1997) 'On words and clocks: Temporal ordering in a ward for autistic youths', in K. Hetherington and R. Munro (eds), *Ideas of Difference*, Sociological Review Monograph. Oxford: Blackwell.
Hetherington, Kevin (1998) 'From blindness to blindness: Museums, heterogeneity and the subject', in J. Law and J. Hassard (eds), *Actor Network Theory and After*, Sociological Review Monograph, Oxford: Blackwell, pp. 51–73.
Hughes Tom, (1983) *Networks of Power: Supply Systems in the US, England* and *Germany, 1880–1930*. Baltimore: Johns Hopkins University Press.
Laclau, Ernesto and Chantal Mouffe (2001) *Hegemony and Socialist Strategy: Towards a Radical Democratic Politics*, 2nd edn. London: Verso.
Latimer, Joanna (1997) 'Giving patients a future: The constituting of classes in an acute medical unit', *Sociology of Health and Illness*, 19(2): 22–53.

Latimer, Joanna (2004) 'Commanding materials: Re-accomplishing authority in the context of multi-disciplinary work', *Sociology*, 38(4):757–775.

Latimer, Joanna (2007) 'Diagnosis, dysmorphology and the family: Knowledge, motility, choice', *Medical Anthropology*, 26: 53–94.

Latimer, Joanna and Rolland Munro (2006) 'Driving the social', in S. Bohm, C. Land and M. Patterson (eds), *Against Automobility*, Sociological Review Monograph, Oxford: Blackwell, pp. 32–53.

Latour, Bruno (1986) 'The powers of association', in J. Law (ed.), *Power Action and Belief: A New Sociology of Knowledge?* Sociological Review Monograph, London: Routledge, pp. 264–280.

Latour, Bruno (1987). *Science in Action: How to Follow Scientists and Engineers through Society*. Milton Keynes: Open University Press.

Latour, Bruno (1991) 'Technology is society made durable', in J. Law (ed.), *A Sociology of Monsters: Essays on Power, Technology and Domination*, Sociological Review Monograph, London: Routledge, pp. 103–131.

Latour, Bruno (1993) *We Have Never Been Modern*, translated by Catherine Porter. Cambridge, MA: Harvard University Press.

Latour, Bruno (1998) 'On recalling ANT', in J. Law and J. Hassard (eds), *Actor Network Theory and After*, Sociological Review Monograph, Oxford: Blackwell, pp. 15–25.

Latour, Bruno (2005) *Reassembling the Social: An Introduction to Actor-network Theory*. Oxford: Clarendon.

Latour, Bruno and Steve Woolgar (1979) *Laboratory Life: The Social Construction of Scientific Facts*. Los Angeles: Sage.

Law, John (1986). 'On the methods of long distance control: Vessels, navigation, and the Portuguese route to India', in J. Law (ed.), *Power Action and Belief: A New Sociology of Knowledge?* Sociological Review Monograph, London: Routledge, pp. 234–263.

Law, John (1991) 'Introduction: Monsters, machines and socio-technical relations', in J. Law (ed.), *A Sociology of Monsters: Essays on Power, Technology and Domination*, Sociological Review Monograph, London: Routledge, pp. 1–23.

Law, John (1994) *Organising Modernity*. Oxford: Blackwells.

Lukes, Steven (1974) *Power: A Radical View*. London: Macmillan.

Lyotard, Jean-François (1991) *The Inhuman: Reflections on Time*. Cambridge: Polity.

Michael, Mike (2000) *Reconnecting Culture, Technology and Nature: From Society to Heterogeneity*. London: Routledge.

Miller, Peter (1992) 'Accounting and objectivity: The invention of calculating selves and calculable spaces', *Annals of Scholarship*, 9: 61–86.

Mingers, John (2002) 'Can social systems be autopoetic? Assessing Luhmann's social theory', *The Sociological Review*, 50(2): 278–299.

Mumford, Lewis (1961) *The City in History*. New York: Harcourt, Brace and World Inc.

Muniesa, Fabian, Yuval Millo and Michel Callon (2007) 'An introduction to market devices', in M. Callon, Y. Millo and F. Muniesa (eds), *Market Devices*, Sociological Review Monograph, Oxford: Blackwell, pp. 1–12.

Munro, Rolland (1995) 'Governing the new province of quality: Autonomy, accounting and the dissemination of accountability', in H. Willmott and A. Wilkinson (eds), *Making Quality Critical: New Perspectives on Organizational Change*, London: Routledge, pp. 127–155.

Munro, Rolland (1996a) 'Alignment and identity work: The study of accounts and accountability', in R. Munro and J. Mouritsen (eds), *Accountability: Power, Ethos and the Technologies of Managing*. London: Thomson International, pp. 1–19.

Munro, Rolland (1996b) 'A consumption view of self: Extension, exchange and identity', in S. Edgell, K. Hetherington and A. Warde (eds), *Consumption Matters: The Production and Experience of Consumption*, Sociological Review Monograph, Oxford: Blackwell, pp. 248–273.

Munro, Rolland (1998) 'Belonging on the move: Market rhetoric and the future as obligatory passage', *The Sociological Review*, 46 (2): 208–243.

Munro, Rolland (1999) 'Power and discretion: Membership work in the time of technology', *Organization*, 6 (3): 429–450.

Munro, Rolland (2001) 'Calling for accounts: Numbers, monsters and membership', *The Sociological Review*, 49 (4): 473–493.

Munro, Rolland (2004) 'Punctualising identity: Time and the demanding relation', *Sociology*, 38 (2): 293–311.

Poulantzas, Nicos (1973) 'On social classes', *New Left Review* I/78, March–April.

Rose, Nikolas (1989) *Governing the Soul: The Shaping of the Private Self.* London: Routledge.
Schillmeier, Michael (2007) 'Dis/ability practices: Rethinking disability', *Human Affairs*, 17(2): 195–208.
Silverman, David (1993) *Interpreting Qualitative Data: Methods for Analysing Text, Talk and Interaction.* London: Sage.
Strathern, Marilyn (1991) *Partial Connections.* Maryland: Rowman & Little.
Strathern, Marilyn (1992) 'Writing societies; writing persons', *History of the Human Sciences*, 5: 5–16
Strathern, Marilyn (1998) 'What is intellectual property after?' in J. Law and J. Hassard (eds), *Actor Network Theory and After*, Sociological Review Monograph, Oxford: Blackwell, pp. 156–180.
Urry, John (2006) 'Inhabiting the car', in S. Bohm, C. Land and M. Patterson (eds), *Against Automobility*, Sociological Review Monograph, Oxford: Blackwell, pp. 17–31.
Weber, Samuel (1995) *Mass Mediauras: Form, Technics, Media.* Stanford, CA: Stanford University Press.

The Ways and Means of Power: Efficacy and Resources

Richard Jenkins

Anthropology, the discipline in which I was originally trained, has a long history of investigating politics. Beginning with early studies of the political institutions of small-scale 'tribal' and 'traditional' societies, followed by interactional studies of micro-politics during the 1950s and 1960s, the emphasis has shifted more recently to the cultural and symbolic construction of relations of domination and resistance. This chapter will not attempt an overview of the political anthropology literature, not least because this would duplicate the efforts of others (Gledhill 2000; Lewellen 2003; Nugent and Vincent 2006; Vincent 2002). Instead, drawing inspiration from political anthropology, I will explore what power is, and how it works, in a way that I hope will resonate across disciplinary boundaries.

My focus is upon the ways and means that people employ in the pursuit of their ends, whatever those are. More specifically, I am interested in the resources upon which people draw as they try to shape present realities and future events. Power, in this approach, is understood as 'efficacy': the many and varied ways in which humans, whether individually or collectively, attempt to achieve their objectives and to assist or obstruct others in the achievement of theirs. This closely resembles Dennis Wrong's definition of power as 'intended and effective influence' (1979: 23). In defining power in this relatively modest and open fashion, I hope to avoid the temptations and pitfalls of the 'totalising' theories of power so roundly, and correctly, criticised by Haugaard (1997). Instead of attempting to differentiate different kinds of efficacy or influence, I will focus on the different kinds of resources that they employ.

This focus upon resources and efficacy opens up new perspectives on existing literatures. For example, as I will discuss in this chapter, 'social capital' can be seen as, among other things, a matter of power. As I will not discuss in this chapter, due to constraints on word length, Erving Goffman, as arguably the greatest sociological explorer of how people get things done in face-to-face interaction, may be revealed as a major, and hitherto unrecognized, theorist of power (and I am sure that the same could be said about other authors).

The arguments that I offer here have two original sources. The first is Max Weber's well-known discussion of legitimacy and domination (1978: 53–4, 212–54). In distinguishing, first, between power and legitimate domination, or authority, and subsequently between charismatic, traditional, and rational-legal legitimacy, Weber acknowledged that people can 'get things done' in a range of ways, drawing on varied resources. Despite the significant criticisms to which his conceptualisation is vulnerable – of which more below – Weber's work provided a cornerstone for all subsequent social science accounts of power (even, arguably, the apparently radically different approach of Foucault; see O'Neill 1986, 1994: 43–63).

The second source, economic anthropology, in particular the debate between formalists and substantivists during the 1960s (Firth 1967; Sahlins 1974), is perhaps less obvious. Formalists argued that the models and assumptions of conventional economics – most specifically, maximising 'economic man', 'the market', and 'scarcity' – could, and should, be applied to all human groups and ways of life. Against this, substantivists insisted that in many contexts formal economics were a flawed and inappropriate ethnocentric imposition. They argued for approaches that interpreted production and exchange, and notions such as 'scarcity', through the lens of local meanings and priorities ('culture'). Among other things, this debate was about what can be defined as resources; in this respect it offers useful insights into efficacy as a practical accomplishment.

Two important aspects of 'how people get things done' will not be discussed here. The first is the spectrum of variation in individual physical or intellectual competences. These competences clearly have an impact on efficacy; indeed, in some respects, 'competence' and 'efficacy' can be regarded as similes. While some of this variation is physiological – impairment that is the product of genetic endowment, illness, accident, or environmental influence – much of it is the product of interactional and institutional factors. Even where, for example, a definite physiological impairment is present, its implications for competence are, at least in part and often in very large part, socially constructed, depending on local definitions and assessments of what counts as competence, local provision for mitigating the impacts of impairment, and local attitudes towards and treatment of those who are defined as incompetent (Ingstad and Whyte 1995; Jenkins 1998).

Second, there are psychological capacities. In the recent words of one intriguing – and heterodox – anthropological discussion of power, this is a matter of 'the existential power of individuals' (Rapport 2003: 3). For example, anyone who has ever spent time in a milieu where a routine means-to-ends is violence knows that the readiness to use violence is not uniformly distributed. Some people reach that point very quickly, some more slowly, and some never at all. Nor are these differences related to physical strength and size.[1] For complex, idiosyncratic reasons, some individuals are more likely to use violence than others. To take another example, aspects of individual psychology make important contributions to 'leadership': not everyone wants to be a leader and not everyone can carry it off, emotionally and performatively. These are not the only reasons why some people become leaders, and not others, but they do matter. And, of course, although the preparedness to use violence and leadership qualities are individual qualities, with complex aetiologies, they are not reducible to individual factors. On the one hand, they are, to some extent, outcomes of socialisation and ongoing experience; on the other, the meanings and practices of violence and leadership are locally and culturally constructed (on violence, see Brown 1975; Marx 1976; and Rapport 1987; on leadership, see Bryman 1992 and 1997).

So, efficacy is, in part at least, influenced by individual variations in competence and psychology. These variations, however, and again at least in part, are emergent products of interaction and institutions. They are socially constructed. Thus a more comprehensive discussion of efficacy would necessarily deal with both of these matters; it is only shortage of space that prevents me from doing so here. I will, instead, work on the simplifying assumption that all human beings are approximately equal in these respects, and, rather than asking why some individuals rather than others come to exercise power, focus on the collectively defined and shaped resources that individuals may bring to bear on achieving their objectives.

POWER AND AUTHORITY

Weber defined *power* as the ability to achieve one's ends in the face of resistance, often, but not necessarily, by means of physical coercion, By contrast, domination, or legitimate rule, he defined as *authority*, the capacity to get others to obey, as a result of discipline and/or habituation. The dominated may collude in their own domination for various reasons: because 'things have always been like this' (tradition), because the ruler is, in whatever respects, a 'special person' (charisma), or because 'we respect the rules' (legal rationality). For Weber, traditional authority and charismatic authority were, in different ways, vested in persons; he saw legal authority as impersonal and vested in organisations. He argued that authority is more sociologically interesting than power.

Weber's model is vulnerable to two basic kinds of criticism. The first says that because, in his scheme, power is conceptualised as the overcoming of resistance, it is overdependent on coercion. By this argument, Weber's approach is, at best, somewhat crude; at worst, it overlooks a range of other significant 'power effects', not least with respect to absences and silences, those things which are neither said nor done. This criticism is implicit in Lukes' 'radical view' of power (1974: 22) and explicit elsewhere (e.g. Gledhill 2000; Wrong 1979). To a considerable extent this point of view depends on, first, taking Weber's distinction between power and authority at face value, second, focusing on what Weber himself described – or dismissed – as the 'sociologically amorphous' dimension of power (1978: 53), and then, third, looping back to conflate power and authority, in order to produce a broader, and apparently more adequate, concept of power. Thus at least part of this criticism is a matter of nomenclature: had Weber distinguished four different kinds of *power*, for example, the matter would probably look rather different.

The second criticism is the more substantial. If we treat Weber's concepts of power and the three kinds of authority – traditional, charismatic, and legal – as variations on the broad theme of efficacy, then it is, in some respects, difficult to differentiate them with clarity. For example, the capacity to mobilise the collective resources that make coercion possible – in particular other people – is likely to depend on being able to exercise traditional, charismatic or legal authority. From a different direction, the law and tradition are not always easy to disentangle. As a last example of the difficulty here, the charisma of a leader often finds expression within 'traditional' meanings, relationships, and practices.

M. G. Smith developed Weber's basic model in the course of a historical study of the Nigerian kingdom of Zazzau, or Zaria (Smith 1960). Proposing that power characterises politics and authority administration, he defined the latter as the *right* to act, and the former as the *ability* to act, regardless of right (*ibid.*: 18–19). For Smith, the exercise of power could 'range from coercion and force through persuasion, influence, manipulations of various sorts and factors, bargaining, to simple suggestion or bluff' (*ibid.*: 19). He was also clear about the need to distinguish the legitimate from the legal (*ibid.*: 20–1). As the following makes clear, however, the difference in practice between power and authority remained a grey area, and unresolved:

> …if A has authority to decide an issue involving B's interests and does so independently of B, A exercises an authority which appears to B as power. If on the other hand B is able to secure from A the decision that B requires, then B has displayed power through A's authority. (*ibid.*: 19fn)

This is an elegant short demonstration of how difficult it can be in practice to distinguish power from authority. Much depends on perspective: one person's authority is another's power. Legitimacy is, almost by definition, in the eye of the beholder, and, as such, likely to be variable and contested. For this reason, exercising power and authority can often look pretty much the same: there is no clear-cut distinction between them, other than how they are evaluated or experienced by those involved.

Some of this problem comes, therefore, from emphasising legitimacy as the fault-line between power and authority. Another part of the problem, however, stems, almost inevitably, from the construction of 'ideal types': 'abstractions from reality…[that] do not describe it in plenitude' (Wrong 1979: 82). Wrong, having extensively typologised power himself, goes on to say that:

> Although it is possible to find "pure" examples of each of the forms of power, most power relations are inevitably mixtures since the taxonomy of forms is largely based on assumptions about the motives of the power subjects and human motivation is almost always a heterogeneous blend of different, often conflicting, impulses and effects. (*ibid.*: 83)

We cannot, of course, simply dispense with ideal types, and any claim to do so would be disingenuous. Rather, in constructing abstract analytical categories, we need to acknowledge their limitations and to ground them – and the echo of Glaser and Strauss (1967) is deliberate – in local 'folk' models (Holy and Stuchlik 1983).

However, in doing so, we need to ask whether Wrong, for example, was sensible to ground his typology of power in individual motivations. It is, at the very least, epistemologically risky to do so, given the inevitability of some uncertainty about the workings of 'other minds'. A similar caution applies with respect to collective canons of legitimacy. Although they are more public than individual motivations, they are, to some extent at least, matters of perception and interpretation, likely to be contested and subject to partisan interpretation. Both legitimacy and motivations are shifting and positional yardsticks. While they are important and worth attending to empirically, they do not offer safe ground on which to construct general analytical categories.

Having said that, Wrong's 'taxonomy of forms' – much like Smith's range of practical ways of exercising power – is of some use, in that it emphasises the diversity and complexity of efficacy. Within his definition of power as 'intended and effective influence', he distinguishes 'force', 'manipulation', 'persuasion', and 'authority'. Force can be 'physical' – itself subdivided into violent and non-violent – or 'psychic', while authority can be 'coercive', 'induced', 'legitimate', 'competent', or 'personal' (1979: 23–64). All of these can be, and are likely to be, combined and inter-related in real life situations.

This section converges on two conclusions. The first is that classifying and distinguishing types or forms of 'power' and 'authority' does not appear to be the best way forward. Better instead to work with a broad category of what I have called 'power as efficacy': how people achieve their ends and fulfil their purposes. The second conclusion is that, even while adopting this position, it is important to recognise that efficacy comes in many colours and speaks with many voices: whatever the context, there are many ways and means that people can apply to the pursuit of their ends. These ways and means – resources for efficacy – provide the rest of this chapter with its subject matter and thematic focus.

RESOURCING EFFICACY

Malinowski's classic study of the Trobriand Islanders of New Guinea, *Argonauts of the Western Pacific* (1922), established the centrality to modern anthropology of intensive fieldwork. Focusing on the inter-island *kula* exchange cycle and ceremonial competitive yam feasting, it also marked the beginning of economic anthropology as a sub-field. Like the other seminal text in this respect, Mauss's *The Gift* (1954), *Argonauts* argued that exchange relationships cannot be understood with reference to materialist or utilitarian criteria alone: *kula* necklaces and armbands, for example, much like gold or paper money, have no intrinsic worth – whatever that might mean – but their exchange established and maintained alliances. 'Stuff' becomes a resource only in the context of what is done with it; in many cases this is a matter of relationships or status rather than subsistence or practicality. Culture, politics, and economics are thus implicated in each other (and the resonances with Marx's approach to political economy are obvious).

Against this disciplinary conventional wisdom – that production and exchange, and what counts as a resource, should be understood substantively, in the context of local frameworks of meaning and relationships between groups and individuals – a school of thought that became known as formalism began to insist, during the 1950s, that universal principles governed these matters; that it was, for example, possible to work with the generic category of economic rationality posited by conventional economics, and that concepts such as 'the market' and 'scarcity' could usefully be applied everywhere. This was, of course, a specialised version of a perennial issue within the comparative social sciences, across the full spectrum of human behaviour (including politics).

The formalist – substantivist debate eventually petered out and is now largely a matter for the textbooks. It is tempting to agree completely with Plattner's assessment of it as a 'non-issue' (1989: 14fn), in that what is necessary is, first, to purge the assumptions and models of formal economics of their ethnocentricities, rather than rejecting them outright, and second, to understand 'rational' behaviour *in context*, where we find it, rather than simply assuming its presence and importance. However, the substantivists' insistence that 'economic behaviour' is not the same everywhere, and is embedded in and shaped by the rest of the human world – and therefore should not be seen as a distinct domain of human activity, governed by values and rules that transcend local mores – was, and remains, sensible. Similarly the notion that, allowing for local circumstances and norms, resources might amount to a much wider spectrum of 'stuff' than the 'land, labour, and capital' of classical economics, also has considerable value. For my purposes, this debate offers two complementary lessons.

The first of these emerges out of the substantivist notion of 'economic spheres': a vision of multi-centric or diverse ways of producing and distributing resources and value, each governed by its own norms and principles. For example, in Bohannan's study (1955) of the Tiv, a Nigerian people, he identified three distinct spheres of production and exchange: first, a barter network of crops, labour and food; second, an open market in cattle and horses in which brass rods served as currency; and third, the exchange of women between lineages. Although differential prestige attached to each – the second and third were the more highly valued – and different yardsticks of value were employed in each, conversions between the three were possible, although sometimes at the expense of public disapproval.

Barth's study (1967) of the Fur of Jebel Marra, southern Sudan – an area that is today in the international news for other reasons – is also exemplary. He described four spheres of production and exchange: the high status exchange of labour and beer, a low status cash market economy, the prestigious holding of feasts in exchange for rank and status, and the exchange of women between kinship groups. Although the exchange of beer or labour for cash, for example, was in principle despised and sanctioned, local practices belied this: the establishment of orchards, as a case in point, allowed for the conversion of beer-mobilised labour into work paid for in cash.

In each of these cases we see people mobilising different kinds of resource to achieve different objectives, informed by different principles and rules. Strategic maximising behaviour, of one kind or another, is present, and some negotiation is possible. It is also clear that these 'resource spheres' are not hermetically sealed; nor are they – and Barth's account makes this very clear – immune to change and evolution. Even bearing these observations in mind, there is, however, a consistent tension within analyses of this kind. Not only are models of separate 'spheres' *ad hoc* and arguably misleading – despite local folk models of them as separate, in practice traffic between them is, as the evidence shows, possible and even likely – but they actually tend to undermine one of the key planks in the substantivist platform, the embeddedness of 'the economic' in the rest of the business of everyday life. Having resisted a universal model of 'the economy' as a self-regulating thing-in-itself, it was replaced by a model of a number of separate 'economies' that was, and is, no more satisfactory.

These shortcomings became clearer in the 1970s and 1980s, when the substantivist agenda began to influence analyses of industrial societies, in the shape of the discovery of the 'hidden' or 'black' economy, an apparently flourishing hive of unregulated industry that artificially inflated unemployment figures and deprived the state of legitimate tax revenues. Other contributions to this view of unemployment and economic life, rooted in broadly similar policy concerns, came from the development studies literature about the 'informal sector' in 'developing' nations (e.g. Bromley and Gerry 1979; Hart 1973; Smith 1989) and discussions in economics about dual or segmented labour markets in the 'developed' world (e.g. Bosanquet and Doeringer 1973; Harrison 1972; Piore 1971).

What emerged was a model of industrial societies as made up of separate economies – there was never any consensus about their number, shape, or detail – in addition to the visible economy that is represented in the state's public accounts. *Inter alia* these included distinct economies of crime, informal barter and reciprocity, gift-giving, domestic labour, and voluntary work (e.g. Davis 1972; Ferman *et al.* 1987; Gershuny 1983; Gershuny and

Pahl 1979; Handy 1984; Henry 1978), which were given a variety of names and sometimes characterised in terms of increasingly complex colour-coding systems. These economies were, apparently, based on different resources and organised according to their own norms and values. Only limited exchange and conversion was possible between them. There is no need to rehearse all of the criticisms of these models, which differed from each other as much as they were in agreement (see Harding and Jenkins 1989, for a comprehensive account). For my purposes, the main points are, first, that models of 'separate economies' do not approximate to the observable realities of what people do, and, second, are not particularly theoretically coherent.

With respect to the first point, evidence suggests that the creation, mobilisation, and exchange of resources – what we can call 'economic activity' – is complex and, if not quite seamless, absolutely not compartmentalised into discrete domains. To take as an example the 'labour market', an apparently clear-cut example of an 'above-ground' formal cash economy, the following resources, among others, may be mobilised when looking for a job or recruiting workers: bureaucratic or legal regulations, formal qualifications, career experience, physical capacity, dress and presentation, various aspects of identity – such as gender, ethnicity or 'race', age, disability, and social status – network connections, membership of voluntary organisations, illicit inducements, and threats (e.g. Beggs and Hurlbert 1997; Blackburn and Mann 1979; Granovetter 1995[1974]; Grieco 1987). These, very heterogeneous, resources can be simultaneously involved in the same complex set of transactions: formal qualifications and 'not what you know, but who you know', for example, may rest on different values but they do not belong to different 'spheres' (Jenkins 1986: 46–79). What's more, a resource in one context, or for one person, might be a disadvantage in another, or for another: a reputation for dishonesty, for example, will facilitate some transactions and prevent others (Hobbs 1988: 119–82; Klockars 1974), as might being 'tidily turned out and well presented' (Jenkins 1986: 54–7).

Moving on to theoretical coherence, there were probably as many different versions of the 'separate economies' model as there were 'separate economists'. At best, it was/is a descriptive approach, at worst, it is irredeemably *ad hoc*; this is probably an unavoidable consequence of the substantivist emphasis on 'the local view'. What was missing was an appreciation that, in seeking to achieve their ends, people routinely improvise, using whatever resources are to hand. What is needed is a theoretical framework that appreciates this – and is also sensitive to local understandings and institutional frameworks – without fragmenting into classificatory profligacy and, in Bourdieu's terms (1990: 39), substituting the 'reality of the model' for a 'model of reality'.

The second lesson to be learned from the debate between substantivists and formalists is that the production, mobilisation, and distribution of resources can sensibly be thought of, for comparative purposes, as generic 'economic activity'. This does not mean that what counts as a resource is universal, or that the local mores which influence the definition and treatment of resources are irrelevant, but it does mean that maximising, husbanding, and investing are recognisable in the basic human strategic repertoire, not least because resources are always in uneven, and imperfectly predictable, supply.

To accept this premise is not to accept that economic activity – the management of resources, if you prefer – either presupposes a universal model of *homo economicus*, or is separate from, or determinate of, the rest of the human world. None of these propositions is true (Harding and Jenkins 1989: 175–7; Jenkins 2002: 47–51). For example, resource management may be a matter of subsistence – to at least nod in the direction of vulgar materialism – but it also contributes to the achievement of many other ends. Put simply, humans need resources, over and above, food and water, in order to do things;[2] indeed, a short-and-to-the-point definition of 'resource' might be 'that which we require to achieve our ends'. It is therefore not surprising that economics and politics are thoroughly bound up with each other: political efficacy depends on resources, and the management of resources is frequently a political matter. What counts as a resource, and what can be done with it, is locally and contextually defined. Both means and ends are locally variable. Maximisation, for example, is one approach to resource management but there are others, such as reciprocity and altruism (Gintis *et al.* 2005; Henrich *et al.* 2004). In a word, means and ends are 'cultural'. Distinguishing the 'economic' from the 'political' from the 'cultural' is thus not easy.

This suggests that power, understood as efficacy in the pursuit of one's objectives, pervades the human world in all of its aspects (much as the management of resources does). To say which is not to accept Foucault's 'power is everything/everything is power' approach, if only because to say that power is everything and everywhere risks defining it away as nothing, and nowhere. But it is an important reminder that power is implicated in all human agency (and, of course, its frustration). In a non-trivial sense, human agency *is* power. Accepting this does not, however, make it easier to understand power: on the one hand, it may simply push the problem on to another overloaded word, 'agency', and on the other, the risk of falling into the Foucauldian trap remains.

In fact, it may be that the concept of 'power' – much like 'the economy', 'culture' and 'politics' – is not a useful analytical category at all. As a feature of everyday talk it is an appropriate object *of* analysis, but that does not make it an intellectual tool that can be used *for* analysis. Which is why I have chosen to focus here on resources. Whatever power/efficacy is, resources are required for its exercise. Resources can, at least, be investigated empirically, as can their management and mobilisation. And it is in the management and mobilisation of resources that efficacy reveals itself. To return to resource management, notions such as maximisation, husbanding and investment sit easily alongside a word such as 'capital'. The next section will examine how this once quintessentially economic concept has been redefined and broadened, to apply to a wide spectrum of human efficacy.

SOCIAL CAPITAL

As Smith and Kylnych remind us, 'The word Capital had been part of legal and business terminology long before economists found employment for it' (2002: 149). For the purposes of this discussion, however, the starting point is Karl Marx. One of the ways in which Marx defined capital was as 'value in process' (1954: 153). In the context of his primary interest in the development and downfall of capitalist society, this largely meant the abstract disembodiment of work – 'dead labour' (*ibid.*: 224) – in the form of money. Mandel expanded upon this, defining capital as 'a value which is increased by a surplus-value, whether this occurs in the course of commodity circulation…or in production' (1970: 30). Metaphors of morbidity aside, it is the emphasis on process, whether circulation or production, that matters here. Capital is a resource, mobilised, or capable of being mobilised, to the achievement of an end. In order to be capital it has to be a resource that is 'use-able' or at least accessible. Capital can be maximised, husbanded, and invested; its value can be increased or decreased.

Since Marx, the notion of capital has, without losing its original monetary sense, been taken up in a range of settings, and in pursuit of a range of intellectual and political projects, acquiring in the process looser and broader meanings. Mainstream economists such as Schultz (1961) and Becker (1964) argued that education and skills are capital of a sort – 'human capital' – and that investment by individuals in their human capital was the solution to the problems of poverty and unemployment. Without going into detail – for a summary see Karabel and Halsey (1977: 307–12) – human capital theory attracted several closely related critiques: it took no account of the organisation and pattern of unemployment and economic activity (unskilled jobs remained to be done and unemployment persisted), it ignored the importance of non-academic or non-skill-based recruitment criteria in the labour market, it assumed a necessary connection between productivity and 'human capital' that did not exist, and it explained a collective problem, unemployment, and poverty, by recourse to the characteristics of individuals. Despite these critiques, and its gradual disappearance from serious analytical economics and educational studies, the expression 'human capital' passed into the international vernacular of politics, policy, and management, referring loosely to education, training, and self-improvement. In so doing, it sowed the seeds for the next variation on the theme to enter social science debates, 'social capital'.

In a well-known article entitled 'Social Capital in the Creation of Human Capital', Coleman (1988) claimed to introduce the concept. Social capital is, however, a notion – certainly an expression – with a longer history than that. Marx may have been the earliest to use it, in 1867, and John Dewey also did so in the early 1900s, while Hanifan developed it, from 1916 onwards, in ways that strikingly resembled later formulations (Farr 2004; Putnam 2000: 18–26). In the background is the long-established social science axiom that, in order to flourish, human beings need sociability and participation in groups. The analytical concept of social capital has been developed recently by a number of people: Bourdieu (1986 [1983]), Coleman (1988), Loury (1977, 1987), and late in the day but perhaps most prominently, Putnam (1993a, 1995, 2000). During the late 1980s and 1990s, it passed into mainstream social science and policy discourses and found a ready political audience (for good introductory surveys of the field, see Field 2003; Lin 2001).

One of the more interesting things here is how independent of each other's works many of these authors appear to have been in their development of the notion of social capital. As a result, each views the concept slightly differently. Bourdieu, for example, is reasonably precise, focusing on relationships and ties and emphasising their largely negative role in the reproduction of élite privilege. Coleman is more vague, often seeming to mean particular values as well, and focusing on the potential benefits of social capital for disadvantaged populations. For Putnam, by contrast, social capital is a matter of 'networks, norms, and trust', and a generic aspect of human community.

In all cases, however, social capital is understood, albeit with differing emphases, as simultaneously an aspect of institutional pattern and collective organisation ('social structure') and a resource to which individuals have differential access and which they can use. On the one hand, there is '*social* capital as *social glue*', on the other, 'social capital as *capital*' (Phillips 2006: 135, italics in the original). Social capital is a shorthand way of talking about social connections and the character of communal life as resources upon which people draw, which – in conjunction with other kinds of resources – help to explain stratification patterns and may be a means by which people can improve their lives and develop their neighbourhoods and communities.

Exemplified by a long-standing American concern with the nature of civil, or civic, society and enthusiasm for the relationship between democracy and community (see also Bellah *et al.* 1985, 1991, for example), an important theme in many discussions of social capital, even if it is sometimes implicit, is that a 'good society' necessitates living with people who you know or who are at least identifiable to you, who know you or can at least identify you, and with whom you have some relationships. This is an image of community – and social capital – as a matter of social networks. However, mutual personal knowing within networks is not just, or even necessarily, a matter of face-to-face relationships. While networks include family, friends, and acquaintances, they also, crucially, include 'friends of friends'. You don't actually have to know someone personally to be in the same network, although you do know *about* them and, through mediators, *potentially* know them.

The origin of the social network concept may be traced back at least as far as Barnes' anthropological research in northern Norway in the early 1950s. Sitting on the village pier, watching the fishing nets drying, he conceived of a metaphor for understanding collectivity as the 'more-than-sum-of-the-parts' which emerges out of relationships between individuals but is not individually centred (Barnes 1954). Over the next couple of decades, the network model of the human world was mainly developed by anthropologists, studying, for example, gendered family relations in urban Britain (Bott 1971 [1957]), rural – urban migration in East Africa (Mayer 1961; Mitchell 1969), local-regional-national politics in Mediterranean societies (Blok 1974; Boissevain 1974), and family and kinship in urban black neighbourhoods in the USA (Stack 1974). Sociological network analyses also developed, particularly in the context of labour-market studies, looking at how people secure jobs (Granovetter 1995 [1974]; Grieco 1987). The technical possibilities for the quantitative analysis of networks were appreciated quite early (e.g. Niemeijer 1973) and, aided by advances in computing, quantitative approaches have dominated empirical research into social networks over recent decades (Scott 2000; Wellman 1999).

The common themes in this diversity of substantive topics and analytical approaches are first, access to resources, and second, security and predictability in the face of uncertainty. Whether it be support and knowledge at the end of migration to a strange place, influence and patronage in delicate micro-political games, informal reciprocal child-care when other resources are unavailable, or knowledge of job vacancies and a recommendation when applying, networks are in large part concerned with *information* about resources and about connections to resources. Access to information depends on 'who you know', which is part of 'who you are' and, no less important, who other people *think* you are.

That social capital and identity are bound up with each other is a theme explored by Portes, during a critical overview of the sociological use of the notion of 'social capital' (1998). He defines social capital in terms of closed networks (for husbanding scarce resources collectively), shared obligations between more than two people, reciprocity norms, and surveillance and sanctions. Social capital is thus a matter of 'enforceable trust' (*ibid.*: 8). He outlines three functions of social capital: social control, family support, and network support. In self-conscious opposition to the celebratory tone of much of the literature – it is telling that he regards Bourdieu's model as 'the most theoretically refined' (*ibid.*: 3) – Portes marshals research evidence to document the potential negativities of social capital: the exclusion of outsiders, excessive demands on group members, restrictions on individual freedom, and 'downward levelling' (and it is worth noting that Putnam [1993b] also considered the anti-social aspects of social capital).

Community and civic participation aside, the literature on social capital suggests several observations about resources and power/efficacy. First, social networks offer access to resources and, as such, can be considered a resource in their own right. This offers at least a riposte to those commentators who, for various reasons, doubt whether social capital should be thought of as 'capital' at all (Farr 2004: 26; Smith and Kulynych 2002). It also suggests that means and ends may not always be easy to distinguish with any clarity: any individual's social network may clearly be means and ends simultaneously. Second, the resources to which social networks offer access are many and varied, from intangibles such as self-esteem, to the materiality of jobs and money. Third, harking back to Marx's definition of capital, unless something can be done with it, unless it can be set in motion, a resource is not a resource. Social networks facilitate that motion, potentially allowing people the efficacy to do things. Fourth, access to resources is as much a matter of exclusion as inclusion. The same is more generally true of the management of resources. The playing field is never level: individuals, groups and categories of people can thus be said to have more or less social capital. Finally, an emphasis on social networks – which tend to subvert formal institutional boundaries, and can be thought of as ill-defined regions in the one great network that constitutes the human world (Watts 2003) – serves to counter the fragmentation induced by models of separate economies or economic spheres, on the one hand, and the typologising of power, on the other.

The last comment notwithstanding, the extension of the notion of 'capital' to 'non-economic' aspects of human life – and it should be said at this point that one of the greatest virtues of the concept of social capital is that it undermines the axiomatic, and, as I argue, misleading, distinction, between the economic and the non-economic – was not exhausted by the appearance of social capital on the scene. If anything, it opened the way to further conceptual proliferation, and the discovery of other capitals. It is to this that I will now turn.

OTHER CAPITALS

The major contributor to the extension and proliferation of the notion of 'capital' has been Bourdieu, keen perhaps to retain at least a metaphorical sense that economic factors are the 'bottom line' of social stratification, no matter how much inequality and domination may be produced and reproduced by education, cultural distinctions, and symbolic boundaries. His definition of social capital came, in fact, fairly late to his theoretical scheme of things. In a series of works published in French from 1970 onwards, dealing with the Kabyle of Algeria and the French class system (in their English versions: Bourdieu 1977, 1984, 1986, 1988, 1990, 1991, 1993, 1996; Bourdieu and Passeron 1977) he developed the concepts of 'symbolic capital' and 'cultural capital'.

Cultural capital, part of a broader field of 'informational capital' (Bourdieu 1998: 45), is primarily legitimate knowledge of one kind or another, and in this sense closely resembles the notion of human capital, discussed earlier. It is, however, considerably broader, in that it also takes in such things as 'taste' and 'refinement', as revealed in consumption patterns. A similar emphasis on a broader-than-educational understanding of cultural stratification can be seen in the work, for example, of Lamont (1992; Lamont and Fournier 1992).

Symbolic capital was never clearly defined by Bourdieu, and it may be that he did not achieve a final, definite vision of the concept himself (Bourdieu and Wacquant 1992: 119fn). It looms largest in his analyses of Kabyle ethnography and can be thought of as approximating to prestige and social honour, in which case it bears more than a passing resemblance to Weber's concept of 'status'. It appears to accrue to individuals at least in part because of their skilful and, in context, *appropriate* accumulation and use of other kinds of capital. Each type of capital – given the strong implication that economic capital is the elemental form, so to speak, of which the others are allotropes – finds its sources and most appropriate uses in particular social fields. Individual or collective levels of capital in one field may or may not match those in other fields, and conversion between fields and capitals is one of the main themes of practical strategising.

What Bourdieu was pointing to here is that, in addition to money, property, and social connections, people in the strategic pursuit of their ends exploit cultural distinction and knowledge, interactional style, information, and reputation (although, given his robust rejection of any notion of rational decision-making as a force in human affairs, that is not a way of putting it with which he would have been comfortable). In a word, all of these things are resources.

So far, so good; and useful. That the resources that enable efficacy are multiple, and not confined to money and property, is one of the central themes of this chapter. However, and in this respect resembling typological approaches to power and substantivist models of economic spheres, Bourdieu's work had a tendency to descriptive *ad hoc* model building. In addition to economic, social, cultural/informational, and symbolic capital, the following all make an appearance in his work at one point or another: linguistic capital, political capital, judicial capital, educational capital, academic capital, scientific capital, personal capital, and professional capital. What's more, cultural or informational capital apparently exists in three sub-forms: embodied, objectified, and institutionalised (Bourdieu and Wacquant 1992: 119). This is improvisatory classificatory complexity masquerading as analytical subtlety. It can only encourage further elaboration in others, as witnessed by the recent appearance of 'spiritual capital' (Romberg 2003).

We need to ask whether models of such complexity are necessary if we are to understand the relationships between efficacy and resources. In adopting such an approach, do we obscure rather than illuminate how power/efficacy works? I will now turn to these questions, in closing.

POWER, EFFICACY, AND RESOURCES

Beginning with a critical exploration and rejection of the conventional distinction between power and authority, I have argued for a simpler view of power as efficacy. The emphasis is on the generic human capacity to *act* – rather than merely behave – and the resources that people draw upon and mobilise in order to achieve their objectives. This recognises the ubiquity of power in the human world, while attempting to avoid the problems inherent in 'totalising' theories of power, as outlined by Haugaard (1997).

Efficacy and means – ends relationships come in many shapes and forms. The creation, mobilisation, and exchange of resources is complex, is not exhausted by the conventional subject matter and models of economics, and is embedded in the 'social', 'cultural', and 'political' lives of human beings. While maximising, husbanding, and investing are important aspects of human behaviour in general, so are reciprocity and altruism (and, although there is no time to explore this here, maximisation and altruism, for example, may, depending on the situation, be complementary rather than contradictory). These are all matters to be explored and understood in local contexts, without taking for granted the assumptions that western economics brings to the table.

That local mores and practices are distinctive, and demand to be understood, first, in their local contexts, does not mean that we should abandon our generalising mission, in Leach's words becoming 'anthropological butterfly collectors' (1961: 2). In this respect, one consistent issue throughout this chapter has been the problem of 'classificatory *ad hoc*-ery', manifest in typologies of kinds of power, the discovery of more and different 'economies', and ever-widening elaborations of the notion of 'capital'. Describing the substantive diversity and complexity of the human world seems to have overwhelmed attempts to understand process or generate relatively simple propositions that apply across a range of contexts. As Leach pointed out, there are at least two related causes for concern (*ibid*.: 3). First, this approach knows no constraint: the number of 'capitals', for example, or separate 'informal' or 'hidden' economies, is in principle infinite. Second:

> the typology makers never explain why they choose one frame of reference rather than another…this is equivalent to saying that you can arrange your butterflies according to their colour, or their size, or the shape of their wings…but no matter what you do this will be science. (*ibid*.)

While this latter may be a slightly harsh judgement, in that typological principles may be explained, the general point – that typologising tends to arbitrariness as well as potentially infinite regression – is well taken.

Typological enthusiasm of this sort has several likely unhelpful consequences for our better understanding of power/efficacy. First, practices that in context, from the perspective of actors, are broadly similar or part of a unitary, even if complex, strategy, may end up in different classificatory boxes. Second, as a result, such continuity as characterises everyday life becomes vulnerable to analytical fragmentation, and 'power' may become reified, seen as something over and against everyday life, rather than integral to it. Finally, and perhaps most problematic, analytical generalisation becomes increasingly difficult.

These considerations suggest that we do not need ever more complicated models of types of power or capital in order to understand how people, individually or collectively, exercise agency with differing degrees of efficacy. We do not, for example, need to add 'embodied' or 'physical capital' to Bourdieu's catalogue in order to grasp the centrality to efficacy of the forceful capacities of human bodies (which is true if only because all 'capitals' are produced and mobilised by real people). Although it seems likely, given that it has become established in widespread use, that the term 'social capital' will remain with us at least in the medium term, there is no need to adopt any of its near relatives.

What we do need, I suggest, in order to permit generalisation and comparative analyses that do not submerge local perspectives under external conceptual frameworks, are some relatively simple generic propositions about the relationship between power/efficacy and resources. Here is a tentative list of propositions that may encourage further debate in this respect:

- Power is a matter of efficacy, the capacity of individuals and groups to achieve their own ends and/or frustrate those of others.

- Power/efficacy depends on the availability of resources.
- Resources come in many forms, and in principle – and often in practice – offer different ways and means to achieve ends.
- Resources vary from context to context, and should be first understood in the context of local mores.
- Resources may be maximised, husbanded, invested in, and shared reciprocally or altruistically, depending on context and project.
- Specific resources may be oriented towards, or more appropriate for, the achievement of particular ends.
- Resources may be combined, depending on context and objective.
- Means and ends are locally defined, but in practice the distinction between means and ends is not always clear-cut.
- Individuals and different groups of actors will have access to differing resources in differing degrees and in differing combinations.
- In practice it may not always be easy to tease out different resources from each other (network connections and status and prestige are closely linked, for example, as are material wealth and the capacity to mobilise embodied human resources).

In this approach, people are understood to adopt problem-solving approaches to their lives, and to draw on available resources as and when it is locally appropriate to do so. Organisations – from a hunter-gatherer band, to a small business, to a large public sector organisation, to a transnational corporation, to a nation-state – are institutionalised ways of managing resources; they are thus 'power containers', in the sense in which power is understood here.

It may be objected that, in foregrounding efficacy, the approach to power that I adopt in this chapter focuses too much on agency, ignoring Lukes' emphasis (1974) on silences and absences as key outcomes of the exercise of power. In many respects, Lukes' position resembles Bourdieu's argument that the production and reproduction of domination 'works' because alternatives become invisible and silent, cloaked and muffled by the axiomatic apprehension of the *status quo* as inevitable or natural that is inculcated during socialisation (Bourdieu and Passeron 1977).

The first response to this objection must be that silences and absence do not 'just happen'. At the least, they reflect an existing balance of power, with a history; and histories are made by people and are what people make of them. At the most, even silences have to be orchestrated sometimes. What is more, silences can be broken; change is possible and human agency has some part to play in its making. The outcomes of change may be unpredictable, of course, and revolutions may be played out in their unintended consequences, but that is a different issue. While human agency may often be inaccurate, clumsy, stifled, or even 'out of control', it is not to be underestimated either.

The second response is epistemological, returning us to Bourdieu's distinction, referred to earlier, between the 'model of reality' and the 'reality of the model'. Unless we place human agency at the heart of our analyses, attending closely to what people are doing and what they think they are doing, then the silences and absences to which Lukes refers are likely to be filled by our own politics, preferences, and perspectives, rather than those of the people whose lives supply our data. This temptation – the patrician lure of intellectual ventriloquism – has dogged social theory and research ever since the enterprise began. The necessary struggle to achieve at least 'good enough objectivity' demands that we accept that, in some senses at least, people know what they are doing better than we do.[3] If they did not, there would be no point in asking them anything at all.

ACKNOWLEDGEMENTS

I am grateful to Mark Haugaard and David Phillips for their comments on an earlier draft of this chapter.

NOTES

1 Gender dimorphism, the fact that men are, on average, taller, heavier and stronger than women, does, however, make a difference, making at least some contribution to the systematic pattern of violence, of men against women, that underpins patriarchy (Jenkins 2002: 121–5).
2 It must also be recognised that humans have many species-specific needs over and above the basic requirements for bodily survival and reproduction (de Swaan 2001: 1–16; Doyal and Gough 1991).
3 This is not an argument for the superiority of common sense over sociological sense (see Jenkins 2002: 27–31).

REFERENCES

Barnes, J. A. (1954) 'Class and committees in a Norwegian Island parish', *Human Relations*, Vol. 7: 39–58.
Barth, F. (1967) 'Economic Spheres in Darfur', in R. Firth (ed.) (1967) *Themes in Economic Anthropology*, London: Tavistock.
Becker, G. S. (1964) *Human Capital*, New York: National Bureau of Economic Research.
Beggs, J. J. and Hurlbert, J. S. (1997) 'The social context of men's and women's job search ties: membership in voluntary organizations, social resources, and job search outcomes', *Sociological Perspectives*, Vol. 40: 601–22.
Bellah, R. N., Madsen, R., Sullivan, W. M., Swidler, A. and Tipton, S. M. (1985) *Habits of the Heart: Individualism and Commitment in American Life*, Berkeley: University of California Press.
Bellah, R. N., Madsen, R., Sullivan, W. M., Swidler, A. and Tipton, S. M. (1991) *The Good Society*, New York: Knopf.
Blackburn, R. M. and Mann, M. (1979) *The Working Class in the Labour Market*, London: Macmillan.
Blok, A. (1974) *The Mafia of a Sicilian Village 1860–1960*, Oxford: Basil Blackwell.
Bohannan, P. (1955) 'Some principles of exchange and investment among the Tiv', *American Anthropologist*, Vol. 57: 60–9.
Boissevan, J. (1974) *Friends of Friends: Networks, Manipulators and Coalitions*, Oxford: Basil Blackwell.
Bosanquet, N. and Doeringer, P. B. (1973) 'Is there a dual labour market in Great Britain?', *Economic Journal*, Vol. 83: 421–35.
Bott, E. (1971) *Family and Social Network*, second edition, London: Tavistock, (first published, 1957).
Bourdieu, P. (1977) *Outline of a Theory of Practice*, Cambridge: Cambridge University Press (published in French, 1972).
Bourdieu, P. (1984) *Distinction: A Social Critique of the Judgement of Taste*, London: Routledge and Kegan Paul (published in French, 1979).
Bourdieu, P. (1986) 'The Forms of Capital', in J. G. Richardson (ed.) *Handbook of Theory and Research for the Sociology of Education*, New York: Greenwood (published in French, 1983).
Bourdieu, P. (1988) *Homo Academicus*, Cambridge: Polity (published in French, 1984).
Bourdieu, P. (1990) *The Logic of Practice*, Cambridge: Polity (published in French, 1980).
Bourdieu, P. (1991) *Language and Symbolic Power*, Cambridge: Polity Press.
Bourdieu, P. (1993) *The Field of Cultural Production*, Cambridge: Polity.
Bourdieu, P. (1996) *The State Nobility: Elite Schools in the Field of Power*, Cambridge: Polity (published in French, 1989).
Bourdieu, P. (1998) *Practical Reason*, Cambridge: Polity Press (published in French, 1994).
Bourdieu, P. and Passeron, J.-C. (1977) *Reproduction in Education, Society and Culture*, London: Sage (published in French, 1970).
Bromley, R. and Gerry, C. (eds.) (1979) *Casual Work and Poverty in Third World Cities*, Chichester: Wiley.
Brown, R. M. (1975) *Strain of Violence: Historical Studies of American Violence and Vigilantism*, New York: Oxford University Press.

Bryman, A. (1992) *Charisma and Leadership in Organizations*, London: Sage.
Bryman, A. (1997) 'Leadership in organizations', in S. R. Clegg, C. Hardy and W. R. Nord (eds.) *Handbook of Organization Studies*, Thousand Oaks: Sage.
Coleman, J. S. (1988) 'Social capital in the creation of human capital', *American Journal of Sociology*, Vol. 94 Supplement: S95–S120.
Davis, J. (1972) 'Gifts and the UK economy', *Man* (n.s.), Vol. 7: 408–29.
de Swaan, A. (2001) *Human Societies: An Introduction*, Cambridge: Polity.
Doyal, L. and Gough, I. (1991) *A Theory of Human Need*, Basingstoke: Macmillan.
Farr, J. (2004) 'Social capital: a conceptual history', *Political Theory*, Vol. 32: 6–33.
Ferman, L. A., Henry, S. and Hoyman, M. (eds.) (1987) 'The informal economy', *Annals of the American Academy of Political and Social Science*, vol. 493: passim.
Field, J. (2003) *Social Capital*, London: Routledge.
Firth, R. (ed.) (1967) *Themes in Economic Anthropology*, London: Tavistock.
Gershuny, J. I. (1983) *Social Innovation and the Division of Labour*, Oxford: Oxford University Press.
Gershuny, J. I. and Pahl, R. E. (1979) 'Work outside employment: some preliminary speculation', *New Universities Quarterly*, Vol. 34: 120–35.
Gintis, H., Bowles, S., Boyd, R. and Fehr, E. (eds.) (2005) *Moral Sentiments and Material Interests: The Foundations of Cooperation in Economic Life*, Cambridge, MA: MIT Press.
Glaser, B. and Strauss, A. (1967) *The Discovery of Grounded Theory: Strategies for Qualitative Research*, New York: Aldine de Gruyter.
Gledhill, J. (2000) *Power and Its Disguises: Anthropological Perspectives on Politics*, second edition, London: Pluto.
Granovetter, M. (1995) *Getting a Job: A Study of Contacts and Careers*, second edition, Chicago: University of Chicago Press, (first published, 1974).
Grieco, M. (1987) *Keeping It in the Family: Social Networks and Employment Change*, London: Tavistock.
Handy, C. (1984) *The Future of Work: A Guide to a Changing Society*, Oxford: Basil Blackwell.
Harding, P. and Jenkins, R. (1989) *The Myth of the Hidden Economy: Towards a New Understanding of Informal Economic Activity*, Milton Keynes: Open University Press.
Harrison, B. (1972) *Education, Training and the Urban Ghetto*, Baltimore: Johns Hopkins University Press.
Hart, K. (1973) 'Informal income opportunities and urban unemployment in Ghana', *Journal of Modern African Studies*, Vol. 11: 61–89.
Haugaard, M. (1997) *The Constitution of Power: A Theoretical Analysis of Power, Knowledge and Structure*, Manchester: Manchester University Press.
Henrich, J., Boyd, R., Bowles, S. and Camerer, C. (eds.) (2004) *Foundations of Human Sociality: Economic Experiments and Ethnographic Evidence from Fifteen Small-Scale Societies*, Oxford: Oxford University Press.
Henry, S. (1978) *The Hidden Economy: The Context and Control of Borderline Crime*, Oxford: Martin Robertson.
Hobbs, D. (1988) *Doing the Business: Entrepreneurship, the Working Class, and Detectives in East London*, Oxford: Oxford University Press.
Holy, L. and Stuchlik, M. (1983) *Actions, Norms and Representations: Foundations of Anthropological Inquiry*, Cambridge: Cambridge University Press.
Ingstad, B. and Whyte, S. R. (eds.) (1995) *Disability and Culture*, Berkeley: University of California Press.
Jenkins, R. (1986) *Racism and Recruitment: Managers, Organisations and Equal Opportunity in the Labour Market*, Cambridge: Cambridge University Press.
Jenkins, R. (ed.) (1998) *Questions of Competence: Culture, Classification and Intellectual Disability*, Cambridge: Cambridge University Press.
Jenkins, R. (2002) *The Foundations of Sociology: Towards a Better Understanding of the Human World*, Basingstoke: Palgrave Macmillan.
Karabel, J. and Halsey, A. H. (eds.) (1977) *Power and Ideology in Education*, New York: Oxford University Press.
Klockars, C. B. (1974) *The Professional Fence*, London: Tavistock.
Lamont, M. (1992) *Money, Morals and Manners: The Culture of the French and the American Upper-Middle Class*, Chicago: University of Chicago Press.
Lamont, M. and Fournier, M. (eds.) (1992) *Cultivating Differences: Symbolic Boundaries and the Making of Inequality*, Chicago: Chicago University Press.
Leach, E. R. (1961) *Rethinking Anthropology*, London: Athlone Press.
Lewellen, T. C. (2003) *Political Anthropology: An Introduction*, third edition, Westport: Praeger.

Lin, N. (2001) *Social Capital: A Theory of Social Structure and Social Action*, Cambridge: Cambridge University Press.
Loury, G. C. (1977) 'A dynamic theory of racial income differentials', in P. A. Wallace and A. LeMond (eds.) *Women, Minorities and Employment Discrimination*, Lexington: D. C. Heath.
Loury, G. C. (1987) 'Why should we care about group inequality?', *Social Philosophy and Policy*, Vol. 5: 249–71.
Lukes, S. (1974) *Power: A Radical View*, London: Macmillan.
Malinowski, B. (1922) *Argonauts of the Western Pacific: An Account of Native Enterprise in the Archipelago of Melanesian New Guinea*, London: Routledge and Kegan Paul.
Mandel, E. (1970) *An Introduction to Marxist Economic Theory*, New York: Pathfinder.
Marx, E. (1976) *The Social Context of Violent Behaviour: A Social Anthropological Study in an Israeli Immigrant Town*, London: Routledge.
Marx, K. (1954) *Capital, Volume One*, London: Lawrence and Wishart.
Mauss, M. (1954) *The Gift: Forms and Functions of Exchange in Archaic Societies*, London: Cohen and West.
Mayer, A. (1961) *Townsmen or Tribesmen*, Cape Town: Oxford University Press.
Mitchell, J. C. (ed.) (1969) *Social Networks in Urban Situations*, Manchester: Manchester University Press.
Niemeijer, R. (1973) 'Some applications of the notion of density', in J. Boissevain and J. C. Mitchell (eds.) *Network Analysis: Studies in Human Interaction*, The Hague: Mouton.
Nugent, D. and Vincent, J. (eds.) (2006) *A Companion to the Anthropology of Politics*, Malden: Blackwell.
O'Neill, J. (1986) 'The disciplinary society: from Weber to Foucault', *British Journal of Sociology*, Vol. 37: 42–60.
O'Neill, J. (1994) *The Poverty of Postmodernism*, London: Routledge.
Phillips, D. (2006) *Quality of Life: Concept, Policy and Practice*, London: Routledge.
Piore, M. J. (1971) 'The dual labour market: theory and implications', in D. M. Gordon (ed.) *Problems in Political Economy: An Urban Perspective*, Lexington: D. C. Heath.
Plattner, S. (1989) 'Introduction', in S. Plattner (ed.) *Economic Anthropology*, Stanford: Stanford University Press.
Portes, A. (1998) 'Social capital: its origins and applications in modern sociology', *Annual Review of Sociology*, Vol. 24: 1–24.
Putnam, R. D. (1993a) *Making Democracy Work: Civic Traditions in Modern Italy*, Princeton: Princeton University Press.
Putnam, R. D. (1993b) 'The prosperous community: social capital and public affairs', *The American Prospect*, Vol. 13: 35–42.
Putnam, R. D. (1995) 'Bowling alone: America's declining social capital', *Journal of Democracy*, Vol. 6: 65–78.
Putnam, R. D. (2000) *Bowling Alone: The Collapse and Revival of American Community*, New York: Simon and Schuster.
Rapport, N. (1987) *Talking Violence: An Anthropological Interpretation of Conversation in the City*, St Johns: ISER, Memorial University of Newfoundland.
Rapport, N. (2003) *I Am Dynamite: An Alternative Anthropology of Power*, London: Routledge.
Romberg, R. (2003) *Witchcraft and Welfare: Spiritual Capital and the Business of Magic in Modern Puerto Rico*, Austin: University of Texas Press.
Sahlins, M. (1974) *Stone Age Economics*, London: Tavistock.
Schultz, T. W. (1961) 'Investment in human capital', *American Economic Review*, Vol. 51: 1–17.
Scott, J. (2000) *Social Network Analysis: A Handbook*, second edition, London: Sage.
Smith, M. E. (1989) 'The informal economy', in S. Plattner (ed.) *Economic Anthropology*, Stanford: Stanford University Press.
Smith, M. G. (1960) *Government in Zazzau 1800–1950*, London: Oxford University Press, for the International African Institute.
Smith, S. S. and Kulynych, J. (2002) 'It may be social, but why is it capital? The social construction of social capital and the politics of language', *Politics and Society*, Vol. 30: 149–86.
Stack, C. B. (1974) *All Our Kin: Strategies for Survival in a Black Community*, New York: Harper and Row.
Vincent, J. (ed.) (2002) *The Anthropology of Politics: A Reader in Ethnography, Theory and Critique*, Malden: Blackwell.
Watts, D. J. (2003) *Six Degrees: The Science of a Connected Age*, London: William Heinemann.
Weber, M. (1978) *Economy and Society: An Outline of Interpretive Sociology*, in G. Roth and C. Wittich (eds.) Berkeley: University of California Press.
Wellmann, B. (ed.) (1999) *Networks in the Global Village*, Boulder: Westview.
Wrong, D. H. (1979) *Power: Its Forms, Bases and Uses*, Oxford: Basil Blackwell.

9

Powerful Geographies: Spatial Shifts in the Architecture of Globalization

John Allen

INTRODUCTION

Geographers, it could be argued, have a particular disadvantage when it comes to addressing a broad social science audience, namely that much of the readership already appears to have fairly well developed views on what space and place contribute to the institutional workings of something like power, especially in terms of its scope and reach. There are certain time-honoured traditions, for instance, which, it has been pointed out, have shaped spatial vocabularies, as for example in the case of state sovereignty where bounded territories and defined distances have long played a part in demarcating the jurisdictional limits of political authority (see Agnew, 1994, 1999, 2005; Biersteker and Weber, 1996; Ferguson, 2004; Hudson, 1999; Walker, 1993). In contrast, at the risk of caricature, a number of writers have tended to stress the constant mobility and flow of all things social – from people and ideas to goods and capital – as a counterweight to settled notions of any kind of authority or easy territorial fix (see, for instance, Appadurai, 1990; Castells, 1996, 2000; Kellner, 2002; Ohmae, 1991; Urry, 2000a, b).

More often than not, though, in response to the challenges of globalization, there appears to be an urge among writers of different hues and backgrounds to merge or piece together the two vocabularies: to hold in some sort of tension, for example, the territorial impulses of nation states and other embedded institutions with the more fluid, networked powers of business and other transnational actors (see, for instance, Held et al., 1999; Hirst, 2005; Mann, 2003; Rosenau, 2003; Taylor, 2004; Wolf, 2004). In this more ill-defined landscape of power, scaled-up, territorial bodies may be tentatively fused with the more fluid, networked activities of economic corporations and social movements to provide what appears to be a more plausible account of the scope and reach of today's globalized actors. Such views of the characteristics of space and spatiality, more generally, broadly represent an attempt to come to terms with the changing dynamics of globalization, but in so doing, perhaps unwittingly, they tend to assume its geography rather than problematize it. In practice, it is assumed that the powerful geographies of the actors involved can be sketched against, what is often, in effect, a *given* global backdrop largely composed of territorial fixity and networked flows.

In this chapter, I want to pursue a different line of thought. The significance of wider geographies to how power exercises political, economic and cultural institutions, the manner in which events elsewhere are folded into the here and now, are part of a geographical reconfiguration of power that, arguably, the tension between fixity and flow strains to convey. Whilst it is not true to say that the fusion of two spatial vocabularies – territorial on the one hand, networked and fluid on the other – has led to a more impoverished understanding of power and its contemporary workings, it is true up to a point. Indeed, the idea that we can add together fragments of our contrasting experience of global change is particularly insensitive to recent spatial shifts in the architecture of globalization. It is as if our grasp of such shifts – the ways in which social proximities are established over physical distances, absent others interleaved with those present, the global folded into the local and, more straightforwardly, space compressed by time – has yet to catch up with our experience of them.

Without wishing to overstate the case, the urge to piece together what we know about territorial and network logics of power represents the limits of conventional geometric thinking about space and time. It pushes up against a *topological* world in which fixed distances and well-defined proximities are perhaps not the best indication of the powerful ties and relationships drawn between individuals, groups and organizations. Topological accounts disrupt our sense of what is near and what is far and loosen defined times and distances; in so doing they call into question the very idea that power may be simply distributed or extended over a given territory, or that it can be regarded as something which flows through extensive networks (Amin, 2002; Amin and Thrift, 2002; Allen, 2003; Gregory, 2004; Murdoch, 2006). Topological thinking suggests that individuals, groups and organizations may exercise power at-a-distance through a cross-cutting mix of distanciated and proximate actions, often reaching out through a succession of mediated relationships or drawing distant others within close reach through the effective use of real-time connections (Allen, 2004). On this view, the so-called 'distant powers' of monolithic institutions or footloose corporations are rarely that, yet neither can the presence of a close and powerful body simply be assumed to deliver authority and control. Broadly speaking, power is more spatially ambiguous than is often recognized.

As I see it, there is no 'given' global backdrop against which the powerful geographies of institutions and governments may be sketched, but rather different groups, decision makers and organizations caught up in spatial and temporal arrangements that often combine anything from the erosion of choice, the manipulation of outcomes and the threat of coercion with the closure of possibilities, the assent of authority and the open-ended qualities of seduction and persuasion. It is often overlooked that power comes in more guises than simply domination and authority, and recent topological shifts in the architecture of globalization have arguably enabled corporate institutions and government bodies, along with non-governmental organizations, to bridge the gap between here and there in ways which exhaust our geometric descriptions of them. Defined territories, mapped connections, measurable distances, and fixed geographical scales, to my mind, no longer capture much of the way in which power is exercised in an increasingly globalized world. In what follows, I first consider two recent attempts to capture what is distinctively new about power and globality: Ulrich Beck's *Power in the Global Age* (2005) and Saskia Sassen's *Territory, Authority, Rights: From Medieval to Global Assemblages* (2006). Both practice a spatial sensibility that is not always present in globalization debates. Moreover, both recognize that a new geography of power is in the making, in which the global is instantiated in the national every bit as much as the national inhabits the global. It is at this point, however, that I wish to show how both push up against the *limits* of geometric thinking around territory, distance and geographical scale, with different abilities to see beyond it. After that, through a number of illustrations, I try to show what difference geography, or rather a topological appreciation of space and place, can make to our understanding of the workings of power in the present global era. More pointedly, I hope to show why geographers are more than simply cartographers of power, mapping already given global distributions of domination and authority.

BECK'S HAZY SPACES OF POWER

Globalization, for Ulrich Beck, has brought forth new spaces and frameworks for acting, in which the old power-plays between territorially defined actors have given way to a more open-ended play for domination and authority between state, business and civil society actors who are no longer subject to the same boundaries as before. It is this latter group of actors who occupy the new, 'hazy power space of global domestic politics' (2005, xi) which, according to Beck, are already at work here and beyond anything that can be pinned down as either national or international. In *Power in the Global Age*, this geographically nebulous state of affairs has come about because capital in particular, in the shape of individual companies, finance houses and commercial entities, under an emergent neo-liberal regime is said to have broken out of the confines of the zero-sum power game set up by the old nation-state international institutional order. In its place, a new deterritorialized game of power politics has taken shape where the enhanced mobility of business and capital is said to give it an edge over territorially bound states.

Meta-power

Under this new game of power politics, globalization, above all, has set in train a means for brokering power which has altered its conventional bases. For Beck, the new power struggle has led to a renegotiation of the very boundaries, rules and territories upon which it is taking place – a game which *goes beyond* the old territorial, institutional rules: a meta-power game.

> A *meta-power game* is in progress in the relationship between global business and the state, a power struggle in which the balance of power and the rules of power governing the national and international system of states are being radically changed and rewritten. It is the world of business in particular that has developed such meta-power by breaking out of the cage of the territorial nation-state-organized power

game and mastering new strategies of power in the digital domain in contrast to territorially rooted states. (2005: 52)

The basis of global business' meta-power is taken to be its mobility and extensive networked capabilities; its ability to take advantage of space-shrinking telecommunications technologies to exploit opportunities wherever and whenever they arise. Beck refers to this ability as a form of 'translegal' or transnational domination, whereby corporate actors do not so much act above the law or authority of nation states as act alongside them in their domestic sphere, influencing the rules and regulations by which economic activity is conducted. In one sense, corporations make their 'own' law through deterritorialized forms of private authority relating to contracts, labour standards, international arbitration and such. The extensive, diffuse power of global business actors enables them to 'threaten' states through their non-involvement, rather than their direct engagement. The possibility of exit, investment and finance moving to territories where authority and regulation works in their global interests, underpins their meta-power (see also Beck, 2001).

Whilst there is nothing especially new about the mobile and footloose characteristics of business and capital, what today is distinctive about their actions for Beck is the fact that they inhabit an arena of 'global domestic politics' – where the mutually exclusive distinctions between the national and the international no longer apply. A form of 'transnational politics' is said to apply where 'nation state politics becomes the site where transnational politics is worked out' (2005: 113). Global business actors, according to Beck, are able to influence the outcome of political decisions taken by governments so that their economic interests are prioritized over others. This is not domination in the 'old' sense of command and control, but rather domination through market usurpation: leaving governments little choice but to go along with the rhythms of deterritorialized global markets.

States and global business are not the only actors engaged in this new transnational politics, however. Beck also considers a variety of actors drawn from civil society, in particular NGOs and social movements engaged in environmental, human rights and consumer campaigns, for example, which are able to effectively mobilize across international borders to realize their goals. Strategic in the sense that they are able to raise public awareness around issues that are packaged as universal and for the 'good of all', such civil society groups are able to exert influence in the domestic sphere of nation states previously held to be beyond outside interference. Leaving to one side the actual success of much transnational activism, the networking abilities of such groups to mobilize around and indeed construct the 'common good' underpins their meta-power, according to Beck. It is this cosmopolitan quality that legitimizes their right to politically interfere in the domestic affairs of states, as for example in respect of the demands of human rights activists or the environmental movement.

The sweep of the analysis, if at times a little over-generalized when it comes down to the actors involved and their powers, does nonetheless point to the increasing interpenetration of somewhat previously discrete national and international spaces. Governments too, often in tandem with NGOs or other forms of civil society protest, can also be seen to exert influence beyond their own borders as they also, in Beck's terms, learn to master the rules of the new meta-game of world politics. Instead of the old zero-sum game of power played out within the borders of the national, he sees the emergence of a more cosmopolitan, positive-sum game between states, business and civil society where no single group of players can realize their goals in isolation from the other. They are all dependent on the powers of each being exercised in such a way that their particular, often material, interests may be realized.

> It takes the authority of states to achieve the NGO's goal of establishing a world order based on civil society, for they are the ones who can give this order a legally and politically binding shape. A plural global area is inconceivable without the existence of strong, active states. Even the strategies of capital that are only pursuing their economic interests, remain ultimately dependent both on states and on civil society's moral pronouncements – this is the only way the cultural and political preconditions for the investment freedom they enjoy can be guaranteed. The gap between the *proponents* of the different camps is indeed closing in this general mêlée of mutual instrumentalization. (2005: 288–289)

In a world of transnational politics, the interests of a highly mobile business community may have the edge over that of territorially rooted states, but both have much to gain by pursuing their own goals in tandem. Moreover, according to Beck, all those involved may enhance their power in the process; states may recapture some of their independence, for example, despite gains made by business and capital, and NGOs may find themselves in alliance with either governments or corporations to push forward specific 'universal' agendas around labour and environmental responsibilities, for instance. On this view, the competitive and conflictual nature of power which arises from one side subjecting another to its instrumental will is less on show than the notion of power as a potential force for integration and enablement at the global scale.

What enables Beck to make this observation, however, that there is more to be gained by the actors involved from exercising power *with* rather than *over* others, is the belief that we are witnessing the formation of a dense 'network of transnational interdependencies' between state, business and civil society actors (2005: xv). In short, the trajectories of these different groups on the global stage are thought to be locked together in such a way that collaboration and domination start to resemble two sides of the same coin.

The limits of geometric description

If this is so, however, the kind of complex cross-cutting arrangements that Beck is at pains to convey where the global is instantiated in the national world are often lost in a vocabulary of close-knit networks, global interdependencies and defined territories. The unsettled nature of the new power formations, the reference to 'hazy power spaces' and the acknowledgement that the 'national' and the 'international' are not mutually exclusive domains, suggest that the spatial trappings of Euclidian geometry may not be the appropriate vehicle to capture the new geography of power that is taking shape. The interpenetration of the national and the global, rather than described as 'hazy' in outline, would perhaps be better understood, I would have thought, if some form of spatial topology were at the heart of the analysis. Although Beck does acknowledge in passing that many 'contacts between different locations in the world are established in the immediate present' and that the distinction between 'here and there' is losing its constitutive meaning in the power-plays between nation-state and global business (2005, 139), the logic of the analysis is not followed through to the point where a topological approach suggests itself.

Whilst it is not necessary to endorse oversimplistic versions of the world getting smaller, the use of real-time technologies to create a simultaneous presence in a variety of global settings is only one way in which our sense of space and time has been jolted, and powerful relationships refashioned to take account of the fact that proximity and distance now play across one another in diverse ways. Likewise, the 'lifting out' and 're-embedding' of aspects of social life, where events elsewhere are folded into the here and now, has the potential to alter how we see the actors of transnational social movements or the cross-border workings of corporate organizations. Power plays are not simply enacted over flat territories, across defined distances and measured connections, but knowing that is not the same thing as being able to articulate or conceptualize it. As indeed Beck's account of 'hazy spaces' reminds us.

It is not simply the rigidity of our geometric descriptions that is at stake, however. A topological appreciation of power in a global age might also have revealed a richer, more varied account of power as it is currently practised between agencies and institutions; that is, over and above that of domination and authority. If there is a new geography of power in the making, then such equally rigid characterisations of the exercise of power may also be open to question. Before we turn to that, however, I want to consider a further attempt to pin down what is new about power and globality which also pushes up against the limits of geometric thinking, but does so in a way that leaves us with a less nebulous geography than Beck, although with much the same restricted sense of the different registers of power in play today.

SASSEN'S OVERLAPPING GEOGRAPHY OF POWER

Early on in *Territory, Authority, Rights: From Medieval to Global Assemblages*, Saskia Sassen makes the exacting point that globalization, in its current manifestation and shape, cannot be adequately grasped through the notion of growing interdependence and the formation of global systems. She makes the point forcefully because she wants to convey what Beck fails to grasp: namely, that there is more to the interpenetration of the national and the global than a web of connections between diverse actors. There is the overlapping *mix of spaces and times* to consider too. If this sounds geographically cryptic, what she means by this is that when the global is conceived as something that is 'lodged' in the national, rather than as an external force acting upon it, we also have to consider the *interaction* of the often quite different time frames and spatial orders of the actors involved. As, for Sassen, the contours of a new geography of power arise out of such interactions, it is important to be clear about what is at issue.

Assemblages of power

Like Beck, Sassen refuses to polarize the domains of the national and the global, and both represent the national setting as the site within which the forces of globalization are played out. Instead of the 'hazy' power space of global domestic politics, however, Sassen is altogether more precise in identifying the emergence of what she refers to as a new *spatio-temporal assemblage*. By this, she has in mind a novel configuration of territory, authority and rights that combines older elements of the legal and bureaucratic system of governance, for example, with new economic capabilities and norms. Part private, part public, with bits and pieces of institutional authority, legal rights and territorial infrastructure, the emergent assemblage which is neither national nor global represents an unstable power formation in the making. It is unstable not only because different economic, political and legal elements may co-exist in novel arrangements, but also because such elements may operate according to a different temporal rhythm and institutional pace which come together in both enabling and contested ways. In short, the mix of time-spaces embedded in the material practices of the different actors and agencies involved – state authorities and jurisdictional agencies, corporate firms and supranational institutions, civil society movements and transnational activists – may work to disassemble and reassemble elements of territorial exclusivity, public authority and civil rights, for instance, in ways that found a new kind of organizing logic and a new, refashioned geography of power.

Notwithstanding Sassen's tendency to be over-schematic in her analysis and rather short on substantive detail outside of the United States, the sense in which power and globality have demonstrated a more cross cutting nature since the 1980s is, for her, evident from the altered nature of state power. In opposition to arguments which stress the loss of state authority in the wake of deregulation, privatization or the enhanced mobility of capital, Sassen emphasizes the active role of the state in regulating its own withdrawal *and* setting up new frameworks of authority through which the globalization of economic and other activities is fostered. The shift of functions to the private sector and the development of new forms of private authority governing such things as property rights, commercial arbitration, contractual agreements and cross-border transactions are geared not towards national but transnational agendas. A redistribution of power within the state is said to have taken place, where a number of public and quasi-public authorities start to function as the institutional home for powerful, transnational actors and global markets.

> The capacity to privatize and denationalize is predicated on changes in specific components of territory, authority, and rights as these have been constituted historically in the national state. The new privatized institutional order for governing the corporate global economy has governance capabilities and a type of specialized and partial narrative authority. That is to say, we see an emergent new normativity that has incorporated elements of what was once state authority. At the same time, once constituted, this new normativity of the world of private power installs itself in the public realm where it reappears as public policy...In so doing, these state institutions reorient their particular policy work or, more broadly, state agendas toward the requirements of the global economy. (2006: 412)

More pointedly for Sassen, this disembedding of state functions and the growing authority of non-state actors in the public realm opens up spaces within the formerly exclusive territory of nation states where global firms are subject to extraterritorial forms of authority. Parts of global cities such as New York and London, for example, where financial and corporate actors are said to operate in an accelerated time-space, are seen to be detached, in partial and variable ways, from the geographically circumscribed authority of the state. This, however, is not a geography where some parts of national territory hover or float above it, autonomous from the reach of the state, but rather that such economic spaces remain firmly embedded in national territories, yet subject to wider geographical authorities when it comes down to regulation and control. Whilst states remain the final authority over their expansive territories, the prevalence of such authority should not, as Sassen notes, be confused with dominance. On this understanding, states are both confronted by and are part of a new geography of power that does *not* have territorial exclusivity as its defining characteristic.

Business and global corporations, as part of the world of private power, benefit from the shifts in authority to non-state actors within the public realm, but as in Beck's analysis there is something of a positive-sum game involved. The actual balance of power rests with the new business interests, especially those corporate economic actors involved in global markets and highly digitized sectors such as banking and finance, yet for Sassen that advantage comes less from their potential hypermobility and more from their ability to insert themselves inside the national state as part of a quasi-global regime of flexibility and openness. Such firms and financial networks may operate according to a heightened spatial and temporal order quite different from much of the surrounding economy or, indeed, polity, but to do so they require an active state to relinquish its territorial hold on authority for the benefit of all, realized in the form of privatized growth and efficiency.

Sassen is clear that the new space-shrinking digital technologies can translate into additional power on the part of capital in its negotiations with governments, more through embedded practices than anything technical, but she is equally clear that such electronic networks only work if they have a territorial base. Near instantaneous transmissions across financial networks, for example, are only possible if supported by state-of-the art environments and vast concentrations of not-so-mobile infrastructure. The new information and communications technologies may be global in scope, but they are not postnational; rather they are part of new assemblages of power that have reconfigured state territory and authority, not displaced it. The stress upon *fixity* is critical for Sassen – that people, institutions and agencies are place-based – for it dovetails with her previous argument (Sassen, 1991) that global cities are precisely the kind of economic spaces which operate globally inside the national. Only this time around, the analysis is taken a step further by referring to powerful global cities as constituting a distinct kind of non-geographical territory operating largely according to their own distinctive rhythms and spatial practices.

The kind of global cities that Sassen has in mind are not the large, cosmopolitan or diverse, complex 'ordinary cities' of the less developed world (see Robinson, 2006) which preoccupy much postcolonial analysis, but the few cities with the capabilities to 'run' the economic networks through their concentration of resources and expertise. New York, Tokyo and London are the obvious main contenders, as part of a wider global network of financial centres, but they are less in evidence here than the fact that such centres represent part of a novel geography of authority comprised of territories *without* geographical borders.

If the global network of financial centres has led to a greater concentration of power in selective cities with capital markets, Sassen, like Beck, also notes an opposing trend: the greater distribution of power within global civil society facilitated by transnational activist networks. Again the evidence is largely limited to human rights and other social justice movements, but her claim is that the new web-based, digital technologies have enabled local actors – and she stresses their local base – to bypass national state authorities by gaining direct access to other local actors in the same country or across borders. The multiplication of local transactions laterally through global networks has enabled transnational solidarities and alliances to form which are able to contest or 'jump' the territorial, jurisdictional authority of states and their legal constraints. In a loose parallel to the unbound geography of authority thought to be enjoyed by global financial centres, local activists are said to inhabit 'microenvironments with global span' (2006: 387), that are neither explicitly national nor global, but rather assemblages of each. As with global cities, these emergent global publics are said to operate with temporal and spatial horizons that sit uneasily alongside the slower, more bureaucratic time-spaces exercised routinely by a significant number of public authorities.

The limits of territorial thinking

What is clear about the thrust of Sassen's account of the new geography of power is that territorial thinking and, more broadly, a conception of globalization as growing interdependence, fails to capture the spatial and temporal dynamics of power in play. The mix of spaces and times that inhabit the national setting are, for her, at the heart of a new overlapping geography of power within which different actors jostle, co-exist and interrupt one another to gain advantage. Globalization itself is reshaping much of the regulatory landscape but not in defined territorial ways where authority is divided neatly along geographical lines. Rather, in the complex institutional assemblages that she envisages, authority becomes detached from territory as corporate and transnational logics circulate through the national frame and emerge as domestic policy. From one angle, this may look like the blurred, 'hazy space' of global domestic politics, where it is often hard to discern the fluid interactions involved, but from where Sassen stands such detachment and re-embedding of authority makes perfect sense if it is understood in non-territorial terms.

Such an understanding, however, requires that we suspend belief in the assumption that state power and authority are extensive with the borders of the nation, as well as capable of uncomplicated geographical reach. The detachment of authority from territory also brings into question the idea that borders are always at the *edges* of any given territory. For Sassen, this is patently not the case and she goes further to argue that borders are not so much redrawn as re-embedded *within* the national geography, in line with the form of authority under consideration (see also Sassen, 2000). The cross-cutting spaces of business, corporations, NGOs, public agencies and solidarity movements, and their different spatial and temporal rhythms, produce territorial detachments of a kind barely conceivable in terms of exclusive geometric spaces.

> ... this detachment today assumes two forms broadly speaking. One is that the border is embedded in the product, the person, and the instrument: a mobile agent endogenizes critical features of the border. The other is that there are multiple locations for the border, whether inside firms or in long transnational chains of locations that can move deep inside national territorial and institutional domains. Global cities account for a disproportionate concentration of such border locations; the latter are mostly institutional locations that assume a territorial correlate, for example, the large concentration of international banking facilities in New York City. Institutional locations in principle need not have territorial correlates. (2006: 416)

Overlapping geographies of power, where rule-making authorities are detached from territories and bordered within firms and transnational organizations, take us a long way from simple territorial logics. They push up against a world of exclusive spaces, defined networked connections and fixed geographical scales to suggest an altogether different geography from the conventional global backdrop. In common with Beck, Sassen considers the global to be instantiated in the national every bit as much as the national inhabits the global, but unlike Beck she problematizes the geography of the national rather than assume its familiar co-ordinates. As such, she reaches the limits of geometric thinking around territory, distance and space; but in terms of sketching a new geography of power in the making, her focus upon nationalizing the global, so to speak, leads her towards a place-based account of disaggregated authority. Whilst the territorial geography of the national is problematized, the networked geography of the global largely escapes scrutiny. Extensive reach, proximity and presence are taken as givens, as if they make little or no difference to the exercise of power at-a-distance. The 'work' of the network, as Bruno Latour (1987, 1999, 2005) continually reminds us, more or less eludes her.

To be fair, Sassen recognizes that supernational networks, in particular digital networks, have the ability to destabilize existing hierarchies of geographical scale but her concern is with the new types of territory that they may bring about, not with the potential transformation of powerful relationships within the networks or their mediation through those physically distant in space and time. The 'lifting out' and 're-embedding' of authority that she has in mind seems to occur within national settings, not between them, or between different time periods. A topological understanding of the spatial shifts that characterize the current phase of globalization would problematize what happens in between 'here and there', as much as the capabilities of the different actors 'lodged' in the nation state. It would also enable us to see more than a reworked geography of authority, and perhaps bring into view the practices of arms length manipulation or extensive inducement deployed by corporations and NGOs alike, for instance, which arguably have been made easier by the topological shifts in the architecture of globalization.

DISTANT PROXIMITIES OF POWER

Both Beck and Sassen are acutely aware of the unsettled nature of the power formations they seek to describe, and Sassen more than Beck is aware that globalization – as a reworking of spatial and temporal dynamics – lies behind much of the inconstant landscape. Where Beck tends to conflate the dynamics of globalization with the capabilities of the actors involved, so for example speed and mobility become attributes of capital and business, Sassen grasps the fact that a reworking of space and time has taken place which is *separate* from the networked 'logic' of capital or the changing functions of the state. When Beck talks about the 'new asymmetry between rooted and winged forms of power that facilitates the unwarlike conquests of global business' (2005: 73), he treats the machinery of the state as largely fixed and capital as essentially mobile. He may not wish to convey this asymmetry in quite such a stereotypical fashion, but in doing so he makes it that much harder to consider the spatial shifts that have altered the architecture of globalization.

As I see it, such topological shifts have made possible a blend of more proximate and far-reaching *practices of power* that have effectively changed the relationships between corporate institutions and government bodies, non-governmental organizations and supranational agencies, transnational actors and jurisdictional agencies. It is not so much about which actors have become more or less mobile, more or less networked, as how certain practices of proximity and reach have enabled a broad range of actors and institutions to make their presence felt in ways hitherto largely unrecognized. The so-called hazy, cross-cutting, overlapping spaces of power that have apparently colonized the national setting may be better understood through a topological rather than a geometric lens. In much conventional geometric thinking about time and space, distances more often than not are there to be overcome, territories are made 'porous' and global scales are 'jumped' by powerful actors (see, for instance, Brenner, 2004; Smith, 2004; Swyngedouw, 2000). In a topological world, in contrast, the distanciated relationships, direct ties and real-time connections of the powerful and not so powerful actors come to the fore.

Powers of reach

A key part of Sassen's novel geography of authority in global cities like London and New York is the co-existence of different financial, corporate and government actors operating within different spatial and temporal frameworks. The combination of old and new forms of governance, authority and rights that is said to restructure the balance of power between the different interests is one that works itself out *in situ*; that is, there is little sense that events or actors distant in space and time are part of the equation. It would be odd, however, if that were the case and indeed that the powerful interplay between economic and political agencies was not, in some way, mediated by those physically absent, as well as by those present in place. Financial and corporate business, regardless of their headquartered location, for instance, are likely to be part of institutional arrangements which arguably mix *far-reaching* with more *proximate* modes, *circuitous* with more *immediate* styles of power, to establish and maintain an influential presence in one or more global cities.

Consider, for instance, the significant increase in private equity transactions around the globe since 2000, but especially in the US, Europe and Asia. Unlike the previous boom in private equity deals in the late 1980s, this time around the scope of transactions is global, effectively giving governments little choice but to engage in the process (Reserve Bank of Australia, 2007). The private equity business profits – from management fee income and a portion of the incremental gains realized – by buying publicaly traded companies, taking them into private hands, raising their operational performance and, after a brief period, typically three to five years, and selling them on at an appreciable profit (Freeman, 2005). A key feature of private equity firms is that they finance a high proportion of their purchases through a mix of debt and funds raised through institutional investors, in particular, banks, insurers, pension funds and various endowments and foundations. In turn, the equity risk attached to such ventures is often sold on by investors, multiplying the number of economic actors involved. For example, a private equity takeover of a major UK high street chain in 2007 led by US investors, KKR (Kohlberg Kravis Roberts), witnessed a catalogue of banks – Citigroup, Barclays Capital, Deutsche Bank, J P Morgan Cazenove, Bank of America, Royal Bank of Scotland, UniCredit and Merrill Lynch – involved in the syndication of risk and the debt financing arrangements for the purchase (*Financial Times*, 2007a). Consortia, trusts, joint partnerships are the norm in this type of high investment economic activity, with KKR involved with the world's largest private equity firm, Blackstone, in purchases worldwide, together with Europe's largest fund, CVC Capital Partners. The latter has offices spread across Europe and Asia, Blackstone has recently opened offices in London, Hamburg and Mumbai and KKR has backed acquisitions across Europe, Australia and Asia. Together, with other significant funds such as the Carlyle Group, Terra Firma, Texas Pacific, Permira and the Apollo Group, a complex geography of financial networking and investment has enabled the mobilization of funds over space to be used to acquire a range of domestic assets from catering outlets, water utilities and transport infrastructure to manufacturing, drug and healthcare companies. The ability to manage and control funds at a distance in this way is a form of distanciated power, in Anthony Giddens' (1984) sense of the term, but it is the *reach* into homely domestic spaces which gives this type of capital its powerful presence.

Much of what private equity groups do involves little more than long-established financial engineering, using debt to lever up profitable returns, rather than the techniques of anything resembling 'fast capitalism'. Practically, such groups act as intermediaries, folding in actors distant in space and time by enrolling them into financial arrangements that offer the inducement of substantial returns (Fenn, Liang and Prowse, 1995). The key to this arrangement, following Latour (1996), is the ability to 'hook up' others to the process of circulation, to draw others into the network of meanings in such a way that it extends and reproduces itself through spaces and time. As such, it involves a *mediated* exercise of power, where distances are bridged by the successive enrolment of actors to form something akin to a single will. Holding the arrangement together is a more tenuous affair than often understood, requiring powers of inducement and persuasion on the part of private equity firms, but what gives them their extensive reach inside domestic spaces, as Sassen perceptively observed, is the ability to work through institutional 'borders', at locations well within the national domain.

The consortia, and their allied banks, although made up of economic actors drawn from far and wide, are able to be more or less *present* in the here and now of western economies. The lifting out of economic relations from one context to another made possible by an extended circuit of institutional actors at a distance provides a kind of arm's length reach into national economies, but the ability to establish near instantaneous reach through a variety of telecommunication and media technologies also gives the consortia the added possibility of exercising an influential presence in real time. The point is less about speed and hypermobility as it is about the reduction of uncertainty and the leverage that co-presence can afford when structuring a deal and working with different interest groups and government bodies. Simultaneous exchange at ever greater distances has nothing to do with power moving faster, it is merely a medium that enables certain practices and not others, such as the inducement and persuasion of governments and shareholders that their interests are, for the present at least, best served by private equity deals (see Blackburn, 2006).

Government reaction to the increased number of private equity acquisitions in the UK for example, where the value of such deals exceeded 89 billion dollars in 2006 (Thomson Financial, 2007), has largely focussed on the perceived efficiency gains that private ownership can bring, tempered by a concern for potential job losses. When companies are taken out of public scrutiny and the short-term requirements of shareholder accountability, the potential efficiency gains realized through the restructuring of management and labour provide a strong inducement for public authorities to back the ownership changes, especially where they involve newly privatized setups as is the case with many infrastructure deals. In any such interplay of forces, however, where actors are mobilized and positioned through particular practices, the possibility of manipulation as much as inducement is always in play. The strong reaction from trades union bodies in the UK to increased private equity deals, for instance, has been to draw attention to the manipulative ploys exercised by private equity firms, where their excessive fees are concealed from view and potential returns exaggerated. If the erosion of job security that private deals foster is the price to be paid for greater economic efficiency, the trades unions have questioned whether the returns from the performance of private equity are in fact any higher over time than that of publicly quoted companies (*Financial Times*, 2007b). Indeed, most studies suggest that the returns over time are roughly similar, although it is difficult to obtain an accurate picture (Samuelson, 2007).

In Beck's analysis, then, what may appear to be a positive-sum game between governments and global private equity consortiums, where the goals of both are realized in tandem, may perhaps be better understood as an instance of 'organizational outflanking'. In Michael Mann's (1986) sense of this term, governments comply not because they perceive their interests to be shared but because they are so embedded in existing economic arrangements that they have little choice other than to go along with the private equity option – for the present, that is. Put another way, government bodies are outflanked by a form of global capital in this instance because the sheer scale of the private equity business holds the potential to 'rejuvenate' a large number of sizeable companies and, as such, cannot be simply sidelined. In the UK, the prospect of a more dynamic and efficient business sector gives private equity the edge over government, not the fact that the later is believed to be territorially 'rooted' in its capabilities.

More to the point, in this scenario, inducement and manipulation can be seen to play across one another in an arrangement that involves far reaching powers intersecting with more proximate modes. As a cameo of the new geography of power in the making, private equity operates neither as a force external to the nation state nor one internal to its boundaries, but rather one with *powers of reach* that enable them to make themselves present in different economies through mediated and real time connections. Power may be believed to be seeping away from states, but public and private authorities are also part of a topological world that is shifting in terms of its global architecture. They too, through the newly privatized institutional order described by Sassen, are engaged *directly* with transnational institutions and their counterparts in other nation states. The changing relationship between government, business and civil society actors, the regulation and enforcement of standards that takes place between them in different national contexts, owes less in this respect to the assumed capabilities of each and rather more to the expanded workings and practices of power made possible by a shift in the spatial and temporal dynamics of globalization.

Powers of connection

It is not only the relationship between government and business that has taken particular twists and turns as a new geography of power is fashioned; NGOs, and civil society actors are also part of the topological equation. For Beck, as well as Sassen, the growth of social movements – networks of actors in environmental, feminist, human rights, labour and consumer alliances – have tilted the balance of power. The ability to mobilize across borders, to conduct transnational campaigns through extensive activist networks and to 'jump' the territorial, jurisdictional authority of states, has, it would appear, empowered many across the globe who previously found themselves constrained in some kind of zero-sum game (see, for example, Della Porta and Tarrow, 2005). Such empowerment, in part, is viewed as a product of newly forged connections: the ability to span the globe from a local base or to 'jump' from the local to the global and back again (McDonald, 2006). Obviously the new media and communications technologies have played a significant part in facilitating such networked mobilisations, but such connectivity in and of itself fails to capture quite how transnational activists have been able to exert an influence often way beyond their means. The power of connections amounts to more than just lines on a map and speaks to the ways in which NGOs and civil society campaigners have been able to make 'publics' *present* across a range of global social justice issues.

The mobilization of distant and dispersed 'publics' around issues of global justice and the ability to bring pressure to bear upon governments and corporations in various parts of the world, but especially in the wealthier parts of Europe, Asia and the US, has been greatly enhanced by the topological shifts in global architecture. The ability, for instance, to link the actions of governments or corporations *directly* to the abuse of poor communities elsewhere in the world or to issues faced collectively such as climate change, ecological disasters, food risks and sweatshop exploitation, is, in practice, a topological tactic. The stress upon practice is deliberate, because the connections between citizen and environmental tragedy or between consumer and corporate exploitation on the far side of the globe have to be made – they are not given.

In many consumer campaigns, for example, civil society movements have been able to *draw closer* events such as sweatshop exploitation in far off locations by fixing directly upon company logos (in the case of sweatshop exploitation, Nike, Gap, Adidas, Puma and Reebok have all figured) and linking the actions of branded retailers directly to abuse overseas. In doing so, they established an immediate connection between exploitation 'over there' and corporate decisions 'back home'. More pointedly, NGOs and campaigning groups were able effectively to erase from view the majority of global supply chain connections that separate factory workers from consumers: the buyers and suppliers, trading companies and sourcing agents, subcontractors and subassembly firms. In other words, they cut out the very agencies and ties which comprise much of the global market machinery that frequently passes for economic interdependence. The power of connection in this instance, therefore, derives from the ability of activists to dissolve, not traverse, the gap between 'near' and 'far' by lifting out exploitation and re-embedding it among those affluent consumers who benefit from it (see Allen, 2006).

Moreover, by framing the issue of sweatshop exploitation as one that involves us all, NGOs, like Oxfam and Christian Aid, used the fact of 'connection' to oblige consumers to take responsibility for events elsewhere. By virtue of being part of an economic system which reproduces exploitation, western consumers were made to feel responsible (but not to blame) for the harm and injustice meted out in their name on factory floors distant in both space and time (see Young, 2003, 2004). The success of this mediated exercise of power, whereby NGOs enrolled consumers to confront retail corporations directly with the consequences of their (indirect) actions, has however less to do with solidarities produced through the new telecommunications technologies and rather more to do with the ability of social movements to persuade, manipulate and influence action at-a-distance.

If folding in events directly from elsewhere is a key tactic adopted by transnational activists, the reaction of those targeted, corporations and government agencies in the main, has been to *distance* themselves from abuses elsewhere. The alliances between NGOs and states or business and civil society movements that Beck sees as critical to the realization of mutual goals is exemplified by the forms of corporate responsibility recently adopted by many global companies operating in sensitive environmental and consumer-orientated fields (see Hartman et al., 2003). What may appear as an exercise of power with rather than over others, however, may from another angle look like a displacement of responsibility onto others, as liabilities are offset or obligations contracted out. In a topological world, the kind of connections which underpin economic interdependence can be stretched just as easily as they can be compressed or erased. The ability of corporations in particular to extend events in time and space, although another instance of distanciated power, is one that involves the mobilization of resources to push events further away rather than draw them closer. The corporate codes of conduct and the extensive monitoring of overseas factory outlets conducted by the retail giants was certainly seen in this light by the NGOs involved in the antisweatshop movement (see Jenkins, et al., 2002).

All of this, it seems to me, makes it difficult to convey the interplay of forces as merely one of domination, authority and resistance, whether seen as transnational or otherwise. Corporate business may attempt to dominate much of what happens elsewhere through their ability to close down choices and constrain possibilities, as often appears to be the case with overseas factories and global supply chains, but it can also be seen to engage in manipulation, persuasion and inducement every bit as much as NGOs and governments do. The ability to do so, on the part of all parties, is enhanced by the topological shifts that have given shape to globalization, although the different registers of power in play are not reducible to them.

Indeed, a topological appreciation of power in the contemporary global era would have drawn attention to the fact that neither social justice movements nor any other type of global actor actually 'jump' scale, they merely connect more or less directly with others elsewhere. Distanciated relationships, direct ties and real-time connections displace the notion of geometric scale and the idea that actors move up and down them, from the local to the global and back. When the global union, UNI, which draws its representation from 150 countries, used the 2007 Davos economic forum in Switzerland as the site from which to lobby against the 'corporate greed' of private equity firms, it did not 'jump' scale as much as make a direct connection to the world's media outlets. How successful it was in constructing a dispersed 'public' around its political goal is a debatable issue, but the intervention itself assumed a topological world as a matter of course; that is, something that has been with us for a while, even if not fully recognized.

CONCLUSION

In making the case for a topological appreciation of the workings of power in the present global era, the sub text of my argument is the fact that the topological shifts that I have outlined are more widespread than many would appear to acknowledge. It is not that the use of real-time technologies to create a simultaneous presence in a variety of global settings is a particularly novel observation or that the compression of space by time is unknown by either Beck or Sassen. It is just that the label topological is rarely used to describe such spatial and temporal shifts. Why this should be so I am not quite sure, but it is evident to me that the writings of both Beck and Sassen do push up against the limits of geometric thinking around territory, distance and geographical scale. The loosening of defined distances and times that appears at various moments in their work, however, is not taken a step further and incorporated into their analyses of the reconfiguration of power and authority. Beck's hazy spaces of power remain that and Sassen's more insightful spatio-temporal assemblages of power only ever shape the domestic setting. The new geography of power that Sassen speaks about is not especially global.

The powerful geographies that I have sketched in the final section separate out the reworking of the spatial and temporal dynamics of globalization from the so-called territorial and mobile characteristics of states, civil society actors and the business world. In doing so, I believe that it becomes easier to grasp the difference that such dynamics make to the powers of reach and connection variously exercised by economic corporations, government authorities and social movements. The ability to draw distant others within close reach or construct the close at hand at-a-distance are indicative of the cross-cutting mix of distanciated and proximate actions that is central to an understanding of the global workings of power today. If little else, such a topology of power relations helps to show why a focus upon how power is exercised and practised can be more useful than one fixated on the territorial and networked capabilities of all those involved.

REFERENCES

Agnew, J.A. (1994) 'The territorial trap: The geographical assumptions of international relations theory', *Review of International Political Economy*, 1: 53–80.
Agnew, J.A. (1999) 'Mapping political power beyond state boundaries', *Millennium*, 28: 499–521.
Agnew, J.A. (2005) 'Sovereignty regimes: Territoriality and state authority in contemporary world politics', *Annals of the Association of American Geographers*, 95(2): 437–461.
Allen, J. (2003) *Lost Geographies of Power*, Oxford: Blackwell Publishing.
Allen, J. (2004) 'The whereabouts of power: Politics, government and space', *Geografiska Annaler*, 86B: 19–32.
Allen, J (2006) 'Claiming connections: A distant world of sweatshops', in Barnett, C., Robinson, J. and Rose, G. (eds), *A Demanding World*, Milton Keynes: The Open University.
Amin, A. (2002) 'Spatialities of globalization', *Environment and Planning A*, 34(3): 379–568.
Amin, A. and Thrift, N. (2002) *Cities: Reimaging the Urban*, Cambridge: Polity.
Appadurai, A. (1990) 'Disjuncture and difference in the global cultural economy', in Featherstone, M. (ed), *Global Culture; Nationalism, Globalization and Modernity*, London, Newbury Park, New Dehli: Sage.
Beck, U. (2001) 'Redefining power in the global age: Eight theses', *Dissent*, Fall, 83–89.
Beck, U. (2005) *Power in the Global Age*, Cambridge: Polity.
Biersteker, T. J. and Weber, C. (eds) (1996) *State Sovereignty as Social Construct*, Cambridge: Cambridge University Press.
Blackburn, R. (2006) 'Finance and the fourth dimension', *New Left Review*, 39: 39–70.
Brenner, N. (2004) *New State Spaces: Urban Governance and the Rescaling of Statehood*, Oxford: Oxford University Press.
Castells, M. (1996) *The Rise of Network Society*, Oxford: Blackwell.
Castells, M. (2000) 'Materials for an exploratory theory of the network society', *British Journal of Sociology*, 51(1): 5–24.
Della Porta, D. and Tarrow, S. (eds) (2005) *Transnational Protest and Global Activism*, Lanham: Rowman and Littlefield Publishers.
Fenn, G. W., Liang, N. and Prowse, S. (1995) *The Economics of the Private Equity Market*, Washington: The Federal Reserve Board.
Financial Times (2007a) 'Boots' £9bn debt issue unfazed by anxiety in credit markets', *Financial Times,* June 30.
Financial Times (2007b) 'Change needed in a powerful industry before it is demonised', *Financial Times,* February 17.
Freeman, R. (2005) 'Venture capitalism and modern capitalism', in Nee, V. and Swedburg, R. (eds), *The Economic Sociology of Capitalism*, Princeton and Oxford: Princeton University Press.
Giddens, A. (1984) *The Constitution of Society: Outline of a Theory of Structuration*, Cambridge: Polity.
Gregory, D. (2004) *The Colonial Present*, Oxford: Blackwell Publishing.
Hartman, L. P., Arnold, D. G. and Wokutch, R. E. (2003) *Rising Above Sweatshops: Innovative Approaches to Global Labor Challenges*, Westport, CT: Praeger.
Held, D., McGrew, A. G., Goldblatt, D. and Perraton, J. (1999) *Global Transformations: Politics, Economics and Culture*, Cambridge: Polity.
Hirst, P. (2005) *Space and Power: Politics, War and Architecture*, Cambridge: Polity.
Hudson, A. (1999) 'Beyond the borders: Globalisation, Sovereignty and extra-territoriality'. in Newman, D. (ed) *Borders, Territory and Postmodernity*, London: Frank Cass.
Jenkins, R., Pearson, R. and SeyFang, G. (2002) *Corporate Responsibility and Labour Rights: Codes of Conduct in the Global Economy*, London: Earthscan.
Kellner, D. (2002) 'Theorizing globalization', *Sociological Theory*, 20(3): 285–305.

Latour, B. (1987) *Science in Action*, Cambridge, MA: Howard University Press.
Latour, B. (1999) 'On recalling ANT' in Law, J. and Hassard, J. (eds), *Actor Network Theory and After,* Oxford: Blackwell.
Latour, B. (2005) *Reassembling the Social*, Oxford: Oxford University Press.
Ohmae, K. (1991) *The Borderless World: Power and Strategy in the Interlinked Economy*, London: Fontana.
Mann, M. (1986) *The Sources of Social Power, Vol 1: A History of Power from the Beginning to AD 1760*, Cambridge: Cambridge University Press.
Mann, M. (2003) *Incoherent Empire*, London and New York: Verso.
McDonald, K. (2006) *Global Movements: Action and Culture*, Oxford: Blackwell Publishing.
Murdoch, J. (2006) *Post-structuralist Geography*, London, Thousand Oaks and New Dehli: Sage.
Reserve Bank of Australia (2007) 'Private equity in Australia', *Financial Stability Review*, March, 59–73.
Robinson, J. (2006) *Ordinary Cities: Between Modernity and Development*, London and New York: Routledge.
Rosenau, J. N. (2003) *Distant Proximities: Dynamics beyond Globalization*, Princeton and Oxford: Princeton University Press.
Samuelson, R. J. (2007) 'The enigma of private equity' *Newsweek*, March.
Sassen, S. (2000) 'Territory and territoriality in the global economy', *International Sociology*, 15(2): 372–93.
Sassen, S. (2006) *Territory, Authority, Rights: From Medieval to Global Assemblages,* Princeton and Oxford: Princeton University Press.
Smith, N. (2004) 'Scale bending and the fate of the national', in Sheppard, E. and McMaster, R. (eds), *Scale and Geographic Inquiry*, Oxford: Blackwell.
Swyngedouw, E. (2000) 'Authoritarian governance, power, and the politics of rescaling, *Environment and Planning D: Society and Space,* 18(1): 63–76.
Taylor, P. (2004) *World City Network: A Global Urban Analysis*, London and New York: Routledge.
Thomson Financial (2007) Year-End Report: Foreign Private Equity Investments.
Urry, J. (2000a) *Sociology Beyond Societies: Mobilities for the Twenty-first Century*, London and New York: Routledge.
Urry, J. (2000b) 'Mobile Sociology,' *British Journal of Sociology*, 51(1): 185–203.
Walker, R. B. J. (1993) *Inside/Outside: International Relations as Political Theory,* Cambridge: Cambridge University Press.
Wolf, M. (2004) *Why Globalization Works,* New Haven, CT: Yale University Press.
Young, I. M. (2003) 'From guilt to solidarity: Sweatshops, and political responsibility', *Dissent*, Spring: 39–44.
Young, I. M. (2004) 'Responsibility and global labour justice', *Journal of Political Philosophy*, 12(4): 365–388.

… PART II

Power and Related Analytic Concepts

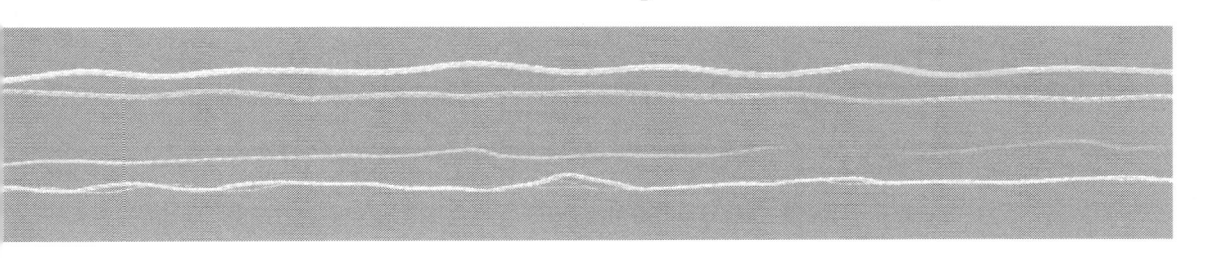

10

Three Conceptions of the Relationship between Power and Liberty

Mitchell Dean

The chapter outlines three different conceptions of the relationship between power and liberty found in social and political thought and uses them to illuminate distinctive rationales for contemporary public policy and styles of governing. The three conceptions include two orthodox ones: the inverse, quantitative, conception; and the juridical conception. The third is derived from Michel Foucault's analytics of government and thus can be called a 'governmental' approach. The chapter essays or 'tests' these conceptions against two distinctive rationales and styles of government, which it calls 'neo-liberalism' and 'neo-paternalism', with which we commence. It concludes that the orthodox conceptions, by virtue of their normative understanding of the relationship and their use of coercion/consent binary, are of much less help than the 'governmental' conception in making intelligible how the practices of public policies operate in contemporary liberal democracies.[1]

NEO-LIBERALISM AND NEO-PATERNALISM

Small, local problems can illustrate and illuminate much larger issues in such a way that our sense of scale might be reversed. The 'big' issue at stake here is the relationship between power and liberty (or freedom) in political and social thought. The 'small' problem which this issue is used to evaluate is posed by the different rationales for many areas of public policy and ways of governing in contemporary liberal-democracies.

To take a recent example: in mid-2007 the Australian government intervened directly in remote aboriginal settlements in the Northern Territory ostensibly in response to a report on pervasive child sexual abuse in these communities. The interventions in those communities included the use of the Australian army to police and bring order to them. By the time legislation had been passed in the Australian parliament in August, it included measures such as the banning of pornography and alcohol in these communities, the requirement that parents send their children to school and present them at medical clinics under the threat of fines, and that those receiving welfare spend half their income on food (Johnston 2007). The legislation also allowed the government to lease aboriginal town land for its own purposes. This was clearly an example of Power with a capital P which had little concern for the individual or collective liberty of the aboriginal population, and marked one event in the long series of governmental interventions which moved away from earlier policy rationales of self-determination (Watson 2004). It is clearly distinct from those approaches to the government of Indigenous communities which sought to govern through forms of Indigenous governance, whether at national level or at the level of local problems such as petrol-sniffing (O'Malley 1998).

A suitably hubristic social or political theorist might be tempted to dub this intervention as the 'death of neo-liberalism' in that it no longer envisaged a form of governing through the freedom of the governed. Yet we know that things are often more partial, more multiple and less prone to major rupture than this formulation would suggest. We also know that the attempt to enforce what is considered proper behaviour through policing, law and conditions on welfare benefits, has been applied to delinquent youth and their parents, 'deadbeat dads' failing to pay child support, 'welfare moms' having children to several fathers, those addicted to drugs and alcohol, teenagers at risk of pregnancy, homeless men, and a host of other 'problematized' behaviours, in widely varied jurisdictions and political contexts.[2] In the United Kingdom, there is now widespread use of Anti-social Behaviour Orders (ABSOs) and Acceptable Behaviour Contracts (ABCs) to deal with conduct likely to cause harassment, alarm or distress to people (see Home Office, 2006), and the notion of 'anti-social personality disorder' has become a legitimate psychiatric term found in the DSM-IV.[3]

If we take a slightly wider view, these are fragments of at least one pole of the changing nature of contemporary forms of authority and ways of governing in contemporary liberal democracies. They are components of the way the previously separate problems of the provision of social support and of social order are being both reoriented and latched together in many of these societies. Briefly, social support is becoming more conditional on the performance of certain activities. The paradigmatic cases of this are what are variously called 'workfare', 'welfare-to-work' or 'work-for-the-dole' programs in which recipients of benefits are required to work in subsidized jobs or community schemes or to undertake various other tasks. The principle of such programs is often expressed as a 'mutual obligation' between the individuals who require support and the communities and institutions that provide that support. According to this principle, it is only right that those who receive benefits and services undertake various activities in return. These may include participation in not only the work projects we have just mentioned but also in training and education activities, and in literacy and numeracy programs. They may include the performance of actions thought to be involved in responsible and equitable parenting. The claimant of social assistance is thus required to participate in such activities or execute them so that she or he will learn to exercise personal responsibility and, by doing so, overcome the psychological and social consequences of what is called 'welfare dependency', including demoralisation, loss of self-esteem, isolation from social networks, loss of work habits, and so on. These activities are also designed to prevent intergenerational reproduction of these bad habits as a culture of dependency (see Schram 2000; Peck 2001).

Until recently, there has been a standard rationale for this requirement which runs as follows (Dean 1995). In order to achieve the objective of fostering the personal responsibility of the claimant, and hence to combat the effects of dependency, it is necessary that the claimant be required to take an active role in participating in these activities. Thus he or she may be asked to agree to a contract that sets out a plan of action and to show proof that he or she undertakes the activities set out on such a plan. Another version is that he or she is provided with knowledge and required to avail him-herself of services provided on a particular market which, incidentally, may be formed through specific governmental policies. The question here is of fostering the 'responsible autonomy' of those who would claim social assistance by shaping the options in which he or she makes choices about the kinds of activities of services which are in his or her best interest. For the purpose of the current discussion, I shall refer to this way of thinking about the organization and reform of the provision of social welfare as 'neo-liberal'. We should note, however, that there is more than one, if not several, versions of this neo-liberalism.

For the last couple of decades, however, certain aspects of the theory and practice of mutual obligation have begun to move beyond such a rationale to incorporate what has been called the 'new paternalism' (Mead 1997a). The notion of the new paternalism entails that there are some populations who, for one reason or another, cannot practise this form of responsible autonomy and need to be closely supervised and directed to do what is right. As one key writer has put it (Mead 1997b: 23):

> To live effectively people need personal restraint to achieve their long-term goals. In this sense, obligation is the precondition of freedom. Those who would be free must first be bound. And if people have not been effectively bound by functioning families and neighborhoods in their formative years, government must attempt to provide limits later, imperfect though they must be.

For this approach, the problem is not simply that the claimants for social assistance and other dependent or irresponsible populations need to be presented with such choices as enable them to exercise their 'responsible autonomy'. It is, rather, that social and political conditions and institutions have so eroded their capacity for personal responsibility that they cannot make the right choice for themselves even when they know what that choice would be. Thus, according to this view, the problem for many of the poor is not that they do not share the work ethic with the rest of the population or want to properly care for their children but that they do not know how to integrate getting and retaining a job and properly and regularly caring for their children into their lifestyle (Mead 1997c: 57, 65). They find it easier to depend on social assistance. With respect to work, they may have developed a fear of getting a job, or they have lost the habits (e.g., of punctuality and regularity) that would enable them to retain a job. According to this view, it may be that these individuals do not even know what their own best interests are; it is more likely, however, that they have lost the ability to follow them even if they do know them. They are the ones, particularly among the youth of these groups, who are likely to engage if not in crime at least in anti-social behaviour and petty infractions, such as vandalism, public drunkenness, harassment and so forth.

According to this view, the condition of the improperly socialized and supervized poor becomes not simply one of poverty but also of social order. There are many antidotes to such behaviour including new forms of policing (epitomized by 'zero-tolerance' policing) and increased used of surveillance ('target hardening') in high-risk areas and on risky populations (Stenson 2005). One solution, which we now find taken up and generalized to entire communities in the Aboriginal case in remote Australia, is closely to supervize claimants for benefits, and to establish effective and well-publicized systems of sanctions, so as to make mandatory activities such as work and daily responsibility for one's children, their health, behavior and education. Thus, this argument contends, we need to compel these individuals to adopt a lifestyle and activities consistent with broadly acceptable community standards. Their obligation to perform such activities is a condition of them becoming free and autonomous individuals in the sense in which such freedom and autonomy is understood in terms of the supposed values and norms of the wider community. The accession to such a status, however, can be almost indefinitely deferred.

I contend that what we witness in these distinctive rationales for social policy is the emergence and use of different concepts of liberty, and different ways of thinking about the relation between power and liberty. On the one hand, power is held to operate by the shaping of liberty and through the exercise of choice. This is particularly clear in the recent revival of the language of consumerism as a way of thinking about the relationship of clients to service provision in education, health, social security and community services. On the other hand, with the movement to a more coercive direction, such as evidenced by the 'new paternalism' and in the drive for a law and order state, we find an exercise of power that seeks to shape a specific form of freedom by means of close supervision and detailed administration of the individual, rather than through freedom itself.

The broad distinction between 'neo-liberalism' and 'neo-paternalism' raises interesting questions on a number of fronts, including whether we are witnessing the emergence of a new political formation better described as authoritarian liberalism than advanced or neo-liberalism (Dean 2002, 2007). Now, however, I want to turn to some theoretical questions raised by these practices and the rationale they offer for their existence. These concern the relationship between two very basic and contested concepts, power and liberty.

THE INVERSE AND QUANTITATIVE CONCEPTION

It would be surprising if concepts such as power and liberty were not contested and did not vary historically in their use. In that thought which calls itself Western there are certainly many concepts of both power and liberty, as well as many conceptions of their relationship. Two conceptions of the relationship between liberty and power stand out as forming something of an orthodoxy in recent social and political science.

The first presents itself as an empirical description of the relationship. It is entailed in the definition of power proposed by Max Weber and contained in Stephen Lukes' influential book *Power: A Radical View* (1974). For Weber, power is defined as 'the chance of a man or of a number of men to realize their own will in a communal action even against the resistance of others who are participating in the action' (1972: 180). The sense in which the exercise of power concerns the ability of one party to realize its will by blocking or frustrating the ability of another to achieve its will thus implies the view that the exercise of power by one party subtracts from the freedom of another. A similar conception of power is also found in the influential work of Lukes (1974: 15, 24), who, despite recognising the 'essentially contested' and 'eradicably evaluative' nature of the term power, claims that 'the absolutely basic common core to, or primitive notion lying behind, all talk of power is the notion that A in some way affects B', although he adds that the effect must be conceived as being significant.

Now this appears rather straightforward. Power is a kind of essence of effectiveness. It is a capacity to realize one's will against the will of others, and thus limit the possibility of others realising their wills. A particular understanding of liberty complements such definitions of power. Take Berlin's famous lecture on 'Two concepts of liberty' (1997). Berlin's lecture is concerned to identify an essential conception of liberty, one that John Stuart Mill called the 'only freedom which deserves the name' (1985: 72). Berlin finds this conception in a notion of negative freedom in which freedom is enjoyed so long as 'I am not prevented by others from doing what I would otherwise do' (1997:194). He contrasts this conception with a positive conception of freedom as freedom 'to lead one prescribed form of life' (Berlin 1997: 203) and which includes notions of freedom as individual self-mastery, and freedom as collective self-government.

Berlin's notion of negative freedom is thus defined against coercion, which entails 'the deliberate interference of other human beings within the area in which I wish to act'. This notion of liberty is found not only in Mill's essay *On Liberty* (1985) but also in Hobbes's *Leviathan* (1996). According to Hobbes a 'Free-man, is he, that in those things, which by his strength and wit he is able to do, is not hindred to do what he has a will to' (1996: 146). For Berlin, as much as for Mill or Hobbes, I am free to the extent that I am not prevented in realising my will, i.e., there is no interference in the area in which I wish to act.

Now if we use the word 'power' to cover all those occasions in which one party affects another in a significant manner, after Lukes, then the relationship between power and liberty in this version of the orthodox conception becomes clear. By significantly affecting another, one party interferes in the area in which the other would act, after Berlin. Thus, as Weber puts it, one party realizes its will even against the opposition of another, and thereby limits the possibility of others achieving their will. The exercise of power by some entails the subtraction of liberty of others. Power and liberty are in this sense antithetical. They are linked in an inverse and quantitative relationship. To be free is to be free from power. To exercise power is to limit the area of freedom of others; thus, there is a quantitative and inverse conception of the relation between power and liberty.

Even in this version, however, power and liberty do not form a stable opposition. If we refer to Hobbes again, we find a conception of power that suggests an identity between power and liberty. He states: 'The Power of a Man is his present means to obtain some future apparent Good' (1996: 62). Power is the capacity of individuals to achieve their purposes. In this sense of power as a capacity, I am free to do what I will when I can exercise my power. As we have seen, liberty is also the capacity to do what I will. In this regard, power and liberty are simply different perspectives on the same essential quality, the capacity to achieve our will or, to use Mill's phrase, 'pursuing our own good in our own way' (1985: 72).

Now return to the neo-liberal and neo-paternalist rationalities. According to the inverse view, both cases would qualify as the exercise of power of one party (the government or its agents) seeking to affect another (social welfare clients) in a significant manner (by getting them to undertake certain acts as a condition of receiving support). Both the 'neo-liberal' and the 'neo-paternal' approach claim to be seeking to get social welfare clients to exercise their freedom responsibly and in a manner consistent with their obligations to the broader community and its agreed-upon norms and values. In both cases, from Berlin's perspective, it would be nonsense to regard this as the 'essential' form of liberty (or negative liberty) as defined by himself and Mill. When both neo-liberalism and neo-paternalism talk about freedom, they talk about the performance of a specific form of life defined by self-mastery, a version of what Berlin calls the positive conception of freedom.

Berlin's lecture can be used effectively to break down the steps in the argument involved here. Both neo-liberalism and neo-paternalism assume that the recipients' dependence on welfare for their maintenance is *prima facie* a case of lack of self-mastery. Notions of self-mastery assume a division between a higher and a lower self, or higher and lower parts of the self, in which the higher self or higher part of the self is engaged in a struggle to subdue or harness and direct the impulses and inclinations of the lower self or part of the self. Freedom in this sense consists in following what the real, ideal or true self or part would do in the absence of these lower impulses or inclinations. The notion of 'community' acts much like earlier notions of a social whole – the State, Church, society, etc. – in that it defines a collective arena of norms and values that can be identified with this 'true self'. To speak of mutual obligation or mutual responsibility is to speak of a way in which one party can be coerced to act in a certain way according to a conception of collective norms and values embodied in the notion of 'community'.

If, however, we remove the idea that those practices relied upon by neo-paternalists or neo-liberals (e.g. enforced work regimes) are aimed at forming or restoring the true freedom of their clients, then what are we to make of claims concerning freedom that might act as their rationale from the perspective of the inverse conception of power and liberty? On the 'neo-paternalist' rationale, no such claims arise. Therefore all talk of freedom is either not relevant to the analysis of these practices or, as we have said, to speak of it is nonsense and, given Berlin's critique of construing notions of self-mastery as positive freedom, dangerous nonsense. In the neo-liberal variant, nevertheless, the attempt to shape the conditions under which choice is exercised might be regarded as contracting the area in which liberty operates, by leaving the individual to make up his or her mind which option is most appropriate for him or herself. Thus, this form of the exercise of power is compatible with a notion of negative freedom, although the area in which that freedom is exercised is severely circumscribed. In the 'neo-paternalist' version, however, the clients are stopped from doing what they would otherwise do, and directed to do something else. While some, or even the majority of people in a given society, might regard this something else as 'in their best interests' or compatible with a specific conception of what is good for them, not even paternalists would represent their practices as operating through freedom.

THE JURIDICAL CONCEPTION

If we take a longer view of the history of 'Western' thought, however, we can identify another, equally orthodox conception of the relationship between power and liberty.

This conception allows us to use a notion of freely given consent to distinguish between different legitimate and illegitimate forms of power.

If we begin with the power side, we can agree with Barry Hindess (1996) that power is often understood not simply as a quantitative capacity but as a capacity and a right. As he notes, this understanding of power is most often found in our understandings of a particular form of power, sovereign power, 'the power that is thought to be exercised by the rule of a state or by its (central) government' (1996: 12). In this conception of power, the sovereign issues commands over its subjects which these subjects are expected to obey as binding obligations. The most usual form in which these commands are issued is in law and thus I shall call this a 'juridical' conception of the relation between power and liberty. In this conception, the sovereign – whether the monarch, or the executive drawn from the elected representatives of the people – is held to have a right to govern by virtue of some prior or continuing consent of the governed.

We can see that this conception of power is most commonly used in discussion of the government of the state. We can also see that it is not inconsistent with the idea of power as a simple capacity to affect others. However the notion that the right of the sovereign rests upon some presumed consent of its subjects suggests quite a different picture of the relation between power and liberty to that of the inverse one we have just considered. In most modern conceptions of the basis of the subject's obligation we find the idea that the subjects' consent to sovereign power is provided freely. Most modern political discussion has assumed that the legitimacy of sovereign power rests on free acts of consent on the part of autonomous individuals who are members of a political community. The image of the contract between the citizens and the state found in the early modern political thought of Hobbes and Locke is perhaps the clearest example of this view. Moreover, the ideal of a community of autonomous citizens freely giving their consent to the binding commands of their sovereign remains an influential and pervasive normative ideal by which we can distinguish between legitimate and illegitimate power. In twentieth-century sociology it is found in critical theorists, such as Marcuse and Habermas, and indeed lurks behind much of the discussion of power in social and political science, including the famous 'community power debates' in the USA and Lukes' 'third dimension of power'.

According to the juridical conception, power and liberty are still opposites in that the subjects give up a portion of their liberty to the sovereign. However they are now linked in at least two major ways. First, it is the act or acts of consent on behalf of citizens that renders the power of the sovereign legitimate. Second, as we can see in the image of Leviathan, the power of the sovereign can be far greater than that of any one individual or group of individuals because it can draw upon the capacities of each of the subjects it commands. Thus while power may still detract from our individual liberty, we can use our liberty to constitute a form of power which is far greater than the sum of our individual capacities.

In both neo-liberalism and neo-paternalism, it is the sovereign, its agents or contractors that exercise power over the social welfare client; but how does liberty fit into the types of social policy practices these discourses seek to justify? In the first instance, we should note that the juridical conception makes reference to the binding obligations, not to the liberty, of those subject to the commands issued by the sovereign. The liberty invoked in this conception is not the liberty of those subject to the sovereign's command but the liberty of the community or of each individual citizen to consent or withdraw consent to the right of the sovereign to issue such commands. If the community has indeed consented to placing compulsory demands upon those receiving social welfare benefits, then the question of the liberty of the recipients of these benefits does not enter into the equation.

In the case of constitutional democracies, the most common way in which that consent is regularly obtained is by means of a popular vote on the basis of which executive government can claim a mandate for the laws it issues and policies it pursues. However, there is a second way in which this community of autonomous individuals may be presumed to have given consent to the actions of sovereign power. This is the case when the laws and policies issued by the sovereign are thought to be consistent with the norms and values of the political community itself. In the case of social welfare law and policy, these norms and values might be that all who can, should, work; that single parenthood should not be rewarded by unconditional welfare benefits; that the children of welfare recipients be sent to school and taken to health clinics, and so on. If the sovereign exercises its right in a manner presumed to be consistent with the values of the political community that constitutes this right, then, according to this view, it is legitimate to command certain citizens to adopt a particular form of life and to exercise their freedom in a particular way. The notion of consent can be used then to legitimate the promotion of a positive conception of freedom in Berlin's sense.

An example of the way in which consent can be given to questions of morality is found, according to Hindess (1996: 58), in Locke's 'law of opinion or reputation'. By approving or disapproving of the actions of their fellows, the members of a community can provide what Locke calls a 'secret and tacite consent' to matters of moral standards that are independent of the authorisations of their rulers (Hindess 1996: 60). While Locke does not go into the relation between the laws of the commonwealth and the law of opinion or reputation there are indications that he would expect them to broadly coincide.

It is salient, then, that the term community – and not the state or society – is often invoked in these discussions of the obligations of the social welfare recipient. We might tend to think that the vogue for this term rests on an appeal to an organic, local and traditional form of the social bond, which is undoubtedly a part of what is condensed in the term. However, community also stands in part for the community of citizens who freely consent to the legitimate exercise of power by the state. If this is correct, then the term 'community' is invoked to suggest that such operations of coercion by the sovereign are legitimated by something like the operation of this 'secret and tacite consent'.

The account I have given of the juridical conception of the relation between liberty and power suggests how power such as that exercised by sovereign bodies or their agents may be held to be legitimized by tacit consent of the members of the community of citizens or by the tacit consent contained within their everyday norms, beliefs and values. It does not suggest, however, why sovereign bodies or their agents would need to act upon individuals so that they might conform to or indeed choose the norms and values held by the community. Again, Hindess' reading of Locke provides a useful exemplar (1996: 76–80). In Locke's account of political power we find a community of autonomous citizens separate from the government of the commonwealth to which they belong. In this account, Locke is concerned to distinguish political power from paternal power, the latter being the power exercised by a parent over a child. Paternal power is justified because, while all have a right to their natural freedom, they are also born ignorant and without the use of their reason. Thus paternalism is justified as a form of power over those who have not yet acquired their reason.

In the cases we are examining, however, most of the individuals involved are not children, although the language of youth may be used to suggest some association of certain client populations with childhood. The existence of persons of legal majority within a political community who cannot be trusted to be fully autonomous suggests a different view of individuals and the community of which they are a part than does the juridical theory of power that rests on the consent of a community of autonomous persons. It suggests that while some, or perhaps most, members of the population beyond a certain age have achieved a condition of autonomy and responsibility, that some have not. It is not surprising that political and social theorists have recognized the existence of such populations. Locke himself attributed the growth of the poor to 'nothing else but the relaxation of discipline and corruption of manners' (1969: 378). More generally he provides an account of human individuals as creatures of habit that are formed in their interactions with others. In such a context, rational and autonomous individuals can only be produced by the effective training in habits of rational thought and behaviour. In this regard we might think that neo-liberal and neo-paternal training or forced work measures towards the long-term unemployed, for example, could be justified as means of producing the habits and work-ethic appropriate to entering or re-entering the paid workforce.

The argument so far suggests that the two orthodox conceptions of power and liberty allow us to say very little about the views of social policy we have termed neo-liberalism and neo-paternalism and the practices to which they are linked. Basically these orthodox conceptions are caught between and often confuse two forms of analysis. The first is the unexceptional analysis that these social policy regimes are forms of the exercise of power over certain individuals and populations which, in their effects, either significantly contract these subjects' sphere of liberty or almost entirely abolish it. The second, somewhat more complex conception, restricts the analysis of the relation to the question of the provision of consent to power or – as we might say after Weber and Talcott Parsons – 'legitimacy' and thus emphasizes consent as the founding act of political liberty of subjects.

Indeed the two models of the relation are not as distinct as this analysis has suggested and much of twentieth-century social theory is concerned with the manner in which rule operates through coercion and consent. For example, the Italian Marxist, Antonio Gramsci (1971), held that the rule of the bourgeoisie in advanced capitalist societies is based on both coercion and consent, but that consent is given by those who do not know that it is in their interests to overthrow the system of capitalist production. Similarly, while holding to the idea of power as a simple quantitative capacity over particular parties, Lukes's central thesis concerning the discovery of a 'third-dimension of power' sketches precisely such a situation. He asks 'is not the supreme and most insidious example of power to prevent people, to whatever degree, from having grievances by shaping their perceptions, cognitions (sic) and preferences in such a way that they accept their role in the existing order of things?' (Lukes 1974: 24). In other words, Lukes indicates the existence of a form of power over individuals which so shapes their outlook that they can no longer effectively consent to the exercise of political power.

It is this conception of a form of power, whose action occurs through 'socially structured and culturally patterned behaviour' (Lukes 1974: 22), and whose effect has been to undermine the possibility of a community of autonomous citizens, which has shadowed political critique and theory for much of the twentieth century. Locke's image of a community, of civil society, and its integrity or otherwise, remains the key to understanding critical political thought. Taking another example from contemporary critical theory, Habermas' notion of an 'ideal speech situation', and his more recent exploration of deliberative democracy (1996), may be read as attempts to establish the conditions under which such a community of consent-giving persons can be constituted.

A GOVERNMENTAL APPROACH TO THE RELATION BETWEEN POWER AND LIBERTY

We can now begin, with the help of Michel Foucault, to vary the fundamental assumptions we have identified in these two orthodox conceptions of the relation between power and liberty. First, let us assume that rather than an inverse, quantitative relationship between power and liberty, that the exercise of power presupposes liberty in the sense that it is possible for the subject of power to act in more than one way. Such a notion is entailed in Foucault's various approaches to relationships of power as 'strategic games between liberties' (1988: 19) and as forming 'a total structure of action brought to bear upon the actions of others' (1982: 220). Such conceptions of power are interesting because they presuppose the existence of free subjects, i.e. subjects are able to act in a number of ways even while they are acted upon.

Power in this regard is an aspect of all social relations and may take the form of open and reversible relationships. Nevertheless, it does not rule out the possibility that these relations of power may take a relatively fixed, irreversible and hierarchical form. When such a form is combined with a high degree of circumscription of the possibilities of action because the 'margin of liberty is extremely limited' we have what Foucault calls 'domination' (1988: 12). Thus Foucault uses the term domination to designate 'what we ordinarily call power' (1988: 12), and argues that power should be viewed as an aspect of all social relationships. Indeed, one of the consequences of this approach is that we cannot say very much at all about power in general, and that our investigations should concentrate on 'what happens' in social and political relationships and focus on the means by which power is exercised. For Foucault, 'power as such does not exist' (1982: 217).

After having varied these assumptions of the orthodox model of power and liberty, a few preliminary consequences begin to emerge for our analysis of contemporary social policy regimes and rationalities. Neo-liberalism can now be described not as a contraction of the sphere of liberty but as the attempt to establish a structure – sometimes by ensuring the provision of public and community services, often in the form of a 'quasi-market' – in which the actions of individuals can be acted upon. Neo-liberal programs in this sense are ones that try to shape the actions of individuals by establishing the conditions under which choice is made. While choice may be limited, it is not this limitation which is their primary goal but rather the exercise of choice through a specified range of options; and while neo-liberal programs may have in mind a particular set of outcomes, such as increasing the economic competitiveness of the population, there is no attempt to define the performance of a single kind of acceptable life as Berlin's positive conception of liberty might suggest.

Programs working according to a neo-paternalist schema, on the other hand, are not simply about the removal of liberty. They might still be regarded as components of relations of power in Foucault's sense, in so far as they still presuppose the liberty of the governed. Neo-paternalism argues quite simply that certain individuals and populations have used their liberty irresponsibly in the past and hence have to be closely directed and supervized in the appropriate form of action in the present. While individuals are still free in that they might simply stop turning up to the service provider to collect benefits (one of the noted effects of neo–paternalist policies [Mead 1997c: 66]), the return to supervision and close direction, together with the use of sanctions, suggests the presence of a high degree of 'domination' and a limitation of 'the margin of liberty' in Foucault's language.

By varying some of our basic ideas of the relation between power and liberty we can thus conclude that neo-paternalism will generally depend to a greater extent on states of domination than neo-liberalism, to use Foucault's terms, which is not a spectacular reward for the theoretical work. Foucault's displacement of these conventional concepts of power and domination are clearly interesting but they do not amount to the principal value of his thinking in this area. The latter arises from his displacement of the juridical conception of the relation between power and liberty.

Before moving to this, we should note in passing that there are fundamental similarities between Lukes' radical view of power and neo-paternalism. In both cases, the effects of culture and social and political institutions are viewed as undermining the capacity of certain individuals to appreciate and act upon their own interests. In the radical view of power, however, as in Gramsci's understanding of the hegemony of the bourgeoisie, and in most theories of ideology and false consciousness, this lack of capacity for autonomous action is found across the entire population. For the new paternalism it applies at most to a significant minority and is best exemplified by those who apply for social assistance.

Let us now vary aspects of the second, juridical, conception. If we remove the privilege given to questions of consent in this relation, two important things follow. First, a particular way of focusing on the exercise of power by the state comes into focus. The move is encapsulated in Foucault's suggestion that in political theory 'we need to cut off the King's head' (1980: 121). The significance of this metaphor, it should be emphasized, is to encapsulate the idea that we need to move beyond the question of *who* holds the power exercised within the centralized, privileged domain of the state. It is not to preclude the analysis of the government of the nation, or the state, within domestic and international relations of power, or a consideration of the nature of sovereign power, as Foucault's lectures themselves amply demonstrate (2003, 2007).

Foucault's displacement of the privilege accorded the state is present also in his general view of government as 'the conduct of conduct', i.e. as the various ways different agencies attempt to direct the behaviours of individuals and groups for specific ends (1982). Thus, while we might analyse the government of the state, we can also discuss the government of an organisation (as Weber does in his definition of politically oriented action)[4] or the government of a school, a church, or of children, and so on.

While this move has important methodological implications, attested to by the now large and varied empirical literature employing the term government in such a way,[5] it is not perhaps the most important effect of removing the privilege of the notion of consent. Of greater significance is the abandonment of the normative question of the distinction between legitimate and illegitimate power as the central question in our discussion of power or, as we are now tending to term it, the discussion of government. For, once this is done, we stop analysing neo-liberalism and neo-paternalism, and other such formations, as providing an account of the normative foundations of certain practices and begin to regard them as components of the explicit and often programmatic ways in which we think about governing, that is as components of what Foucault called *governmentality* (2007). They are distinctive kinds of 'rationalities of government' which bear a certain kinship with one another. By rationalities of government I mean the more or less systematic ways of thinking about problems to be addressed, the means by which they can be solved, the actors and identities involved, and the goals sought in so doing. That is, these rationalities of government should be approached not as a description of the way things *should* work between power and liberty in a proper constitutional framework but as ways of rendering certain states of affairs problematic and providing solutions to such problems.

There are detailed tools for analysis of such rationalities of government, and the problematizations, technologies, ends and objectives to which they are linked, cannot be gone into here (Dean 1999). I will be content simply to mention some of the consequences of this displacement of the question of government. One is that we should attend to the vocabulary and language of governmental rationalities with a view not to what they mean but to the kinds of action they provide a rationale for, the way they constitute problems, and so on. While the normative principles of neo-liberalism and neo-paternalism might diverge, their language does not place them in a position of fundamental opposition. In the sphere of social policy, both are responses to the way in which certain forms of conduct are seen to be deviant. Such deviant conduct is regarded as evidence of 'welfare dependency', to address which both approaches employ the calculative rationality of risk to divide populations, use similar techniques of governing, and invoke the goal of ensuring the individual fulfils his or her obligations to the community or institutions that provide support.

A second point is that government as 'the conduct of conduct' is not purely or even primarily about these rationalities or ways of thinking about government. While the element of more or less rational calculation distinguishes government from among the broader field of relationships of power, rationalities of government are linked to practices and techniques for the realisation of their objectives. While much could be said about these, an elementary point can be made here. Neo-liberalism and neo-paternalism may simply be different ways of describing and imagining the operation of the same practices, instruments and techniques of government, and of investing them with different purposes. According to variants of neo-liberalism, the use of measures such as contract and case-management aim to elicit the agreement of client populations to the performance of certain activities, so that they might overcome welfare dependency (Dean 1995). Neo-paternalists, however, argue, positively, that these same measures enable the close supervision and management of client populations and the effective publicity of sanctions (Mead 1997c: 61–3). Indeed, it might be that the two opposing ways of thinking about and reforming a regime of practices are essential to the functioning of those practices. The paradigmatic example of this would be Foucault's argument (1991) that over two centuries penal practice focused on the prison was caught between programmes calling for more effective and stringent punishment and those calling for the rehabilitation of the prisoner. On this analogy, neo-liberalism and neo-paternalism are twin and privileged poles in the debate over various practices of social policy such as workfare and are necessary to its functioning.

One reason why neo-liberalism and neo-paternalism are twins is linked to a third point. This concerns the relation between government (and power more generally) and the subject. In the orthodox conception, power subtracts from the liberty of the subject, and the salient form of liberty of a political subject is to consent to or refuse to consent to power. Thus the subject has only two relations to power: one of consent or refusal, and one of coercion. By contrast, when we focus on practices of government, we find practices that try to shape the conditions under which choice is made, work on or through the freedom of individuals and groups, or attempt to produce specific forms of freedom. We might want to say that by 'conducting conduct', forms of government try to produce different kinds of identity and freedom among specified individuals and populations. In this sense the ways in which we come to understand and act upon ourselves as subjects is itself an objective of specific relationships of power, which is as true for neo-paternalism as for neo-liberalism. Neo-paternalism seeks to prescribe particular forms of life and identity for those populations that have shown themselves unable to act in what the neo-paternalists define as the best interests of those whom they target. Neo-liberalism, by contrast, attempts to define the field of possibility for the forms of life of the entire population by establishing a structure for the choices and actions of those it regards as responsible. It hardly needs to be said that there is no inconsistency between these two rationalities of government once populations have been assigned identities around the opposition between the responsible and irresponsible uses of liberty. It is in this sense that both rationalities are necessary to the operation of contemporary practices of social welfare and social order.

CONCLUSION

The discussion raises many theoretical questions, but I shall briefly address only two. The first concerns whether the 'governmental' conception of power as proposed by Foucault is in some way similar to the insidious and supreme form of power detected by Lukes. The second is whether a conception of liberty as shaped through liberal forms of government does not amount to an endorsement of a positive conception in Berlin's sense.

Practices of government in Foucault's sense are similar to the third dimension of power in that they seek to shape the preferences of individuals and, with certain reservations, may be said also to shape their 'perceptions and cognitions'. They are not insidious, however, in Lukes' sense, because they do not refer to something that operates through 'socially structured and culturally patterned behaviour' but to more or less explicit, thought-out, calculated attempts to direct conduct. Most often, they are not about shaping perceptions and thoughts but about habits and choices. In this regard, rather than being something that occurs behind social actors' backs, they are something that occurs under their noses, in their faces.

Because they are more or less rational, calculated and explicit they are publicly available and open to singular analysis – hence the term an 'analytics of government' widely used in the Foucauldian literature. Furthermore, there is no assumption that they are effective on individuals. The definition of power as a game between liberties allows the ever-present possibility or resistance, evasion, non-compliance and subversion of practices of government. Foucault (2007: 201–3) himself broaches the possibility of counter-conducts. Government as the conduct of conduct entails not simply A affecting B, but the thought-out but tenuous attempt by A to act upon the actions of B for diverse and varying ends, with specific means and instruments. It also entails the possibility that B is subject to many such attempts and may act on him or herself in a manner which is counter to A's strategic intention. As two central contributors to this study of government have put it, government is a 'congenitally failing' operation (Miller and Rose 1990: 10), not simply because of the multiplicity of diverse governmental programs and practices, or the technical problems of insufficient knowledge or poor implementation, but because of the ever-present possibility of resistance and the formation of counter-conducts, i.e. the exercise of freedom in a way not envisaged by or in opposition to the goals of a particular program.

Let us turn now to the question of whether this governmental approach amounts to an endorsement of a positive conception of liberty of the kind identified by Berlin. The question of the status of the distinction between positive and negative conceptions of freedom can be set aside for another discussion. Here, I want to suggest that there is a fundamental difference between the aim of the literature concerned with governmentality and Berlin's perspective. While the latter is concerned to unmask false uses of the notion of liberty (and thus engages in a kind of normative project of its own) the study of governmentality is an attempt to examine how various governmental practices construct and seek to work through forms of freedom. In this regard, to show how social policies and programs work through, repress or aim to produce specific forms of freedom on the part of certain individuals and populations is to do nothing more than show how preferences, choices and actions, as well as forms of life, have become the objects and objectives of forms of government. Freedom is not used in a normative sense in this analysis so there is no respect in which the forms of what is called freedom in these practices receive a normative endorsement.

From the point of view of the governmental approach, Berlin goes too far in distinguishing between legitimate and illegitimate conceptions of liberty. The former study examines the kinds of social action that are constituted by or in relation to particular discourses concerning freedom, liberty, choice, activity and so on without judging the legitimacy of such concepts. If, however, the concept of negative liberty is taken to define the fundamental meaning of the term, Berlin's resistance to the specification of particular forms of freedom does not go far enough. To make this point, consider this from an interview with Foucault (Martin 1988: 15):

> What I am afraid of about humanism is that it presents a certain form of our ethics as a universal model for any kind of freedom. I think that there are more secrets, more possible freedoms, and more inventions in our future than we can imagine in humanism as it is dogmatically represented on every side of the political rainbow.

Berlin attempts to justify a commitment to a particular form of freedom, freedom as freedom from the interference of others in the realm in which an individual would act or freedom to pursue one's self-defined purposes. On this view, Berlin's conception of freedom assumes that to be free is to be autonomous, where autonomy is defined as a matter of not being subject to another. From the perspective of power as a ubiquitous aspect of relationships in which we act upon each other's actions, autonomy defined in this way is illusory. It follows from this that there is no principle with which to distinguish between a 'true' negative conception of freedom and a 'false' positive one. Thus, there can only be historically specific versions of what it is to be free. Freedom in general, much as power in general, simply does not exist. There are only different forms of freedom and historically different conceptions of freedom.[6] Freedom is always exercised in the singular.

Foucault's concepts of power and liberty raise new questions about rationalities such as neo-paternalism and neo-liberalism. We might, for instance, ask whether a neo-paternalist rationality of government reveals aspects of our treatment of the long-term unemployed or single parents that are in some way obscured by a neo-liberal rationale. In particular, it poses clearly the question of the uses of states of domination in contemporary social policies, or the degree of coercion, surveillance and detailed administration that can be held to be necessary.

Alternatively, the existence of multiple rationales for similar, if not the same, governmental practices, raises questions about the relationship between the operation of these practices and the rationales that are given for them. Rather than the 'tactical polyvalence of discourses' noted by Foucault (1979: 100–2), this seems to be a case of the 'rational polyvalence of the practices'. Different rationales enable us to think about how practices of social policy may be made to operate for different purposes, whether at certain times and places or in regard to specific populations. Such rationales might then have effects in the reform, implementation and operation of such practices.

The analytics of government attempts to clarify how we think and act upon ourselves and others without being constrained by the shadow of the normative distinctions of conventional notions of power and liberty. While it does not necessarily stem from any particular set of values or principles it does, as Max Weber suggested, stand in the service of 'moral forces' (Weber 1972: 152). By making clear what is at stake when we try to govern in a particular way and employ particular ways of thinking and acting, such a study allows us to accept a sense of responsibility for the consequences and effects of thinking and acting in these ways. Perhaps even more fundamentally, in its concern for freedom, and in its refusal to specify the form and content of the undefined work of freedom, such an analysis of power displays an orientation to the possibilities of freedom without prescribing the form that such freedom will take.

NOTES

1 The substantive part of the following argument was originally published in the Proceedings of the 1999 Conference of the Australasian Political Studies Association, University of Sydney, September 26–29.

2 See the various chapters advocating 'welfare reform' along the neo-paternalist lines described below in Mead (1997a) and Saunders (2000). Of particular relevance to the discussion is the chapter in the latter by Noel Pearson (2000) a key Indigenous advocate of paternalist policies who played a pro-government role in the 2007 interventions.

3 The text of the entry for Anti-social Personality Disorder in the *Diagnostic and Statistical Manual of Mental Disorders, Fourth Edition*, can be found at http://www.behavenet.com/capsules/disorders/antisocialpd.htm Downloaded 7 September, 2007.

4 Weber defines 'politically oriented action' as that which 'aims to exert influence on the government of a political organisation; especially at the appropriation, redistribution or allocation of the powers of government' (1968: 55).

5 See, for example, the various contributors to Gordon et al. (1991), Barry et al. (1996), Dean and Hindess (1998), Larner and Walters (2004), and Dean and Henman (2004).

6 Take two examples of historically varying conceptions of freedom quite different from those considered here. First, there is the notion of the civil freedom of individuals as only possible within a self-governing civil association, found in the 'neo-roman' theory of free states developed in early-modern Britain (Skinner 1997). Secondly, there is the ancient Greek notion of *sophrosyne*, a state in which one could attain freedom in relation to the practice of pleasures and thus not be a slave to them (Foucault 1985, ch. 4).

REFERENCES

Barry, Andrew, Osborne, Thomas, and Rose, Nikolas (eds) (1996) *Foucault and Political Reason: Liberal, Neo-liberalism and Rationalities of Government.* London: UCL Press.
Berlin, Isaiah (1997 [1958]) 'Two concepts of liberty', in *The Proper Study of Mankind.* London: Chatto and Windus.
Dean, Mitchell (1995) 'Governing the unemployed self in an active society', *Economy and Society* 24 (4): 559–83.
Dean, Mitchell (1999) *Governmentality: Power and Rule in Modern Society.* London: Sage.

Dean, Mitchell (2002) 'Liberal government and authoritarianism', *Economy and Society* 31(1): 37–61.
Dean, Mitchell (2007) *Governing Societies: Political Perspectives on Domestic and International Rule*. Maidenhead: Open University Press.
Dean, Mitchell and Henman, Paul (eds) (2004) 'Governing society today', *Alternatives: Global, Local, Political*, 29(5), special issue.
Dean, Mitchell and Hindess, Barry (eds) (1998) *Governing Australia: Studies in Contemporary Rationalities of Government*. Cambridge: Cambridge University Press.
Foucault, Michel (1979) *The History of Sexuality. Vol. One: An Introduction*. London: Allen Lane.
Foucault, Michel (1980) *Power/Knowledge: Selected Interviews and Other Writings* 1972–1977, C. Gordon (ed.). Brighton: Harvester.
Foucault, Michel (1982) 'The subject and power', in H. Dreyfus and P. Rabinow (eds), *Michel Foucault: Beyond Structuralism and Hermeneutics*. Brighton: Harvester.
Foucault, Michel (1985) *The Use of Pleasure*. New York: Pantheon.
Foucault, Michel (1988) 'The ethic of the care of the self as a practice of freedom', in J. Bernauer and D. Rasmussen (eds), *The Final Foucault*. Cambridge, MA.: MIT Press.
Foucault, Michel (1991) 'Questions of method', in Colin Gordon, Graham, Burchell and Peter Miller (eds), *The Foucault Effect: Studies in Governmentality*. London: Harvester Wheatsheaf.
Foucault, Michel (2003) *Society Must be Defended*, trans. D. Macey. New York: Picador.
Foucault, Michel (2007) *Security, Territory, Population*, trans. G. Burchell. Houndmills: Palgrave.
Gordon, Colin, Burchell, Graham and Miller, Peter (eds) (1991) *The Foucault Effect: Studies in Governmentality*. London: Harvester Wheatsheaf.
Gramsci, Antonio (1971) *Selections from the Prison Notebooks*. London: Lawrence and Wishart.
Habermas, Jürgen (1996) *Between Facts and Norms: Contributions to a Discourse Theory of Law and Democracy*. Cambridge: Polity Press.
Hindess, Barry (1996) *Discourses of Power: From Hobbes to Foucault*. Oxford: Blackwell.
Hobbes, Thomas (1996 [1651]) *Leviathan*. Cambridge: Cambridge University Press.
Home Office (2006) *A Guide to Anti-social Behaviour Orders*. HMSO.
Johnston, Tim (2007) 'Papunya journal; far-reaching policy for Aborigines draws their fury', *New York Times*, August 24.
Larner, Wendy, and Walters, William (eds) (2004) *Global Governmentality: Governing International Spaces*. London: Routledge.
Locke, John (1969 [1697]) 'Report to the Board of Trade respecting the relief and employment of the poor', in J. Axtell (ed.), *The Educational Writings of John Locke*, Cambridge: Cambridge University Press.
Lukes, Stephen (1974) *Power: A Radical View*. London: Macmillan.
Martin, R. (1988) 'Truth, power, self; an interview with Michel Foucault', in L. H. Martin, R. Gutman and P. R. Hutton (eds), *Technologies of the Self: A Seminar with Michel Foucault*. London: Tavistock.
Mead, Lawrence (ed.) (1997a) *The New Paternalism: Supervisory Approaches to Poverty*. Brookings Institution.
Mead, Lawrence (1997b) 'The rise of paternalism', in L. Mead (ed.), *The New Paternalism: Supervisory Approaches to Poverty*. Brookings Institution.
Mead, Lawrence (1997c) 'Welfare employment', in L. Mead (ed.), *The New Paternalism: Supervisory Approaches to Poverty*. Brookings Institution.
Mill, John Stuart (1985 [1859]) *On Liberty*, Harmondsworth: Penguin.
Miller, Peter and Rose, Nikolas (1990) 'Governing economic life', *Economy and Society*, 19 (I): 1–31.
O'Malley, Pat (1998) 'Indigenous governance', in M. Dean and B. Hindess (eds), *Governing Australia: Studies in Contemporary Rationalities of Government*. Cambridge: Cambridge University Press.
Pearson, Noel (2000) 'Passive welfare and the destruction of indigenous society in Australia', in Peter Saunders (ed.) *Reforming the Australian Welfare State*. Melbourne: Australian Institute of Family Studies.
Peck, Jaime (2001) *Workfare States*. New York: Guilford Press.
Saunders, Peter (2000) *Reforming the Australian Welfare State*. Melbourne: Australian Institute of Family Studies.
Schram, Sanford F. (2000) *After Welfare: the Culture of Postindustrial Social Policy*. New York: New York University Press.
Skinner, Quentin (1997) *Liberty before Liberalism*. Cambridge: Cambridge University Press.
Stenson, Kevin (2005) 'Sovereignty, bio-politics and the local government of crime', *Theoretical Criminology*, 9 (3): 267–87.

Watson, Virginia (2004) 'Liberalism and advanced liberalism in Australian Indigenous affairs', *Alternatives: Global, Local, Political,* 29 (5): 577–98.
Weber, Max (1968) *Economy and Society: An Outline of Interpretive Sociology,* in G. Roth and C. Wittich (eds). New York: Bedminister Press 3 Vols.
Weber, Max (1972) *From Max Weber,* in H.H. Gerth and C. W. Mills (eds). London: Routledge, p. 941.

Power and Identity

Nigel Rapport

> The individual is something quite new which creates new things, something absolute; all his acts are entirely his own.
> Ultimately, the individual derives the value of his acts from himself; because he has to interpret in a quite individual way even the words he has inherited. His interpretation of a formula at least is personal, even if he does not create a formula: as an interpreter he is still creative.
>
> Friedrich Nietzsche
> *The Will to Power*

INTRODUCTION: THE HUMAN AND THE STATUS OF CULTURE

Are human beings the same *inasmuch as* they all inhabit different cultural worlds, or is their being human something that exists *over and against* their inhabiting such worlds? Do they become human within culture or does their humanity transcend cultural particularities? Clifford Geertz (1973: 22) has called this the 'recurrent dilemma' of social science: how to square generic human rationality and the biological unity of mankind ('humanism') with the great natural variation of cultural forms and social structures ('structuralism'). The history of social science in its entirety may, according to George Stocking (1992: 347), be viewed as 'a continuing (and complex) dialectic between the universalism of "anthropos" and the diversitarianism of "ethnos"', between recognizing human consciousness as foundationally individual and free, and as collective and culturally given.

If consciousness, its form and content, is not separate from the symbolic discourses and social practices in which it is culturally and socially embedded, then not only may identity – human, individual, whatever – be seen as subordinate to cultural matrices (which may remain unconscious), but the notions of 'humankind', 'humanism', 'human nature', 'human dignity' and so on, may be deemed historically contingent and culturally specific products. 'Man', as Michel Foucault put it, 'is only a recent invention, a figure not yet two centuries old' (1972: 115). However seriously one takes Foucault's historical claim, the implication is clear: humankind and humanism are ethnocentric (mythical, teleological) concepts ripe for deconstruction. Far from being transcendent, humanistic values, methods and truths are part of particular discourses which have created the world in a certain image so as to serve certain interests and ends. 'Humankind' – 'the subject' or 'subject-effect', better – is ever, inevitably and inextricably enculturated: hence multiply and partially constructed, conditioned, elicited, politicized and gendered. Even the existential certainties of the Western humanist – whereby, in David Lewis's words (1982: 55), '[m]y distinctness, my being me, is quite unmistakeable to me, there can be nothing of which I am more certain' – amounts to a culturally derived (and rather unusual) 'metaphysics of presence'.

There are a number of possible responses to this structuralist (or 'culturalist') critique. One is simply to say that treating 'ethnos' as an absolute is plainly wrong. Science, medicine, history, literature, diplomacy, the market and travel prove the existence of a universal humanity, and of an inherent individuality of consciousness and experience through which it is embodied (cf. Rapport 1997a). Another response, as adumbrated philosophically by Richard Rorty (1992), is to admit that a humanist perspective is historically recent and culturally specific but to argue, notwithstanding, that as a way of knowing the world it offers the best prospectus for a diversity of cultural world-views being able to live peaceably alongside and through one another: it is the most powerful way of construing ontologically secure human identities. In what she calls a 'tactical humanism', Lila Abu-Lughod (1991: 138) arrives at a similar position. Humanism may be a local discourse (despite its erstwhile claims) but it still has more global reach than any other and it carries most moral force as a language of equality. Of course, the discourse has suffered from being misapplied and abused. In the past, promoting and celebrating 'heroic' individual identities has occurred at the same time as an ignoring of others' systematic oppression; positing individuals' autonomy has co-occurred with a masking of the inequalities of social-structural positioning; placing humankind at the centre of the world has co-occurred with a justifying of an exploitation of nature; and respecting a universality of human dignity and individual integrity has co-occurred with a denying of humanity to specified 'others' (women, children, natives, slaves, Jews). However, this abuse notwithstanding (and no discourse, finally, can protect itself from abuse), humanism offers social science the best hope for describing both the universality and the universal particularities of human experience, and for speaking truth both to the social-structurally powerful and the powerless. In particular, humanism offers an escape from concepts which can become imprisoning essentialisms. 'Culture', 'society', 'community', 'nationality', 'ethnicity', 'gender' and 'race' structure the world according to certain fixed and determinate notions of identity. So-called 'identity-politics' impose sameness, categorizing people as alike and stereotyping their collective characteristics; equally, identity-politics make and maintain alterity, creating differences between people, and implying fundamental separations which inexorably translate into hierarchy and inequality (Amit and Rapport 2002).

To write 'against culture' (and other such homogenizing categorizations) is to eschew regarding people as 'typical examples of a genus' (Watson 1992: 139). It is, in Abu-Lughod's phrasing (1991: 157), to produce humanistic 'ethnographies of the particular': precise narratives of the existence of particular individuals in particular times and places. Paradoxically, *the very particularity of human lives* is a property they hold in common, over and against their cultural and other differences. The individual discloses the human. 'Humanistic narratives' portray the efforts to make meaning that are common to the lives of everyone. Through the stories of particular lives, of individuals amid the histories of their own particularities, social science can offer a global authority to the possible authenticity of individually conducted lives. Counterpoised to the identity politics of structurally over-determined identities can be lodged the 'existential power' (Rapport 2003) of individual practice.

The above paragraphs demonstrate the reflexive nature of the social sciences: the way in which information and value overlap (Bateson and Ruesch 1951); and the way in which models, theories and analyses are consequential upon the social life they observe, re-entering the world as participatory components that give rise to new structurations (Giddens 1990). Interpretations of the nature of the human, the cultural, of identity and power, are to be regarded as much as pragmatic and strategic instruments as matters of information. What is the most powerful way to regard identity, and for what purposes? How is power to be identified, and to what ends?

The style of this chapter is perspectival. It provides a point of entry into current debates. At the same time it argues for a particular stance in these debates. The consequences of a humanist perspective on the nature of power and identity are such, I argue, that it best provides for fulfilment, dignity and satisfaction – the realizing of individual capacities for life – both as regards individuals in themselves, and in their relationships with others. The chapter is in two main parts. The first elaborates on the nature of power and its origin; the second examines the nature of identity, the relational character of both power and identity, and the consequences of a politics of identity.

THE NATURE OF POWER: HUMANIST AND STRUCTURALIST PERSPECTIVES

Power can be conceived of existentially as an inherent attribute of individuals as active beings, beings who, through their ongoing activity-in-the-world, create and recreate meaningful environments in which they live. Ralph Waldo Emerson and Friedrich Nietzsche refer in this connection to individuals' native 'force', John Dewey to their 'impulse', Max Weber to their 'will'. Residing within individuals, and lent to the relations and groupings to which they lend their allegiance, a notion of 'existential power' compasses the force, the will, the energy, in a word the agency, whereby individuals produce effects in their worlds – effect worlds, in fact. Such existential power is at once something metabolic, physiological, something pertaining to individuals acting as embodied physical organisms, and something more particularly intelligent, pertaining to the capacity to sense and make sense (cf. Barnes 1988: 4).

Gregory Bateson defines individuals as 'energy sources' (1973: 126). While individuals' bodily boundaries are permeable, and while they may be dependent on energy-transfers across these borders, inasmuch as they exist, individuals have an inescapable physical and experiential separateness which differentiates and distinguishes them from the rest of the world. As discrete centres of energy, individuals begin, from before birth, to become distinctly themselves: to accrete identities and personalities. This takes place through activity-in-the-world, through movement and through assessment of what the senses relay to be the results of that movement. Bateson refers in this connection to the individual 'organism-plus-environment' and 'organism-in-its-environment' (1973: 423, 426), and James Fernandez to a human 'phenomenological subjectivity' (1992: 127, 134–5). Activity-in-the-world leads to a development of a personal, environing 'sensorium' in which individual human beings dwell.

Two things are further to be stressed: not only does the energy behind this activity-in-the-world remain individually based, it is also individually directed. From the moment the individual energy source begins moving in its environment and becoming itself (its selves), a unique history of embodiment, of worldly engagement, unfolds and grows which compasses its own logics, its own habits, its own ways of doing and being, and its own purposes. Of course, the individual organism-plus-environment is not alone in the world. It is discrete but not alone. It has embarked upon its distinct voyage of activity-in-the-world (-in-*its*-world) and sense-making, but it is surrounded by a plurality of other things-in-the-world, inorganic and organic, some engaged in comparable voyages to its own. On this view, social science might be broadly described as the study of the effects that human beings as energetic things-in-the-world have upon one another. This is a far from singular or easily generalizable matter (which is why a respect for the individual case goes to the very heart of social science as a project). Since each individual centre-of-energy is driven by its own metabolism, within its own embodiment, along its own historical course of activity-in-the-world, how each will react to other things is not determinable; more specifically, it is difficult, if not impossible, to predict how one human being will affect another human being with whom it comes into contact. This is so for three reasons: first, to repeat, because each is set upon its own life-course, each is engaged in furthering a life-world whose direction and logic has been distinct from the moment 'it' began; secondly, because each engages with others from the position of outsider: each is dependent on bodily sense-making apparatuses which are discrete and distinctive to itself, which imbue it with its own perspective on the world and no other, and thirdly, because the sense-making procedures of each is characterized by a creativity – a 'randomness' even (Rapport 2001) – which makes their generation of perspectives unpredictable even to themselves.

An appropriate way to conceive of human social life, Emerson suggests, is as a proportionate meeting between individuals' 'native force' and social conventions: '[l]ife itself is a mixture of power and form' (1981: 280). Georg Simmel speaks therefore of a 'reciprocal influence' between sociocultural form and individuals' vital 'impulse' (1971: 24). However, as they deal with and employ conventional social and cultural forms as means and modes of expression and communication, it is individuals' native force which drives them to accrue and maintain senses of themselves and their worlds, and it is an individual intelligence which determines what that exchange of forms signifies. This means that the forms of social exchange cannot be treated as things-in-themselves. 'The sociocultural' is not a distinct ontological domain so much as a phenomenological space shot through – continuously affected and effected – by the diversity of individual interpretation and intention. The fact that there is unpredictability and that the consequences of individual meetings may be unintended must not, *contra* Giddens (1976: 155–60), lead us to conceptualize 'action', 'pattern' or even 'structure' as distanced and distinguishable from individual actors and moments. It is always by way of the latter that the social forms are animated, given complexity and depth (cf. Rapport 1990).

A 'prosperous' social life, Emerson concludes, depends on how 'sweetly' individuals are able to effect the meeting between their intrinsic force and personal interpretations of the surface conventions which act as both buffers and points of contact between themselves and others: '[w]e live amid surfaces, and the true art of life is to skate well on them' (1981: 280).

The power of the institutional

The above introduces a very different concept of power to that characteristically presumed by a structuralist social science. The latter might posit power as something residing in, and deriving from, abstract and impersonal entities and forces such as 'social structures', 'languages', 'discourses', 'unconscious drives' 'habituated practices' and 'institutions', and from categorial designations such as 'class', 'gender', 'ethnicity', 'nationality'. These abstractions are seen to be responsible for real effects, and as controlling those individual human 'functionaries' that live within their compass, whether or not the latter are aware of their so being controlled. Indeed, recent 'post-humanist' thought has claimed that such impersonal forces are responsible for giving rise to the consciousness of human beings *tout court* – responsible for our conceiving of the possibility of there being something called 'individuals' or 'persons' with 'experience' and 'power'– thus collapsing any distinction between social structure and agent, cultural form and will. Under a structuralist dispensation, the impersonal often becomes an 'anthropomorphized agent', assuming many shapes – 'vector, instrument, technology, technique, discourse' (Kurtz 2001: 29) – but always eluding the control of human agents.

Nor is this conclusion so far removed, in outcome, from more traditional functionalist and structuralist theorizations which saw social order as emanating from a system of normative control (a set of external sanctions or a system of interiorized morality), and where the power of one individual over another derived from the institutional contexts and practical routines by which they found themselves encapsulated. 'Interactional', 'organizational' and 'structural' 'modalities' condition the settings and contexts in which individuals exercise their potency and capability, Eric Wolf concludes (1999: 5). Timothy Earle (1998: 951) speaks even more plainly: 'four sources of power exist: social, military, ideological and economic', and maintaining a social position 'depends on using one or more of these power sources' – of which 'the economic is primary'. At best, a hierarchy of kinds of power is admitted in a structuralist social science in which existential 'modalities' come to be thoroughly overwritten. Questions such as how individuals deal with life, how they make meaning in the midst of everyday routine and change, suffering and good fortune, become questions largely of social determination. As Michael Jackson sums up, in the rush to depict the 'political power' of techniques of influence and oppression, a recognition of the 'existential power' to act and constitute identity is lost (1996: 22); a focus on 'institutional processes of governance' eschews a broader conceptualization of 'the power to do, the capacity to achieve things or projects' (Eves 1998: 20–1). Under a structuralist dispensation, in short, individual agency comes to be overwritten, more or less vulgarly, by social structure and institutionalism, hierarchy and history, *habitus* and hegemony.

A different place to begin, in considering such seemingly impersonal, structural or institutional facets of power, is with the vital distinction between the forms of social reality and the force, the will, behind them and the significance, the meaning, they carry. There is no way that such experiential dualities (form and force, form and meaning) can properly be elided or eschewed. Form should never be seen as overwriting content; they are, as Simmel insisted (1971), 'co-present dualisms'.

There are both political or institutional *and* existential or personal manifestations of power. The distinction is clearly borne out by the different ways individual incumbents of the same political office, functionaries of the same institution, fulfil (define, maintain, extend, subvert, personalize, anonymize) their role; but the relationship between the institutional and the existential is not a mutual one: not a relationship between equal things, between things that are equally things. Rather, there is a fundamental sense in which the institutional can be understood as conditional upon the existential.

The structuralist argument regarding the power of the institutional is often framed in terms of language. The power of language over its individual speaker-hearers – individuals as 'inhabitants', willy-nilly, if not prisoners, of discourses, language games or symbolic codes – is taken to be paradigmatic of the institutional or structural as such (cf. Ray 1989). By contrast, an existentialist appreciation might begin with a description of language as an institution whose very nature is to function in 'ironic mode' (Martin 1983: 415), there being no certain or necessary accordance between what individuals appear to say and actually say, between the linguistic meanings of different individual users, or between linguistic expression and the way the world is. Linguistically formulated social structures, norms and codes are dependent on and determined by their being continually animated by individual speaker-hearers for particular purposes at particular moments (cf. Rapport and Overing 2000: 117–26).

Of course, there is significant give-and-take between the two emphases. Without the institution of language individuals would not have the medium through which to express and hope to communicate their meanings and to metacommunicate notions of register and code; perhaps they would not have the means even to formulate such meaning, certainly not with the same ease. Notwithstanding, there is something ontologically and qualitatively distinct in the agency with which each individual is responsible for imbuing language with meaningfulness, relevance and validity, through their continued, intentioned use of it – without which the institution would simply remain inert cultural matter – and so maintaining language's role as a synthesising process in social life. To claim for the institutional something akin to its own animating force and function is hypostatization (cf. Haugaard 1997: 165). It is humanity that speaks – in the shape of individual utterances of individual language-users – not language as such.

George Steiner (1975) offers an apposite formulation (echoing Simmel and Emerson) when he describes social life as exhibiting a 'dual phenomenology'. In social interaction there is a common surface of speech-forms and notations, of grammar and phonology – the conventions of collective public exchange – resting upon a base of private meanings and associations, meanings which derive from the 'irreducible singularity' of personal consciousness, from the specificity of an individual's ongoing, articulate somatic and psychological identity (Steiner 1975: 170–3). Speaking a language does not translate into that language possessing agency or achieving hegemony, determining or causing meaning, or eliminating the interpretive work of individual speaker-hearers. Linguistic norms and routines may institutionalize (also hierarchicalize) certain conventional avenues of expression but they in no wise determine what is meant as individuals partake of the language from within the personalizing contexts of their world-views (cf. Rapport 1993: 161–77).

Linguistic usage is never unmediated by a creative individual improvization of its conventions. Individuals at once partake of language's rules and routines (take part in the continuing constitution of socio-cultural milieux to which linguistic interaction gives rise), and make these into instruments of their own ongoing, changing understanding and use. Whatever the order and sense – the power – purportedly instantiated by the institutional logic of the language as such, the individual speaker-hearers partaking of its rules and routines animate them according to their own mental and bodily (verbal and behavioural) presence in those routines. Individuals in interaction can thus be seen to be both assisting in a continuing collective performance – in the performance of an institution – and, at the same time, creating, extending and fulfilling ongoing agendas, identities, world-views, life-projects, of their own. There can be worlds of difference between shared grammatic-cum-paradigmatic competency – shared institutional membership – on the one hand and shared cognition or mutual comprehension on the other.

Likewise, there can be worlds of difference between individuals' constructions of themselves and how they are described by others. These may bear little relation; others' interpretations are beyond individuals' capacity directly to control, even possibly to influence. And while the structuralist inference is that here, therefore, individuals are subsumed by the logic of an impersonal domain, an institutional *habitus* which itself acts in the effecting of an autonomous, public world of meaning (Derrida 1982: 316), there is no call, to repeat, for such hypostatization. The fact that it is within the gift of others to make of individuals 'heroes' or 'terrorists' (Leach 1977), 'innovators' or 'deviants' (Haugaard 1997: 175), does not alter the nature of original, individual acts of self-authorship, nor the ongoing individuality of serial acts of interpretation by others. 'The public' is no more a thing-in-itself than 'the social' (cf. Rapport 1994: 26–8). One continues to distinguish conceptually, absolutely, between self-knowledge and other-knowledge and posits the relationship between these as indeterminate: unpredictable, oblique, random, ultimately unknowable. A 'public reputation' is not something individuals can control; nor is it something that controls them: public exchange is never unmediated by continuing acts of individual interpretation. All manner of affirmation and of delegitimization, of affection and of violation, may be visited upon the individual by others, but none, barring death, touch upon the absolute capacity (necessity) of individuals to make their own sense. Individual speakers and hearers, actors and others, are 'condemned', in Jean-Paul Sartre's elaboration (1975: 352), to go on making their own sense.

A dialectical relation exists between the existential and the institutional, but the existence of such relations should not obscure our recognition of the ontological priority of the existential, also its qualitative distinctiveness. The existential possesses an instrumental priority, inasmuch as the power of the institutional is dependent on the animating work of individual functionaries (individuals who are active in the world, *inter alia* as institutional role-players). The role-player is never to be seen as subsumed within the logic of the institutional – the 'content' collapsed into the 'form', in Simmel's terminology – for the individual always possesses the power – the existential awareness, the ironic capacity and proclivity – to say, '*Here I am partaking of an institution, playing a particular language-game*'. Sometimes individuals 'play' better at some games rather than others, and sometimes the playing is more trying, intrusive, than at others, but there is no moment at which individuals do not possess the capacity – and experience the mixed emotions – of recognizing both where the logic of the institution (as personalized by fellow-players) would take them, and the distinctive, individual place they nevertheless stand, emotionally and cognitively, in relation to it. It may not always be a simple matter determining how to reconcile these positions – how to act, what to say, how to seem – both as institutional players and as themselves. However, it is never difficult for individuals to see themselves both present and detached. They are conscious players in the game – however reluctant, however conventionally disempowered – but never played unconsciously by it. To begin to understand the 'power' of institutions – to categorize, normativize, hierarchicalize, exclude – is to see institutions being worked, and resisted, and negated, for all manner of purposes and in every moment, by wilful individuals. 'We human beings', as Victor Turner summed up, 'are all and always sophisticated, conscious, capable of laughter at our own institutions' (cited in Ashley 1990: xix).

One needs to have a conception of existential power as a 'real quality', a 'concrete thing', prior to and independent of anything else (Helms 1993: 9). The individual energy, will and force which underlie the work of interpretation in linguistic usage underlie equally the extent to which institutions as such gain animation in public life, and continue to manifest a structural power.

THE RELATIONALITY (OR EXTENSIVENESS) OF IDENTITY AND OF POWER

Alfred Whitehead (1925) was sufficiently blunt when he wrote:

> The misconception that has haunted philosophical literature throughout the centuries is the notion of 'independent existence'. There is no such mode of existence; every entity is to be understood in terms of the way it is interwoven with the rest of the universe.

Under a structuralist dispensation, the above is interpreted as meaning that there can be no autonomous individual actor subsisting as a free-thinking and sovereign entity. There is an insistence that people only assume the identity of individuals (to the extent that they do) within a socio-cultural milieu, as a result of socialization and enculturation: as part-and-parcel of the ways in which processes of structuration engender a reproduction of other socio-cultural identities – languages, modes of production and practice, systems of exchange, institutions and organizations, cosmologies and ecologies. People are the sum of their social exchanges, of the natures elicited from them by their relationships.

A short riposte to this is that it confuses *individuality* with *individualism*. It conflates a particular sociocultural conceptualization of individual identity and the universal, biological nature of selfhood (Rapport and Overing 2000: 178–95). 'Individualism' pertains to a particular ideology of identity, concerning the value and dignity of the human individual, his or her rationality and self-knowledge, right to privacy, freedom of conscience and of contract (cf. Lukes 1990). 'Individuality', by contrast, refers to a universality of the human condition whereby individuals engage with others by virtue of discrete sense-making apparatuses (nervous systems and brains), possessing discrete centres of consciousness in discrete bodies. There is a distinctiveness that pertains universally to an individual's unique position vis-à-vis the rest of the world, a unique intentionality. Not only is an individual's being-in-the-world universally mediated by very particular interpretative prisms which distance him or her from it, then, but while intrinsically 'of the world', the individual also inexorably comes to know the world as 'other'.

To agree with Whitehead's prescription, then, is not necessarily to adopt a structuralist perspective. One can agree with an emphasis on the relational nature of identity while insisting that the forces directing and interpreting relations are individual ones; there is always a relationship between individual and world but it is, first and foremost, of ongoing individual construction and interpretation. (Social science, to repeat, may be described as the study of the effects, intended and unintended, direct and tangential, which human beings have upon one another as energetic things-in-the-world.) The individuality of consciousness and of agency is a human universal, whatever may be the status of individualism as a social norm.

Power as embodied

Recognition within social science of the relational qualities of power and its exercising is widely attested. Edmund Leach (1977) spoke of power as transactional, something pertaining to that liminal interface or contact zone between human beings; while Richard Adams (1977) described power as the ability to influence the conduct and decision-making of others through the control over energetic forms in the latter's environment. Power *as a relationship* is basic to the way many theorists have sought to define power as such.

For Floyd Hunter (1970):

> [Power describes] the acts of men [sic] going about the business of moving other men to act in relation to themselves or in relation to organic or inorganic things.

For Max Weber (1947):

> Power is the probability that one actor within a social relationship will be in a position to carry out his [sic] own will despite the resistance of other participants.

And for Robert Dahl (1957):

> A has power over B to the extent that he [sic] can get B to do something that B would not otherwise do.

There is insufficient appreciation in these definitions, however, that perhaps the first and paradigmatic relationship in the exercise of power concerns individuals' relations with themselves. Before effecting relations with other 'organic and inorganic things' (Hunter) and 'overcoming others' resistance' (Weber), an exercise of power may be said to effect the identity of individuals as such. Paradigmatically, power concerns relations between two or more distinct states of consciousness within the individual (cf. Rapport 1997a: 30–42). Viewed existentially, the individual body is the paradigmatic site of that 'liminal interface or contact zone' (Leach) between two states of being, the original site of 'getting something done' (Dahl). Here is situated a 'controlling' of 'energetic forms' such that individuals may have effects on environments (Adams). Fundamental to our understanding of power, in short, might be an appreciation of those processes of identification whereby individuals effect a change to themselves: to their conscious senses of self and world, to the personal sensorium that is their relations with the world.

The exercise of power may well entail a relationship, but it is to be recognized that the relationship may be of two, very different kinds: with individuals' own selves; with others. The former, I would argue, is foundational inasmuch as it may proceed without the latter but not the other way around. An individual may attend wholly to the self – may intend the self – and have an impact upon others not at all or only indirectly. To engage with others and seek to wield power over them is epiphenomenal upon a prior relationship an individual has with himself or herself. For, only as a self, active in the world towards an ongoing accruing of meaning and identity, does an individual construe otherness and relate, consciously and intentionally, to other things-in-the-world.

Rather than the simple (structuralist) proposition that power entails a relationship between social things, a number of more complex possibilities now suggest themselves. Through the exercise of existential power the individual identifies the self and also particular relationships with an environing world: the individual achieves selfhood and construes otherness; but the relationship with otherness may be of a variety of kinds. It is possible for individuals to exercise their power by endeavouring to use others, but also by using only themselves. It is possible for individuals to use others in such a way that it becomes impossible for these others ever to use themselves, but also to use others in such tangential or accidental ways that it neither assists nor even affects others' use of themselves. It is possible for individuals to use others in ways these others can find comprehensible, but also to use others such that the usage is impossible to understand. It is possible for individuals to model their intended use of others upon their use of themselves, and alternatively upon criteria very different or diametrically opposed.

In short, individuals may wield power over themselves, in the advance of their ideas, their sensibilities or their strength, *independently of* – with effects quite distinct and in manners quite different from – attempts to influence others (in advance of their reputation, their wealth or their patronage). Moreover, the relationship between individuals' effecting of power over themselves and their affecting of others cannot be easily specified or determined. There is no logic, to repeat, *intrinsic* to the effects which energetic things-in-the-world have upon one another: their relationship takes no *necessary* form, for its significance is a matter of interpretation. In important respects power *per se* is a matter of interpretation, residing in the eye of a beholder.

It is necessary to treat the power of the individual on the one hand, and the identities and relationships to which that power gives rise on the other – both within the individual body and without – as phenomenally and analytically distinct. Existence, as per Sartre's (1956) famous summary, precedes essence. This is not to take issue, to repeat, with an emphasis on the relational nature of identity or the extent to which, in Bateson's words (1973), 'things are epiphenomena of the relations between them', but rather to insist (as Bateson also does) that it is the 'energy sources' of individual physical organisms which possess the intrinsic power responsible for construing relationships and perceiving things in the first place. The things and relationships which are identified in this way will be many and varied (human and non-human, organic and inorganic) and changeable (things and relationships will come and go), but the exercise of individual power that goes into their making continues to exist for the lifetime of the energetic body.

Identity as extensive

The word 'identity derives from the Latin, '*identitatis*', whose root is '*idem*': 'the same'. Identity suggests that something is the same as itself. To make sense of this notion is to consider a thing as intrinsically plural – at the least dual. The concept of identity, one might say, treats thingness *extensively*. Insofar as something comes to have an identity, a thing is recognized as containing within it the potential, even the necessity, of extension.

The extensiveness of identity might be of a number of kinds. It might be temporal; in spite of the passing of time, one recognizes that something has retained its identity: '*I have the same dribbling skills in football as I did 20 years ago*'. Extension might be spatial: '*Radio reception is as bad in the bedroom as in the kitchen*'. Extension might be situational: '*Emilie is as composed engaging the University Principal as she is undergraduates*'. Whatever the nature of the extension, identity posits a claim to sameness between two or more existential moments where – it is also claimed – difference might be anticipated as occurring. Identity might be described as a relationship which is consequent upon the power of construing sameness.

Identity entails acts of judgement, then: '*I adjudge this thing (person/object/relationship/situation) to be the same as that*'. In turn, such judgement calls for criteria of assessment and distinction: '*I know that this is the same as that, and also different from another, in this way*'. In saying this, moreover, a third figure has necessarily entered the picture. If the thingness of identity presumes at least a dual phenomenology, then the act of distinguishing between whether the second thing is the same as the first or different introduces a third figure. Most commonly, indeed, attributions of identity are found in full fields, or systems, of classification that individuals and groups construct around themselves. The fullness and diversity, the particularity and historicity of these systems of classification was, indeed, the place this essay began. 'Culture' is the term social scientists have employed to convey the multiplicity of human systems of classifying identity and their complexity. Cultural systems of symbolic classification compass specific ranges of samenesses and differences. The systems can possess great historical depth. They can represent generations of hard-won practical experience; they can also represent traditional flights of human fancy tied to human imaginations religiously passed on ('This is the number of angels that can dance on the head of a pin'; 'This is the physiological feature responsible for the essential distinction between Male and Female/between White and Black/between Human and Animal'). The ways in which human individuals and groups have allocated identity to the world and its things, and have made and adjudicated their claims are legion.

The particularity of our species turns on our creative capacity for making the world into different kinds of places by our symboling work and by our own malleability: our capacity to form *ourselves* into the kinds of being who could exist in the very different systems of symbolic classifications of identity which we continue creating.

The consequences of identity

The particular way in which human beings do come to construe identity is not merely incidental. Flights of fancy they may be, traditions of imaginative creation, but such is the adaptability of the species, its capacity to live in a world which goes beyond both the seeming limits of an instinctual animality and the seeming limits of a natural ecology (we repress libido, we modify genes, we make deserts bloom), that our acts of construing identity and of constructing cultural systems, are responsible, in large, for the worlds we actually inhabit. Our decisions on how to act and why derive from our reliance on systems of classification: '*It is "good" not to "associate" with "evil" "folk"*'; '*"Meat" "affords" a "healthy diet" for "children"'*; *'"British citizens" are "subject to" the "sovereign"'*. Significantly, we *evaluate* our own identities and those of others on the basis of the identifications we and they decide to make in the world. *'We know right from wrong: they do not'*; *'We only holiday in Cannes'*; *'We could never vote Conservative'*. In short, systems of classification translate into significant distinctions between proper and improper, insiders and outsiders, better and worse. They are powerful means of manifesting human identities, individual and collective, to oneself and to others. From our identifications we accrue the contents of selfhood, and justifications for action.

The lesson from ethnography is the relativity and contingency of these identifications: systems of classification are multiple and contradictory (Rapport 1997b). Even the same individual, the same group, will invest at once in a number of different modes of assigning identity. Between individuals and groups the contrariety increases exponentially. We must be wary of this relativity: the human capacity to live any number of different lives under the aegis of different classificatory systems does not make such systems all equal, or always necessary. Nietzsche referred to the systems as 'illusions'. Art, religion, even a science of discrete things, offered comforting *illusions* concerning the world's patterning and constancy; it was thus that human beings overcame a potential nausea in the face of the world's actual randomness, chaos, entropy, meaninglessness, absurdity (cf. Rapport 1999).

All the same, we should not be taken in by our own fictions, Nietzsche urged. We should adopt an 'ironical' stance even in regard to values and vocabularies we deem 'final' and of absolute value in our lives (cf. Rorty 1992). We might then oscillate or zigzag between identifying with clear-cut systems of classification – benefitting from the proportion, direction, ambition, progress and propriety which they give to individual and collective lives – and, alternatively, recognizing the truth of their fanciful and contingent status. The true constancy of the world, Nietzsche concluded, beyond identifiable things was entropy and flux: 'the real immortality, that of movement' (1994: 125). As well there was the constant capacity of human beings, together and alone, to go on creating the illusion of identity, of systems of classification, to suit their purposes of leading proportionate, directional, progressive lives.

Identity politics

Aware of the dangers of forgetting the illusionary, constructed nature of systems of classification and identity – the homogenising of identity, the stereotyping, hierarchicalizing and othering – Ernest Gellner has wondered whether 'categorization [even] between consenting adults [is] to be allowed to all?' (1993: 3). His point is a serious one: 'We are all human (...). Don't take more specific classifications seriously'. The power to construe identity in a world of movement, entropy and flux is a fundamental human capacity. We must be wary, however, of the achievement of identity giving onto the 'fundamentalism' of an unironical performance of social life (cf. Kateb 1984: 351).

'Culture', explains Gellner (1995: 6), may be defined as,

> a collectivity united in a belief (...). That is what the term means. More particularly, a collectivity united in a false belief is a culture. Truths, especially demonstrable truths, are available to all and sundry, and do not define any continuity of faith. But errors, especially dramatic errors, are culture-specific. They do tend to be the badges of community and loyalty. Assent to an absurdity is an intellectual *rite de passage*, a gateway to the community defined by that commitment to that conviction.

Like Nietzsche, Gellner would preserve a space – experiential, practical, moral – beyond the illusions of culture. Our true humanity, our constancy in a world of flux, is to be found in our existential capacities to go on creating meaning. This we might truly value.

The irony is that as social science has called for deconstruction of a conceptualization of culture inherited from German Romanticism – ultimately from Johann Herder – which posits essentialist collective identities (in analogy with natural species), so the political currency of 'culture' and commensurate categorizations ('ethnicity', 'nationality', 'religiosity', 'gender') as symbolic capital has spread. We have entered an era of 'culture wars': political lobbying and violence on the basis of exclusive ascriptions and their 'rightful' entailments. This is not coincidental. Notions of culture, race, tribe, nation, religion, gender and class as bespeaking intrinsic homogeneousness and solidarity, delimitation and differentiation, reflect widespread anxieties concerning people's ability to grasp and influence forces that impact upon their life-worlds:

> Cultural and ethnic identity have become the catchwords for many of those disadvantaged by colonial and postcolonial inequalities in the distribution of power, (...) imagin[ing] they can recapture something of the integrity and authenticity they feel they have *personally* lost. [Jackson 2002:107]

Eliding the personal and social, the biographical and historical in this way empowers the anonymized, the historically marginalized and excluded: embedding individual being in a transcendent field of Being.

How is social science to respond to this? Does one applaud the politicization as 'romantic authochthonization' (Malkki 1995: 52–63)? Or does one insist that essentializing arguments concerning identity threaten a free and mobile society, our individual capacities to construe and practice newly achieved identities on a continuing basis? In place of 'an ironing out of difference in the name of some notion of common humanity' (Jackson 2002: 114), existing inequalities come to be reversed, and new discriminations devised: a kind of 'inside-out colonialism' (Gellner 1993). Kinds of cultural fundamentalism are deployed in community- and nation-building, dividing the world into true belongers and believers – and foreigners, infidels and apostates – on the basis of different origins and essences. Here are reified categories which admit neither synthesis nor resolution.

'Any kind of identity thinking is insidious', Michael Jackson concludes (2002: 115), 'because like all reification, it elides the line that separates words and worlds, language and life'. Reducing the world to simplistic, generalized, category oppositions abolish vast areas of *human* experience and capacity. Collective nouns and identity terms traduce the open-endedness and ambiguity of life, spawning dangerous illusions of essential difference and threatening inhumanity and intolerance being visited on iconic others (cf. Sen 2006).

CONCLUSION: DECOLONIZING THE HUMAN SUBJECT

There is nothing 'primordial' or necessary in the way that discontent with the liberal world flows into fundamentalism and chauvinism, Brian Barry explains (2001:4), merely a political expediency. The tendency towards identities of an absolutist and exclusivist kind – fundamentalist religion, ethnic nationalism – represents a highly contemporary, 'modern', choice: the strategic use of purist thinking (cf. Bauman 1998, Zizek 2005). Lobbying on the basis of such essentialism has reaped political and statutory rewards. It is also – to recall the hermeneutic circle of human reflexivity – a kind of social modelling which works well in a particular kind of milieu: a world constructed on the basis of clear-cut classificatory structures. It is the efficacy of essentialism as an instrument of a kind of identification, one might say, to *presage and reinforce* this kind of world; but what if one wished to practise and to secure a different kind of being-in-the-world, one more attuned to what one deemed the fullness of human capacities?

The issue is moral as well as epistemological. It comes down to the nature of the anthropological concrete, where this chapter began. What can one assert as being the constituent units of humanity, ontological and agential, and potentially rights-bearing? Distinct, cohesive cultural communities, or individual members of milieux (communitarian and other, cultural and other)? Is membership of a cultural community a contingent relationship, an option, and 'culture' a possible instrument – an idiom, a rhetoric, a resource, a vehicle – for social synthesis and self-expression? Or is cultural membership foundational and determinate? The position taken in this chapter has been that it is proper, descriptively, analytically and morally, to treat the power of the human individual on the one hand, and the social relationships and communities to which that power gives rise on the other, as distinct. Individual power is ontologically prior to its effects, distinct from the 'essences' of sociocultural identity, relationship, system and change that it creates. Classes and categories, the matter they are seen to contain and the relations they are seen to exhibit, should never be confused or conflated with the energy and will behind them, the power that speaks through them. By way of the particular forms of things and relationships, individuals express and effect any number of personal states of affairs, make and remake the identities of their personal sensoriums. This is at once an ontological state of affairs and a matter about which we must be politically correct.

It is apposite to recall a distinction which Isaiah Berlin (1990) urged between 'negative' and 'positive' freedoms. Negative freedom was freedom from imposition; positive freedom was freedom to gain particular goods (health, wealth, spiritual purity). Negative freedom was more fundamental, Berlin concluded, since it avoided any conceptual imposition concerning what freedom might entail. This chapter has dwelt on distinctions that might, equally, be ranked: existential power over and against structural power; identity as extensive over and against identity as essential. A recognition of power as a human, individual energy – a *capacity to act* in and on the world – and of identity as an achievement of sameness and difference – an *ongoing interpretation* – are foundational of appreciating power and identity in their varied *sociocultural* conceptualizations.

Anthony Cohen (1994: 180) has advocated a social-scientific championing of the individual as the anthropological concrete which he calls 'decolonizing' the human subject:

> We must make deliberate efforts to acknowledge the subtleties, inflections and varieties of individual consciousness which are concealed by the categorical masks which we have invented so adeptly. Otherwise, we will continue to deny people the right to be themselves, deny their rights to their own identities.

Michael Jackson concurs: it is necessary to 'annul' the use of culture as discursive means to classify, define and explain human experience. Culture is to be deemed 'an idiom or vehicle of intersubjective life, but not its foundation or final cause' (Jackson 2002: 118–25). To do justice to our existential power – our human nature – to make sense of the world, and to go on doing so, is perhaps to constitute individuals as 'migrants of identity' (Rapport and Dawson 1998). A constitutional pluralism based on human-individual capacities to move between selves, communities, systems of classification, within a liberal-democratic framework, establishes the rights of people, individually as well as collectively, to create and develop identities of an ongoing diversity, strangeness and vitality.

REFERENCES

Abu-Lughod, L. (1991) 'Writing against culture', in R. Fox (ed.), *Recapturing Anthropology*, Sante Fe: School of American Research Press.
Adams, R. (1977) 'Power in human societies', in R. Fogelson and R. Adams (eds)., *The Anthropology of Power*, New York: Academic.
Amit, V. and Rapport, N. (2002) *The Trouble with Community: Anthropological Reflections on Movement, Identity and Collectivity*. London: Pluto.
Ashley, K. (1990) 'Introduction', in K. Ashley (ed.), *Victor Turner and the Construction of Cultural Criticism*. Bloomington: Indiana University Press.
Barnes, B. (1988) *The Nature of Power*. Cambridge: Polity.
Barry, B. (2001) *Culture and Equality*. Cambridge: Polity.
Bateson, G. (1973) *Steps to an Ecology of Mind*. London: Intertext.
Bateson, G. and Ruesch, J. (1951) *Communication*. New York: Norton.
Bauman, Z. (1998) 'Postmodern religion?', in P. Heelas (ed.), *Religion, Modernity and Postmodernity*, Oxford: Blackwell.
Berlin, I. (1990) *The Crooked Timber of Humanity*. London: Murray.
Cohen, A. P. (1994) *Self Consciousness*. London: Routledge.
Dahl, R. (1957) 'The concept of power', *Behavioral Science*, 2(3): 201–15.
Derrida, J. (1982) *Margins of Philosophy*. Brighton: Harvester.
Earle, T. (1998) 'Political domination and social evolution', in T. Ingold (ed.), *Companion Encyclopedia of Anthropology*. London: Routledge.
Emerson, R. W. (1981) *The Portable Emerson*. Harmondsworth: Penguin.
Eves, R. (1998) *The Magical Body*. Amsterdam: Harwood Academic.
Fernandez, J. (1992) 'What it is like to be a Banzie: On sharing the experience of an equatorial microcosm', in J. Gort, H. Vroom, R. Fernhout and A. Wessels (eds), *On Sharing Religious Experience*. Amsterdam: Rodopi.
Foucault, M. (1972) *The Archaeology of Knowledge*. New York: Harper.
Geertz, C. (1973) *The Interpretation of Cultures*. New York: Basic.
Gellner, E. (1993) 'The mightier pen? Edward Said and the double standards of inside-out colonialism', *Times Literary Supplement*, February 19: 3–4.
Gellner, E. (1995) 'Anything goes: The carnival of cheap relativism which threatens to swamp the coming *fin de millenaire*', *Times Literary Supplement*, 4811: 6–8.
Giddens, A. (1976) *New Rules of Sociological Method*. London: Hutchinson.
Giddens, A. (1990) *The Consequences of Modernity*. Stanford: Stanford University Press.
Haugaard, M. (1997) *The Constitution of Power*. Manchester: Manchester University Press.
Helms, M. (1993) *Craft and the Kingly Ideal*. Austin: University of Texas Press.
Hunter, F. (1970) 'Community power structure', in E. Keynes and D. Ricci (eds), *Political Power, Community and Democracy*. Chicago: Rand-McNally.
Jackson, M. (1996) 'Introduction: Phenomenology, radical empiricism, and anthropological critique', in M. Jackson (ed.), *Things As They Are*. Bloomington: Indiana University Press.
Jackson, M. (2002) *The Politics of Storytelling*. Copenhagen: Museum Tusculanum Press.
Kateb, G. (1984) 'Democratic individuality and the claim of politics', *Political Theory*, 12(3): 331–60.
Kurtz, D. (2001) *Political Anthropology*. Boulder: Westview.
Leach, E. (1977) *Custom, Law and Terrorist Violence*. Edinburgh: Edinburgh University Press.
Lewis, H. D. (1982) *The Elusive Self*. London: Macmillan.
Lukes, S. (1990) *Individualism*. Oxford: Blackwell.
Malkki, L. (1995) *Purity and Exile*. Chicago: University of Chicago Press.

Martin, G. (1983) 'The bridge and the river. Or the ironies of communication', *Poetics Today*, 4(3): 415–35.
Nietzsche, F. (1968) *The Will to Power*. New York: Random House.
Nietzsche, F. (1994) *Human, All Too Human*. Harmondsworth: Penguin.
Rapport, N. (1990) 'Ritual speaking in a Canadian suburb: Anthropology and the problem of generalization', *Human Relations*, 43(9): 849–64.
Rapport, N. (1993) *Diverse World-views in an English Village*. Edinburgh: Edinburgh University Press.
Rapport, N. (1994) *The Prose and the Passion: Anthropology, Literature and the Writing of E. M. Forster*. Manchester: Manchester University Press.
Rapport, N. (1997a) *Transcendent Individual: Towards a Literary and Liberal Anthropology*. London: Routledge.
Rapport, N. (1997b) 'The "contrarieties" of Israel. An essay on the cognitive importance and the creative promise of both/and', *Journal of the Royal Anthropological Institute*, 3(4): 653–72.
Rapport, N. (1999) 'Problem-solving and contradiction: Playing darts and becoming human', *Self, Agency and Society*, 2(1): 81–101.
Rapport, N. (2001) 'Random mind: Towards an appreciation of openness in individual, society and anthropology', *The Australian Journal of Anthropology*, 12(2): 190–220.
Rapport, N. (2003) *I Am Dynamite: An Alternative Anthropology of Power*. London: Routledge.
Rapport, N. and Dawson. A. (eds.) (1998) *Migrants of Identity: Perceptions of Home in a World of Movement*. Oxford: Berg.
Rapport, N. and Overing, J. (2000) *Social and Cultural Anthropology: The Key Concepts*. London: Routledge.
Ray, W. (1989) *Literary Meaning*. Blackwell: Oxford.
Rorty, R. (1992) *Contingency, Irony and Solidarity*. Cambridge: Cambridge University Press.
Sartre, J.P. (1956) *Being and Nothingness*. New York: Philosophy Library.
Sartre, J.P. (1975) 'Existentialism is a humanism', in W. Kaufman (ed.), *Existentialism from Dostoevsky to Sartre*. New York: New Arena Library.
Sen, A. (2006) *Identity and Violence*. London: Allen Lane.
Simmel, G. (1971) *On Individuality and Social Forms*. Chicago: Chicago University Press.
Steiner, G. (1975) *After Babel*. Oxford: Oxford University Press.
Stocking, G. (1992) *The Ethnographer's Magic and Other Essays in the History of Anthropology*. Madison: University of Wisconsin Press.
Watson, C. W. (1992) 'Autobiography, anthropology and the experience of Indonesia', in J. Okely and H. Callaway (eds.), *Anthropology and Autobiography*. London: Routledge.
Weber, M. (1947) *Theory of Social and Economic Organization*. New York: Oxford University Press.
Whitehead, A. (1925) *Science and the Modern World*. New York: Macmillan.
Wolf, E. (1999) *Envisioning Power*. Berkeley: University of California Press.
Zizek, S. (2005) 'Beyond discourse analysis', in *Interrogating the Real*. London: Continuum.

12

Culture and Power

Fredrik Engelstad

Emperor Julian: He who shall rule must rule over the wills, over the minds of men.

Henrik Ibsen, *Emperor and Galilean*, II, 4 (1873)

A politician appealing to voters for support. A sermon celebrating communion with God. A TV channel sending weather forecast, news, soap operas and advertisements. The models on the catwalk eliciting admiring glances and desires. A teacher instructing his students in an established corpus of knowledge.

These situations are all instances of power in a cultural framework, articulated through a variety of expressive forms. But expressive forms do not function in isolation. They are embedded in complex configurations of semantic codes, interactive preconditions and organizational efforts. The analysis of such configurations is the common task of studies of culture and power. The concepts of culture and power are both elusive and highly contested, however, and their combination not less so. In the present context the answer to this is not to go into fine-grained conceptual discussions, but to take as a point of departure the core meaning of concepts under discussion, unfold their relevant behavioral mechanisms, and then see whether important empirical problems remain unanalyzed within the given framework.

The concept of culture used here refers to meaning, norms and aesthetic/ritual practices in a broad sense. It coincides with the understanding of culture as manifested in generalized patterns of communication and interpretation, in line with the thinking of Clifford Geertz (1973). Culture is 'there', as given, forcefully shaping perceptions and modes of interpretation. But it has to be enacted and interpreted by social actors in order to retain its force. For analytical purposes culture cannot be grasped as a totality, however, it has to be broken down into patterns or pieces, what Wendy Griswold (1987) has termed cultural objects: messages in the form of utterances, pictures, narratives, songs, rituals, games, arguments, tools, buildings – often linked into broader patterns, such as styles, aesthetic doctrines, theological systems and scientific theories. Such carriers of signification are interpreted in the light of constitutive rules, classification systems, genres and grammars.

For the purposes of the present chapter, the formula coined by Michel Foucault, delimiting power as a 'set of actions upon other actions' (1983: 220) is sufficient as a general understanding of what power is about. This means that power is treated as a generic concept, the central focus being a pragmatics of power, outlining the relevant mechanisms where power is put into action. Within the framework of culture, power is largely exerted by influencing social actors' interpretations. Crucial in this respect is the distinction between the direct and indirect workings of power. *Direct* power effects are typically achieved by speech acts conveying promises and threats, enunciating prohibitions, issuing orders and making requests (Searle 1969, Bach 1998). *Indirect* power may take the form of persuasion, acting on actors' knowledge and beliefs about the nature of the world, and their conceptions of how the world ought to be, as expressed in norms, values, political loyalties or personal preferences. Moreover, power works indirectly by affecting individuals' opportunity structure. In the cultural realm this includes their possibility to express their views in public, their access to information and to cultural objects, such as books, films, newspapers and cultural institutions. Finally, power shapes the interpretational modes of those to be influenced, by affecting actors' worldviews, and epistemological conceptions, their interpretive skills, as well as their self-esteem and ability to make well-founded judgments.

ASPECTS OF CULTURE AND POWER

Frames of interpretation

The close connection between power and culture was a main theme in the works of Max Weber in the first decades of the twentieth century. But scholars further developing Weber's ideas on power mostly took the path toward rationalist models. Hence, only relatively recently was culture accorded a significant place in mainstream theory of power. A turn took place from the early 1970s with the work of Pierre Bourdieu and Michel Foucault, both focusing specifically on culture–power relationships in modern or early modern European society. Concurrently, the reappraisal of the work of Antonio Gramsci (cf. Lukes [1974]2004, Kurz 1996) contributed to a new combination of Weberian and Marxian approaches, centered on the notion of hegemony. The cultural turn tended to replace a rationalist, individualist conception of power with a structuralist view stressing the ubiquity of power, its unintended as well as hidden modes of operation. Taken to the extreme, ambiguous formulations by Foucault, such as: 'What defines a relationship of power is that it is a total structure of actions brought to bear on possible actions …' (1983: 220), or Bourdieu's theory of practice and habitus, led to crude images of power where social action has vanished out of sight, and social life appears as governed by anonymous forces understood only by a small group with esoteric knowledge.

Structuralism, however, is not a necessary consequence of culture entering power studies. Acknowledging that power exists in all spheres of society, that it often operates covertly and is linked to unintended consequences, may well be combined with an insistence on purposive action as a basic frame of interpretation and explanation (Ortner 2006). If power is ubiquitous, it is because any social relation may engender inequality, but these relations need not have a systems quality. Power relations may appear as opaque because they are diffuse and complex, or because actors decide to conceal them, either as part of a manipulative strategy or due to social tact. Finally, it is a core assumption in the theory of social action that purposive choices in micro often entail unplanned and sub-optimal outcomes in macro. This is true for the cultural realm on a par with other social fields. It is often assumed that these outcomes are to the advantage of powerful actors, but they certainly need not be, as expressed in a main tenet in Marxian dialectics, that the strategies of powerful groups in the long run entail their downfall.

Preconditions for culture and power

Humans are symbolic beings, constantly interpreting the world around them. This is a necessary but not sufficient condition for understanding the place of power in culture. Additionally, human beings are endowed with a set of psychological predispositions which by themselves contribute to homogenous patterns of behavior. Some of them are linked to group functioning in various ways. On the *emotional* level, humans have a disposition for identification with larger groups, such as kinship groups, tribes or nations. Individuals experience themselves as group members and feel sorrow, joy or shame on behalf of the group or some of its members, e.g. a national sports team. On the *cognitive* level, the tendency to avoid cognitive dissonance contributes to the formation or general patterns of opinion. Own beliefs and conceptions are tested against those of others and made to conform to them. When *acting*, humans tend to reduce uncertainty by copying successful actions of others, doing as other people do. And when *acting in concert*, there is a tendency to call for leadership and adapt to hierarchical modes of organization (DiMaggio 1997). Another set of dispositions concerns self-delusion. Humans are only partly rational; they also have a general tendency to rationalize their own behavior, cling to unfounded convictions and adhere to ideologies based on false assumptions (Boudon 1994).

Viewed in isolation, these general dispositions may entail significant cultural patterns without hidden power structures of any sort being involved. At the same time these dispositions serve as material for the exertion of power. Organizing mass movements, shaping the public opinion, elaborating common symbolic systems, to mention a few examples, would hardly be possible without common psychological dispositions. The same is true for seemingly irrational mass behavior. But such dispositions do not function in uniform ways. They are tendencies, not deterministic blueprints, shared to varying degrees among individuals, and they are enacted in greatly different social situations. This means that they serve as common elements in the development of a wide variety of different and often opposing cultural formations, which constitute fields where power is played out.

Legitimacy

Long term, efficient uses of power normally rest on a relatively high degree of legitimacy. Admittedly, history shows that it is indeed possible to maintain control over large societies by means of threat and terror. But the costs of constant surveillance of large groups are formidable, and constitute important impediments to power holders. Hence, autocratic rulers tend to strengthen their regime by legitimizing strategies. Legitimacy is inherently a cultural phenomenon, expressed by signs and arguments, referring to religious or political doctrines, popularized through slogans, publicized through posters, public decorations and monuments. In order to be efficient they have to be conveyed directly or indirectly by power holders and accepted by their subordinates.

A special type is the tale of origin, linked to Weber's (1978 [1922]) concept of traditional authority. A group claims the right to rule because its members in the past victoriously fought a common enemy, developed common resources, founded a kingdom or established a special relationship to a deity. These stories often acquire an elaborate poetic-mythological form, frequently modified to suit new situations, ancient Greek mythology being a prominent example. Another paradigmatic case is the medieval sagas of Norwegian kings, which had the clear goal of supporting the existing king's claims to the throne. Moreover, legitimacy may be based on rational argumentation, Weber pointed out, focusing on established rights, regularized procedures or desirable outcomes. The present government may be accepted even by actors opposed to it if it is supported by a majority of citizens, has come to power in the lawful way, or due to its observed or assumed effects on the level of welfare.

Legitimacy may have non-rational sources as well. Claims to power positions may be legitimized by aesthetic appearances. Elaborate and expensive dress, large palaces, breathtaking cathedrals all reinforce the feeling that the powerful deserve their power (Daloz 2007). Upper classes legitimize their position by referring to their good manners and exquisite taste. Bourdieu (1996[1989]) circles around the attempt to uncover and describe inauthentic versions of legitimacy in a bottom-up perspective. 'Misapprehension' is his central concept. By means of subtle mechanisms of persuasion, members of society are drawn into supporting present power holders against their interests, or at least to abstain from protest. These examples may be interpreted in the light of the 'just world' hypothesis, holding that humans have a tendency to experience present conditions as generally fair and based on good reasons (Lerner 1980), aptly summarized in the Nietzschean 'aristocratic equation': Good = noble = powerful = beautiful = happy = loved by God (Nietzsche 1992 [1887]).

To be avoided in this context is describing established patterns of legitimacy as inherently static. Contestation of legitimacy is one of the core mechanisms in power struggles, and it takes a variety of cultural forms. In democratic societies argumentation may be the dominant form, found in all parts of society, from debates over canonization of works of art as part of national culture to questions of recognition of minority languages. But argumentation is far from the only form. Ridiculing power holders by more or less subtle jokes, parodies, ironic and ambiguous messages is found in most societies, and may be raised to an art form in semi-modern autocracies.

Power in rituals and performative speech acts

A ritual is a social occasion where participants recapitulate an ancient event, a common loyalty or a relationship to a deity. The ritual is stylized and is regularly repeated. Rituals may be informal parts of everyday interaction (Goffman 1967) like a family dinner, or deliberately and minutely designed as a great national or religious parade. Some rituals have strong emotional, even ecstatic components, whereas others may be slow, repetitive, undramatic, even boring to the outsider. The chief concern is that the 'right elements' are present in the right way (Alexander 2004). In both cases, the core of the ritual is the emotional energy elicited, giving participants a sense of commonality and heightened meaning. The power aspect resides in the identification of the participants with the basic values that are represented in the ritual, thereby reinforcing social rules and their legitimacy. Religious communion, parades on the national day, weddings and funerals, all have in common that those present internalize common values, and confirm their overarching position. Uses of poetry, rhythm, music and dance reinforce the relationship (Collins 2004).

Some rituals are centered on the exposition of conflict. Carnivals and feasts may depict the power relations upside down, serving as a sort of security valve in hierarchical societies. In many modern democracies, election campaigns are concluded by television debates where main contenders fight like gladiators over the confidence of their voters (Gomard and Krogstad 2001). Ritual-like patterns of behavior may also be elicited when conflict is put to the extreme. Victor Turner (1974) describes stylized processes with strong narrative components resembling dramas on the stage. Here, the initially weak party in the struggle achieves martyrdom by being killed by his opponent. As a martyr, he settles the conflict to the advantage of his beliefs in a way that he could not do while alive.

A special version of the ritual is the performative speech act (Austin 1962, Searle 1995). A performative speech act is a declaration that establishes a social fact. A meeting is opened when the chairman declares it to be so. When the registrar speaks the words 'I declare you man and wife', the couple is married. The ritualistic element is, again, the presence of 'the right elements'. Whether the declaration is made with some sort of public appeal or not, is of no significance. What matters is that the right words are spoken by the right person within the right framework. There are several implications for power relations in this context. First, the registrar is holding power, as she or he is in the position of possibly denying the performance of the wedding. At the same time, the registrar is acting as a delegate, filling a position that is neither shaped nor set up by him- or herself. The power of the delegate is in one sense connected to the representation of a larger system of social power, i.e. clerical or secular legislation issuing the right to perform certain tasks such as weddings (Bourdieu 1991).

Micro–macro relations

The forms of power outlined above are mainly related to small-scale situations; in direct conversation, or implicitly as part of interaction within families, among friends and in work groups. Even if their occurrence in micro affairs is basic, the overarching challenge for the understanding of power and culture is to build a bridge from micro to macro, from dyads and small groups to organizations and institutions. This may be conceived as a cycle of reciprocal effects: a structure-engendering action, which in turn reinforces structure (Giddens 1984). However, such a general formulation does not capture the actual emergence of structural features, and the way social patterns are purposively shaped to achieve given goals. A more precise conception for the present purposes is Michael Mann's synthesizing treatise on *The Sources of Social Power* (1986), centered around four 'networks' or fields of power – economic, political, military and ideological. His main point is that these power fields differ in technology, logistics and possibilities for control. Hence they develop differently, even if they to some extent are interdependent. Concerning the cultural field, a crucial point is that power aspects of culture to a large extent does not coincide with political or economic boundaries, even though culture to some extent is inscribed in the nation state.

The emergence of macro structures may be conceptualized in terms of clusters of mechanisms (Coleman 1986, Giesen 1987): *Aggregation* refers mainly to spontaneous behavior in large groups, such as street crowds and concert audiences. Goods, information and evaluation may be diffused through *networks*. Action may be shaped by *organizational* means, by building social movements or setting up organizations. Cultural patterns may increase their stability and viability by *institutionalization* of churches, national rituals, museums, festivals.

Crucial in the formation of cultural macro structures is the phenomenon of mediation. Messages are objectified and 'take on their own life' by being reported and commented on by third parties and diffused to larger networks, being shaped into formal speech and written texts, transposed into systems of communication such as money, and stored in archives, museums, on the Internet. These processes are shaped by communication technology as well as organizational forms, which in the terms of Mann (1986) comprise the logistics of cultural power. The diffusion of messages is dependent on the medium and its reproducibility. Messages may be transmitted orally, in written form, in print or by broadcast media. There is a general trend that the number of potential receivers has increased along this line; to take an obvious case, dissemination by radio being more efficient and less expensive than transmission of messages written by hand. But the relationship is in no way linear; the conservation and diffusion of oral messages is easily underrated as demonstrated, e.g. by the oral tradition of Homeric epics over several centuries in Ancient Greece.

POWER IN COMMUNICATION

In order to impinge on the behavior of others, actors must make themselves understood. This does not imply that power holders disclose their true intentions. Strategic behavior mostly presupposes that parts of the actors' intentions remain unexpressed or hidden. In more extreme cases deception is a necessary part of the strategy. But communication is still a necessary part of the strategy.

One exception to the necessity of communication is unexpected violent attacks on individuals or groups. Another is the erection of material obstacles that the target person or group must adjust to. In isolated cases such obstacles are devoid of meaning, but when permanently present they take on a symbolic character. The wall through Berlin was planned only as a material impediment to exit from East Germany, but it soon took on signal functions, serving as a command: Keep away, as well as a warning: If you force your way into forbidden territory you will be arrested, or even shot. In a wider context the Berlin wall became a vigorous symbol of the Cold War. After 1989 its material remains took on purely aesthetical functions, some parts left standing as monuments, whereas small bits became souvenirs for tourists. In its afterlife, the symbolism of the Berlin wall becomes contagious: e.g. the wall between Israeli and Palestinian territory is easily interpreted in similar terms.

Power in direct communication

Speech acts not only consist of the sentences actually spoken, but also of utterances intended to have an effect on the listener. The 'utterance' refers to the meaning implied, but not necessarily directly expressed by the speaker (Grice 1989). The sentence 'The window is open' presumably states a fact, but it may also imply the request 'Close the window', the prohibition 'Don't lean out' or be an answer to the question 'Why is it cold here?' The ability to elicit responses and actions reflects the *force* of an utterance. Speech acts intending to influence the listener directly may state solely what the listener is expected to do (directives, Searle 1969), or make commitments concerning future actions of the speaker herself as well (commissives, Austin 1962). The force of the utterance may have several different sources, based in the utterance itself or in external elements. External sanctions controlled by the speaker may be sufficient to realize her intentions, but in many cases indirect expressions and embellishing elements are necessary conditions if the utterance is to have the expected effect (Thomas 1996).

Threats and *promises* may be expressed head on: 'Give me your money, or I hit you', 'Get going, and I'll give you an apple when you come back'. Their effect is based in the common acknowledgment of the sanctions, which must be credible in order to work. If both parties are well informed about the sanctions, and the relationship is supposed to be upheld, the utterance is often euphemized and transmitted implicitly, as when the sentences above are modified to 'Today I'm in the mood for expensive champagne', 'I just came over a really tasty apple'.

Authority relations usually are legitimate relations of *command* and *subordination*. The normative element in the relationship mitigates the character of direct command and increases the expression of respect vis-à-vis the subordinate, even if commands are an essential part of the relationship, as e.g. in most business enterprises. Sanctions are present, but at some distance. Power relations are softened by indirect expressions, metaphors and humorous allusions to the tasks to be performed. This tendency is increased if subordinates are expected to independently make decisions on behalf of the organization. Without this expressive force, the readiness of the employee to perform the tasks may decrease considerably.

Normative commitments, mostly expressed in the form of *requests*, are basically neutral to the relationship of the communicating parties. When the neighbor asks for help because he has trouble with his car, the listener is bound by the norm 'Help thy neighbor', but has no formal obligation to do so. In this case the force of the request for help is dependent on the expressions of respect and gratitude from the speaker.

Appeals to listeners may evoke their self-esteem, their identity or belonging to a given group. If the implied utterance is 'As a reasonable individual you ought to prefer X' is to be accepted, no normative commitments or sanctions are at work, which means that the efficiency of the appeal is determined by the expressive force alone.

Descriptions of the world, construction of messages

Power may also be exerted indirectly by persuading actors to change their normative conceptions, or their beliefs about the world. The speaker issues no requests or commands, but pre-empts that the listener will make decisions on his own based on the new information.

This form of power in communication may be analyzed along the lines of classical theory of rhetoric, which is the earliest reflection over the preconditions for persuasive power (Pernot 2005). Aristotle distinguished between logos, pathos and ethos of the speech. *Logos* concerns the subject under discussion, how it is presented to give the audience optimal understanding (from the speaker's point of view), and how arguments are shaped. *Pathos* refers to the preemption of reactions in the audience; how to make people listen and arouse interest in the matter. The *ethos* aspect has to do with the confidence in the orator, how the speaker makes him- or herself credible in the eyes of the public.

Core mechanisms in the construction of descriptive messages are framing, selection, valorization and ascription of causality. Typically present in small-scale communication (Blakar and Rommetveit 1979), these aspects of messages are brought to the fore in documents, news and public speeches.

Framing relates to the contexts evoked by the message. Conditionally on the actualized context, a message may radically change its meaning. A simple example is the description of a bottle being half-full or half-empty, both of which are necessarily true at the same time. Depictions of the war in Iraq may alternatively be interpreted within the frame of war on terrorism or within a frame of Western imperialism (Goffman 1974). On a deeper level, frames are anchored in basic classification systems, as pointed out already by Durkheim (1965[1912]). In the wake of Mary Douglas (1991[1969]) this was taken up under the notion of 'boundary work', i.e. setting up distinctions between the worthy and the unworthy, the decent and the indecent, high culture and low culture, the right belief and heresy, national loyalty and treason (Lamont 1990, Lamont and Fournier 1992).

Messages are necessarily *selective*. No photograph is objective in the sense that it gives a complete account of a situation. It is impossible to represent all possible relevant elements in a subject up for discussion. That selected elements are brought to attention, while others remain unmentioned or undercommunicated, is part of any attempt at communication. All messages contain unstated implications, which to varying degrees may be concealed or brought forth. A conversation on future energy sources may emphasize the profitability of coal as an energy source, focus on the possible increases in pollution or point to effects on job mobility, but it cannot simultaneously cover all aspects.

Valorization

Making descriptions of given states and events, actors often have to choose between notions with positive or negative connotations. Generally, actors tend to euphemize their descriptions of self compared to others. The declination 'I am firm, you are obstinate, he is pig-headed' is a classic version of in- and out-group differentiation (Merton 1968 [1936]). In general 'our' boys are brave, the enemy's soldiers are ruthless; we are liberators, they are terrorists. Official documents tend to neutralize concepts with negative connotations, as when the notion of the 'poor' is replaced by 'citizens experiencing pecuniary stress'.

Assumptions about *causality* constitute a core dimension in communication. Any phenomenon is judged according to how it has emerged – how and why did it happen? A common evasion of judgment is the undercommunication of who it was that brought about a certain event. The statement 'Ethnic tensions arising: ten killed' denies or insinuates what happened and who was responsible, depending on the group of which the listener defines him- or herself as a member.

Appeal of messages: efficiency of communication

The appeal of a message reflects its ability to speak to the hearts of the audience. Appeal is raised by evoking matters related to the identity of listeners, or what they detest and are opposed to. The more unified the audience, the easier it is to play on common emotional references. And vice versa, to reach a multiplex audience, it is necessary to frame the message in a relatively generalized and abstract way, something that on the other hand may weaken its intensity and appeal. The difficult balance between these two alternatives lies at the heart of Max Weber's (1922) distinction between 'sect' and 'church', and his notion of 'bureaucratization of charisma'.

In order to elicit the 'right' response from the point of view of a power holder, messages need to be formed as clearly as possible to avoid misunderstandings. However, messages in the form of direct orders or recommendations – 'Don't walk on red', 'Buy local food' – tend to have little appeal in themselves. In addition to employing the poetic functions of words – metaphors and metonyms, rhymes and rhythm, or merging them with images and music (cf. p. 10) – messages acquire a stronger seductive effect when they speak directly to the deep concerns of listeners, mobilizing their well-established frames of interpretation. Charismatic authority has as its core the ability of the power holder to make members of the audience feel that each of them is seen, that their unexpressed hopes and fears are voiced by someone who is able to take care of them, and even link them to a higher reality, whether it be the nation, the class or God.

The deep structure of Erving Goffman's (1959) treatise on the presentation of self also sheds light on some general power mechanisms. One of his main points is that the establishment of any social interaction consists in the delineation of relevant themes, and thereby those to be avoided. The basic reason is found in Goffman's conception of tact: a reciprocal acknowledgment among actors of the common need for saving face and being exposed to social interaction as an acceptable person. Underneath, however, there is also a power theme: interacting parties have a potential 'power over the agenda', by means of knowledge about the other that might be exposed in the open. A special type of avoidance is that of silence or empty spaces, inducing the receiver to 'fill in' according to his or her own impulses. This not only initiates interpretative behavior, but also makes the receiver convey information about herself, thereby reinforcing the power of the other party. The sinner confessing to the priest is an example often cited (Foucault 1980[1976]).

Power and presentation of self

The ethos aspect of communication concerns the speaker presenting him- or herself as a competent and trustworthy person. Claims to trustworthiness may be justified by evoking former experience: I'm the person who has seen or lived through what I'm talking about. Or the speaker may refer to her broad knowledge or specific expertise in the matter under discussion. Moreover the listener may be reminded of former successes: Trust me, I have already demonstrated my ability to cope with similar problems. Alternatively the speaker may point to his official position, being in charge of the problem, and therefore deserving the attention of the audience (Bauhr and Esaiasson 2001). A special case of trustworthiness is based in general prestige. Actors holding a prestigious position in one social field often are allowed to transfer their credibility into other fields, as when the political views of a film star attracts special publicity. This process of transference is the core in Bourdieu's concept of symbolic capital (Bourdieu 1990[1980]).

Goffman's 'theatrical model' may be extended into a more general view of theatrical performances as a constitutive element in social interaction, by drawing the efficiency of communication into the core. Modern societies are permeated by acts of meaning, but to a large extent they take on another form than the traditional rituals outlined above. Political speeches in a wide sense may be interpreted on a par with theatrical performances, not only from the personal point of view, but also connected to the shaping of the 'script' to be performed as well as the effects on the public in a parallel way to that of theater audiences (Alexander 2004).

Politics: varieties of charismatic power

In democratic countries politicians are confronting a set of conflicting expectations. They should appear similar to the citizens that they are representing, while at the same time they have to distinguish themselves, in order to show that they are able to fill their demanding responsibilities. Charismatic presentation of self is a way of bridging this divide, but the way that it is done rests on specific cultural repertoires (Swidler 1986). When the South Korean politician Ban Ki-Moon was elected General Secretary of the United Nations, the question was raised whether his personality was sufficiently charismatic for him to fill the position. Ki-Moon replied by pointing to his roots in Asian culture where charisma takes on a different, more low-key form than in many Western countries (Hoge 2006). A similar point is made in detailed comparative studies of political charisma in different countries, distinguishing an outer-directed, conquering form of charisma from a more inner-directed, compassionate form (Krogstad and Storvik 2007).

In the Scandinavian countries, expectations that politicians appear in a modest way are rather extreme. In Nigeria, at the other end of the spectrum, politicians unconditionally have to demonstrate their power ostentatiously, by their way of dressing, their cars and their residences. The explanation for this difference seems to lie in the arena of politics. In Scandinavian welfare states, politicians act as, and are regarded as, representatives of a formalized system of provisions, whereas in Nigeria, where formal welfare systems are absent, politicians must affirm by their appearance that they are able to collect resources to be distributed among clients and supporters (Daloz 2003, 2007).

Close relations between power and sex also come out in politicians' presentation of self, in Scandinavia mostly very implicitly, in a larger country like France quite openly. In the age of mass television credibility is intimately linked to personal attractiveness, and lack of sex appeal easily translated into a lack of political appeal. Being at the head of a large nation presupposes a will to conquest in a double sense of the word: conquest of the position at the national level, and taking a conquering stand in the competition on the international scene. This takes on both a political dimension and a gender dimension. Hence, women encounter special problems in shaping charismatic images of self when entering high power positions, in making femininity go together with charismatic dominance. In Scandinavia, where charismatic elements are played out in a more low-key manner, however, there seems to be more room for the exposition of femininity in power positions (Krogstad and Storvik 2007).

The object as message

The presentation of the political self is not limited to the specifically personal image. At all times, power holders have presented themselves by signs and symbols. Objects draw up and describe boundaries between social groups by means of decor and embellishment of homes, gardens, dress. A related mode of message lies in the uniqueness of the object. Expensive goods accessible only by the happy few, lend luster to their owners and users by their scarcity. Alternatively, scarcity may rest formal monopoly or quasi-monopoly. In European monarchies of the Renaissance, red wine was the color reserved for kings. The ascent of a new king on the throne in pre-revolutionary France was followed by a change in style in furniture and dress, with the exquisite versions reserved for the king himself.

Objects not only are linked to power holders, but also serve as their representation. An extreme case is again the French king, whose utensils were shown the same reverence as his person (Auslander 1996). In societies where power holders have a shorter time horizon in their incumbency, decoration to a greater degree follows the role, not the person. The power of top politicians is underlined by their dwellings being made into national symbols: the White House, Palais de l'Élysée or 10 Downing Street.

Objects also are made sources of legitimacy. The exquisite dress and the stylish home bring forth in spectators feelings of being themselves unworthy, trivial, insufficient or ugly. Thus the beautiful are felt to deserve their powerful position (see also p. 213). As a contrast, objects have been linked to legitimacy due to their roots in mass production. In Marxian theory of commodity fetishism (Marx 1998 [1845]), the industrially produced object exerts a special fascination because it hides its own production history. The shining surface of the brand new automobile, all chrome and lacquer, seems to tell a story of an object engendered by itself, untouched by human hand. Its power lies in its mute but forceful appeal: 'Buy me, I'm all for you'. The exposition of the object as a commodity, framed by the well-filled shop, conceals the circumstances of its creation as a product of exploited labor. Thereby the aesthetic aspects of the commodity contribute to the legitimacy of capitalist production.

Frames of interpretation and aesthetic hierarchy

A distinction between immediate, sensuous and cultivated taste in the evaluation of artistic objects is a theme in the sociology of culture going back to Kantian aesthetic philosophy. The basic difference between the two types is linked to degrees of abstraction. The sensuous taste is concrete, judging pictures as to whether their motifs are recognizable in the real world, music according to whether it is beautiful. The cultivated taste abstracts from immediate impressions, and judges art works according to abstract aesthetic criteria, applied within the context of its place in art history.

In the art world of modern society, this distinction forms a hierarchy. The abstract mode is linked to real artistic achievements, whereas the sensuous mode is connected to popular culture, and is often rejected as reactionary or manipulative, even by Marxist theoreticians of culture. T.W. Adorno's rejection of jazz (1981 [1955]) stands out as a blunt example, but the basic conception is much broader. As opposed to the commercialization of cultural products, true art has been conceived by critical theorists as the only social field in opposition to the prevailing capitalist society, as a 'realm of freedom' foreshadowing liberation from the 'realm of necessity' of existing society (Marcuse 1964).

This theme was turned on its head by Bourdieu in his *Distinction* (1984 [1979]). He attacked the established hierarchy as imposed on the lower classes by the bourgeoisie, with the assumption that the established aesthetic hierarchy is a mode of domination of the lower classes. Because it falls outside the capacity of ordinary people to interpret abstract art or modern music, they are judged as inferior, and to some extent legitimize this judgment by accepting the established aesthetic hierarchy. At the same time, Bourdieu cannot be interpreted as defending popular culture in opposition to high-brow art. He is also skeptical to the mass media, especially television (Bourdieu 1998[1996]), much on a par with Horkheimer and Adorno's (1979 [1947]) criticism of the culture industry from the immediate post-World War II period. However, paradoxically the development of technologies of communication, along with the vast commercialization of cultural production since the 1960s, has contributed to blurring the boundaries between popular culture and high art in film, music and literature. Hence, in the globalized culture of the early twenty-first century the hierarchical relation between aesthetic preferences has lost much of its force.

Communication and social control

When messages increase their appeal by being metaphorical and indirect, the chances for misunderstanding are similarly increased. The possibility of misinterpretation, and even drastic transformation, of messages increases when they are mediated by several steps, as, for example, are rumors in large networks or news transmitted by one mass medium and passed on to others. The feather grows to five hens, or the serious problem ends up being defined as a minor incident. The danger of misrepresentation leads up to measures of control, in the forms of standardization of speech and codes of interpretation, embodied in formalized rules or in informal standards of appropriateness in communication.

Social control in a more direct mode concerns what citizens are allowed to express openly, and what is proscribed, tabooed and can only be uttered implicitly. No society is without prohibitions on what may be said in public, a majority of societies are subject to strong informal restrictions or direct censorship. Traditionally, prohibitions are associated with the reverence of the highest powers: God, the king or the ruling party. A majority of the population in the world – still living in non- or semi-democratic regimes – risks severe punishment for criticism of political leaders or religious beliefs. Regimes legitimized by freedom of expression still prohibit utterances possibly threatening national security. Forbidden themes change over time. In the 1950s, being attacked as un-American might be detrimental to one's social prospects; in Turkey people still may be taken to court for assumed un-Turkish utterances. Western societies in general are becoming more tolerant toward explicit descriptions and images of sexuality, while utterances which may be seen as discriminatory or racist are now forbidden to a larger degree, either informally or directly by legislation.

POWER AND DOMINANCE IN CULTURAL FORMATIONS

Social structures do not act. Social effects are caused by social actors, whether individuals or groups. Social structures form a necessary context for action, actions entail a reconfiguration of structures, and the actions in the next round contribute to shaping the identity of the actors themselves. In many cases it suffices to focus on the structure of the context to interpret and explain social dynamics. This is true when the patterns of action are trivial or highly stylized by role expectations. At the same time, focusing mainly on structural features entails insufficient understanding of social dynamics and social power. This point does not imply a denial of cultural dominance, but an aim at making the emergence of the wide variety of such outcomes understandable.

Structures of dominance may be largely unintended, but nevertheless effective. At the other end of the spectrum, it happens only exceptionally that the dominant ideas are accepted and shared by all members of a society. Even in traditional societies, hostilities between rivaling factions of belief are the rule, rather than the exception. In large, modern societies, it is the rather continuous struggles over values as conceived by Max Weber (1922) that is the normal condition. Thus, in order to understand the phenomenon of cultural dominance it is necessary to lay out the larger set of mechanisms at work (Mann 1986). Below the four sets of micro–macro relations already sketched (p. 7) are put to use: aggregate effects, network diffusion, organization and institutionalization.

Aggregate cultural effects

A much cited type of aggregate effects in the social sciences is a set of simultaneous, individually rational actions entailing unintended, collectively irrational outcomes. Advertising is a pertinent example, where the aggregate effect of individual action is the emergence of a general culture of consumption. Most advertisers are fairly indifferent to the general patterns of consumption. They concentrate on targeting their audiences and developing the most efficient means to persuade them to buy more of a given set of commodities. However, individually rational advertisers include non-rational appeals to the public in order to increase their communicative efficiency. And each actor copies the successes of their competitors (Leiss, et al. 1990). Even if prospective buyers are rational as well, they also respond to appeals to their irrational desires. Hence, the aggregate effect may be the emergence of a commercial culture with significant elements of irrationality. For this to happen, a threshold effect (Schelling 1978) is required, such that consumers encounter appeals to the non-rational part of their personality sufficiently often to adapt to its signals.

Another set of models focuses on individuals and the aggregation of their group based experiences over time. These groups may be linked to social class, to contrasts between urban and rural locales, gender divides or relationships between minorities and the majority. In their everyday life members of, e.g. minorities may encounter slight skepticism or reservations in the behavior of majority members, such that each event seen in isolation must be judged insignificant. When continuously repeated these experiences are easily interpreted by members of the minority group as clear signs of discrimination. Such patterns are reinforced if the dominating group generally is accorded higher social prestige.

Aggregate effects may emerge even when two groups are living peacefully side by side, without one group attempting to dominate the other, e.g. two tolerant religious denominations. In the case where one group is a majority and the other a minority, the sheer fact of being in minority may lead to feelings of being dominated by the majority – 'They are always the ones that count!'. The absence of role models demonstrating that it is possible for members of the minority group or the weak group to attain advantageous social positions on a par with the majority is sufficient for the interpretation of dominance to take root.

A central aspect of the latter models is that no single actor exerts power in a direct way, so nobody needs to feel responsible for the perceived patterns. That may be one reason for their stability.

Models of common goods

Standard theory of collective goods focuses on social phenomena that would be to the benefit of everyone, while at the same time every individual has an interest in being a free rider and not contribute to the erection or maintenance of the good. The result is that the collective good is not produced. The 'tragedy of the commons', where every actor has an interest in overexploiting a common resource base, is an oft-cited example. Related models may be identified in the cultural realm, typical forms of cultural common goods being group equilibria or group integration.

In his discussion of segregated housing patterns, Schelling (1978) demonstrates that a mixed neighborhood may be stable as long as each actor accepts that half of their neighbors may belong to their own group and the other half to the opposite group. But this equilibrium is very vulnerable; a few deviant cases suffice to initiate a chain reaction leading to a strictly segregated pattern even if this is intended by nobody. A handful of individuals may also intentionally influence dominant patterns of interpretation in much larger groups. Openly discriminatory behavior among a small number of people is sufficient to create significant strains between a majority and a minority group, if it entails changes in expectations in the minority. A drastic example of the same pattern is processes of ethnic cleansing, as observed, e.g. in former Yugoslavia. Even rumors set out by a small faction about expected attacks on the own group from the opposite party make each of them ready for pre-emptive attacks on the other; with mass killings as the final result.

Cultural diffusion

Social prestige serves as a crucial motor in the diffusion of cultural patterns. An old, but still pertinent example is found in the world of fashion. The 'trickling down' model describes how new styles originate in the expensive *haute couture* fashion houses, are transposed to restricted and relatively expensive markets, and in the last step transmitted to the mass market and made accessible to ordinary consumers. The point here is that potentially everyone buys into style originated in the most prestigious layers of society (Fallers 1954).

If trickling down effects rest on a sort of consensus across groups with different prestige, cultural encounters may on the contrary be very strenuous. Many societies have a clear hierarchy of dialects, France being a typical example. Given the general recognition of the Parisian dialect, when speakers of the vernacular in the French provinces encounter representatives of the dominant sociolect, they may experience a feeling of distance, insufficiency or even shame of not mastering the official spoken language (Bourdieu 1991). For some people the typical reaction is adapting to the official norm, others respond by withdrawal, even resistance.

More drastic versions of linguistic divides are found in societies where relatively small linguistic minorities use a distinctly different language than the majority or the dominant groups. If the minority is below a certain numerical threshold, it becomes culturally dependent on the majority. When the numbers of speakers of the minority language do not reach a critical mass at which they can sustain separate general news media or publishing houses to fully cover their own needs, the minority are forced to enter the domain of the majority and acquire the majority language, while the majority is not dependent on the minority culture. This pattern is repeated on the international level, where representatives of a few languages struggle over the dominating position in the world, whereas small linguistic communities must adapt to them.

Access, framing, interpretation

A well-known power position is that of the gate-keeper. The secretary of the boss has a special opportunity in filtering information flows and regulating access; which messages will be let through, who is allowed to talk to him, and when. In informal networks of communication similar filtering processes take place. Some persons may serve as messengers or gate-openers to powerful actors if they have their confidence, thereby enhancing their own power positions. A generalized version occurs with increasing amounts and complexity of information, making the majority of actors dependent on opinion leaders to sort and interpret information (Katz and Lazarsfeld 1955).

The degree of information overflow typical in many areas of modern societies entails a professionalization of opinion formation. Interpretation, framing and reframing of facts, norms and aesthetic judgments becomes a specialty for politicians, lawyers, public commentators and intellectuals. To varying degrees their ideas trickle down to a larger public, to become conventional wisdom. Typical examples are relatively recent changes in the interpretation of multi-culturalism, conceptions of gender equality, formulations of class interests or the value of popular culture. In the political field interpretive and reframing activities are increasingly organized on a large scale in think-tanks.

The learned discourse

The intimate relationship between knowledge and power was a main thread in the work of Michel Foucault, who analyzed the emergence of scientific theories by focusing on their underlying premises. His point of departure was that these theories never reach an end stage where they can claim to represent the absolute truth. It is a matter of debate to which degree Foucault took the fully relativistic position that knowledge in the last instance is reducible to power relations, but this position is not a necessary implication of his work. The main point is that the diffusion of scientific theories depends on the general acceptance of a specific theoretical structure, which is accepted as representing the production of scientific truths. In this sense, the idea of the 'force of the better argument' is compatible with Foucault's thinking, even though the (provisional) acceptance of a theory as true is also dependent on power relations.

One way of understanding these power relations is to take an approach relatively close to that described above in the discussion of communicative power in everyday life (p. 13). Foucault (1970 [1966], 1971) inaugurated a new turn in discourse analysis by focusing on the elements taken for granted in scientific theories. Scientific discourse, as he uses the term, refers to the way that the object of the discipline is constituted, how core elements under investigation are to be interpreted, as exemplified by the turn from the humoral to the mechanistic perspective in medicine (Foucault 1981 [1963]). The established 'ways of talking' within a given discipline rests on a set of exclusions. Some things are not discussed, such that the discourse presupposes a common conception of rationality, or that the speaker only has unselfish motives for his or her utterances. Excluded also is a set of prospective participants in the discussion, namely those who are lacking the necessary formal qualifications. To use a crude example, in the 'normal' psychiatric discourse those who are not 'normal' themselves do not have a position. There is no way to enter the learned discourse from their point of departure.

Religious doctrines and cultural struggles

Religious zeal as motivation for organized cultural and political struggles is ubiquitous: from the conquests of Islam, the Medieval crusades, the Thirty Years War, up to the armed conflicts in the latter half of the twentieth century in the Middle East, the Balkans, northern Ireland and Afghanistan. One question is to what extent these conflicts are about religion and to which extent religious zeal serves as a cover for other worldly interests. Examples of people living peacefully side by side, despite wide differences in their creeds, are abundant. Cultural clashes tend to ignite when humans feel they have more to fight over than their beliefs alone. The diffusion of the Christianity in early medieval Europe was largely motivated by attempts to build a rudimentary state in competition with local chiefs who were also religious leaders in their communities. Later, the Reformation was introduced by kings and princes in order to strengthen their own position, both politically and economically, by confiscating papal goods for the crown.

The significance of religion for economic change was highlighted in Max Weber's discussion of the effects of Calvinism on the emergence of capitalism (Weber 1976 [1904]), and his great treatise on the world religions (Weber 1999 [1922]). The existence of general effects of religion on economic behavior is undisputed, but Weber's thesis on capitalism as the outgrowth of Calvinism has not resisted closer scrutiny. One set of counter-arguments is related to the historical process itself. There are strong indications that flowering versions of capitalism appeared in northern Italy and other regions of central Europe well in advance of the reformation (Boudon 1991, Gorski 2006). Even though the motivational mechanism assumed by Weber, that capitalism as an economic system materialized as an unintended consequence of self-delusion among Calvinist merchants, is somewhat strained, the Protestant work ethic undoubtedly was a central force in the growth of capitalism in northern Europe, and even more so in northern America.

A significant case in the modern world is the growth of political islam, which acquires political power more as a force of protest than as an agent of social change. In this respect it is parallel to the position of the Christian churches in the Communist world, which became arenas of resistance to dictatorship, but then lost much of its force after the fall of the Iron Curtain. The crucial difference lies in the goals of political islam, which is not the establishment of individualist freedom, but rather the restoration of pre-capitalist society.

The public sphere

The public sphere is the arena where citizens meet and exchange views on matters of common interest: the Athenian agora and the Roman forum were both market places and arenas for discussion and public speeches. Specific to modern societies is the enlargement and shaping of the public sphere via medialization – by magazines, newspapers and broadcasting, lately also by the Internet. The emergence of the public sphere entailed crucial changes in the power structure of modern societies. By the distribution of the printed word, social and political powers had to face the force of argumentation. In itself the force of the better argument was nothing new, but had its background in the traditions for discussion and disputation in the universities. What came with modern society was that the force of argumentation replaced the sovereign's will as the decisive element in the relationship between citizens and the state. The public sphere in its modern version was rooted in the eighteenth century salons, coffee houses and print-shops. Its emergence was intimately connected to the growth of large market formations, which is a precondition for the distribution of media reaching a large readership. This relationship is ambiguous, however, because the media are commercialized products at the same time.

From different positions Jürgen Habermas and Richard Sennett have described the ambiguities and subsequent changes in the public sphere in Europe. Habermas (1989 [1962]) conceived a decisive turn in the functioning of the public sphere in the growing commercialization of the media, newspapers becoming a product on the market, while being more and more dependent on advertising. In a parallel process politics and the market became intermixed in the latter half of the nineteenth century, restricting the free development of civil society and reducing discussing citizens to a passive audience. In later formulations, however, Habermas (1994) modified his pessimistic view of the passivity of the public, underlining the positive impact of mass education on the formation of public opinion. From a different angle Sennett (1977) outlines what he characterizes as the fall of public man, to the advantage of more unrestrained subjectivity that is the hallmark of the commercialized media. A crucial moment was Émile Zola's intervention in the Dreyfus affair. By putting his 'J'accuse!' on the front page of the newspaper *L'Aurore*, Zola opened up for the subsequent subjectification – dominance of the ethos aspect – of the public sphere, at the cost of rational deliberation, according to Sennett.

Structurally, the changes in the public sphere cover the transformation of communication from dispersed networks to mass circulation, from relatively slow distribution to instant diffusion. In a power perspective, it may be described as a transformation from the effects of the better argument to the effects of the most efficient statement. Actors aiming to disseminate efficient statements are, of course, salesmen and politicians seeking mass sales or mass support. But to the degree that intellectuals wish to influence public opinion, they too are forced to operate from a subjectified position in the medialized public sphere.

At the same time the development of the media is a core condition for democracy, by being a channel for critical comments on the part of citizens vis-à-vis power holders. Both economically and politically the media are dependent on their readers, listeners and spectators (Schudson 1995), something that strengthens the power of the public. But power also flows in the opposite direction. The media cannot dictate their audience which opinions to hold; their power lies in their ability to turn the attention of the public in a given direction by selecting information, shaping perceptions, and evoking core values (McCoombs and Shaw 1972) (see p. 218).

Cultural confrontation: struggles over hegemony

Max Weber's (1978[1922]) conception of modern society as an arena for continuous value struggles was central also to ideas of 'hegemony' and cultural leadership as conceived by Antonio Gramsci. A prominent leader in the Italian Communist movement of the between war era, Gramsci pointed out that struggles between social classes have a strong cultural component, and thus that the traditional Marxian notion of structure and superstructure had to be modified. He interpreted the contradictions between the ruling classes and the working class in terms of a struggle over dominance between the teachings of the Catholic Church and the emerging worldview of the working class built on science, embodied in the technology of modern industry. The existing hegemony of the religious doctrine, upheld by a vast amount of rituals, aesthetic messages, preaches, tracts and a large theological edifice, was the result of an immense organizational activity on the part of the Church. For the working class to gain momentum in the class struggle, it had to organize a competitive cultural movement based on scientific thinking (Gramsci 1973).

Gramsci delineated a struggle between a world view which he regarded as primitive and outdated, and one which heralded the future, representing the rational thinking of the enlightened working class. More than half a century after his death the picture looks different. The cultural basis for broad class solidarity has crumbled. The growth of cultural pluralism opens up for a much more floating and multi-layered situation, where hegemonies become less sharply delineated and less stable over time. Laclau and Mouffe (2001[1985]) reformulated an influential revision of the theory of hegemony within the framework of a philosophy of language, while at the same time underlining the significance of struggle between competing social forces. Freed from its basis in overarching class struggles, the concept of hegemony is more aptly connected to more specific social arenas, and linked up with social movements challenging cultural dominance from various sides, struggling for civil rights, gender equality or environmental concerns. These movements are constituted on the basis members' intuitive reactions to social concerns, which are transformed by the movement organizations into full-fledged ideological justifications of their cause (Tarrow 1998, della Porta et al. 2006).

In struggles over hegemony the chances of success or failure depends on five elements: (i) the ability to set focus on a given problem, (ii) the ability to formulate own interests as consistent with general interests in face of the problem, (iii) an elaborate theory – moral doctrine, theology, scientific theory – ensuring the credibility of argumentation, (iv) access to channels of communication, and (v) ability to mobilize citizen support for own cause. If attempts to change hegemonies do not succeed, additional reasons may be that movements face considerable collective action problems (Olson 1965), or lack sufficient resources to formulate alternative views (Bourdieu 1991). A core role is also held by the credibility of the theoretical justification (point iii above). A few examples show the variation from failure to success: one reason for the emergence of neo-liberal thinking is the decreased support for Keynesian economics. After long struggles with disbelief in the results of climate research movements to stop CO_2 pollution seem to gain terrain. The feminist movement has profited from the strong moral imperative of equal treatment of individuals irrespective of gender.

Cultural institutionalization: social integration by representation

With the emergence of large-scale nation-states in the Western world, mainly during the nineteenth century, the integration of the population by a diversity of institutions became crucial. Searle (1995) points to broad types of institution building, money being his favored example, which may be seen as generalizations of speech acts ('We declare this piece of paper to be a five euro bill'). At the core of such generalization processes are repeated sets of delegation, assigning rights and duties to specific persons. Central institutional phenomena, such as property rights and marriage, are developed from generalized speech acts.

Additional modes of integration of the population lie in the early modern state's ability to make itself visible by cultural representations. In the decades before and after 1900, large-scale 'invention of tradition' took place in Europe (Hobsbawm 1983). National mythologies were construed on the basis of folk music and popular fairytales. Folk dance and national costumes were stylized and formalized into general codes. Public space was given a national signature by being filled with national symbols. Streets and places were named after national heroes or significant events. Monuments and statues were set up celebrating national heroes, local notables and mythological characters to such a degree that one observer characterized the French *Belle époque* as a period of 'statuomania' (Agulhon 1978). Similar processes are found in the United States where George Washington and Abraham Lincoln in particular have been the object of veneration as the founding fathers of the republic. The breath of the interpretation of their lives and acts allows Americans of all political persuasions to view them as the central heroes in national history (Schwartz 1991, 2000). Likewise, festivals and commemoration of crucial events in the history of the nation ensure the cultural continuity of political power (Spillman 1997).

Many more recent monuments of national significance are not surrounded by a comparable consensus. Competing interpretations of the legitimacy of past actions shade into present-day politics. War memorials may evoke contesting interpretations of the war itself, and thereby intense public debate, as demonstrated in the disputes over the memorial dedicated to American casualties in Vietnam (Wagner-Pacifici and Schwartz 1991), or the memorial over the Jewish population in Berlin (Young 2000). The same is true for victims of terrorism, whether on the right or left (Tota 2003). The fall of Communism in eastern Europe led to the dismantling of an enormous number of statues of the founders of Marxism–Leninism, some of them destroyed, others collected in special parks, celebrating the fall from power of the rulers of yesterday (Levinson 1998).

In architecture and city planning power is delineated more abstractly. The solemn character of courthouses and parliamentary buildings bear witness of the presence and power of the state. Typically, the solemn presence of these buildings rests on ancient power symbols, columns from ancient Greece and Rome, often in combination with baroque vaults, as in Washington's Capitol or Berlin's Reichstag. When cathedrals represent the power of spirituality, they do so by the height of their towers, but foremost by the enormous distance from floor to ceiling in the inner space. Confronted by such spaces, humans cannot avoid being aware of their own bodily and personal limitations. In contrast, the skyscraper also repeats and increases the striving upward; its towering profile is turned into a monument to the victory of capitalism, but it does not bring forth in visitors the spiritual awe created by the interior of the cathedral.

Nation-building by cultural institutions

The presence of the state is felt not only in its material monumentality. Arts, sciences and educational institutions constitute a common ground for painting the pictures of the national state as an imagined community (Anderson 1983). Cultural institutions embrace specific public institutions such as museums and universities, but just as much publishing houses and galleries creating and operating in markets for distribution of cultural products, and media for criticism and evaluation of these products in the non-state public sphere.

The relationship of cultural institutions to social and political power is twofold. On the one hand they represent the nation as a whole, and in this capacity dominate the public education from elementary schools to universities. Being German, Yugoslavian or British means that these institutions become a primary horizon for generalized interpretations of the world, linked to mastery of the national language, identification with the nation's history (Hohendahl 1989, Wachtel 1998). Thereby the individual comes to understand him- or herself as a subject in the double sense of being subjected to the state, while also being able to act as a sensible citizen (Engelstad 2003). This homogenization, mainstreaming and disciplining of citizens through a national heritage is felicitously captured in the book title *Peasants into Frenchmen* (Weber 1976).

At the same time, cultural institutions are ambiguous. The arts are never only conformist; often they are openly rebellious. Interpretation of the arts is not static, but changes with the emergence of new historical challenges. Hence, cultural institutions also draw up an arena for contestation and cultural struggles. The arts, foremost literature, become a source for the understanding of the specific national alignments of conflict, between classes, genders, religious denominations, regions, urban and rural ways of life (Griswold 2000, Engelstad 2003). In this sense, integration through culture is a variety of integration through conflict.

Conflict is also a central element in processes of canonization. Bourdieu (1993) sketches a conflictual field of literary criticism segmented into at least three sub-fields, those of popular culture, mainstream art and the avant-garde. Struggles over definition of artistic quality are continuously fought out between segments as well as within each segment. The interpretation and reinterpretation of the significance of stylistic innovation, reader appeal and commercial success is a continuous theme in evaluations of authors and literary works.

These dynamics point to a crucial tension in the cultural basis for modern democratic societies. Core values in democratic societies are equality of opportunity and freedom of expression in a broad sense. These values are institutionalized through public policies, political movements, religious denominations and civic associations. In the educational system the values of freedom and equality are the object of massive indoctrination, to the degree that they appear as self-evident. But in other parts of the world they are far from evident. Democracy is confronted by theocracy as an overarching doctrine. The ideal of equality is standing up against conceptions of essential and ineradicable inequalities between the sexes, between social groups or hierarchical positions. This contrast demonstrates the fact that institutionalized values are neither self-evident, nor the result of logical proofs. In the last instance they can only be defended on the basis of beliefs.

Cultural power in the market

The last decades of the twentieth century saw a shift in cultural power from public institutions to the markets for mass produced commodities in the Western world. Due to growing affluence in large parts of the population, design, advertising and distribution of everyday utensils has acquired a distinct aesthetic and cultural component. Thorstein Veblen's (1994 [1899]) conception of conspicuous consumption, originally alluding to the upper classes, has become relevant for the majority of the population in modern societies. In a parallel move the culture industry has taken off as one of the major industries in the modern economy, creating role models for a large number of people. The result is aesthetization of everyday life on an unprecedented scale.

The main power component here lies in the process of branding of commercial goods, by means of symbolic connotations. Through advertising campaigns the brand name is connoted to youthfulness, playfulness, sophistication or seriousness, depending on the target group. The crucial link in branding is the combination of confidence – the customer presumes that the soft drink will be of the same quality tomorrow that it is today – and identity – the quality and characteristics of the product spill over to the customer herself. These presumptions are reinforced by the observation that large groups of consumers think the same way – aptly illustrated by an old Elvis Presley LP cover announcing in capital letters: '50 million fans can't be wrong'.

These processes lead to a cultural homogenization, but they engender counter-movements as well. The accessibility of objects also drives forth differentiation of tastes and preferences. Visible sub-groups constitute their identity by going against the tide, elaborating competing aesthetic norms in opposition to the establishment. The result is a peculiar dialectic; whereby counter-cultural aesthetics are picked up by mass producers when they have reached a critical mass of adherents.

Social class and cultural power

The significance of cultural power for social class relations, always a central topic in sociology, received a definite turn with Bourdieu's *Distinction* (1984). In the classical Marxian formulation class struggle was conceived as a struggle over power to govern society as a whole. Social classes were constituted by their relations in the social production (class in itself), but their struggle over power would also be determined by the class consciousness of the working class (class for itself) (Marx and Engels 1992 [1848]). This basic conception was also present in Gramsci's later formulation, as mentioned above (p. 227), albeit with a greater emphasis on the necessity of a vision embracing society as a whole, not only reflecting the position of the working class.

Although both Marx and Gramsci still have a status as classics in the social sciences, their conception of class struggles is now obsolete. The framework common to contemporary theories of social classes is that of more or less permanent patterns of inequality, not of transcendence of the capitalist mode of production. In the optics of culture and power the central question concerns the role played by culture in conserving existing inequalities between classes. Here two theoretical strands are distinguished; one holding that culture reinforces existing class inequalities, another that cultural complexities contribute to erasing very clear class differences.

The first view builds on the work of Bourdieu. Very crudely, the theory maintains that class differences not only are reproduced, but even widened due to cultural factors. Members of social classes are differently socialized, due to their specific habitus they have different codes for good manners, different preferences in cultural consumption and different experiences in schools. The system of cultural values, prestige hierarchies and cultural policies systematically works to the advantage of the upper strata, and contributes systematically to the widening of the gap between classes. In addition to being economically disadvantaged, the lower classes are culturally exploited and manipulated into accepting the established class differences as legitimate.

There is no general theory opposing this view, but a set of counter-arguments converging on the presumption that Bourdieu's theory exaggerates the systematic linkage of class and culture. Empirical studies show that the picture painted by Bourdieu for France, does not apply to the United States (Lamont 1992). Others have doubted the systematic class boundaries in cultural consumption patterns, showing that people with high education tend to be culturally omnivorous, enjoying simultaneously hip hop and classical music (Peterson and Simkus 1992).

This research may be complemented by some general observations on the fragmentation of the relationship between class and culture. First, the strong socialization effects implied in the concept of habitus are hardly realistic. Moreover, the occupational structure forming the basis of class boundaries is constantly changing, thereby also blurring the effects of socialization. Second, the dominating culture in modern societies is not that of the upper class or the educated class. It is the culture of the mass media, which has rather strong appeal to members of all classes, despite significant distinctions between cultural segments. Finally, social movements building on identity politics tend to cut across class lines, as pointed out by Laclau and Mouffe (2001[1985]) (see p. 227). The same is true for religious movements. Hence, a theory of static class relations seems less plausible than that of cultural fragmentation and fluid class boundaries. These points do not imply that class boundaries are disappearing, only that they are in change and vary across societies. Cultural power relations possibly contribute more to the fluidity of class boundaries than to their stability.

The sense of self

Power is an active force in the formation of the self, was a main point in Foucault's later work. At the same time he underlined the ambiguity of these effects. Power is not only oppressive; it 'incites, it induces, it seduces', and even though 'in the extreme it constrains or forbids absolutely', power also 'creates things, produces pleasure, shapes knowledge, creates discourse' (Foucault 1980: 119, 1983: 220). Foucault himself did not elaborate this point much further, but this duality of power in shaping the self may be traced in other parts of the literature on power and culture.

The alienated self

That cultural power has a series of alienating effects is a core point in Bourdieu's work (1986). The school system is ascribed general alienating effects, not only because it confronts students from lower classes with a culture that is basically rooted in the upper middle classes, but because it also induces them to take for granted misrepresentations of the culture of their class of origin. Such mechanisms may lead to withdrawal, self-contempt or even self-denial.

The undeserving self
Being continuously confronted by the elegance, riches and good manners of other people leads to a general feeling of the subject being unworthy. The same is true for those with low education, and insufficient knowledge and experience. Typically, the subject may compensate his or her insufficiency by accepting a servant position. This may have the double advantage of protection by the powerful, and emanation of social prestige from the powerful to their subordinates.

The conformist self
A basic tenet of the early Frankfurt school was that the cultural industry reinforces individuals' tendency to self-delusion. The market pressures on the cultural industry make it dependent on reinforcing people's wishful thinking. The most extreme example is the worship of the American Dream. The public is constantly showered by films, talk shows, novels, magazines reporting social success stories, with the message that everyone can 'make it'. These have, according to Horkheimer and Adorno (1979[1947]) the double effect of mobilizing and tranquilizing at the same time. They create support for a capitalist system which promises riches to all but makes it impossible for the majority to attain that goal, while at the same time directing attention away from the real problems created by capitalism.

The commercialized self
In modern societies the labor market, making labor power into a commodity, is a normal phenomenon. In sales and service enterprises, the commodity character tends to spill over to the appearance of the employee. The salesperson is expected to show that he cares for the customer, the air hostess is instructed to demonstrate personal attachment to the passengers. The result is easily that not only labor power, but emotions are commercialized and exploited (Hochschild 1983).

The staged self
A dialectical contrast to the description by Horkheimer and Adorno is a post-modern portrait of the individual with a fluid identity, shaping him- or herself by choosing worldviews and freely combining aesthetical forms of self-presentation procured by the cultural marketplace. The emergence of aesthetic freedom is due to the combination of commercialization, increased consumption power and available role models from the world of film and television (Bauman 2000).

The reflective self
Foucault (1980[1976]) underlined the empowering aspects of self-examination and self-reflection, as enacted for instance in the confession. The confessor gives confidential information about him- or herself to someone who does not reciprocate the intimacy, thereby confirming a hierarchical relationship. On the other hand, the disclosure of inner thoughts and secret actions becomes a material for the confessor, for recognition of his or her own desires and abilities. This image can be generalized to several other situations involving the professions listening to and interrogating their clients.

The protesting self
The basic precondition of social protest movements is not insupportable conditions *per se*, but a belief system or a moral theory explaining why conditions are unacceptable and

how they may be changed. Frame alignment contributes to the development of personal identities; along with political commitment moral intuitions are transformed into broader conceptions of self and society (Tarrow 1998, Benford and Snow 2000).

The empowered self
Within a cultural context, empowerment is closely connected to learning processes. Learning takes place in everyday experience, in addition to disciplining institutions, which have as their goal to shape individuals' capacities, adjust their ambitions, and increase their sense of mastery. Educational institutions are among the most dominant bodies in modern societies, felt by many as laying unbearable restrictions on their freedom. But the other side of the coin is the increase in positive freedom – the ability to mobilize resources for action – which follows from educational discipline.

The condescending self
Exerting power not only affects the subjectivity of subordinates, but often inflates the self-image of actors in superior positions. What is felt as 'natural authority' stemming from a given role, is reinforced by prestige flowing from other arenas, such as family background or special individual traits. An additional source of prestige is spillover effects from one successful role performance to others, where the performance, seen in isolation, actually is less distinguished (Bourdieu 1986).

The aggrandized self
Actors having at their disposition violent power resources, weapons or punishment arrangements, tend to lose the empathy of normal social interaction. This is true for the gangster making threats in a low voice, the judge issuing harsh sentences and the holy warrior alike. History is full of the horrible consequences of powerful zealots bringing the incredulous onto the narrow path. The slogan 'Power corrupts, and absolute power corrupts absolutely' is valid for criminals as well as benevolent actors accepting cruelty against disbelievers when it is justified as being to their own good.

FUTURE PROSPECTS OF CULTURE AND POWER

This chapter has mostly built on assumptions about the workings of culture and power typical of the twentieth century. The dynamics of information technology and the Internet in the twenty-first century certainly present a challenge to this view. There is no lack of daring prophecies about the future, predicting that formation and diffusion of culture will take completely new directions in the decades to come. But the impact of technological change is easily overrated. Cultural homogenization may take place in some domains, while conflict increases in others, and many cultural features remain relatively intact.

Cultural power on a globalized scale

One obvious aspect of changing cultural power relations all over the world is the diffusion of branded consumption goods. The same blue jeans, snickers, hamburgers, soft drinks, watches – or their pirate imitations – are offered from Atlanta to Maputo to Shanghai. The few international corporations controlling the symbolic capital of international brands exert a formidable power in global market segments. This corporate power not only concerns the distribution of goods charged with symbolic messages, their production is globalized in chains of manufacturing as well. Low-wage countries make up long, hierarchical production chains, some links delivering raw materials, others doing actual processing, others again procuring design and control systems, whereas the ultimate control and the profits remain in the corporate headquarters (Gereffi 2005).

The products of the culture industry are diffused in parallel moves. No place on the earth is so remote that they cannot receive the broadcast signals transmitting standardized pop music, action films and soap operas. The operation of the media is to a large extent financed by advertisements for the same globalized products.

These processes are often interpreted as an ongoing homogenization in the form of one-sided influence from the West to the rest of the world. And to a large extent they are. At the same time, the processes of cultural diffusion are much more complex, linking distant parts of the non-Western world together, as is, e.g. the case when Indian films get a large audience in Nigeria (Larkin 2002). Moreover, information technology not only brings civilizations in contact, but also increases the consciousness of crucial cultural differences between regions in the world. Distant cultures take on new meanings when they are looming on the horizon. Religious divides acquire a new and more palpable meaning, feelings of cultural inferiority and oppression become more acute, social aspirations take on new and ambiguous forms, both striving toward modern consumption society and rejecting it. In this perspective a fundamentalist movement like Al-Quaida is not a traditional, but an acutely modern phenomenon (Gray 2004).

The Internet in social change

Similar ambiguities are found in the diffusion of personal messages and general news, and they influence the relationship between the Internet, social movements and the existing public sphere. The Internet has greatly facilitated the organizing of social movements; on the international scene spectacular political manifestations have been coordinated all over the globe. But in this process the Internet has mostly been a facilitator, not a separate way of action. The efficiency of these movements still rests on two other elements: bringing people physically together in mass rallies, and getting broad coverage in the 'conventional' media of television and newspapers (Kolb 2005, della Porta et al. 2006).

A second aspect is what may be termed 'hacktivism' in 'cyberwars', i.e. activism taking part most on the net, by attacks on targeted websites or servers. However, even these seem to be dependent on coverage in the media in order to have significant effects (Vegh 2003).

A third aspect concerns the effects on the public sphere. In autocratic regimes where the public sphere is deficient or even non-existent, an underground public sphere, or set of public spheres, often develops with the support of information technology. A salient question is whether such underground discussion groups, not unlike Habermas' description of the public sphere of the eighteenth century, will emerge into a public sphere on the national level, as in well-established democracies, or remain as dispersed chat-groups with relatively little political effect.

In parallel, questions are raised about the future of the public sphere in democratic societies. Here the Internet seems to permeate the functioning of the old media. Newspapers have their fast growing Internet editions, to an increasing extent television shows feature two-way communication with viewers questioning, commenting and judging performances on the screen. All of this comes in addition to the explosion of chatline communities relating citizens more intensely than ever before. Under one angle, this development is an extension of democracy. Citizens are enabled to channel their activities in new directions, exploiting a new form of freedom. Under another angle, these changes point in the direction of weakening democracy and strengthening tendencies toward populist anarchy, if they impair the legitimacy of democratic institutions and transform the public sphere into a marginal segment in the total flow of communication.

But all of this is speculation. IT bubbles have burst before, and that will happen again. What is certain is that new cultural struggles will develop, leading to new transformations of the public sphere and of the exertion of power, but it is virtually impossible to tell where they will take us. This calls for broad reflections on culture and power, which should be a prominent part of the research agenda of the future. In such an endeavor researchers should foremost avoid depicting the persons they study as cultural dopes, but let them be recognized as social actors in their own right.

REFERENCES

Adorno, Theodor. W. 1981 [1955]. *Prisms*. Cambridge. MA: MIT Press.
Agulhon, Maurice. 1978. La statumanie et l'histoire. *Ethnologie francaise*, 8:145–172.
Alexander, Jeffrey. 2004. Cultural pragmatics: Social performance between ritual and strategy. *Sociological Theory*, 22:527–573.
Anderson, Benedict. 1983. *Imagined Communities*. London: Verso.
Auslander, Leora. 1996. *Taste and Power*. Berkeley: University of California Press.
Austin, John L. 1962. *How to Do Things with Words*. Cambridge: Harvard University Press.
Bach, Kent. 1998. Speech Acts. In E. Craig, ed. *Routledge Encyclopedia of Philosophy*. London: Routledge.
Bauhr, M. and Peter Esaiasson. 2001. Trust me! On the nature of ethos argumentation. In Kirsten Gomar and Anne Krogstad, eds. *Instead of the Ideal Debate. Doing Politics and Doing Gender in Nordic Political Campaign Discourse*. Århus: Aarhus University Press.
Bauman, Zygmunt. 2000. *Liquid Modernity*. Cambridge: Polity Press.
Benford, Robert A. and David A. Snow. 2000. Framing processes and social movements: An overview and assessment. *Annual Review of Sociology*, 26:611–639.
Blakar, Rolv Mikel and Ragnar Rommetveit, eds. 1979. *Studies of Language, Thought and Verbal Communication*. London: Academic Press.
Boudon, Raymond. 1991. *Theories of Social Change: A Critical Reappraisal*. Cambridge: Polity Press.
Boudon, Raymond. 1994. *The Art of Self-persuation*. Cambridge: Polity Press.
Bourdieu, Pierre. 1977 [1972]. *Outline of a Theory of Practice*. Cambridge: Cambridge University Press.
Bourdieu, Pierre. 1986. The forms of capital. In John G. Richardson, ed. *Handbook of Theory and Research for the Sociology of Education*. New York: Greenwood Press.
Bourdieu, Pierre. 1990 [1980]. *The Logic of Practice*. Cambridge: Polity Press.
Bourdieu, Pierre. 1991. *Language and Symbolic Power*. Cambridge: Polity Press.
Bourdieu, Pierre. 1993. *The Field of Cultural Production*. New York: Columbia University Press.
Bourdieu, Pierre. 1996 [1989]. *The State Nobility*. Cambridge: Polity Press.
Bourdieu, Pierre. 1998 [1996]. *On Television and Journalism*. London: Pluto Press.
Coleman, James. 1986. Social theory, Social research, and a theory of action. *American Journal of Sociology*, 91:1309–1335.
Collins, Randall. 2004. *Interaction Ritual Chains*. Princeton: Princeton University Press.
Daloz, Jean-Pascal. 2003. Ostentation in comparative perspective: Culture and elite legitimation. *Comparative Social Research*, 21:29–62.

Daloz, Jean-Pascal. 2007. Political elites, and conspicuous modesty: Norway, Sweden, Finland in comparative perspective. *Comparative Social Research*, 23:173–212.

Daloz, Jean-Pascal. 2007. Elite distinction: Grand theory and comparative perspectives. *Comparative Sociology*, 6:27–74.

della Porta, Donatella, Massimilliano Andretta, Lorenzo Mosca, Herbert Reiter. 2006. *Globalization from Below. Transnational Activists and Protest Networks*. Minneapolis: University of Minnesota Press.

DiMaggio, Paul. 1997. Culture and cognition. *Annual Review of Sociology*, 23:263–87.

Douglas, Mary. 1991 [1969]. *Purity and Danger: An Analysis of Concepts of Pollution and Taboo*. London:Routledge.

Durkheim, Emile. 1965 [1912]. *The Elementary Forms of Religious Life*. New York: The Free Press.

Engelstad, Fredrik. 2003. National literature, collective identity and political power. *Comparative Social Research*, 21:111–145.

Fairclough, Norman. 1995. *Critical Discourse Analysis: The Critical Study of Language*. Harlow: Longman

Fallers, Lloyd. 1954. A note on the 'Trickle effect'. *Public Opinion Quarterly*, 18:314–322.

Foucault, Michel. 1970 [1966]. *The Order of Things*. London: Tavistock.

Foucault, Michel. 1972 [1969]. *The Archeology of Knowledge*. London: Routledge.

Foucault, Michel. 1971. *L'Ordre du Discours*. Paris: Gallimard.

Foucault, Michel. 1973 [1963]. *The Birth of the Clinic*. London: Tavistock.

Foucault, Michel. 1980 [1976]. *The History of Sexuality. Vol. 1, An Introduction*. The New York: Vintage.

Foucault, Michel. 1980. *Power/Knowledge*. New York: Pantheon.

Foucault, Michel. 1983. The subject and power. In Hubert Dreyfus and Paul Rabinow, eds. *Michel Foucault: Beyond Structuralism and Hermeneutics*. New York: Harvester Wheatsheaf.

Geertz, Clifford. 1973. *The Interpretation of Cultures*. New York: Basic Books.

Gereffi, Gary. 2005. The global economy: Organization, governance, and development. In Neil Smelser and Richard Swedberg, eds. *The Handbook of Economic Sociology*. second edition. Princeton: Princeton University Press.

Giddens, Anthony. 1984. *The Constitution of Society*. Cambridge: Polity Press.

Giesen, Bernard. 1987. Beyond reductionism. Four models relating micro and macro levels. In Jeffrey Alexander et al. eds. *The Micro-Macro Link*. Berkeley: University of California Press.

Goffman, Erving. 1959. *The Presentation of Self in Everyday Life*. New York: Doubleday Anchor.

Goffman, Erving. 1967. *Interaction Rituals: Essays in Face-to-Face Interaction*. Chicago: Aldine.

Goffman, Erving. 1974. *Frame Analysis. An Essay on the Organization of Experience*. Boston: Northeastern University Press.

Gorski, Joseph. 2006. Mann's theory of ideological power: Sources, applications and elaborations. In John A. Hall and Ralph Schoeder, eds. *An Anatomy of Power. The Social Theory of Michael Mann*. Cambridge: Cambridge University Press.

Gramsci, Antonio. 1973. *Selections from the Prison Notebooks*. London: Lawrence and Wishart.

Gray, John. 2004. *Al Qaeda: And What It Means to Be Modern*. London: Faber and Faber.

Grice, Paul. 1989. *Studies in the Way of Words*. Cambridge: Harvard University Press.

Griswold, Wendy. 1987. A methodological framework for the sociology of culture. *Sociological Methodology*, 17:1–35.

Griswold, Wendy. 1994. *Cultures and Societies in a Changing World*. Thousand Oaks: Pine Forge Press.

Griswold, Wendy. 2000. *Bearing Witness. Readers, Writers, and the Novel in Nigeria*. Princeton: Princeton University Press.

Habermas, Jürgen. 1989 [1962]. *The Structural Transformation of the Public Sphere*. Cambridge: Polity Press.

Habermas, Jürgen. 1994. Further reflections on the public sphere. In Craig Calhoun, ed. *Habermas and the Public Sphere*. Boston: MIT Press.

Hobsbawm, Eric. 1983. Mass-producing traditions: Europe 1870–1914. In E. Hobsbawm and T. Ranger, eds. *The Invention of Tradition*. Cambridge: Cambridge University Press.

Hochschild, Arlie. 1983. *The Managed Heart: Commercialization of Human Feeling*. Berkeley: University of California Press.

Hoge, Warren. 2006. For New U.N. Chief, a Past Misstep Leads to Opportunity. *New York Times*, December 9, 2006.

Hohendahl, Peter-Uwe. 1989. *Building a National Literature. Germany 1830–1870*. Ithaca: Cornell University Press.

Horkheimer, Max and Theodor W. Adorno. 1979 [1947]. *The Dialectics of Enlightenment*. London: Verso.

Katz, Elihu and Paul Lazarsfeld. 1955. *Personal Influence*. Glencoe: The Free Press

Kolb, Felix. 2005. The impact of transnational protest on social movement organizations: Mass media and the making of ATTAC Germany. In Donatella della Porta and Sidney Tarrow, eds. *Transnational Protest & Global Activism*. Lanham: Rowman & Littlefield.

Krogstad, Anne and Aagoth Storvik. 2007. Seductive heroes and ordinary human beings. Charismatic political leadership in France and Norway. *Comparative Social Research*, 23:213–247.

Kurz, Donald V. 1996. Hegemony and Anthropology. Gramsci, exegeses, reinterpretations. *Critique of Anthropology*, 16:103–135.

Laclau, Ernesto and Chantal Mouffe. 2001 [1985]. *Hegemony and Socialist Strategy*. Second edition. London: Verso.

Lamont, Michèle. 1990. The power-culture link in a comparative perspective. *Comparative Social Research*, 11:131–150.

Lamont, Michèle. 1992. *Money, Morals and Manners. The Culture of the French and American Upper Middle Class*. Chicago: Chicago University Press.

Lamont, Michèle and Marcel Fournier, eds. 1992. *Cultivating Differences. Symbolic Boundaries and the Making of Inequality*. Chicago: Chicago University Press.

Larkin, Brian. 2002. Indian film and Nigerian lovers: Media and the creation of parallel modernities. In Jonathan Xavier Inda and Renato Rosaldo, eds. *The Anthropology of Globalization*. Malden, Mass.: Blackwell.

Leiss, William, Stephen Kline and Sut Jhally. 1990. *Social Communication in Advertising*. London: Routledge.

Lerner, Melvin. 1980. *The Belief in a Just World: A Fundamental Delusion*. New York: Plenum Press.

Levinson, Sanford. 1998. *Written in Stone. Public Monuments in Changing Societies*. Durham, N.C.: Duke University Press.

Lukes, Steven. 2004 [1974]. *Power: A Radical View*. Second edition. New York: Palgrave Macmillan.

Mann, Michael. 1986. *The Sources of Social Power. Volume I, A history of Power from the Beginning to A.D. 1760*. Cambridge: Cambridge University Press.

Marcuse, Herbert. 1964. *One Dimensional Man: Studies in the Ideology of Advanced Industrial Society*. London: Routledge and Kegan Paul.

Marx, Karl. 1998 [1845]. *The German Ideology*. New York: Prometheus Books.

Marx, Karl. 1992 [1867]. *Capital: A Critique of Political Economy*. Vol I. London: Penguin Books.

Marx, Karl and Friedrich Engels. 1992 [1848]. *The Communist Manifesto*. Oxford: Oxford University Press.

McCombs, Maxwell E. and Donald L. Shaw. 1972. The agenda setting function of mass media. *Public Opinion Quarterly*, 36:176–187.

Merton, Robert K. 1968 [1936]. The self-fullfilling prophecy. In *Social Theory and Social Structure*. New York: The Free Press.

Nietzsche, Friedrich. 1992 [1887]. Genealogy of morals. In W. Kaufman, ed. *Basic Writings of Nietzsche*. New York: Modern Library.

Olson, Mancur. 1965. *The Logic of Collective Action*. Cambridge: Harvard University Press.

Ortner, Sherry B. 2006. *Anthropology and Social Theory. Culture, Power and the Acting Subject*. Durham: Duke University Press.

Pernot, Laurent. 2005. *Rhetoric in Antiquity*. Washington D.C.: Catholic University of America Press.

Peterson, Richard R. and Albert Simkus. 1992. How musical tastes mark occupational status groups. In Michèle Lamont and Marcel Fournier, eds. *Cultivating Differences. Symbolic Boundaries and the Making of Inequality*. Chicago: Chicago University Press.

Schelling, Thomas. 1978. *Micromotives and Macrobehavior*. New York: Norton.

Searle, John. 1969. *Speech Acts*. Cambridge: Cambridge University Press.

Searle, John. 1995 *The Construction of Social Reality*. New York: The Free Press.

Schwartz, Barry. 2000. *Abraham Lincoln and the Forge of National Memory*. Chicago: University of Chicago Press.

Schwartz, Barry. 1991. Social change and collective memory. The democratization of George Washington. *American Sociological Review*, 56:221–236.

Sennett, Richard. 1977. *The Fall of Public Man*. New York: Alfred Knopf.

Schudson, Michael. 1995. Introduction: News as Public Knowledge. In *The Power of News*. Cambridge: Harvard University Press.

Spillman, Lyn. 1997. *Nation and Commemoration in the United States and Australia*. Cambridge: Cambridge University Press.

Swidler, Ann. 1986. Culture in action: Symbols and strategies. *American Sociological Review*, 51:273–286.

Tarrow, Sidney. 1998. *Power in Movement*. Cambridge: Cambridge University Press.

Thomas, Jenny. 1996. *Meaning in Interaction. An Introduction to Pragmatics.* London: Longman.
Tota, Anna Lisa. 2003. Collective memories 'at work': The public remembering of the past. *Comparative Social Research*, 21:63–86.
Turner, Victor.1974. *Dramas, Fields, and Metaphors.* Ithaca: Cornell University Press
Veblen, Thorstein. 1994 [1899]. *The Theory of the Leisure Class.* New Brunswick: Viking Penguin.
Vegh, Sandor. 2003. Classifying forms of online activism: The case of cyberprotests against the World Bank. In Martha McCaughey and Michael Ayers, eds. *Cyberactivism. Online Activism in Theory and Practice.* New York: Routledge.
Wachtel, Andrew B. 1998. *Making a Nation, Breaking a Nation: Literature and Cultural Politics in Yugoslavia.* Stanford: Stanford University Press.
Wagner-Pacifici, Robin and Barry Schwartz. 1991. The Vietnam veterans' memorial: Commemorating a difficult past. *American Journal of Sociology*, 97:376–420.
Weber, Eugen. 1976. *Peasants into Frenchmen.* Palo Alto: Stanford University Press.
Weber, Max. 1976 [1904]. *The Protestant Ethic and the Spirit of Capitalism.* New York: Charles Scribner and Sons.
Weber, Max. 1978 [1922]. *Economy and Society.* Berkeley: University of California Press.
Weber, Max. 1999 [1922]. *The Sociology of Religion.* Fourth edition. Boston : Beacon Press.
Williams, Raymond. 1997. *Problems in Materialism and Culture.* London: Verso.
Young, James E. 2000. *At Memory's Edge. After-Images of Holocaust in Contemporary Art and Architecture.* New Haven: Yale University Press.

13

Power and Hegemony

Mark Haugaard

Over recent years the concepts of power and hegemony have become increasingly prevalent in their use in the social sciences. Yet, as I found recently when co-editing a book on power and hegemony (Haugaard and Lenter 2006), there are few works that theorize the relations of the concepts to each other.

As the power debate has developed over the last number of years there has been a general move away from the perception of power based on relations of coercion, to a view of power involving qualified levels of consent on the part of the relatively powerless. Associated with this move has been a conceptual drift away from the idea of power as something dialectically opposed to freedom, from which we should be seeking liberation. Such a generalized paradigmatic shift directly parallels Gramsci's own epistemic move away from a view of bourgeois domination as rooted simply in access to economic and military resources, as a means of coercion, to a more nuanced view of domination as rooted in hegemony, which constitutes a system of dominant ideas that receive consent from the relatively powerless or subaltern groups. While bourgeois hegemony is clearly not normatively desirable, Gramsci believed, he also realized that there is no escape from hegemony; thus, hegemony is also a condition of freedom.

The objective of this article is to explore and make explicit the themes and ideas within the power literature that have strong resonance with the Gramscian concept of hegemony. I shall not be building a new theory, instead exploring existing themes within an existing literature.

In political science and sociology, the power debate began in the 1950s as a debate concerning the extent of democracy in the US. Dahl entered this debate by arguing that critics of American democracy used an unsophisticated view of power, which confused power *resources* and a *reputation* for power with *actual power*. Dahl insisted that a social scientist cannot establish the dominance of any group without basing their analysis upon concrete decisions – by examining who initiated and vetoed specific policy outcomes (Dahl 1958: 466). For Dahl, power is reducible to its *exercise*, whereby 'A has power over B to the extent to which A can make B do something which would not otherwise do' (Dahl 1957: 202–3).

While Bachrach and Baratz (1962) agreed with Dahl that power resources are potential power, rather than actual power, and took the view that power is reducible to its exercise, they argued that Dahl failed to take account of the way in which institutional bias facilitates certain decisions and excludes others. For them the exclusion of issues from the political arena has to have specific identifiable agency in order to constitute power. Within their conceptual vocabulary 'non-decisionmaking' is also a kind of decision.

Lukes (1974) attempted to break the behaviourist link between power and its exercise. There are essentially two interrelated aspects to the third dimension of power. First, against Bachrach and Baratz's insistence on observable behaviour, Lukes argued that 'the bias of the system is not sustained simply by a series of individually chosen acts, but also, most importantly, by the socially structured and culturally patterned behaviour of groups, and practices of institutions, which may indeed be manifest by individuals' inaction' (Lukes 1974: 21–2). Second, Lukes argued that the ultimate form of power is 'false consciousness', in which social actors do not know what their 'real interests' are. Because this third dimension of power is divorced from its exercise and, in the case of false consciousness, only manifest through the subaltern's inability to know their true interests, Lukes departed from Dahl's definition of power. For Lukes, 'A exercises power over B when A affects B in a manner contrary to B's interests' (Lukes 1974: 23).

The departure from power conceived in terms of its exercise to the inclusion of 'socially structured and culturally patterned behaviour' has an implicit open-endedness, which could, in principle, include every aspect of socialization as a manifestation of power. In that case, power would be everything and nothing, an argument that Lukes (2005) was later to make. The 'false consciousness' argument is deeply problematic as it presupposes 'true consciousness'. To Westerners the beliefs of Islamic women may appear as 'false consciousness' (they are certainly relatively disempowering) but any such claim appears ethnocentric as it implies the corollary that Western culture constitutes 'true consciousness'.

Lukes was well aware of these potential criticisms, even from the beginning. In the final chapter of *Power: A Radical View* (1974), entitled 'Difficulties', Lukes attempted to deal with some of these issues. Interestingly, for our purposes, Lukes made use of Gramsci's analysis of hegemony to argue that three dimensional power can be shown to exist when the actions of the dominated show a disjuncture between two conceptions of the world. Disjuncture is manifest in a contrast between 'thought and action, i.e. the co-existence of two conceptions of the world, one affirmed in words and the other displayed in effective action' (Gramsci 1971: 326; quoted Lukes 1974: 47). This hypothesis is followed by a substantive quotation from the *Prison Notebooks*, which concerns the way in which dominated groups may have an incipient world-view that is revealed through social action and constitutes their real interests. They may consciously affirm one that is alien and imposed, while their social practices reveal their 'real interest'. Gramsci wrote of a contrast between theory and practice in the life of the great masses which

> cannot but be the expression of profounder contrasts of a social historical order. It signifies that the social group in question may indeed have its own conception of the world, even if only embryonic; a conception

which manifests itself in action, but occasionally and in flashes – when that is, the group is acting as an organic totality. But this same group has, for reasons of submission and intellectual subordination, adopted a conception which is not its own but is borrowed from another group; and it affirms this conception verbally and believes itself to be following it, because this is the conception which it follows in 'normal times' – that is when its conduct is not independent and autonomous, but submissive and subordinate (Gramsci 1971: 327; quoted in Lukes 1974: 47)

The key to identifying 'real interests' is not simply some objective truth but an alternative world-view, which typically manifests itself in moments of radical rupture. Again quoting Gramsci, Lukes cites how the 'community of the faithful' deserted the Catholic Church in France during the French Revolution and he also gives the example of the way in which Czechs reacted to the 'relaxation of the apparatus of power in 1968' (Lukes 1974: 48). Real interests can also show themselves in 'normal' circumstances when there is a disjuncture between social practices and ostensible beliefs. For instance, within the Indian caste system lower castes frequently emulate behavioural patterns of higher castes without, overtly, rejecting the caste system (Lukes 1974: 48–9).

In the much lengthened second edition of *Power: A Radical View* (2005), Lukes again argues that the third dimension of power is a form of hegemony (Lukes 2005 : 123–31). He tries to distance his position from the 'true' 'false' consciousness dichotomy by invoking reason. He argues that three-dimensional power entails domination, which renders social agents less free '*to live as their nature and judgment dictate*' (Lukes 2005: 114 – italics orig.). Following Spinoza, freedom entails living authentically according to the dictates of one's nature and autonomously according to the dictates of one's judgement, which entails correct reason and 'practical wisdom' – *phronesis* in Aristotlean terminology (Lukes 2005: 115–6). While reason and practical wisdom do *not* necessarily entail some privileged access to a realm of absolute truth, and the idea of human nature does not necessarily presuppose dogmatic essentialist privileging of one way of life, this retheorization of the third dimension of power still places Lukes in difficult waters: the shoals and reefs of essentialism, elitism and ethnocentrism are apparent. Despite these risks, it is evident that the inculcation of demeaning views of deviancy and normalcy are classic instances of power that should not be ignored just because theorizing them entails violating certain current academic taboos.

Part of Lukes' way of distinguishing power from general socialization, both in 1974 and 2005, is to insist upon some kind of *agency* associated with power, which, in 2005, is defined as *the power to mislead* (Lukes 2005: 149 – italics orig.). However, while establishing the existence of this kind of power can be done fairly straightforwardly in the case of deliberate inculcation (brain-washing) and, further, one can concur that this does constitute an important force in modern society (viz. the millions spent on advertising), the most significant form of domination, entailing acquiescence due to 'the socially structured and culturally patterned behaviour of groups' does not entail this kind of intentional agency. To argue that it does has an implication of conspiracy theory.

The crucial problematic for Lukes in his third dimension of power, and for Gramsci in his account of hegemony, is why do subaltern groups frequently appear to *consent* to their own domination? A wider issue of the relationship between consent and power is raised by this question. Three-dimensional power is considered conflictual by Lukes; yet, as an empirical fact, any actor who is subject to this power in effect is consenting to their own domination. The conflict comes from a normative evaluation by the analyst to the effect that the subaltern actor *should* not be so consenting.

In political philosophy, Hannah Arendt developed a Civic Republican perspective, in which power is the 'capacity to act in concert' (1970: 44). In her view, power is primarily 'power to', as opposed to 'power over' and is derived from the fostering of autonomy in collaborative endeavour through virtue politics (Arendt 1958). In fact the very thing which Lukes terms 'power', as distorted reason, in Arendt's hand is the very opposite of power. For Arendt, power is the outcome of undistorted communication between citizens, which allows for a kind of co-dependent autonomy. The latter does not presuppose negative freedom (freedom from others) but is the autonomy of a just Civic Republican polis in which the self derives fulfilment, becomes a true self, through collaboration with others. Going back to the Greek interpretation of humans as essentially 'political animals', our 'human nature' is constituted through power, which enables us to realize our essence as members of a polis by facilitating autonomy through collaboration with others.

This virtual reversal of Lukes and the generally accepted conflictual view of power also found in Weber (1978), Mann (1986) and Poggi (2000) are highly significant relative to the Gramscian concept of hegemony. The usual normative view of power is as something insidious, which has to be escaped from; by contrast the Arendtian view, by following the Greek tradition, conceptualizes power as part of the discourse of virtue. Corrupt forms of power, contrary to actor's interest (what the conflictual power theorists have in mind in their description of power), are viewed as forms of 'violence' – both in the literal (as coercion) and in the metaphysical sense of the word (as violence to human nature). If Arendt is correct, and there is virtuous power, how do we distinguish this from the decadent form, especially if the latter entails consent by the subaltern, as in the third dimension of power?

In Gramsci, under the conditions of bourgeois capitalism hegemony is *not* synonymous with virtue, yet it is substantially *more* virtuous than violence and coercion. Counter-hegemony and consequent proletarian hegemony is entirely virtuous, despite the fact that from a sociological perspective (as distinct from a normative one) both hegemonies represent the same kind of strategic use of social force combined with consent. In *Gramsci's Political Thought*, Femia usefully distinguishes the latter from the former hegemony by calling it 'integral' hegemony as opposed to the former, which is either 'decadent' or 'minimal' hegemony (Femia 1987: 46). What distinguishes 'integral hegemony' from the other two is that it represents a true 'collective will' while the other two forms are in some sense a distortion of the collective will. It echoes Aristotle's distinction between virtuous and corrupt governmental forms in which each corrupt form has its virtuous counterpart but there is no escape from the dualism itself: monarchy is government by one, for the benefit of the many, while tyranny is government by one, for the benefit of one, and so on for aristocracy versus oligarchy and constitutional government versus democracy. Integral hegemony would be the use of the collective will for private interests, rather than for collective interests. This would have close affinity with Arendt's neo-Aristotelian Civic Republican view of power as the capacity to act in concert. However, once one goes beyond the simplistic dichotomy of bourgeois (normatively undesirable) versus proletariat (virtuous), how can one distinguish the two if both entail consent?

In Greek thought, hegemony was also contrasted with empire, and the distinction rested on the degree of autonomy. *Hegemonia* implies leadership, which facilitates the autonomy of the led, while empire implies leadership that facilitates only the autonomy of the leader. Greek thought, of course, was premised upon a principle of continual cycles of virtue and decline. However, due to the Enlightenment concept of 'progress' and the replacement of cyclical conceptions of time with clock time during the early modern period, modern thought is tacitly linear in form. The implication of this is that what was cyclical for the Ancients, as a continual rise and decline, in modern thought can progress from a corrupt to a virtuous form and remain that way through a process of 'overcoming' contradictions. The latter is the ever sought after 'end of history'. For most conflictual theorists the latter would constitute an escape from power, but for Arendt it would be the ultimate dominance of power over coercion and violence. Similarly, for Gramsci successful proletarian hegemony entails the dominance of power through consent over violence and coercion. But, unlike in Arendt, the dominance of hegemony also takes place in the instance of bourgeois hegemony, which Gramsci rejects on normative grounds.

In the work of Foucault we find a similar insistence that power is not a state that is to be escaped. Foucault mirrors Lukes in that both theorists insist that power and knowledge are inextricably interwoven but for Lukes there is an escape from the dualism. Foucault's insistence that there is no escape from power/knowledge is partly a reflection of a deeper epistemological conflict between so-called modern and post-modern social theories, expressing contestation over the central idea of Enlightenment and modern scientific rationality that truth is always out with power. Foucault's recognition that power/knowledge cannot be escaped is not entirely nihilistic in its implications, as post-modern approaches are often acceded to be, because he argues that power is not always negative. However, he refrains from providing us with criteria for distinguishing normatively desirable from undesirable power.

Aside from Arendt there is a highly developed consensual perspective on power in sociological theory. In response to Mill's attack upon the workings of US democracy, Parsons entered the power debate (Parsons 1963). He began from the fundamental insight that power does not simply exist 'out-there' but *has to be created*. Political scientists should approach power in much the same way as economists approach wealth. The latter do not simply analyse wealth's *distribution* but, more fundamentally, they seek to understand *how the economy produces wealth*. Wealth is *non zero-sum* and so is power. Furthermore, in the economy inequality is integral to the effective production of wealth and so, similarly, in the polity the unequal distribution of power may be the key to its effective creation (Parsons 1963).

Parsons developed his account of the creation of power within his structural-functionalist framework. His central re-evaluation of the nature of power is worth emphasizing because it constitutes a significant paradigm shift. Any collective endeavour presupposes the ability to achieve shared goals and that capacity for action is a form of power, as 'power to'. The creation of 'power to' is premised upon complex political organization and that entails the creation of positions of authority, the occupants of which exercise 'power over' others. To the extent to which authority is based upon legitimacy, both 'power to' and 'power over' are premised upon some kind of consent by the governed. Of course, no political system is perceived as entirely legitimate by everyone at all times and, even if it were, there would always be 'free riders' who will try to circumvent the legitimate exercise of 'power over' and, for this reason, those in authority will have recourse to violence and coercion in the case of recalcitrance. However, the use of the coercion entails the failure of legitimate authority. As in Arendt (1970: 56), legitimate power seems to end where violence and coercion begin. Moreover, the use of violence has a negative impact upon the total amount of legitimate power in the system. Dictators who constantly need to send in the tanks in order to control their subjects do so because they lack the kind of power which Parsons has in mind and, by and large, the more often they send in the tanks the less legitimate power they will have. This is the key to Gandhi's concept of 'passive resistance' whereby he orchestrated the effective withdrawal of Indian consent to being governed by the British in India. Similarly it can be argued that hegemony entails effective leadership which augments the power of the led. This entails that the hegemon has authority, which presupposes consent by the subaltern actors, which gives both sets of actors a capacity for action which they would not otherwise have if it were not for the institutionalization of the hegemonic relationship. Hence, hegemony is not something to be replaced but, rather, transferred from one hegemon to the other.

In Parsons the consensual basis of power is derived from consensus on system goals, which may be the case in some instances of simple organizations, but in the case of complex systems of domination is rather implausible. Barry Barnes (1988) follows in Parsons' footsteps in wishing to provide an account of the 'creation of power' but dispenses with the structural-functionalist framework and system goals. In place of these he uses rational choice theory coupled with an extension of Kuhn's characterization of paradigms to cover social knowledge in general. In Barnes, the source of consensus which gives members of a social system an added capacity for action, as 'power to', is rooted in shared social knowledge. Barnes' argument is a significant reversal of Lukes' position where power and knowledge are considered mutually antagonistic forces but it is consistent with the Gramscian idea of hegemony as based upon shared knowledge from which there is no escape.

Consensus on social knowledge is explained in terms of an analogy between self-referring and non self-referring objects (Barnes 1988: 46–53). Imagine that we wish to know if a spherical object is indeed spherical; we will turn it over and examine it from all sides. In contrast, imagine that we wish to know if an outcrop of rock is the top of a mountain, we will not examine the rock in itself but compare it to surrounding rocks, in order to ascertain which is the highest. The latter is a 'ring of reference' that constitutes the mountain top as the summit. To extend the analogy to society, if I see a 'circle' as a 'target', the essence of its 'targetness' is not intrinsic to the circle but externally constituted by the individuals who perceive that 'circle' as a 'target'. In fact, all social objects are similarly constituted through our shared social knowledge and it is that knowledge which enables us to act collectively and in concert. In short, society is conceived of as a massive self-affirming paradigm, which gives actors social 'power to' do things, which they could not otherwise if they were acting singly.

Knowledge also gives actors 'authority', which is similarly constituted through rings of reference situated in the belief systems of the relatively less powerful. When, in everyday speech, we assert that so and so '*is* powerful' the suggestion is that the power is intrinsic to that actor. In reality it is the subaltern who constitutes the ring of reference that confers power upon the powerful. If we say that John is powerful, we are actually saying something about the people around John, rather than John himself. After all, what distinguishes the real Napoleon from the 'napoleons' in psychiatric institutions is not intrinsic to them but externally so – the former had a ring of reference which the latter lacks.

In the Arendt, Parsons and Barnes side of the power debate we have a conceptualization of power which in many respects is entirely at odds with that of Dahl, Bachrach and Baratz, and Lukes' perception. In the latter, power is always 'over others' and, implicitly, to their detriment, while for the former power is a capacity for action that exists for their benefit.

A similar dualism is implicit in Gramsci's account of hegemony. Hegemony is, on the one hand, a source of domination while, on the other, it is based upon consent and, indeed constitutes a form of collective will (Ives 2004: 113, 151). The workings of this duality are clearly implicit in his discussion of political science and sociology, in which he describes the state as follows:

> ...the State is the entire complex of practical and theoretical activities with which the ruling class not only justifies and maintains its dominance, but manages to win the active consent of those over whom it rules...' (Gramsci 1971: 244).

The characterization of a theoretical position as dualist, of course, suggests some kind of unresolved theoretical tension and, as presented so far, the conflictual and consensual power traditions are, indeed, in mutual opposition. One thinker who has attempted to overcome dualism in social theory and replace it with duality is Anthony Giddens, through his theory of structuration (1984). Of course, the dualism which he sought to replace was between subject- and object-centred social theories but, not entirely coincidentally, the resulting theory of structuration also constitutes a conceptual bridge between the consensual and conflictual power traditions.

Giddens was highly influenced by Heidegger's move from epistemology, as the central problematic of philosophy, to ontology. For Heidegger, Western philosophy is premised upon a mistaken dualism whereby the subject is conceptually separated from the object, or the 'world out there', creating the false problematic of building a bridge between the two – Descartes' problem (how do I know that the 'world *out there* exists?'). In reality, there is not a cognising subject and an inert external reality. The world 'out there' exists as meaning given through my interpretation of it in my act of being. If I look out the window, watching a bird on the bird feeder, the window, the bird and the birdfeeder are not external to me, although I experience them that way, but, rather, they are a combination of sense data and interpretation and the latter is purely a reflection of *my* interpretative horizon. The latter is not some external semiotic system which, through an act of will, I choose to project upon the world, but instead is an imposition of my 'being-in-the-world'. The window, the bird and birdfeeder are not some external reality that I am dualistically separated from but are a fusion of my being-in-the-world and incoming data.

The dualism of social theory is between subject-centred social thought, in which the individual is central, and object-centred theory, where the individual exists as an effect of the social world. The former includes hermeneutics and rational choice theory, while the latter includes Marxist and anthropological structuralism, and Parsonian structural-functionalism. Mirroring the Heideggerian problematic of world and subject, in social theory we have social subject versus social structures and system. According to Giddens, in reality social structures do not exist externally to social action but are reproduced in the moment of social action. To take the example of language, linguistic structures can, of course, be perceived in their own right and separately from the speaking subject. However, such a perception is actually a methodological bracketing of the fact that language can live only through speaking subjects. Right at this moment I am using the structures of the English language to structure words into meaningful sentences and that act of ordering contributes to the reproduction of social, linguistic, structures. It is the fact that I, and millions of others, routinely speak or write in English that distinguishes the latter from a dead language such as Norse. Within structuralism structures are always portrayed in terms of constraint with an implicit underlying evaluative characterization of structures as opposed to freedom. Of course, it is correct that these structures constrain my actions but, they are also a condition of meaningful freedom in the sense that they are a precondition of my being able to do what I wish in collaboration with others – in this case explaining power and hegemony. These structures are external as part of a linguistic system and experienced as external through the imposition of norms by others upon me as a speaking subject. If I were to use a singular noun with a plural verb my editor would either insist on verb/noun agreement and continuous experiments with 'alternative grammars' would, in all probability, elicit a response that would convince me that what I was doing was 'wrong'. However, over time, structures are also experienced as internal in the sense that they exist as a tacitly used rule, which I automatically use to order my action and constitute part of my perception of order in the world-out-there. In this sense, from the perspective of the social agent, structures are simultaneously both enabling and constraining, rules and resources, and internal and external. In short agency and structure are characterized by duality, not dualism, which actors reproduce in the moment of structuration, as a form of world-begetting action.

The duality of structure as both a rule and resource parallels Gramsci's discussion of normative and immanent, or spontaneous, grammar. The latter is the grammar that we use almost reflexively to structure our speech, while normative grammar is a derivative which we experience in the 'reciprocal monitoring, reciprocal teaching, reciprocal 'censorship' expressed in such questions as 'what did you mean to say?'... 'Make yourself clearer' etc. and in mimicry and teasing. This whole complex...comes together to create a grammatical conformism, to establish 'norms or judgements of correctness and incorrectness.' (Gramsci 1985: 180; quoted in Ives 2004: 93). While Gramsci considers normative grammar as constraint, it is, of course, necessary for the existence of spontaneous grammar, as illustrated in the above examples concerning 'incorrect' usage. As such, normative grammar is central to the existence of spontaneous grammar as a shared resource, which is both public (as manifest in correction) yet private. The latter meaning of 'private' does not mean 'private' in the sense of being singular to, or the particular property of, the social agent. Extending the Greek idea of the 'idiot' as a 'private individual', Gramsci argues that freedom is not freedom to create your private grammars, which is the freedom of an 'idiot' (Gramsci 1985: 124; Ives 2004: 91). Instead, freedom entails using grammars and systems of meaning in a manner that may be novel but which, none the less, does not transcend them entirely, which, of course, is theoretically consistent with Wittgenstein's private language argument as developed in the *Philosophical Investigations* (1967).

Giddens views power both as 'power to' and as 'power over' (Giddens 1981:50; 1976: 111–2). Power is a capacity for action, which agents derive from the enabling aspect of social structures. 'Power over' is a subset of 'power to', which entails domination. However, domination is not an absolute zero-sum phenomenon but entails mutual autonomy and dependence (Giddens 1982: 39). If an actor A wishes to exercise power over B, A is of course more autonomous than B but A is still somewhat dependent upon B's resources (otherwise B would not be worth exercising power over) and this fact does give B some autonomy. To take a classic Marxist example, in capitalist relations of production, the capitalist has more autonomy than the worker, but he or she still is dependent upon the latter, who has the option of withdrawing their labour. While the capitalist exercises power over the worker, it is also the case that the worker derives some benefit from the relationship, which gives them some, albeit reduced, capacity for action – 'power to'.

The fact that power presupposes autonomy and dependence is of theoretical significance for the concept of hegemony. The meaning of hegemony articulated by ancient Greek historians, including Thucydides, and which also receives emphasis by Gramsci, is a view of hegemony as a power relationship in which both the hegemon and the led retain some autonomy (Fontana 1993 and Haugaard 2006). Unlike empire, hegemony entails an alliance between states in which the hegemon always makes sure to respect the autonomy of the subaltern elements within the hegemonic alliance. The very notion of hegemony in the Greek historians' and Gramscian mode implies that allies or followers possess autonomy, since these subordinates, in giving their consent to leadership or domination, have by implication the ability to refuse inclusion in a hegemonic arrangement. Ancient Athens rose to the position of hegemon, only to lose the Peloponnesian War to Sparta, which became the new hegemon but which failed to retain that position because it engendered hatred from its allies, thus undermining consent and autonomy (Lentner 2006).

In Giddens the consent implicit in power is rooted in a general, tacit, social knowledge lodged in practical consciousness, which is a prerequisite for competent structuration practices. Practical consciousness knowledge, or what Bourdieu terms *habitus*, is the social knowledge which makes ordered interaction possible and, in that sense, is theoretically similar to Barnes' 'social knowledge'. What distinguishes the former from the latter is the fact that Barnes views this knowledge paradigmatically, while Giddens is more Durkheimian in interpreting this knowledge in terms of rules and norms. However, what is absent from all their positions, but which was present in Bourdieu, is the idea that this knowledge may itself be the outcome of power.

Bourdieu takes the view that *habitus* is the outcome of conflict. It is a form of tacit knowledge which the relatively powerful and the relatively powerless reproduce in a continual struggle for prestige and status. Bourdieu is influenced by Elias' view of *habitus* as an outcome of struggle between classes who use culture as a mode of distinction and exclusion, with which the dominant group defines their particular culture as 'civilized' (Elias 2000). In *Distinction* (1984), Bourdieu documents how the bourgeoisie reify their particular manners as 'natural' and, thus, manage to define what constitutes the 'correct' socialization for those of the upper echelons of society. Once a particular *habitus* is 'naturalized', as superior to the *habitus* of others, it constitutes 'cultural capital' which becomes another resource beyond economic and coercive capital. Gramsci described the capitalist system as defended by endless fortifications and ditches (Gramsci 1971: 238) and, arguably 'cultural capitals' constitutes many such ditches. An excellent example is found in the unification of Italy. Prior to unification there was no singular Italian language but a multiplicity of minor Latin-based languages spoken in the Italian peninsula. A political decision was taken to make Florentine the official language of Italy because it was associated with high culture and literature and thus known to the educated classes, although it was spoken by as few as two per cent of the population in everyday speech. Consistent with his understanding of the workings of hegemony, Gramsci opposed this (see Ives 2004) because he perceived this as a hegemonic move by the elite. Using Bourdieu's terminology, it could be argued that the Italian bourgeoisie created cultural capital for themselves by making their everyday speech Italian – the official language of state and education.

Bourdieu's account of habitus and cultural capital is framed within the orthodoxies of Marxism, whereby class and the economy are still privileged as part of an essentialist discourse. In contrast, in Foucault these essentialisms are absent. Social actors are considered part of systems of thought that shape historically specific relations of domination. In contrast to Lukes, the opposition between true and false consciousness is absent. Instead it is social consciousness *per se* that lies at the centre of Foucault's problematic.

Foucault is essentially a meaning holist (see Foucault 1989: 99). The categories of meaning by which social actors make sense of the world are relationally constituted. For instance, the Renaissance episteme should be seen as a system of knowledge in which everything mirrors everything else through resemblance, such that it makes sense to argue that the face mirrors the heavens – Venus is the mouth as it gives passage to kisses, etc. (Foucault 1970: 17). Within such a system of thought, the mouth and Venus may have the same signifier as in the modern system, but as concepts they are significantly different because their relational context is altered. The importance of context, of course, is the central insight of hermeneutics but in Foucault it is coupled with the perception that social actors themselves constitute signifiers within these systems of thought which define who or what they are, thus making meaning entirely political.

Foucault contrasts two models of power, which he sometimes refers to as 'Reich's hypothesis' and 'Nietzsche's hypothesis', respectively (Foucault 1980: 91). The former corresponds to the negative conflictual view of power while the latter is a positive constitutive power. It would be too simplistic to say that the latter is identical with consensual power in the Arendt, Parsons and Barnes tradition, as this form of power does not have the positive normative connotations which it has for those theorists. However, it shares with them the insights that power is created by the social system, is not reducible to coercive power and, as in Barnes, is derived from shared social knowledge. Foucault's negative normative judgement comes from a double deception at the core of power. The first deception is the assumption that power is identical with conflictual coercive power. This has the effect that positive power is invisible to social actors and, as a consequence, they are easily subjected to it. Second, in the relationship between power and knowledge there exists a self-deception that truth is somehow exempt from power – Lukes' third dimension of power would be an example of this deception. In Foucault, truth performs a special reifying function in the creation of regimes of power/knowledge.

Foucault distinguishes between what he calls 'deep' and 'shallow' conflicts. A shallow conflict is one that essentially reproduces a system of meaning, while a deep one subverts that system and central to it is a conflict over truth. In essence, a system of thought becomes dominant when it can establish a link to truth and, in the process, prove different systems of thought arbitrary. Again this has clear parallels with Gramsci's account of a truly counter-hegemonic strategy, which would be the conceptual equivalent of Foucault's deep conflict. In Gramsci, this kind of deep conflict is a war of position in which the core of a hegemonic system or block is replaced. Much to the chagrin of Marxists, Foucault once claimed that the conflict between Marx and the classical economists was a storm in a teacup (Foucault 1970: 262), meaning that it constituted a shallow conflict, which took place within an existing system of meaning. Similarly, Gramsci claimed that the key to the overthrow of existing relations of domination was not the replacement of those in charge of the existing centres of power, rather there had to be an undermining of bourgeois hegemonic social practices.

Echoes of the positions can be found in the famous debates between Miliband and Poulantzas in the 1970s.

Foucault formulates his view of positive constitutive power in terms of a reversal of Clausewitz's assertion that war is politics continued by other means. According to this model, power is '...the reign of peace in civil society...' where the purpose of power is not to end the conflict of war but, instead, is to reinscribe the effects of war '...in social institutions, in economic inequalities, in language, in the bodies themselves of each and everyone of us.' (Foucault 1980: 90). Much like Arendt, Foucault argued that violence reveals the absence of power but without the Arendtian consequent assumption that power is consequently benign.

Again this opposition between power and violence, politics and war, is reminiscent of Gramsci's insistence that hegemony is not reducible to coercion. In fact the strength of the bourgeoisie is manifest in their lack of a need to coerce. While Gramsci's distinction between a war of manoeuvre and a war of position (Gramsci 1971: 229) is a military metaphor, his point is that war of manoeuvre, which is a final military confrontation, is superficial compared to war of position, which entails the creation of a new hegemonic block.

While Foucault argues that there is no escape from power/knowledge, he argues that some forms of domination are more effective than others (Foucault 1980: 93). In particular he is interested in the contrast between the modern system of power and the pre-modern sovereign complex. The former is power as most people take it for granted, as coercive power, while the power of the disciplinary prison regime is positive constitutive power. In his genealogical analysis, modernity is characterized by a particular fabric of power/knowledge in which the social subject is objectified. Objectification facilitates the creation of a grammar of normality and abnormality, which social agents find themselves drawn into. The workings of the modern regime of power/knowledge is illustrated by the contrast between the horrors of the execution of Damiens in 1757 and the modern prison timetable of 80 years later (Foucault 1979). The former was hanged, drawn and quartered, with a number of added sadistic flourishes. In contrast, the objective of the prison is to inflict as little pain as possible on the body, but to maximize control over its movements. The common sense explanation for the change is an increase in civilization and leniency. Foucault's hypothesis is, however, that the change is a consequence of a different economy of power. In the pre-modern, Sovereign, model of punishment the objective is to create a ritualized representation of war between the Sovereign, as the embodiment of the body politic, and the criminal who, by their criminal act, has, in effect, broken the social contract, and stepped out of society to make war upon it. By the extremity of the punishment, which is a virtual carnival of violence, the Hobbesian Sovereign demonstrates his monopoly of violence (the criminal's resistance is made useless as his body is mutilated, pulverised and thrown to the winds) as the ultimate source of social order. In contrast, the criminal of the modern period is not someone whom society declares war against but is an object of failed socialization that has to be resocialized. As one contemporary commentator put it: 'Punishment, if I may so put it, should strike the soul rather than the body' (Quoted in Foucault 1979: 16). The paradigmatic representation of the form of punishment is Bentham's Panopticon, which is a circular building, with glass on the outside, and the prisoners in a doughnut like shape around a watchtower. The prison-guard, sitting in the central watchtower, can at all times observe the prisoners' everyday movements, while the prisoners can observe no-one except themselves. The result is a one-way judgemental monologue by the 'normal' concerning the 'abnormal'. The only option for freedom on the part of the prisoner is to internalize this judgement and, in effect, objectify themselves in the eyes of reason. So, power/knowledge holds the promise of freedom but only as a form of domination.

Bentham intended the Panopticon not only as a model for the prison but as a generalized architectural design which could be used for schools, factories or any other large institutional complexes. As such, it was a model for society itself. In the pre-modern system those who had power were the objects of knowledge (the local prince and aristocracy), while the relatively powerless were invisible. In modernity this is reversed, it is school children, the insane, patients, the marginal and the working population who are the objects of knowledge. These relations of visibility parallels the Kantian world-view in which the source of knowledge is to be found in the human mind as the ultimate source of the categories of interpretation. If the mind is the source of truth, then the creation of social order presupposes social subjects who can internalize the truths upon which that order is based. The distinction between 'right mind' and 'insanity, 'normality' and abnormality', become the key political question, not who holds the monopoly of violence. Of course violence is still present, we have to restrain the objects of socialization if they try and run away but the routine reproduction of social order is premised upon the internalization of shared truths concerning normality and abnormality. To the extent to which disciplinary power is successful it makes coercion superfluous. Thus, it is a reversal of the Arendtian normative position, whereby the most insidious power is the one that is most successful at supplanting violence with consent.

As argued by Fontana (2006), Gramsci held two perceptions of the state. The first is common to everyday liberal and bourgeois discourse where the state is conceptualized as a neutral arbiter holding the monopoly of violence for the purposes of the rule of law. Beyond this there is 'civil' society which embodies the, so called, 'private realm'. However, for Gramsci this distinction is essentially a legitimating ideology, which masks the fact that 'civil society' is not separate from the state but is inextricably intertwined in it. For instance, the idea of the 'private realm' in it itself presupposes a system of bourgeois domination, so what appears like a limit to state power, is actually a rationalization for a specific mode of domination. The myth of the neutral state, which maintains this distinction, is not actually neutral because it is inextricably bound up with a particular mode of domination. If a revolution were to take place in a developed bourgeois society, controlling the state would not actually change the system if the legitimating mindset, which distinguishes between public and private, were not also changed. There are direct parallels with Foucault's distinction between deep and shallow conflicts. A conflict which reproduces an existing discourse may change who is in charge but fails to change the nature of domination. Pre-modern social order is not reinforced by discourse in the same manner. The state, or its embodiment in the body of the King, is a monopoly of violence which maintains itself in opposition to the criminal as a revolutionary subject. The dysfunctionality of this system is that it presupposes a discourse in which it is, in effect, legitimate for the subject to decapitate the King if they have the means of violence to do so or, indeed, if the King fails to protect the subject from the violence of others outside the body politic (Hobbes' sole condition for legitimate revolution). The concept of the Sovereign making war upon the recalcitrant subject has implicit in it the reversal of the relationship in the form of revolution.

The Sovereign is rendered as relatively weaker than modern systems of domination in which the recalcitrant citizen is someone who, effectively, has failed to recognize the truth and, by implication, is not of 'right' mind. In this context it is worth observing that in his account of the overlapping consensus which underlies liberal democratic society, Rawls argues that those who do not commit themselves to this overlapping discourse are 'unreasonable' (Rawls 1993: 58–66).

If the modern system of domination and the state is protected by a system of power which goes beyond simple access to coercive resources, this explains why it is (counter-intuitively so) the case that a revolution is easier to realize in a pre-modern society than a modern bourgeois one. In his reflections upon the success of the Russian revolution, in contrast to the failure of communist parties to mobilize the masses in modern bourgeois democracies, Gramsci wrote the following:

> In the East the State was everything, civil society was primordial and gelatinous; in the West, there was a proper relation between Sate and civil society, and when the State trembled a sturdy structure of civil society was at once revealed. The state was only an outer ditch, behind which there stood a powerful system of fortresses and earthworks. (Gramsci 1971: 238)

The description of civil society as primordial and gelatinous is intended to imply that it is so highly underdeveloped as to be almost absent and the powerful system of fortresses and earthworks are, of course, not only civil society but also the sources of domination within civil society that make bourgeois hegemony possible (Fontana 1993). The big question is, of course, what exactly these sources are.

In a discussion of philosophy, Gramsci claimed that everyone is actually a philosopher in the sense that our very interpretative horizons, which make us who we are, imply some kind of philosophical commitment. His exact words are as follows:

> It must first be shown that all men are 'philosophers',...This philosophy is contained in: (1) language itself, which is a totality of determined notions and concepts and not just of words grammatically devoid of content; (2) 'common sense' and 'good sense'; (3) popular religion and, therefore, also in the entire system of beliefs, superstitions, opinions, ways of seeing things and of acting,... (Gramsci 1971: 323)

Within this framework, so-called, 'organic intellectuals' perform the task of stitching this philosophy of everyday life to specific systems of domination. Consequently, a counter-hegemonic strategy would entail replacing this bourgeois philosophy of everyday life with another, linked to an alternative social order. Gramsci argued that this type of order would be commensurable with the social practices of the proletariat. Gramsci's hypothesis is that under bourgeois domination 'organic intellectuals' perform the task of endowing the proletariat with a philosophy of everyday life which is particular to the task of legitimating the social practices pertinent to capitalism. In consequence the proletariat develops an essentially disjointed view whereby their philosophical world is out of step with or in opposition to their everyday practical activities (Gramsci 1971: 333), a disjuncture that manifests itself in those moments when practice diverges from theory, revealing an underlying tension, symptomatic of domination. As argued earlier in the context of Lukes, this can give an insight into a tension existing between the way the dominated believe themselves to think, and an alternative interpretative horizon or everyday philosophy, which is more commensurable with their social practices. In this context, the key to overcoming domination is the promulgation of an alternative philosophy that brings theory and practice back into unity, which entails a radical philosophical engagement with subaltern social agents. For Gramsci, this is the key to distinguishing normatively desirable power, based upon consent, from its opposite, which is also based upon internalized consent.

The fact that Gramsci describes everyone as a philosopher and includes in that philosophy, 'common sense', language and popular religion (which is interpreted in a wide sense), suggests that what he has in mind includes our wider social interpretative horizons. It includes Lukes' third dimension of power (as Lukes argues), Barnes' concept of social knowledge, Giddens' practical knowledge, Bourdieu's *habitus*, and some aspect, if not the totality, of Foucault's understanding of power/knowledge and discourse. Because these theorists have benefited from a knowledge of theoretical developments and empirical research in the social sciences which has taken place since Gramsci's death, an understanding of their work gives us a more profound knowledge of the 'earthworks and ditches' of the modern system of domination than would have been available to Gramsci.

Further content to these earthworks and ditches is given by Clegg in *Frameworks of Power* (1989), in which he seeks to replace the modernist agent-centred analysis of power with a vocabulary more reminiscent of the post-modern age. Central to this is a vocabulary based upon electronic 'circuits of power'. The first, and most economical circuit of power, is episodic power, which includes the behavioural emphasis of Robert Dahl. However, as observed by Clegg, if an agent exercises power over another, this momentary episodic phenomenon is a manifestation of a deeper power, which defines who the social agent *is*. To take an analogy with chess, if we observe a queen taking a pawn this observation is only relatively superficial if we do not understand what makes a queen a queen and a pawn a pawn. The deeper understanding defines the second circuit of power, which is dispositional circuit. It defines meaning and membership and is reified by conflicts over truth – as in Foucault. Building upon Laclau and Mouffe's (1985) concept of quilting points, Clegg argues that these constitute 'obligatory passage' points through which all traffic must pass (Clegg 1989: 207). It is at the level of dispositional power that the concept of hegemony could be theorized, which Clegg implicitly acknowledges. However, Clegg prefers to distance himself from Gramsci because the strongly Marxist discourse implies an arrogant privileging of the intellectual. In this sense he would agree with Lukes that three dimensional power is a form of hegemony but, taking account of the problems associated with distinguishing 'true' from 'false consciousness', Clegg wishes to distance himself from such a dichotomy (1989: 165).

Dispositional power does not, of course, exist in a vacuum, but is a reflection of a deeper system of relations of domination, which Clegg refers to as the third circuit of power, which is both a source of system change and stability. Essentially dominant groups 'organizationally outflank' (a term borrowed from Mann 1983) each other in a process whereby the existing system remains stable as long as the existing dominant elite succeed in organizationally outflanking any attempts to change the order of things (1989: 220–1). Conversely, if another elite manages to organizationally outflank the older elite, the system changes – for instance, the bourgeoisie organizationally outflanked the feudal aristocracy. Clegg is at pains to emphasize that such outflanking does not necessarily presuppose human agency – the humble rat, in the form of the bubonic plague, contributed to the organizational outflanking of the feudal system.

In his later work (Clegg et al. 2006), Clegg builds upon the insights of Bauman and actor network theory to argue that changes within the post-modern world have contributed to a change in power which makes it essentially post-Foucauldian. The image of the Panopticon presupposes a form of engagement between actors (prisoner and prison guard), which the new mobile elites tend to avoid (see also Bauman 2000). The centres of power are no longer fixed and the key to being in power is to be mobile while subaltern groups remain tied to space, suggesting hegemony is no longer relational in the way it was in the modern world. If there is such a group as 'organic intellectuals', in post-modern domination they keep the subaltern distracted by media events and local identities while the global elite move companies and resources around the world within a system of domination premised upon disengagement with people but control of fluid organizational nodal points.

In Clegg's second circuit of power there is a tacit assumption of conflict, while in Haugaard (1997, 2003 and 2006) these systemic elements are also consensually based. Like Gramsci, I frequently methodologically bracket coercive power and violence. Central to this project is the idea that social structures are reproduced collaboratively between social actors in interaction and, consequently, any social interaction presupposes the possibility of refusal on the part of the subaltern actor. The latter possibility is only overcome if social structures are either not discursively reflected upon, existing as practical consciousness knowledge (*habitus*), or are perceived of a lying beyond social convention. Various techniques of reification are entailed, which include primordialist myths (nationalism), appeals to nature ('natural differences'), essentialism, appeals to God, science, 'truth' and whatever constitutes a 'rock of certainty' within a given social order. In this work we also see a deliberate merging of the ideas of modernist thinkers, such as Lukes, and Giddens, with post-modern concerns, especially Foucault and Clegg.

In the work of Flyvbjerg, Hayward and Gordon, we find that coercion is not so much replaced by consent, but with reason, which is not really reason in the objective scientific sense but closer to 'rationalisation'. Flyvbjerg's work (1997 and 2001) is dominated by a theoretical confrontation between the ideas of Foucault and Habermas. For Flyvbjerg, Habermas' 'ideal speech' situation is an imposition of a particular type of reason, which is a 'rationalization' of modern modes of domination. Following Foucault, Flyvbjerg argues that 'ideal speech', as a conceptualization of truth as divorced from power, is deception that legitimates modern forms of domination. In a detailed study of the debates over the location of a bus station in Aalborg, Denmark, Flyvbjerg shows how what is 'rational' and what is 'true' is the outcome of minute political struggles. Similarly, in Gordon's ethnographic work on the New South Wales Police Force, these rationalizations become internalized within the complex organization, as local truths, which are carefully guarded by the elite within that organization (Gordon 2007).

Hayward's *De-facing Power* is largely a dialogue with the three-dimensional power debate, in which the author argues that the third dimension of power is not sufficiently radical. In an ethnographic account of two schools, Hayward describes the process by which the two groups of children internalize very different modes of rationality. In 'North End Community School' children learn 'unreflective rule-following and deference to authority' (2000: 177), while in Fair View a form of critical thinking is encouraged which is central to autonomy. If we take the schoolteacher as example of the organic intellectual, Hayward's study could be interpreted as account of the way in which hegemony is reproduced in the contemporary world.

Looking at the power debate as a whole, it is dominated by a number of overlapping Janus faced dualities: theories which divorce power from truth versus those which see the two as inextricably bound; those that emphasize 'power over' versus those who consider 'power to'; and those that perceive power as primarily based upon coercion and violence versus those who consider it consensual. These dualities are also intrinsic to hegemony and what emerges as central, as indeed it also was for Gramsci, is the idea that sophisticated power relations are based upon deep systemically generated sources of consent or the appearance thereof which renders the sword-wielding image of the King of Hobbes' Leviathan obsolete.

REFERENCES

Arendt, Hannah (1958) *The Human Condition*. Chicago: University of Chicago Press.
Arendt, Hannah (1970) *On Violence*. London: Penguin.
Bachrach, Peter and Morton S. Baratz (1962) 'The two faces of power', *American Political Science Review*, vol 56 – reprinted in Haugaard (2002).
Bauman Zygmunt (2000) *Liquid Modernity*. Cambridge: Polity.
Barnes, Barry (1988) *The Nature of Power*. Cambridge. Polity.
Bourdieu, Pierre (1984) *Distinction*. London: Routledge.
Clegg, Stewart (1989) *Frameworks of Power*. London: Sage.
Clegg, Stewart, David Courpasson and Nelson Phillips (2006) *Power and Organizations*. London: Sage.
Dahl, Robert (1957) 'The concept of power', *Behavioural Science*, 2: 201–215.
Dahl, Robert (1958) 'A critique of the ruling-elite model', *American Political Science Review*, 52: 462–469.
Elias, Norbert (2000) *The Civilizing Process*. Oxford: Blackwell.
Femia, Joseph (1987) *Gramsci's Political Thought*. Oxford: Clarendon Press.
Flyvbjerg, Bent (1997) *Rationality and Power*. Chicago: University of Chicago Press.
Flyvbjerg, Bent (2001) *Making Social Science Matter*. Cambridge: Cambridge University Press.
Fontana, Benedetto (1993) *Hegemony and Power*. Minneapolis: University of Minnesota Press.
Fontana, Benedetto (2006) 'State and Society: The Concept of Hegemony in Gramsci' in Mark Haugaard and Howard Lentner (eds) *Hegemony and Power*. New York: Lexington Books, pp. 23–44.
Foucault, Michel (1970) *The Order of Things*, London: Routledge.
Foucault, Michel (1979) *Discipline and Punish*. Harmondsworth: Penguin.
Foucault, Michel (1980) *Power/Knowledge*. Colin Gordon, (ed.) Brighton: Harvester Press.
Foucault, Michel (1989) *The Birth of the Clinic*. London: Routledge.
Giddens, Anthony (1981) *A Contemporary Critique of Historical Materialism*. London: Macmillan.
Giddens, Anthony (1982) *Profiles and Critiques in Social Theory*. London: Macmillan.
Giddens, Anthony (1984) *The Constitution of Society*. Cambridge: Polity.
Gordon, Raymond (2007) *Power, Knowledge and Domination*. Copenhagen: Business School Press.
Gramsci, Antonio (1971) *Selections from the Prison Notebooks*. Quintin Hoare and Geoffrey Nowell Smith (eds), Lawrence and Wishart.
Haugaard, Mark (1997) *The Constitution of Power*. Manchester: Manchester University Press.
Haugaard, Mark (2002) *Power: A Reade*. Manchester: Manchester University Press.
Haugaard, Mark (2003) 'Reflections on seven ways of creating power', *European Journal of Social Theory*.
Haugaard, Mark (2006) 'Power and hegemony in social theory', in Haugaard and Lentner (2006): pp. 45–67.
Haugaard, Mark and Howard Lentner (eds) (2006) *Hegemony and Power*. New York: Lexington Books.
Hayward, Clarrisa Rile (2000) *De-facing Power*. Cambridge: Cambridge University Press.
Ives, Peter (2004) *Language and Hegemony in Gramsci*. London: Pluto.
Laclau, Ernesto and Chantal Mouffe (1985) *Hegemony and Socialist Strategy*. London: Verso.
Lentner, Howard (2006) 'Hegemony and power in international politics' in Haugaard and Lentner (2006).
Lukes, Steven (1974) *Power: A Radical View*. London: Macmillan.
Lukes, Steven (2005) Second Edition of *Power: A Radical View*. Basingstoke: Palgrave Macmillan.

Mann, Michael (1986) *The Sources of Power*, Vol 1. Cambridge: Cambridge University Press.
Mann, Michael (1986) *The Sources of Social Power*. Cambridge: Cambridge University Press.
Parsons, Talcott (1963) 'On the concept of political power', *Proceedings of the American Philosophical Society*, Vol. 107 – reprinted in Haugaard (2002).
Poggi, Gianfranco (2000) *Forms of Power*. Cambridge: Polity Press.
Rawls, John (1993) *Political Liberalism*, New York: Columbia University Press.
Weber, Max (1978) *Economy and Society* (2 Vols). Berkeley: University of California Press.
Wittgenstein, Ludwig (1967) *Philosophical Investigations*. Oxford: Oxford University Press.

14

Power and Legitimacy: From Weber to Contemporary Theory

Ray Gordon

The chapter provides a comparative review of literature pertinent to power and legitimacy in social systems. The review will trace a specific path from the work of Max Weber to contemporary times. A comprehensive assessment of all contributions to the literature is outside the scope of the review. Instead, the focus is restricted to the comparison of three key bodies of literature, namely, mainstream functionalist approaches, critical approaches, and pragmatic approaches. A small sample of contemporary work that specifically centres on power and the construction of legitimacy in organizations will also be reviewed.

The chapter will begin by illustrating how Weber's work acts as a founding voice for much of the literature. Any discussion of power and legitimacy cannot leave Weber's counterpart Karl Marx out of the picture, however; hence, Marx's contribution is also addressed. The objective is not to analyse Weber's and Marx's writings in detail, as numerous other writers have done so already, but to illustrate how particular accounts of the nature of power and legitimacy have emerged from their work.

The first body of literature that the chapter concentrates on relates to mainstream functionalist approaches to power and legitimacy. The review reveals that contributors to this path have a preoccupation with 'rationality', adopting a rational approach to power and legitimacy in social settings which is largely grounded in a 'first dimensional' and 'resource dependency' model of power. In this approach, legitimacy is necessarily linked to the formally sanctioned use of power. More specifically authority is legitimate and power is illegitimate.

The chapter then examines critical theorists' discussions of power and legitimacy. Legitimacy within this body of literature is related to the effects of domination. While Weber's work rattles away in the background, Marx is the primary influence in this literature. For these writers, Marxian constructs such as hegemony, false consciousness and alienation are of central concern when considering legitimacy.

A body of literature that represents an alternative intellectual tradition is then investigated. Once again Weber's work echoes within this literature, particularly in more contemporary contributions, but it is the voice of earlier writers, Niccoló Machiavelli and Friedrich Nietzsche, that are the primary influences. The work of Michel Foucault also features prominently in this literature, as does the work of more contemporary writers such as Stewart R. Clegg, Cynthia Hardy, Mark Haugaard and Bent Flyvbjerg. The difference between this body of literature and the others is that the construction of legitimacy has a far more pragmatic orientation.

Finally, the chapter explores the similarity and differences between the aforementioned bodies of literature, and shows how contemporary writers, such as David Courpasson, Stewart R. Clegg, Martin Kornberger and Ray Gordon have traced a similar path through the power and legitimacy literature. The chapter illustrates how these writers have applied the subsequent theory to empirical settings to reveal a link between, what Weber termed, 'structures of dominancy', and the social construction of legitimacy.

THE VOICE OF WEBER

Weber's view of power was embedded in a sociological vision that stressed the centrality of the project of rationalization, which has framed modern times. This 'project of rationalization' derived from the Enlightenment movement, resulting in European entities imposing what they considered to be a superior form of reason, and hence social practice, on the rest of the world. Other social groups, such as Indigenous peoples, were considered inferior savages that could only benefit from adopting European social ways and general laws of reason (Clegg et al., 2006). As Clegg (1989) argues, in the mid to latter half of the twentieth century, Weber's work was used as a warrant to legitimize the process of rationalizing less 'rational' forms of life out of existence (Clegg, 1989).

Weber did not have an affinity for the rationalization process; indeed, his views are marked by a world-weary cultural pessimism. The rationalization process is seen as a corollary of fundamental transformations stemming from the Industrial Revolution and the epistemic shift to modernity; a response to the changing environment of the times marked by an increasing complexity of social and organizational structures and systems (Touraine, 1988) that were radically changing the fabric of society. Noticeably absent from the mainstream literature was the pessimism inherent in Weber's theory and observations: he was concerned that the 'rationalization of the world would produce for modernity a bureaucratic "iron cage" of bondage' (Clegg, 1990: 28). Weber saw the 'discipline' of bureaucracy encroaching upon all spheres of social life as a result of its technical superiority over any other forms of social organization (Weber, 1948: 214).

In regard to power, Weber adopted a different approach to Marx. Marxian theory provided little room for discretion and opportunities for strategic agency, with power relations reduced to those who owned capital and those who did not. Weber acknowledged that while power was *derived* from owning and controlling the means of production, it was not *reducible* to ownership and non-ownership because power is additionally derived from the knowledge of 'how' production can be achieved. For Weber, power relations also reflected the differential ability of people to control methods of production (Hardy and Clegg, 1996). In contrast to Marx, Weber saw people in relations of production not as victims of their own 'false consciousness' or as being deceived by the ruling class but as members of an organization with the capacity to make strategic use of their own skills and knowledge of the production process.

In short, Weber's view of power is more complex than Marx's, with all organizational members being recognized as having access to varying degrees of power. Organizational members exercise some control over their ability to use this power, both to challenge and reinforce the formal organizational structure in which differential powers are vested, legitimized and reproduced. Thus, the foundation and maintenance of positions of dominance are not simply grounded in economically defined class relations, as Marx had argued (Weber, 1978: 942), but are subject to the strategic action of individuals operating under socially constructed 'structures of dominancy'. Weber used the term 'structure of dominancy' to refer to those socially constituted norms that gave rise to a 'prevailing authority', which is considered legitimate because it is efficacious authoritative action with respect to norms (Clegg, 1975).

Weber viewed abstract labour power as representing a capacity embodied in a person to exercise discretion in the application of their overall capacities at work. As the power of labour was embodied in employees, who held ultimate discretion over themselves, there was always a potential for them to offer resistance to projects of managerial control (Hardy and Clegg, 1996: 624). Accordingly, the provision of strategies for managers to control, deflect or defeat labour's discretionary power is evident in much of the early mainstream organization theory literature. The most important strategy, the use of rule systems, is the mainstay of Weberian analysis of organizations as bureaucracies.

Weber and Marx's work focuses on the way in which power is derived from owning and controlling the means of production, a power reinforced by organizational rules and structures. Collectively, the work of Weber and Marx represents the foundation of the modern era's approach to power and legitimacy. It is an approach fundamentally characterized by ideal views about how power 'ought' to be in organizations. The differences in their views however, provide a 'fork in the road' in regard to the development of alternative bodies of literature that discuss the relationship between power and legitimacy. The first of these draws directly from Weber's work by linking power and legitimacy to rationality. The second, while resonating with Weber, primarily draws from Marx's work and associates power and legitimacy with the emancipation of peoples who are unaware that their lives could be different. The chapter will now explore these two bodies of literature.

MAINSTREAM FUNCTIONALIST ACCOUNTS OF POWER AND LEGITIMACY

Weber is often acclaimed for providing the foundation for much of organizational and management theory. More specifically, the pursuit of rationality and subsequently Weber's construction of *rational legal authority* is central to the field. However, it is important to note that Weber not only discusses *rational legal power* (authority) but also *traditional power* (historic customs, blood lines etc.) and *charismatic power* (personal power). In terms of legitimacy, the mainstream organizational theory and management literature implicitly assumes that rational legal authority is *the* appropriate form of power for organizational environments. Interestingly, and as noted earlier, the field omits Weber's pessimism in regard to his construction of rational legal authority.

Clegg (1975) argues that, in a sociological sense, early organizational theory and management writers adopted a relatively narrow approach to organizations. The approach can be traced back to the impact that the work of functionalist theorists, in particular Talcott Parsons, had on the social sciences throughout the mid twentieth century. The translation of Weber by Parsons and Henderson (1948) has been subjected to negative feedback with writers such as Gouldner (1976), Banton (1972) and Clegg (1975) arguing that the interpretation was flawed. Clegg (1975) highlighted that the key problem with Parsons and Henderson's interpretation lies with their translation of the word *Herrschaft* to mean rational authority. In discussing the relationship between power and authority, however, Weber provides examples of *Herrschaft* that indicate the word had two meanings. First, Weber discusses *Herrschaft* in a way that suggests the word's English translation means rational authority. Clegg (1975: 56–66) points out that Weber also used the word to describe unobtrusive forms of domination. These two meanings will now be explained in further detail.

Weber viewed the efficacy of authority as being contingent upon its social acceptance. Whether authoritative action was efficacious was contingent on whether it was considered as being rational by those subject to it. An individual attempting to exercise authority needs do so on the basis of a:

> legal norm…established by agreement or by imposition, on grounds of expediency or value rationality or both, with the claim to obedience, (to those)…who stand on certain social relationships or carry out forms of social action which in the order governing the organization have been declared to be relevant (Weber, 1968: 217)

The use of the term 'the order governing the organization' encompasses formally sanctioned rules and positions of authority as well as socially constituted norms. Thus, the obedience of a person to an attempt to exercise authority depends on both the formal design and whether this person's 'right to power' is perceived as legitimate with respect to the norms of the social system (Clegg, 1975). In this sense, quite differently to Parsons and Henderson's interpretation, Weber acknowledges that the legitimacy of rationality has a contextual, historical and value laden dimension.

Weber's discussion of 'structures of dominancy' supports the argument that his use of the word *Herrschaft* does not simply refer to sanctioned authority. According to Clegg (1975; Clegg et al. 2006), Weber explains, through reference to practical examples, that the norms underpinning the interpretation of rationality in social systems are actually imbued with power. These norms reflect differential power relations which, through customary social practice, result in the constitution of 'structures of dominancy'. Weber explains why people orient themselves towards a particular form of social order:

> Without exception, every sphere of social order is profoundly influenced by structures of dominancy. In a great number of cases, the emergence of a rational association from amorphous social action has been due to domination and the way in which it has been exercised. Even where this is not the case, the structure of dominancy and its unfolding is decisive in determining the form of social action and its orientation towards a 'goal' (Weber, 1968: 942).

In this extract, Weber suggests the rationality that emerges from discursive social action is subject to both social norms and structures of dominancy. These structures of dominancy are taken for granted norms that are socially constituted over time through recurring practices, and unobtrusively privilege certain ways of thinking and doing things. Adherence to the norms constitutes social relations in which certain individuals and groups are privileged and others are marginalized. Weber elaborates that the actions of people in positions of dominance, because of the privilege invested in such positions, contributes to both the constitution and reinforcement of the norms. Thus, the constraining nature of a system's norms is likely to reflect a historically constituted 'structure of dominancy'. While this description of a structure of dominancy may appear somewhat similar to the Marxian concept of hegemony, Weber does not see people as being victims of 'false consciousness' but playing an active role in the formation of these structures of dominancy.

It is evident that Weber's definition of *Herrschaft* extends beyond Parsons and Henderson's (1948) translation of 'formally sanctioned authority'. Weber's work indicates that *Herrschaft* can mean *legitimate* authority in specific contexts of action; thus, this concept of legitimacy problematizes the assumption that emanates from Parsons and Henderson's interpretation that formal authority is rational. Weber considered *Herrschaft* in terms of both authority and domination; domination in the sense that authoritative action would be considered legitimate with respect to social norms that were not only imbued with, but also reinforced by, historically constituted structures of dominancy (Clegg, 1975). Parsons and Henderson's account of authority disconnects itself from Weber's 'deeper' level consideration of structures of dominancy and thus constructs an interpretation of power in organizations that, comparatively, lacks depth. Their account suggests that the legitimacy of formal authority is seen as being the way things 'ought' to be.

Many social, political and, in particular, organizational and management writers have embraced Parsons and Henderson's work and adopted an approach that links power and legitimacy to hierarchy. However, Hardy and Clegg (1996) point out the acceptance of formal authority as legitimate power means that social theorists:

> have rarely felt it necessary to explain why it is that power should be hierarchical. In other words, in this stream of research, the power embedded in hierarchy has been viewed as 'normal' and 'inevitable' following from the formal design of the organization. As such, it has largely been excluded from analyses, which have, instead, focused on 'illegitimate' power, i.e. power exercised outside formal hierarchical structures and the channels that they sanction (Hardy and Clegg, 1996: 624).

Hardy and Clegg highlight that contrary to what Weber actually says, mainstream social and organizational theory largely separates power and authority: authority, because of its taken for granted legitimacy, is viewed as something different to power; power is reserved for action that is not sanctioned with authority. Key studies within the mainstream literature leading up to the early 1970s (see Thompson, 1956; Dubin 1957; Bennis 1959; Mechanic, 1962; Crozier, 1964; French and Raven, 1968; Hickson et al., 1971; Pettigrew, 1973; Pfeffer and Salancik, 1974) conceptually separate power from authority. These studies show that the exercise of power was attributed to political action on behalf of organizational members who were not formally sanctioned with authority and that such action was illegitimate, dysfunctional and thus, irrational. Interestingly, throughout this period, while management writers set about representing power in such terms, the problematic nature of 'legitimate' systems of authority were under-explored. Consequently, the focus of management writings was on the use of authority as a means to defeat conflict (Hardy and Clegg, 1996) brought about by the 'illegitimate' exercise of power. From this assumed 'purely rational' viewpoint it follows that in a social system where there is legitimate authority, those who are not sanctioned with authority have a duty to obey; when one has a duty to obey, one 'should' not engage in conflict. According to this view, in any social system where there is legitimate authority there 'should' be no conflict. In short, such a view amputates much of the workings of power, conflict and legitimacy from the theoretical and interpretative horizon.

Many mainstream social and organizational theorists have therefore associated power with conflict situations in which individuals engaged in political activities to realize their own vested interests at the expense of the organization's interest as a whole:

> It is clear that political activity is activity, which is undertaken to overcome some resistance or opposition. Without opposition or contest within the organization, there is neither the need nor the expectation that one would observe political activity (Pfeffer, 1981: 7).

Here, in one of his earlier accounts of power, Pfeffer implies that the only reason managers engage in politics is to overcome worker resistance that has caused an inefficient and ineffective use of an organization's resources. In doing so, Pfeffer privileges managers with an intellectual superiority and relegates power to episodic conflict scenarios. He implies that power and politics would not even occur if workers did not resist management.

Other writers hold similar viewpoints in regard to power (see Gandz and Murray, 1980; Enz, 1988). For example, Mintzberg (1983) has written:

> Politics refers to individual or group behaviour that is informal, ostensibly parochial, typically divisive, and above all, in the technical sense, illegitimate – sanctioned neither by formal authority, accepted ideology, nor certified expertise (Mintzberg, 1983: 172)

Mintzberg's approach to power sees politics and resistance premised on the assumption that organizations are rational arenas and managers are purely rational beings. The implication is that organizations and managers exist free from the influence of contextual pressures and individual interests respectively. While the literature aligns legitimacy with respect to the organization's best interests, it is somewhat problematic that the organization's interests and the interests of those sanctioned with authority are assumed to be one and the same. Hardy and Clegg point out, 'the possibility that managers might seek to serve their own vested interests [in a given context] is largely ignored' (1996: 629).

As indicated above, Weber viewed the functioning of power as embedded in an organization's structures of dominancy, which are unobtrusive in the sense that they reflect the outcomes of political struggles played out in the organization's past. The outcomes privilege certain ways of knowing and doing things and thus help to shape the meaning actors attribute to things in the present. Parsons and Henderson's exclusion of Weber's discussion of these deeper level structures of dominancy masks important sociological variables pertaining to power and legitimacy in social systems. The result is that to this day, many management writers continue to consider formal structure as a legitimate equilibrium starting point from which to promulgate how power 'should' be in organizations, a starting point that misrepresents the complex nature of power and legitimacy in organizations (Hardy and Clegg, 1996; see also Clegg, 1989; Deetz, 1985; Knights and Willmott, 1992).

CRITICAL ACCOUNTS OF POWER AND LEGITIMACY

Similar to both Weber and Marx, the critical theorists were concerned with the link between power and domination. More specifically, the critical theorists pondered why there was so little resistance from subordinate groups in social settings, and why these groups appeared to consent to their own subjugation (Clegg et al., 2006).

The work of the critical theorists emerged indirectly from what became known as the Community Power Debates of the 1950s and 1960s. Political theorists, such as Dahl (1957; 1961) and Polsby (1963), focused their research on how decisions made in a community illustrated the nature of power relations in that context. Two opposing theories of what constituted 'good' government emerged – *elitism* and *pluralism*. If the same groups or individuals were found to make most of the decisions in the key decision making arenas, the community was said to be *elitist*; if decisions were made in different arenas by different groups, the community was said to be *pluralist*.

Dahl (1957, 1961, 1968) is recognized as the main contributor to the Community Power Debate literature. In a series of publications, he mapped out a behavioural science oriented response to what he described as the much less rigorous work of the 'elitist' theorists of Hunter and Mills. Dahl regarded the work of the elitist theorists as methodologically slack. Therefore, he focused on the construction of a methodological approach that could capture and provide a formal model of power. To acquire precision, Dahl employed the principles of mechanics and focused on cause and effect relationships between forms in motion: the power of 'A' could be measured through the response of 'B' (Clegg, 1989).

These debates led to a critique by Bachrach and Baratz (1962) who questioned the pluralists' implicit assumption that decision-making processes were accessible to all members and that non-participation reflected satisfaction with the decision-making process and its outcomes by non-participants. These authors, and others (Lukes, 1974; Clegg, 1975; Saunders, 1979), asserted that unobservable conflict did not equate with no conflict and that interests and grievances could remain unspoken and outside of the decision arena (Gaventa, 1980; Saunders, 1979). At this point, research turned to how full participation in decision processes might be constrained (Hardy and Clegg, 1996).

Earlier, Schattschneider (1960) had argued that the inaction of people to acts of power could be due to the suppression of information that might inform their interests and needs and thus limit their knowledge and compound their ignorance. Building on this insight, Bachrach and Baratz (1962; 1963; 1970) developed the idea that power could also be linked to how decisions were *not* made. This has become known as the 'second dimension of power'. Bachrach and Baratz (1962; 1963; 1970) argued that a variety of previously unconsidered options were available to the more powerful members of an organization to prevent subordinates from participating in decisions. For example, through a form of negative decision-making brought about by endless committees, enquiries or co-optations, the powerful may not 'hear' the viewpoints or demands of the less powerful (Parry and Morris, 1974).

Furthermore, non-decision making could also operate through what Friedrich's (1937) had earlier observed as a 'rule of anticipated reaction' where B anticipates A's likely opposition and consequently does not raise an issue. In short 'potential protagonists remain mute, from the expectation that they would invoke strenuous opposition' (Clegg, 1989: 79).

Resonating with the 'rule of anticipated reaction' is Schattschneider's (1960) 'mobilization of bias':

> which refers to those situations where dominant interests may exert such a degree of control over the way in which a political system operates, and over the values, beliefs and opinions of less powerful groups within it, they can effectively determine not only whether certain demands come to be expressed and needed, but also whether such demands will ever cross people's minds...Crucial issues thus never emerge for public debate, and to study the course of contentious issues (as Dahl did in New Haven) is merely to study what happens to the political crumbs strewn carelessly about by an elite with its hands clasped firmly around the cake (Saunders, 1979: 30–31).

Suppression of crucial issues is an example of what Bachrach and Baratz (1962) refer to as a non-decision making process. Thus, when it comes to the construction of legitimacy, 'Latent' power conflicts remain hidden from the public face of power, which is confined to 'the dominant values and the political myths, rituals, and institutions which tend to favour the vested interests of one or more groups' (1962: 950).

Lukes (1974) maintained that Bachrach and Baratz's research was limited. He argued that they focussed too much on how 'decisions' were made, albeit 'non-decisions' (Ranson et al., 1980: 8), and doubted the necessity of assuming that parties must be in conflict for non-decision-making power to be evident. Lukes built on the work of Bachrach and Baratz to develop a theory in which power could be used to prevent conflict from occurring through the 'management of meaning'. Today this approach is known as the 'third dimension of power'. The management of meaning occurred by shaping people's

> perceptions, cognitions and preferences in such a way that they accept their role in the existing order of things, either because they can see or imagine no alternative to it, or because they view it as natural and unchangeable, or because they value it as divinely ordained and beneficial (Lukes, 1974: 24).

Lukes maintained that power could not be confined to observable conflict, the outcomes of decisions, or the suppression of information; it must also consider the question of political acquiescence (Hardy and Clegg, 1996). In this sense, Lukes was concerned with how, through the natural order of things, people might be 'duped, hoodwinked, coerced, cajoled or manipulated into political inactivity' (Saunders, 1980: 22). For Lukes (1974; 2005), this use of power helped elite groups and individuals to sustain their dominance and reduce the likelihood of subordinates exercising their discretionary power. Along these lines, one may observe that the exercise of 'power is most effective when it is unnecessary' (Ranson et al., 1980: 8).

Accordingly, Lukes (1974; 2005) was concerned with identifying mechanisms which perpetuated the status quo. His approach was characterized as a liberal reflection on a Marxian heritage (Clegg, 1989): 'liberal' because he wanted to separate power from fate and structural determination, 'Marxian' because of his use of Gramsci's concept of 'ideological hegemony' to describe situations where 'a structure of power relations is fully legitimized by an integrated system of cultural and normative assumptions' (Hyman and Fryer, 1975: 199). The right to power of elite individuals or groups to make decisions becomes reified over time through the routine normalcy of their exercise of such power. The perceived superiority and right to dominance of social elites, such as owners, leaders and managers, becomes part of the natural order of things. Lukes (1974; 2005) viewed power as operating when people have no awareness of, let alone the desire to realize, their own 'real interests'.

It is Lukes' concept of 'real interests' that renders his third dimension of power problematic. Benton (1981) identifies a paradox in Lukes' idea that one can know other people's 'real interests' and likens the paradox to the 'central problem' with which Marx has been confronted:

> In its simplest form this is the problem of how to reconcile a conception of socialist practices as a form of collective self-emancipation with a critique of the established order which holds that the consciousness of those from whom collective self-emancipation is to be expected is systematically manipulated, distorted and falsified by essential features of that order. If the autonomy of subordinate groups (classes) is to be respected then emancipation is out of the question; where as if emancipation is to be brought about, it cannot be self-emancipation. I shall refer to this problem as the 'paradox of emancipation'. (Benton, 1981: 162)

In short, people need autonomy to achieve self-emancipation but if, as Lukes and Marxist theory suggests, people are being 'hoodwinked' by the social order in which they exist to the point that they are unaware of their 'real interests', then such autonomy cannot lead to self-emancipation. Similarly, if people unaware of their 'real interests' are emancipated by others, neither can this be self-emancipation.

When Lukes suggests (1974: 33) that it is possible for power to be exercised over people against their perceived preferences but in their 'real interests', Benton (1981: 164–165) argues that such people would be unable to recognize these real interests because of their lack of relative autonomy and democratic participation. The lack of autonomy and democratic participation means that those exercising the power must have made a judgement of what these people's real interests are or should be. To make such a judgement requires one to deny a position of moral relativism; it assumes an absolutist position that, as Haugaard (1997) points out, adopts a self-acclaimed intellectual superiority from which to enact a position of sovereign power.

Clegg (1989: 102) notes that Lukes' moral position on one's real interests is of little value in determining people's sociological reality or, even more problematically, their sociological unreality. According to Barbalet the consequence of Lukes' moral relativism is as follows:

> If to be subject to power is to have one's real interests contravened, and if real interests can be identified only outside of a subordination of power, then it is impossible ever to determine whether one is subject to power, except when it ceases to matter. (Barbalet, 1987: 8)

Clegg (1989: 103) contends that Lukes' three-dimensional view of power is problematic because Lukes does not explain how there might be an epistemological possibility of determining 'real interests'. The three-dimensional approach does not succeed, as many have claimed, in delimiting a space in which a comprehensive view of power can be located. Despite the significance of these criticisms, Lukes' work does make a major contribution, particularly with respect to how, through the management of meaning, the exercise of power does not necessarily have to be linked to conflict.

In summary, the Community Power Debates represent what is known as the first dimension of power. The main criticism of these debates is that full participation in decisions is assumed. Bachrach and Baratz's work began the second dimensional view of power, which focuses on the study of non-decision-making or how decisions are prevented from being made. The main problem with this approach is that it assumes the exercise of power is grounded in conflict situations. Lukes' work initiated the third dimensional view of power, which argues that people can manage the perceptions of others so that conflict does not occur and thereby influence the nature of the decision process and hence what is considered legitimate. In this third dimension, Lukes (1974) draws upon Marx's concept of 'false consciousness' and Gramsci's concept of 'ideological hegemony' to argue that the power of dominant groups is legitimized by an integrated system of cultural and normative assumptions. Common to the critical theoretical approach that underpins this body of literature is a concern for differentials in power within social systems and how these differentials result in some people being privileged and others marginalized. In this sense, the literature is underpinned by a concern with domination and the pursuit of democracy. The critical theorists show an obvious link to Marx through their concern for people's 'real interests'. An assumption exists that others know the real interests of people better than the people do themselves. Such an assumption embodies the adoption of a sovereign position of power which is somewhat contrary to its grounding in the pursuit of democracy.

PRAGMATIC ACCOUNTS OF POWER AND LEGITIMACY

The pragmatic literature constitutes an alternative intellectual discipline that was largely ignored by mainstream social and organizational theorists until recent times. Many contributors to the previous bodies of literature adopt a normative approach to power and legitimacy, where power is something that is held and exercised by people and import is placed upon whom has more or less of it; they aspire to some grand idealist view of how power 'should' be in a social system and who should have how much of it. For the rational theorists the ideal is rational, for the critical theorists the ideal is democracy. In contrast, contributors to the alternative intellectual tradition do not adopt any such idealist starting points. They are not concerned with telling people how power 'ought' to be used; rather they are concerned with studying 'how' power actually is in a social system. While the founding voices of the pragmatic literature are Machiavelli and Nietzsche, with Foucault's work holding a prominent position, Weber's work, especially his concept of structures of dominancy, also resonates.

For Machiavelli, the achievement of order in organizations does not emanate from a commitment to an ideal form of governance through a benevolent sovereign, but is secured by a strategically minded Prince (Machiavelli, 1958). The Prince's

> focus is on strategies, deals, negotiations, fraud and conflict in which myths (ideals) concerning moral action become game players' resources (tools or weapons) rather than a topic which frames what the game should be (Clegg, 1989: 30).

Rather than adopt a normative starting point, Machiavelli conceived power in terms of strategy and practice and as distinctly empirical (Bauman, 1982). Machiavelli (1958: 91) maintained that 'a man who neglects what is actually done for what should be done (pursuit of ideals) learns the way of self-destruction'. Similarly, but much later, Nietzsche (1968) argued that ideals are myths and lies, claiming that people have a will to power more than their will to ideals, morals and values. In regard to the virtues of rationality, Nietzsche further argues that 'rationality at any cost...in opposition to instincts has itself been no more than a form of sickness' (1968: 34).

Reflecting on the provocative nature of these statements, one can gain an appreciation as to why Machiavelli and Nietzsche's work has been considered vulgar and divisive. However, rather than dispel what Machiavelli and Nietzsche have had to say about power and legitimacy, one might consider the value of their work on two fronts. First, the statements act as beacons that remind us that people cannot divorce themselves from context and time. Secondly, their work indicates that having faith in the way things 'ought' to be, risks blindness to the way things actually are. In this sense, the work of Machiavelli and Nietzsche can be seen as a check to the blind pursuit of ideals, including the modern ideals of 'rationality', 'truth' and 'democracy' (Flyvbjerg, 1998; 2001).

In more recent times, a number of writers in the field of organizational studies have been influenced by the work of the French theorist of ideas, Michel Foucault, who in turn, was clearly influenced by Machaivelli and, even more so, by Nietzsche. Like Machiavelli and Nietzsche, Foucault was interested in the micro-dynamics of power and focused on the relationship between power and knowledge in social systems.

In his archaeological phase, Foucault uses history to show how things become taken for granted in everyday life: how things that people 'take for granted' are accepted as being part of reality and thus legitimate. Foucault highlights how different historical periods, such as the Renaissance, the classical and the modern periods (or 'epistemes') constituted different versions of knowledge and thus legitimacy: what was taken for granted as being legitimate in one episteme would not necessarily be considered legitimate in another. The significance of the argument becomes more apparent when one considers the constitution of knowledge in a cultural sense. Foucault added that reality is not only time specific but also culturally specific, being historically constituted in both periods of time and cultural settings. One can appreciate what Foucault means by recognizing the differences in the systematic organization of knowledge reflected upon by some cultures. For example, in Indigenous cultures such as those of different clans of Australian Aborigines, knowledge is based on myths, stories and legends – the Dreamtime. This differs from that of members from another culture who reflect upon knowledge constituted by religious doctrines, and differ again from most western societies, that reflect upon knowledge based on the principles of science. Each culture has its own set of historical antecedents and thus constitution of knowledge. If people from different cultures are reflecting on different bodies of knowledge when they make sense of the world, it is highly likely that their perceptions of legitimacy will also differ.

The non-uniformity of knowledge implies, whether in a historical or present period, that in a culturally diverse world the perception of reality and thus legitimacy will have a plurality. Haugaard (1997: 43) observes that, 'hence, there is no "true" or "correct" interpretation based upon the discovery of the truth'. Idealists may critique Haugaard's observation by asking 'how can it be true that there is no truth?' Such a question however, is distinctly modern as it seeks absolutism and misses the point of Foucault's message, much as, to a certain degree, do Haugaard's observation. Foucault, one would suggest, would have altered Haugaard's observation slightly so that it read 'hence, there is no *single* "true" or "correct" interpretation based upon the discovery of truth' (Gordon, 2007). Foucault acknowledged that people do have a perception of 'truth', but the perception comes from reflection upon their meaning systems which are underpinned by a culturally specific constitution of knowledge: different cultures have different histories, different versions of knowledge, and therefore, viewpoints about 'truth'. Thus, there are *multiple* 'true' and 'correct' interpretations based on the discovery of 'truth'. Incidentally, as Haugaard (1997) points out, there is no culture on earth that does not believe that its 'truth' is not 'true' (Haugaard, 1997). Consequently, it is difficult for people not to privilege their version of 'truth' over others, including ideals about how power and legitimacy 'ought' to be.

By way of further explanation, Foucault's 'archaeology of knowledge' shows how cultural settings are actually historically constituted meaning systems – a meaning system being a historical *a priori* system of order that makes it possible for individuals to make sense of their world (Foucault, 1970). Language plays an important role in the transfer of meaning, but Foucault argues that language alone does not constitute meaning. In a way this is not dissimilar to Weber's (1968) explanation of 'structures of dominancy': Foucault shows, through comparing what was constituted as 'truth' within different historical periods and different cultural settings, that there is a deeper more unobtrusive level of a social system with rules and codes of order that govern the construction of meaning. He attributes the unobtrusive nature of these codes of order to their acceptance by people as being part of everyday life. For example, in regard to social action, actors in the presence of leaders behave with deference, with this being the expected form of behaviour because leaders, over time, have come to be considered 'superior' to their followers. A more analytic example in regard to language is that statements gain their meaning from their relationship with other statements but these meanings are not timeless. Over time, actions and statements are used in different contexts and within knowledge bases that change. For example, many people are familiar with the sentence 'dreams fulfil desires'. Foucault notes that this statement 'may have been repeated throughout centuries; but it is not the same statement in Plato and in Freud' (Foucault, 1989: 103).

Haugaard (1997) offered a further interpretation of the 'codes of order' that govern the construction of meaning. He stated that these codes are not spoken, nor deliberately created, but exist because of the experience of an unobtrusive order that makes it possible for actors to understand their world. One can appreciate that for people to have their viewpoints considered as making sense by other members of the cultural system in which they exist, knowledge of the system's formally sanctioned rules may not be enough; they will also need to know the unobtrusive codes of order that are part of the system's historically constituted knowledge. If they do not know these codes they may find it difficult to make sense of what is going on around them and, if what they say and do does not resonate with these codes, they may be seen as making non-sense, being illegitimate and effectively disempower themselves.

Foucault's work makes the approach to power adopted by both the rational and critical theorists, to employ one of his own phrases, 'groan with protest' (Foucault, 1980: 54). By using history to understand how the present has come to be, he destabilizes the principles that have underpinned much of the modern era. In particular, he challenges the idea that the human body and human mind form the locus of control and the source of knowledge and truth, which is evident in the view that power is something that is held by people. Foucault's archaeology of knowledge questions the concepts of 'identity' and 'self'. It decentres the 'self' by suggesting that there is no core self; rather, one's perception of self has been socially constructed. People cannot hold a perception of self without reflecting on their knowledge and this knowledge, which has been socially constituted over time, acts as a reciprocal source that both constrains and enables their perception of self.

The work that constitutes Foucault's archaeology phase provided an alternative view of power, but, as he later acknowledged, it was fundamentally problematic. The idea of a meaning system *determining* what is considered as truth and thus, valid knowledge, does not explain how things change. In short, if the past determined the present, then things would not change and knowledge could not be extended within such a system. Further, if nothing changed, one's own concept of time and space would cease too. Addressing this problem led Foucault (1980) into his genealogical phase.

Genealogy is the study of the strategies and conflict that comprise the creation of a meaning system. For Foucault, learning and the dynamic of knowledge, which he refers to as 'truth production', are situated in a theory of power. He argued ' "truth" is linked in a circular relation with systems of power which produce and sustain it, and to the effects of power that induce and extend it' (Foucault, 1980: 133). In accordance with Foucault, it is the exercise of power constrained by a social system's archaeology of order, which shapes the production of new 'truths' and subsequently extends knowledge within this system.

It follows that the production of 'truth' (the creation of knowledge) in any social system is the consequence of a struggle for power. Haugaard (1997: 68) interpreted the notion of this struggle as suggesting that there will be a disqualification of some representations of knowledge (as idiocy), and a qualification or acceptance of others as legitimate, all in the name of 'truth'. Foucault (1980) added that when the struggle for power gives rise to a representation being seen as 'truth', and therefore established as legitimate knowledge, there has been a positive outcome of power. This is what Foucault means by power in a positive form. He does not see this as positive in the sense that it is something people should welcome but positive because it introduces change into a system by virtue of creating new realities, truths and knowledge (Haugaard, 1997).

The strategies people employ to realize their perceived interests in a given situation are central to Foucault's genealogy. He points out that these strategies are both constrained and enabled by a social system's constitution of knowledge. People reflect upon their knowledge to make sense of what is happening in their world and to decide how they will position themselves strategically with respect to these happenings. In other words, people position themselves to acquire legitimacy for their viewpoint or preferred course of action.

For Foucault, '…it is not possible for power to be exercised without knowledge, it is impossible for knowledge not to engender power' (Foucault, 1980: 52). This power/knowledge nexus places people within a web of power relations from which there is no escape (Hardy and Clegg, 1996). Thus, what is ordinarily taken to be knowledge in a social system is the outcome of a struggle for power that is grounded in context. The constitution of knowledge is not only culturally significant but also contextually significant. Knowledge can only be partially fixed as it is both discursive and plural. A corollary to this is that if the ideals people aspire to reflect their constitution of knowledge, ideals must also be both discursive and plural (Gouldner, 1976).

Furthermore, Foucault's genealogical analysis indicates that while all interpretations are open for relative testing, not all interpretations are equal. In social systems, the acceptance of an interpretation must be built upon a claim of validity, part of which is acquiring legitimacy over alternative interpretations. While interpretations may well be influenced by *a priori* knowledge (people's ideology and values would reflect this knowledge), the process by which one interpretation gains legitimacy over others indicates that the representation of interpretations is subject to the influence of contextual variables. The process of acquiring legitimacy illustrates that the means by which an interpretation acquires validity is not simply ideologically grounded (i.e. based on some preconceived idea of how things 'ought' to be) but has a discursive dimension that is distinctly political, strategic, empirical and, thus, context dependent.

Foucault's work essentially destabilizes the literature that constitutes the idealist approaches to power and legitimacy. Many theorists have built upon and critiqued his work, with some of the more notable in social science generally applicable to organizational studies including Giddens (1984), Laclau and Mouffe (1985), Barnes (1988), Clegg (1989), Hindess (1996), Haugaard (1997) and Flyvbjerg (1998). In the next section of this chapter, the work of Clegg (1989; Clegg et al. 2006), Haugaard (1997), Flyvbjerg (1998) and Courpasson (2000) will be focused on due to their more direct contribution to the debate on power and legitimacy in social systems.

CONTEMPORARY WORK ON POWER AND LEGITIMACY

In more recent times writers such as Clegg (1989), Haugaard (1997); Flyvbjerg (1998) and Courpasson (2001, 2006) have drawn on the work of Weber, Foucault and other theorists to explore the complex workings of power and legitimacy in social systems. Using a comprehensive account of Weber's account of authority and rationality, Clegg (1975, 1989; Clegg et al., 2006) has shown that the functioning of an organization is subject to both formal structures and unobtrusive structures of dominancy. The legitimacy of formal structures and rule-based authority cannot be taken for granted; rather it has to be regarded as a contingent variable dependent on local and temporal circumstances. In other words, the efficacy of authority is not simply based on formally sanctioned rules and positional power but also socially constituted norms. Thus, whether or not people will obey a person attempting to exercise authority depends on both the formal design of the organization and whether this person's 'right to power' is perceived as legitimate with respect to the norms of the social system. In short, 'structures of dominancy' both constrain and enable the exercise of power and the construction of legitimacy in social systems.

Findings from a recent empirical study conducted by Courpasson (2006) on three French organizations adds further insight into the effects of structures of dominancy on the construction of legitimacy in social systems. The organizations were attempting to move from traditional hierarchical and bureaucratic forms of governance to what Courpasson and others term contemporary forms of 'soft' control and coordination (Barker, 2002). Such forms of control are characterized by flatter organically oriented structures and entrepreneurial forms of governance aimed at facilitating participative management practices through the empowerment of workers. What is interesting about Courpasson's research is that it does not just provide empirically grounded insight into power and legitimacy but also offers an informative critique of the current organization and management literature's inherent assumption that 'soft' management practices and policies have supplanted hierarchical and bureaucratic control, and that the entrepreneurial form of governance is pervasive (du Gay, 1996).

Courpasson (2006) argues the organizational leaders in his study faced the problem of elaborating and reproducing specific resources of legitimacy within an alternative form of governance. His data shows that contrary to their intention,

> 'contemporary tools and strategies of soft control and coordination are not the opposite of hierarchical and bureaucratic governance…soft governance is fused with and is itself governed by legitimate authority' (2000: 142).

He goes on to demonstrate how previous legitimate authority unobtrusively perpetuates itself within soft practices, with the result that it continues to legitimize certain actions while de-legitimizing others.

Gordon et al. (2008), drawing on Courpasson's work, conducted an ethnographic study in power and legitimacy within a police organization that was undergoing a radical organizational redesign aimed at introducing 'soft' control systems. The authors propose that depending on the nature of how a structure of dominancy constrains and enables the thinking, feeling and doing of the people, it will, to some degree constitute an unobtrusive structure of legitimacy. They draw on the work of Weber, Foucault, Clegg, Haugaard, Flyvbjerg and ultimately Courpasson to show how a historically constituted 'rule of anticipated reaction' established a 'mobilization of bias' in the police organization in question. Despite the introduction of change initiatives to achieve otherwise, this mobilization of bias resulted in the views and preferred courses of action of those who had historically held positions of dominance to more easily acquire legitimacy. They augment Flyvbjerg's (1998) observation that actors in positions of dominance go largely unchallenged and are subsequently freer to 'rationalize their own version of rationality' to argue that legitimacy is largely based on the nature of power and rationality embedded and constituted within a social system's structures of dominancy. The authors acknowledge, arguably, that this might not be a problem if those in positions of dominance were capable of completely rational thought and action but of course they are always subject to contextual pressures and their own self-interests and bias. Therefore, legitimacy does not simply derive from rationality but from the rationalization of a certain rationality that is sanctioned by organizational members. Gordon et al. (2008), like Courpasson (2000), advocate the use of the term 'legitimization of legitimacy' to describe the process by which members of a social system legitimize certain forms of legitimacy and exclude others. In their case, the process was problematic due to the existence of a mobilization of bias; organizational members did not legitimize the public discourse of change or the discourse of internal change initiatives and agents; rather, the historically constituted structure of legitimacy undermined these discourses.

CONCLUSION

In both the mainstream functionalist and critical approaches to power and legitimacy, power is linked to the 'body' in that power is something that is held by people. Both bodies of literature adopt a normative approach to legitimacy by advocating opposing views in regard to who 'should' have more or less of the power. For the functionalist theorists, it is those people formally sanctioned with authority that should have power: resistance to this power is considered dysfunctional and illegitimate. For the critical theorists, resistance is a good thing: it results in creative agency, the exercise of discretion for workers and, above all, it is more democratic.

The approach adopted by the pragmatic theorists is very different. Foucault's work, in particular, challenges normative views of legitimacy, suggesting that they are a result of power, are culturally significant and context dependent. For Foucault and his followers, power does not involve

> 'taking sides, identifying who has more or less of it, as much as seeking to describe its strategic role – how it is used to translate people into characters or articulate an organizational morality play' (Hardy and Clegg, 1996: 631).

Rather than normative, contributors to the pragmatic body of literature take a strategic approach to the construction of legitimacy.

In comparison to the pragmatic body of literature, the functionalist literature amputates much of the complex working of power in the construction of legitimacy in a social system. Contributors to the functionalist approach adopt equilibrium starting points that de-contextualize their theoretical frameworks and limit the study of power and legitimacy to an episodic and causal level. The pragmatist body of literature, in particular the work of Foucault and his followers, by incorporating deeper, more unobtrusive dimensions to power, provide further insight into the balance of power and the subsequent construction of legitimacy in social systems.

The pragmatic approach views social systems as complex arenas of negotiation, contest and struggle, rendering them:

> subject to multivalent powers rather than monadic sites of total control…It is in these struggles that power and resistance [and legitimacy] are played out in dramatic scenes that those approaches influenced by Foucault seem best able to appreciate because they are not predisposed to know in advance who the victorious and vanquished dramatis personae 'should' be (Hardy and Clegg, 1996: 63).

It is this approach to power and legitimacy that is currently being applied in empirical settings. The work of Courpasson in particular clearly demonstrates that tying legitimacy to preconceived ideas of how things 'should' be is problematic. Just as Weber argued, the work of Courpasson illustrates that legitimacy is contingent upon social efficacy. Whether action is considered efficacious depends on whether it is interpreted as being rational by those subject to it. The construction of rationality is subject to structures of dominancy and where a structure of dominancy facilitates a mobilization of bias, a structure of legitimacy is formed: those in positions of dominance are not only free to rationalize their own versions of legitimacy but also, in a social sense, free to legitimize their version of legitimacy. The behaviour of powerful individuals and groups in recent times highlight the significance and problematics associated with such phenomena. One need only recall the accounts of unethical behaviour and corruption that were rationalized as legitimate in companies such as Enron and OneTel, not to mention government officials and agencies throughout the world.

REFERENCES

Bachrach, P. and Baratz, M.S. (1962). 'Two faces of power', *American Political Review*, 56: 947–52.
Bachrach, P. and Baratz, M.S. (1963). 'Decisions and non-decisions: An analytical framework', *American Political Review*, 57: 641–51.

Bachrach, P. and Baratz, M.S. (1970). *Power and Poverty: Theory and Practice*. Oxford: Oxford University Press.
Banton, M. (1972). 'Authority', *New Society*, 22 (512): 86–8.
Barbalet, J.M. (1987). 'Power, structural resources and agency', *Perspectives in Social Theory*, 8: 1–24.
Barker, J. (2002). 'Tightening the iron cage: Concertive control in self-managing teams'. In S.R. Clegg (ed.), *Central Currents in Organization Studies II: Contemporary Trends, Volume 5*. London: Sage, originally published in *Administrative Science Quarterly*, 1993, 38: 408–37.
Barnes, B. (1988). *The Nature of Power*. Cambridge: Polity Press.
Bauman, Z. (1982). *Memories of Class: The Pre-history and After-life of Class*. London: Routledge and Kegan Paul.
Bennis, W.G. (1959). 'Leadership theory and administrative behavior: The problems of authority', *Administrative Science Quarterly*, 4: 259–301.
Benton, T. (1981). ' "Objective" Interests in the Sociology of Power', *Sociology*, 15(2): 61–184.
Clegg, S.R. (1990). *Modern Organizations: Organizations in the Post Modern World*. London: Sage.
Clegg, S.R. (1989). *Frameworks of Power*. London: Sage.
Clegg, S.R. (1975). *Power, Rule and Domination*. London: Routledge and Kegan Paul.
Clegg, S.R., Courpasson, D. and Phillips, N. (2006). *Power and Organizations*. Thousand Oaks, CA: Sage.
Courpasson, D. (2000). 'Managerial strategies of domination: Power in soft bureaucracies', *Organization Studies*, 21(1): 141–62.
Crozier, M. (1964). *The Bureaucratic Phenomenon*. London: Tavistock.
Dahl, R.A. (1957). 'The concept of power', *Behavioural Science*, 2: 201–5.
Dahl, R.A. (1961). *Who Governs? Democracy and Power in an American City*. New Haven: Yale University Press.
Dahl, R.A. (1968). 'Power', in *International Encyclopaedia of the Social Sciences*, New York: Macmillan, pp. 405–15.
Deetz, S. (1985). 'Critical-cultural research: New sensibilities and old realities', *Journal of Management*, 11(2), 121–36.
Dubin, R. (1957). 'Power and union-management relations', *Administrative Science Quarterly*, 2: 60–81.
du Gay, P. (1996). *Consumption and Identity at Work*. London: Sage.
Eisenhardt, K. (1989). Building theory from case study research. *Academy of Management Journal*, 14(4), 532–550.
Enz, C.A. (1988). 'The role of value congruity in interorganizational power', *Administrative Science Quarterly*, 33, 284–304.
Flyvbjerg, B. (1998). *Rationality and power: Democracy in Practice*. London: University of Chicago Press.
Foucault, M. (1970). *The Order of Things*. London: Routledge.
Foucault, M. (1977). *Discipline and Punish*. London: Allen Lane.
Foucault, M. (1980). *Power/Knowledge: Selected Interviews and Other Writings 1972–1977*, C. Gordon (ed.) Brighton: Harvester Press.
Foucault, M. (1989). *The Archaeology of Knowledge*. London: Routledge.
French, J. and Raven, B. (1968). 'The bases of social power', in D. Cartwright (ed.), *Studies in Social Power*. Ann Arbor, MI: Institute for Social Research.
Friedrich, C.J. (1937). *Constitutional Government and Democracy*. New York: Gipp.
Gandz, J. and Murray, V.V. (1980). 'The experience of workplace politics', *Academy of Management Journal*, 23(2), 237–51.
Gaventa, J.P. (1980). *Power and Powerlessness: Quiescence and Rebellion in an Appalachian Valley*. Urbana: University of Illinois Press.
Giddens, A. (1984). *The Constitution of Society: Outline of the Theory of Structuration*. Berkeley: University of California Press.
Gordon, R.D. (2007). *Power, Knowledge and Domination*. Liber: Copenhagen Business School Press.
Gordon, R.D, Kornberger, M. and Clegg, S.R. (2008). 'Power, rationality and legitimacy', *Organisation Studies*. forthcoming.
Gouldner, A.W. (1976). *The Dialectic of Ideology and Technology: The Origins of Grammar, and the Future of Ideology*. London: Macmillan.
Hardy, C. and Clegg, S.R. (1996). 'Some dare call it power', in Clegg, S.R., Hardy, C. and Nord W.R. (eds), *Handbook of Organization Studies*. London: Sage, pp. 622–41.
Haugaard, M. (1997). '*The constitution of power: a theoretical analysis of power*', Hindess, B (1996). *Discourses of Power: From Hobbes to Foucault*. Oxford: Blackwell.
Hickson, D.J., Hinings, C.R., Lee, C.A., Schneck, R.E. and Pennings, J.M. (1971). 'A strategic contingencies theory of intra-organizational power', *Administrative Science Quarterly*, 16: 216–29.

Hyman, R. and Fryer, B. (1975). 'Trade unions: Sociology and political economy', in J.B. McKinlay (ed.), *Processing People: Cases on Organizational Behaviour*. London: Holt, Rinehart & Winston.

Knights, D. and Willmott, H. (1992). 'Conceptualizing leadership processes: A study of senior managers in a financial services company', *Journal of Management Studies*, 29, 761–82.

Laclau, E. and Mouffe, C. (1985). *Hegemony and Socialist Strategy*. London: Verso.

Lukes, S. (1974). *Power: A Radical View*. London: Macmillan.

Machiaveli, N. (1958). *The Prince*. London: Everyman.

Mechanic, D. (1962). 'Sources of power of lower participants in complex organizations', *Administrative Science Quarterly*, 7: 349–64.

Mintzberg, H. (1983). *Power in and around Organizations*. Englewood Cliffs, NJ: Prentice Hall.

Neitzsche, F. (1968). *The Will to Power*. New York: Vintage Books.

Parry, G. and Morris P. (1974). 'When is a decision not a decision?', in I. Crewe (ed.), *British Political Sociology Yearbook, Vol 1: Elites in Western Democracy*. London: Croom Helm. pp. 317–37.

Parsons T. and Henderson, A.M. (1948). *Weber: The Theory of Social and Economic Organization*, translated by Tacott Parsons and A.M. Henderson. New York: Free Press.

Pettigrew, A.M. (1973). *The Politics of Organizational Decision-making*. London: Tavistock Publications.

Pfeffer, J. and Salancik, G. (1974). 'Organizational decision making as a political process', *Administrative Science Quarterly*, 19: 135–51.

Pfeffer, J. (1981). *Power in Organizations*. Marshfield, MA: Pitman.

Polsby, N. (1963). *Community Power and Political Theory*. New Haven: Yale University Press.

Saunders, P. (1979). *Urban Politics: A Sociological Interpretation*. Harmondsworth: Penguin.

Schattschneider, E.E. (1960). *The Semi-sovereign People: A Realist's View of Democracy in America*. New York: Holt, Rinehart & Winston.

Thompson, J. D. (1956). 'Authority and power in identical organisations', *American Journal of Sociology*, 62: 290–301.

Touraine, A. (1988). 'Modernity and cultural specificities', *International Social Science*, 118: 443–57.

Weber, M. (1948). *The Theory of Social and Economic Organization*, trans. Talcott Parsons and A.M. Henderson. New York: Free Press.

Weber, M. (1968). *Economy and Society: An Outline of Interpretive Sociology*, edited and with an introduction by Roth. G. and Wittich, C. New York: Bedminster Press.

Weber, M. (1978). *Economy and Society: An Outline of Interpretive Sociology*. Berkeley: University of California Press.

Wood, J.R.T. (1997). *Royal Commission into Corruption in the New South Wales Police Service*. Sydney: The Government of the State of New South Wales.

15

Collective Violence and Power

Siniša Malešević

INTRODUCTION

Although collective violence and war has been a near universal feature of human history and a decisive component in the formation of the modern social order, most classical and contemporary sociology has tended to shy away from the study of the gory origins and nature of modernity. This is perhaps most apparent in the sociological accounts of power where collective violence has generally either been ignored or reduced entirely to its strategic dimension. In other words, while the consensualist approaches to power have principally neglected its violent underpinnings, the conflict and competition oriented theories were inclined to treat violence as a mere means to acquire or uphold power. However, once in action collective violence regularly attains its own dynamics which, in turn, can change the dynamics of the entire social order. Collective violence in its widest and historically most prevalent form, warfare, generates its own dialectics of unpredictability. It is this autonomy and contingency of violence, or what Clausewitz (1997: 66–9) calls the friction of war, that transforms social life for good. Hence, violence is often, if not always, much more than just a tool of power. It is one of the essential constituents of human subjectivity, and of modern subjectivity in particular, since modernity as we know it would be unthinkable without violence.

This chapter explores the intrinsic structural vibrancy between power and violence in modernity. As in the modern era violence tends to be almost exclusively monopolized by the state apparatuses, the particular focus is on the relationship between violence and state power. The first part of the chapter reflects briefly on the classical sociological understandings of power and violence, with a particular spotlight on the contributions of

Weber, Treitschke, Hintze and Schmitt. The second part provides a critical survey of the leading contemporary approaches in the field including those of Tilly, Mann, Poggi and Collins. The final part of the chapter briefly sketches an alternative sociological account of coercion and power by stressing the ideological underpinnings of this relationship.

POWER AND VIOLENCE IN CLASSICAL SOCIAL THOUGHT

Despite the vast epistemological differences espoused in classical sociological theories of modernity, there was a near universal consensus that the progression of modernity entailed the inevitable diminishing of collective brutality and mass killing. Inspired by Enlightenment ideals, sociology envisaged the birth of a new social order built on reason, truth and progress where there was no room for large scale human sacrifice. For this reason alone classical sociology exhibited little or no analytical patience for the study of collective violence. This neglect was not confined only to culturalist or consensualist perspectives exemplified by the work of Comte, Durkheim, Simmel or Mead, but was also integral to the more materialist and conflict oriented theories such as those of Marx, Pareto and even Spencer and Weber.

While Marx clearly adopted a militarist discourse of collective (class) struggle and revolutionary violence as essential to class conflict, these were largely seen as linked to dialectical laws of history operating outside of individual or collective will. As class struggle was linked to the transformation in the modes of production and their ownership, so the central focus was not on killing or incapacitating the bourgeoisie, as in real war, but rather on appropriating and redistributing their possessions. The language of violence was used either as metaphor (i.e. 'class war' or 'cheap prices as the heavy artillery of bourgeoisie' [Marx and Engels, 1998: 41–2]) or in the context of the extraordinary processes accelerating the inexorable arrival of a peaceful communist order. Collective violence was associated almost exclusively with the brief final stage of revolutionary upheaval: 'when the class struggle nears the decisive hour, the process of dissolution going on within the ruling class... assumes such a violent, glaring character...' (Marx and Engels, 1998: 45).

Similarly Pareto, Spencer and Weber devoted little attention to the analysis of collective violence. Spencer did develop an influential typology that distinguished militant from industrial societies, while Pareto discussed the use of force by 'lions' in his theory of the circulation of elites, and Weber became renowned for his coercive definition of the state, yet none of these thinkers showed much interest in the extensive study of the complex relationships between power and violence. While for Spencer collective violence was confined to the militant stage of human evolutionary development, which for him was seen as evaporating with the arrival of industrialism, for Pareto violence was nothing more than one available means utilized by various elites to acquire or maintain a hold on power. Finally, despite Weber's emphasis on the coercive character of social and political life, there is little empirical and even less theoretical exploration of collective violence in his work. For example, in his account of modernity we find not physical carnage and irrationality but an abundance of rules and the overproduction of rationality. In other words a great majority of classical sociologists were either ignorant of the study of collective violence – seeing it as a phenomenon of pre-industrial epochs – or they simply reduced violence to no more than a particular method or resource for pursuing some other economic, political or cultural goals.

Collective violent action is never analysed as a *sui generis* process but only as a second order reality; an instrumental or strategic device for accomplishing specific individual or group interests.

The only prominent exception to this rule was the so called German/Austrian militaristic tradition of social thought.[1] Grounded in Leopold von Ranke's historical romanticism and idealism and underpinned by the peculiar geopolitical position of Germany, and particularly Bismark's Prussia in the nineteenth century, a number of influential German intellectuals became preoccupied with the role of power and violence in the historical processes of state creation. Ranke's legacy imprinted an intellectual hostility upon the Enlightenment's universalism and rationalism, including its scientific methodology and causality which were firmly rejected in favour of historical uniqueness; however, the Prussian statist heritage moulded these intellectuals so as to be in reverence of the state and to place emphasis on the importance of foreign policy in understanding social relations. Some of these authors were also directly or indirectly influenced by the emerging Darwinian and Lamarckian paradigm of universal evolutionary struggle for survival, such as L. Gumplowicz or G. Ratzenhofer while others such as F. Oppenheimer and A. Rustow attempted to reconcile their analytical and historical statist analyses with their open political or ethical anarchism and anti-statism. Although there were many influential representatives of this bellicose tradition of thought, three social thinkers in particular stand out in terms of their direct influence on the contemporary historical sociology: Heinrich von Treitschke, Carl Schmitt and Otto Hintze.

Treitschke was both an academic and a prominent public figure whose ideas left their mark on several generations of German intellectuals in the late nineteenth and early twentieth centuries. For Treitschke power is for the most part equalized with the ability of the state to pursue its will. In fact the state is defined as power: 'the state is the people legally united as an independent power' or 'the state is the public power of offence and defence' (Treitschke 1914: 9, 12). In this view the state is completely anthropomorphized, reified and essentialised as it acquires fixed and unchangeable human like abilities – personality, will, and needs. In his own words: 'if we remember that the essence of this great collective personality is power, then it is in that case the highest moral duty of the State to safeguard its power' (Treitschke, 1914: 31). In this understanding not only is there no power outside of, or above the state, but also the state's *raison d'etre* is the accumulation, maintenance and utilization of power. As he emphasizes 'Power is the principle of the State, as Faith is the principle of the Church, and Love of the family.' (Treitschke 1914: 12). In this account the state performs two essential functions: within its borders it administers justice while outside of its borders it fights wars. As a sovereign entity its power has no limits either internally or externally as the state can declare wars or suppress rebellions when and how it pleases. Moreover 'without war there would be no state at all' as states are created exclusively through warfare (Treitschke 1914: 21). Contrary to Enlightenment principles Treitschke (1914: 39) argues that states are not created on the basis of people's sovereignty but in fact 'against the will of the people'. It is the experience of war that moulds individuals into nation-states: 'only in war a people becomes in very deed a people' (Davis, 1915: 150). And in the final instance it is the possession of the army that defines the state. As Treitschke (1914: 100) puts it succinctly: 'the state is no Academy of Arts, still less a Stock Exchange; it is power, and therefore it contradicts its own nature if it neglects the army'. As with other representatives of the Prussian historical school that were deeply influenced by Hegelian teleology, such as Droysen or Duncker, Treitschke understands history as an ethical process where the success of a particular state, defined largely by its ability to win wars, is interpreted as an indicator of its higher morality. The state is a moral absolute that stands above individuals, that possesses omnipotent powers, and that shapes its existence through eternal conflict with other states.

Otto Hintze was a student of Treitschke which is evident in the way his early work occasionally exhibits 'a mystical belief in the state as a higher entity with a life of its own' (Gilbert 1975: 13). However, despite his strong emphasis on state power and the importance of foreign policy and warfare in the formation of modern order, Hintze developed a much more sophisticated approach to the study of power and collective violence. Unlike Treitschke's normativist militarism and glorification of state and war, Hintze begins to explicate what is essentially a historical sociology of power transformation. Tracing the historical development of the constitutional state Hintze (1975: 181) argues that 'all state organization was originally military organisation, organisation for war'. The roots of representative political institutions such as assemblies are to be found in the congregation of warriors as membership in a political community was determined by one's ability to fight wars. By extensive exploration of the structure and origin of the ancient Greek and Roman political institutions, the European feudal system, the thirteenth- and fourteenth-century *Standstaat*, and the absolutist orders of the eighteenth and early nineteenth century, Hintze concludes that the two determining historical factors of state creation are the structure of social classes and the external ordering of the states. Both of these factors are linked to warfare as external and internal conflicts are regularly inversely proportional. As Hintze (1975: 183–4) points out with respect to the example of Rome: 'wherever the community was sufficiently adaptable, as in Rome, the pressure of the foreign situation forced a progressive extension of the citizenry with political rights, because greater masses of soldiers were needed. It was at heart this joint operation of external pressure and internal flexibility that enabled Rome to progress from city-state to world empire'. He identifies three dominant historical moments in the transformation of state and military power: (a) the tribal and clan system where 'the state and the army are virtually identical units', often underpinned by kin solidarity and a substantial degree of social equality; (b) the feudal epoch which changed the nature of warfare through a shift from a non-professional mass infantry to the heavily armed professional cavalry, while a looser central authority with a multiple pyramid structure gave way to a rigid hierarchical and eventually hereditary social structure; and finally (c) the age of militarism where the expansion of warfare created habitual fiscal crises thus prompting tax and state centralization, the development of the universal military service ('a nation in arms') and the constitutional state structure defined by new egalitarian principles where 'the division between warriors and the citizenry – the fighters and the feeders – was overcome (Hintze, 1975: 207). In this view the modern, or as he calls it the militarist, era is even more prone to collective violence as individuals do not fight as mercenaries or servants of a monarch but are socialized to see their nation-state as a supreme moral authority, 'a community, a corporate collective personality' worth dying for. In other words, for Hintze (1975: 199), just as for Treitschke, it was the 'power politics and balance-of-power politics' that created 'the foundations of modern Europe'.

Although Carl Schmitt was a jurist and legal rather than social theorist his theory of the political is an integral part of the militarist tradition. Just like Treitschke and Hintze Schmitt emphasizes the conflictual, coercive and power driven nature of social life. However, unlike the other two thinkers he understands power and the political in much broader terms than state power alone. Not only is it that political action historically precedes state formation but also once democratization takes off, and state and society fully develop, they permeate each other and, in this situation, 'what had been up to that point affairs of state become thereby social matters, and, vice versa, what had been purely social matters become affairs of state' (Schmitt 1996: 22). For Schmitt the political can not be defined only negatively – as an antithesis of the religious, the cultural or the economic – but it requires its own positive definition. Echoing Treitschke's principle association between faith and church, love and family, and power and state Schmitt (1996: 26) argues that if the realm of morality is characterized by a distinction between good and evil, economics by profitable and unprofitable, and aesthetics by beautiful and ugly, than the concept of the political also necessitates an absolute categorical distinction. In his view this ultimate distinction of the political is between friend and enemy. In other words the political is to be disassociated from the ethical and studied in its own terms: 'The political enemy need not be morally evil or aesthetically ugly; he need not appear as an economic competitor...but he is, nevertheless, the other, the stranger;...existentially something different and alien, so that in the extreme case conflicts with him are possible' (Schmitt, 1996: 27). The two are understood by Schmitt not as symbols or metaphors but as essential and existential categories of social action. Political action is embedded in antagonisms and in the last instance politics is a form of warfare:[2] if there is no external threat to maintain the friend-enemy distinction at the level of sovereign states this polarization is likely to replicate itself in the domestic sphere where party politics becomes deeply antagonistic. However the ultimate potency of the political is rooted in its potential virulence: 'The friend, enemy, and combat concepts receive their real meaning precisely because they refer to a real possibility of physical killing. War follows from enmity. War is the existential negation of the enemy' (Schmitt, 1996: 33). Hence as power politics and conflict are cornerstones of social life one can never eradicate the friend/enemy distinction without obliterating political life itself.

Deemed in part to be responsible for the ideological justification of the expansionist and blinkered policies of the German state in two world wars, this bellicose tradition of social thought was largely rejected, suppressed and seen as ethically unsustainable in the post-WWII context. More than anything else mainstream social theory and sociology remained convinced that such militarism has no explanatory relevance in the contemporary world. As a result, for most of the second half of the twentieth century, sociological theory was dominated by varieties of non-pugnacious theories of social change such as structural functionalism and neo-Marxism. It seemed that the militarist tradition was no more than an obscure tangent in the history of social thinking. However, if the arguments developed by Treitschke, Hintze, Schmitt and other representatives of this school of thought, are read and interpreted as sociology rather than ontology or ethics, then they still have much to offer in explaining the historical bonds between power and collective violence. In other words, if one removes the trappings of essentialism, reificatory and moralist discourse, and the determinist logic of argumentation, it is possible to build on the insights of this tradition to articulate a potent historical sociology of power and violence. And in fact, much more implicitly than explicitly, this has occurred in the works of some leading contemporary historical sociologists. From early in the 1980s and onwards, that is, as the Marxist and functionalist paradigms were exhausted, sociology witnessed a significant revival of 'militarist' thought. However in contrast to the normative or ontological militarism of the late nineteenth and early twentieth century, this was an explanatory militarism which attempted to move away from overly economistic and culturalist interpretations of social change by emphasising the violent foundations of modernity.

THE CONTEMPORARY SOCIOLOGY OF POWER AND VIOLENCE

The most influential contemporary historical sociologists of power such as Michael Mann, Charles Tilly, Randall Collins and Gianfranco Poggi rarely if ever make direct reference to Treitschke, Schmitt, Hintze or any other representative of militarist thought. Instead if a link to intellectual predecessors is made, then it is regularly to Max Weber as a 'founding father' of both the comparative historical method and a macro social theory which goes beyond narrow economism and culturalism, thus placing coercion at the heart of social theory. In this context they all uphold Weber's definitions of power and state – both of which underline the coercive nature of these social entities. However, although Weber emphasizes the forceful, almost zero sum, character of power relations, and describes the state in terms of the monopoly of physical force,[3] he does not provide either a coherent sociological theory of state power nor of collective violence. Weber did develop a highly influential typology of power stratification which forms a backbone for some of the contemporary theories of power. Nevertheless, apart from a few fragmentary notes, there is too little analysis to account for a full blown theory of collective violence and the state power in the way it is invoked by leading contemporary historical sociologists. Rather, Weber's definitional emphasis on the role of violence was less his own creation than a reflection of his times, together with the *esprit de corps* of German academia, which was heavily influenced by militarist thought. In some respects Weber provided a morally acceptable face to the militarist tradition: lending to it his impeccable intellectual credentials through which the key arguments of the militarist tradition were 'smuggled' into and revived in the contemporary context, and with little or no apparent consequences. It is much safer and morally responsible to be an intellectual descended of Weber than Treitschke. However it is Treitschke, Hintze and Schmitt's emphasis on the military origins of state, the view of state power as autonomous and omnipotent, the decisive role of warfare in historical transformations, and the conflictual nature of human sociability that lie at heart of the contemporary historical sociology of power. Despite his Nietzschean invocation concerning the will and glory of the state's power prestige, Weber (1978: 910–11) largely ignores the broader geopolitical context in which states emerge and operate. Although he defines state power in terms of territoriality and a monopoly of violence he does not explore the exogenous context in which they transpire. However, the modern state does not appear or function in a geopolitical vacuum, and its very existence is premised on the mutual recognition from other such states. And it is from this very angle, which is rather more Treitschkeian than Weberian, that contemporary theories of state power develop. Hence, if we examine their arguments closely it is possible to see that there is a direct link between contemporary historical sociologists of power and the classical militarist tradition of thought.

Charles Tilly's (1975, 1985, 1992) entire life work is built upon the task of explicating the relationship between the birth and expansion of state power with the use of large scale violence. Although he defines power in relational terms by insisting on its 'incessantly negotiated character', his focus is firmly on the conflictual and asymmetrical dimension of power relations: 'Power is an analyst's summary of transactions among persons and social sites: we can reasonably say X has power over Y if, in the course of a stream of interaction between X and Y, (1) a little action from X typically elicits a large response from Y, and (2) their interaction delivers disproportionate benefit to X' (Tilly, 1999: 344). More specifically, his focal point is on what he sees as a dominant form of power in modernity – the power of the nation-state. Throughout human history, although enormous power was often concentrated in the hands of a few individual despots, tyrants and emperors, it is the arrival of modernity that, for the first time, provided structural and organizational capabilities not only for the concentration of, but also for a monopoly over, the coercive power channelled through the institutions of the nation-state. To explain the gradual emergence and eventual dominance of this form of power Tilly traces its historical origins to seventeenth century Europe where the sheer cost of prolonged military campaigns on the part of European monarchs led to the rapid centralization, territorialization and bureaucratization of rule. In other words, directly echoing Hintze, Tilly (1985: 170–2) argues that 'war makes states', or more precisely, that 'war making, extraction, and capital accumulation interacted to shape European state making'. As with Treitschke, Tilly (1992: 1) analyses states primarily as 'coercion-wielding organisations' which possess ultimate power over a particular territory. In early modernity warfare proved to be the most efficient mechanism of social control, state expansion, capital accumulation and the extraction of resources. As a consequence modernity was a witness to the proliferation of mass scale violence with wars gaining in intensity and brutality, with twentieth century – with its 250 wars, causing over 100 million deaths – by far the bloodiest in recorded history (Tilly 2003: 55). Following in the footsteps of Treitschke and Hintze, Tilly sees war making as the most important state activity through which state power acquired unprecedented autonomy and external geopolitical strength, while simultaneously pacifying its domestic realm. The monopoly over the legitimate use of violence within a particular territory develops as a direct outcome of intensification of inter-state warfare. The Schmittian distinction between friend and enemy emerges fully only in the context of modern state-building, as enmity becomes displaced outside of the borders of a nation-state and as private violence is largely eradicated through severe policing and social delegitimization. War and the preparations for war are potent generators of dramatic social change, the offshoot of which is the development of both an extensive state apparatus as well as a vibrant civil society. Through warfare the state advanced its fiscal administration, courts and other legal institutions, regional administration and financial infrastructure, whereas greater popular mobilization, including universal conscription, led towards the steady extension of various political and social rights to a wider population, thus enhancing civil society. To sum up, for Tilly, as with Hintze and Treischke, the concentration and monopolization of power in the institutions of the modern nation-state was a direct product of extensive war making.

Although Michael Mann (1986, 1993) has been nearly universally regarded as a neo-Weberian sociologist,[4] his theory of state power owes as much to Treitschke, Hintze, and Schmitt as it does to Weber. Similar to Tilly, Mann moves the focus of sociology from society to state as state autonomy and its geopolitical environment largely determine the condition of existence of a particular society. Instead of a unitary and inflexible notion of society that dominates much of social science, Mann (1986: 2) prefers to speak of 'multiple overlapping and intersecting power networks'. In other words in a Treitschkean vein, but with much more in the way of reflexivity, and much less in the way of teleology Mann posits social power and state expansion at the centre of societal change. A social world is ordered first and foremost as a conglomerate of intertwined power networks. More specifically social power is analysed along the axis of four central and interrelated sources: political, economic, military and ideological power. Although they are treated as autonomous institutional and organizational forms, Mann (1986: 2) also contends that they are 'overlapping networks of social interaction' that 'offer alternative organizational means of social control'. Unlike Weber, although much as Hintze, Mann separates the political and the military, thereby treating militarism as a distinct organizational capacity. As he recently puts it, by military power he means 'the social organization of concentrated lethal violence' (Mann 2006: 351). Even though states have originated and developed their organizational might primarily through warfare, state power is not to be reduced to its military capabilities. While the primary function of states throughout history was to fight wars and balance geopolitical arrangements, and though this is still a potent generator of state activity and its authority, historically the administrative and military modes of control have rarely acted as one indivisible entity. As a result the modern nation-state is a forceful war making machine, but this is not its only source of strength. In other words the omnipotence of a nation-state in modernity is derived from its military might, economic control of material resources and ideological legitimacy. However, most of all its institutional supremacy is rooted in its territorialized organizational potency. For Mann (1993: 9, 2006: 352), just as for Treitschke and Schmitt, and again very unlike Weber, 'political power means state power'. The ascendancy of the political arises from the state's monopolistic, centralized and institutionalized control over a particular territory. The steady rise of this administrative power of state is linked to the historical process of what Mann (1986: 112–14) calls social caging, whereby rulers have gradually imposed restrictions on individual freedoms in exchange for economic resources and political and military protection, in this way simultaneously generating mechanisms of social stratification and triggering the long term process of institutional and administrative centralization. While in the early historical periods social caging was fostered by the artificial irrigation of agriculture in enclosed river-valley civilizations, in the early modern era this process reinforced tight administration of nation-states which eventually created an institutional shell for the arrival of democracy. In a profoundly Hintzean way, Mann (1988) argues that citizenship rights were historically shaped by the interests of economic, political and military elites who controlled the state, whereby extension of civil and political rights was directly linked to deep fiscal crises of the state and the introduction of universal conscription. The democratization of the state in modernity, including the extension of the universal franchise and welfare reforms, was in many respects a direct outcome of the mass mobilization of warfare. According to Mann (1986), the political power, that is state power, has two main forms – despotic and infrastructural. Whereas despotic power stands for the rulers unconstrained action exercised without negotiation with civil society (i.e. the unlimited powers of Roman Emperor), infrastructural power is reflected in a state's ability to permeate society through its institutional mechanism of control, such as its capacity to tax without consent, to conscript its citizenry in times of war, to store and use information on individual citizens, to enforce its laws on the territory it controls, and so on. With the expansion of modernity, the processes of democratization, and liberalization, the state gradually transforms from being despotically strong and infrastructurally weak into being despotically weak and infrastructurally strong.

Even though Gianfranco Poggi is nominally considered as one of the most Weberian of all contemporary political sociologists, and regards himself as such (Poggi 2001: 12–14), his account of power and violence is really much closer to Schmitt and Treitschke than Weber, while his understanding of the origins of state power is distinctively Hintzean. Even though he follows Weber's tripartite division between political, economic and ideological power, for the most part, his interpretation of social power overemphasizes the coercive character of domination and as such is only partially Weberian. Unlike Weber, who stresses the administrative and juridical foundations of state power and attributes great importance to the contents of various religious doctrines and especially to the distinctive form of rationalization that emerged in medieval Christian Europe, Poggi concentrates almost exclusively on the violent sources of social power; and whereas Weber writes about political power in general terms, including its various modalities (domination, legitimacy, authority, status, coercion etc.), for Poggi (2001: 30) political power is constituted and exercised exclusively in reference to coercive actions: 'What qualifies the power...as political is the fact that it rests ultimately upon, and intrinsically...refers to, the superior's ability to sanction coercively the subordinate's failure to comply with commands'. In other words political power cannot be properly defined without reference to organized violence. Or as he recently put it, and in very stark terms: '[ancient Greeks] did not subscribe to my own bloody-minded identification of politics with violence' (Poggi 2006: 137). While for Weber violence is by and large just a means of politics, for Poggi violence is its essence. Reminiscent of Treitschke, Poggi (2001: 31) writes about 'the harsh material basis of primordial political experience' and echoing Schmitt, he argues that political power is anthropologically grounded in a capacity to inflict physical pain, suffering and death and so, in the last instance politics is unthinkable without violence.[5] In this view all forms of political power, including 'even discursively generated laws' ultimately require coercive sanctioning. In other words to command obedience presupposes the threat of violence. The development of technology expands the capability of human beings to kill and injure other humans both in terms of scope (i.e. a fiercest tiger can only kill a handful of animals with his teeth and claws in one go, while by detonating a nuclear bomb a single human can annihilate millions) and form (i.e. devising a variety of strategies and methods for slaughter). This expansion of violence directly affects political power, as in Poggi's account the two are intrinsically connected, thus simultaneously extending the range and modes of political domination. With the birth of modern state structures political power, being rooted in the monopolistic and legitimate control of violence, multiplies exponentially. The fact that rulers in modern nation-states (in the West) are institutionally constrained in their use of violence while pursuing political goals does not mean that violence disappears with modernity. Instead as Poggi (2001: 53) argues 'the political system's superior capacity to use violence as a means of enforcement is assumed and kept in the background by institutionalization...[and] such settled social circumstances are in turn the product of wanton and brutal violence, however occasionally exercised'. Adopting Hintzean analysis Poggi (2004: 99) understands the modern state-making process through the prism of evolving warfare: 'From the beginning, the modern state was shaped by the fact of being essentially intended for war-making, and primarily concerned with establishing and maintaining its military might'. With his accentuation of violence as a central feature of both social power and state building, Poggi's account remains inextricably wedded to the classical militarist tradition of social thought.

Randall Collins is almost unique among contemporary historical sociologists in his attempt to reconcile the macro and micro levels of power analysis as he integrates large-scale structural historical study of state formation and geopolitical changes with the face-to-face interactional exploration of social conflict. Situating conflict at the heart of social relations, Collins (1975, 1986, 1999) explains social action with reference to technological change, available resources, shared experiences of privilege, communication and cooperational networks and collective subjective perceptions, but most of all, to status struggle. Adopting a very Machiavellian position (though with a Weberian twist); Collins tells us that 'Life is basically a struggle for status in which no one can afford to be oblivious to the power of others around him and everyone uses what resources are available to have others aid him in putting on the best possible face under the circumstances' (Collins 1975: 60). In his most recent book Collins (2008) attempts to reconcile this bellicose macro structural view with the neo-Durkhemian and neo-Goffmanian analysis of the micro foundations of violence. For a sympathetic criticism of this project see Malešević (2008). Nevertheless his understanding of political and state power is fully in tune with Tilly, Mann and Poggi, and thus with the classical militarist thought, in the way he interprets politics almost exclusively through the prism of violence. Echoing Tretschke even more so than Weber, Collins (1975: 352) defines the state though its unimpeded capacity to pursue its will by relying on the means of coercion: 'The state is, above all, the army and the police, and if these groups did not have weapons we would not have a state in the classical sense'. In this account political power relates to warfare, while coercive threats and politics more generally, as with Schmitt chiefly concern force and the organization of violence. According to Collins (1975: 351–3), in pre-modern social orders private violence and politics are more or less identical, while the modern nation-state monopolizes its means ('the state consists of those people who have the guns or other weapons and are prepared to use them'), which leads to a situation where 'much politics does not involve actual violence [anymore] but consists of maneuvering around the organization that controls the violence'. Hence in the modern age the dominant form of political power becomes state power. The might of a particular state is determined by its ability to secure high power prestige both internally (through the penetration and successful mobilization of civil society groups) and externally (by raising and maintaining its geopolitical standing). Drawing on Weber directly and on Hintze indirectly, Collins (1986, 1999) argues that the state's geopolitical status is grounded in the military experience of its population whereby war victories raise the prestige of state rulers and enhance the power and legitimacy of the state, whereas military defeats do the opposite. War is seen as a catalyst of social and political change in history and a prime mover of state formation. To fully grasp the political power of the state one has to understand the military and other coercive apparatuses of a particular social order. The fact that modern liberal democracy allows more voice, dissent, popular representation and, consequently, power sharing, is far from being a reliable indicator of a relentless march forward. Instead this historical contingency is deeply rooted in the coercive structure of its social order. It is the relatively balanced dispersal of resources – coercive and otherwise – among well organized and independent social groups able to mobilize different interests that have created a distinctly multi-polar social and political environment. 'In a recent work (2004: 284–88) Collins argues that the Weberian definition of power still requires its micro level 'translation'. He distinguishes between D-power (deference or order-giving power) and E-power (efficacy power). Collins contends that the D-power is much more formal and thus ritualistic, has strong social significance, 'is consequential for meaningful social experience' since it shapes the 'culture' of personal relations but it does not guarantee efficiency. In contrast E-power is trans-institutional, operating through macro social networks, much less formal and hierarchical and potentially more dispersed but resulting in efficient outcomes. He argues that in contemporary world the D-power has become milder and generally is on the decrease while E-power, exemplified by mega-mergers of world leading corporations, is becoming more hierarchical 'where chains of financial resources and other forms of influence ripple far and wide throughout social networks, such that what few individuals do may have some effects upon the life of millions'.

As is evident from this brief analysis, despite their almost exclusive identification and self-identification with the Weberian approach the leading contemporary historical sociologists of power are deeply grounded in German militarist social thought. However, perhaps because they are profoundly wary of the ethical implications of building on this highly contested tradition, modern historical sociologists rarely make direct reference to Treitschke, Hintze and Schmitt. This is perhaps a form of internalized concealment which is largely unnecessary as they, for the most part, successfully de-essentialize, historically contextualize and remove the normative proto-fascist baggage from classical militarism, thus providing a much more sophisticated and explanatory potent account of power and collective violence. What in the works of the German militarists starts as teleology, ontology and apology of violence and the omnipotence of state power, ends up in the writings of Mann, Tilly, Collins and Poggi as a refined epistemology of social conflict and a highly persuasive historical sociology of domination. In this way, by drawing on classical bellicose thought, contemporary historical sociology has managed seriously to undermine the hegemony of the Marxist and other economistic theories of history by shifting its explanatory emphasis from the control of the means of production towards something far more important in understanding the power – the control of the means of destruction. As Collins, Poggi, Mann and Tilly convincingly argue and empirically prove one cannot explain the transformation and continual importance of political power without reference to violence and one cannot understand the origins of state formation and the current, almost indisputable, institutionalized supremacy of the nation-state system in the world, without intense engagement with the coercive nature of social life. Although these contemporary accounts are highly convincing in underlining and analysing the intrinsically coercive character of politics, they nonetheless seem less convincing when addressing the popular legitimization of power. In other words whereas these theoretical models extensively, and for the most part adequately, elucidate political power, there seems to be too little explanatory space for an understanding of ideological power.

THE MISSING LINK: POWER, VIOLENCE AND IDEOLOGY

Despite the hopes and aspirations of the Enlightenment that the new era would bring about a world without violence, where conflicting interests and values would be accommodated through rational argumentation, dialogue and debate, modernity turned out to be the most violent epoch in recorded history. Underpinned by grand vistas of an ideal social order, well equipped with the latest scientific and technological discoveries, and highly adept in mobilizing an enormous popular base, modern, democratizing, constitutional states proved to be incomparably vicious and much more efficient as war machines than any of their despotic and non-egalitarian predecessors. Notwithstanding the cruelty of pre-modern rulers, no tyrant of agrarian civilization could match the brutal efficiency of mass slaughter in concentration camps or the scope and speed of carnage caused by machine guns, aerial bombardment or nerve gas. There is no historical equivalent to tally all the revolutions, total wars and genocides of modernity. Yet it is this era more than any previous epoch that proclaimed the emancipation and liberation of the human subject as its central and core value. As direct heirs of the Enlightenment, modern constitutional orders, including both rulers and citizens, enshrine ideas of reason, justice, liberty, equality and humanity as self-evident[6] principles on which all social life should rest.

The situation whereby modernity is normatively built on the principles that glorify reason and human life and despise violence, while at the same time witnessing more bloodshed and mass killing than ever before, may seem to be a puzzling paradox. However, if one engages with the form, content, and structure of ideological power in the modern age then this particular outcome seems less mysterious. Although Poggi, Mann, Collins and Tilly adroitly explain why modernity was born and structurally remains reliant on violence, for the most part they provide no answer to the question: 'Why modern self-reflexive beings, socialized in the environment that abhors the sacrifice of human life, nonetheless tolerate and often tacitly support murder on a massive scale?' To answer this question properly one needs to take ideological power much more seriously than contemporary historical sociologists have done.

Although Mann, Poggi, Collins and Tilly all acknowledge the importance of collective values and beliefs they nevertheless still essentially treat ideology either as a second order reality or almost exclusively reduce ideological power to religious doctrines. Thus for example Poggi (2001) identifies ideological/normative power as one of the 'three basic power forms' together with political and economic power. He sees it as important but 'of derivative nature' and associates it almost exclusively with religion. In his own words 'religious power [is seen] as a prime and indeed primordial manifestation of ideological/normative power' (Poggi 2001: 71). Similarly Collins (1975: 369, 371) does not see much difference between traditional religions and modern secular ideologies: 'secular ideologies operate in most respects like religious ones', or 'modern ideologies are variants of the same basic set of conditions, new forms appropriate to modern conditions of the same appeals for moral solidarity and for obedience to the organization stretching beyond individuals that make up the social essence of religion'. Tilly (1985, 2003) devotes even less attention to ideology seeing it as an epiphenomenon shaped by political, military and economic forces. It is only in the work of Mann (1986, 1993) that ideological power receives more attention as he identifies ideology as one of the four central pillars of social power and conducts extensive historical analysis of worldwide ideological transformations.

By ideological power Mann (2005: 30) understands 'the mobilization of values, norms, and rituals in human societies that surpasses experience and science alike, and so contains nontestable elements'. He distinguishes between its transcendent and immanent forms whereby transcendent ideologies largely correspond to the autonomous and universalist doctrines capable of generating a large scale support base by transcending the existing institutions and projecting 'sacred' authority. Immanent ideologies refer to more dependent sets of beliefs and values that serve to strengthen the solidarity of existing power networks and organizations. However, even here, ideology is perceived in both of its forms as a weak force and rarely if ever figures as a key explanandum. Not only does Mann argue that premodern ideological doctrines 'had no general role of any significance, only world-historical moments' (Mann, 1986: 371), and that the impact of ideas generated in the French revolution on the European states was much smaller than generally assumed, but more importantly, he argues that since the nineteenth century the power of ideology, and religion in particular, has been very much in decline.[7] In addition Mann adopts a very instrumentalist understanding of ideology which focuses almost entirely on the function and means of ideological movements, and thus has little to say about the ends and contents of ideological messages (Hobson 2004; Gorski 2006).

The apparent neglect of ideology among contemporary historical sociologists of power was not shared by their militarist predecessors. Treitschke, Schmitt and Hintze were well aware that the successful proliferation and institutionalization of collective violence requires potent mechanisms of justification. Moreover they properly understood that the collapse of the old monotheistic universe of traditional order and their replacement with competing doctrines of universalist and egalitarian principles of modernity opened up the possibility for much fiercer bloodshed. To echo Dostoyevsky's Ivan Karamazov – once god is dead everything is permissible. As Schmitt (1996: 54) argues, ideas such as humanity, justice, progress or civilization are especially potent ideological devices as they allow one side in a conflict 'to usurp a universal concept against its military opponent' and treat him not as a disliked though nonetheless respected adversary, but rather as a something outside the norms of humanity. That is, as a monster; and monsters have no place in the world of humans – they unconditionally deserve annihilation. As President Truman put it in justifying his decision to drop atomic bombs on Japan: 'When you have to deal with a beast, you have to treat him as a beast. It is most regrettable but nevertheless true' (Alperovitz, 1995: 563). Consequently wars have 'decreased in number and frequency' but have 'proportionally increased in ferocity' (Schmitt, 1996: 35).

Although classical militarists often approach ideological power more from a normative, prescriptive position rather than an explanatory one – glorifying as they do omnipotent state power, militarist ethic, rigid nationalism and overt or covert racism – they also demonstrate that one cannot easily separate violence from ideology. To fully understand the proliferation of violence in modernity one has to study its ideological underpinnings. In other words any successful attempt to draw on the classical militarist tradition requires engagement with both the coercive and the ideological nature of power. To succeed any power requires legitimation and coercive power much more so.

The accounts of ideology presented in the works of contemporary historical sociologists suffer from two pronounced weaknesses. First, there is a degree of conceptual confusion whereby ideology is treated either too widely, when used as a synonym for culture (i.e. Mann 1986, 1993, 2006), or too narrowly and historically inaccurately, when reduced to traditional religious doctrines (Poggi 2001; Collins 1975; Mann 1986). As I have argued elsewhere (Malešević 2002: 58–61) although in modernity religious doctrines often acquire ideological attributes and can act as fully fledged ideologies, pre-modern religions lacked the institutional and organizational resources to function as modern ideologies. Not only did they operate in a context where there was no mass public literacy, standardized vernacular languages, state sponsored public education systems and printing capitalism (Anderson 1991), but traditional religions also lacked sophisticated mechanisms for the swift dissemination of information and the efficient bureaucratic organizational structure, all of which are essential for ideological power. As they appeal to reason and offer a rational explanation of social reality, normative ideologies require a fully formed literate public. Ideologies were born in a post-Enlightenment secular environment where what had formerly been a largely undisputed religious (Christian) monopoly was suddenly substituted by ideological pluralism. In this new historical context religious doctrines found themselves competing with the secular *weltenschauungen*. Unlike pre-modern religious doctrines, modern ideologies are often underpinned by the authority of science, humanist, and other secular ethics, and collective interests that are grounded in principles that stand in stark opposition to theological worldviews. Unlike religions, ideologies are deeply rooted in earth and not heaven. As Gouldner (1976) points out, the mass appeal of ideology in our age comes only with the creation of a modern human subject who 'must be more interested in the news from this world than in the tidings from another'. Against the promise of an afterlife, ideologies articulate competing blueprints for the transformation of the existing social reality. Liberalism, socialism, anarchism, scientific racism and many other ideologies offer secular blueprints and political grand vistas of social change capable of mobilizing millions of individuals. Since Machiavelli we know that secularized politics, unconstrained by religious ethics, is able to do both – to generate mass popular appeal and to be extremely ruthless in the implementation of its ideological goals. In this context ideologies appear as a much more potent generator of social action than traditional religions could ever be.

This leads us to the second problem of the contemporary historical sociologists – their perception of ideology as an explanatorily weak force. As Mann (2006: 346–7) puts it bluntly 'ideas can't do anything unless they are organized'. But this view can just as easily be turned on its head as all organizations are built and run on particular ideas and without ideas organizations cannot do anything. This is not to say that human actions are ultimately governed by ideas and values rather than material or political interests – the general mistake of all idealist epistemologies – but that the apparent success of coercive power in modern age cannot be adequately explained without understanding the justificatory power of modern ideologies. In other words ideological power is not the only, and not necessarily the primary generator of social action, but its social significance lays in its legitimizing capacity. When ends are perceived as ultimate truths, underpinned by unquestioned scientific authority and the ethical certainties of humanism, then all means become valid. In this context the question of the use of violence is often transformed into a question of mere efficiency. A decision to drop a uranium-235 20,000- ton nuclear warhead on a large urban congregation, which will inevitably kill hundreds of thousands of human beings, becomes a matter of precision and effectiveness. The first words of captain William Sterling Parsons after dropping a bomb on Hiroshima reveal this only too well: 'Results clear-cut, successful in all respects. Visible effects greater than any test. Conditions normal in airplane following delivery (Truman papers: 1945: 7)'. Similarly implementing a blueprint of the racially pure society entails the use of gas chambers as the most rational means for speedy, functional and efficient disposal of 'human waste'.

In the same vein, establishing an ideal classless social order may necessitate the rapid and total extermination of kulaks and other 'leeches' and 'vampires' that suck the blood of 'our proletarian people' and so on. Modern ideological doctrines with their inclusive, universalist rhetoric of collective solidarity provide the most potent but also the most uncompromising social mechanism of group mobilization able to justify the most extreme forms of violence (Malešević 2006, 2007). As possessors of ultimate secular truths, liberated from curbs of sanctimonious virtuosity and equipped with institutional structures and mass armaments of the modern state, ideologies appear simultaneously as powerful mobilizers of collective action and as legitimizers of that action. Although modern self-reflexive men and women are socialized to revere human life much more than any of their predecessors they also possess more powerful narratives for the justification of mass slaughter in terms of ideological doctrines. While an individual human life is sacred in principle, no price is too high when ideological goals are at stake: killing hundreds of thousands of human beings becomes 'regrettable' but acceptable when 'safeguarding democracy', 'attaining or fighting communism', 'establishing our own sovereign and independent nation', 'creating an ethnically or racially pure society' or setting up a Sharia-based pan-Islamic caliphate. Once buttressed by compelling ideology there is no limit to coercive power.

CONCLUSION

Despite being perceived as an abomination in the modern age, violence was and remains an indispensable ingredient of social and political life. Although modern states have managed to successfully monopolize its control, thus making it virtually invisible, they have not eradicated violent action. On the contrary, the enormous power that nation-states acquire in modernity, becoming the pre-eminent political actors within their societies as well as in the international geopolitical arena, is essentially derived form this largely unchallenged monopoly of the control of violence. As Collins puts it so aptly, the state is 'above all the army and the police'. Put more bluntly violence and power are inherently linked as there is no power which in some way is not grounded in the manipulation of violence. However the relationship between the two is not one-sided whereby coercion exists only as a means of political power. Instead what I would argue is that once unleashed, collective violence becomes its own master operating on its own tracks and creating new social realities. This is most evident in modern warfare where, on the one hand, the use of systematic violence radically transforms social institutions and human relations, thus generating new social and political orders, while on the other hand it dramatically expands the scale of human sacrifice and bloodshed. It is only in the wake of two devastating total wars and a couple of brutal revolutions that the liberal, democratic, constitutional, welfare inclusive social order has emerged. Regardless of its distaste for violence, sociology cannot afford to ignore the other, vicious, face of the modern Janus. Although classical militarist thought and contemporary neo-bellicose traditions of historical sociology have revitalized the importance of collective violence for the study of power, there is still need for greater analytical engagement with the ideological processes through which coercion becomes legitimized. This is highly significant since, sociologically speaking, coercive power without ideology is blind while ideology without coercion will always remain feeble.

NOTES

1 H. Joas (2003: 141–162) disputes the existence of such a militarist tradition in Germany or Austria by attempting to show that there was little in common a between number of individual thinkers taken to be representatives of this tradition. However, despite obvious diversity in their political views and their disciplinary interests, their research focuses on war, violence and state power, as well as their distinct bellicose approach to social life, distinguishes these authors as representatives of a particular intellectual tradition.

2 Schmitt (1996: 34f) incorporates Clausewitz's dictum that war is the continuation of politics by other means into his friend/enemy distinction by arguing that 'war, for Clausewitz, is not merely one of many instruments, but *ultima ratio* of the friend-enemy grouping. War has its own grammar…but politics remains its brain. It does not have its own logic'.

3 Weber's (1978: 53–4) often cited definitions of power and state are as follows: (1) power is 'the probability that one actor within a special relationship will be in a position to carry out his own will despite resistance, regardless of the basis on which this probability rests' and (2) the state is 'a compulsory political organisation with continuous operations…insofar as its administrative staff successfully upholds the claim to the monopoly of the legitimate use of physical force in the enforcement of its order'.

4 For example see most chapters in J.A. Hall and R. Schroeder (eds) 2006.

5 In a rare direct reference to Schmitt in his early work on state formation Poggi (1978: 5–13) acknowledges the ontological importance of Schmitt's account of politics: 'Much as one might discount Schmitt's view as demoniac or fascist, history has repeatedly born him out. Once the dangerousness and the ultimate disorderliness of social life are recognized, their implications remain utterly amoral and – today more than ever – utterly frightening'.

6 As for example stated in the preamble to American constitution : 'We hold these truths to be self-evident, that all men are created equal, that they are endowed, by their Creator, with certain unalienable Rights, that among these are Life, Liberty and the pursuit of Happiness'.

7 In recent writings Mann (2006: 345) has acknowledged this problem and now seems to accept that late modernity has been and still is highly ideological.

REFERENCES

Alperovitz, G. (1995) *The Decision to Use the Atomic Bomb*. New York: Albert Knopf.
Anderson, B.(1991) *Imagined Communities*. London: Verso.
Collins, R. (1975) *Conflict Sociology*. New York: Academic Press.
Collins, R. (1986) *Weberian Sociological Theory*. Cambridge: Cambridge University Press.
Collins, R. (1999) *Macro History: Essays in Sociology of the Long Run*. Stanford: Stanford University Press.
Collins, R. (2004) *Interaction Ritual Chains*. Princeton: Princeton University Press.
Collins, R. (2008) *Violence: A Micro-Sociological Theory*. Princeton: Princeton University Press.
Clausevitz, C. von (1997) *On War*. Ware: Wordsworth.
Davis, H. W.C. (1915) *The Political Thought of H. von Treitschke*. New York: Charles Scribner's Sons.
Ferrill, A. (1988) *The Origins of War: From the Stone Age to Alexander the Great*. London: Thames and Hudson.
Gilbert F. (1975) 'Introduction'. In F. Gilbert (ed.), *The Historical Essays of Otto Hintze*. New York: Oxford University Press.
Gorski. P. (2006) 'Mann's theory of ideological power: Sources, applications and elaborations'. In J.A. Hall and R. Schroeder (eds), *An Anatomy of Power: The Social Theory of Michael Mann*. Cambridge: Cambridge University Press.
Gouldner, A. (1976) *The Dialectic of Ideology and Technology: The Origins, Grammar and Future of Ideology*. London: Macmillan.
Hall, J.A. and Schroeder, R. (eds) (2006) *An Anatomy of Power: The Social Theory of Michael Mann*. Cambridge: Cambridge University Press.
Hintze, O. (1975) *The Historical Essays of Otto Hintze*. New York: Oxford University Press.

Hobson, J. (2004) *The Eastern Origins of Western Civilisation*. Cambridge: Cambridge University Press.
Joas, H. (2003) *War and Modernity*. Cambridge: Polity Press.
Keegan, J. (1993) *A History of Warfare*. New York: Vintage Books.
Malešević, S. (2002) *Ideology, Legitimacy and the New State*. London: Frank Cass.
Malešević, S. (2006) *Identity as Ideology*. New York: Palgrave Macmillan.
Malešević, S. (2007) 'Between the Book and the New Sword: Gellner, Violence and Ideology'. In S. Malešević and M. Haugaard (eds) *Ernest Gellner and Contemporary Social Thought*. Cambridge: Cambridge University Press.
Malešević, S. (2008) Solidary Killers and Egoistic Pacifists: Violence, War and Social Action. *Journal of Power*, 1(2): 207–216.
Mann, M. (1986) *The Sources of Social Power I*. Cambridge: Cambridge University Press.
Mann M. (1988) *States, War and Capitalism*. Oxford: Blackwell.
Mann M. (1993) *The Sources of Social Power II*. Cambridge: Cambridge University Press.
Mann, M. (2005) *The Dark Side of Democracy*. Cambridge: Cambridge University Press.
Mann, M. (2006) 'The sources of social power revisited: A response to criticism'. In J.A. Hall and R. Schroeder (eds), *An Anatomy of Power: The Social Theory of Michael Mann*. Cambridge: Cambridge University Press.
Marx, K. and Engels, F. (1998) *The Communist Manifesto*. London: Verso.
Poggi, G. (1978) *The Development of the Modern State*. Stanford: Stanford University Press.
Poggi, G. (2001) *Forms of Power*. Cambridge: Polity.
Poggi, G. (2004) 'Theories of state formation'. In K. Nash and A. Scott (eds), *The Blackwell Companion to Political Sociology*. Oxford: Blackwell.
Poggi, G. (2006) 'Political power un-manned: A defence of the Holy Trinity from Mann's attack'. In J.A. Hall and R. Schroeder (eds), *An Anatomy of Power: The Social Theory of Michael Mann*. Cambridge: Cambridge University Press.
Schmitt, C. (1996) *The Concept of the Political*. Chicago: Chicago University Press.
Tilly, C. (ed.) (1975) *The Formation of National States in Western Europe*. Princeton: Princeton University Press.
Tilly, C. (1985) 'War making and state making as organized crime'. In P. Evans, D. Rueschemeyer and T. Skocpol (eds), *Bringing the State Back In*. Cambridge: Cambridge University Press.
Tilly, C. (1992) *Coercion, Capital and European States*. Oxford: Blackwell.
Tilly, C. (1999) 'Power: Top down and bottom up', *The Journal of Political Philosophy*. 7(3): 330–352.
Tilly, C. (2003) *The Politics of Collective Violence*. Cambridge: Cambridge University Press.
Treitschke, H. von (1914) *Selections from Treitschke's Lectures on Politics*. London: Gowans & Gray.
Truman Library (1945) Draft Statement on Dropping of the Bomb. President's Secretary's File. *Truman Papers*. http://www.trumanlibrary.org/index.php.
Weber, E. (1978) *Economy and Society, I–II*. New York: Bedminster Press.

PART III
Power and Substantive Issues

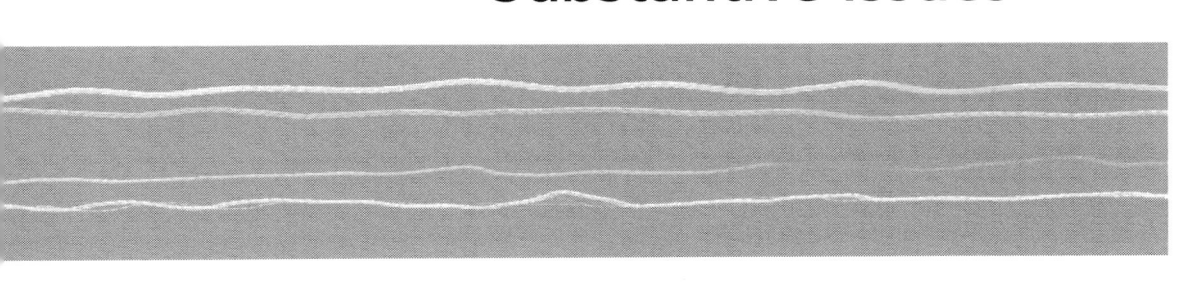

16

Gender and Power

Amy Allen

INTRODUCTION

At least since the inception of the second wave of feminism, power has been a central concept in feminist theorizing about gender. Early second wave feminist theory and activism were fueled largely by a desire to reveal, critique, and overturn specific relations of power: namely, gender domination and subordination. Later on, largely in response to criticisms from women of color, feminists attempted to broaden their focus to include the interlocking structures of race, class, gender, and sexuality based oppression and subordination. Despite the centrality of the concept of power to these endeavors, power as such is rarely explicitly thematized by feminists in their discussions of gender, race, class and sexuality (exceptions include Allen 1998, 1999; Hartsock 1983, 1996; Yeatmann 1997; Young 1992). As a result, how power is conceptualized in various feminist analyses of gender often must be reconstructed from discussions on a variety of different topics. This poses a challenge for critically assessing these conceptions of power. Moreover, despite their common aim of understanding, critiquing, and overturning an interlocking set of power relations, feminist theorists have employed a wide variety of different – and sometimes incompatible – theoretical strategies and conceptions of power in their critique of existing gender relations.

These differing conceptions of the relationship between power and gender that underpin different approaches to feminist theory have been further complicated by a fundamental lack of agreement on the definition of power. While many feminists have understood power in terms of domination, oppression, subordination – thus, they have implicitly defined power as the exercise of a certain form of power-over others[1] – others have rejected this definition in favor of a notion of power as individual and/or collective empowerment or transformation – thus, they have implicitly (and occasionally explicitly) redefined power as power-to or power-with. Interestingly, some of these latter feminists have argued against the former conception of power (power as a dominating form of power-over) on the grounds that this is a masculinist understanding of power. As such, they have suggested that the former conception of power is itself shaped by power relations, specifically, masculine domination. In this way, feminists have echoed Steven Lukes's contention that

> how we think about power may serve to reinforce and reproduce power structures and relations, or alternatively it may challenge and subvert them. It may contribute to their continued functioning, or it may unmask their principles of operation, whose effectiveness is increased by their being hidden from view. To the extent that this is so, conceptual and methodological questions are inescapably political... (Lukes 2005, 63).

This observation leads Lukes to conclude that power is an essentially contested concept (Lukes 1974, 2005; see also Connolly 1983).[2] If this is correct, then fundamental disagreement over how to define power will not be unique to feminist theory. However, in the case of feminist theory, the lack of agreement over the definition of power, lack of explicit attention to how power is being theorized, and the sheer centrality of the notion of power to feminist conceptions of gender all combine to create an exceptionally muddy conceptual terrain.

In what follows, I shall do my best to clarify this terrain. I begin by briefly rehearsing the history of the various second-wave feminist accounts of the relationship between gender and power, noting the differing definitions of power that underpin such accounts. Next, I turn to what is now arguably the predominant conception of the relationship between gender and power: the poststructuralist approach that is associated most closely with the work of Judith Butler. (Though I discuss how this conception emerged out of a critical engagement with the earlier, second-wave feminist views, I set aside the question of whether or not this approach is emblematic of a so-called third wave of feminism.) I argue that through the ambivalent notion of subjection, the poststructuralist approach integrates in interesting and insightful ways two definitions of power that previous feminist theorists had kept separate – power-over and power-to – though it neglects a crucial third dimension – power-with. Although the influence of the poststructuralist approach has been mainly limited to scholars working in the humanities, it is interestingly similar to the ethnomethodological conception of 'doing gender' that has been influential in sociology. A common strength of both of these accounts of gender and power is that they enable us to theorize the reciprocal and interrelated construction of femininity and masculinity within relations of power and, crucially, the way that hegemonic structures of gender position these two forms of identity as the only acceptable options for viable, intelligible, socially acceptable ways of doing or performing gender. As such, these approaches prompt a reorientation of theoretical inquiry: away from what now seems like a narrow and problematically essentialist focus on the situation of 'women' vis-à-vis power relations and toward a much broader consideration of the interconnected and power-saturated construction of femininities, masculinities, sexual dimorphism, and normative heterosexuality.

However, both the poststructuralist and ethnomethodological accounts have also been subject to criticism, often on similar grounds. Critics have charged these accounts with failing to offer a satisfactory conception of agency and resistance to prevailing relations of dominance and subordination and with paying insufficient attention to the macrostructural and institutional dimensions of power. Moreover, neither account has enough to say about collective power-with and the crucial role that it plays in making individual empowerment and resistance possible. Finally, neither account as it stands seems fully able to illuminate the interlocking and intersecting of relations of power along the lines of gender, race, class and sexuality. After considering these and related criticisms of the poststructuralist and ethnomethodological approaches, I conclude with a discussion of intersectionality. My contention is that the challenge of how to make sense of intersecting and cross-cutting axes of power – along lines of gender, race, class, and sexuality – across all three dimensions of power – power-over, power-to and power-with – remains the crucial challenge for feminist theories of gender and power.

SECOND-WAVE FEMINIST CONCEPTIONS OF POWER

The watershed text that is widely credited with launching second-wave feminist theory on both sides of the Atlantic is Simone de Beauvoir's *locus classicus*, *The Second Sex* (1974). Beauvoir offers a brilliant and groundbreaking analysis of the situation of women: the social, cultural, historical, political and economic conditions that define their existence. Beauvoir's basic diagnosis of women's situation relies on the distinction between being for-itself – self-conscious subjectivity that is capable of freedom and transcendence – and being in-itself – the un-self-conscious things that are incapable of freedom and mired in immanence. She argues that although all human beings are, by virtue of their ontological structure, capable of transcendence, throughout history women have been relegated to the status of the immanent Other while the status of transcendent Subject has been reserved for men. As Beauvoir puts it in a famous passage from the Introduction to *The Second Sex*: 'She is defined and differentiated with reference to man and not he with reference to her; she is the incidental, the inessential as opposed to the essential. He is the Subject, he is the Absolute – she is the Other' (Beauvoir: xxii).

This distinction – between man as Subject and woman as Other – is the key to de Beauvoir's phenomenologically based conception of power as domination or oppression. She writes,

> every time transcendence falls back into immanence, stagnation, there is a degradation of existence into the *en-soi* – the brutish life of subjection to given conditions – and liberty into constraint and contingence. This downfall represents a moral fault if the subject consents to it; if it is inflicted upon him, it spells frustration and oppression. In both cases it is an absolute evil (Beauvoir: xxxv).

Although Beauvoir suggests – quite controversially – that women are partly responsible for their situation to the extent that they have often willingly submitted to the status of the Other in order to avoid the anguish of authentic existence (see Beauvoir: xxvii), she also – perhaps somewhat paradoxically – maintains that women are oppressed because they are compelled to assume the status of the Other, thus, doomed to immanence (ibid.: xxxv). For Beauvoir, women's situation is thus marked by a basic tension between transcendence and immanence – as self-conscious human beings, women are capable of transcendence, but they are compelled into immanence by cultural, social, and political conditions that deny them that transcendence (see Beauvoir: chapter 21) – and power is understood as a relation of domination in which an individual or group of individuals is systematically prevented from exercising their inherent, ontological capacity for freedom and transcendence.

Despite the undeniable influence of Beauvoir's work on later generations of feminist theorists, in the early 1970s, when the women's movement emerged out of new left social movements and became a potent political force in its own right, the main theoretical reference point was not phenomenology but Marxism. According to the traditional Marxist account of power, domination is understood on the model of class exploitation. Domination is first and foremost an economically rooted phenomenon that results from the capitalist's appropriation of the surplus value produced by the workers. As many early second wave feminist critics of Marx pointed out, however, Marx's categories are sex/gender blind (see, for example, Firestone 1970; Hartmann 1980; Rubin 1976). Because he focuses solely on economic production, Marx completely overlooks women's reproductive labor in the private sphere and thus fails to see how this labor is both crucial for the functioning of capitalist relations of production and exploited within those relations. As a result, Marx ignores the ways in which class exploitation and gender subordination are intertwined. Because of this gender-blindness, early Marxist-feminists argued that Marx's analysis of class domination must be supplemented with or expanded by incorporating a feminist critique of patriarchy in order to yield a satisfactory account of women's oppression (see, for example, Eisenstein 1979; Hartmann 1980). The resulting theoretical framework came to be known as dual systems theory.[3]

While some feminists responded to the hegemonic status of Marxism as a critical tool for analyzing society by seeking to expand Marxist categories to correct for their gender-blindness, others took a different tack. So-called radical feminists developed a critique of patriarchy which they understood as a structural system of male domination from which racism, class oppression and heterosexism were derived. Such feminists sought not to expand Marx's analysis of class oppression to encompass issues of sex and gender but instead to use Marxism as a methodological model for developing their own theoretical perspective and calls for revolutionary change. For example, Shulamith Firestone, in her classic but now tragically underappreciated book *The Dialectic of Sex*, argues for a radical feminist revision of the historical materialism of Marx and Engels, as she puts it, 'a materialist view of history based on sex itself' (Firestone 1970: 6). As Firestone understands it, the subordination of women is rooted in their subordinated role in the biological family. On her view, 'the biological family is an inherently unequal power distribution' (Firestone 1970: 8) because the female role in biological reproduction renders women responsible for the care of infants and thus dependent on men for their physical and economic survival. Although Firestone admits that this power relation is rooted in biological nature, she does not see this as an obstacle to revolutionary, emancipatory social change. In her view, we have already begun to 'outgrow nature,' (Firestone 1970: 10), so we ought not shy away from the implication that overturning patriarchy will require 'the elimination ... of the sex distinction itself' through the abolition of biological reproduction (Firestone 1970: 11). With this move, 'the tyranny of the biological family would be broken. And with it the psychology of power' (Firestone 1970: 12).[4]

Psychoanalytic feminists pursued a different, though not unrelated, line of inquiry, seeking to uncover the ways in which the gendered division of labor within the heterosexual, nuclear family generates gendered personality structures that reinforce that division of labor and thus reinforce men's dominance and women's subordination. Nancy Chodorow's *The Reproduction of Mothering* (1978) argued that the institution of primary female parenting creates developmental and psychological conditions that perpetuate a stark separation of male and female identities, personality characteristics, and roles, all of which help to reproduce that very institution. As Chodorow put the point, 'families create children gendered, heterosexual, and ready to marry. But families organized around women's mothering and male dominance create incompatibilities in women's and men's relational needs' (Chodorow 1978: 199). Specifically, 'as a result of having been parented by a woman, women are more likely than men to seek to be mothers, that is, to relocate themselves in a primary mother-child relationship, to get gratification from the mothering relationship, and to have psychological and relational capacities for mothering' (Chodorow 1978: 206). These psychological and relational capacities include a sense of self as fundamentally in relation to and continuous with others, and a greater capacity for empathy. Chodorow claimed that, as a result of the practice of female parenting, women tend to develop these capacities and men do not, instead experiencing themselves as separate and distinct from others. In other words, women tend to define and experience themselves relationally while men tend to suppress relational capacities and needs (see Chodorow 1978: 207). This primes us psychologically to assume our respective roles in the gender division of labor – women doing unpaid and undervalued care-giving work in the home and men working for pay outside it – and thus in the system of gender-based subordination.

Despite important differences among these theoretical perspectives – phenomenological, Marxist, radical-feminist, and psychoanalytic – in their precise understanding of domination, oppression, or patriarchy, all of the approaches considered up until now have in common the assumption that power can be safely equated with domination. Since domination is a form of power-over – specifically, a power-over relation that is illegitimate and harmful rather than legitimate and beneficial to the one over whom power is exercised – they also share an implicit commitment to the definition of power as power-over. Although Chodorow's psychoanalytically inspired account of the relationship between power and gender was subject to harsh criticism from some quarters (see Young 1990 and Spelman 1988), her work also served indirectly as inspiration for the development of an alternative feminist conception of power. Carol Gilligan's enormously influential *In a Different Voice* (1982) used Chodorow's work as a jumping-off point, and the ethics of care that Gilligan developed in turn inspired feminist theorists of the 1980s and 1990s to develop an alternative conceptualization of power, one that focused not on masculine domination as a form of power-over, but instead on women's power, defined as empowerment, or power-to. For example, drawing on care ethics, Virginia Held argues against what she regards as the masculinist definition of power as 'the power to cause others to submit to one's will' (Held 1993: 136). Held further suggests that women's unique experiences as mothers and caregivers can serve as the basis for new insights into power. As she puts it, 'the capacity to give birth and to nurture and empower could be the basis for new and more humanly promising conceptions than the ones that now prevail of power, empowerment, and growth' (Held 1993: 137). According to Held, 'the power of a mothering person to empower others, to foster transformative growth, is a different sort of power from that of a stronger sword or a dominant will' (Held 1993: 209). On Held's view, a feminist analysis of power leads to a reconceptualization of power as the capacity to transform and empower oneself and others.[5]

Held, in her attempt to shift the definition of power from domination or control to empowerment, makes the provocative charge that the prevailing conception of power is itself reflective of and rooted in existing power relations – namely, relations of gender subordination. In a similar vein, Nancy Hartsock argues that 'social understandings of domination itself have been distorted by men's domination of women' (Hartsock 1983: 1). Hartsock criticizes mainstream political theory for understanding and conceptualizing power from the position of the dominant – the ruling class and men. The feminist task in analyzing power, according to Hartsock, is to reconceptualize power from a specifically feminist standpoint, one that is rooted in women's life experiences. Conceptualizing power from this standpoint can, according to Hartsock, 'point beyond understandings of power as power over others' (Hartsock 1983: 12).

However, despite the sophisticated nature of this insight into the ways in which our theoretical conceptions of power can themselves be a product of pernicious power relations, these alternative feminist conceptualizations of power remain unsatisfactory. As one-sided and perhaps even masculinist as it may be to define power solely in terms of power-over or, even more narrowly, domination, how useful is it to redefine power in such a way that gender, race, class, and sexual subordination can no longer be seen as relations of power at all? Is such a theoretical move really necessary in order to enable us to make sense of and highlight the possibilities for individual and collective empowerment and transformation? The feminist conceptions of power that I have discussed in this section seem to leave us with an unsatisfying and overly simplistic choice: either we understand power as the exercise of power-over others (usually in the form of domination), or as an empowering, transformative capacity or power-to act, but not both. In the next section, I shall argue that one of the most important insights of both poststructuralist and ethnomethodological approaches to the relationship between gender and power is that they enable us to understand these two aspects of power as inherently and complexly intertwined.

POSTSTRUCTURALISM AND ETHNOMETHODOLOGY

As Mary Hawkesworth has noted, over the course of the 1990s, the concept of gender became, somewhat paradoxically, both 'the central analytic concept in women's studies' and 'a highly contested concept within feminist theory' (Hawkesworth 1997: 650). The contestation over the concept of gender came from two distinct and not entirely reconcilable directions: first, from the experiences of feminists of color and lesbian-feminists who argued that the centrality of the category of gender obscured the intersectional and interlocking nature of relations of subordination based on race, class, gender, and sexuality; second from poststructuralist feminists who argued that the concept of gender is a 'totalizing fiction ... that create[s] a false unity out of heterogeneous elements' (Hawkesworth 1997: 651). Such critiques fueled a widespread sense of gender skepticism, a term coined by Susan Bordo to refer to 'a new skepticism about the use of gender as an analytical category' (Bordo 1993: 216).[6] Although it is important not to conflate these two positions, it is also important to point out that both the intersectional- and poststructuralist-feminist accounts of power and gender are motivated by similar concerns about the ways in which the concept of gender itself served within academic feminist discourse as a mechanism of exclusion, thus, as a tool of power. As Christine di Stefano puts it:

> the achievements of feminist theory consist of our various successes in naming, analyzing, and contesting illicit power as it impact upon and constitutes women. By contrast, our failures lie with inadequate analyses of power and also with our complicity with illicit power (di Stefano 1991: 87).

The point is here related to the one made by Held and Hartsock above: feminist conceptions of the relationship between gender and power can function and all too often have functioned as mechanisms of domination.

Both the intersectional and poststructuralist conceptions of gender and power highlight the failures of previous feminist approaches and attempt to develop conceptions of the relationship between power and gender that avoid repeating those failures. I return to a fuller discussion of the intersectional approach in the next section. For now, I focus on the poststructuralist account of the relationship between power and gender, comparing this approach, which has been so influential in the humanities, particularly in cultural studies, literary theory, and philosophy, with the sociologically grounded ethnomethodological account of 'doing gender'.

Most poststructuralist feminist work on power takes Foucault's analysis of power as its point of departure. In his middle-period works (Foucault 1977, 1978, 1980), Foucault analyzes modern power as a mobile and constantly shifting set of force relations that emerge from every social interaction and thus pervade the social body. As he puts it, 'power is everywhere, not because it embraces everything, but because it comes from everywhere' (1978: 93). Foucault offers a 'micro-physics' of modern power (1977: 26), an analysis that focuses not on the concentration of power in the hands of the sovereign or the state, but instead on how power flows through the capillaries of the social body. He is critical of previous analyses of power (primarily Marxist and Freudian accounts) for assuming that power is fundamentally repressive, a belief that he terms the 'repressive hypothesis' (1978: 17–49). Although he does not deny that power sometimes functions repressively (see 1978: 12), Foucault maintains that power is primarily productive; as he puts it, 'power produces; it produces reality; it produces domains of objects and rituals of truth' (1977: 194). Quite provocatively and controversially, Foucault argues that one of the most important effects of this productive power is the individual subject; as he puts it, 'the individual is not the vis-à-vis of power; it is, I believe, one of its prime effects' (1980: 98). The complicated and ambivalent relationship between the subject and power is captured by Foucault's use of the term 'subjection', a term that highlights Foucault's contention that individuals are constituted as subjects in and through their subjection to power relations.

This Foucaultian notion of subjection is central to the work of Judith Butler – undoubtedly the most influential poststructuralist theorist of gender. For example, in her early book, *Gender Trouble* (1990), Butler notes that

> Foucault points out that juridical systems of power *produce* the subjects they subsequently come to represent. Juridical notions of power appear to regulate political life in purely negative terms...But the

subjects regulated by such structures are, by virtue of being subjected to them, formed, defined, and reproduced in accordance with the requirements of those structures (1990: 2).

As Butler sees it, the implication for feminist theorists is that 'feminist critique ought also to understand how the category of "women", the subject of feminism, is produced and restrained by the very structures of power through which emancipation is sought' (1990: 2). This Foucaultian insight into the nature of subjection forms the basis for Butler's trenchant critique of the category of women as an inherently totalizing and exclusionary category, and for her call for a subversive performance of the gender norms that govern the production of gender identity. In *The Psychic Life of Power* (1997), Butler expands the Foucaultian notion of subjection, bringing it into dialogue with a Freudian account of the psyche. In the introduction to that text, Butler highlights the paradoxical nature of subjection as a form of power. It has an element of domination and subordination, to be sure, but, she writes

> if, following Foucault, we understand power as *forming* the subject as well, as providing the very condition of its existence and the trajectory of its desire, then power is not simply what we oppose but also, in a strong sense, what we depend on for our existence and what we harbor and preserve in the beings that we are (1997: 2).

Although Butler credits Foucault with recognizing the fundamentally ambivalent character of subjection, she also argues that he does not offer an account of the specific mechanisms by which the subjected subject is formed. For this, Butler maintains, we need an analysis of the psychic form that power takes, for only such an analysis can illuminate the passionate attachment to power that is characteristic of subjection.

As should be clear from this brief sketch of Butler's position, the poststructuralist approach not only poses the question of the relationship between gender difference and relations of dominance and subordination (as second-wave feminists attempted to do as well), it also suggests that the category of gender itself is power-laden, that it can serve as a mechanism of exclusion. For Butler, this suggestion stems from a broader belief about the repressive nature of all identity categories; as she puts it: 'Identity categories are never merely descriptive, but always normative, and as such, exclusionary' (Butler in Benhabib et al 1995: 50). It also stems from her acceptance of the Foucaultian idea that there is no outside to power, which means that the social critic or genealogist or theorist of power always necessarily thinks and writes from a position within power relations. As Butler puts it, 'power pervades the very conceptual apparatus that seeks to negotiate its terms, including the subject position of the critic' (39). Moreover, Butler contends that the attempt to articulate a theoretical or philosophical starting point that is pure or outside of or unaffected by power relations 'is perhaps the most insidious ruse of power' and constitutes a 'forceful conceptual practice that sublimates, disguises, and extends its own power play through recourse to tropes of normative universality' (39).

The ethnomethodological approach to gender is laid out in Candace West and Don Zimmerman's seminal article 'Doing Gender'.[7] Although West and Zimmerman propose their approach as a 'distinctively sociological' understanding of gender, as we shall see, it bears striking similarities to Butler's poststructuralist notion of the performativity of gender. Drawing on the work of Harold Garfinkel and Erving Goffman, West and Zimmerman argue that gender is 'not a set of traits, nor a variable, nor a role' (West and Zimmerman, 2002: 6), but instead should be understood as a 'routine, methodical, and recurring accomplishment,' an 'achieved property of situated conduct' (West and Zimmerman, 2002: 4). Gender is not a matter of what one *is*, it is something that one *does*; it is accomplished through ongoing social interactions. Key to this account of doing gender is the idea of accountability. For ethnomethodologists, accountability is central to the organization of social interaction. As actors, we regularly hold others accountable for their adherence to (or deviation from) social norms, and we expect to be held accountable in return. Thus, to do gender is to be held accountable in ongoing social interactions for one's adherence to or transgression of social norms of gender. A West and Zimmerman note, 'to "do" gender is not always to live up to normative conceptions of femininity or masculinity; it is to engage in behavior *at the risk of gender assessment*' (West and Zimmerman 2002: 13). However, since one's faithfulness to gender norms can be relevant in virtually any situation or context – public or private, hetero or homosocial – and since doing gender in some way or another is socially expected in virtually all interactions, the doing of gender is both omnirelevant and unavoidable.

The omnirelevance and unavoidability of gender mean that women and men are 'hostage to its production' and, we might add, ongoing reproduction (West and Zimmerman 2002: 4). Thus, although West and Zimmerman do not emphasize the connection between gender and power, they clearly recognize it:

> doing gender...renders the social arrangements based on sex category accountable as normal and natural, that is, legitimate ways of organizing social life....Thus, if, in doing gender, men are also doing dominance and women are doing deference, the resultant social order, which supposedly reflects 'natural differences', is a powerful reinforcer and legitimator of hierarchical arrangements (West and Zimmerman, 2002: 21).

However, they do not view this as a hopeless situation. Although we all are expected to (and expect each other to) do gender and are held accountable (and hold others accountable) for failing to do it appropriately or correctly, we are capable of doing gender differently, perhaps even of undoing gender. West and Zimmerman recognize that, on an individual level, this is difficult to accomplish, inasmuch as 'if we fail to do gender appropriately, we as individuals – not the institutional arrangements – may be called to account'. However, collective social movements such as the feminist movement 'can provide the ideology and impetus to question existing arrangements, and the social support for individuals to explore alternatives to them' (West and Zimmerman 2002: 22).

The most obvious similarity between these two approaches lies in the shared assumption that gender is not a function of who or what one is but of something that one does.[8] Both approaches reject the idea that gender reflects one's essential, fixed nature; instead, they view it as a performance or an interactional accomplishment. To be sure, there are important differences in the specifics of these two approaches, namely, in how they understand the doing of gender. As Moloney and Fenstermaker put it, 'In Butler's theory, gender is *discursively* constituted; gender is "performed" through discourse, broadly defined. In West and Fenstermaker, gender is *interactionally* produced; gender is "done" in interactions, broadly defined' (Moloney and Fenstermaker 2002: 194). What remains unclear is the extent of overlap between the domains of discourse and interaction. I suspect that these notions are not as far apart as they might initially seem, especially given, on the one hand, the importance of conversational analysis for ethnomethodology and, on the other hand, the importance of both speech act theory and the maintenance and reproduction of social norms for Butler's theory of performativity. Although there is no doubt that these two approaches use different terminologies and draw on distinct research traditions, they seem to be talking about the same thing. Be that as it may, another interesting similarity between the two approaches is that they not only argue against the naturalness or essential nature of gender and sex categories, they also offer important insights into how the sense of naturalness that adheres to these categories is produced. As West and Zimmerman put it: 'doing gender means creating differences between girls and boys and women and men, differences that are not natural, essential, or biological. Once the differences have been constructed, they are used to reinforce the "essentialness of gender" ' (West and Zimmerman 2002: 13). Similarly, Butler closes *Gender Trouble* by envisioning a future in which cultural configurations might 'confound ...the very binarism of sex, and expose ...its fundamental unnaturalness', which, in turn, 'might lead to the denaturalization of gender as such' (Butler 1990: 149).

Perhaps because of these similarities, these two approaches have been subjected to similar sorts of criticisms. For instance, both poststructuralist and ethnomethodological approaches have been criticized for offering deterministic accounts of gender that have difficulty making sense of agency, empowerment, resistance to prevailing norms, and/or social change. With respect to Butler, for example, Seyla Benhabib maintains that 'the theory of performativity...presupposes a remarkably deterministic view of individuation and socialization processes...' (Benhabib in Benhabib et al. 1995: 110). Similarly, Barrie Thorne complains that the ethnomethodological approach analyzes 'social phenomena with a functionalist tilt, emphasizing the maintenance and reproduction of normative conceptions but neglecting countervailing processes of resistance, challenge, conflict, and change' (Hill Collins et al. 2002: 88).[9]

However, I would argue precisely the opposite of these critics. What is distinctive and crucially important about both of these approaches, at least from the point of view of the theoretical exploration of the relationship between gender and power, is the way in which they illuminate the complex intertwining of domination (as a form of power-over) and empowerment (or power-to). For Butler the meeting point of these two conceptions of power is the notion of subjection: she envisions the individual as empowered as a subject in and through a process of subjection to power. This enables Butler to preserve the possibility of agency, but to offer an account of agency that recognizes its inherently ambivalent nature, the fact that it is always situated in existing relations of power and in relation to prevailing norms. Although Butler often talks as if she equates power with domination, her use of the notion of subjection also implies a broader understanding of power that encompasses empowerment as well. This is evident in her reflections on the notion of subjection in the introduction to *The Psychic Life of Power*:

> Power acts on the subject in at least two ways: first, as what makes the subject possible, the condition of its possibility and its formative occasion; and second, as what is taken up and reiterated in the subject's 'own' acting. As a subject *of* power (where 'of' connotes both 'belonging to' and 'wielding'), the subject eclipses the conditions of its own emergence; it eclipses power with power (Butler 1997: 14).

Although Butler does not explicitly distinguish domination (as a form of power-over) from empowerment (or power-to), one could easily read this distinction back into what she says (and, indeed, doing so has the advantage of making what she is saying seem much less mysterious).

Similarly, the ethnomethodological approach theorizes the intertwining of domination and empowerment through its emphasis on the notion of accountability. It is true that this approach conceives of gender as an ongoing accomplishment of individuals, but this accomplishment is structured by prevailing norms of acceptability and accountability, which, in turn, are a function of existing structures of gender dominance. Although the ethnomethodological approach has been faulted for not focusing enough on the power relations that underpin the doing of gender (see Hill Collins et al. 2002), I would argue that these theorists have offered an enormously useful framework for understanding the interplay between individual capacities or power-to – specifically, the abilities of individuals to accomplish or do gender appropriately in particular contexts – and mechanisms of social control and domination – the subordinating gender norms to which we are held and hold ourselves and others accountable. Moreover, because they understand the maintenance and reproduction of relations of domination as dependent upon the ongoing interactional accomplishments of individuals, ethnomethodologists are in a better position than many previous theorists of gender and power to make sense of resistance and change. As Fenstermaker and West put it: because gender is 'done', 'there is both activity (including resistance) and agency at its foundation' (2002: 99). In other words, understanding how gender is 'done' is the key to figuring out how it can be 'undone'.[10]

This way of understanding the distinctiveness of these approaches highlights the extent to which they constitute a major theoretical advance over the second wave approaches discussed in the previous section. Second wave feminist theories – whether phenomenological, Marxist, radical, or psychoanalytic – have been frequently criticized for overemphasizing the subordinate status of women, thus, implying that they are helpless, passive victims. Indeed, so-called third wave feminists have taken to referring to second-wave feminism as 'victim feminism' and referring to their new approach as 'power feminism', to emphasize their focus on women's empowerment. However, the theorists of empowerment that I discussed above leave themselves open to the charge that, by revaluing women's experiences and capacities as caregivers and viewing these as sources of empowerment, they are simply, as Catharine MacKinnon put it, affirming 'the qualities and characteristics of powerlessness' (MacKinnon 1987: 39). The poststructuralist and ethnomethodological approaches, by contrast, avoid both of these problems, by emphasizing the active and creative role played by individual subjects/actors in the maintenance and reproduction of subordinating social norms. Thus, these approaches are able to understand individuals as empowered to act in and through their adherence to the existing structure of gender domination. Although this may offer a somewhat more ambivalent and limited conception of empowerment than we might have been hoping for, it nonetheless seems utterly realistic. Empowerment does not arise in a vacuum; it is a capacity that is produced within the context of the very power relations that we would like to use it to challenge and eventually overturn. Insofar as both the poststructuralist and ethnomethodogical approaches theorize the ways in which relations of domination can only be maintained and reproduced through the performances or doings of individual actors, they do a much better job than previous approaches have done of carving out a space for empowerment without naively envisioning it as something that stands wholly outside of existing relations of dominance and subordination.

To be sure, both of these approaches could do even more along these lines. In particular, both approaches would benefit from more sustained reflection on a third definition of power: power-with, or collective power, power understood as 'the human ability not just to act but to act in concert' (Arendt 1970: 44). Collective power can generate important conceptual, normative and psychological resources for individual empowerment and resistance and, thus, is an important motor of social change (Allen 1999). The ethnomethodologists, as I noted above, at least recognize that this is an important point, though they do not devote much space to discussing it nor do they do much work to connect their analysis up with the vast social movement literature. Butler, unfortunately, seems not only uninterested in but downright suspicious of the notions of collective power or solidarity (see Butler 1990). As I have argued elsewhere (Allen 1998), this constitutes a serious limitation to her analysis of power.

A second common criticism of both of these approaches concerns their overemphasis on microlevel interactions and performances and a relative lack of attention to macrolevel institutional and structural patterns or systemic relations of power. For example, with respect to the ethnomethodological approach, Lynn Weber argues that 'because of its exclusive attention on face-to-face interaction, macro social structural processes such as institutional arrangements, community structures, and even family systems are rendered invisible' (Hill Collins et al. 2002: 89). Similarly, Nancy Fraser complains that whereas 'Butler's approach is good for theorizing the micro level, the intrasubjective, and the historicity of gender relations', 'it is not useful…for the macro level, the intersubjective, and the normative' (Benhabib et al. 1995: 164; quoted in Moloney and Fenstermaker 2002: 195). I am not convinced, however, that these charges entirely hit their mark. With respect to the ethnomethodological approach, precisely what these authors are trying to understand is the contact point between individuals and larger institutions or structures. West and Zimmerman make this point clear in their initial formulation of the approach when they note that doing gender 'links the institutional and interactional levels' (West and Zimmerman 2002: 22). Similarly, Moloney and Fenstermaker point out in defense of the ethnomethodological approach that the notion of accountability provides a bridge between the institutional and interactional levels (Moloney and Fenstermaker 2002: 195). One might make a similar case for Butler, whose use of the concept of citationality arguably fulfills a similar function to that of accountability – that is, it relates individual performances to broader social norms and structures of power (on this point, see Allen 1998).

However, this response is convincing only up to a point, as it is clear that neither approach gives a complete account of the macro level in its own right, nor does either approach even indicate what sort of macro structural approach it might favor.[11] This lack of an independent account of the macro-structural level explains the serious difficulties that both of these approaches have in making sense of class oppression. Butler, for her part, does not even try to analyze class, and it is difficult to see how she could without seriously expanding or perhaps modifying her understanding of power (for a critique of Butler on this point, see Fraser 1997). West and Fenstermaker do attempt to extend the ethnomethodological approach to explain class stratification in their essay 'Doing Difference', but, as several critics have pointed out, the results are very weak (see Hill Collins et al. 2002). This brings us back to the challenge of how to produce a feminist account of gender and power that also sheds light on the multiple and interlocking systems of oppression along lines of race, class, and sexuality. That is to say, it brings us back to the issue of intersectionality.

INTERSECTIONALITY

As I noted above, the motivation behind the poststructuralist and intersectional approaches is in some respects similar: both are rooted in a concern over the ways in which the concept of gender itself has functioned as a mechanism of exclusion, thus, as a way for the relatively powerful (middle-class, white, heterosexual academic feminists) to ignore or discount the lives and experiences and concerns of the relatively powerless (working class women, women of color, and lesbians). However, it is important not to conflate these two approaches. As Leslie McCall argues, while the work of poststructuralist feminists tends to be 'critical of categorization per se', intersectional theorists have tended to be critical only of 'broad and sweeping acts of categorization' (McCall 2005: 1779; for a similar point, see Bordo 1993). In other words, 'feminists of color have steered a middle course [between poststructuralism and identity politics], consistently engaging in both theoretical and empirical studies of intersectionality using finer intersections of categories' (McCall 2005: 1780). Moreover, some intersectional theorists are highly critical of poststructuralism, on the grounds that the image of power as a network ultimately obscures rather than illuminates power relations along lines of race, class, and gender.[12] Although, as I argued above, I do not think it is fair to accuse these approaches of failing to illuminate power relations, it is true, as Christine di Stefano observes, that 'all too often, the postmodern critique is allied or conflated with that of women of color who have no use for or interest in postmodern theory' (di Stefano 1991: 86).

As Leslie McCall notes, one might argue that intersectionality 'is the most important theoretical contribution that women's studies, in conjunction with related fields, has made so far' (McCall 2005: 1771). Yet, unfortunately, it seems to me that the promise of intersectionality – understood as the attempt to think through the relationships between multiple and interrelated dimensions of social/political subordination along lines of race, class, gender, and sexuality – remains largely unfulfilled. As I indicated above, the notion of intersectionality originally arose out of the criticisms of feminists of color of existing feminist accounts of power and gender (for classic statements of intersectionality, see Crenshaw 1991a, b; King 1988; for more recent assessments, see McCall 2005; Ward 2004). As Kimberle Crenshaw argues in her early statement of intersectionality, non-intersectional approaches to feminist theory presuppose single-axis frameworks for thinking legal discrimination and social subordination. A single-axis framework treats race and gender as mutually exclusive categories of experience and analysis. In so doing, such a framework privileges the perspective of the most privileged members of oppressed groups (e.g. sex- or class-privileged blacks in race discrimination cases; race or class privileged women in sex discrimination cases) (for a similar point, see Spelman 1988). Thus a single-axis framework distorts or, worse, completely ignores the experiences of black women, who are simultaneously subject to multiple and intersecting systems of subordination. As Crenshaw puts it, 'the intersection of racism and sexism factors into Black women's lives in way that cannot be captured wholly by looking at the race or gender dimensions of those experiences separately' (Crenshaw 1991b: 1244).

However, it is crucially important to point out that intersectionality is not only relevant to the experience of black women or others who are subject to multiple oppressions, even though the initial formulation of the framework was inspired by such experiences. One of the cornerstones of the intersectional approach is that one cannot adequately understand the power relations within which, for example, white, middle-class, heterosexual women are positioned without understanding how their race, class, and sexual *privilege* shapes that positioning.

Some theorists of intersectionality have maintained that this notion refers primarily to the formation of individual identity and social positioning – both micro-level processes – and that a full analysis of the intertwining of racial, gender, sexual, and class-based subordination requires a macro-level concept that corresponds to intersectionality Thus, Patricia Hill Collins has introduced the notions of intersectionality (as a micro-level concept) and interlocking systems of oppression (as a macro-level concept). As she puts it

> the notion of interlocking oppressions refers to the macro-level connections linking systems of oppression such as race, class, and gender. This is the model describing the social structures that create social positions. Second, the notion of intersectionality describes micro-level processes – namely, how each individual and group occupies a social position within interlocking structures of oppression described by the metaphor of intersectionality. Together they shape oppression (Hill Collins et al. 2002: 82).

Were this framework to be more fully developed and worked out, it would go quite a long way toward making sense of the complex and interrelated relations of domination along lines of race, class, gender, and sexuality.

As things stand now, however, this remains an unfulfilled promise in feminist reflections on power. Moreover, even were this – admittedly large and difficult task – to be fulfilled, more work would still remain to be done. The remaining challenge would be to extend the intersectional framework for understanding domination to encompass intersectional models of individual and collective empowerment, and to theorize the complicated interconnections between these different modalities of power. To that end, given the ways in which they highlight the interconnections between domination and individual empowerment, the poststructuralist and ethnomethodological models can be useful. However, in response to the criticisms of those models that I discussed above, it would also be necessary to situate the poststructuralist and ethnomethodological analyses of power in the broader institutional and macrostructural contexts that shape the ongoing discursive and interactional production and reproduction of our social world. Doing so is particularly important for developing a model of power that can make sense of class stratification, which is ultimately a product of macrostructural economic relations (on this point, see Fraser 1997). In addition, the poststructuralist and ethnomethodological analyses need to be expanded to encompass the notion of collective power (power-with). Without some account of power-with, we cannot make sense of either collective or individual empowerment and resistance to domination, inasmuch as the power that emerges from collective social movements generates normative, conceptual and psychological resources that make individual empowerment and resistance possible. What is needed, then, is an account of power that draws on the insights of these three research programs – poststructuralism, ethnomethodology, and the intersectional approach – in order to articulate a complex and differentiated conception of power – encompassing and theorizing the interconnections between domination (understood as a form of power-over) and individual and collective empowerment (power-to and power-with, respectively) – that will be capable of illuminating the intersecting and cross-cutting axes of power along lines of gender, race, class, and sexuality.

NOTES

1 It is important to note that power-over and domination are not the same thing; domination a form of power-over others. We can at least analytically distinguish exercises of power-over others that point toward beneficial or transformative ends from those that aim at domination or oppression. On this point, see Wartenberg (1990). I shall return to this point below.

2 However, even this point is contested. For alternative points of view, see Morriss (2002) and Wartenberg (1990).

3 For a trenchant critique, see Young (1990).

4 For a moving and surprisingly plausible fictional account of such a possible world, see Piercy (1976).

5 Similar criticisms of the notion of power-over as masculinist and alternative conceptions of power as empowerment or as a transformative capacity can be found in the work of lesbian feminists (see Hoagland 1988), eco-feminists (see Starhawk, 1987), and French feminists (see Irigaray 1985 and Cixous 1977). I discuss these conceptions of power in Allen (2005).

6 For a related discussion, see di Stefano (1991). For defenses of gender as an analytical category, see Hawkesworth (1997) and Scott (1986).

7 This approach is subsequently expanded and elaborated in Fenstermaker and West (2002).

8 For helpful discussion of the similarities and differences between these approaches, see Moloney and Fenstermaker (2002).

9 Thorne also suggests that Butler's account compares favorably to the ethnomethodological account on this point, inasmuch as Butler 'emphasizes possibilities for transgression' (Hill Collins et al. 2002: 88).

10 Interestingly enough, the title of one of Butler's recent books is *Undoing Gender* (2004), though there is no indication that this title is intentionally referring to the ethnomethodological literature, or even that she is aware of that literature.

11 Moreover, Butler's adherence to poststructuralism might be taken as indication that she rejects the very idea of macrostructural social analysis.

12 On this point, see Hill Collins's remarks in Hill Collins et al. (2002).

REFERENCES

Allen, Amy (1998) 'Power trouble: Performativity as critical theory', *Constellations*, 5 (4): 456–471.
Allen, Amy (1999) *The Power of Feminist Theory: Domination, Resistance, Solidarity*. Boulder, CO: Westview Press.
Allen, Amy (2005) 'Feminist perspectives on power', *Stanford Encyclopedia of Philosophy*, http://plato.stanford.edu/entries/feminist-power/
Arendt, Hannah (1970) *On Violence*. New York: Harcourt, Brace, and Co.
Beauvoir, Simone de (1974) *The Second Sex*, trans. H.M. Parshley. New York: Vintage Books.
Benhabib, Seyla, Judith Butler, Drucilla Cornell and Nancy Fraser (1995) *Feminist Contentions: A Philosophical Exchange*, Linda Nicholson (ed.). New York: Routledge.
Bordo, Susan (1993) 'Feminism, postmodernism, and gender skepticism', in *Unbearable Weight: Feminism, Western Culture and the Body*. Berkeley, CA: The University of California Press.
Butler, Judith (1990) *Gender Trouble: Feminism and the Subversion of Identity*. New York: Routledge.
Butler, Judith (1997) *The Psychic Life of Power: Theories in Subjection*. Palo Alto, CA: Stanford University Press.
Butler, Judith (2004) *Undoing Gender*. New York: Routledge.
Chodorow, Nancy (1978) *The Reproduction of Mothering: Psychoanalysis and the Sociology of Gender*. Berkeley, CA: The University of California Press.
Connolly, William (1993) *The Terms of Political Discourse*, Third Edition. Princeton, NJ: Princeton University Press.
Crenshaw, Kimberle (1991a) 'Demarginalizing the intersection of race and sex: A black feminist critique of antidiscrimination doctrine, feminist theory, and antiracist politics', in Katharine T. Bartlett and Rosanne (eds), *Feminist Legal Theory: Readings in Law and Gender*. Boulder, CO: Westview Press.
Crenshaw, Kimberle (1991b) 'Mapping the margins: Intersectionality, identity politics, and iolence against women of color', *Stanford Law Review*, 43 (6): 1241–1299.
Eisenstein, Zillah (1979) 'Developing a theory of capitalist patriarchy', in Zillah Eisenstein (ed.), *Capitalist Patriarchy and the Case for Socialist Feminism*. New York: Monthly Review Press.

Fenstermaker, Sarah and Candace West (eds) (2002) *Doing Gender, Doing Difference: Inequality, Power, and Institutional Change*. New York: Routledge.
Firestone, Shulamith (1970) *The Dialectic of Sex: The Case for Feminist Revolution*. New York: William Morrow and Company.
Foucault, Michel (1977) *Discipline and Punish: The Birth of the Prison*, trans. Alan Sheridan. New York: Vintage.
Foucault, Michel (1978) *The History of Sexuality, Volume 1: An Introduction,* trans. Robert Hurley. New York: Vintage.
Foucault, Michel (1980) 'Two Lectures' in Colin Gordon, (ed.), *Power/Knowledge: Selected Interviews and Other Writings, 1972–1977*. New York: Pantheon.
Fraser, Nancy (1997) *Justice Interruptus: Critical Reflections on the 'Postsocialist' Condition*. New York: Routledge.
Gilligan, Carol (1982) *In a Different Voice: Psychological Theory and Women's Development*. Cambridge: Harvard University Press.
Hartmann, Heidi (1980) 'The unhappy marriage of marxism and feminism: Toward a more progressive union', in Lydia Sargent (ed.), *Women and Revolution*. Boston: South End Press.
Hartsock, Nancy (1983) *Money, Sex, and Power: Toward a Feminist Historical Materialism*. Boston: Northeastern University Press.
Hartsock, Nancy (1996) 'Community/sexuality/gender: Rethinking power', in Nancy J. Hirschmann and Christine di Stefano (eds), *Revisioning the Political: Feminist Reconstructions of Traditional Concepts in Western Political Theory*. Boulder, CO: Westview Press.
Hawkesworth, Mary (1997) 'Confounding gender', *Signs: Journal of Women in Culture and Society*, 22 (3): 649–685.
Held, Virginia (1993) *Feminist Morality: Transforming Culture, Society, and Politics*. Chicago: University of Chicago Press.
Hill Collins, Patricia, Lionel A. Maldonado, Dana Y. Takagi, Barrie Thorne, Lynn Weber and Howard Winant (2002) 'Symposium on West and Fenstermaker's "Doing Difference"', in Fenstermaker and West (eds), *Doing Gender, Doing Difference*. New York: Routledge.
King, Deborah (1988) 'Multiple jeopardy, multiple consciousness: The context of a black feminist ideology', *Signs: Journal of Women in Culture and Society*, 14 (1): 42–72.
Lukes, Steven (1974) *Power: A Radical View*. London: Macmillan.
Lukes, Steven (2005) *Power: A Radical View*, 2nd expanded edition. London: Macmillan.
MacKinnon, Catharine (1987) *Feminism Unmodified: Discourses on Life and Law*. Cambridge: Harvard University Press.
McCall, Leslie (2005) 'The complexity of intersectionality', *Signs: Journal of Women in Culture and Society*, 30 (3): 1771–1800.
Moloney, Molly and Sarah Fenstermaker (2002) 'Performance and accomplishment: Reconciling feminist conceptions of gender', in Fenstermaker and West (eds), *Doing Gender, Doing Difference*. New York: Routledge.
Morriss, Peter (2002) *Power: A Philosophical Analysis*, 2nd edition. Manchester: Manchester University Press.
Piercy, Marge (1976) *Woman on the Edge of Time*.
Rubin, Gayle (1976) 'The traffic in women: Notes on the political economy of sex', in Rayna Reiter (ed). *Toward an Anthropology of Women*. New York: Monthly Review Press.
Scott, Joan (1986) 'Gender: A useful category of historical analysis', *The American Historical Review*, 91 (5): 1053–1075.
Spelman, Elizabeth (1988) *Inessential Woman: Problems of Exclusion in Feminist Thought*. Boston: Beacon Press.
di Stefano, Christine (1991) 'Who the heck are we? Theoretical turns against gender', *Frontiers: A Journal of Women's Studies*, 12 (2): 86–108.
Ward, Jane (2004) '"Not all differences are created equal": Multiple jeopardy in a gendered organization', *Gender and Society*, 18 (1): 82–102.
Wartenberg, Thomas (1990) *The Forms of Power: From Domination to Transformation*. Philadelphia: Temple University Press.
West, Candace and Sarah Fenstermaker (2002) 'Reply – (Re)Doing difference', in Fenstermaker and West (eds), *Doing gender, Doing Difference*. New York: Rouledge.
West, Candace and Don H. Zimmerman (2002) 'Doing Gender', in Fenstermaker and West (eds), *Doing Gender, Doing Difference*. New York: Routledge.

Yeatmann, Anna (1997) 'Feminism and power', in Mary Lyndon Shanley and Uma Narayan (eds), *Reconstructing Political Theory: Feminist Perspectives*. University Park, PA: The Pennsylvania State University Press.

Young, Iris Marion (1990) *Throwing Like a Girl and Other Essays in Feminist Philosophy and Social Theory*. Bloomington, IN: Indiana University Press.

Young, Iris Marion (1992) 'Five Faces of Oppression', in Thomas Wartenberg (ed.), *Rethinking Power*. Albany, NY: SUNY Press.

17

Managing Power in Organizations: The Hidden History of Its Constitution

Stewart R. Clegg

INTRODUCTION

Management as a practice of power involving the imposition of will is directed at framing not only the conduct of others but also oneself. It is a form of government linking 'how to mandate' with 'how to obey'. Managing implies power because it involves governing the conduct of oneself and others. Managing in any epoch will be a particular skill that involves execution and doing. It will be active, a practice. Moreover, it will not merely be a practice of the self – one doesn't just learn how to be a manager – but it is also a practice of the many others who are to be managed. Others must learn to be managed just as those who will manage them must learn that which constitutes managing in any given place and time.

While managers originally were constituted as the delegated 'servants' of 'masters', and indeed various Masters and Servants Acts still frame employment relations, modernity saw servants become employees. In US English, Jacques (1996: 68) tells us that the term employee first occurs in the context of a discussion of the railways in which context it stays until the 1870s, when it started to be used more generally. By the early years of the twentieth century, employee had become the accepted and most commonly used term, carrying a weight of semantic meaning: being a permanent worker belonging to an organization; being subordinated; being assigned to tasks to which one is fitted and for which one is paid a wage; being subject to the expertise of a managerial specialist and the panoply of management knowledge, all of which, finally, enables one to become a specialist producer and consumer (Jacques 1996: 70–86). The employee was one half of an emerging binary division for which the other half was the manager – a specialist in authority – overseeing the employee – a specialist in obedience. The division is significant because they both constitute a systemic unity. The worker is power (energy to work), the manager is knowledge (authority by science to conduct behaviours), comprising the essential unity between power-knowledge, the base of modernity (Ibarra-Colado 2001). What is distinctive about being an employee is that one is presumed, as someone in receipt of a wage, to be an *obedient subject,* who in return for an income is expected to be responsible to the control of another higher in a chain of command, one of the key concepts of early management theory.

Traditionally, power over those who were subject to supervision was bundled up unequivocally with authority: in the guild system, for instance, the apprentice learnt from a Master, became a journeyman after the period of indenture as an apprentice was completed, and learnt from other Masters whom he encountered in his journeying. Traditional organization meant that there was continuity between task and status structures. One moved up the status hierarchy by displaying mastery of tasks.

In such situations power and knowledge were indivisible: with increased knowledge, in principle, came increased power. Early forms of manufactory did not differ greatly although, as innovations in technology were introduced, the nexus between the operatives' knowledge, the task structure and the status structure began to dissolve. Thus, the emergence of industrial society began to break the nexus between task and status structure and, in doing so, made the power/knowledge relationship in organizations more discontinuous as status and task structures became increasingly unaligned as power became embedded in routines in organizations and social programs evolved to buttress power at work.

The use of close supervision of people was very much an engrained habit of pre-modern society, if only because practices of rule were invariably tightly coupled spatially, as the vast majority of people were, literally, placed in a specific locality in a here-and-now that they rarely transgressed or moved away from. For the majority of people life was lived in and around the limits of a walk that might take a day or so to undertake. Being settled they were subject to frequent informal as well as occasional formal scrutiny. Settled life, if it were interrupted, would most likely be because of being pressed into military service of some kind, often literally, as the press-gangs roamed the streets of ports seeking to press available young men into the service of the navy, or recruiting sergeants sought out young village labourers for a life of adventure. Once pressed into service they would meet much more formal management than in the fields or village. They entered an institutional space.

On board ship what they entered was more or less a total institution (Goffman 1961) where they could not escape a particular fusion of power and knowledge, oversight and insight, embodied in the person of the bo'sun. The bo'sun was a boatswain, or petty officer, who controlled the work of other seamen. He knew what was to be done and how it should be done and would ensure that whatever was to be done would be done his way, often using harsh punishment, if necessary, to discipline the recruits. The recruits could not escape – that is what it means to say that they were in a total institution – it was an organizational space that wholly contained them. Their time was enveloped by a single space, that of the ship. Whilst on board they were contained within a disciplinary framework of shifts, work, punishments, and provisions that were totally outside their control. The insights of those who managed and handled sailors enabled them to learn skills that they needed for survival in a harsh and dangerous environment. There would be gaps, for instance when the ship docks, those seaman allowed shore leave would gain a temporary degree of freedom. (Of course some were forbidden leave; others may go ashore only under supervision.)

Those who were pressed into military service on land were barely more fortunate. Admittedly, the environment was slightly less total, in the way that a garrison affords more freedom than a ship. Yet, they were more regimented. Being regimented meant not only assuming a regimental identity and the uniform that went with it; it also meant learning a uniform mode of behavior, taught through drill (on which see Foucault 1977).

There are some scholars who suggest that the main basis for early management ideas came from the lessons learned in such garrisons, especially as it pertained to the assembly and disassembly of muskets and the drilling of soldiers in the use of these and other weapons on the parade ground (Dandeker 1990). These methods were first applied to muskets by French gunsmiths, and brought from France to the United States at the time of the American Revolution, where they led, in a way mediated by Charles Davies' position at the West Point Military Academy, to the 'disciplining' of America through the new science of engineering, in which F. W. Taylor was to play a key popularizing role.[1]

MANAGING BODILY ORDER AT WORK

Frederick Winslow Taylor produced the first modern technology of power, one oriented to constituting a political economy of the body. In an ideal organization, one constructed according to the principles that Taylor advocated and as they were to be developed subsequently, people did exactly what they were supposed to do. Innovation was not favoured; instead, strict obedience to the plan was rewarded. As far as one is concerned with management, the maturation of modernity is marked, programmatically, by Taylor, for he was responsible for creating the individual and responsible employee not just as a creature of religion such as the Protestant ethic – or habit – but as a consciously designed utilitarian project.[2] Taylor's (1911) preface to *The Principles of Scientific Management* makes this quite clear when he stresses the need for national efficiency. His utilitarianism can be seen in a number of characteristics of his thought. First, it is teleological in its orientation to means. What is important is securing the desired consequences. Second, in Taylor's philosophy, actions can be judged only by their consequences, such that a dogged empiricism is allied to an unquestioned grasp of the ends to be served. Third, ends are defined in terms of efficiency (primarily for the factory owners) but are represented as the common good. Taylor took utilitarianism from a program for dealing with the marginal and abnormal, the other, and transposed it into a program for dealing with the everyday and the normal, the worker.

Individual actions were conceptualized as entailing a whole within which comparison and differentiations must be made. Individuals were differentiated from one another; their attributes were to be measured in quantitative terms, their abilities were to be hierarchically arranged. The expected range of normal output at work was to be codified and then used as a mechanism of feedback, enforcement and further normalization. Through fusing an economic function with one that is social, the organizational workplace became a huge laboratory for the perfection of techniques of management. Disciplinary programs were created with the power to shape people, to shape work, and to shape the organization's technical and human system. Of course, programs are not projects that are perfectly accomplished – they are always situated in the future perfect, designs for a world that would be made if there were no obstacles to its unfolding as such. Yet there are always such obstacles, always resistance to the projects of power, always unanticipated consequences of social action. In many ways these resistances, these imperfections in specific power projects, only serve to heighten the resolve and the perception of need for the failed project to try again. The problems that it was designed to address are evidently still there and so the project needs to be revised, perfected and enacted again – and again. It is this recurrence that comprises the specific nature of management knowledge, a set of *savoirs* produced by everyday practices of power. The power that is at work in programs of management, a pragmatic science of immediate practical consequence shaping the existence of people in their everyday life, is highly specific. It is not merely a repressive or prohibitory power; it does not just involve the possibility of imposing one's will upon the behaviour of other persons through prohibiting behaviour that they would otherwise normally be disposed to. Rather, it works in a more positive way by shaping the dispositions that define what we take, normally, to be true. The calculations subjects make about effort, disposition, and demeanour, for instance, are both subject to, and resources for, this pragmatic science. Managing means constituting central aspects of identity through relations of power; thus, when one is managing this implies that one is exercising power – over both other people and things. Managing means making things happen through the exercise of initiative and agency – and that means power.

Taylor's concern with productivity and performativity provided the intellectual and social context within which management was first defined. It was a context riddled with power at every turn. Assumptions about the natural order of things underlay Taylor's idea that some were born to manage and direct, while the fate of others was to be managed and directed. Efficient management was based on reforming power/knowledge relations, taking them out of the hands of the workers and systematically refashioning them so that they could be placed in the hands of management. Once these reformed relations were in management's remit then managers would be obliged to obey the precepts of science and respect a liberal mentality, much as should efficient employees in general. Once the one best way was devised, any deviation from it should be regarded with anathema. The purity of power consisted in its eternal return as repetition, as the same routine.

Power – getting others to do what one wanted them to do, even against their will – was inscribed as the normalcy of the new system of scientific management. In this system one should always do just as one was told; one should never be where one does not belong, and what one should do and where one should be were not to be left to chance but should be determined, authoritatively, by the science of productive efficiency and management. The new system of rule could be denoted as a regime of impersonal authority which served no interest other than the general interest in utilitarian efficiency, an interest from which all, with the exception of lazy people who refused to change their behaviour, might prosper. The poor but honest labourer could enrich himself through the dignity of his own exertions in a system designed to maximize the rewards that flowed. So could the employer in the counting house, amassing profits from the same principles. In principle, all would be for the best in the best of all possible worlds.

After Taylor, the individual workman need not exist merely as a creature of habit, tradition or craft but could become an *object* of scientific knowledge and a *subject* produced by the application of that knowledge. The worker became a utilitarian subject. Taylor marks a significant break not because he was some unique innovator or discoverer of truths previously unknown but because he popularized ideas that, although they had been practiced previously, had not been collected, synthesized, documented, and marketed as specific ways of intervening into the everyday organization of work. They had not been 'made up' into a bundled program, designed to regulate conduct and to order the spaces within which things are thinkable, utterable, and doable. It was the achievement of this that marks the emergence of modern management as the application of rational means to everyday practice and measurable ends.

Taylor's utilitarian calculus was oriented to the problem of making employed, rather than idle, hands busier in the service of the greatest good of national efficiency and for the better reward of both hands and the businesses that employed them. In fact, one of Taylor's biographers, Kanigel (1997), suggests that efficiency became iconic for almost all American organizations, and increasingly, those of other industrialized nations. It had to be worshipped, feted and widely represented in cultural artefacts of the age. Taylor's (1911) *Principles of Scientific Management* was such an artefact. It helped persuade people that efficiency was desirable as an end in itself and that all legitimate means should be oriented towards it.

A key feature of Taylor's work was use of a stopwatch to time his observations of work – in a less than perfect attempt to impose exactness – whose accuracy was later to be improved greatly by the use of film by some of his associates. In many respects, Taylor was an acute, if somewhat one-dimensional, ethnographer. Taylor was a detailed chronicler of life in the factory. He wanted to know exactly how workmen did what they did when they worked, which entailed detailed ethnographic observation, for which he developed a system of denoting and coding. However, it was an ethnographic method devoid of understanding and input from the subject it objectified.

Taylor's ethnographic interests were not anthropological; he did not wish merely to describe accurately the customs and rituals of those whom he encountered in work but sought to reform the nature of that work, guided by a concern only to increase efficiency. He sought to redesign work so that it was conducted in the most efficient way that he could imagine, based on his detailed empirical ethnographies and timings of how it was actually done, as well as how it might be done differently, according to his redesign. The approach constituted management as a science premised on the dangerous conviction that a single view, based on efficient ends, was to be esteemed above any grasp of interpretive understandings that might be found in the context being studied.

Taylor stressed three techniques in the design of work. Empirical examination, division of labour, and individual competition were his themes for the analysis of work in the factory. Examination was conducted through the detailed observation, note-taking and timekeeping of the methods engineer. The redesigned work that would flow from this close inspection and examination was premised on a radical division of labour, with a strict separation between the mental labour of oversight, intended to see the strict dictates of the system were followed, and the manual labour of the production worker, which followed the formalized plan of the engineer. Finally, each individual employee competed against all other employees to maximize the pieces that they could make and thus the piece rate that they could earn such that they could become a 'high-priced man' (Taylor 1911: 60)

Timing and redesign were the panoptical mechanisms that Taylor designed. All work practice were subject to hundreds of observations and timings, through which he sought to establish what he thought of as the one best way in which to do any given task. Taylor's primary objective in doing a time study was to ascertain an appropriate production rate to use as a basis for an incentive payment. What he sought was the fastest rate and then he wanted to be able to decompose its elements so that he could understand how it was possible, and how it could become the standard for all operatives.

Expensive measurement and observation instruments and pre-printed notepads were used to develop the standards. Observations were made with care for precision, up to a thousandth of a minute in some cases. Taylor compartmentalized productive activities into elements. For each job, elements were defined in such a way that activity within the element could not easily be interrupted. They were the micro-components of work, the smallest unit of task time complete in themselves.

Taylor's procedure made time study much easier, making it possible to produce detailed descriptions for production planning, using the central notion of standard data. If elements were properly designed, according to Taylor's rules, it became possible to determine a standard for the process by describing the process in terms of its pre-rated elements. Taylor's system was based on a standardized description of every job, abstracted from what was determined as the 'one best way', then recorded on cards and filed, and used as the measure for anyone doing the task in question. A lack of task variability and the repetitious nature of the tasks involved in the occupations studied extended the usefulness of the approach.

The innovation with which Taylor is most associated is *the linking of efficiency to power through the medium of the human body*. The program sought to drill efficiency into the nature of being, starting with the individual body (anatomical politics), moving to the collective body of/in the organization (bio politics), and generally percolating into the societal body by economizing society (social politics), all in the name of efficiency.

Efficiency means achieving desired effects or results with minimum waste of time and effort; through minimizing the ratio between effective or useful output to the total input in any system. It was Taylor's practical experience, rather than theoretical knowledge gained from engineering, that enabled him to begin the enquiries for which he became famous. These started with a practical problem of how workmen might best use lathes to cut metal when they were powered by the new invention of electricity. As Jacques (1996: 105–106) notes, Taylor's innovations with the lathe were a result of applying mathematics, creating quantitative tables, and using slide rules to shape new practices.

The central focus of Taylor's system was the body of the individual labourer and its relation not only to other bodies but also to the material artifacts that formed the labourer's immediate work environment. What Taylor produced may be characterized as a political economy of the body.[3] As such, Taylor was the symbolic icon and the visible point of an epoch and a mentality. In this way, the overall contribution was made by a broad movement in which several individuals made an important contribution building this management of bodies (Taylor, of course, but also the Gilbreths, Münsterberg, Gantt and others who responded to the structural conditions provided by the new factory system powered by electricity, by producing new mechanisms for managing bodies in the factory and beyond [see Nelson 1975; Watts 1991]).

Canguilhem (1992: 63) points out that Taylorism established a mode of work premised not only on the subjection of the worker's body to the superior intelligence of the managers' mind, but also to industrial machinery. The human body was measured as if it functioned like a machine. For the former, Taylorism represented a working out of Cartesian dualism – the split between mind and body – as a social relation, as Braverman (1974) was to argue; but it is how this was done that interests us as it was through new disciplines focused on the individual human body that Taylor's (1911) practice sought to produce its effects. The new disciplines, the subjection of the body to new rigours, were clearly justified by productive economic practices. Foucault defined a discipline as a 'unitary technique by which the body is reduced as a 'political' force at the least cost and maximized as a useful force' (Foucault 1977: 221). It was in this context that Foucault introduced the idea of anatomical politics, related to the disciplinary regime of the individual body. It was in this sphere that Taylor's major contributions were made. Taylor was the founder of the discipline dealing with the design of machines and equipment for human use, and the determination of the appropriate human behaviours for the efficient operation of the machines, which has subsequently and variously been called human factors, human engineering and ergonomics (the latter of which could, in fact, be seen as an example of what Foucault [1977] refers to as 'bio-power' – the government of the social body – while Taylor was more concerned with the management of individual actions rather than the use of knowledge and categorizations to manage populations). Discipline targeted the human body, with the goal of simultaneously exploiting it and rendering it docile and cooperative. For instance, in his experiments with shovels at Bethlehem Steel, Taylor focused on the body of the men; for instance, he told a worker that the most efficient method of shovelling was to put the right arm down by the right hip, hold the shovel on the left leg, and throw the weight of the body forward when digging the shovel into a pile, instead of using the arms and just pushing the shovel into a pile.

What Taylor did was to routinize power. Management intervention, in terms of an explicit exercise of power, was designed to handle situations where routines were not working. These routines were premised on a hierarchy: Organizations should be arranged in a hierarchy, based upon systems of abstract rules and impersonal relationships between different categories of employees. Taylor's framework for organization thus created a seemingly scientific basis for a clear delineation of authority and responsibility, based on a separation of planning from operations, a high degree of task specialization (although this was subsequently to be developed to new heights by Henry Ford), and a system of incentive schemes for workers. Management knowledge was designed to order and control what was known, protecting and insuring it against the uncertainty of the unknown, to the greatest extent possible (Yates 1989; Brown and Duguid 2000). The less that management had to exercise power the better power was embedded in the routines.

At the end of the nineteenth century the conditions of possibility for building new practices and knowledge with which to discipline bodies had produced, as we have seen, a new economy of the body. Now, while this was newly applied to factory work, it was not a new occurrence. Foucault (1977: 28) discussed the development of a political anatomy where 'power seeps into the very grain of individuals, reaches right into their bodies, permeates their gestures, their posture, what they say, how they learn to live and work with other people', in relation to earlier forms of drill observed in the bodies of marching soldiers and the posture of school children became cases for analysis. With Taylor, their non-institutionalized parents, if they worked in the factory, could also be reformed through an inspectorial urge.

MANAGING THE MORAL ORDER

Hitherto, with Taylor, the regulation of work had stayed within the organization and its disciplinary practices. It soon expanded outside, into the streets, the homes, the bars and savings accounts of industrial workers. The stimulus was Henry Ford's introduction of the moving assembly line and attempts to ensure that only deserving workers received the high wages that Ford's factories were paying.

In 1913, 30 years after Taylor installed his first system, a revolution in manufacturing occurred when Henry Ford introduced the assembly line as a new way of producing automobiles, modelled on the Chicago slaughterhouses. The assembly line of production borrowed heavily from that of death. It vastly simplified production through running at a constant speed by which the workman must measure his pace, so that products are delivered at a constant production rate. Each job on the line had to be completed in an amount of time commensurate with this production rate. Each job became known by a precise description of the task it comprised; however, there were many thousands more jobs involved in the making of a car compared to the killing and butchering of a pig, with the job description manuals coming to resemble telephone directories.

The relations of power in these organizations were shaped by ever more elaborated definitions of routines, embedded less in traditional craft and practice but more in the creation and specification of new workplace relations and routines. They reached their zenith in the new workshops and factories of the automobile industry, especially the Ford Motor Company, which in the 1920s was seen as the very harbinger of what modernity was all about. The power of mass production was seen as the greatest productive power that had been unleashed by the modern world, but behind the glittering automobiles, behind the assembly lines of modern times, there was another more complex and subtle moral machinery of power at work.

While it is important to know how much time each element requires to be accomplished, other aspects of time study techniques were not appropriate for assembly line manufacturing. Individual incentives were not appropriate because every operator was tied to the speed of the line and they were not needed because of the discipline the line imposed. What remained from the Taylor system was the elemental decomposition of jobs. Jobs were small, repetitive and routine. In fact, routine became such a problem among Ford's workers that, in the first year of full assembly line operation, the company experienced about 900 percent turnover (see Williams et al. 1992). Between October 1912 and October 1913, Ford hired 54,000 workers in order to maintain a work force of 13,000. The annual turnover rate settled at around 400 percent and daily absenteeism ran between 10 and 20 percent. It was for this reason that on January 5, 1914, the Ford Motor Company announced the five-dollar, eight-hour day for all production workers, irrespective of pieces produced (which was determined by the speed of the line anyway, not individual effort). What the company announced was not a plan to pay workers an hourly rate equivalent to five dollars a day but a plan that allowed workers to share in the company profits, which, in principle, would amount to a five dollar day. This represented a considerable sum of money for production work in contemporary terms, doubling incomes and, with the possibilities afforded by hire-purchase, a new innovation, meant that having consumer goods such as cars became something to whose ownership it was feasible to aspire. Ford's innovation reflects the relentlessly upbeat, optimistic, culture of consumption, premised on the five dollar day, which became a significant feature of American life and American world-wide culture.

In 1914 Ford established the Sociological Department to investigate the home lives of workers (Marcus and Segal 1989: 236–238). It was a remarkable example of an ultimately failed attempt to institute meta-routines governing societal politics. The five dollar day was designed to include only those who were 'worthy' and who would 'not debauch the additional money'. The rules governing eligibility were demonstrating that, if one were a man, one lived a clean, sober, industrious and thrifty life, while women had to be 'deserving' and have some relatives solely dependent upon them. After a probationary period, subject to a recommendation from their supervisor, worker eligibility would be investigated. About 60 percent were found to be eligible. Investigators from the Sociological Department visited workers' homes and suggested ways to achieve the company's standards for 'better morals', sanitary living conditions, and 'habits of thrift and saving'. Employees who lapsed were removed from the system and given a chance to redeem themselves. Long-term failure to meet Ford Motor Company standards resulted in dismissal from the company.

Meyer (1981) reports a 1917 Sociological Department report. Fifty-two investigators visited 77 districts throughout Detroit and its suburbs. Each district contained an average of 523 workers. Each investigator had an average caseload of 727 workers making 5.35 regular investigations each day, five 'absentee calls' and 15 'outside calls'. For each investigation Ford maintained a record consisting of every available source of information from churches, civic organizations and the government. The company wanted to know whether or not the worker was purchasing a home, whether he had a savings account and whether he had debt. It required the bank account number, name of the bank and balance of any accounts; for debts, the company needed to know the holder of the debt, its reason and the balance (Meyer 1981: 130).

There was a degree of racism at work in these sociological investigations, paralleling Ford's well-documented anti-Semitism (Lee 1980). After the Civil War, black people had been leaving the sharecropper society of the Deep South in droves, fleeing a culture rooted in slavery; and, after hitting Highway 61, they headed for the burgeoning factories of the north, in Chicago and Detroit, in the latter of which Ford began hiring African Americans in large numbers in 1915, paying them the same wages as his white employees. The material basis of the jazz age for the many black people who headed north was provided by working in the factories and assembly plants. By 1923, Ford employed 5,000 Detroit-area black men, far more than in other plants.

The influx of black people into northern cities and jobs was the occasion for middle-class white anxieties. Indeed, at the time they were a source of what Stanley Cohen (1972: 9) has referred to as a 'moral panic'. A moral panic occurs when some 'episode, condition, person or group of persons' is 'defined as a threat to societal values and interests'. Such moral panics are based on the perception that some individual or group, frequently a minority, is dangerously deviant, and poses a menace to society. They often occur as a result of a fear of a loss of control when adapting to significant changes. Typically, as Cohen suggests, authorities create 'stylized and stereotypical' representations, raise moral fears, and 'pronounce judgment'.

Moral panic fed in to the work of Ford's Sociological Department. They wanted to ensure that Ford employed were sober, disciplined men, whose energies would be conserved and their minds wholly focused on the necessity of being excellent five dollar a day men. Workers who wasted money on booze, dope, and vice were not welcome as Ford employees, as members of the Ford family. Decent white folk knew the type of person most likely to be wasteful of their energies and the kinds of excesses in which they would be wasted. African Americans, jazz and intoxication of various kinds became inexorably intertwined in the popular imagination of, as well as some experience in, black culture. The scapegoating of black cultures, such as jazz, was emblematic of a deep-seated paranoia.

> Jazz received a fair amount of negative press in the late 1910s and then became the object of a moral panic during the 1920s. Some whites feared jazz because it was rooted in black culture, because it played a role in facilitating interracial contact, and because it symbolized, in racially coded terms, the intrusion of popular tastes into the national culture... (Porter 2002: 9).

The moral panics that grew in the 1920s and 1930s around 'jazz' were barely coded concerns for the contagion of white society by black bodies and black culture. As Lopes (2005: 1468) suggests, from the Jazz Age of the 1920s 'the sordid world of jazz and the deviant jazz musician became a common trope in the popular press, pulp fiction, and Hollywood film. Jazz in general served as a trope for the darker side of the American urban experience'. For Ford, establishing a Sociological Department (as well as employing Pinkerton's to spy on potential trouble makers and unionists and to break up union meetings) to ensure the moral probity of these new employees seemed a small investment to make to ensure an efficient, reliable and certain workforce, untroubled by an inability to save, invest and consume. Such irrationalities were to be expected of people who made jazz their culture.

It is not surprising that jazz played this role; first, it was associated by respectable white society with unrespectable black society; second, it infused the body with passion, rhythm, movement and a lack of disciplined sobriety. It was wild dance music and its main feature was its exuberant ability to move its fans and musicians to shake their bodies, dance and beat the rhythm. As Appelrouth (2005: 1497) suggests, 'manners of the body share the potential for becoming a stage on which the struggle for social legitimacy and control is dramatized'. In the body may be seen the larger social order and its struggles to impose good order, taste and discipline on nature. Pollution of the body is a metaphor for the disruption of the boundaries that shape 'legitimate' society, as Douglas (1996) suggests. Thus, following Appelrouth (2005: 1497) 'we should not be surprised to find anxieties concerning social disruptions expressed through a body-centred discourse. During periods in which challenges are posed to existing social divisions and schemes of classification, attempts to define the body publicly take on heightened significance'. As the *Ladies Home Journal* saw it,

> Jazz disorganizes all regular laws and order; it stimulates to extreme deeds, to a breaking away from all rules and conventions; it is harmful and dangerous, and its influence is wholly bad ...The effect of jazz on the normal brain produces an atrophied condition on the brain cells of conception, until very frequently those under the demoralizing influence of the persistent use of syncopation, combined with inharmonic partial tones are actually incapable of distinguishing between good and evil, right and wrong (Faulkner 1921: 16; from Appelrouth 2005: 1503).

Degenerate brains, an inability to follow rules, and a general lack of moral qualities were not what Mr. Ford required in his employees, so the Sociological Department had much to do as a private moral police for the Jazz Age and, even though the Department did not last long, it hardly mattered. After 1921 it was discontinued and rolled into the notorious Service Department, run by ex-boxer and security chief Harry Bennett, who formed it into a private army of thugs and gangsters to terrorize workers and prevent unionization. Ford's Service Department would grow to be the largest private police force in the world at that time. Its major work was spying such that no one who worked for Ford was safe from spies, intent on seeing that the five dollars was not being wasted, both literally and metaphorically.

A trope was at work at this time. The Jazz Age viewed through 'respectable' white eyes was characterized by anxieties about the association of blackness, jazz, booze and dope. The latter was a particularly significant trope, as was alcohol. Despite the fact that, as its name suggests, marijuana first came into the US from Mexico, jazz and marijuana became inextricably linked with black people and black music in the popular imagination. The first recorded use of marijuana in the US was in Storyville in 1909 (Abel 1980), which was the red light district of the port of New Orleans and the birthplace of jazz. Foundational jazz musicians, such as Jelly Roll Morton, honing their craft in the bordellos, created incidental accompaniments to the central commerce conducted there. Rather than drink, dope was the preferred drug. Marijuana didn't slow down the reflexes and improvization the way that alcohol could; also it seemed to heighten the creative impulse. Jazz and dope were not exactly the stuff of a rationalizing impulse.

Increasing societal support developed for Ford's 'sociological' and 'service' projects. First in the ranks was the project of Prohibition, the doomed attempt to ban alcohol consumption from a number of US states, which started in 1920, and which Ford had long supported and promoted, also intensified a prohibitory gaze that sought to ensure that employees could resist temptations to vice. In fact, the struggle against liquor was also a struggle against jazz with which it was associated in licentiousness. Gramsci explicitly made the connection to moral panics.

> The struggle against alcohol, the most dangerous agent of destruction of laboring power, becomes a function of the state. It is possible for other 'puritanical' struggles as well to become functions of the state if private initiatives of the industrialist prove insufficient or if a moral crisis breaks out among the working masses (Gramsci 1971: 303–304).

Power in the organization was now effectively buttressed by power in the wider society; in order to ensure the most efficient routines at work, some control over the type of person that was employed was required. Initially, the new power of surveillance over private life was vested in and an extension of the organization; latterly, as Fordist modernity became characteristic of modernity in general, in workshops large and small, the state took over the functions that private capital had hitherto assumed.[4] Small employers or those new to business could not develop their own Sociological Departments, but the state, as an ideal total moralist, supplemented the work of surveillance over those in whom the churches and associated temperance movements had not succeeded in instilling a governmental soul. Power shifted its focus from the individual to the collective.

MANAGING THE COLLECTIVE SOUL

The analytics of power, focused on a political economy of the body, sought to create workers as precision instruments. Task decomposition, the reformation of tasks and their physical undertaking according to methods, and the use of imposed sequences were all important. However, as time passed it became increasingly evident that the body alone was not what was employed at work: the worker's body, to be truly disciplined at work, required disciplining in life. Ford's Sociological Department went some way towards achieving this. The body, though always individuated, houses a social being; one with a culture and an identity, as well as passions and interests transcending the working week. The conceptualization of this managerial problem was a natural progression of the moral projects that sought to reform the employee through political economy aimed at the body. If projects of power were to overcome the limited efficacy of their efficiency concerns to date, then they had to address both body and soul; they had to recognize the place of the *being* in the body as a social subject.

The Hawthorne Studies provided Mayo with the opportunity to argue that small groups had their own sources of positive power, derived from group morale. When Mayo (1933) looked at the findings from the Hawthorne Laboratory investigations he thought that the results showed that employees had a strong need for shared cooperation and communication. Merely by asking for their cooperation in the test, Mayo believed the investigators had stimulated a new attitude among the employees. The assemblers considered themselves to be part of an important group whose help and advice were being sought by the company. He believed that if consultation between labour and management were instituted it would give workers a sense of belonging to a team. Here we can see the transformation produced in the modes of surveillance. A new strategy of government of the body/soul in the factory was to be based on the construction of a sentiment of freedom (and responsibility) without – apparently – any kind of surveillance:

> The improvement in production, they believe, is not very directly related to the rest pauses and other innovations. It reflects rather a freer and more pleasant working environment, a supervisor who is not regarded as a 'boss,' a 'higher morale.' In this situation the production of the group insensibly lifts, even though the girls are not aware that they are working faster. Many times over, the history sheets and other records show that in the opinion of the group all supervision has been removed. On occasion indeed they artlessly tell the observer, who is in fact of supervisory rank, very revealing tales of their experiences with previous 'bosses'. Their opinion is, of course, mistaken: in a sense they are getting closer supervision than ever before, the change is in the quality of the supervision (Mayo 1975: 75).

These studies changed the landscape of management from Taylor's engineering approach to the political economy of the body to a social sciences approach that focused on the interior life, the mental states, the consciousness and unconsciousness – the 'soul' – of the employees. Worker productivity would, henceforth, be interpreted predominately in terms of patterns of culture, motivation, leadership and human relations (Maslow 1978). The locus of power shifted from the engineering expert, designing the job, selecting and training the right worker and rewarding performance, to the manager, responsible for leading, motivating, communicating and counselling the individual employee as well as designing the social milieu in which work takes place.

Mayo developed what became known as the Human Relations School. The emphasis of this approach was on informal work group relations, the importance of these for sustaining the formal system, and the necessity of the formal system meshing with the informal system. In the informal system special attention was to be paid to the satisfaction of individual human needs, focusing on what motivates different people, in order to try and maximize their motivation and satisfaction. Mayo thought the manager had to be a social clinician, fostering the social skills of those with whom she or he worked. Workers who argued with their managers and supervisors were expressing deep-seated neuroses lodged in their childhood history.

Therapeutic interviews were recommended as a management tool, to create better-adjusted workers, and training in counselling and personnel interviews was touted as an essential management skill. The advice was simple. Pay full attention to the interviewee and make it clear that this is the case; listen carefully to what they have to say; do not interrupt; don't contradict them; listen carefully for what is being said as well as any ellipses in terms of what is left unspoken; try and summarize carefully what has been said by the speaker as feedback for the interviewee, and treat what has been said in confidence (Trahair 2001).[5]

An ideal interview would be a form of confessional, working through positive power. The individual subjects who are interviewed will reveal themselves to themselves through these interviews; 'they will reflexively turn in upon themselves as an object of truth', as Haugaard (1997: 90) suggests, but the presentation of truth will be one which mere employees 'are not competent to interpret so the expert [the manager] is needed to weave a discourse of truth out of their deepest desires and most secret longings'.

The body having been re-engineered it was now time to get to work on the soul – or at least that secular synonym for it – the unconscious. Trained dispositions are disciplined and responsible and will conduct the body through self-control. Mayo contributed to the new technologies of the self and counselling (Rose 1996; also see Baritz 1974). With Mayo, power moves from a focus on the body of the worker to the voice of the worker; the signs of the unconscious that are interpretable through eliciting employee participation in therapeutic counselling. Now, it is evident that this is not a meeting of equals. These sessions are to be neither friendly chats nor a meeting of equals but a meeting of clinical expertise lodged in superior power, claiming the mantel of authority, with human weakness, frailty and illness.

Just as Taylor's focus on disciplining the body was tempered in practice by Ford's concern with the morality of his five dollar a day workers, so the theoreticians of management shifted their focus from the body to the soul (consciousness and unconsciousness). The locus of the moral being was defined as one who not only is but also wants to be an obedient subject. The self became 'an object of reflection and analysis, and, above all, transformable in the service of ideals…' (van Krieken 1990: 353). The ideals were only too clear, given that the meta-routine that had already been established was efficiency. What was under construction here was an attempt to establish patterns of spontaneous obedience as similar meta-routines that could be depended on utterly.

Mayo unequivocally unleashed a program for reforming the individual as an object of reflection, analysis, and transformation, and much of subsequent management was to extend this technology of power by normalizing it as simply the constitution of management. Rose (1989: 2) noted that the 'management of subjectivity' became 'a central task for the modern organization' and those who profess expertise about them.

What was crucial about the Hawthorne Studies was that it reconstituted subjectivity not as a unique quality of the individual's psychology but as a phenomenon of the group and a resource for the organization.

> The group represented a field for thought, argument, and administration that was genuinely supraindividual and yet not of the order of the crowds or the mass. The group would exists as an intermediary between the individual and the population, it would inhabit the soulless world of the organization and give it subjective meaning for the employee, it would satisfy the social needs of the atomic and fragmented self isolated with the rise of the division of labor and the decline of community, it would explain ills and could be mobilized for good, it could bring about damage in its totalitarian form and contentment and efficiency in its democratic form. In the medium of the group a new relay was found where administration in the light of psychological expertise could come into alignment with the values of democracy (Rose 1996: 136).

The attitudes of employees; their feelings of control over their working lives; the sense of cohesion within the work group, and their belief in the good dispositions of bosses and supervisors towards them created 'a range of new tasks' that 'emerged to be grasped by knowledge and managed in the factory' (Rose 1996: 138). Things that were not known had to be made knowable, to be given shape and form. Non-directive interviews were used to find a 'way into the emotional life of the factory, the emotional significance of particular events in the experience of the worker' (Rose 1996: 139). These could then be slotted into the emergent discourse of functionalism that Parsons and others at Harvard were developing: manifest and latent functions could be distinguished so that one could analyze problems scientifically, in terms of underlying causes rather than apparent explanations.

Human relations approached these matters through more psychobiological constructs, preparing the way for organizational behaviour to emerge as a self-referential discourse, while functionalism goes on to define contingency theory as the triumph of organization studies. Organizationally, knowledge of existing patterns of relations could be incorporated into change programs to make them more efficacious; interviews could fulfil therapeutic functions by making latent issues manifest. Managers could then manage in full knowledge of those sentiments and values belonging to their employees and act upon them appropriately. Specialized functions, such as personnel management, emerge to deal with these issues, through counselling, easing adjustments to change, planning and collecting data. Other new disciplines such as organizational communications also emerge as instruments for realigning misaligned values within organizations. Definitions of the situation could be arrived at that were shared in management's terms rather than being opposed by worker's terms. A culture of commitment could be built and its builders should be leaders. Groups needed leaders. Leadership prowess was evaluated on the basis of an ability to get others to do what it was that the leaders wanted them to; and when they did this they could be seen to be leaders who cheapened the costs of surveillance greatly (Bavelas and Lewin 1942). Such leaders learned how to use the democratic potential of groups to manage so that they could relax their vigilance in consequence. Group dynamics, leadership, sensitivity could all become the object of training and the subject of a new disciplinary apparatus that could be forged, just like a science, in the laboratory (Cartwright and Zander 1953).

Political economy shaded into moral economy as the 1930s developed. Slowly, it became evident that efficient routines could only be founded on the social and cultural rehabilitation of the worker as a whole person rather than merely their perfection as an instrument of political economy. The political economy project was doomed by one simple substantive fact. What people ordinarily know and do – sometimes in ways that a theory never captures – is essential to how organizations are able to do what they do. The one best way could never be entirely prescribed and where it was attempted then, by definition, something close to a non-learning organization would be instituted. Even scientific managers could realize this in the main lesson of the Hawthorne studies. It was a realization that became the impetus for Mayo's moral economy project.

The moral economy project was not really as radical as some of its prophets, such as Mayo, assumed. It built on what Taylor bequeathed. It didn't deconstruct the legacy. Contemporary theory builds on the legacy of both of these schools. In this approach, the ordinary knowledge of ordinary people is regarded as a neglected resource that managers must access, use and routinize. They will do this through the simple strategies of building social capital (brought into focus primarily through the work of Robert Putnam [1993, 1995]) and through the use of those coactive power strategies that Mary Parker Follett recommended for building such capital. Once social capital has been identified, then new routines can be constructed. Social capital takes care of the coactivity while knowledge management will structure the new routines. It is tempting to see the former as a continuation of the concern with the moral economy and the latter as a simple extension of scientific management – to incorporate the mind as well as the body and soul of the employee.

MANAGING SOCIAL CAPITAL

Social capital has been defined in management as 'the sum of actual and potential resources embedded within, available through, and derived from the network of relationships possessed by an individual or social unit' (Nahapiet and Ghoshal 1998: 243). Firms are 'understood as a social community specializing in the speed and efficiency in the creation and transfer of knowledge' (Kogut and Zander 1996: 503). Organizations, designed to bring people together for task completion, supervision and coordination, result in frequent and dense levels of social contacts, creating coactive power in Follett's terms. Social capital, as Follett realized, makes it possible for ends to be achieved that, in its absence, could otherwise only be achieved at additional cost.[6]

Social capital concept privileges the worker as a 'knowledge worker' with embrained rather than embodied knowledge (Blackler 1995). Such employees are potentially mobile and can go to another employer; thus, they must be kept loyal by avoidance of coercion (which, much as the use of tight contracts, destroys trust) and by use of soft power (see Fox [1974] on power and trust relations).

Trust and control can be viewed as structures of inter-related situated practices that influence the development of different forms of expert power in particular organizational contexts. In this view, trust and control relations are generative mechanisms that play a role in the production, reproduction and transformation of expert power. Trust is based on predictability of behaviour, where some type of control or self-control mechanism influences such predictability. Trust and control are closely associated (Reed 2001; Maguire, Phillips and Hardy 2001). Many organizations attempt to 'manage' trust as a means of control (Knights, et al. 2001). Maguire, Phillips and Hardy (2001) have suggested several ways in which this happens, including actively manipulating the employee using rewards, acquiring information about the employee and thus rendering him/her more predictable and hence controllable, and active manipulation of the goodwill of the employee by increasing his/her identification with the organization.

The rhetoric of 'trust' often sits uncomfortably in the context of all the routines constituting a 'low trust' workplace of design of technologies and of work by standardized procedures. Contemporary labour process studies carried out or reviewed by Thompson and Ackroyd (1995), Thompson and Ackroyd (1995) and Thompson and Warhurst (1998) suggest that we need to untangle the managerial rhetoric and intention with the realities of the situation.

MANAGING KNOWLEDGE

Knowledge management is another new idea with deep roots that go back to Frederick Taylor and scientific management. Two aspects of knowledge management are relevant here. First, there is the treatment of knowledge as a commodity, through the mechanization and objectification of knowledge creation, diffusion and storage. Treated this way it increases management's sense of control. Second, there is soft domination of the knowledge worker by identification-based control. The highest degree of trust is when the person completely identifies with the organization, in which case his/her self-image is aligned with managerially determined objectives (Alvesson and Willmott 2002). What knowledge management seeks to do is to draw from the tacit knowledge of individuals and the social capital of the group to construct new and improved routines. The thrust of scientific management and the many subsequent clones spawned from its political economy, such as knowledge management, was that routines produce increased efficiency where the correspondence between relations of knowledge is closed, where the worker does exactly what the scientific manager prescribes. Taylor and his heirs sought to make workers functionaries of knowledge relations defined externally to the 'being there' of the workers. Yet, paradoxically, as the Hawthorne Studies first revealed, efficiency is determined by the extent to which individual knowledge and expertise is accessed and utilized (Grant 1996a: 380).

In the most current clone of scientific management – which is knowledge management – efficiency is based on *common knowledge* as a prerequisite to the communication of direction and routine. Translating specialist information depends on the sophistication and level of common knowledge. Second, the *frequency and variability of task performance* changes the efficiency of knowledge integration (Nelson and Winter 1982). The efficiency of comprehending and responding appropriately among employees involved in tasks is a function of frequency of task performance. Third, *organizational structure* that reduces the extent and intensity of communication to achieve integration assists efficiency and to do this the employee has to be integrated into the enterprise as an obedient rather than resistant subject. Knowledge management grows out of the cross-pollination of scientific management and human relations theory to make obedient subjects creative.[7]

Knowledge management is an instrument producing new routines that result from acquiring and distilling knowledge of tacit experiences and action that is embedded in social and institutional practice (Spender and Kijne 1996; Brown and Duguid 1991). Individual public performances draw on private parts of the self – the soul in Follett's terms – in interactions. Thus, as recent theory has it, 'the primary role of the firm is in integrating specialist knowledge resident in individuals into goods and services' (Grant 1996b: 120). Knowledge management institutes what Garrick and Clegg (2000) have referred to as an 'organizational gothic' at the heart of organizational life, a capacity to suck the vitality from the individual body and soul in order to enhance the vitality of the corporate body for increased efficiency and reduced costs, through greater co-active power. The secret is in extracting creativity from the individual through the use of co-active power and instilling it into the body corporate, where the body corporate retains its vitality by sucking out the vitality of those members that compose it (Garrick and Clegg 2000). The allusion to Dracula is intended; the practice seems as gothic as any Hammer horror movie.

MANAGING POWER/KNOWLEDGE

Individuals share uniquely held knowledge on the basis of what is held in common among them. Common knowledge refers to the 'common cognitive ground' among employees that facilitates knowledge transfer through promoting dialogue and communication (what Nonaka and Takeuchi [1995: 14] term redundancy). Redundancy creates an intentional overlap of information held by employees that facilitates transferring and integrating explicit and tacit knowledge. Knowledge about elements not directly related to immediate operational requirements that arises from images in tacit knowledge can be shared through redundant information about business activities, management responsibilities, the company, products and services (Nonaka and Takeuchi 1995: 81–82). Competitive, individuated, relations of power make this knowledge difficult to surface. Coercive power leads to zero-sum games, win/lose scenarios, power/resistance and resource dependency (see Chapter five). It creates power effects more akin to rape than seduction, as Nonaka and Takeuchi (1995) argue. The rape and seduction analogy suggests that seduction would seek to elicit expert knowing representing a rich and anchored context, whereas rape absconds with the partial acquisition of knowledge without context, and thus, lacking situated meaning, promotes only a wrenching of something unwillingly given. That is why the projects of knowledge management and social capital are seeking to become aligned. First, use co-active power to seduce knowledge that can become the basis for the new routines. Then, when the new routines are established they take on a coercive power of their own, as individuals can be held accountable to them. The major problem with the knowledge management project is that we all carry a great deal of redundancy around in our heads. If you don't know what you know until you need to know it, how can you know what you have stored away in the junk room, so to speak, as 'redundant knowledge'? When the time is ripe relevant knowledge surges forth unbidden, but you cannot take an inventory of the 'redundant' when the time isn't ripe. There has to be someone knowing something in some context before knowledge can be known, let alone abstracted. The study of knowledge management should really be a study of power/knowledge management because its processes are indivisible from those of power:

> At the core of management is the legitimation, extension, and normalization of dominant property rights, the practical disciplining of the everyday organizational life of members, and the framing of knowledge that can be ascribed a key role in extending, limiting, and otherwise shaping these rights. I call this the discourse of power/knowledge – a discourse that, in academic terms, functions as a surrogate for discussion of sovereignty (Clegg 2003: 536).

All forms of organization are forms of organization of social relations. All social relations involve power relations. Power is evident in relations not only of ownership and control but also of structuration and design. These relations take many forms. They may be embodied as financial capital, intellectual capital, or social capital. Such relations are likely to be both differentially distributed and socially constructed as well as exist in differential demand in differentiated markets. Power is also evident in the various forms of knowledge that constitute, structure and shape these markets and organizations, what is referred to today as knowledge management. What is novel in knowledge management is its variation on the repertoire of scientific management is the orientation to the brain rather than the body, the fusion with the moral economy of social capital, and the combination of coactive with coercive power. It frames the new combinations of power/knowledge that are so evident in soft power today, as we explored further in Chapter 12.

CONCLUSION

In management and organization theory power is embedded in practices that, very largely, do not theorize it as such. Little of what has been addressed as constituting the 'standing conditions' legitimating regimes of power, entered greatly into subsequent accounts of power by management and organization scholars (Clegg, Courpasson and Phillips 2006). Where it does so enter then it was as an assumption of 'authority', defined in terms of legitimate power, which could be safely bracketed as an unproblematic set of relations requiring no address. The marginalization of power was a trend strengthened further by the fillip that the Second World War gave to all matters related to personnel and organization design in the most advanced military of the day, the US forces, as well as in American factories involved in the war economy. In fact, power was being written into a corner where it was destined to become the antithesis, the other, to authority. The ascendance of a concern with authority went hand in hand with a view that resistance was counter productive and identified with organizational power; thus, power was expunged from authority. Perhaps this is one reason why the discourse of knowledge management has grown, so uncritically, with little or no address of power.

Bodies had been disciplined; new subjectivities were being constituted through new disciplines, frames, and practices that early pioneers talked and wrote into being; but, simultaneously with their talking and writing these practices into being there was a surprising silence about the nature of what was being created as, explicitly, practices of power. In large part this was because the intellectual apparatus that would enable one to make an explicit interpretation in power terms had yet to be constructed.

Formal acknowledgement of power, as a concept in its own right at the heart of organization practice, was something that waited in the wings where it had scuttled with the neglect of Follett's work for most of the century. The late translation of Max Weber's work into English from the late 1940s onwards saw it reappear but not in quite the way that its progenitor seemed to have intended. In the time and the space between scientific management and human relations, political and moral economy, after Weber but barely touched by his concerns, a concept of power emerged in theory, hesitantly, but with distinct characteristics, which, by and large, failed to address the historical constitution of power addressed in this chapter. When, from the 1970s onwards, the study of power and resistance developed out of labour process theory, the mechanics researched were very much workplace-focused and missed the broader canvas on which these relations had already been prepared and constituted (see Fleming and Spicer 2007). Meanwhile, as I have argued elsewhere, the post-war theoretical mechanics of mainstream organization theory became increasingly fixated on power defined as deviations from authority (see Clegg, Courpasson and Phillips 2006; Hardy and Clegg 1996), predicated on strategic resource control. What I have sought to do in this chapter is to capture some of the hidden history of power as it was constituted rather than merely provide a description of existing accounts which are, as I have argued elsewhere, fundamentally limited (Clegg, Courpasson and Phillips 2006).

NOTES

1 Hoskin and Macve (1988) note that from 1817 up to the 1840s, West Point was the prime conduit from France to the US through which the emergent disciplines of mathematics and engineering were introduced to US practice. It was, throughout that period, America's leading engineering and scientific school, and both the material taught, and the pedagogy used to deliver the material, derived initially from the French model of education developed in the late eighteenth century at the *École Polytechnique*. French techniques, in turn, have their roots in the methods pioneered by the masters of the Venetian Arsenal in warship building and crossbow manufacture.

2 Taking etymology as a guide, it seems that there is something distinctive in the emergence of management as a characteristic of the modern era, an era that literally means 'of our time'. The literal meaning is too imprecise, however. More specifically, one can think of modernity as a specific quality that first emerged in Western civilization (Sayer 1991). In general, it is a period of time and a quality of culture that the world has been experiencing for at least the last two centuries. While there are many different ways of dating, defining and characterizing modernity, we will take the modern world as being born at the point where the individual emerges as a conscious reflecting and reflected subject opposed to the 'universal, social body of customs and laws' (Kolb 1986: 67). Bauman (1997: 1) characterizes modernity as an obsession with order. Modernity, among other things, represents the cutting off of the individual from traditional ways of life; it inscribes the use of reason to govern and limit uncertainty.

3 Even perceptive observers of the body, such as Dale (2001) and Turner (1984) fail to recognize Taylor's contribution in terms of a political economy of the body.

4 Prohibition dealt with drink, at least until its failure and its creation of a criminal economy was acknowledged by its repeal in 1933. In consequence, the moral panic shifted from alcohol to dope during the 1930s, enacted by the banning of cannabis in seventeen states. The Federal Bureau of Narcotics was established in 1930. In 1937 the Marijuana Tax Act effectively banned cannabis throughout the United States. One presumes that the new intensification of work was a significant reason for the panic, in addition to its association with the moral corruption of white society from black culture. Taylorized and Fordized workers could hardly be both intoxicated by recreational drug use and expect to be the new men of the industrial age, eager to earn their five dollars a day.

5 Mayo's intent was clearly manipulative. Contemporary forms of workplace counseling are handled off site, away from work, and confidentially. Mayo's interest in counselling was not about helping employees but helping managers better manage these employees through control and manipulation.

6 Social capital as it is conceptualized most often in organization theory has three dimensions: structural, cognitive and relational. The discussion of structural and relational concepts is drawn from network theory, favouring separation. Structural elements comprise the overall patterns of connection (Burt 1992). These are to be found in the presence or absence of network ties, network configuration, and morphology, such as patterns of linkages. Density, connectivity and hierarchy characterize the linkages. Networks that are created for one purpose may be used for another (Nahapiet and Ghoshal 1998; Coleman 1988). The relational dimension of social capital captures references to assets created and leveraged through relationships. Among these are trust, trustworthiness, norms and sanctions, obligations and expectations, identity and identification. Relational embeddedness refers to the kind of personal relationship that people have, such as respect and friendship, which influence their behaviour in fulfilling socially ascribed motives (Blum and McHugh 1971). The cognitive element refers to resources that provide shared representations, interpretation and systems of meaning among parties (Nahapiet and Ghoshal, 1998).

7 Not too creative though: it is a creativity that remains highly framed. Grant (1996b) identifies four mechanisms for accessing the creativity of, and simultaneously framing, specialized knowledge in organizations. The first three integrate knowledge while reducing the need and cost of communication and learning, while the fourth is dependent on interaction and cross-over learning in the decision process. The first mechanism stresses rules and directives involve direct forms of coordination (impersonal coordination including plans, schedules, forecasts, rules, policies, procedures, social norms and etiquette) and indirect forms (education and training) (de Boer, Van Den Bosch and Volberda 1999). Standardized information and communication systems are supposed to govern interaction and reduce the quantity of directions in communication necessitated by specialist knowledge and roles (Demsetz 1991; de Boer, Van den Bosch and Volberda 1999). Teece, Pisano and Shuen (1997: 520) press Mayo's discovery of culture into service by arguing that culture is a de facto governance system mediating the behaviour of individuals. Second, sequencing activities and inputs allow individual specialist activity to be coordinated continuously, reducing communication. Activity independence varies depending on the product and technologies involved such as sequential, overlapping or concurrent. Third, routines as simple sequences of an automatic nature will be differentiated by supporting complex patterns of interactions among individuals, permitting transfer, recombination or creation of specialized (tacit) knowledge (Dyer and Nobeoka 2000). Highly interdependent changes in one routine, or a higher-level system or architecture, result in new routines required to integrate and coordinate related routines (Teece, Pisano and Shuen 1997). They occur between individuals in the absence of rules, directives or significant verbal communication and are expressed via a repertoire of responses (Grant 1996b: 115). Fourth, group problem-solving and decision-making supports low communication and direct transfer of knowledge arising from first three mechanisms. As task complexity increases, the need for interpersonal communication, interaction in decision-making and group input for non-standardized coordination also increases: meetings and open forums should be arranged in which consensus on unusual, complex and important tasks involving mutual adjustment can be achieved. Devices that decentralize knowledge integration serve to increase participation and thus increase the scope and flexibility of knowledge integration (de Boer, Van den Bosch and Volberda 1999: 387).

REFERENCES

Abel, E. L. (1980) *Marihuana: The First Twelve Thousand Years.* New York: Plenum.
Alvesson, M. and Willmott, H. (2002) 'Identity regulation as organizational control: Producing the appropriate individual', *Journal of Management Studies*, 39 (5): 619–644.
Appelrouth, S. (2005) 'Body and soul: Jazz in the 1920s', *American Behavioral Scientist*, 48(11): 1496–1509.
Baritz, L. (1974) *The Servants of Power. A History of the Use of Social Science in American Industry.* Westport, CT: Greenwood Press.
Bauman, Z. (1997) *Postmodernity and its Discontents.* Cambridge: Polity.
Bavelas, A. and Lewin, K. (1942) 'Training in democratic leadership', *Journal of Abnormal and Social Psychology*, 52(1): 163–176.
Blackler, F. (1995) 'Knowledge, knowledge work and organizations: An overview and interpretation', *Organization Studies*, 16(6): 1021–1046.
Blum, A. F. and McHugh, P. (1971) 'The social ascription of motives', *American Sociological Review*, 36: 98–109.
Braverman, H. (1974) *The Labor Process and Monopoly Capitalism.* New York: Monthly Review Press.
Brown, J. S. and Duguid, P. (1991) 'Organisational learning and communities of practice: Toward a unified view of working learning and innovation', *Organisation Science*, 2: 40–57.
Brown, J. S. and Duguid, P. (2000) *The Social Life of Information.* Boston: Harvard Business School Press.
Burt, R. S. (1992) *Structural Holes: The Social Structure of Competition*, Cambridge, MA: Harvard University Press.
Canguilhem, G. (1992) 'Machine and organism', in J.Crary and S. Kwinter (eds), *Incorporations.* New York: Zone Press, pp. 45–69.
Cartwright, D. and Zander, A. (1953) *Group Dynamics: Research and Theory.* London: Tavistock.
Clegg, S. R. (2003) 'Managing organization futures in a changing world of power/knowledge', in H. Tsoukas and C. Knudsen (eds), *The Oxford Handbook of Organization Theory.* New York: Oxford University Press, pp. 536–567
Clegg, S. R., Courpasson, D. and Phillips, N. (2006) *Power and Organizations.* Thousand Oaks, CA: Sage.
Cohen, S. (1972) *Folk Devils and Moral Panics.* London: Routledge.
Coleman, J. S. (1988) 'Properties of rational organisations', in S. M. Lindenberg and H. Schreuder (eds), *Interdisciplinary Perspectives on Organisation Studies.* Oxford: Oxford University Press, pp. 79–90.

Dale, K. (2001) *Anatomising Embodiment and Organization Theory.* London: Palgrave.
Dandeker, C. (1990) *Surveillance, Power and Modernity: Bureaucracy and Discipline from 1700 to the Present Day.* Cambridge: Polity.
de Boer, M., Van den Bosch, F. A. J. and Volberda, H. W. (1999) 'Managing organisational knowledge integration in the emerging multimedia complex', *Journal of Management Studies*, May, 36(3): 379–398.
Demsetz, H. (1991) 'The theory of the firm revisited', in O. E. Williamson and S. Winter (eds), *The Nature of the Firm.* Oxford University Press, New York, pp. 159–178.
Douglas, M. (1966) *Purity and Danger.* London: Routledge & Kegan Paul.
Dyer, J. H. and Nobeoka, K. (2000) 'Creating and managing a high-performance knowledge-sharing network: The Toyota case, *Strategic Management Journal*, 21: 345–367.
Fleming, P. and Spicer, A. (2007) *Contesting the Corporation.* Cambridge: University of Cambridge Press.
Foucault, M. (1977) *Discipline and Punish: The Birth of the Prison.* London: Allen & Lane.
Fox, A. (1974) *Beyond Contract: Work, Trust and Power.* London: Tavistock Press.
Garrick, J. and Clegg, S. R. (2000) 'Organizational gothic: Transfusing vitality and transforming the corporate body through work-based learning', in C. Symes and J. McIntyre (eds), *Working Knowledge: The New Vocationalism and Higher Education*, Buckingham: The Society for Research into Higher Education and Open University Press, pp. 153–171.
Goffman, E. (1961) *Asylums.* Harmondsworth: Penguin.
Gramsci, A. (1971) *From the Prison Notebooks.* London: Lawrence and Wishart.
Grant, R. M (1996a) 'Prospering in dynamically competitive environments: Organisational capability as knowledge integration', *Organisational Science*, July–August, 7(4): 375–387.
Grant, R. M. (1996b) 'Toward a knowledge-based theory of the rirm', *Strategic Management Journal*, 17: 109–122.
Hardy, C. and Clegg, S. R. (1996) 'Some dare call it power', in Stewart R. Clegg, Cynthia J. Hardy and Walter R. Nord (eds), *The Handbook of Organization Studies.* London: Sage, pp. 622–641.
Haugaard, M. (1997) *The Constitution of Power.* Manchester: Manchester University Press.
Hoskin, K. and Macve, R. (1988) 'The genesis of accountability: The West Point connections', *Accounting, Organizations and Society*, 13; 1: 37–73.
Ibarra-Colado, E. (2001) 'Foucault, gubernamentalidad y organización: una lectura de la triple problematización del sujeto', in *Iztapalapa*, 21(50): 321–358.
Jacques, R. (1996) *Manufacturing the Employee: Management Knowledge from the 19th to 21st Centuries*, Thousand Oaks, CA: Sage.
Kanigel, R. (1997*)* *The One Best Way: Frederick Winslow Taylor and the Enigma of Efficiency*, New York: Viking.
Kogut, B. and Zander, U. (1996) 'What do firms do? Coordination, identity and learning', *Organisation Science*, 7: 502–518.
Kolb, D. (1986) *The Critique of Pure Modernity: Hegel, Heidegger and After.* Chicago: University of Chicago Press.
Lee, A. (1980) *Henry Ford and the Jews.* New York: Stein and Day.
Lopes, P. (2005) 'Signifying deviance and transgression: Jazz in the popular imagination', *American Behavioral Scientist*, 48(11): 1468–1481.
Maguire, S., Phillips, N. and Hardy, C. (2001) 'When silence = death, keep talking: Trust, control and the discursive construction of identity in the Canadian HIV/AIDS treatment domain', *Organisation Studies*, 22(2): 285–310.
Marcus, A. and Segal, H. P. (1989) *Technology in America.* New York: Harcourt Brace Johanovitch.
Maslow, A. H. (1978) 'A theory of human motivation', in Victor H. Vroom and Edward L. Deci (eds), *Management and Motivation*, Harmondsworth, Penguin Books, pp. 27–41.
Mayo, E. (1933) *The Human Problems of an Industrial Civilization*, New York: Viking.
Mayo, E. (1975) *The Social Problems of an Industrial Civilization.* London: Routledge and Kegan Paul.
Meyer, S. (1981) *The Five Dollar Day: Labor Management and Social Control in the Ford Motor Company, 1908–1921.* Albany: State University of New York.
Nahapiet, J. and Ghoshal, S. (1998) 'Social capital, intellectual capital and the organisation advantage', *Academy of Management Review*, 23(2): 2–266.
Nelson, D. (1975) *Managers and Workers: Origins of the New Factory System in the United States, 1880–1920*, Madison: University of Wisconsin Press.
Nelson, R. R. and Winter, S. G. (1982) *An Evolutionary Theory of Economic Change.* Cambridge, MA: Harvard University Press, Belknap Press.

Nonaka, I. and Takeuchi, H. (1995) *The Knowledge Creating Company*. Oxford: Oxford University Press.
Porter, E. (2002) *What Is This Thing Called Jazz? African American Musicians as Artists, Critics, and Activists*. Berkeley: University of California Press.
Putnam, R. D. (1993) 'The prosperous community: social capital and public life', *American Prospect*, 13: 35–42.
Putnam, R. D. (1995) 'Bowling alone: America's declining social capital', *Journal of Democracy*, 6: 65–78.
Reed M. J. (2001) 'Organization, trust and control: A realist analysis', *Organization Studies*, 22(2): 201–228.
Rose, N. (1989) *Governing the Soul*. London: Routledge.
Rose, N. (1996) *Inventing Our Selves: Psychology, Power, and Personhood*. Cambridge: Cambridge University Press.
Sayer, D. (1991) *Capitalism and Modernity: An Excursus on Marx and Weber*. London: Routledge.
Spender, J. C. and Kijne, H. J. (eds) (1996) *Scientific Management: Frederick Winslow Taylor's Gift to the World?* Boston: Kluwer Academic Publishers.
Taylor, F. W. (1911) *Principles of Scientific Management*. New York: Harper.
Teece, D. J., Pisano, G. and Shuen, A. (1997) 'Dynamic capabilities and strategic management', *Strategic Management Journal*, 18(7): 509–533.
Thompson, P. and Ackroyd, S (1995) 'All quiet on the workplace front? A critique of recent trends in British industrial sociology', *Sociology*, 59(4): 615–633.
Thompson, P. and Warhurst, C. (eds) (1998) *Workplaces of the Future*. London: Macmillan.
Trahair, R. (2001) 'George Elton Mayo', *Biographical Dictionary of Management*, Thoemmes Press: http://www.thoemmes.com/
Turner, B. S. (1984) *The Body and Social Theory*. Oxford: Blackwell.
van Krieken, R. (1990) 'The organisation of the soul: Elias and Foucault on discipline and the self', *Archives Europeénes de Sociologie*, 31(2): 353–371.
Watts, S. L. (1991) *Order against Chaos: Business Culture and Labor Ideology in America 1880–1915*. New York: Greenwood Press.
Yates, J. (1989) *Control through Communication: The Rise of System in American Management*. Baltimore: Johns Hopkins University Press.

18

Cultures of Resistance in the Workplace

David Courpasson and Françoise Dany

INTRODUCTION

Talking about resistance largely means addressing the processes through which a taken for granted phenomenon (for instance, managerial hegemony) is more or less suddenly unveiled by certain social actors and made questionable and thinkable by the same social actors. The unravelling of the taken for granted (Ewick and Silbey 2003) sometimes enables, under certain conditions, the up-ending of the domination of social and power structures, so that maybe surprisingly, relatively 'powerless' people, can sneak into these structures and find a way to do things differently or simply, to express a contest. The differences created mark acts of resistance that are contextually and culturally dependent on these specific conditions. Recently, Spicer and Böhm (2007) offer a synthesis of diverse interpretations of resistance activities in the workplace. They suggest that four frameworks have been mobilized in order to study resistance: (1) reappropriation (Ackroyd and Thompson 1999), where resistance aims to reappropriate the critical goods 'stolen' by the labour process, (2) micro politics (Thomas and Davies 2005), through which employees contest the 'colonization of their subjectivity', (3) hegemonic struggle (Laclau and Mouffe 1985), seeing the hegemonic discourse of management as the center of a web of social relations which imply a struggle around the 'incompleteness' of managerial schemes (Spicer and Böhm 2007: 1671), and (4) Social Movements (Zald and Berger 1978; Zald 2005), through which collective challenges are held together by a sense of common purpose, solidarity, across time and space by relatively resilient organizational forms of contestation. This synoptic vision is very helpful for understanding how individuals and collective resist managerial discourse. It offers a plural vision of how resistance is enacted either in collective movements or in infra-political conduits in a more informal way.

In this chapter, we are going to highlight that resistance in today's companies is marked by the hybridizations between those frameworks of resistance. A better grasp of those hybridizations can help us to understand how and why certain individuals trigger change in the contemporary workplace, sometimes without even knowing and wanting it. In particular, through a story of individual resistance we shall analyze how infra-political individual acts of resistance, importing external valuable resources such as those mobilized by social movements, manage to propagate cognitive shifts among invisible collectives of peers and eventually transforms an initial isolated protest into an informal collective 'insurgency' against management through an escalation of resistance. From this story, we defend two major ideas: first, that infra-political resistance can actively engage with official centres of power through contesting concrete managerial decisions; second, that individualistic forms of management like those developed in post-bureaucratic or post-modern 'high commitment' organizations do not prevent isolated resistance from generating wider movements because their structures of 'soft power' (Courpasson 2006) offer many opportunities to operate transitions between infra-political strategies, the workplace and civil society.

To illustrate this perspective, we first tell the story of Jean-Paul. The story is about an organizational exit, through which a young and promising executive decides to refuse the promotion offered by the management. The story illustrates what led one of the most compliant employees of the company to decide to 'send his supervisor packing' and how, a largely private decision generated cognitive shifts in the company, among his peers as well as people feeling confronted with similar types of situations. Second, we discuss this story by stressing in particular the process of escalation of resistance and a vision of what we call creative resistance which is a hybridization of the diverse forms highlighted by Spicer and Böhm (2007). We discuss creative resistance as based on the conscious reassertion, by a given individual or collective, of specific values against the values of management, an assertion which does not need to be sustained by an overt struggle. This reassertion is rendered necessary by a managerial decision utterly mirroring the underlying values of contemporary management. To conclude we explain why we believe that this form of resistance is typical of new forms of management like the post-bureaucracy (Hecksher and Donnellon 1994) as it is triggered by the practice of empowerment and of institutionalized dialogue within the company, the central features of contemporary post-bureaucracies.

THE STORY OF JEAN-PAUL

Jean-Paul is 33 year old. He graduated from a prestigious French school of engineering and then he obtained an MBA from a prestigious business school in England. He worked for three years in a big consulting firm and has been working for two years as head of department in a building trade company, located in Toulouse, in the south-west of France. He has been married for three years, and has just received the most exhilarating promotion an ambitious executive in his thirties can expect: he has become the father of little Elodie, 2 month old.

The story begins in February, a normal Friday evening at around 10 pm. After two long and boring days of visits in the south-western area of the company, Jean-Paul is comfortably seated with his wife, Helen, in the living room, absent-mindedly watching some TV show. The phone rings, bringing Jean-Paul back to the real world. Louis is calling, the direct supervisor of Jean-Paul. Louis is 40, and a big 'fan' of Jean-Paul. He thinks the latter has got the calibre to go high in the company, to become, perhaps, the future CEO.

The call has a simple objective: Louis has just got out of a meeting with the Board, and he has got something wonderful to announce to Jean-Paul: he managed to convince the whole board that Jean-Paul is the right person to take over an important corporate project. The project is about acquiring and integrating a big Scottish laboratory. The project concerns engineering and R&D developments, but mostly it is a social project, possibly involving dismissals and tough negotiation with unions. It is a proper test to 'measure' and confirm Jean-Paul's managerial capacities!

The problem is, so to speak, that if he accepts the challenge, he has to fly to Scotland the following Tuesday, in 72 hours time, for an uncertain duration of between six to nine months, maybe more, 'depending on your capacity to move things forward quickly', according to Louis. Louis enthusiastically gives Jean-Paul 24 hours to make a decision, of which he says, 'that's something you should talk about with Helen', but he advises Jean-Paul that it is a decision to make quickly anyway, as other candidates are queuing up to get the project. The reward for success will be enormous for Jean-Paul: nothing less than managing the North American business unit, the biggest of the company, at less than 35 years old!

Jean-Paul is presented with a very classical dilemma in business organizations, qualified as an 'obedience dilemma' (Courpasson and Dany 2003). Obedience, because what is actually tested is the 'level of compliance' of a given individual: what are they inclined to sacrifice for the sake of career and simultaneously, for the sake of the success of an important project? Put differently, the company managers want to know whether Jean-Paul is someone reliable: is he ready for sacrifice? Jean-Paul might be the right person, but there are presumably other people who could fit the job within the company. So there is both choice and agency (as Jean-Paul is free to take the offer or not) as well as social pressure, because the consequences of a refusal, even if uncertain, are likely to be significant.

Having got the offer, Jean-Paul is not just thinking about refusing or accepting, in a binary perspective. He is thinking about contesting the very rationale of the dilemma, the reasons why he has been asked to move to Scotland and to make such a difficult decision. He does not sleep very well indeed, even if he has already made his decision: he won't go to Scotland. Later he invokes three major reasons:

- He does not want to admit that his company places people in such undecidable situations, what is more, with a sort of 'affable generosity'. 'Business requires clear rules of the game: either you are generous or you try to trap people and test people' he says. Accordingly, Jean-Paul situates his refusal on the terrain of a moral contestation: what is at stake is the process used by the company to make him believe that he has a choice and that the company managers care about this choice.
- The trap is crude. What worries Jean-Paul a lot is having been selected for the Scottish project while everyone knows he has just got a newborn child. This really means that being a key person in this company requires to be entirely dedicated to one's career. In this perspective, Jean-Paul knows that refusing to sacrifice his private life, like a 'standard' would-be leader, means that he is therefore contesting the underlying model of leadership which looms behind the dilemma. He refuses to see his managerial life as necessarily

antagonistic to his personal life, as being a struggle between the private/intimate spheres and the public sphere. Louis orders something which is unacceptable for Jean-Paul: choosing between the private and the public.
- He does not like Scotland: 'it is cold and far away!'

Jean-Paul calls Louis on Saturday at 10 pm. Louis is having dinner with some friends; the conversation has to be short, as usual. Jean-Paul takes time anyway to explain that he is not going to go to Scotland. Louis takes the decision with his usual smile, he does not sound surprised. He says thanks to Jean-Paul for having decided quickly and adds: 'see you on Monday; we shall talk about all that'. Jean-Paul puts down the handset, remaining silent for some long minutes, realizing from this very moment what he has just done: his days are numbered in the company. If he sees it through, he should even number them himself – so, to be coherent with the moral argument he put forward in his choice, he has to leave the company.

Jean-Paul left the company three months later. He gave the letter of resignation on the following Monday to Louis. The latter accepted it uncomplainingly and unsmilingly. Jean-Paul will rapidly find a job as business unit manager in a competing company. Three years after the story, there was some talk of his being project director in the United States, one of his dreams.

Most interpretations of this type of story would see Jean-Paul's decision as a story of resignation rather than as a story of resistance. Indeed, Jean-Paul does not try to convince the company that he is right. Likewise, he does not search for the support and encouragement of his peers. At first glance, he chooses the exit rather than starting a difficult and time-wasting struggle with managers. Yet we suggest it is actually a story of resistance, since Jean-Paul is challenging a managerial rule about the career of would-be leaders that he simply refused to take for granted. While he does not oppose it overtly, he refuses its legitimacy and chooses to escape. We think it is not a mere exit; it is a way to voice its values and to fully live them, to demonstrate that one can live according to different values, without wanting to change the system.

Resistance is not restricted to disobedience. It is also a form of obedience, which allows people to live according to their values while they discover along their way that those values are opposed to those of management. This is basically what we could call affirmative resistance: officially claiming the superior legitimacy of given values without wanting to engage in a political struggle against competing values.

While the company missed the boat, we think that several 'messages for management' are contained in this relatively commonplace story of refusal of what should not be refused. The company did not see them and has simply buried them in the neutral and administrative acceptance of the resignation. Yet, others did see it, especially among Jean-Paul's peers: that there is something wrong with selecting people on the basis of private tests of commitment, which, moreover, are hidden behind the façade of other arguments rather than on the basis of competence or passion for the job. That Jean-Paul's resistance suggests that the company does not respect people's lives, that it uses them for an uncertain and ill-defined common good. Thus, the refusal triggers a number of ambivalent feelings in Jean-Paul's co-workers and would-be peers of the leaders: was he right? Is he a coward? What would I do if I were him?

In Jean-Paul's circle, two interpretations of his act circulate. First, some executives think that it is the proof of an exaggerated ego and individualism. They are interpreting the decision in a 'he did not share the strategic purposes of the organization – we knew that for a long time – that is just a confirmation' mode. They distance themselves from Jean-Paul and do not see him as part of their 'group'. One of the colleagues taking this stance accepts the Scottish project later on. Three months later he returned to France having overseen a social conflict which involved the personnel of the local lab as well as the local municipality and some town councillors. Other colleagues take Jean-Paul's side. They feel at one with him and blame the company management for having coldly let Jean-Paul exit. The decision is interpreted in a 'one does not have the right to confront someone that dryly and quickly with such a personal dilemma' mode. Four of them are going to follow Jean-Paul and leave the company in the following twelve months.

Put differently, the act of resistance displayed by Jean-Paul won't remain neutral. Even if his decision was definitely shaped on private grounds, referring to personal stakes and conditions, it obliges employees and managers to explore the significance of the exit regarding critical issues like: is our company a good company? Does it manage its employees in a fair way? It triggers and fuels a series of discussions, deliberations and debates within the company, over which the company management won't have any hold. Those processes generate cognitive shifts because they show that several individuals sharing certain beliefs and certain ideas about what is and is not acceptable in a company find the oportunity to claim their views explicitly, and by doing so, oblige managers to find ways of making sense of the exits.

In this perspective the very feature of resistance is to produce well-targeted signals and to set a precedent stipulating that there are rules that are worth questioning in the company, and even that there is room for alternative interpretations of those rules: for instance, this would be the first time a promising executive had decided to 'give the company management the finger', according to Philippe, a close colleague of Jean-Paul.

More specifically, the story of Jean-Paul offers a vision, in which resistance is both stemming from asymmetrical power relationships and is contributing to reshaping these very relationships. It is neither only a struggle for reappropriation of stolen goods or resources, nor a defensive micro-political strategy of identity protection. It is not exclusively a struggle against the discursive and practical hegemony of management, and it is not a social movement. It is a hybridization of those forms. Put differently, Jean-Paul represents a category of resisters who see themselves as more rational and more competent than power holders when confronted with a given problem, but who are not contesting management per se. On the contrary, as the story suggest, they are using the discourse of management to sustain a refusal. There is something like a temporary and provisional power inversion which enables them to claim their right (to exit) but which is not materialized as a struggle for something or against something. Resisters sneak into a decision-making area which is not normally theirs; they break a taken for granted political situation according to which being offered an upward career is something for which 'normal people' should be thankful. Therefore, the issue is largely in the hands of power holders who have to decide whether they accept this temporary up-ending and political inferiority, or whether they counter-resist it. Through this story, we therefore invert the classical power separation in which studies of forms of resistance are 'stuck', by addressing situations in which resisters are potentially and temporarily stronger than management oligarchs, even if, in the upshot, oligarchs retain power either by admitting and authorizing resistance as a fact, or by discrediting the decision itself. The following question is therefore about the subsequent effects of the initial act of resistance, and how this act can result in concrete changes through escalation processes.

FROM ISOLATION TO ESCALATION

Broadly, the literature offers two ways of understanding the effects of resistance activities in the workplace. First, from the acknowledgment of situations of inequality, which are seen as triggering political responses from deprived groups or people, these responses being a function of power relationships. In that perspective, power 'serves for the development and maintenance of the quiescence of the non-elite' (Gaventa 1982: 4) or it enables subordinate elements of a given polity to mitigate or deny claims made on them by superdordinate fractions of the same polity (Scott 1985:290). According to this view, resistance is not capable and even intended to fundamentally alter power structures and the status of power holders. It allows people to defy temporarily the taken-for-granted hierarchies of statuses and privileges, but does not modify it. Second, resistance is understood as the process by which power structures and relationships are modified, altered and power bested. In this second perspective, resistance can be thought of as a major ingredient for changing patterns of managerial authority in contemporary organizations. In other words, resistance is seen as an act of power.

This second vision puts forward that the possibility of effecting changes in organizations is based on the intricate relations between structures of power and individual or collective strategies of resistance. It is the creative face of resistance. For example, Fleming and Spicer (2007) aptly develop this notion by juxtaposing what they term a 'fourth face' of power with new strategies of resistance in and around the workplace. The fourth face of power is identified as *subjectification*, a state which occurs when actors are attached to a form of identity which is actually derived from a structure of domination, (see also Hardy and Leiba-O'Sullivan 1998). Seeing subjects as being in a state of subjectification is a departure from traditional visions in which resistance is identified with overt 'industrial struggles' (Fleming and Spicer 2007: 42). The fourth face of power, conceived as subjectification, opens the way to more various and ambiguous forms of subversion, in which resistance is a set of 'subtle' creations allowing people to construct 'counter spheres within forms of domination...[through which they]... quietly challenge power relations without necessarily leaving them' (Fleming and Spicer 2007: 43). Resistance under these conditions consists of creating alternative identities and systems of representation within structures of domination that are hardly negotiable. Consequently, resistance is synonymous with tactics which enable people to infuse existing structures of domination with unexpected ingredients: rescripting official cultures (Kondo 1990), cynically parodying them (Butler 1998), or over-identifying (Fleming and Sewell 2002).

In this approach, creative resistance is not very different from what Scott (1990) calls a hidden transcript, that is to say, the process through which people exhibit surface compliance while refusing to internalize the ideological arguments asserted from above. However, it differs in one important aspect illustrated for instance by Kondo (1990), according to whom resistance is productive of sensemaking, turning managerial directives to the employees' advantage instead of, as with Scott's peasants, being capable of 'masking' resistant interpretations whose covert existence marks a whole authentic and autonomous self. The story of Jean-Paul provides another example of creation: it is a situation in which individual subjects engaged in resistant acts obtain an immediate relief or benefit, but more interestingly, engage a broader process of cognitive shifts within their peers' group (in this case, the group of 'would-be leaders'), thus progressively altering the ongoing relationship between this group and the dominant group and the managerial authorities. They oblige management people and other employees to 'think intensely'. Although this process is not intentional, it is interesting because it offers a description of how a non-intentional, non-organized and isolated act of resistance can trigger a progressive redefinition of the position of a certain group relative to the dominant group. In the story of Jean-Paul, resistance is creative via the process through which an isolated individual produce long-term improvements in its social position and relationship to the dominant group, without intending it, by creating a temporary political asymmetry that leads other similar executives to make sense of it, and to invent their own response and interpretation of the event. New meanings about executive career rules and principles are not the result of a struggle between resisters and authorities. They rather stem from the interaction between the initial resister, leading the process initially, the rest of the executive community, because Jean-Paul's peers know that they might be confronted to the same dilemma sooner or later, and the company managers who are going to be obliged to react, in particular in order to find alternative solutions (replacing Jean-Paul and his exiting peers) and above all, to find compelling explanations of the situation to the rest of the company, in order to save face, and to show that this decision is not creating a problem for the company because it can be fixed easily.

In this case, the question is to understand how individualistic and isolated modes of contestation are likely to generate unexpected new political constituencies within the organization and by doing that, to produce political implications of a broader scale than those permitted by the isolated personal commitment of individuals like Jean-Paul. How Jean-Paul's decision is triggering alternative modes of invisible collective action is the most complicated part of the story we tell here.

In our example, this issue stems in particular from the succession of several exits of successful colleagues after Jean-Paul's decision. Our hypothesis is that there is a connection between the initial exit, decided on individualistic grounds, and an unobtrusive collective decision to leave the company, made by four other executives without apparently collusion or deliberation of any sort between them. Therefore, we do not suggest that these subsequent exits have been scheduled intentionally, but that they have a political significance in that they imply individuals belonging *de facto* to a same invisible group, and having been engaged in a political struggle without having the project of organizing and collectivizing their acts. Consequently, the significance of (small) acts of resistance like Jean-Paul's exit does not lie in their own localized and temporary effects. Rather, it lies in their capacity to transform local acts in primary locations for protest against management methods and criteria into an alternative collective framework about how a given individual should handle his/her career in this very company, based on a collective reference for action. The act of resistance shapes a shared consciousness within a given interpretive community of relatively comparable employees, of what is acceptable and not, and how a refusal can be managed or not in a given company. While in the everyday life of overburdened managers, the idea of a threshold in what is acceptable or not is overshadowed by the promise of a bright future and by the lack of availability to think and act politically, Jean-Paul's defiance sort of breaks off the normal managerial script and reveals that certain things are still possible.

Moreover, this act is politically significant because resistance here touches a crucial tenet of managerial hegemony: the system is attacked through a central prerogative of company leadership, namely the criteria of promotion of executives, that is to say, through the very politics of managerial elite reproduction. Jean-Paul and his remote followers do not negotiate structures of domination themselves: they 'simply' contest the validity of a specific rule of the game in a specific context, this rule being an important fulcrum of the structure of domination; but they do not intentionally target this pillar of management hegemony: it is 'offered' to them by the managerial decision to promote Jean-Paul. This story reveals a situation where domination is not only up-ended and contested per se, but transformed and eventually lessened at the level of 'local practice' (Rubin 1996: 242).

In this account, the act of resistance has nothing to do with the ruses and tricks of the weak. It is the result of a decision entailing an initiatory individual power over ongoing relational logics within the organization. It is because the individual feels trapped that he produces a shock, thus claiming that he is actually part of the same 'interpretive community' (McCann and March 1996: 222) as power holders. Through his decision, the resister directly challenges existing relations because he has infiltrated the 'dominant text' (Ewick and Silbey 1992: 27) which in the case of Jean-Paul, is about the criteria of promotion of the best executives in the company, something which is not supposed to be discussed by employees, even high potentials, but a major prerogative of managerial oligarchs.

Through his refusal, Jean-Paul opens another black box of management: the box of culture and values. In other words, he confronts alternative visions of managerial culture and of life projects; he sends a message which is symbolically powerful: an ambitious executive can renounce honours, power and rewards when personal values are at stake. To better understand this cultural confrontation, we turn now to a rapid examination of how the literature has addressed resistance as an outcome of cultural confrontations, as a means to confronting alternative values and beliefs.

CULTURES OF RESISTANCE

The literature on resistance shares at least one idea: that acts of resistance are contextually and socially embedded. Resistance mirrors specific 'behind the scenes' cultural backgrounds and claims. Put differently, the peasants of Scott (1990), the skilled workers of Vallas (2006) or the bankers of Weeks (2004) have something in common: they act within a given structure of power and within a given culture of power. For Weeks (2004), the culture of complaint in the bank explains the reproduction of power structures but also some elements of adaptation (Weeks 2004); for Vallas' (2006) skilled workers the culture of parochialism and traditionalism, or the culture of craft and expertise, explain diverse action orientations of subgroups towards management initiatives, while for Scott's (1990) peasants, the distinctive subculture of cohesion (the 'community of fate') and the realities of power of subordinate groups explain that much of their political action is founded on interpretation, precisely because they are acting in a culture of opacity, where the message of power holders is

Table 18.1 Cultures of resistance in the workplace

	Cultures of defiance	Cultures of appropriation	Cultures of contestation
	Fantasia 1988 Burawoy 1979	Vallas 2006	Lipset et al. (1956); Osterman (2006); Marquis and Lounsbury (2007)
Power as	Oppressive acts	Managerial imperatives and obligations, Hegemony of management ideas	Oligarchy: entrenched leadership and conservative transformation
Agency	Oppositional values, Suspicion, reject of newness 'Street-savvy' behaviours	Skilful interpretation of working rules, Struggling for knowledge superiority between contending groups	Member's sense of their own self-worth, High social status in the membership, Being assertive
Form of resistance	Cohesion, Contesting legitimacy of new rules and outsiders' values	Contesting through entering into the [managerial] system	Connection through social training, Skill development and behavioural modelling, Scepticism toward authority
Outcome	Reproduction of insularity and of the power elite	Development of unexpected forms of cooperation, Gaining control over a given management process	Individual transformation through training, Keeping members' commitment and innovativeness

cryptic and ambiguous (Scott 1990). Therefore, acts of resistance can be analyzed through the diversity and the combination of cultures of resistance. We outline three major cultures in the following table (Table 18.1).

The culture of defiance is probably the most studied context of resistance. It stigmatizes groups of subordinates that systematically refuse what comes from above, because it comes from above and because it threatens the traditional values of a given cohesive community or class. What is hierarchically imposed is suspected of depriving class members of their material resources; therefore, it is a very contentious culture that is based on indignation and the reaffirmation of workers' values and skills against the dominant vision of expertise and status recognition (see Vallas 2006: 1697–1701 and the description of what he calls 'populist defiance'). The culture of defiance is made up of discourses and stories but also of open contests between workers and hierarchies based on a passionate critique of the adversary's values and claims. The defiant culture is not only aimed at organizational elites but more broadly, at any kind of 'untrustworthy' outsider. It is a culture of resistance through closure of ranks. The outcome is more often than not the reproduction of the closure and of the management stereotype of the rigid-thinking worker: localized resistance tends, therefore, to reproduce the dismissive authority structure it contests, by confirming the very reasons why organizational elites strive to change the workplace. It affirms and reproduces the vicious cycles that it produces. Such resistance is thus recursive of existing power relations, affirming rather than changing them.

The fulcrum of the *culture of appropriation* is contestation constituted through engagement in the new managerial rules of the game. As Vallas put it (2006: 1701), people demand the right to play the new game. The resistance comes from their fear of being excluded from crucial transformations and new duties; therefore, it derives from struggles around the occupational boundaries that frame a territory of expertise and knowledge. The example given by Vallas is the struggle between technicians and engineers to gain control over strategic aspects of the production process: he calls this pattern 'craft usurpation'. The culture of appropriation is therefore less protective and closure-oriented than the culture of defiance: it produces acts of resistance pushing people to enter into the adversary's arena rather than being excluded from it. It raises claims to be integrated in the change process.

The *culture of contestation* offers a third interesting alternative for thinking resistance as a cultural confrontation. For instance, Osterman (2006: 628) suggests that an organization (a social movement organization in his paper) can create the underlying conditions shaping the two conditions of a culture of contestation: the growth of political skills and the feelings of self-worth. Resistance derives also from an assertive organizational culture which is created by specific channels of action, demonstrating that culture does not only rely on values and ultimate purposes but can also be crafted and designed. For Swidler, for instance, culture is also the result of strategies of action based on 'tool kits' (1986: 273–276, quoted in Osterman 2006). A culture of contestation is therefore the result of the informal codes of behaviour that members deploy toward power in their day-to-day life. Contest is not only authorized but encouraged as a portion of the culturally accepted codes of conduct. For Osterman, such cultures seek to avoid the effects of oligarchy and to maintain the commitment of members, despite the entrenching process of leadership. People are encouraged to become more assertive members, sceptical toward authority, and trained to refuse unilateral power. Developing a culture of contestation is aimed at resisting the potential development of illegitimate and internal unilateral powers. In its form, it offers a unitary vision of organizational functioning rather than one that sees it comprised of subcultures. In the upshot the specificity of this culture of resistance is that it generates patterns of compatibility and creative interaction between oligarchical political structures and members' participation and agency.

Embedding resistance within specific cultures is important for two reasons. First, the outcomes of acts of resistance should be different according to the cultural context in which they take place. For instance, cultures of defiance are more likely to result in reproducing patterns of power than cultures of contestation. Second, it confirms that resisting without having a clear political project is possible as long as the act of resistance is based on a substantive confrontation of values rather than on the exclusive project of overthrowing the leaders. The resistance is creative because it is culturally embedded, that is to say, it can be read and interpreted and rationalized by every executive in the business world. Creative resistance requires a clear mobilization of external values (the values of the family and the respect of private life) which, imported in the managerial realm, make sense for a majority of people. This cultural backscene is partly what contemporary versions of resistance are missing.

Indeed, contemporary debates about resistance, in particular those deriving from Foucauldian accounts and the so-called emergence of subjective forms (Fleming and Sewell 2002), seem to neglect the cultural embeddedness of acts of resistance. To be short, they depict resistance as mostly individualistic. Resisting is the business of everyone, like managing one's career. In this over-subjectivized environment, those employees who follow overt and classical forms of resistance, such as an industrial dispute, are doomed to failure because of the development of complex and deeply pervasive forms of (neo)managerial control like those underlying the self-concerted teams (Barker 1993). Therefore, workers would/should find new ways of resisting, mostly through subjectivation and cynical distancing, but those infra-political micro-actions are not fundamentally altering the structures of power, nor the discourses of management, and do not even change the personal situation of resisting individuals, precisely because they miss the substantive cultural arguments that resisters are likely to push and oppose to taken for granted managerial arguments.

The story of Jean-Paul leads to analyzing the effects of resistance from the content of resistance more than from the form of resistance adopted. First, it exemplifies how resistance can be creative through the connection it establishes between the initial isolated refusal and the subsequent behavioural modifications in a group of peers. The creative side of resistance is not based on a political intentional project of overthrowing the leaders, but on a simple personal arbitration between what is seen acceptable and not acceptable by Jean-Paul. The arbitration is simple but it is based, once again, on a substantive confrontation and comparison between systems of beliefs about, say, managing one's life. The underlying idea is that, paradoxically, contemporary managerial 'soft domination' (Courpasson 2006) tends to facilitate the emergence of acts of resistance which are not politically shaped and formalized, but which take progressively a political form through the unexpected and unintended effects they provoke within an invisible collective of peers. Indeed, regimes of soft domination are partly based on the power given de facto to people (especially 'key' people) to make their own choices and to feel entirely accountable for the consequences of those choices. It is also based on the capacity to mobilize networks of actors to trigger debates and deliberations among comparable people, through the democratization of the business firm (Ackoff 1994). People can talk, exchange, confront and they are 'entrepreneurs', therefore they have the right and the duty to be individual and collective decision-makers. The production through an initial act of resistance, of knock-on effects on a larger community of young executives is therefore partly generated by new managerial regimes of power. Because in the latter, people are likely to appropriate the practices of management to their advantage (Vallas 2006). Second, these effects oblige management to take a clear position toward individual and collective acts of resistance, because they come from key players, resourceful people who the company do not want to lose, and because these key players could jeopardize managerial beliefs as they found their resistance on an alternative belief which proves to be credible. Through the story of Jean-Paul, we see individuals who are capable to tell rationally and pragmatically about their own experiences, and potentially capable of accumulating and spreading different examples of similar resistance within the group of peers, which highlight the possibility of contesting taken for granted hegemonic situations.

Here the taken-for-granted 'thing' is that people like Jean-Paul are supposed to share and to have incorporated a common vision of the identity and of the actions of an ambitious executive 'pegged' as a would-be leader. Those people do not refuse challenges in their career, they accept and even enforce for themselves the 'career tournament' rules in order to achieve their goals. Jean-Paul, and later his colleagues, are altering considerably this vision because they shed light on an alternative. It is not only the possibility of refusal, but the content of the arguments which are decisive. In other words, Jean-Paul mobilizes external values and beliefs, that is to say, values and beliefs produced outside the workplace, to legitimize their resistance: the importance of family and of children, the respect of private life, and what is more, an implicit suggestion that it might be possible to conceive another process of producing performance. Maybe Jean-Paul would have been even more involved and successful in the company if the management had accepted his refusal and had seen the signs of a strong personality (confirming, by the way, the choice of the company of having put Jean-Paul in the 'would-be leaders, box') behind this decision.

THE CONDITIONS OF A CREATIVE RESISTANCE IN THE WORKPLACE

Let's get back to Jean-Paul's story for a while. What do we learn from this story? On one hand, there is nothing really new under the sun. First, we see an individual confirming that people are sceptical realists about managerial discourses and decisions, that they are not passive recipients of an elite-generated model and notion of what is good and bad in the workplace. Second, we acknowledge that people learn, through their workplace experience (Vallas 2006), about how managerial imperatives and official texts are actually operated and are acted upon. Put differently, Jean-Paul's defection is having effects because of this accumulated experience and because of the very fact that he has been groomed within the company as a compliant leader, as someone capable of making informed decisions, including for his sake – which he does – as a father and husband.

On the other hand, the story of Jean-Paul tells us something more about the opportunity grasped by a potential leader developing an oppositional ethical and ideological claim about what makes a deserving manager. In other words, his story offers an alternative interpretation of the significance of micro-acts of resistance. First, this type of act is consequential because it enables people to display an active sense of dignity and autonomy, which is not given in the usual managerial work. To put things differently, there is a significant existential sense to these acts of creative resistance (McCann and March 1996: 226). The refusal of Jean-Paul is effectively a demand for recognition of his own needs and personal/private identity. He sends a message to the company managers, and in doing so, he proves capable of shifting the agenda from the requests of power holders to his own demands; he asserts his own frame of what is essential and what is unessential. The interesting point here is that this assertion is producing something for the others, because it is provoking a cognitive shift in the group of comparable individuals in the company, through the very discussions triggered by Jean-Paul's exit and the disagreements arising in a supposedly homogenous group.

Another aspect is that it is not a story relating an experience of powerlessness, in Gaventa's terms. First, the defiant action is successful because it opens surprising means to create a role inversion between superordinate and subordinate powers. Here, Jean-Paul does not act because he has accumulated experiences of entrapment and deprivation in his career; quite the contrary. He is neither confused nor resigned. He acts because he feels autonomous and skilled enough to interpret the dilemma he sees as one that is unfair or wrongly spelled out, as a proof of the fragility and illegitimacy of certain dominating patterns of decision-making in the company. Second, Jean-Paul imports external variables into the company. He is likely to use those resources because he has a clear and strong private position, because his familial resources are as strong and influential as his organizational resources: in other words, there is symmetry between the private and the public spheres. Therefore, he can be personally and politically ambitious and, at the same time, give sense to resistance in the eyes of others because he uses external values which are understandable by anybody, enemies and allies alike. As Ewick and Silbey put it (2003: 749), 'resistance, to the extent that it constitutes forms of consciousness, ways of operating and making do, may prefigure more formidable and strategic challenges to power'. Bringing his private arguments into the public managerial sphere enables Jean-Paul to constitute a form of consciousness which can be transmitted and explained to other comparable persons, including the company managers.

To sum up, this isolated and apparently mundane act of resistance is likely to escalate politically and turn into a layer and more significant political event for several reasons:

- The subsequent fate of Jean-Paul and his personal status, the concrete outcome of the act of resistance. The message is clear: exiting means getting more from another competing company. Refusing the evidence of management power can be more profitable.
- The reactions of his colleagues and the fact that the company managers have actually set up for several years internal networks of potential leaders in particular through executive education programs. Thanks to these programs, people talk to each other, they interpret closely what happens when one of their 'peers' is affected by a crucial decision. Would-be leaders are not constituting a closed community, but they are capable of knowing what happens to the others, especially when it is collectively significant.
- There is also a contextual specificity, which is that the Scottish project, a couple of year after Jean-Paul's refusal, is seen as a failure. Notwithstanding, the correlation between the refusal of Jean-Paul and the eventual failure is an easy one to make (including on humorous grounds).

The story also shows the importance of material resources in the ability to actually resist management decisions: Jean-Paul is politically strong, he could tip the balance and at any rate he does find another job. The symbolic resource provided by the implicit status of 'would-be leader' is also important: the invisible membership of a *high potential* band of brothers *within* a discursive community (executives taking part to management seminars in particular), where a specific language and rhetoric about career and success are used as socializing events, fosters a sense of shared identity, which in turn will reflect pre-existing inequalities among managers and highly qualified people in the workplace. Being action- and agency-oriented depends highly on the individual's position within pre-existing social and symbolic hierarchies. The act of resistance stems directly from the resilience of those hierarchies; Jean-Paul is resisting successfully because he is located high in the scale of internal status. His act is so to speak a by product or, a side-effect of this scale. The creative resistance is therefore both a production from above (organizational hierarchies) and a production from below (personal interpretations of the rules managing careers): actors interact with the resources and hierarchies shaped by the company to strengthen and legitimize their very acts of resistance. They use the discourse of management which is part of the toolkit of managerial power to act as empowered agents, deliberating privately about their future and the congruence between their beliefs and the purposes of the organization they are working in.

In this story, there is also a particular structure of opportunity, in the sense of social movement theory: access to extra-organizational (values) and intra-organizational resources (executive seminars), and associational factors linking individual efforts of the presumably 'weak' actor with some general preoccupations (justice, privacy, defining a good leader) is influential. Jean-Paul's resistance is not a negation of power. It is not separating the 'life of power' from the 'life of resistance'. It is creating a new opportunity for shaping an alternative way of being a potential leader in the company.

Third, the singularity of the story is that it does offer an alternative interpretation of the necessity of associational bonds among subordinate people to create significant movements of resistance. Social movement theory strongly suggests that the significance of resistance is directly linked to the capacity of mobilizing and connecting otherwise isolated and marginalized people. Scott confirms this view, developing the idea that cultural bonds linking oppressed groups are a necessary ingredient of the elaboration of 'hidden transcripts', or the culture of solidarity depicted by Fantasia (1988). We definitely find this ingredient of resistance in the cultures of defiance and appropriation (Table 18.1).

Our story offers a different version of the associational ingredient. Jean-Paul is part of an invisible group we called 'would be' leaders, a category which is mostly a managerial invention, in the identification of those also pegged as 'high potentials'. Their identification as such does not inform us about the existence of any kind of associational or cultural bond. Those young executives have common points, no doubt, the least being to compete for the same scarce resources and to share common social and training events, but this does obviously not create a culture of solidarity. Rather, those people are loosely connected through episodic events. They constitute a fragmented polity in which an isolated act has an important impact. They are competing with each other. Nothing very solidaristic at first glance. So we cannot argue that the individualistic modes of resistance impede the creation of a political collective action over time. Indeed, the search for privacy and peace that we see in the story of Jean-Paul does not preclude the progressive constitution of an invisible forum overtly contesting the prevalent managerial values on leadership and promotion in the company.

CONCLUSION

In this chapter, we have suggested that the relationships between local resistance and processes of organizational transformation can be observed in forms that are less visible than open rebellions and protests, but nevertheless contribute to reshape relations of power. Thus the question of when local acts of resistance are likely to 'connect up' to broader transformations and when they are not is important because it has several implications.

First, this direction of analysis obliges to complete the definition of resistance that most literature keeps unchanged for ages. Seeing resistance as any action that opposes the regular processes and systems of power is unsatisfactory. We have to include all complex forms of human action and interaction which dramatizes the outcomes of a subordinate relationship (McFarland 2004) and which therefore, involve aspects of consciousness and explicit challenges to structures of power, entailing a conscious or unconscious intent among a given group of people to challenge certain aspects of broader structures, like the evidence of leaders' profiles and preferences, in the case we develop in this chapter. Put differently, the initial act of Jean-Paul permits eventually to generate concrete acts of resistance, but it was not resistance *per se*, because Jean-Paul was initially not intending to challenge managerial power, but to defend his contextual interests and those of his family. Resistance arises from the unobtrusive and unexpected deliberations among peers who feel concerned exceedingly by Jean-Paul's acts, and who fuel their own exits with a collective consciousness that Jean-Paul unwittingly prepared.

Second, a proper definition of resistance should include visions according to which resistance systematically articulate broader and collective challenges to power, which allow the penetration of the hegemonic system through some of its crucial channels like in our case, the regulation of elite production and perpetuation. The story of Jean-Paul offers an interesting example of how locations labelled private (the family, the birth of a child) are capable to upend some key functions of managerial power.

Third, the story of Jean-Paul invites to think how neo-managerial regimes of power founded on the idea of 'empowerment' in particular, produce socially the possibility for resourceful people to defy the systems by which they have been groomed and trained. We follow Vallas (2006) by confirming that the culture of institutionalized dialogue entailed in post-bureaucratic work systems, the discourse of subversion spread out by certain management gurus, the emergence of less controllable networks of peers enabled by new technologies, and periodically sustained by corporate investments in executive education, help the spreading of a culture of contestation amongst the normally most compliant groups of employees. Without necessarily seeing in this type of story the emergence of a new political category of 'managerial activists', we offer an alternative framework to think the incredibly complex interlinkages between power structures and acts of mundane resistance in the contemporary workplace.

REFERENCES

Ackoff, R. L. (1994) *The Democratic Corporation*. New York: Oxford University Press.
Ackroyd, S. and P. Thompson (1999) *Organizational Misbehavior*. London: Sage.
Barker, J.R. (1993) 'Tightening the iron cage: Concertive control in self-managing teams', *Administrative Science Quarterly*, 38: 408–437.
Burawoy, M. (1979) *Manufacturing Consent: Changes in the Labor Process Under Monopoly Capitalism*. Chicago, IL: University of Chicago Press.
Butler, J. (1998) *The Psychic Life of Power: Theories in Subjection*. Stanford, CA: Stanford University Press.
Courpasson, D. (2006) *Soft Constraint: Liberal Organizations and Domination*. Liber: Copenhagen Business School Press.
Courpasson, D. and F. Dany (2003) 'Indifference or obedience ? Business firms as democratic hybrids', *Organization Studies*,
Ewick, P. and S. S. Silbey (1992) 'Conformity, contestation, and resistance: An account of legal consciousness', *New England Law Review*, 26: 731–749.
Ewick, P. and S. S. Silbey (2003) 'Narrating social structure: Stories of resistance to legal authority', *American Journal of Sociology*, 108(6): 1328–1372.
Fantasia, R. (1988) *Cultures of Solidarity: Consciousness, Action, and Contemporary American Workers*. Berkeley: University of California Press.
Fleming, P. and G. Sewell (2002) 'Looking for the good soldier, Svejk: Alternative modalities of resistance in the contemporary workplace', *Sociology*, 36(4): 857–873.
Fleming, P. and A. Spicer (2007) *Contesting the Corporation*. Cambridge: Cambridge University Press.
Gaventa, J. (1982) *Power and Powerlessness: Quiescence and Rebellion in an Appalachian Valley*. Urbana: University of Illinois Press.
Hardy, C. and S. Leiba-O'Sullivan (1998) 'The power behind empowerment: Implications for research and practice', *Human Relations*, 51(4): 451–483.
Hecksher, C. and A. Donnellon (eds) (1994) *The Post-bureaucratic Organization: New Perspectives on Organizational Change*. London: Sage.
Hodson, R. (1995) 'Worker resistance: An underdeveloped concept in the sociology of work', *Economic and Industrial Democracy*, 16 :79–110.
Hodson, R. and T. A. Sullivan (1995) *The Social Organization of Work*. Belmont, CA: Wadsworth/Thomson.
Kondo (1990) Crafting Selves: Power, Gender, and Discourses of Identity in a Japanese Workplace.
Laclau, E., and C. Mouffe (1985) *Hegemony and Socialist Strategy*. London: Verso.

Lipset, S. M., M. Trow and J. S. Coleman (1956) *Union Democracy: The Internal Politics of the International Typographical Union*. New York: Free Press.

Marquis, C. and M. Lounsbury (2007) 'Vive la resistance: Competing logics and the consolidation of US community banking', *Academy of Management Journal*, 50 (4): 799–821.

McCann, M. W. and T. March (1995) 'Law and everyday forms of resistance: A socio-political assessment', *Studies in Law, Politics and Society*, 15: 207–236.

McFarland, D. A. (2004) 'Resistance as a social drama: A study of change-oriented encounters', *American Journal of Sociology*, 109(6): 1249–1318.

Osterman, P. (2006) 'Overcoming oligarchy: Culture and agency in social movement organizations', *Administrative Science Quarterly*, 51(4): 622–649.

Rubin, J. W. (1996) 'Defining resistance: Contested interpretations of everyday acts'. In Sarat, A. and S.S. Silbey (eds), *Studies in Law, Politics and Society*. JAI Press, pp. 237–260.

Scott, J. C. (1985) *Weapons of the Weak: Everyday Forms of Peasant Resistance*. New Haven, CT: Yale University Press.

Scott, J. C. (1990) *Domination and the Arts of Resistance: Hidden Transcripts*. New Haven, CT: Yale University Press.

Spicer, A. and S. Böhm (2007) 'Moving management: Theorizing struggles against the hegemony of management', *Organization Studies*, 28(11): 1667–1698.

Swidler, A. (1986) 'Culture in action: Symbols and strategies', *American Sociological Review*, 51: 273–286.

Thomas, R. and A. Davies (2005) 'Theorizing the micro-politics of resistance: New public management and managerial identities in the UK public services', *Organization Studies*, 24(9): 1487–1509.

Vallas, S. P. (2006) 'Empowerment redux: Structure, agency, and the remaking of managerial authority', *American Journal of Sociology*, 111(6): 1677–1717.

Weeks, J. R. (2004) *Unpopular Culture: The Ritual of Complaint in a British Bank*. Chicago: University of Chicago Press.

Zald, M. N. (2005) 'The strange career of a idea and its resurrection: Social movements in organizations', *Journal of Management Inquiry*, 14(2): 157–166.

Zald, M. N. and M. A. Berger (1978) 'Social movements in organizations: Coup d'etat, insurgency, and mass movements', *American Journal of Sociology*, 83: 823–861.

Power and Exclusion

Kevin Ryan

The close of the twentieth century bore witness to a number of impressive proclamations concerning the triumph of liberal democracy, the end of history, and the arrival of a new world order. A brave new world of peace and prosperity was predicted, and yet the social and political problems associated with modernity show little sign of abating. The problems themselves have long been framed by specific normative evaluations and political strategies, such as the imperative to secure and defend what Karl Popper (1966) called the 'Open Society' against its internal and external enemies or, from another perspective, to confront authority in a bid for emancipation, justice and equality. Though both the problems and the normative evaluations endure, questions of social difference and political division have given rise to a new category of thought and action: exclusion. Now pervasive in policy debate and academic research, the concept of exclusion has been stretched over the social so as to encompass the more specific problems of poverty, domination, discrimination, exploitation, solidarity and cohesion, all of which connect up with, in a variety of ways, the question of power. When coupled to exclusion and emplaced within the context of democracy, 'power' has a tendency to invoke dark images of repression and heroic narratives of struggle and resistance. There are of course good reasons why the relationship between power and exclusion can be, and has been, examined in this way. However, in this chapter what I want to do is place exclusion, power, and that particular mode of social organization we call democracy together without first drawing conclusions as to the inherent goodness or badness of what is, as we shall see, a complex relation.

The chapter begins with two statements which take us back to the beginning of the twentieth century, both of which are anchored in the authority (and legitimacy) of science. We will return to these statements in due course and move beyond them to the present. Their initial purpose however is to map the contours of a specific problematic which is the subject of this chapter.

POWER, ORDER AND EXCLUSION: INITIAL REFLECTIONS

In 1901 Francis Galton delivered a lecture to the Anthropological Institute on the topic of 'the possible improvement of the human breed under the existing conditions of law and sentiment'. In this paper Galton argued that 'we cannot doubt the existence of a great power ready to hand and capable of being directed with vast benefit as soon as we shall have learnt to understand and to apply it' (1901: 665). Galton of course was a pioneer in the field of eugenics, which is among the technologies of life that Michel Foucault called 'biopower'. With its strategic aim of modification, and often deploying techniques such as sterilization and sexual segregation, eugenics is a crude example of how biopower seeks to direct the forces, propensities and capacities of a living population (Foucault, 2003: 248–9, 268). A more sophisticated example would be the public and social services provided by the state in the name of security and welfare. Either way, biopower acts upon life and, when Galton wrote this paper, the dominant biopolitical concern was whether and to what extent the historical trajectory of the population – measured as intelligence, vitality, morality – was one of improvement or degeneration. Galton ended his lecture with a flourish, explaining that 'to no nation is a high human breed more necessary than to our own, for we plant our stock all over the world and lay the foundation of the dispositions and capacities of future millions of the human race' (Galton, 1901: 665). Here biopower is pressed into the service of empire and presented as the agent of human progress. It is also a specific mode of exclusion, for the 'we' that Galton writes of – the 'nation' – is placed at the top of a hierarchy with spatial and temporal dimensions, simultaneously homogenizing that which it includes while othering that which it excludes. We will return to this a little later.

Twenty two years after Galton's lecture, another British eugenicist, Cyril Burt, published a paper on 'delinquency and mental defect', in which he argued that 'the foundations of character, it is true, rest upon certain innate tendencies; but character itself is not innate' (Burt, 1923: 170). The question of 'character' has long intrigued liberal thinkers and reformers: is human nature mutable; can the subject of Reason be engineered from the raw materials of life? At the end of the eighteenth century one answer to this question (discussed in more detail below) took the form of a technical innovation which was partly architectural and partly administrative. Jeremy Bentham's panopticon poorhouse (or school, prison, or factory – the model was flexible) was designed to remove indigents from the general population by classifying, segregating, and placing all those who were a burden on society under surveillance and corrective influences (Bentham, 1995). Though never built strictly according to Bentham's specifications, the modality of power he envisioned spirals through the nineteenth century, from the monitorial schools of Andrew Bell and Joseph Lancaster, to Robert Owen's 'institute for the formation of character' at New Lanark, to experiments in preventative and reformatory education. The nineteenth century spawned a carceral net that acted as a sieve upon the general population, with those individuals coded as defective and delinquent subjected to various forms of treatment modelled on panoptic principles of hierarchical observation and normalising judgement (Foucault, 1977). By the early twentieth century the problem of defective character was in the hands of professionals such as Cyril Burt, who would have agreed with Bentham on at least one crucially important point: the subject of a liberal order could indeed be made. Between Bentham and Burt lies the birth and consolidation of a specifically social apparatus which positions the individual to be corrected within a grid of disciplinary powers; and while not without frequent disagreement and dispute, it is still possible to identify a strategic objective that connects the authority of science to the coercive instruments of the state and unites an otherwise heterogeneous field of practitioners and practices: each and all must be trained in 'the art of living' (Glueck, 1925). From this arises the question of what to do with those who cannot or will not be disciplined. The answer is varied at the level of specifics, but at the general level it exhibits a pervasive logic: remove problem individuals from the circuits of association and procreation so that they can be made available for specific types of reformatory and curative intervention. This is a second mode of exclusion: the construction of a margin that bounds order from within.

Two modes of power then: biopower and disciplinary power, which are both connected to the sovereign power of the state and yet neither is equivalent to it. We should note too that Galton and Burt were writing in a context wherein psychology was fighting for recognition, and while the discipline had achieved a certain status at this time it still lacked its place within an order of authorities which was entangled in the state yet more or less outside of the law (Rose, 1985: 112–45). This order of authorities, which includes medicine, education and social work, can be conceptualized, from Foucault, as 'government'. To govern is to deploy a whole range of technologies, programmes, knowledges and calculations, some of which aim to act directly upon the body or the mind of individuals, while others seek to act indirectly upon the capacity for action which conjoins the individual and the social (Foucault, 1991; Rose, 1999; Dean, 1999). It is important to be specific here, to distinguish 'government' and 'power' from images of repression and coercion. In Foucault's own words:

> A man who is chained up and beaten is subject to force being exerted over him, not power. But if he can be induced to speak, when his ultimate recourse could have been to hold his tongue, preferring death, then he has been caused to behave in a certain way. His freedom has been subjected to power. He has been submitted to government (Foucault, 2000: 324)

To be governed is to be free to articulate a certain type of discourse: it is to think, to speak, to act within an order of possibilities and limitations which is also a regime of truth; and this – together with the modes of power and exclusion sketched above – is among the conditions of possibility for Popper's Open Society, which is to say an order both liberal and democratic. In exploring this in more detail I want to bring us back, very briefly, to the end of the feudal era, the purpose of this detour being to trace an outline of recent changes in the arts of government. It is by no means trivial that in the closing decades of the twentieth century the exclusions underpinning the authority of Galton and Burt's statements have been made explicit and contested. I also wish to emphasize that the aim of this chapter is not to describe a series of different types of society but rather to conduct a genealogy of a specific relation. Foucault once characterized this relation as a sovereignty-discipline-government 'triangle' (1991a: 102), and I will use this figure as a signpost in organizing the analysis.

THE PROBLEM OF ORDER: SOVEREIGNTY UNBOUND

In his *Treatise of Orders and Plain Dignities*, first published in 1610, Charles Loyseau considered the estates general of France: those who pray, those who fight, and those who labour (Duby, 1980). As Loyseau reflected upon this tripartite world he noted that 'the most perfect division is into three species', and here lies the crux of the matter, for perfection was to be found in the precise combination of division and hierarchy. What Loyseau looked for in 'the disorderly jumble of the sublunary world' (the phrase is George Duby's) was the essence of worldly perfection: 'in all things there must be order, for the sake of decorum and for their control' (Loyseau, 1994: 5, 118).

Consider the nature of Loyseau's enterprise. Today we might call this 'history', though history as we understand it does not exist at this time. Instead the past is a resource for moral discourse, which in Loyseau's *Treatise* concerns the order of things. We could also say, consistent with the truth of the feudal world, that order was understood as God's will and design, entrusted to his prelates and princes on earth, but, as Zygmunt Bauman has argued, this is already to project the concerns of the present onto the past. In the words of Loyseau we see not a transformation in how the problem of order is understood, but the discovery of order as an object of conscious thought and reflection (Bauman, 1991: 5–6). Loyseau confronted an entirely novel question: order must be made and defended, but in whose name or to what end? The answer which slowly came into focus was 'the State'. This is already evident in the *Treatise*: 'sovereign lords command all those in their state, addressing their commandments to the great, the great to the intermediate, the intermediate to the minor, and minor to the people; and the people, who obey all of these, are again divided into several orders and ranks' (1994: 5). Loyseau modelled the 'well ordered state' on martial principles of discipline and rank, because order necessitated inequality between the 'species of dignity': those who command and those who obey.

The *Treatise* was written in a context wherein sovereign power was becoming 'unbound' (*absoluta*) from the estates of the feudal world, which also rendered political authority highly unstable (Opello and Rosow, 2004: 87). Between Jean Bodin – an older contemporary of Loyseau – and Thomas Hobbes half a century later, the concept of sovereignty was elaborated as absolute and indivisible power, and yet it was also split between existing theological and emerging rationalist justifications: between the doctrine of divine right and the notion of a 'common power' derived from the sovereign's subjects (Hobbes, 1996). The source of sovereign power was thus both external to the body that wielded it (monarch or assembly) and centred in the body politic, and within the space of this division emerged a rationality of rule that was neither equivalent to the personage of the prince nor the doctrine of a divinely ordained order. With its root in the writings of Machiavelli this would be known as reason of state (*raison d'état*), a mode of rule concerned explicitly with the 'things' that Loyseau sought to order and control (see Dean, 1999; Foucault, 1991a; Meinecke, 1957). Foucault noted that the metaphor of the ship looms large in this literature, which he distilled in the following passage:

> What does it mean to govern a ship? It means clearly to take charge of the sailors, but also the boat and its cargo...it consists in that activity of establishing a relation between the sailors who are to be taken care of and the ship which is to be taken care of, and the cargo which is to be brought safely to port, and all those eventualities like winds, rocks, storms and so on (Foucault, 1991a: 94).

Deferring neither to the wisdom of God nor to the strategies of the prince, reason of state is government by reason alone, and it combines the art of self-government (morality), the art of governing a family (economy), and the art of governing a state (politics): an order of three nested domains which gradually displaced the feudal world of three orders. The aim of government was to bolster the state: to augment its strength and foster its greatness by holding out and protecting itself against competition with other states. Yet enduring and standing fast would not be enough, for it was imperative that the state grew in strength and stature, which was only possible if its strength could be known. To this end the arts of government would gradually harness the techniques of statistics and political arithmetic and bring them to bear on 'life'. This concern with the government of life, or population, would become the target of specific disciplinary and pastoral powers (Foucault, 2000: 298–325).

Europe at this time was rife with religious wars and confessional civil wars, with armies often recruited from mercenaries without fixed political allegiance. It was in this context that the disciplinary society envisaged by Loyseau began to emerge, with territorial states raising large standing armies. Techniques of drill and regiment – rediscovered from the Roman Legions – moulded individuals into a corporate body directed to specific ends, which, as it transpired, could be applied equally well to the organisation of bodies in asylums, factories and schools. The soldier became an interchangeable cog in a disciplinary machine: part of a uniform surface upon which was inscribed the signs of the state's power and legitimacy (Opello and Rosow, 2004: 58–60; Foucault, 1977).

At the same time, in securing the internal order of the state, various authorities issued 'police' ordinances (Dean, 1999: 88–90). As an art of government, police (*Polizeiwissenschaft*) aimed to regulate all the disorders, agitations and disobediences that had gone unregulated in the feudal world, so that 'by means of a wise police, the sovereign accustoms the people to order and obedience' (Vattel, 1768, cited in Foucault, 1977: 215). Police was a condition to be achieved, with the meaning of 'good police' synonymous with the 'happiness' and 'good order of a community' (Small, 1909: 317, 442; Pasquino, 1991: 109–10; Oestreich, 1982). The organization of the state was to mirror the household economy so that, in providing for the welfare of each and all (*omnes et singulatim*), the state would exercise a form of surveillance and control over the population as encompassing as that which the head of the household exercised over his family and his goods (Foucault, 1991a: 92).

Here the sovereignty-discipline-government triangle becomes manifest. The government of a state combines disciplinary and pastoral powers, the twin ends of which are to ensure the strength and security of the state and secure the happiness and prosperity of the population. By the end of the eighteenth century the tension between these objectives had become acute, in no small part because the contested notion of sovereignty cut right through them. With a nod to Rousseau and natural rights theorists such as Locke, Jacques Donzelot characterizes the problem as follows: 'if the state is the embodiment of the general will, the active synthesis of individual sovereignties and powers, there is nothing left to oppose it, and nothing can contest it'; however, 'if right resides solely in the individual, the individual can always repudiate and paralyse the intervention of the state' (1991: 171). This is what Donzelot calls the 'infernal circle of the metaphysics of sovereignty'.

It is also here that a point of disagreement appears in the literature. Certainly Foucault is correct in identifying the relation between government and population. However Mitchell Dean's meticulous research suggests the need to distinguish between pre- and post-Malthusian conceptions of population (Dean, 1991). In the pre-Malthusian world 'population' is an index of the wealth and strength of the state, 'police' is an ideal to be sought by government, 'economy' is the art of household management, and 'family' is contiguous with political authority. At the end of the eighteenth century all of these were recast: no longer the sum of inhabitants within a territory, population became 'a reality *sui generis* with its own forces and tendencies'; police a force deployed by the state in defence of domestic security; economy a quasi-autonomous reality subject to its own laws and regularities, and family a private realm external to government (Dean, 1999: 95–6; cf. Elias, 1978: 40–5). Faced with the task of governing these forces, tendencies and limits, the post-Malthusian world discovered an ineliminable gap between population and subsistence, an essential scarcity which redefined the relation between state and economy. The 'social question' would arise within the space of this fracture, giving discursive form to what is without doubt the central and enduring problem of government: how to govern the relation between each and all.

LIBERAL ORDER: SOVEREIGNTY DIVIDED

In the world of three orders and in the order of three domains, sovereign power – the power of the sword (and later the cannon and musket) – was essentially negative and deductive: the power to take life or let live; the power to enforce submission to duties of labour; the power to subtract taxes and tolls; the power to demand blood as a sign of loyalty in times of war or as punishment for crimes committed (Foucault, 2003: 240–1; Dean, 1999: 105). Yet already in the arts of government we see this negative power supplemented by a positive mode of power, a power that aims to strengthen life and foster the conditions of life. This would become a specifically liberal mode of government, which seeks to act upon action, or 'structure the possible field of action of others' (Foucault, 1983: 220–22, also Rose and Miller, 1992). During the nineteenth century sovereignty was reformulated and slowly democratized as the rights of the legal and political subject of rule were elaborated. Yet this subject was both the individual and the nation, ensuring that the tension within the sovereignty-government-discipline triangle – Donzelot's 'infernal circle' – would endure.

Liberal government and the social question

Earlier I mentioned Bentham's panopticon: an administrative machine designed to create the subject of a utilitarian order. The machine was never built according to Bentham's specifications, yet certain elements of his design did find their way into an important legal and administrative innovation in the United Kingdom in the early decades of the nineteenth century: the Poor Law Amendment Act of 1834. I want to use this as a starting point in examining how law and science combined to institute the powers of liberal order. Driven in part by a Malthusian-inspired discourse calling for total abolition of public assistance, the Act of 1834 did not abolish so much as reorganize the provision of poor relief on the basis of a distinction between poverty and pauperism (Dean, 1991; Poynter, 1969; Polanyi, 2001). It was Bentham who had formulated this distinction, reasoning that poverty was the source of productive labour and the motor of progress, unlike indigence (pauperism), which was a fetter on both (Bentham 2001: 3). It was also Bentham who designed the mechanism that would become the state-administered 'workhouse test' or 'less eligibility principle', intended to render conditions inside the workhouse less eligible (desirable) than any form of paid employment outside (Bentham 2001: 39; Checkland and Checkland, 1974: 334–5). The logic of this was that the poor would govern themselves in accordance with the utilitarian calculus of pleasure and pain. In other words, the able-bodied poor would volunteer to enter the workhouse only if this increased their happiness and reduced their suffering. If they could support themselves through their own labour then they would feel compelled, by reason, to do so. Here discipline takes the form of a precision tool: a mode of administration which facilitates the creation of a national labour market (Dean, 1991). The Act of 1834 limited the scope of sovereign intervention by acting upon the rational and voluntary decisions of free individuals. Leaving the economy untouched, public assistance was organized in such a way that it was deliberately punitive, yet it would not be forced upon the pauper. However, not all people were able or willing to conform to this ideal of the self-governing subject, and here we can locate the illiberal exception within Bentham's design for a liberal order. Bentham noted that beggars set a bad example to the industrious poor and caused pain on the part of the charitable, thus depressing the quantity of happiness in society. His proffered solution was to apprehend beggars and subject them to the discipline of labour within the workhouse. Furthermore, he enlarged this class so that it included 'insolvent fathers, chargeable bastards, and disreputable mothers' (Bentham, 1843: 8: 404). It must be noted that this illiberal exception is not just consistent with liberal government, it is also necessary. This is because the problem of beggary, or in legal terms, vagabondage, is quite specific.

Drawing together legal definitions and socio-political significance, the pauper and the vagabond can be conceptualized as two sides of a single problem, the meaning of which is split between forms of conduct deemed to be either too dependent (and thus insufficiently free) or too free (and thus insufficiently constrained). The two sides of this problem do not carry equal weight however, for liberal self-government operates between the rule of a law which is enforced by the state and the laws of the market which define the limits of legitimate government, and pauperism – unlike vagabondage – renders this relation governable. While it includes those unable to labour because of sickness or infirmity (those who qualify as 'deserving' of public assistance), the question of pauperism is essentially one of surplus labour, which is manageable, because the surplus can be absorbed either by the workhouse or by the labour market. Either way the figure of the pauper can be fixed in social space. The vagabond however represents unconstrained mobility, and this threatens to subvert the very possibility of a liberal order. It is for this reason that Bentham deemed it necessary to apprehend those who sought alternatives both to the disciplinary design of the workhouse and the disciplinary effects of the labour market (see Ryan, 2007).

As it turned out it was not only the public authorities that sought ways of governing those who are both more and less than surplus labour. The mixed workhouse created by the Act of 1834 quickly became the symbol of 'contagion', exposing innocent children, the deserving poor, and impressionable young women to debilitating and demoralizing influences. Philanthropists, social inquirers and statistical societies (as well as religious orders, though I will not deal with this dimension here) all staked a claim in this problem by designing novel approaches to the government of the 'dangerous and perishing classes' (Carpenter, 1968), among them ragged schools, industrial schools, reformatory schools, refuges for 'fallen' women and home visiting associations. Organized under the banner of social economy (Procacci, 1991), this heterogeneous field of innovation and intervention fused the pastoral ethos of Christianity with a new scientific paradigm of social inquiry. Located between state and market, this marks the constitution of 'society'.

The 'social question' as it would later be called brought the powers of liberal order – sovereign, disciplinary, bio – into alignment, though it would remain an unstable relation, riddled with disagreement, conflict and struggle (Ryan, 2007). The social is also where the liberal axiom of self-government meets with external constraints, which in turn is how liberal order expands by excluding those judged unfit to be free (Valverde, 1996: 360). As noted above, the primary symbols of disorder at this time were the pauper and the vagabond. Pauperism could be governed by the rational calculation of pleasure and pain (the workhouse test), while vagabondage threatened to render the liberal mode of administration ineffective by seeking out alternatives to both public assistance and wage labour. A deficiency of independence on the one hand, and an excess on the other: between pauperism and vagabondage was everything that threatened to subvert liberal order, but this also made such an order possible. Here we might note Bentham's concern with 'improvement', meaning the perfectibility of knowledge and the reformation of morals (Bentham, 1988), for the birth of liberal order was in part made possible through the discovery of a distinctly linear conception of history which was to have an important bearing on how the relation between power and exclusion was configured.

The limits of liberal order

In his essay on *The Subjection of Women* published in 1869, J.S. Mill addressed the inequalities experienced by women by arguing that 'between subjection to the will of others, and the virtues of self-help and self-government, there is a natural incompatibility' (1991: 253). Compare this with his earlier work on *Representative Government*, where Mill considered the case of people who lack the 'spring of spontaneous improvement'. If such people were to 'advance', then it was necessary that they be governed by a 'good despot' who would train them 'in what is specifically wanting to render them capable of a higher civilisation' (1991: 453–4). Or again, in the introduction to his *On Liberty*, Mill noted that the doctrine of liberty had definite limits:

> We are not speaking of children, or of young persons below the age of which the law may fix as that of manhood or womanhood. Those who are still in a state to require being taken care of by others, must be protected against their actions as against external injury. For the same reasons, we may leave out of consideration those backward states of society in which the race itself may be considered as in its nonage...Despotism is a legitimate mode or government in dealing with barbarians, provided the end be their improvement, and the means justified by actually effecting that end' (Mill, 1991: 14–15).

Mill challenged the exclusion of *some* women: those in the same stage of 'improvement' as the men of 'civilised society'. Other women, as with other men, inhabit the world in its primitive or child-like state, which is to say that they are analogous to the children of a civilized order. Neither is (yet) capable of self-government.

What exactly should we make of this well known exception at the heart of Mill's liberalism? Mariana Valverde argues that 'advocating despotism for most of the world peoples was not for Mill a case of making a contingent exception, but was an integral part of the definition of liberty itself' (1996: 360). Liberalism makes universal claims derived from human reason, from natural (or more recently, human) rights, and the equal moral worth of all individuals. Yet this claim to the universal also codifies the exception which legitimizes exclusion. Everything beyond liberal order is an inferior reflection of that order – in a rudimentary stage of evolution or historical development – and in this way people who are perceived to be primitive and infantile are made available to be acted upon in the name of Reason, Civilization and Progress. The power of liberalism's discourse lies in the way it orders social knowledge into truth; a very specific mode of in/exclusion which constitutes and circumscribes the field within which liberal self-government is possible (see Foucault, 1991b: 82; 1980: 131; Laclau and Mouffe, 2001: 111). Because some people are not capable of practising the kind of freedom which accords with a liberal order, or indeed willing to practice it even if they are, so there is an exception to the axiom of incompatibility between subjection and self-government. Some people must be subjected to reformatory influences, and if they are indeed capable of self-government then they will, in time, benefit from the freedoms and autonomy that a liberal order bestows upon its subjects. Freedom may be granted, but it is contingent on the willingness and ability to learn, that is, to comply and conform. However, liberalism manages to disavow its illiberal foundation by projecting difference onto a temporal axis, with the hierarchical difference between civilized and primitive peoples, between progressive and backward cultures structured not by power/knowledge but by historical distance (Jacques, 1997). All people everywhere will eventually be self-governing, but not yet.

As noted by Valverde, Mill's optimism was by no means unusual. This was the post-Enlightenment age of Progress, and while it was occasionally disturbed it remained largely untroubled as it looked to a distant horizon of perfection. In the second half of the nineteenth century however the theme of degeneracy loomed large, which concerned the existence of a 'residuum' or residual population of paupers, vagabonds, prostitutes, delinquents and defectives: all those deemed unfit to compete in the struggle for existence. Anchored in discourses of race and fitness and a context marked by national rivalry, this saw the basis of normative judgements transformed, so that what had previously been a question of morality now became a matter of pathology and social defence. And the key concept was heredity (Stedman Jones, 1971; Rose, 1985; Foucault, 1998: 118–19).

In terms of practical effects, the theory (or rather theories) of degeneracy made a crease in Mill's discourse and enlarged its scope, folding it back onto the domestic population and opening out a space for the development of programmes to detect the primitive and the infantile within. Liberalism's 'outside' began to encircle the behaviours, dispositions and relations that were seen to pose a threat to liberal order from the 'inside'. Arranged around a normative centre – 'autonomy', 'civilization', 'progress' – the questions and problems squeezed through the grid of power/knowledge and consigned to the margins of order become the focus of programmes concerned with examining, curing, training and reforming. Defined in the negative, the margin gives symbolic form to what is perceived to be lacking, to what is desired, and what it is that 'society' wills to know, to experience and to accomplish, and in this way the negative residuum is given a positive function in the orders of discourse: pauperism is both a state of dependency on the part of the individual and a social burden that threatens the productive life and wealth of the nation; vagabondage is a state of excessive liberty and mobility which threatens the safety and security of society; unmarried motherhood is the consequence of an act which undermines 'morality' and is coded in various contexts as a sin or a symptom of mental deficiency; juvenile delinquency and mental defectiveness together define the limits of what can be accomplished through education and vocational training. All of these signs and symptoms are, to paraphrase Foucault, an incitement to discourse, and all articulate a strategic objective: what Galton, in the quote above, called 'the possible improvement of the human breed. As a mode of exclusion that bounds order from within, the margin gives discursive form and substance to the quest for ordered perfection.

Exercised over children and child-like adults – or in the words of Mill, those who lack the spring of spontaneous improvement, those who must be taken care of by others, and those who must be protected against their own actions – despotism is a legitimate mode of government provided it is exercised for the improvement of the individual and the improvement of society. Individual progress and social progress must somehow coincide, which for Mill is 'the ideal perfection of utilitarian morality' (1991: 148). The prison is reserved for those who have breached the law and must be subject to the rigour and letter of the law. Far more encompassing – far more productive – are those interventions born from social economy that look for petty departures from the norm and operate under the auspices of care and cure, education and training.

Power and exclusion between law and norm

Within the sovereignty-discipline-government triangle is constituted something which connects the social disciplines directed at individual minds and bodies to the biopolitical regulation of the social body: the norm (Foucault, 2003: 252–3). Unlike the rule of law, which is codified and constrained insofar as it is reserved for those who breach the code, the norm derives its authority and legitimacy from scientific measurement and claims to objectivity. Distilled from a body of living persons as they are examined, aggregated and arranged along a distribution (and the growth of statistics and social mapping would establish specific ways of enumerating and visualising the practice, see Hacking, 1990; Joyce, 2003), this is at once the realm of the 'normal' and the basis of normalizing practices. Some persons exceed the range of the normal, others fall short of it, but once the distribution has been constructed then no individual corresponds exactly to the standard of 'average man' (Quetelet, 1848). Again, to contrast this with the rule of law, then we can note that law presides over, judges, and acts in the name of justice by taking property or liberty from those who transgress its rule (Foucault, 1998: 144). With the nineteenth century came a trend which Foucault called a 'phase of juridical regression', which is not to say that the law was supplanted so much as incorporated into a disciplinary continuum, from the prison to the workhouse, factory, asylum, hospital, school and family. Invested with concrete disciplinary and regulative powers, the normal implements the panoptic principles of examination, hierarchical observation, and normalising judgement, together 'manifesting the subjection of those who are perceived as objects and the objectification of those who are subjected' (Foucault, 1977: 184–5).

Liberal order deploys law and norm in dividing the population and excluding certain people from the status of the autonomous and rational individual (Dean, 1999: 132). For Bentham this was the stock of idle and defective 'hands'; for Mill it was those who existed in a state of 'nonage'; and at the end of the nineteenth century it was the 'residuum' or bottom tenth of the population that threatened to pull society into a downward spiral of regressive evolution (Booth, 1969; Booth, 1890). Excluded are those who define 'reason' through their insanity, those who define 'independence' through their pauperism, and those who define 'morality' through their criminality, licentiousness, intemperance and delinquency; but there is also another dimension to this grid of divisions: the responsible use of freedom requires appetites, impulses and drives to be mastered, and by tutoring its subject in the arts of civility, manners and self-restraint, liberal order divides the individual against his or her self (Foucault, 1983: 208; Elias, 1978).

Unlike the subject of liberal*ism* (i.e. a political ideology or philosophy), the subject of liberal order is made within a tapestry of disciplinary and biopolitical powers: medicine, psychiatry, education, social work, charity, child rescue – all converge on the individual body and the social body as a single strategic aim: self-government. Liberal order is in fact an order of authorities and powers (plural) which is modelled on the 'good despot'. Alert for defective minds, deficient bodies, malformed character, for dangerous dispositions, pathological desires and forms of biological and moral contagion that might corrupt the individual and degrade the 'national livestock' (Bentham's phrase), the objects of this normalizing gaze present a tricky question: what should be done? Defective stock can be left to its own devices in the hope that it will eventually die out. It can be plucked from the social body and placed in special holding pens, sexually segregated so that the risk of procreation is removed. There is the discredited option of extermination, either through selective sterilization or else on a much larger, industrial scale. Or another option: it can be classified into distinct groups, each a specific class of abnormal body or mind to be subjected to treatment and training. The strategies are not mutually exclusive and they share two things: firstly the combination of sovereign power, disciplinary power and biopower, and secondly the quest for order (Bauman, 1991; Foucault, 2003: 258–63; see also Broberg and Roll-Hansen, 1996; Castel, Castel and Lovell, 1982; Rafter, 1988). At this point we return to the statements of Galton and Burt: the interrelated themes of a great power to be directed and a subject to be made, which warrants a few words on the relation between liberal government and social government.

To begin, we could take the case of England and ask why Eugenics ran into a cul-de-sac well before the science was discredited by the Holocaust. Could it have something to do with context: the liberal order of individual freedoms and rights was simply incompatible with the negative imperative of eugenics? The evidence fails to support this, for eugenic practices were instituted in England, such as the use of the Mental Deficiency Act to control female sexuality (Walmsley, 2000). The answer lies less in the failure of a single eugenic strategy than a struggle between competing strategies. Eugenics shares something with the sovereign power that characterized the world of three orders and the order of three domains: it is negative and deductive, seeking to subtract the pathological from the normal, and in this way it leaves the 'normal' untouched. Competing with this was what Nikolas Rose calls a 'neo-hygienist strategy', which did not foreclose on the deductive technique of eugenics so much as incorporate it into an apparatus much greater in scope; one that inaugurated social government and crossed from the abnormal to the normal, encompassing the family and the child *as such* (Rose, 1985: 112–45). Connecting the family to the school to the clinic to the legal and administrative functions of the state, this was less a coercive intervention than a type of pedagogy which placed the family under a specific form of tutelage, the strategic aim of which was to convert social norms into subjective desires (also Donzelot, 1979). Here disciplinary power and biopower are more or less fused within the institutional apparatus of the state, with the social state of welfare and security a direct outgrowth of this particular articulation of pastoral power and sovereign power.

Notwithstanding differences between welfare regimes (Esping-Anderson, 1990), it is nonetheless possible to speak of a generic social state in the way that risk was socialized during the twentieth century, with social rights bolstering the status of citizenship and offsetting the inequalities created by a market economy (Marshall, 1992); and yet the central problem of government – how to govern the relation between each and all – endured, as did the modes of exclusion. More recently the social state has been undermined by structural dislocations and challenged by a variety of political forces, some championing the free market, some attacking the 'nanny' state, and others exposing the technologies of cure and care as forms of domination. Add to this the disastrous long-term effects of industrialization, which now cloud the future, then it is perhaps unsurprising that the post-Enlightenment themes of progress and perfection have all but vanished. In the remainder of this chapter I want to look not at the detail of this transformative process but at its effects, and in particular the emergence of what may be a new, or at the very least modified, mentality of government. Nikolas Rose calls this 'advanced' liberalism.

ADVANCED LIBERAL ORDER

One noticeable effect is the way that exclusion has become the explicit focus of political thought and action. In fact it is more correct to speak of inclusion rather than exclusion, for a whole arsenal of programmes and strategies have been mobilized in the name of social inclusion. Encoded in the language of empowerment, the inclusive society bypasses that unified field of objects and relations we have come to know as 'society' and deploys strategies which attempt to govern social problems through the autonomous decisions of individuals and various types of community (Rose, 1996, 1999). As with the subject of classical liberal government, the subject of advanced liberal order is positioned within a conjunction, or 'weave', of disciplinary and regulatory powers, but this is now orchestrated through novel technologies of life. On the one hand the body (individual and social) continues to be disciplined, regulated and administered through practices such as education and medicine. On the other hand, autonomy is increasingly acted upon by recording, monitoring and measuring the performance of decision-making actors and entities, the strategic objective of which is to promote a specific, disciplined and responsible mode of autonomy; and the recording, monitoring and measuring may be done by agencies which are part state, part market and part civil society. All of this has followed from, even as it augments, the trend in decarceration which characterized the closing decades of the twentieth century, and we will consider this in due course. First I want to sketch the broad contours of advanced liberal order.

Performance and auditing: the control of control

It might be wise to begin with a word of caution on terminology. As with 'progress' and 'development', the word 'advanced' (i.e. advanced liberalism) seems fatally infused with normative connotations. It is not used here to suggest something which is better or more complete, but to indicate a combination of continuity and change in the arts of liberal government. For reasons of brevity it will also be necessary to gloss contextual differences, although I will at times refer specifically to the USA and the UK.

Perhaps the first, and most general, trend to note is the widespread emergence of the enterprise state, with business practices identified as the model for public sector reform (Osborne and Gaebler, 1992; Verheijen and Coomes, 1998). In the bid to bolster the legitimacy of the state, the old bureaucratic model of organization has, to a greater or lesser extent, been remodelled in the image of competitive markets. At the same time, the offices responsible for the management and provision of public services are subject to ever greater scrutiny, with transparency, accountability, and value for money becoming the watchwords of public management (Power, 1997: 44; Rose, 1999: 147). One of the ways of engineering accountability – in fact the principal way if Michael Power's thesis is correct – is through the technique of audit. Power notes that the audit is both an idea and a practice, on the one hand applied, in the practical sense, to a whole variety of organizational contexts, and on the other providing a normative response to 'demands and aspirations for accountability and control' (1997: 6). It is through the combination of these practical and normative dimensions that the technology of audit has the capacity to shape our understanding of the problems for which it is posed as the solution (Power, 1997: 7).

The audit prises open what Rose calls the old 'enclaves of power' – public agencies and private professions such as teaching and medicine – so that authority becomes a measurable and contestable relation, with auditable standards of performance the means and the measure of legitimacy. As a general rule against which the organization or agency is assessed, the audit renders performance both visible and verifiable through acts of certification, reporting and comparison (Power, 1997: 125–6). At the other side of this relation are the clients and consumers of public and private goods and services. By participating in the exercise of authority, the newly empowered consumer-citizen is no longer, strictly speaking, subject to it.

Advanced liberal order not only remakes the subject of government, it also recasts the terrain of government, with the unified field long known as 'society' fragmenting into relatively discreet zones and networks. Adopting something of a supervisory role, the state facilitates cooperation between state-funded providers, voluntary agencies and the private sector, acting upon the action of stakeholders as they are organized into partnership and plugged into 'webs of knowledge and circuits of communication' (Rose, 1999: 147; also Torfing, 2005). While there is clearly an empowering dimension to this, it is also a mode of subjectification, with actors and agencies both monitored from central points in relation to standards of performance as well as being required to evaluate, and report on, their own performance (Rose, 1999: 152). In this way the power of decision-making is simultaneously devolved and made visible, which also reconfigures the state by instituting new methods of control which attempt to keep observational practices under observation (Power, 1997: 129; Rose, 1999: 146–7). Taken together, the logic of performance and the technology of audit recalibrate the strategic objectives of disciplinary power and biopower, and it is here that we can see how the problem of governing social exclusion assembles a disciplinary apparatus around questions such as employability and dependency.

T. H. Marshall famously characterized welfare as a social right which filled out the status of citizenship and offset the inequalities created by a market economy (1992). This has changed. It used to be fashionable, at least among social democrats, to refer to welfare as the social wage. Advanced liberalism drops the phrase but enforces the underlying logic by tying public assistance to designated responsibilities and obligations. Welfare must be earned, and the most acceptable – in the sense of officially and socially recognized – way of earning welfare is to take charge of one's own employability (Rose, 1999: 162–4). The problems associated with long-term unemployment, for example those whose skills and credentials have become obsolete, are to be banished in the name of 'active' welfare. The implementation of the idea differs from context to context, but the message is reasonably consistent, and is generally known as workfare: the unemployed must be taught that paid work is the norm, while dependency and passivity are choices which will no longer be tolerated. And if there really are no jobs available, then there is still no justification for idleness, for the experience of unemployment can and should be made to resemble work (Mead, 1993; Torfing, 1999; Bewick, 1997). Even training schemes offering little in the way of remuneration or career prospects can subject participants to the rudiments of a work ethic. There is a trace of the old pauper-vagabond complex in this: the subject may exhibit an excess or deficiency of freedom, and so dispositions and conduct must be somehow engineered, which in the current context means learning to govern one's self as an enterprise (Rose, 1996; O'Malley, 1992). The self-governing subject of the inclusive society anticipates and offsets the risks of lived life, not only by keeping skills and credentials up to date, but also by keeping insurance policies up to date: health insurance, mortgage protection, life assurance, income protection, the list is potentially endless. This is one indication of how the subject of advanced liberal rule is positioned within the sovereignty-government-discipline triangle. We might call this the core of inclusion, but what happens to those who are unable or unwilling to enterprize their self in this way?

The rule of inclusion

There are in fact two dominant strategies. One, most prominent in the USA, is characterized by David Garland as 'mass imprisonment'[1] (Garland, 2001b). Yet even alongside this surge in what Garland calls 'punitive segregation' can be found another strategy, one deploying a range of techniques from contracts and shaming punishments to preventative partnerships. In this section I want to focus on the second strategy, though without entirely losing sight of the first.

Stanley Cohen was among the first to notice that the trend towards decarceration – well established by the 1980s – did not herald the end of social control so much as the emergence of a new inclusionary mode of control: control in the 'community' (1985). Notwithstanding the important fact of the renewed enthusiasm for incarceration, Cohen's analysis has withstood the test of time, with an actuarial mode of crime prevention – or what Cohen called 'the new behaviourism' – rising to prominence in the context of advanced liberal government.

For Garland, this is part of a trend that he calls 'the new criminologies of everyday life' (2001a: 127–31). Characterized by an atheoretical and practical approach to crime, and known by names such as routine activity theory and situational crime prevention, the basic premise is that crime is a normal and commonplace aspect of modern society, and so successful crime-prevention means moving away from a retrospective focus on individual crimes committed, to a prospective calculation of aggregate risks and preventative measures. The new criminologies might focus on strategies to manipulate the social environment so as to reduce opportunities for crime, or on more specific problem-solving strategies which aim to increase the difficulty of committing crime (Clarke, 2000: 99). Either way, as noted by

Jock Young, the aim is to avoid trouble rather than understand it, so that it no longer really matters whether the offender is 'bad or mad' (1999: 66–7). The conceptual framework finds its practical application in new modes of control: in efforts to create unobtrusive situational constraints which, in the words of Garland, 'guide conduct towards lawful outcomes' (2000: 1). At the most general level it involves strategies to dissolve the boundaries between state and civil society, to devolve responsibilities to individuals and communities, and to design situational controls which can be built into the fabric of routine social life. More specifically it entails 'hardening' potential targets (for example by fitting locks to the steering columns of cars), improving 'natural' surveillance (such as neighbourhood watch schemes, or better street lighting in problem housing estates), and deflecting offending from settings in which crime is likely to occur (one tried and tested example is closing streets to stop people cruising for prostitutes). The aim is not to correct conduct or reform character; instead it is about redesigning things and reconfiguring contexts: replacing cash with credit cards, placing closed-circuit television cameras in hot spots and trouble spots, coordinating the closing times of rival pubs and clubs, obliging local authorities to conduct periodic audits of crime, and organizing crime reduction strategies by creating partnerships between public and private agencies (Garland, 2001a). The last of these is codified in England and Wales by the Crime and Disorder Act of 1998, which recruits citizens into crime prevention strategies through the organizational innovation noted above: governing through partnership.

Adam Crawford (2003) identifies something very specific in all of this: the emergence and proliferation of a contractual mode of governance, or 'modes of control that mimic and deploy contracts and agreements in the regulation of deviant conduct and disorderly behaviour'. We tend to associate contracts with voluntary decisions and agreements. However, an individual can also be subjected to a contract as a condition of freedom. Putting this slightly differently, a person can be drawn into the voluntary acceptance of imposed obligations so that she or he enters into a set of constraints (a relation of 'partnership') which narrows the scope of future choices and actions (Crawford, 2003). As a flexible technology to regulate self-regulation, the contractual form structures the boundary conditions within which freedom is exercised, thus reformulating disciplinary power. Discipline takes the form of a transaction, the strategic aim of which is to secure compliance on the part of those who are to be tutored in the arts of self-government.

Contractual governance looms large in the battle against 'anti-social' behaviour, a strange discourse which in some respects is wholly new and in other respects rediscovers the residuum of the nineteenth century (Squires and Stephen, 2005). In some cases the anti-social individual is subjected to the spectacle of shaming punishment, which is also an attempt to reintegrate the offender into the community. In Western Australia for example, graffiti artists have been made to erase their work in front of an audience (Pratt, 2000). A more concrete, and possibly controversial, manifestation of contractual governance is the anti-social behaviour order (ASBO) in the UK, which was introduced under the Crime and Disorder Act of 1998. I will not go into the detail of the ASBO here, suffice to note that it aims to regulate behaviour that has caused or is 'likely' to cause 'harassment, alarm or distress to one or more persons' (Ramsay 2004). The ASBO is customized to fit the precise circumstances of a given anti-social individual, limiting the scope of his or her choice by prohibiting behaviours specified in the order. Critics of the ASBO focus on, among other things, its hybrid nature, which is to say that it is served in a civil court but breaching the ASBO is a criminal offence, and may lead to a custodial sentence (Padfield, 2004; Jones and

Sagar, 2001). It is for this reason the ASBO can be conceptualized as a switching mechanism or transmission point: it attempts to regulate conduct without removing the individual from the space of liberties, yet at the same time it constrains the exercise of freedom, and it does this with a mixture of the carrot and the stick. Surrounded by coercion, the ASBO is a mode of regulated freedom: a technology that can quickly remove the anti-social individual from the zones of inclusion and pass her or him over to the coercive apparatus of sovereign power. An explicitly punitive example of the contractual form, the ASBO marks the edge between inclusion and exclusion.

Other applications of the contract are less punitive, an example (again from the UK) being the Acceptable Behaviour Contract (ABC). The ABC is a voluntary written agreement whereby the anti-social individual takes responsibility for his or her actions and enters into a partnership with local authorities, such as the police, housing and school authorities. Less punitive again is the automatic referral order provisioned for under the Youth Justice and Criminal Evidence Act 1999, which covers all 10–17-year-old offenders who plead guilty on a first offence. Here the individual is subjected to principles of restorative justice – restoration, reintegration, and responsibility – with the contract organising the offender, victim, family and members of the wider community into a forum wherein the crime and its consequences are discussed (Crawford, 2003). At the same time, a supervisory panel monitors compliance with the terms of the contract.

Mirroring the way that government seems to have abandoned the project of 'society', contractual governance discards the fiction of the social contract as the basis of order, with citizenship itself fragmenting into zones and circuits of inclusion, each with tentative and revocable rights of membership (Crawford, 2003: 499–500, also von Hirsch and Shearing, 2000: 85). Consider the subject of the ASBO, the subject of the ABC, and the subject of the youth referral order. All are positioned within what Adam Crawford calls a 'parochial mode of control', yet each is configured differently with respect to governing authorities, freedoms and constraints, rights and obligations.

In a context marked by the intersection of value pluralism, the apparent failure of big government, and a proliferation of demands for greater autonomy, advanced liberal government acts upon freedom indirectly by intensifying and directing the 'forces that bind individuals into…groupings and relations' (Rose, 2000: 1398–9). Such forces can be specified as shame, responsibility, obligation, trust, but these only become governmentalized – being both a mentality and a technology – when they are organized and programmed into the texture of social relations. In other words they have to be embodied and enacted by the subject of rule. At the core of advanced liberal order are those subjects capable of and willing to practice a type of autonomy which is both disciplined and responsible. At the margin are those less willing and/or less capable. Whether they are to be empowered or disciplined, these are the subjects who are subjected to the rule of inclusion; and if they breach this code, then they can be sequestered within the walls of the penitentiary.

CONCLUDING REFLECTIONS

Drawing on the governmentality literature, I have attempted to show how a specific type of (liberal democratic) order was assembled through a blend of pastoral and disciplinary powers. To conclude, I would like to consider the question of whether or not advanced liberalism enlarges or diminishes the scope of sovereign power. In contrast to the perfectionist impulse of classical liberal government and post-war social government, advanced liberal order shifts to a strategy of management, which recalibrates the relation between power, order and exclusion. While those people coded as criminal and dangerous are still excluded from the circuits of freedom in the name of safety and security, government aims to recruit the 'marginalized', the 'disadvantaged', and those at 'risk' of exclusion into the task of governing their self. It is in this context that we find the power of contract at work, which brings those who are unable or unwilling to practice responsible autonomy under specific forms of surveillance and tutelage, teaching them how to comply with the rule of inclusion. Acting upon technologies of control are the actuarial logic of performance, the organizational power of partnership, and the regulatory power of auditing and accounting. Performance, partnership, audit, and contract together secure order. In the wings, now as in the past, is the penal sanction, or the power to exclude. Sovereign power certainly retains its place in the triangle of sovereignty-government-discipline, yet this complex relation is being remodelled as a whole, which also reassembles the subject of rule. In other words, and to mix metaphors, understanding power and exclusion today requires the triangle of powers to be examined in the round rather than focusing on one of its points.

NOTE

1 At the time of publishing his *Mass Imprisonment*, Garland was predicting a total inmate population of 2 million (in jails and prisons) in the USA by the end of 2001.

REFERENCES

Bauman, Zygmunt (1991) *Modernity and Ambivalence*. New York: Cornell University Press.
Bentham, Jeremy (2001) *Writings on the Poor Law: The Collected Works of Jeremy Bentham Volume I*. Michael Quinn (ed.), Oxford: Clarendon Press.
Bentham, Jeremy (1995) [1787] *Jeremy Bentham: The Panopticon Writings*. Miran Božoviè (ed.), London and New York: Verso.
Bentham, Jeremy (1988) [1776] *A Fragment on Government*. Cambridge: Cambridge University Press.
Bentham, Jeremy (1843) *Works: Volume 8*. edited by J. Bowring. Edinburgh: William Tait.
Bewick, Tom (1997) 'The poverty of US welfare reform: Lessons from California', *Working Brief*: August/September: 21–26.
Booth, Charles (1969) *Charles Booth's London: A Portrait of the Poor at the Turn of the Century Drawn from His 'Life and Labour of the People of London'*. Albert Fried and Richard M. Elman (eds). London: Hutchinson.
Booth, General William (1890) *In Darkest England and the Way Out*. London: William Burgess Carlyle Press.
Broberg, Gunnar and Nils Roll-Hansen (eds) (1996) *Eugenics and the Welfare State: Sterilisation Policy in Denmark, Sweden, Norway, and Finland*. Michigan: Michigan University Press.
Burt, Cyril (1923) 'Delinquency and mental defect (II)', *British Journal of Medical Psychology*, 3: 168–78.
Carpenter, Mary (1968) [1851] *Reformatory Schools for the Children of the Perishing and Dangerous Classes and for Young Offenders*. London: Woburn.
Castel, Robert, Françoise Castel and Anne Lovell, (1982) [1979] *The Psychiatric Society*. New York: Columbia University Press.
Checkland, S. G. and E. O. Checkland (eds) (1974) *The Poor Law Report of 1834*. Harmondsworth: Penguin.
Clarke, Ronald V. (2000) 'Situational crime prevention, criminology and social values', in A. von Hirsch, D. Garland and A. Wakefield (ed.), *Ethical and Social Perspectives on Situational Crime Prevention*. Oxford and Portland, Oregon: Hart.
Cohen, Stanley (1985) *Visions of Social Control*. Cambridge: Polity.

Crawford, Adam (2003) "'Contractual governance" of deviant behaviour', *Journal of Law and Society*, 30: 4: December: 479–505.
Dean, Mitchell (1999) *Governmentality: Power and Rule in Modern Society*. London: Sage.
Dean, Mitchell (1991) *The Constitution of Poverty: Toward a Genealogy of Liberal Governance*. London and New York: Routledge.
Donzelot, Jacques (1979) [1977] *The Policing of Families*. Baltimore and London: John Hopkins University Press.
Donzelot, Jacques (1991) 'The mobilisation of society', in G. Burchell, C. Gordon and P. Miller (eds). *The Foucault Effect: Studies in Governmentality*. Hertfordshire: Harvester Wheatsheaf.
Duby, Georges (1980) *The Three Orders: Feudal Society Imagined*. Chicago: University of Chicago Press.
Elias, Norbert (1978) *The Civilising Process: the Development of Manners*. New York: Urizen.
Esping-Anderson, Gøsta (1990) *The Three Worlds of Welfare Capitalism*. Cambridge: Polity.
Feeley, Malcolm and Jonathan Simon (1994) 'Actuarial Justice: The emerging new criminal law', in David Nelken (eds), *The Future of Criminology*. London: Sage.
Feeley, Malcolm and Jonathan Simon (1992) 'The new penology: Notes on the emerging strategy of corrections and its implications', *Criminology*, 30: 4: 449–74.
Foucault, Michel (2003) *Society Must be Defended: Lectures at the Collège de France 1975–1976*, New York: Picador.
Foucault, Michel (2000) [1994] *Power: The Essential Works of Foucault 1954–1984 Volume III*, James D. Faubion (eds). New York: The New Press.
Foucault, Michel (1998) [1976] *The History of Sexuality Volume One: The Will to Knowledge*. London: Penguin.
Foucault, Michel (1991a) 'Governmentality', in G. Burchell, C. Gordon and P. Miller (eds), *The Foucault Effect: Studies in Governmentality*. Hertfordshire: Harvester Wheatsheaf.
Foucault, Michel (1991b) 'Questions of method', in G. Burchell, C. Gordon and P. Miller (eds), *The Foucault Effect: Studies in Governmentality*. Hertfordshire: Harvester Wheatsheaf.
Foucault, Michel (1983) 'The subject and power', in Hubert L. Dreyfus and Paul Rabinow (eds), *Michel Foucault: Beyond Structuralism and Hermeneutics*, Second Edition. Chicago: University of Chicago Press.
Foucault, Michel (1980) *Power/Knowledge: Selected Interviews and Other Writings 1972–1977*, Colin Gordon (ed.). New York: Pantheon.
Foucault, Michel (1977) [1975] *Discipline and Punish*. London: Penguin.
Galton, Frances (1901) "The possible Improvement of the human breed under the existing conditions of law and sentiment", The Second Huxley Lecture of the Anthropological Institute', *Nature*, 64: 1670: 659–65.
Garland, David (2001a) *The Culture of Control*. Oxford: Oxford University Press.
Garland, David (Ed) (2001b) *Mass Imprisonment: Social Causes and Consequences*. London: Sage.
Garland, David (2000) 'Ideas, institutions and situational crime prevention', in A. von Hirsch, D. Garland and A. Wakefield (eds), *Ethical and Social Perspectives on Situational Crime Prevention*. Oxford and Portland, Oregon: Hart.
Glueck, Bernard (1925) 'The significance of mental hygiene in child guidance', *Annals of the American Academy of Political and Social Science*, 121: 53–56.
Hacking, Ian (1990) *The Taming of Chance*. Cambridge: Cambridge University Press.
Hobbes, Thomas (1996) [1651] *Leviathan*. Cambridge: Cambridge University Press.
Jacques, Carlos T. (1997) 'From savages and barbarians to primitives: Africa, social typologies, and history in eighteenth-century French philosophy', *History and Theory*, 36: 2 May: 190–215.
Jones, Helen and Tracy Sagar (2001) 'Crime and Disorder Act 1998: Prostitution and the Anti-social Behaviour Order', *Criminal Law Review*, November: 873–85.
Joyce, Patrick (2003) *The Rule of Freedom*. London and New York: Verso.
Laclau, Ernesto and Chantal Mouffe (2001) *Hegemony and Socialist Strategy, Towards a Radical Democratic Politics*, 2nd edn. London: Verso.
Levitas, Ruth (1996) 'The concept of social exclusion and the new durkheimian hegemony', *Critical Social Policy*, 46; 16: 5–20.
Loyseau, Charles (1994) [1610] *A Treatise of Orders and Plain Dignities*, Howell A. Lloyd (eds), Cambridge Texts in the History of Political Thought. Cambridge: Cambridge University Press.
Marshall, T. H. (1992) [1950] *Citizenship and Social Class*. London: Pluto.
Mead, Lawrence M. (1993) 'The logic of workfare: The underclass and work policy', in W. J. Wilson (ed.), *The Ghetto Underclass*. London: Sage.

Meinecke, Friedrich (1957) *Machiavellism: The Doctrine of Raison D'Etat and its Place in Modern History*. New Haven: Yale University Press.
Mill, John Stuart (1991) *On Liberty and Other Essays*. Oxford: Oxford University Press.
O'Malley, Pat (1992) 'Risk, power and crime prevention', *Economy and Society*, 21; 3 August: 252–75.
Opello, Walter C. and Stephen J. Rosow (2004) *The Nation-state and Global Order*. London: Lynne Reinner.
Oestreich, Gerhard (1982) *Neostoicism and the Early Modern State*. Cambridge: Cambridge University Press.
Osborne, David and Thomas Gaebler (1992) *Reinventing Government: How the Entrepreneurial Spirit is Transforming the Public Sector*. Reading Massachusetts: Addison-Wesley.
Padfield, Nicola (2004) 'The Anti-social Behaviour Act 2003: The ultimate nanny-state act?', *Criminal Law Review*, September: 712–27.
Pasquino, Pasquale (1991) 'Theatrum politicum: The genealogy of capital – Police and the state of prosperity', in G. Burchell, C. Gordon and P. Miller (eds), *The Foucault Effect: Studies in Governmentality*. Hertfordshire: Harvester Wheatsheaf.
Polanyi, Karl (2001) [1944] *The Great Transformation*. Boston, MA: Beacon Press.
Popper, Karl (1966) [1945] *The Open Society and its Enemies*, Volume 1, 5th edn. London: Routledge and Kegan Paul.
Power, Michael (1997) *The Audit Society: Rituals of Verification*. Oxford: Oxford University Press.
Poynter, J. R. (1969) *Society and Pauperism: English Ideas on Poor Relief, 1795–1834*. London: Routledge and Keegan Paul.
Pratt, John (2000) 'The return of the wheelbarrow men: Or, the arrival of postmodern penality', *British Journal of Criminology*, 40: 127–45.
Procacci, Giovanna (1991) 'Social economy and the government of poverty', in G. Burchell, C. Gordon and P. Miller (eds), *The Foucault Effect: Studies in Governmentality*. Hertfordshire: Harvester Wheatsheaf.
Quetelet, M. A. (1848) *A Treatise on Man and the Development of his Faculties* (1968 reprint). New York: Burt Franklin.
Rafter, Nicole Hahn (1988) *White Trash: The Eugenic Family Studies 1877 –1919*. Boston: Northeastern University Press.
Ramsay, Peter (2004) 'What is anti-social behaviour?', *Criminal Law Review*, November: 908–25.
Rose, Nikolas (2000) 'Community, citizenship, and the third way', *American Behavioral Scientist*, 43; 9 June/July: 1394–1411.
Rose, Nikolas (1999) *Powers of Freedom*. Cambridge: Cambridge University Press.
Rose, Nikolas (1996) 'The death of the social? Re-figuring the territory of government', *Economy and Society*; 25; 3: 327–356.
Rose, Nikolas (1985) *The Psychological Complex: Psychology, Politics and Society in England, 1869–1939*. London: Routledge and Keegan Paul.
Rose, Nikolas and Peter Miller (1992) 'Political power beyond the state: Problematics of government', *British Journal of Sociology*, 43; 2 June: 173–205.
Ryan, Kevin (2007) *Social Exclusion and the Politics of Order*. Manchester: Manchester University Press.
Small, Albion (1909) *The Cameralists: The Pioneers of Social Polity*. Chicago: University of Chicago Press.
Squires, Peter and Dawn E. Stephen (2005) *Rougher Justice: Anti-social Behaviour and Young People*. Devon: Willan.
Stedman Jones, Gareth (1971) *Outcast London*. Middlesex: Penguin.
Torfing, Jacob (2005) 'The Democratic Anchorage of Governance Networks', *Scandanavian Political Studies*, 28; 3: 195–218.
Torfing, Jacob (1999) 'Workfare, Danish-style', *Centre for the Study of Democracy*, 6; 2 Summer 11–13 (published online at: http://www.wmin.ac.uk/sshl/pdf/CSDB62.pdf).
Valverde, Mariana (1996) ' "Despotism" and Ethical Liberal Governance', *Economy and Society*, 25; 3 August: 357–72.
Verheijen, Tony and David Coomes (eds) (1998) *Innovation in Public Management: Perspectives from East and West Europe*. Cheltenham: Edward Elgar.
von Hirsch, Andrew and Clifford Shearing (2000) 'Exclusion from public space', in A. von Hirsch, D. Garland and A. Wakefield (eds), *Ethical and Social Perspectives on Situational Crime Prevention*. Oxford and Portland, Oregon: Hart.
Walmsley, Jan (2000) 'Woman and the Mental Deficiency Act of 1913: Citizenship, sexuality and regulation', *British Journal of Learning Disabilities*, 28: 65–70.
Young, Jock (1999) *The Exclusive Society: Social Exclusion, Crime and Difference in Late Modernity*. London: Sage.

20

The State and Power

Bob Jessop

The state and state power are hypercomplex and changeable phenomena and no single theory or theoretical perspective can fully capture and explain their structural and strategic dynamic. Moreover, despite recurrent tendencies to reify them as standing outside and above society, the state and political system belong to a broader set of social relations. We cannot adequately describe or explain the state apparatus, state projects, and state power without referring to their differential articulation with this ensemble. A distinctive type of theoretical orientation is called for that can take account not only of the state's historical and institutional specificity as a distinctive accomplishment of social development but also its role as an important element within the overall structure and dynamic of social formations. This chapter advocates a suitable approach, which treats the state in 'strategic-relational' terms; enabling us to explore the nature of state power as the material condensation of a changing balance of political forces. First explicitly proposed by the Greek political theorist, Nicos Poulantzas (1974, 1978), it needed much elaboration. Indeed, the strategic-relational approach (hereafter SRA) in its state-theoretical application could be described as the meta-theoretical, theoretical, and empirically informed process of elaborating the implications of Poulantzas's initial proposition.

WHAT IS THE STATE?

No definition of the state is innocent because, as the SRA implies (Jessop 2007), every attempt to define a complex phenomenon must be selective (for one review of attempts to define it, see Ferguson and Mansbach 1989). Moreover, as Bartelson remarks about attempts to define the state:

> If we accept that the state concept is foundational and constitutive of scientific political discourse, we should not be surprised to find that it cannot easily be subjected to the practices of definition [i.e. making stipulations about its meaning and reference within a given context of employment and according to given criteria], since the term state itself figures as a positive and primitive term in the definitions of other, equally central, concepts. This is what makes clarification both seem so urgent and yet so difficult to achieve. Hence, and as a consequence of its centrality, the concept of the state cannot be fully determined by the character of its semantic components or by its inferential connections to other concepts, since it is the concept of the state that draws these components together into a unity and gives theoretical significance to other concepts on the basis of their inferential and metaphorical connections to the concept of the state, rather than conversely (Bartelson 2001: 11).

These problems of centrality and ambiguity, of the foundational nature of the state for political discourse and the constitutive nature of definitions of the state for political imaginaries and political practice, pose real difficulties for rigorous analysis. Indeed the variety of attempts to solve (or dissolve) them could be used to organize a critical review of state formation, the historical semantics of the state, and political practices oriented to the state (cf., on historical semantics, Brunner et al., 1990; Koselleck 1988; Luhmann 1990; Skinner 1989). Serious questions are also posed for historians, political geographers, and social scientists who have been concerned with state formation and transformation and political practices oriented to the state, both in Europe (where the 'modern state' first arose) and in other historical-geographical contexts. The same problems occur in more prosaic forms in everyday discourses, ordinary politics, and routine statal practices (cf. Bratsis 2006; Painter 2006). We turn to these first.

Everyday language sometimes depicts the state as a subject – the state does, or must do, this or that. Sometimes it treats the state as a thing – this economic class, social stratum, political party, or official caste uses the state to pursue its projects or interests; but the state is neither a subject nor a thing. So how could a state act *as if* it were a unified subject and what could constitute its unity as a 'thing'? Also, how do social actors come to act *as if* the state were a real subject or a simple instrument? Coherent answers are hard to find because the state's referents vary so much. It changes shape and appearance with the activities it undertakes, the scales on which it operates, the political forces acting towards it, and the circumstances in which it and they act, and so on. When pressed, a common response is to list the institutions that comprise the state, usually with a core set of institutions with increasingly vague outer boundaries. From the political executive, legislature, judiciary, army, police, and public administration, the list may extend to education, trade unions, mass media, religion, and even the family. Such lists typically fail to specify what lends these institutions the quality of statehood. Finding this essence is hard, because, as Max Weber famously noted, there is no activity that states always perform and none that they have never performed (1948: 77–78). Does a theory of the state require a theory of state failure? Finally, who are the principals and who are the agents in the activities that states undertake? Are the principals restricted to 'state managers' or do they include top advisors and other direct sources of policy inputs? Likewise, where does the boundary lie between (a) state managers as principals and (b) state employees as routine agents or executants of state programmes and policies? Also, do the agents include union leaders involved in policing incomes policies, for example, or media owners and media workers who circulate propaganda on the state's behalf?

An obvious escape route from these problems is to define the state in terms of its formal institutional features and/or the foundational instruments or mechanisms of state power. The *Allgemeine Staatslehre* (general state theory) tradition pursues the first approach. It focuses on the articulation of three key features of the state: state territory, state population, and state apparatus. Max Weber largely follows the second approach. This is reflected in his celebrated definition of the *modern* state as the 'human community that (successfully) claims the *monopoly of the legitimate use of physical force* within a given territory' (Weber 1948: 78, parenthesis and italics in original; cf., more elaborately, 1978: 54–56). Yet other definitions highlight the modern state's formal sovereignty vis-à-vis its own population and other states. This does not mean that modern states exercise power largely through direct and immediate coercion – a sure sign of crisis or state failure. For, where state power is regarded as legitimate, it can normally secure compliance without such recourse. Indeed, this is where the many state-theoretical traditions concerned with the bases of political legitimacy and/or social hegemony are so important in exploring the character of the state projects that endow the state with some institutional and operational unity as well as the nature of the societal projects that define the nature and purposes of government in relation to the social world beyond the state and/or interstate systems. Nonetheless, organized coercion is a legitimate last resort in enforcing decisions. Even when blessed with political legitimacy, of course, all states reserve the right – or claim the need – to suspend the constitution or specific legal provisions and many also rely heavily on force, fraud, and corruption and their subjects' inability to organize effective resistance. Indeed, for theorists such as Carl Schmitt, it is the effective power to declare a state of emergency that defines the locus of sovereignty within the state system (Schmitt 1921, 1985; for a critique, see Agamben 2004).

Another solution is to regard the essence of the state (pre-modern as well as modern) as the territorialization of political authority. Such action involves the intersection of politically organized coercive and symbolic power, a clearly demarcated core territory, and a relatively fixed population on which political decisions are collectively binding. Thus, the key feature of the state would become the historically variable ensemble of technologies and practices that produce, naturalize, and manage territorial space as a bounded container within which political power can be exercised to achieve various, more or less integrated and changing policy objectives. It should nonetheless be emphasized that a system of territorially exclusive, mutually recognizing, mutually legitimating national states exercising formally sovereign control over large and exclusive territorial areas is a relatively recent institutional expression of state power that is historically contingent rather than an inevitable and irreversible result of social development (Teschke 2003, 2006). The existence of such an inter-state system is also the source of the increasingly artificial division between domestic and international affairs (Rosenberg 1994; Walker 1993). This is reflected in recent debates about the future of the national territorial state and attempts to define emergent forms of political organization of a statal, semi-statal, or non-statal character. For other modes of territorializing political power have existed, while some still co-exist with the so-called Westphalian system with its individual sovereign states in an anarchic inter-state system (allegedly established by the Treaties of Westphalia in 1648 but realized, as Teschke notes, only stepwise during the nineteenth and twentieth centuries) and new expressions are emerging and yet others can be imagined. Earlier modes include city-states, empires, protectorates, enclaves, the medieval state system, absolutism, and modern imperial-colonial blocs. Emerging modes that have been identified, rightly or wrongly, include cross-border regional cooperation, a new medievalism, supranational blocs (e.g., the EU), a western conglomerate state, and an embryonic world state. Nonetheless, while state forms shape politics as the 'art of the possible', struggles over state power also matter. State forms have been changed before through political activities and will be changed again.

While there are significant material and discursive lines of demarcation between the state *qua* institutional ensemble and other institutional orders and/or the lifeworld, the SRA stresses that its apparatuses and practices are materially interdependent with other institutional orders and social practices. In this sense it is socially embedded. Indeed, as Tim Mitchell argues,

> [t]he state should be addressed as an effect of detailed processes of spatial organization, temporal arrangement, functional specification, and supervision and surveillance, which create the appearance of a world fundamentally divided into state and society. The essence of modern politics is not policies formed on one side of this division being applied to or shaped by the other, but the producing and reproducing of this line of difference (1991: 95; on the construction of sovereignty, see also Bartelson 1995).

These detailed processes also divide the globe fundamentally into *different* states and societies and thereby create a more or less complex inter-state system within an emerging world society. Some consequences of this are addressed below.

States do not exist in majestic isolation, overseeing the rest of their respective societies, but are embedded in a wider political system (or systems), articulated with other institutional orders, and linked to different forms of civil society. A key aspect of their transformation is the redrawing of the multiple 'lines of difference' between the state and its environment(s) as states (and the social forces they represent) redefine their priorities, expand or reduce their activities, recalibrate or rescale them in the light of new challenges, seek greater autonomy or promote power-sharing, and disembed or re-embed specific state institutions and practices within the social order. Such fluidity holds for the international as well as national dimensions of state relations. The state's frontiers may display a variable geometry and its temporal horizons regarding the past, present, and future are also complex. There are also continuing attempts to redesign its institutional architecture and modes of working to enhance state capacities to achieve particular political objectives.

Two conclusions follow. First, the distinction between the state apparatus and the wider political system makes a real difference and is defined (and redefined) materially and discursively. Thus, analysing its constitution and its effects is a central task for any theorist of the state. Second, as some systems theorists argue, the political system is self-substituting, i.e., a crisis in the political system does not normally lead to its demise but its reorganization. Clearly, a fundamental part of such reorganization includes the redefinition (or restructuring) of the forms of institutional separation between the economic and political systems and their relationship to the lifeworld and, in this context, the redefinition of the 'line of difference' between the state and the political system. These redefinitions are especially clear for the European Union insofar as it is a polity in the course of (trans)formation and this process is being contested by many different social forces. Indeed, the process of state formation in Europe provides a real-time experiment in the complexities and contingencies of state formation.

One implication of the above is that an adequate theory of the state can only be produced as part of a wider theory of society, but it is precisely in the articulation between state and society, however, that many of the unresolved problems of state theory are located. For the state involves a paradox. On the one hand, it is just one institutional ensemble among others within a social formation; on the other, it is peculiarly charged with overall responsibility for maintaining the cohesion of the social formation of which it is merely a part. Its paradoxical position as both part and whole of society means that it is continually called upon by diverse social forces to resolve society's problems and is equally continually doomed to generate 'state failure' since so many of society's problems lie well beyond its control and may even be aggravated by attempted intervention. Many of the differences among state theories derive from contrary approaches to various structural and strategic moments of this paradox and further development of state theory requires addressing the overall logic (or, perhaps, 'illogic') of this paradox.

In this context it should be noted that 'societies' (or, better, 'imagined human communities') can be dominated by different principles of societal organization (*Vergesellschaftung*). These can be associated with different projects and priorities (e.g., economic, military, religious, political, social ranking, cultural), reflected in the state as a key site where social power relations may be crystallized in different forms (Mann 1986) and, indeed, where struggles over these principles of societal organization are often conducted because of the part-whole paradox in which the state is so heavily implicated. Thus, a state could operate principally as a capitalist state, a military power, a theocratic regime, a representative democratic regime answerable to civil society, an apartheid state, or an ethico-political state. There are competing principles of societalization linked to different functional systems and different identities and values anchored in civil society and, in principle, any of these could become dominant, at least for a while. There is no unconditional guarantee that the modern state will always (or ever) be essentially capitalist – although exploration of state forms may indicate certain strategically selective biases in this regard. Moreover, even where capital accumulation is the dominant axis of societalization by virtue of structural biases and/or successful political strategies, state managers typically have regard to the codes, programmes, and activities of other functional systems and the dynamic of the lifeworld in their efforts to maintain a modicum of institutional integration and social cohesion within the state's territorial boundaries and to reduce external threats. However, such structural coherence and social cohesion is necessarily limited insofar as it depends on the displacement and/or deferral, through one or more spatio-temporal fixes, of the effects of certain contradictions and lines of conflict beyond its socially constituted spatio-temporal boundaries and action horizons. Different kinds of fix exist and they depend on specific forms of government, governance, and metagovernance ('governance of governance') (Jessop 2002, 2004).

DEFINING THE STATE

Given the preceding remarks, I now define the state as a 'rational abstraction' to be respecified in different ways and for different purposes as strategic-relational analysis proceeds. In short, in order to initiate the analysis rather than pre-empt further exploration, the *core of the state apparatus* can be defined as a distinct ensemble of institutions and organizations whose socially accepted function is to define and enforce collectively binding decisions on a given population in the name of their 'common interest' or 'general will' (Jessop 1990: 341). This broad definition identifies the state in terms of its generic features as a specific form of macro-political organization with a specific type of political orientation; it also indicates that there are important links between the state and the political sphere and, indeed, the wider society. Thus, not all forms of macro-political organization can be classed as state-like nor can the state simply be equated with government, law, bureaucracy, a coercive apparatus, or another political institution. Indeed this definition puts the contradictions and dilemmas entailed in political discourse at the heart of work on the state, because claims about the general will or common interest are a key feature of the state system and distinguish it from straightforward political domination or violent oppression (contrast Tilly 1973). The approach can also serve as a basis for describing specific states and political regimes and exploring the conditions in which states emerge, evolve, enter into crisis, and are transformed. This initial cluster definition is also compatible with diverse analytical approaches to the state and with recognition of what Mann (1986) terms the polymorphous crystallization of state power associated with alternative principles of societalization.[1]

This said, six qualifications are required to make this multi-dimensional definition useful in orienting a strategic-relational research agenda:

1. Above, around, and below the core of the state are found institutions and organizations whose relation to the core ensemble is uncertain. Indeed the effective integration of the state as an institutional ensemble pursuing relatively coherent policies is deeply problematic. This is where governmental rationalities, administrative programmes, and political practices oriented to achieving such integration become significant. Moreover, while statal operations are most concentrated and condensed in the core of the state, they depend on a wide range of micro-political practices dispersed throughout society. States never achieve full closure or complete separation from society and the precise boundaries between the state and/or political system and other institutional orders and systems are generally in doubt and change over time. In many circumstances this ambiguity may even be productive in pursuit of state policies. Similar problems emerge in relation to inter-state relations in the emerging world political system.

2. The nature of these institutions and organizations, their articulation to form the overall architecture of the state qua institutional ensemble, and its differential links with the wider society will depend on the nature of the social formation and its past history. The capitalist type of state differs from that characteristic of feudalism, for example;[2] and political regimes also differ across capitalist social formations.

3. Although the socially acknowledged character of its political functions is a defining feature of the normal state, the forms in which this legitimacy is institutionalized and expressed will also vary. Indeed the whole point of describing such political functions as 'socially acknowledged' is to stress that their precise content is constituted in and through politically relevant discourses. The contested discourses about the nature and purposes of government for the wider society and their relationship to alternative hegemonic projects and their translation into political practices become significant in this context.

4. Although coercion is a state's ultimate sanction, states have other methods to secure compliance. Violence is rarely the state's first resort (especially in consolidated capitalist societies) and would often be counterproductive. A full account of the state must consider all the means of intervention at its disposal, their capacities and limitations, and their relative weight in different contexts. This is especially important for evolving forms of statehood in an increasingly interdependent world society.

5. The society whose common interest and general will are administered by the state should no more be interpreted as an empirical given than the state itself. The boundaries and identity of the society are often constituted in and through the same processes by which states are built, reproduced, and transformed. Indeed it is one of the more obvious conclusions of the state-centred approach that state- and nation-building are strongly influenced by the emergent dynamic of the emergent international system formed through the interaction of sovereign states. An effect of globalization and its associated relativization of scale is the increasing difficulty of defining the boundaries of any given society – to the extent that some theorists claim that only one society now exists, namely, world society (Luhmann 1982, 1997; Richter 1996; Stichweh 2000). Interestingly, the tendential emergence of world society reinforces the importance of national states in many areas of social life (Meyer et al. 1997).

6. Whatever the political rhetoric of the 'common interest' or 'general will' might suggest, these are always 'illusory' insofar as attempts to define them occur on a strategically selective terrain and involves the differential articulation and aggregation of interests, opinions, and values. Indeed, the common interest or general will is always asymmetrical, marginalizing or defining some interests at the same time as it privileges other. There is never a general interest that embraces all possible particular interests (Jessop 1990). Indeed, a key statal task is to aid the organization of spatio-temporal fixes that facilitate the deferral and displacement of contradictions, crisis-tendencies, and conflicts to the benefit of those fully included in the 'general interest' at the expense of those more or less excluded from it. In turn, this suggests clear limits to the possibility of a world state governing world society because this would exclude a constitutive outside for the pursuit of a 'general interest' or require a fundamental shift in social relations to prevent social exclusion.

These qualifications indicate the limitations of a general definition of the state that is presented once-and-for-all and never respecified as the analysis unfolds. Allegedly Marx was once asked why *Capital* did not begin with a definition of the capitalist mode of production and answered that such a definition could only be provided at the conclusion of the work. Apocryphal or not, such a response would be very apt for any request to define the state once-and-for-all when we are attempting to get to grips with actually existing states. For an adequate understanding of the state should address not only the nature and limits of the state apparatus (see above) but also the modalities of state power and this takes us well beyond the state (however defined) to the changing balance of social forces within the state, oriented to the state, and, indeed, operating at a distance from the state.

AN EXCURSUS ON POWER

State theorists have long debated how best to define state power. These debates are reflected in heated ontological debates that reveal the essentially contested nature of power (classically Lukes 1975) and related epistemological and methodological debates about how to identify and measure power as a social relation (Clegg 1989; Haugaard 1997; Isaac 1987). The SRA focuses initially on power as capacity rather than power as the actualization of such capacity. At its most basic, power is the capacity of a given force to produce an event that would not otherwise occur. Such a capacity is inherently relational because it depends on the reciprocal correspondence between capacities *and liabilities* – the capacities of the causal force, the liabilities of that on which this force operates. In the social world there is at least a *double* contingency at work, signified in the master-slave relation, in the sense that each party to a social relation has capacities and liabilities. In most cases the number and range of relevant forces is far wider.

Where social relations are mediated through the instrumentality of things, then the affordances of the latter also matter. Not everything that is possible is actualized; and not everything that is possible is compossible, i.e., can be actualized at the same time as other possibilities. The more strongly structured are social relations, the more constraints there are on compossibility and on potential sequences of events. This is what enables study of durable patterns of domination (*Herrschaft*), their development, and radical ruptures therein. When examining state power we are typically interested in the actualization of *socially structured* capacities and liabilities rather than *socially amorphous* (or random) acts of power. Hence it is crucial to focus on capacities grounded in structured social relations rather than in the properties of individual agents considered in isolation. Moreover, as these structured social relations entail enduring relations, there are reciprocal, if often asymmetrical, capacities and vulnerabilities. A common paradigm here is Hegel's master-slave dialectic – in which the master depends on the slave and the slave on the master. Marx's equivalent paradigm case is, of course, the material interdependence of capital and labour.

At stake in both cases are enduring relations of reproduced, reciprocal practices rather than one-off, unilateral impositions of will. One interesting implication of this is that power is also involved in securing the continuity of social relations rather than producing radical change. Thus, as Isaac notes, '[r]ather than A getting B to do something B would not otherwise do, social relations of power typically involve both A and B doing what they *ordinarily* do' (1987: 96). The capitalist wage relation is a particularly useful example here. For, in voluntarily selling their labour-power for a wage, workers transfer its control and the right to any surplus to the capitalist. A formally free exchange thereby becomes the basis of factory despotism and economic exploitation. Nonetheless, as working class resistance in labour markets and the labour process indicate, Marxists note that the successful exercise of power is also a conjunctural phenomenon rather than guaranteed by unequal social relations of production. The actualization of capacities to exercise power and its effects, if any, is always and everywhere contingent on circumstances. Moreover, as capacities to exercise power are always tied to specific sets of social relations and depend for their actualization on specific circumstances, there is no such thing as power in general or general power but only specific types and forms of power.

The SRA has fundamental implications for the analysis of the most basic features of social order. These include structure and conjuncture, structural constraints and conjunctural opportunities, the complex, overdetermined nature of power relations, the vital role of specific mechanisms and discourses of attribution in identifying the agents responsible for the production of specific effects within a particular conjuncture, the significance of specific capacities and modes of calculation in framing individual and collective identities, the relational and relative nature of interests, and the dialectical relation between subjective and objective interests (cf. Jessop 1982: 252–8). In particular, it reveals that structures do not exist outside of specific spatial and temporal horizons of action pursued by specific actors acting alone or together and in the face of opposition from others. Likewise, actors always act in specific action contexts that depend on the coupling between specific institutional materialities and the interaction of other social actors. The meaning of terms such as structural constraint, power, or interests in specific conjunctures derives from the overall articulation of elements. Structural constraints comprise those elements in a situation that cannot be altered by agent(s) in a given time period and will vary according to the strategic location of agents in the overall matrix of the formation. This matrix involves a complex hierarchy of potential powers determined by the range and determinacy of opportunities for influencing elements that constitute constraints for other agents. The potential for power depends not only on the relations among different positions in the social formation but also on the organization, modes of calculation, and resources of social forces. In turn the actual balance of power is determined, *post hoc,* through the interaction of the strategies or actions pursued by these forces within the limits imposed through the differential composition of structural constraints. The interests advanced or harmed through the exercise of power must also be assessed relationally. For interests depend on the conjunctural opportunities in a given period and hence on the potential balance of power. All this has major implications for calculating political strategies over different time periods and also highlights the importance of a conjunctural, relational approach to such issues as the nature of state power (cf. Jessop 1982: 2007).

Over time there is a tendency for reflexively reorganized structures and recursively selected strategies and tactics to co-evolve to produce a relatively stable order but this may still collapse owing to the inherent structural contradictions, strategic dilemmas, and discursive biases characteristic of complex social formations. Moreover, because structures are strategically selective rather than absolutely constraining, there is always scope for actions to overflow or circumvent structural constraints. Likewise, because subjects are never unitary, never fully aware of the conditions of strategic action, never fully equipped to realize their preferred strategies, and may always meet opposition from actors pursuing other strategies or tactics, failure is an ever-present possibility. The approach is intended as a heuristic and many analyses of the state can be easily reinterpreted in strategic-relational terms even if they do not explicitly adopt these (or equivalent) terms; but a strategic-relational *research programme* requires detailed comparative historical analyses to retroduce the specific selectivities in different types of state, state forms, political regimes, and particular conjunctures (for an illustration, see Jessop 2002).

Strategic analysis can be taken further if we allow for a measure of self-reflection on the part of some actors regarding the identities and interests that orient their strategies. The SRA implies that they reflect on their identities and interests, are able to learn from experience and, by acting in contexts that involve strategically selective constraints and opportunities, can and do transform social structures. Thus actors may create new resources, new rules and new knowledge with all that this implies for the rearticulation of constraints and opportunities. They may also (re)formulate their strategies in the light of changing experience and knowledge about the strategic contexts in which they perform. In turn, structural analysis can be taken further by investigating the path-dependent structural coupling and co-evolution of different operationally closed (or autopoietic) systems (cf. Luhmann 1995). For this will enable better understanding of the emergence and subsequent reproduction of structured coherence (or institutional integration) and of the relative importance of different institutional orders and principles of societalization.

If structures are relativized and relational complexes of social constraints/ opportunities, then the analysis of power will involve the attribution of responsibility to specific acts by specific agents for the realization of a specific range of effects in specific temporal and spatial horizons. If power involves an agent's production of effects that would not otherwise occur, it is essential both to identify the structural constraints and conjunctural opportunities confronting these agents and the actions that they performed which, by realizing certain opportunities rather than others, 'made a difference'. The SRA nonetheless challenges orthodox accounts of power in two respects. It not only sees the exercise of power as an *explanandum* rather than as a *principle of explanation* but also radically relativizes it by treating it as an issue of attribution. For the scope of the explanandum will vary with the relative tightness of the spatial and temporal definition of the conjuncture in which particular agents 'made a difference' and of the field of possible effects and repercussions rippling out over social time and space. Moreover, if analyzing power relations poses issues of attribution, i.e., identification of those social forces or actions allegedly responsible for realizing a specific set of effects, it also means absolving other forces of responsibility. But such analyses can be overturned by redefining the conjuncture in which an alleged exercise of power occurred (widening or further tightening its scope) and/or by focusing on the prior formation of the agents whose actions are alleged to have made a difference. This does not mean that individual actions do not 'make a difference' but it does undermine unqualified, non-contextualized talk about power. Nor does the SRA mean that social forces cannot realize intended effects to a significant extent. They may do so within a circumscribed context in which they can shape conjunctures and so constrain the actions of others. It goes without saying, of course, that the resulting repercussions will sooner or later escape not only the control but also the cognizance of the actors who set the scene for their initial realization.

A STRATEGIC-RELATIONAL APPROACH TO STATE POWER

Following this excursus, we return to the state and state power, starting with the divisions between the state and other parts of a given social formation. How these divisions are drawn, reproduced, and changed influences political processes and state capacities. These are always strategically selective. First, although the state apparatus has its own distinctive resources and powers, which underpin its relative autonomy, it also has distinctive liabilities or vulnerabilities and its operations depend on resources produced elsewhere in its environment. Second, state structures have a specific, differential impact on the ability of various political forces to pursue particular interests and strategies in specific contexts through their control over and/or (in)direct access to these state capacities – capacities whose effectiveness also depends on links to forces and powers that exist and operate beyond the state's formal boundaries. Third, the nature and extent of the realization of these capacities and liabilities – hence the nature and impact of state power – depend on the structural relations between the state and its encompassing political system, on the strategic ties among politicians and state officials and other political forces, and on the complex web of structural interdependencies and strategic networks that link the state system to its broader social environment. Together these considerations imply that, from a strategic-relational perspective, the state's structural powers or capacities, their structural and strategic biases, and their realization do not depend solely on the nature of the state as a juridico-political apparatus – even assuming its institutional boundaries could be precisely mapped and prove stable. They also depend on diverse capacities-liabilities and forces that lie beyond it. Putting states in their place like this does not exclude (indeed, it presupposes) specifically state-engendered and state-mediated processes. It does require, however, that they be related both to their broader social context and to the strategic choices and conduct of actors in and beyond states (Jessop 1990, 2002).

It is important to explore the properties of the state as an institutional ensemble and their implications for the strategic selectivity of state power, a mode of inquiry introduced by Nicos Poulantzas, who derived the idea from Marx's claim that capital is a social relation. Marx argued that

> property in money, means of subsistence, machines and other means of production, does not as yet stamp a man as a capitalist if there be wanting the correlative – the wage-worker, the other man who is compelled to sell himself of his own free-will. ...capital is not a thing, but a social relation between persons, established by the instrumentality of things (1887: 717).

The same argument runs through his and Engels's reflections on the state and can be paraphrased to read that state power is a social relation between political forces mediated through the instrumentality of juridico-political institutions, state capacities, and political organizations (cf. Marx 1843, 1850, 1852, 1871).

Poulantzas expressed this intuition in his thesis that state power is an institutionally mediated condensation of the balance of forces in political class struggle. The argument dissolves more orthodox Marxist approaches that tend to regard the state as a thing or a subject that is external to the capitalist mode of production. Instead it refocuses attention on the social nature of capitalist production and its complex economic, political and ideological preconditions. The state and state power must assume a central role in capital accumulation, even in those apparently counterfactual cases characterized by a neutral, laissez-faire state, as well as those where the state is massively involved in the organization of production. Moreover, because the state is seen as a complex institutional system and the influence of classes is seen to depend on their forms of organization, alliances, etc., it is also necessary to reject a crude instrumentalist approach. It is no longer a question of how pre-existing classes use the state (or the state itself acts) in defence of capitalism defined at an economic level. Henceforth it is a question of the adequacy of state power as a necessary element in the overall reproduction of the capital relation in different societies and situations. Also, state power in turn must be considered as a complex, contradictory effect of class (and popular-democratic) struggles, mediated through and conditioned by the institutional system of the state. In short, the effect of these studies is to reinstate and elaborate the idea that the state is a system of political domination (cf. Jessop 1990: 45).

Several strategic-relational theorists have systematically elaborated the insight that the state is a system of political domination (in addition to Jessop, see Bertramsen et al., 1991; Brenner 2004; Hay 2002; Marsh et al., 1999). In different ways, they are all concerned with different states' *structural selectivity* and *strategic capacities*. The SRA argues that the exercise and effectiveness of state power is a contingent product of a changing balance of political forces located within and beyond the state and that this balance is conditioned by the specific institutional structures and procedures of the state apparatus as embedded in the wider political system and environing societal relations. A strategic-relational analysis would examine how a given state apparatus may privilege some actors, some identities, some strategies, some spatial and temporal horizons, and some actions over others as well as the ways, if any, in which political actors (individual and/or collective) take account of this differential privileging by engaging in 'strategic-context' analysis when choosing a course of action. It involves exploring the ways in which the state as an ensemble of institutions had a specific, differential impact on the ability of various political forces to pursue particular interests and strategies through access to and control over given state capacities – themselves dependent for their effects on links to forces and powers beyond the state (on this concept, see especially, Offe 1972; Poulantzas 1978). The SRA also studies variations in these capacities, their organization, and exercise, and emphasizes how the relational nature of state power has effects on states' capacities to project their power into social realms well beyond their own institutional boundaries.

Strategic-relational theorists have also introduced a distinctive *evolutionary* perspective into the analysis of the state and state power in order to discover how the generic evolutionary mechanisms of selection, variation, and retention may operate in specific conditions to produce relatively coherent and durable structures and strategies. One implication is that opportunities for reorganizing specific structures and for strategic reorientation are themselves subject to structurally inscribed strategic selectivities and therefore have path-dependent as well as path-shaping aspects. For example, it may be necessary to pursue strategies over several spatial and temporal horizons of action and to mobilize different sets of social forces in different contexts to eliminate or modify specific constraints and opportunities linked to particular state structures. Moreover, as such strategies are pursued, political forces will be more or less well equipped to learn from their experiences and to adapt their conduct to changing conjunctures.

On this basis, we can elaborate four guidelines for analysing the state as a concrete-complex object of inquiry: (1) the state is a set of institutions that cannot, qua institutional ensemble, exercise power; (2) political forces do not exist independently of the state: they are shaped in part through its forms of representation, its internal structure, and its forms of intervention; (3) state power is a complex social relation that reflects the changing balance of social forces in a determinate conjuncture; and (4) state power is capitalist to the extent that it creates, maintains, or restores the conditions required for capital accumulation in a given situation and it is non-capitalist to the extent that these conditions are not realized (Jessop 1982: 221). Some fundamental substantive concepts for analyzing the state's institutional architecture, its social bases, state projects, and the organization of hegemony can be elaborated on the basis of these guidelines.

The first and third guidelines are often misunderstood. They rest on the sound strategic-relational arguments that (a) the state is neither a unified subject nor a neutral instrument but an asymmetrical institutional terrain on which various political forces (including state managers) contest control over the state apparatus and its distinctive capacities; and (b) class power depends less on the class background of those nominally in charge of the state or their subjective class identities and projects than on the differential class relevance of the effects of the exercise of state capacities in a complex and changing conjuncture, a view that does not reduce state power to class power. Nor does it exclude the influence of the core executive, the military, parliamentary deputies, or other political categories, in all their complexity, in the exercise of state power or the determination of its effects. Nor again does it exclude that the state's role as a system of political class domination could sometimes be secondary to its role as a system of official domination over 'popular-democratic forces' or, indeed, secondary to its institutional mediation of the relative dominance of another principle of societalization (such as theocracy, 'racial' apartheid, or genocide). However, such issues can only be adequately explored by refusing a radical distinction between state power and class power.

It also follows that, as an institutional ensemble, the state does not (and cannot) exercise power: it is not a real subject. Indeed, rather than speaking about *the* power of the state, one should speak about the various potential structural power*s* (or state capacities), in the plural, that are inscribed in the state as an institutional ensemble. The state is an ensemble of power centres that offer unequal chances to different forces within and outside the state to act for different political purposes. How far and in what ways their powers (and any associated liabilities or weak points) are actualized depends on the action, reaction, and interaction of specific social forces located both within and beyond this complex ensemble. In short, the state does not exercise power: its power*s* (always in the plural) are activated through the agency of definite political forces in specific conjunctures. It is not the state that acts: it is always specific sets of politicians and state officials located in specific parts and levels of the state system. It is they who activate specific powers and state capacities inscribed in particular institutions and agencies. In doing so, they may well take account of the prevailing and, perhaps, future balance of forces within and beyond the state (including beyond its territorial borders as well as its domestic juridico-political boundaries). Moreover, as in all social action, unacknowledged conditions influence the success or failure of their actions and there are always unanticipated effects.

THE STATE AS STRATEGY

Treating the state in relational terms and linking it to issues of strategy enables three main arguments to be advanced:

1. The state system is the site of strategy. It can be analysed as a system of *strategic selectivity*, i.e., as a system whose structure and *modus operandi* are more open to some types of political strategy than others. Thus a given type of state, a given state form, a given form of regime, will be more accessible to some forces than others according to the strategies they adopt to gain state power; and it will be more suited to the pursuit of some types of economic or political strategy than others because of the modes of intervention and resources which characterize that system. ... this notion of strategic selectivity is more fruitful than that of structural selectivity because it brings out more clearly the *relational* character of this selectivity. For the differential impact of the state system on the capacity of different class(-relevant) forces to pursue their interests in different strategies over a given time horizon is not inscribed in the state system as such but in the relation between state structures and the strategies which different forces adopt towards it. ...

2. The state is also a site where strategies are elaborated. Indeed one cannot understand the unity of the state system without referring to political strategies; nor can one understand the

activities of the state without referring to political strategies. Marxists often argue that the capitalist state has an essential institutional and/or class unity but none of the reasons put forward for this are convincing. At best they establish the *formal* unity of the state system (e.g., as a sovereign state with a centralized hierarchy of command) but this cannot guarantee its *substantive* operational unity. For the state is the site of class(-relevant) struggles and contradictions as well as the site of struggles and rivalries among its different branches. Its being such a site poses the problem of how the state comes to act, if at all, as a unified political force. It is here that the role of state managers (both politicians and career officials) is crucial for understanding how a relative unity is imposed on the various (in)activities of the state and how these activities acquire a relative autonomy from the conflicting pressures emanating from civil society. Thus we must examine the different strategies and tactics that state managers develop to impose a measure of coherence on the activities of the state.

3. The structure and *modus operandi* of the state system can be understood in terms of their production in and through past political strategies and struggles. These strategies and struggles could have been developed within that system and/or at a distance from that system; and they could have been concerned to maintain it and/or to transform it. In this sense the current *strategic selectivity* of the state is in part the emergent effect of the interaction between its past patterns of *strategic selectivity* and the strategies adopted for its transformation. In turn the calculating subjects that operate on the strategic terrain constituted by the state are in part constituted by the *strategic selectivity* of the state system and its past interventions (1990: 260–2). The current institutional order should always be seen as the product of strategies pursued within the constraints imposed by existing forms of class domination as well as the prevailing balance of forces. In the absence of this it would be impossible to distinguish adequately between strategies that are 'arbitrary, rationalistic, and willed' and those that stand some chance of becoming 'organic' (Jessop 1985: 343–345).

CONCLUSIONS

This chapter has emphasized the difficulties of studying the state (cf. Abrams 1988) and suggested several ways in which to resolve some of these difficulties. In particular, whilst far rejecting the idea that there can be only way to approach such a hypercomplex and changing phenomenon, it has elaborated the key Poulantzasian insight that the state is a social relation. This elliptical phrase is best re-stated as 'state power is an institutionally-mediated condensation of the changing balance of political forces'. Starting from this insight, I have presented some key features of the strategic-relational approach to the state and state power. This approach recognizes different patterns of condensation, corresponding to the dominance of different principles of societalization (economic, military, religious, 'racial', etc.) and can therefore be used far beyond its initial Marxist theoretical framework. Indeed, such extensions are essential to analyse effectively the variety of states and political regimes and the polymorphous crystallization of state power (Mann 1986). However, comparative institutional and historical analysis also requires a common set of orienting concepts to facilitate description and explanation and these can be found in the strategic-relational approach to the state and state power. Moreover, because the state and state power cannot be studied in isolation from the wider sets of social relations in which the state is embedded, the SRA is especially suitable to this end thanks to its broader concerns with domination, hegemony, and resistance.

NOTES

1 The arguments in this and the next paragraph derive from Jessop (1990: 341–343).
2 Types of state are theoretical constructs that define which forms of political organization might correspond to the basic elements of different modes of production: they facilitate the analysis of states in specific social formations. Engaging in this sort of theoretical exercise does not imply that every state in a capitalist society will correspond to the capitalist type of state (cf. Poulantzas 1978: 147–167). On the capitalist type of state, see also Jessop 2002, especially 36–45

REFERENCES

Abrams, P. (1988) 'Notes on the difficulty of studying the state', *Journal of Historical Sociology*, 1 (1), 58–89.
Agamben, G. (2004): *State of Exception*. Chicago: University of Chicago, Cambridge University Press.
Bartelson, J. (1995): *A Genealogy of Sovereignty*. Cambridge: Cambridge University Press.
Bartelson, J. (2001): *A Critique of the State*. Cambridge: Cambridge University Press.
Bertramsen, R.B., Thomsen, J.-P.F. and Torfing, J. (1991): *State, Economy, and Society*. London: Unwin Hyman.
Bratsis, P. (2006): *Everyday Life and the State*. London: Paradigm.
Brenner, N. (2004): *New State Spaces: Urban Restructuring and State Rescaling in Western Europe*. Oxford: Oxford University Press.
Brunner, O., Conze, W. and Koselleck, R. (1990): 'Staat und Souveränität', in *Geschichtliche Grundbegriffe. Historisches Lexikon zur politisch-sozialen Sprache in Deutschland*. Band 6, Stuttgart: Klett-Cotta, 1–153.
Clegg, S.R. (1989): *Frameworks of Power*. London: Sage.
Ferguson, Y.H. and Mansbach, R.W. (1989): *The State, Conceptual Chaos, and the Future of International Relations Theory*. Boulder: Lynne Rienner.
Haugaard, M. (1997): *The Constitution of Power*. Manchester: Manchester University Press.
Hay, C. (2002): *Political Analysis. A Critical Introduction*. Basingstoke: Palgrave.
Isaac, J.C. (1987): *Power: A Realist Analysis*. Ithaca: Cornell University Press.
Jessop, B. (1982): *The Capitalist State: Marxist Theories and Methods*. Oxford: Martin Robertson.
Jessop, B. (1985) *Nicos Poulantzas: Marxist Theory and Political Strategy*. Basingstoke: Macmillan.
Jessop, B. (1990): *State Theory: Putting the State in its Place*. Cambridge: Polity.
Jessop, B. (2002): *The Future of the Capitalist State*. Cambridge: Polity.
Jessop, B. (2004): 'Multi-level governance and multi-level meta-governance'. In I. Bache and M. Flanders, (eds), *Multi-level Governance*. Oxford: Oxford University Press, 49–74.
Jessop, B (2007): *State Power: a Strategic-Relational Approach*, Cambridge: Polity.
Koselleck, R. (1988): *Critique and Crisis: Enlightenment and the Pathogenesis of Modern Society*. Dedington: Berg.
Luhmann, N. (1982): The world society as a social system. *International Journal of General Systems*, 8: 131–138.
Luhmann, N. (1990): 'State and politics: Towards a semantics of the self-description of political systems'. In *Political Theory in the Welfare State*. Berlin: Walter de Gruyter, 117–154.
Luhmann N. (1995): *Social Systems*. Stanford: Stanford University Press.
Luhmann, N. (1997): 'Globalization or world society? How to conceive of modern society', *International Review of Sociology*, 7 (1): 67–75.
Lukes, S. (1974): *Power: A Radical Analysis*. Basingstoke: Macmillan.
Mann, M. (1986): *The Sources of Social Power. Volume I. A History of Power from the Beginning to AD 1760*. Cambridge: Cambridge University Press.
Marsh, D. et al., (1999): *Postwar British Politics in Perspective*. Cambridge: Polity.
Marx, K. (1843): Contribution to a Critique of Hegel's *Philosophy of Law*. MECW 3. London: Lawrence & Wishart (1975), 3–129.

Marx, K. (1850): *Class Struggles in France*. MECW 10. London: Lawrence & Wishart (1978) 47–145.
Marx, K. (1852): *The Eighteenth Brumaire of Louis Bonaparte*. In T. Carver. (ed.), *Marx: Later Political Writings*. Cambridge: CUP (1976), 31–127.
Marx, K. (1871): *The Civil War in France*. MECW 22. London: Lawrence & Wishart (1986), 307–57.
Marx, K. (1887): *Capital, Volume I*. London: Lawrence & Wishart. (1976).
Meyer, J., Boli, J., Thomas, G.M. and Ramirez, F. (1997): 'World society and the nation-state', *American Journal of Sociology*, 103 (1): 144–81.
Mitchell, T.J. (1991): 'The limits of the state: Beyond statist approaches and their critics', *American Political Science Review*, 85 (1): 77–96.
Offe, C. (1972): *Strukturprobleme des kapitalistischen Staates*. Frankfurt: Suhrkamp.
Painter, J. (2006): 'Prosaic geographies of stateness', *Political Geography*, 25: 752–74.
Poulantzas, N. (1974): *Fascism and Dictatorship: The Third International and the Problem of Fascism*. London: New Left Books.
Poulantzas, N. (1978): *State, Power, Socialism*. London: Verso.
Richter, D. (1996): *Nation als Form*. Opladen: Westdeutscher Verlag.
Rosenberg, J. (1994): *The Empire of Civil Society*. London: Verso.
Schmitt, C. (1921): *Die Diktatur*. Berlin: Duncker & Humboldt.
Schmitt, C. (1985): *Political Theology: Four Chapters on the Concept of Sovereignty*. Cambridge: MIT Press.
Skinner, Q. (1989): 'The state. In T. Ball, (ed.), *Political Innovation and Social Change*. Cambridge: Cambridge University Press, 90–131.
Stichweh, R. (2000): *Die Weltgesellschaft. Soziologische Analysen*. Frankfurt: Suhrkamp.
Teschke, B. (2003): *The Myth of 1648. Class, Geopolitics and the Making of Modern International Relations*. London: Verso.
Teschke, B. (2006): 'Debating *The Myth of 1648*: State formation, the interstate system and the emergence of capitalism in Europe – A rejoinder', *International Politics*, 43 (4), 531–73.
Tilly, C. (1973): 'Reflections on the history of European state-making'. In C. Tilly, (ed.), *The Formation of National States in Western Europe*. Princeton: PUP, 3–83.
Walker, R.B. (1993): *Inside/Outside: International Relations as Political Theory*. Cambridge: Cambridge University Press.
Weber, M. (1948): 'Politics as a vocation'. In M. weber (ed.), *Essays from Max Weber*. London: Routledge and Kegan Paul, 77–128.
Weber, M. (1975): *Essays in the Methodology of Social Sciences*. Glencoe: Free Press.

21

Reconfiguring Power in a Globalizing World

Philip G. Cerny

INTRODUCTION

The concept of power has traditionally played a central and crucial role in the analysis of International Relations and World Politics. It has been seen as the key factor, variable, driving force or 'currency' in relations among states. Indeed, this role has been seen by many observers since Thucydides as the defining attribute of the international system itself. This interpretation of the role of power is said to derive from the understanding that no seriously effective level of organized, authoritative or legitimate governmental or sociopolitical structure exists above the level of the state that does not itself emanate from and, in the last analysis, remain responsible to autonomous, sovereign states – i.e., that there is no genuinely *supranational* power structure or political process in world politics. Therefore in order to explain what happens in world politics – as distinct from politics *within* states – it is necessary to privilege (a) power-seeking actions of states (taken as structurally coherent 'unit actors' in and of themselves: Waltz 1979) and of 'state actors' (actors acting through or on behalf of states) and (b) structured, ongoing relations of power between and among states, over the claims of other potential causal variables. This interpretation is usually labelled the 'realist' – or, in a revised version that has become widespread in academic International Relations since the 1970s, 'neorealist' – paradigm, derived originally from the thought of such political theorists as Machiavelli and Hobbes and central to the nineteenth century German concept of *Realpolitik*.

In this understanding of the world, there is no agreed, overarching political forum in which individuals, economic interests and social groups can systematically and effectively express their views and pursue their goals – in other words, engage in collective action – other than through the level of the state and of those international institutions and (international 'regimes' or mis-named 'global governance' institutions) and less formal processes licensed by sovereign states and ultimately constrained by them in terms of the basic structural dynamics of the system. In the words of Aristotle, 'justice' and 'friendship' on a social level can only exist *within* the *politeia* or political community. Aristotle argues that people are essentially 'social animals'; however, that sociability stops at the border, or the proverbial 'water's edge'. All other people and communities are by definition *outsiders* – foreigners – and relationships with them, even if they are relatively peaceable most of the time, are in the last analysis, when external threats to the polity are perceived, dominated by asocial relations of force. Therefore, despite claims that an 'international society' or 'world society' has developed that includes and sometimes transcends the power-based relations of states (Bull 1977; Hurrell 2007); despite assertions that the world order is essentially rooted in capitalist economic structures (Gill and Law 1987); and despite the hypothesis that a 'global civil society' is developing from below, indeed relations of power among states still constitute the bottom line of world politics.

As a result, traditional analyses of international relations assert, such goals as justice, fairness, equality, democracy, redistribution and the like are ultimately trumped by power rivalries and only stabilized by *balances of power* among states (Little 2007). Indeed, the very definition of power in the international arena power is constituted by the *relative* power of states *vis-à-vis* each other – even if exercised by states themselves in some sort of collective fashion through inter-state institutions and bargaining. Power *as such* in the international arena concerns the relative power of different states, rooted in relations of force, and because states as endogenously entrenched collective action organizations have clear, historically, geographically, economically and socially derived imperatives and priorities in the international arena – the core of which are national defence and the promotion of 'national interests' in the wider world – these imperatives and interests will trump any international or transnational 'public good' or 'general interest' when push comes to shove.

Power in its international manifestation has therefore been seen since Ancient Greece as fundamentally distinct from its internal or domestic manifestation. Power as a means to pursue the 'highest good' within the polity (Aristotle again) is, in contrast, externalized in the form of the state's power to pursue national interests over, above and against the national interests of other states in an anarchic world. Higher ends like social justice, economic welfare or even civil peace itself are subordinated to the underlying requirements of survival, national self-interest and 'self-help' (Waltz 1979). Those higher ends are not forgotten, but are only effectively operationalized internationally through the medium of state action – where they are subordinated to underlying relations of force. Indeed the dominant power imperative of world politics therefore prioritizes and privileges qualitatively different kinds of ends, requires quite different means, and justifies radically different standards of conduct by actors – such as killing and repressing enemies – from government leaders down to ordinary people, especially, but not exclusively, when they become soldiers.

However, this traditional conception of power has always had a range of critics:

- believers in transcendent religious, spiritual, moral and/or ethical values, whether metaphysical or humanistic;
- economic liberals, who see market forms of exchange as entailing imperatives of growth, efficiency and prosperity that ultimately expand onto a transnational or global scale;

- Marxists, who, in contrast, see the same capitalism as creating ever-evolving means for an increasingly internationalized ruling class to expand its domination, and ultimately look to its replacement by socialism;
- liberal democratizers who seek to expand democracy not only within a growing number of nation-states but also across borders in more democratic and/or pluralistic institutions, legal principles and political processes (Held 1995); and
- political science pluralists who see political behaviour as increasingly driven by transnational interests, values and identities rather merely domestic ones (Cerny 2006).

Today, realism and neorealism are being challenged and revised in the light of these critiques. In particular, each of the latter does not merely involve interpreting the deep-rooted and historically robust debates about international politics in general as reflected in the history of political philosophy since Aristotle, Thucydides, Machiavelli, Hobbes, Smith, Marx and the rest. In addition, and more importantly for this book, each critique also carries with it an underlying understanding of how the structure of the international system has been undergoing fundamental change and transformation over time – particularly in the light of developments in the late twentieth and early twenty-first centuries, usually called globalization. All sorts of economic, political and social relationships that cut across borders are today seen from a range of diverse perspectives as undermining – or at least potentially undermining – the 'realist' inside/outside distinction that has been constituted historically not only through international relations theory but also through practices of war, diplomacy, economic competition and the like.

In these critiques, the world is seen as being constituted more and more through revived, emerging and even hegemonic cross-cutting linkages and loyalties of friendship, justice, class, economic self-interest, identity and/or belonging – the traditional stuff of domestic political philosophy and politicking. These increasingly densely structured linkages do not merely constrain the actions of states but, more importantly, enable social, economic and political actors to develop modes of 'transnational' action, creating webs of collective action that are different not merely in degree, but also in kind, from the crude relations of force characteristic of traditional international relations. States are being cut across, run around, manipulated and reshaped by complex transnational and 'glocal' (global-local) linkages that are transforming state behaviour itself.

This chapter will first outline in greater detail the traditional conception of power in International Relations, and then consider a number of contemporary trends that challenge that conception. We will look in particular at cross-cutting or 'horizontal' forms of power, including international institutions, regimes and 'global governance', non-state and transgovernmental actors, the changing structure of the global economy, evolving transnational social and cultural bonds, the loosening of frontiers and borders, the emergence of transnational pluralism, the restructuring of the state itself, and the growing 'civilianization' of power in a world of complex interdependence.

Earlier modes of all of these trends have existed since time immemorial. Indeed, the era of a clearly defined states system – a historically contested concept, normally dated back to the 1648 Peace of Westphalia but in many ways more recent – and of the 'high nation-state' from the mid-nineteenth to the mid-twentieth centuries has been relatively short in the *longue durée* of history. However, in the global era these trends are taking new forms that can be interpreted as heralding a fundamental structural transformation of world politics and society. Indeed, this chapter will argue, world politics is close to reaching a 'tipping point' (Gladwell 2000) whereby the very nature of power in world politics is being transformed into something much more closely resembling the traditional 'domestic' version, but spread not only among states ('inter-nationally': Hirst and Thompson 1996) but also transnationally among cross-border economic interests and 'global civil society', and 'translocally' (Spruyt 1994), among world cities, ethnicities, economic 'clusters', *aficionados* of internet social websites and the like.

THE TRADITIONAL CONCEPTION OF POWER IN INTERNATIONAL RELATIONS

There are four main ways in which power is seen as different in the international context from power in domestic political systems. All four of these ways can be seen as different dimensions of what is often called the 'inside/outside distinction' or the 'levels of analysis distinction' (Hollis and Smith 1990) which forms the core of the realist paradigm but is important for the other approaches as well. The inside/outside distinction means that politics, and even the nature of society itself, are different when looking inside a *politeia* or political society, on the one hand, and when looking outwards, on the other. In Roman times, this distinction – and the inherent yet schizophrenic connection between the two levels – was symbolized by the god Janus, the god of the city. Janus, whose statue was placed at the city gates, had two faces, looking in opposite directions – one looking inside the city, and one looking outside, the first seeking to nurture social bonds, solidarity and community, the second prepared to fight invaders and pursue the city's external interests against aliens by force. This division of world politics into inside and outside requires a dual role for the state and state actors, the city-state in Greek times and the nation-state in modern times. This dual role is today often called 'two-level games' (Putnam 1988).

The first of the four main dimensions of the inside/outside distinction derives, as noted above, from the oft-noted (and oft-qualified) statement that there is no world government, no overarching authority structure or international political process to define norms, make decisions and impose sanctions on those transgressing those norms or defying those decisions. States and state actors cannot appeal to a higher authority either to pursue their own goals or to prevent others from pursuing theirs. As in Thomas Hobbes's state of nature, the international world is a potential 'war of all against all', in which 'defection' – the willingness and incentive to opt out of cooperative arrangements when a state's fundamental national interests are seen to be threatened – is the 'default' state of affairs. Self-defence and what Kenneth Waltz, the leading theorist of the neorealist school of International Relations, calls 'self-help', constitutes the bottom line of world politics (Waltz 1979).

This kind of self-regarding imperative is indeed said to be the only *legitimate* course of action in a world made up of sovereign states accountable only to their own 'people'. In this world, there is no use trying to appeal to a higher authority, whether supranatural or supranational; states are the bottom line because in the last analysis, that's all there is. Indeed, because of the primordial priority of power as force, such appeals can be dismissed either as hopeless idealism and impractical romanticism, on the one hand, or as a mask for ulterior motives of external (or even domestic) power-seeking, on the other. Samuel Johnson was reported as saying: 'Patriotism is the last refuge of a scoundrel.' For realists, however, it is the espousal of supranational idealism that marks the real scoundrel. Only actors who effectively pursue the genuine national interests of their states can be truly moral as well as practical (Morgenthau 1949; Pin-Fat 2005).

The second of dimension, which follows from the first, is that the goals states pursue will be fundamentally different on the 'outside', international level from those that state authorities and political actors pursue 'inside' the domestic political system. In particular, in this context, it is not only exceedingly difficult but regarded as *illegitimate* for states to impose their social values on other independent sovereign states. Pursuing and enforcing norms of social and economic justice, the distribution and redistribution of wealth or other resources, and furthering elemental social bonds among 'the people' can only be done within states, unless there is a process of alliance, emulation or interactive economic growth in which other states voluntarily adopt the same values. In other words, in Aristotelian terms, the principles of 'justice' and 'friendship' only operate within states; all others are outsiders.

This dimension therefore rests on an apparent philosophical paradox. Each state is entitled to possess a different internal moral, ethical and socio-economic system, although the extent of this autonomy is historically uncertain. Indeed, in this context what one might call moral realists argued paradoxically that peace could only be promoted through non-interference and mutual recognition of the ultimate sovereignty of states to determine their own priorities and national interests. The existence of a plurality of different kinds of states with different values and interests can therefore be seen to be a guarantee of a kind of state-based pluralism based on mutual recognition of those differences (Hurrell 2007), almost a kind of vertically containerized international multiculturalism. The Peace of Westphalia was in fact fundamentally a religious truce between Protestant and Catholic European monarchs after centuries of religious warfare and complex institutional conflicts between monarchs (and between them and the Papacy), with each agreeing not to interfere in the others' choice of religion within their 'own' states. This principle was later extended to other choices, including modern ideologies – except, of course, that in the twentieth century in particular, those ideologies themselves often became internationalized.

Nevertheless, such sovereign autonomy often masked desires for conquest, as demonstrated by the history of European imperialism and colonialism, while Nazis, Fascists and Communists attempted to spread their values forcefully by conquering or promoting revolution in other states. In this sense, therefore, the notion of power as sovereign autonomy on the one hand and power as the use of force to pursue national interests on the other has always represented a complex dialectic or contradiction within the traditional conception of power in world politics – one which was summed up by the Roman writer Vegetius in the famous maxim: 'If you want peace, prepare for war.' As has often been pointed out, however, preparation for war often leads to the vicious spiral known as the 'security dilemma' (Herz 1950), potentially leading to arms racing and the possibly unintended outbreak of war. Thus the history of the modern world has been one of an unstable dialectic of war and peace stemming directly from the clash of national interests – interests which cannot be fully insulated from external factors even without full-blown globalization – and outwardly-oriented, even universalistic, ideological goals, on the one hand, and the unstable foundations of the interstate system in relations of force and balances of power, on the other.

The third dimension, again following from the first two, is that power is *organized* differently within the state's internal domain from its external environment. Neorealists in particular label 'inside' politics as 'hierarchical', in the sense that there is some sort of vertical, centralized structure that can be authoritarian or liberal democratic – with all shades in between. In principle, however, more domestically liberal and pluralist forms of this centripetal state allow competing actors to co-exist with each other, relating and interacting through a range of 'horizontal' processes such as elections, shared and/or competing economic interests, multiple social institutions including churches, families, etc. Different groups, factions, individuals and interests, whether pursuing their economic self-interest or attempting to further social values – what V.O. Key called 'sectional' and 'value' groups (Key 1953) – accept (at least up to a point) common 'rules of the game' and conflicts are resolved through common procedures and processes, whether through political institutions and parties, courts and the legal system, rule-governed bureaucracies and/or shared social norms.

Nevertheless, whether hierarchical or pluralistic – domestic polities are always a complex mix of the two – the role of power within a state tends to concern the use of power as a *means to a 'higher' end* rather than an end in itself. Although power struggles, corruption and domination by particular individuals and groups over others is ever crucial to domestic policy processes and institutions, one of the main trends of the past few centuries in the developed countries, and today increasingly in developing countries (although there are always steps backward too, as in Kenya in early 2008) has been the institutionalization of power as a stabilizing force. Power has moved from the foreground – as it has been when tribal elites, medieval nobles, mafias and 'warlords' of various stripes have used brute force for the direct expropriation of wealth and assertion of control – to the background; this process is an essential part of what is generally seen as progress, modernization or development. Naked exercises of power are seen as illegitimate, and power is only seen as legitimate when it is applied in the service of social stability, development, social values (both individualistic and collectivist) and the 'public interest'. In this context, as Weber argued, what keeps the state together is its 'monopoly of legitimate violence', but the key word here is 'legitimate' – constitutionally constituted forms such as the 'police power', courts, political institutions and the like.

However, it is often said that 'politics' of this sort nevertheless 'stops at the water's edge'. Because the international system is, in contrast, 'anarchical' – a description accepted by a range of different approaches to International Relations, meaning not chaotic and disordered but simply without an effective overarching system of government or governance – the state is dominated by the *imperatives built into the international system itself* to act *as if it were a single, fused unit* in foreign policy. The 'outside' state needs to act as if it were genuinely organized 'vertically' – as if it were at one and the same time both an effective 'container', bottling up internal politics and preventing it from spilling over into the international sphere (see Brenner et al., 2003), on the one hand, while at the same time constituting a genuine, relatively efficient command system for effectively coordinating and mobilizing potential domestic material and human resources and capabilities for the pursuit of power on the international level.

Not only is the state, to use Waltz's term, required to act as a 'unit actor' *vis-à-vis* other states analogously organized, but leading politicians have to act like 'statesmen' representing a holistic 'national interest', and the outward-facing state is organized through command hierarchies like armed forces, intelligence agencies and foreign policymakers rather than competitive political processes or economic markets. This capacity has often been seen to be stronger in authoritarian than in democratic states – as reflected in Vladimir Putin's address to the Presidential State Council of Russia on 8 February 2008 – or in states with strong, autonomous executives – as in the 'unitary executive' theory of the George W. Bush Administration (Savage 2007) – although this has been contested throughout history (see Pericles's oration to the Athenians as reported by Thucydides). It is also at the core of contemporary debates about transatlantic relations, summed up in the statement that 'Americans are from Mars; Europeans are from Venus' (Kagan 2003; Sheehan 2008).

The result, as noted by Rosenau, is to separate out in organizational terms domestic policymaking – left to 'parochial' interests and actors – from foreign policy, which is effectively the preserve of 'cosmopolitan elites' (Rosenau 1961). Of course, this means that foreign policy can be manipulated for domestic purposes (Cerny 1980). More importantly, however, it means that there is a continual tension within even the most democratic of polities between accountability and transparency, on the one hand, and control and secrecy, on the other. The effect is to create a kind of dual state, reflecting the Janus image mentioned earlier. Centralized command powers – legitimated, as noted above, by perceived external imperatives and the logic of solidarity (i.e., the dialectic of threats and national interests, of wanting peace but preparing for war, etc.) rather than by social values and the logic of peaceful individual and/or group competition within a relatively acceptable set of rules of the game – are thus structurally hegemonic whenever a serious perceived threat arises leading to a dispute between them and 'civilian' values.

The fourth dimension, then, that of raw power – the use of force and violence – is the ultimate arbiter of international relations, the 'currency' of world politics. The influence of a particular state depends upon its basic stock of potential power resources or 'capabilities', its ability to mobilize people and resources to fight, and its capacity to use – or threaten – force in order to impose its will beyond its borders. The concepts of 'resources' and 'capabilities' in this context are extremely fungible, however. As the Russian Empire learned in 1905 and 1914, having biggest fleet and the largest army are not much help against a better organized and more highly motivated opponent. 'Hard' capabilities themselves are often difficult to assess and measure except in battle. For example, guerrilla warfare has classically been able to counter much larger conventional forces; the apparent technological superiority of American forces in Iraq and Afghanistan today is sometimes said to be an actual disadvantage against the improvised methods of insurgents; and major weapons systems like nuclear missiles may be only useful to the extent that they are *not* used, as in the doctrine of deterrence and 'mutually assured destruction'.

Even more problematic are the 'soft' capabilities of strategic planning, tactical skill, efficient organization, communication, and the general psychological state of the armed forces. However, these themselves are dependent upon the existence not only of an economic infrastructure that can provide the required finance, technological and production capabilities, workforces, etc., to supply the armed forces with effective equipment and weaponry, but also of a social and human infrastructure – the sense of identity, loyalty and belonging to the 'nation' rather than to ethnic, family or religious ties, warlords or mafias, particular subnational or cross-national geographical regions and the like. In addition, political resources are necessary too – reliable and effective leadership, legitimate and efficient political institutions, and inclusive political processes. Solidarity must exist from the bottom up, not just from the top down.

The effective building, marshalling and use of traditional forms of power are highly problematic. In the traditional understanding of international power relations, the international system itself is defined as a structure of relative power based on: (a) how many strong or weak states there are, or the polarity of the international system; and (b) how great are the disparities among them, or the degree of hierarchy of the system (Waltz 1979). A system with more than three strong powers is multipolar; a system with two dominant powers is bipolar; and a system with only one hegemonic power is unipolar. Alliances are precarious: a Chinese or Asian proverb has it that: 'The enemy of my enemy is my friend.' In this context, the main stabilizing – and potentially destabilizing – mechanism is a balance of power among states (Little 2007).

However, balances of power are ultimately contingent. They emerge from wars, and conditions change over time. Old powers decline, new ones arise, and various kinds of re-equilibration occur. In the last analysis, even when there is relative peace and stability, those conditions emerge from and are maintained by underlying relationships of force. In the last analysis, they depend on the effectiveness of states both in being capable of developing, continually modernizing and using – *as well as not using* – force in circumstances where the very use of force has counterproductive effects: where miscalculated aggression leads to defeat; where overambition leads to 'imperial overstretch' (Kennedy 1987); where 'planning for the last war' proves useless in the face of technological and organizational advances; where force triggers multiple layers of conflict such as civil wars; where domestic opposition leads to defeat at home; and where the very structure and foundations of the state are threatened with destabilization, disintegration and state failure; and as we will argue below, all four of the traditional dimensions of international power outlined above are increasingly coming under pressure in a globalizing world.

BEYOND ANARCHY AND HIERARCHY: CROSS-CUTTING FORMS OF POWER IN THE WORLD ORDER

The traditional conceptualization of power as described above – one which is most characteristic of the 'realist' school of International Relations theory, a label derived from nineteenth Century German concept of *Realpolitik*, but often taken for granted by practitioners, mass publics, and many who would offer only a partial critique – has nevertheless been challenged at many levels. 'Idealists', 'liberal internationalists' and 'liberal (or sometimes neoliberal) institutionalists' argue not only that growing interdependence among states since the First World War has led to the uneven development of a range of institutions such as the United Nations and the World Trade Organization, but also that a raft of smaller specialized regimes, along with transgovernmental networks, together constitute an important and relatively autonomous superstructure that increasingly leads to cooperative outcomes (Keohane 1984; Ruggie 1993; Slaughter 2004). Marxists have of course long argued that the inherently internationalized infrastructure of capitalism, rooted in the relations of production, constitutes an authoritative socio-political superstructure too – a superstructure that in the era of globalization takes on an even more transnationalized form which Gill calls the 'new constitutionalism' (Gill 2003).

New critiques also challenge the image of the inside/outside structuring of international power relations. Postmodernists perceive a fragmentation of traditional 'narratives' of the state and the states system, but with no emerging alternative conception of power except the interaction of micro-'circuits of power' (Foucault 1981). Economic liberals and neoliberals argue that transnational market forces and new forms of market friendly regulation at multiple levels – transnational, regional, national and local – are creating a range of norms, practices, policies and institutional reforms that spin new webs of power within and below – as well as across – borders.

Indeed, the 'global' is sometimes not seen as a distinct level at all, but one which is immanent and embedded in the local, whether in terms of the organization of geography and space (Brenner et al., 2003) or the dynamics of social and political relations at the micro-level (Sassen 2007) – the macrocosm within the microcosm. Transnational pluralists assert that those interest groups which have the most clout today are those that can coordinate a range of multi-level transnational linkages (Cerny 2006). And constructivists and other ideas-oriented theorists argue that transnationally oriented ideologies, especially neoliberalism, are becoming increasingly embedded and hegemonic, shaping globalization on the one hand (Cerny 2008a) but also engendering potential resistance on the other (Gills 2000).

In all these cases, analysts argue that the traditional inside/outside distinction and the vertically organized forms of power intrinsic to it are being not only eroded but also systematically cross-cut by horizontal linkages, organizational forms and power relationships, whether political, social or economic, in increasingly complex forms of transnational interdependence (Keohane and Nye 1977; Halperin 2007; Cerny 2008b). Whether or not this rapidly evolving state of affairs leads to or constitutes a coherent system of 'global governance' is of course highly contested (Prakash and Hart 1999); but its increasingly 'multi-layered', 'multi-level' or 'multi-nodal' structure requires a reconfiguration of our very conception of how power is structured and how it is wielded by actors in practice – the structure and dynamics of power. This reconfiguration involves all four dimensions of power discussed earlier.

In terms of the first dimension, debates among academic political scientists, international relations theorists, international political economists – as well as among practitioners, policymakers, politicians, international bureaucrats, economic and financial commentators, military experts, etc. – focus more and more on whether, as noted above, some sort of system of global governance is in fact emerging. This does not constitute the equivalent of world government, of course. Indeed, the very concept of 'governance' as it was previously used in political theory connoted not formal institutionalized structures and processes, but informal practices, indirect processes of social control, and loose and fungible structures of power such as the 'self-organizing networks' analyzed by policy network theorists (Rhodes 1996), economic sociologists, marketing specialists and political economists (Thompson et al., 1991; Castells 1996; Henderson et al., 2002).

It is certainly true, of course, that the underlying structures of these institutions and processes are still highly intergovernmental. They are set up by states, their decision-making members are appointed by states, their voting arrangements most of the time reflect the relative power of states – often as determined by funding arrangements which give sometimes disproportionate power to the largest donor governments – and governments are often not bound by their decisions and have at least some sort of powers of veto and/or are able to dilute and avoid complying with institutional decisions. Nevertheless, the crystallization of new formal and informal structures, institutions and processes is widely seen to enable the development of cooperative arrangements that are not as subject to defection as in the case of direct intergovernmental relations, not as dominated by purely national interests as unmediated foreign policy-making processes are, and not as dependent on self-defence and self-help as neorealist unit actors would be.

In some cases, institutionalized processes have become relatively independent from the control of states, especially where autonomous legal processes give decision-makers formal insulation from governments. Probably the most advanced of these regimes is the World Trade Organization's Dispute Settlement Mechanism. Of course, even here there are limitations. Only member states have legal standing to bring actions against other states for violating the requirements of membership by imposing trade protection measures, and there is no process for directly compelling compliance with the decisions of WTO panels – the only sanction is to permit the injured party or parties to impose retaliatory measures. However, outside groups and organizations are widely consulted in the dispute settlement process – for example, some international organizations have formal observer status – and compliance can usually be negotiated rather than imposed, often *before* a formal adjudication is reached (Wolfe 2005). The result is a semi-autonomous political process that pursues the goal of freer trade, for better or worse depending on your viewpoint, on as close to a supranational basis as it is possible to reach in a world of still formally sovereign states. The clamor of states to join the WTO beyond the original 123 who participated in the Uruguay Round negotiations, including China, and with Russia and the Ukraine among several waiting in the wings – there are 151 members as of July 2007 – indicates that there is a strong consensus among the overwhelming majority of states that the benefits of membership and compliance with the rules significantly outweigh the costs.

Of course, most international regimes are less inclusive, more constrained by member governments, and/or much narrower in their remits. States often engage in 'venue shopping' and 'forum shopping' to find the organization they think will most likely support their national position. However, the fact that they participate in such processes on a regular basis and formulate strategies and tactics around such international and transnational 'rules of the game' is a strong indicator that states themselves generally act to reinforce rather than to undermine the process. Thus, many analysts argue, there are several characteristics that lead to the conclusion that the development of international regimes has reached some sort of 'critical mass' in developing towards a more coherent form of global governance with significant supranational potential, at least in specific, but often structurally important, issue-areas. The resistance of the George W. Bush Administration in the United States to join certain organizations such as the Kyoto Protocol on climate change has been widely seen across the world as the deviant behaviour of an arrogant, warmongering regime – behaviour which is, however, likely to change after the 2008 presidential elections, whichever party wins.

The main variable propelling this process of change is usually seen to be the nature of the policy issues and challenges that face both states and international organizations today – challenges like global economic growth, climate change and pollution, cross-border civil and insurgent wars, increasing relative inequality, and the growing public salience of poverty and uneven development, not to mention a range of significant issues concerning particular transnationally networked economic sectors, cross-cutting transportation and infrastructure issues, technological changes with global implications such as governing the internet, and the like. The enmeshing of public and private sector organizations, especially in issue-areas requiring international regulation, further reinforces the formal and informal roles of international regimes. Also the development of regional organizations, especially what many analysts would regard as the semi-sovereign European Union, has taken regime development and institutionalization to a very high level on a range of issues, rules and practices. Nevertheless, despite the EU's relatively high level of integration, not only are some of the same questions as we have asked of other international regimes still relevant – especially the role of EU member states in key decision-making processes – but other regional organizations have also proved much weaker and more internally conflict-prone, making regionalization a rather uneven process in global context.

These characteristics of a wide range of international regimes are therefore widely thought to be leading to ever-increasing potential 'absolute gains' for participating actors, rather than the zero-sum 'relative gains' of autonomous nation-states pursuing their national interests in the traditional way (Keohane 1984). In other words, in addition to the development of a complex if often fragmented international decision-making superstructure, new if still embryonic forms of transnational *quasi-authority* are emerging that are increasingly rooted in cross-cutting, post-national forms of legitimacy that are less rooted in national structures of accountability (see http://www2.warwick.ac.uk/fac/soc/csgr/activitiesnews/conferences/conference2007/ for a range of papers on the issue of legitimacy). However, global governance advocates also would accept that operating in such a changing world is leading to new problems of management and control, what Lake has called 'the privatization of governance' (Lake 1999; Kahler and Lake 2003) and the increasing importance of 'private authority' in international affairs (Cutler et al. 1999; Ronit and Schneider 2000; Hall and Biersteker 2003). Institutions and processes of global governance do not, of course, have the direct sanctioning power that has been at the core of state development and power in the modern era – especially in the form of Weber's 'monopoly of legitimate violence', whether domestic or international. Their sovereignty is to some extent 'pooled' rather than compromised by the development of these institutions and processes. Nevertheless, the inside/outside distinction is being increasingly – and systematically – transgressed in many significant ways, and nation-states themselves are being enmeshed in transnational webs of power.

In terms of the second dimension, the goals of social, political and economic actors increasingly reflect social, economic and political values other than mere national defense, the pursuit of national interests or the position of the state in an international pecking order as determined by relations of force and balances of power. The key to this change lies in the same driving force that is reinforcing the practical impact and quasi-authority of international regimes – i.e., the changing nature of the cross-cutting challenges that states, regimes, interest groups, value coalitions, private sector actors and the like face in the global era.

The increasing integration of transnational economic markets has led to the emergence of cross-border interest groups, both formal and informal, including groups representing such economic or 'sectional' interests as multinational corporations; financial market actors, banks, accountants, auditors, investors, bondholders, and today social groups affected by the US subprime mortgage crisis; coalitions of farmers, small businesses and the like affected by the need to operate in global markets; and even trade unions and other social groups affected by global economic change. Furthermore, international awareness of and concern about issues of social justice, poverty and the power of abusive and/or corrupt elites have led to the rapid growth of 'value' groups (Key 1953) or 'advocacy networks' (Keck and Sikkink 1998), now widely referred to as 'global civil society', often with close relationships with more socially oriented international regimes.

Among the most potent themes of global civil society groups are human rights and human security. In other words, these groups have been successfully redefining two of the most important social and political issue-areas of the modern world for the traditional legitimation of nation-states themselves – stemming from the Enlightenment – as having a primordially international and even global dimension. Human rights – the international equivalent of civil rights, one of the most important value issue-areas where democratic states have in the past claimed to represent the most elemental underlying interests and values of their citizens – are now being internationalized. Also security, since time immemorial the overwhelmingly predominant rationale for the state retaining and pursuing power in the international arena, is being reclaimed for the world as a whole – a qualitative leap beyond the rather crude and often stalemated twentieth century notions of 'collective security' represented by the League of Nations and the United Nations, and perhaps most salient of all, given the recent growth of concern with issues like climate change and the increasingly obvious effects of global warming, have been environmental groups. These groups have come to occupy a particularly central place in the claim to represent people in general across borders, not only transcending the nation-state but calling for global solutions to deal with a growing, imperative crisis.

Cross-cutting forms of power and influence are therefore being, and will continue to be, used more and more to pursue goals of fairness (Kapstein 2006), transnational economic regulation (Jordana and Levi-Faur 2004), 'green' environmental policy (Kütting 2004), human rights, multiculturalism, corporate governance (Gourevitch and Shinn 2005), criminal behaviour by governments (the International Criminal Court), the excessive use of force (the Ottawa Convention on the banning of landmines), and many others. The pursuit of social justice and even social and economic redistribution is no longer limited to the arena or 'container' of the nation-state, and new forms of political and social action requiring the linking of local, national, regional and international interest and value groups across borders (Tarrow 2005) and the building of transnational coalitions to push for transnational polices and solutions are becoming increasingly significant. Political, social and economic power is being harnessed transnationally in ways previously disqualified by the inside/outside distinction.

In terms of the third dimension, therefore, power is clearly increasingly being *organized* in cross-cutting, transnational ways. In addition to the proliferation and expansion of international regimes and global governance – the most obvious but problematic public face of this reorganization process – transnational circuits of power are increasingly organizing around *sectors* and *issue-areas* rather than around holistic national interests. Of course, many of these organizational trends are still embryonic, and nation-state-based actors play key roles, but the general direction of change is clear.

In economic sectors characterized by the growing significance of multinational or transnational corporations, the ability of these corporations to coordinate their own actions across borders – whether in pressing for regulatory changes, playing off tax jurisdictions, etc. – is just the tip of the iceberg. Even small firms that seem ostensibly 'local' are not immune, being dependent upon 'foreign' raw materials, export markets, investment finance, migrant labour and the like, and increasingly both form parts of wider networks and coordinate their actions.

As a result, in addition to the journalistically salient phenomenon of 'offshoring' of jobs and its impact on local employment in downsized firms, ordinary people are becoming enmeshed in increasingly complex and subtle ways international production processes, technological developments, markets and consumer preferences. In other words, the organization of the world of work – once embedded in the Fordist factory system – increasingly depends upon flexible, complex transnational economic activities and circuits of political-economic power. Ordinary people are growing more and more aware that their fates depend not so much on decisions taken at national level but on wider developments and transformations at international, transnational and translocal levels (Hobson and Seabrooke 2007).

Less formal networks and more formal interaction among firms, 'private regimes', 'alliance capitalism' and the ability of non-state actors generally to develop a range of formal and informal interconnections, both economic and political, has led to significant degrees of policy convergence both across states and in terms of shaping the evolution of global governance more generally (Higgott, Underhill and Bieler 1999). The linking of financial markets and institutions across borders has led to far-reaching changes in market organization, including cross-border mergers and convergence of practices. Financial crises have played a large part in catalyzing these organizational changes, as demonstrated by global fallout from the recent subprime mortgage crisis in the United States. Significant issue-areas such as accountancy, auditing and corporate governance have led to ongoing negotiation processes among firms, sectoral private sector organizations, governments and international regimes to reconcile conflicting standards and move towards a more level playing field (Mügge 2006).

In this context, not only have government agencies redefined their aims and objectives in the light of transnational experience – interacting increasingly through 'transgovernmental networks' among governmental agencies and public/private policy communities (Slaughter 2004) – but value-oriented as well as sectoral pressure groups organized across borders have, as noted above, also come to the fore in a number of key issue-areas such as the attempt to expand 'corporate social responsibility' agreements and standards (Lipschutz 2005). These processes are uneven but ongoing. In this context, the organization of power is increasingly *horizontally stratified* according to issue-area, mainly structured through economic and social linkages across borders, and therefore less amenable to control and centralization through the state (Cerny 1995). Indeed the 'splintered state' (Machin and Wright 1985) or 'disaggregated state' (Slaughter 2004) is increasingly characterized by horizontal cross-border power relationships too.

The fourth dimension – the use of force and violence – has also undergone fundamental change (Cerny 2000). The end of the Cold War did not result so much from the breakdown of a particular balance of power as from the increasing ineffectiveness of interstate balances of power generally to regulate the international system. Both superpowers became weaker in systemic terms because traditional forms of power could not cope with the challenges of the late twentieth-century international order. This change has entailed not merely the replacement of interstate competition for military security by new forms of interstate competition, e.g. for 'economic security', but rather a realization that security based on the simple interaction of unitary nation-states itself is becoming a cause of even greater insecurity, represented not only from above by a general threat of uncontrollable nuclear annihilation – the core problematic of the bipolar balance of the Cold War itself – but also from below, by the rise of civil wars, tribal and religious conflicts, terrorism, civil violence in developed countries, the international drugs trade, state collapse, etc.

The provision of security itself as a public good – the very *raison d'être* of the Westphalian states system – can no longer be guaranteed by that system. Changing payoff matrices are creating a range of incentives for players – especially non-state players – to defect from the states system itself unless restrained from doing so by the constraints of complex interdependence. Attempts to provide international and domestic security through the state and the states system are becoming increasingly dysfunctional, both increasing 'imperial overstretch' and provoking severe backlashes at both local and transnational levels – what has been called 'blowback' (Johnson 2000). These backlashes interact with economic and social processes of complex globalization to create overlapping and competing cross-border networks of power, shifting loyalties and identities, and new sources of endemic low-level conflict. A combination of economic interpenetration and low-level conflict – along with the post-Vietnam 'body bag syndrome' in the most powerful countries (including the United States in the wake of the Iraq War), leading to popular revulsion at more ineffective forms of state-based military action – are taking over the kind of systemic regulatory role played by interstate conflict and competition in the Westphalian system. Emerging mechanisms of stabilization are therefore highly uneven, riddled with structural tensions, and suboptimal in terms of effective governance, although in quite different ways from traditional balances of power and the old inter-state 'security dilemma'.

The future of military force as the bottom line of power is itself being questioned once again, but in a rather different way from earlier forms of extra-governmental pacifism and anti-war protest. As noted above, a rather different model of the pursuit of power by *states themselves* has potentially been emerging as the result of long-term change in and experience of international war and power relations over the past 50–100 years. In particular, there has been a transformation in European attitudes and foreign policy across the board as the result of having been the cradle of two devastating world wars and the geographical epicentre of the Cold War. This transformation involves a shift towards a combination of multilateralism – reinforced by the regionalism of the European Union, but primordially rooted in the experiences of European nation-states – towards a combination of demilitarization and multilateralism as the new, main organizing principles of the international system (Sheehan 2008; Moravcsik 2007).

Europe's identity as a new model 'civilian superpower' (Galtung 1973), reflected not only in the foreign policies of Germany and other states but also in the attitudes of elites and mass publics (Harnisch and Maull 2001), is an expression of a widespread normative perspective that the use of force in international relations is just as immoral and counterproductive as the use of force by private actors domestically. Although there is as yet no equivalent of Weber's 'legitimate monopoly of violence' at the international level, the use of traditional forms of power by states is becoming increasingly delegitimized. For example, the counterproductive use of force by the United States in the 'global war on terror' in the name of state security and the *heimat* (homeland) has paradoxically been a catalyst in expanding calls for what might be labelled the 'domestication of power' in the international system. It is widely held outside the US – and increasingly inside, too – that terrorism is fundamentally a 'law and order' question that is best addressed by police powers and legal methods, rather than by labelling terrorists as 'enemy combatants' and pursuing them as if they constituted a traditional state-like international threat. The drive for American hegemony and empire that is represented by the George W. Bush Administration may prove to be the 'last hurrah' for the use of traditional methods of power and force in the international arena.

CONCLUSIONS

Power at the international level has traditionally been seen as constituting the underlying structural dynamic of the international system – beyond and outside the bounds of domestically rooted relationships of 'friendship' and 'justice', and ultimately manifested in the real or latent use of force, i.e. through war or the threat of war. Power in this traditional sense has been embodied by and embedded in nation-states, the fundamental building blocks and unit actors of international relations. That conception of power has been seen as stemming from or reflecting the lack of world government and therefore the 'anarchy' of a system the highest authorities within which have been states themselves, pursuing their national interests and seeking to affirm their place in the international pecking order. It has involved a limited form of power – power in and of itself, organized by states, rooted in the use of force, rather than a means to a higher collective end.

Today, the international system is undergoing a fundamental process of structural change that is transforming the way power is conceived, shaped, built up, organized and used. This process of the reconfiguration of power increasingly cuts across state borders – embedded in new but still embryonic forms of global governance, reflecting the sort of 'higher' normative values that domestic actors have always pursued at home, shaped by transnational interests and global civil society rather than interstate conflict, organized through transnational and transgovernmental networks rather than unified foreign policy elites and military command structures, and informed by a growing sense that the use of force is becoming increasingly counterproductive in an international system characterized by complex interdependence – and indeed, that international power must be 'civilianized' and domesticated in order to be both effective and legitimate in a globalizing world.

REFERENCES

Brenner, Neil, Bob Jessop, Martin Jones, and Gordon MacLeod (eds) (2003). *State/Space: A Reader*. Malden, MA and Oxford: Blackwell.
Bull, Hedley (1977). *The Anarchical Society: A Study in World Politics*. Basingstoke: Macmillan.
Castells, Manuel (1996). *The Rise of the Network Society*. Oxford and Cambridge, MA: Blackwell.
Cerny, Philip G. (1980). *The Politics of Grandeur: Ideological Aspects of de Gaulle's Foreign Policy*. Cambridge: Cambridge University Press.
Cerny, Philip G. (1995). 'Globalization and the changing logic of collective action', *International Organization*, 49; 4 (Autumn): 595–625.
Cerny, Philip G. (2000). 'The new security dilemma: Divisibility, defection and disorder in the global era', *Review of International Studies*, 26; 4 (October): 623–646.
Cerny, Philip G. (2006). 'Plurality, pluralism, and power: Elements of pluralist analysis in an age of globalization', in Rainer Eisfeld, (ed.), *Pluralism: Developments in the Theory and Practice of Democracy*. Opladen: Barbara Budrich, 81–111.
Cerny, Philip G. (2008a). 'Embedding neoliberalism: The evolution of a hegemonic paradigm', *Journal of International Trade and Diplomacy*, 2; 1 (Spring):
Cerny, Philip G. (2008b). 'Neoliberalism and place: Deconstructing and reconstructing borders', in Bas Arts, Henk van Houtum and Arnoud Lagendijk (eds), *State, Place, Governance: Shifts in Territoriality, Governmentality and Policy Practices*. Berlin: Springer.
Cutler, A. Claire, Virginia Haufler and Tony Porter (eds) (1999). *Private Authority and International Affairs*. Albany, NY: State University of New York Press.

Foucault, Michel (1981). *Power/Knowledge: Selected Interviews and Other Writings, 1972–1977*. Colin Gordon (ed.). New York: Longman.
Galtung, Johan (1973). *The European Community: A Superpower in the Making*. London: HarperCollins.
Gill, Stephen (2003). *Power and Resistance in the New World Order*. London: Palgrave Macmillan.
Gill, Stephen and David Law (1987). *The Global Political Economy: Perspectives, Problems and Policies*. Upper Saddle River, NJ: Prentice-Hall.
Gills, Barry K. (ed.) (2000). *Globalization and the Politics of Resistance*. London: Palgrave Macmillan.
Gladwell, Malcolm (2000). *The Tipping Point: How Little Things Can Make a Big Difference*. Boston: Little, Brown.
Gourevitch, Peter A. and James Schinn (eds) (2005). *Political Power and Corporate Control: The New Global Politics of Corporate Governance*. Princeton, NJ: Princeton University Press.
Hall, Rodney Bruce and Thomas J. Biersteker (eds) (2003). *The Emergence of Private Authority in Global Governance*. Cambridge: Cambridge University Press.
Halperin, S. (2007). '"Horizontal" Connections and Interactions in Global Development', in P. Wagner and N. Karagiannis (eds), *Varieties of World-making: Beyond Globalisation*. London: Liverpool University Press, pp. 133–53.
Harnisch, Sebastian and Hanns W. Maull (eds) (2001). *Germany as a Civilian Power? The Foreign Policy of the Berlin Republic*. Manchester: Manchester University Press.
Held, David (1995). *Democracy and the Global Order: From the Modern State to Cosmopolitan Governance*. Cambridge: Polity Press.
Henderson, Jeffrey, Peter Dicken, Martin Hess, Neil Coe and Henry Wai-Chung Yeung (2002). 'Global production networks and the analysis of economic development', *Review of International Political Economy*, 9; 3 (August): pp. 436–464.
Herz, John H. (1950). 'Idealist internationalism and the security dilemma', *World Politics*, 3; 2 (January): pp. 157–80.
Higgott, Richard, Geoffrey R.D. Underhill and Andreas Bieler (eds) (1999). *Non-state Actors and Authority in the Global System*. London: Routledge.
Hirst, Paul and Grahame, Thompson (1996). *Globalization in Question? The International Economy and the Possibilities of Governance*. Oxford: Polity Press.
Hobson, John M. and Leonard Seabrooke (eds) (2007). *Everyday Politics of the World Economy*. Cambridge: Cambridge University Press.
Hollis, Martin and Steve Smith (1990). *Explaining and Understanding International Relations*. Oxford: Clarendon Press.
Hurrell, Andrew (2007). *On Global Order: Power, Values and the Constitution of International Society*. Oxford: Oxford University Press.
Johnson, Chalmers (2000). *Blowback: The Costs and Consequences of American Empire*. New York: Metropolitan Books.
Jordana, Jacint and David Levi-Faur (eds) (2004). *The Politics of Regulation: Institutions and Regulatory Reform for the Age of Governance*. Cheltenham: Edward Elgar.
Kagan, Robert (2003). *Of Paradise and Power: America and Europe in the New World Order*. New York: Alfred A. Knopf.
Kahler, Miles and David A. Lake (eds) (2003). *Governance in a Global Economy: Political Authority in Transition*. Princeton, NJ: Princeton University Press.
Kapstein, Ethan B. (2006). *Economic Justice in an Unfair World: Toward a Level Playing Field*. Princeton, NJ: Princeton University Press.
Keck, Margaret E. and Kathryn Sikkink (1998). *Activists Beyond Borders: Advocacy Networks in International Politics*. Ithaca, NY: Cornell University Press.
Kennedy, Paul (1987). *The Rise and Fall of the Great Powers: Economic Change and Military Conflict from 1500 to 2000*. New York: Random House.
Keohane, Robert O. (1984). *After Hegemony: Cooperation and Discord in the World Political Economy*. Princeton: Princeton University Press.
Keohane, Robert O. and Joseph S. Nye, Jr. (1977). *Power and Interdependence*. Boston: Little, Brown.
Key, V.O. Jr. (1953). *Politics, Parties, and Pressure Groups*. New York: Thomas Y. Crowell.
Kütting, Gabriela (2004). *Globalization and the Environment: Greening Global Political Economy*. Albany, NY: State University of New York Press.

Lake, David A. (1999). 'Global Governance: A Relational Contracting Approach', in Aseem Prakash and Jeffrey A. Hart (eds), *Globalization and Governance*. London: Routledge, pp. 31–53

Lipschutz, Ronnie D. (2005). *Globalization, Governmentality and Global Politics: Regulation for the Rest of Us?*, with James K. Rowe. London: Routledge.

Little, Richard (2007). *The Balance of Power in International Relations: Metaphors, Myths and Models*. Cambridge: Cambridge University Press.

Machin, Howard and Vincent, Wright. (eds) (1985). *Economic Policy and Policy-making Under the Mitterrand Presidency, 1981–1984*. London: Frances Pinter.

Moravcsik, Andrew (2007). 'Make way for the quiet superpower: The year ahead offers the perfect chance to remake transatlantic relations', *Newsweek,* (international edition), 31 December 2007.

Morgenthau, Hans J. (1949). *Politics among Nations: The Struggle for Power and Peace*. New York: Alfred A. Knopf.

Mügge, Daniel (2006). 'Private-public puzzles: Inter-firm competition and transnational private regulation', *New Political Economy*, 11; 2 (June):

Pin-Fat, Véronique (2005). 'The metaphysics of the national interest and the 'mysticism' of the nation state: Reading Hans J. Morgenthau', *Review of International Studies*, 31; 2 (Summer): 217–236.

Prakash, Aseem and Jeffrey A. Hart (eds) (1999). *Globalization and Governance*. London: Routledge.

Putnam, Robert D. (1988). 'Diplomacy and domestic politics: The logic of two-level games', *International Organization*, 42; 2 (Summer 1988): 427–460.

Rhodes, R.A.W. (1996). 'The new governance: Governing without government', *Political Studies*, 44; 4 (September): 652–667.

Ronit, Karsten and Volker Schneider (eds) (2000). *Private Organisations in Global Politics*. London: Routledge.

Rosenau, James N. (1961). *Public Opinion and Foreign Policy: An Operational Formulation*. New York: Random House.

Ruggie, John Gerard (ed.) 1993. *Multilateralism Matters: The Theory and Praxis of an Institutional Form*. New York: Columbia University Press.

Sassen, Saskia, (ed.) (2007). *Deciphering the Global: Its Scales, Spaces and Subjects*. London and New York: Routledge.

Savage, Charlie (2007). *Takeover: The Return of the Imperial Presidency and the Subversion of American Democracy*. New York: Little, Brown.

Sheehan, James J. (2008). *Where Have All the Soldiers Gone? The Transformation of Modern Europe*. Boston: Houghton Mifflin.

Slaughter, Anne-Marie (2004). *A New World Order*. Princeton, NJ: Princeton University Press.

Spruyt, Hendrik (1994). *The Sovereign State and Its Competitors: An Analysis of Systems Change*. Princeton, NJ: Princeton University Press.

Tarrow, Sidney (2005). *The New Transnational Activism*. Cambridge: Cambridge University Press.

Thompson, G., Jennifer Frances, Rosalind Leva I and Jeremy C. Mitchell (eds) (1991). *Markets, Hierarchies and Networks: The Coordination of Social Life*. London and Thousand Oaks, CA: Sage Publications.

Waltz, Kenneth N. 1979. *Theory of International Politics*. Boston: Addison Wesley Longman.

Wolfe, Robert (2005). 'See You in Geneva? Legal (Mis) Representations of the Trading System', *European Journal of International Relations*, vol. 11, 3 (September), 339–365.

22

Discourse of Power

Stewart R. Clegg and Mark Haugaard

Writing a conclusion to such a large and varied volume as this was a task that demanded some consideration. Obviously, we had commissioned the pieces that we did because we thought that the authors invited were the best able to address the topics that they were invited to address. Yet, we wanted to engage with the contributors in this conclusion, not to treat them irreverently but not to treat them too reverently either. We wanted to engage in tribute and critique of their efforts, in the most positive and constructive sense of these terms; tribute as praise, review, as acknowledgement. In doing this we pay tribute to our contributors, in attempting to probe and understand the limitations both of the concept itself and the contributors' understandings of it. We seek to deploy reasoned judgement in our readings, drawing on a broad background of analysis, one that is capable, we hope, of the interpretive leaps needed for seasoned and systematic inquiry into the conditions and consequences of the use of a concept as central and as contested as 'power'.

Having made this decision, there was the question of how we should organize our ideas. When we started to write the conclusion we were on opposite sides of the earth, so the opportunities for face-to-face discussion were precluded. Mark suggested that we might try and conduct a conversation by e-mail, as a dialogue about the chapters, pulling out the points and implications that seemed significant. So this is what we did. The conversation started with Mark.

MARK:

In the introduction we began by observing that there is no single concept of power which can be deemed the 'correct one'. Rather, power is a 'family resemblance' concept where the extent to which a specific usage serves as a useful conceptual tool for the matter at hand is the test of utility. If the concept works for the task in hand, it is a commendable usage. Clearly, not all contributors agree with this essentially Wittgensteinian reading. For instance, in his chapter on 'power to' and 'power over', Göhler makes the case for replacing these concepts with 'transitive' and 'intransitive power'.

For Göhler, 'power to' is interpreted as being somehow 'independent of others', a distinction that parallels the difference between power as defined in terms of its *exercise* or as a *capacity* concept. I have always assumed that the fundamental distinction lies between power which actors resist (power over) and that which they do not (power to), while the 'capacity' versus 'exercise' issue was a separate debate whereby both concepts could exist as capacity or as exercise.

STEWART:

Well, interesting that you should say this. I am not so sure that 'power over' requires resistance. One may turn up for work on time and go through the motions of what one is supposed to be doing, whilst occasionally imagining oneself in another place, doing other things, whilst one does what one has to do to pay the bills. Now, unless we go the way of Cohen and Taylor (1976) and label imagination and day-dreaming as an 'escape attempt', it is hard to see this mundane compliance as 'power over' if resistance has to be coupled with it. One is at work, ostensibly in situ and in role, however semi-detached one might actually be, while doing what is required of one. One might rather be surfing or lying in someone's arms, but one is at work, dulled by the rhythms of everyday acquiescence and organization, externally imposed. Now, unless you want to maintain that the acceptance of a job involves a bargain in which you compel yourself to labour for the other freely (irrespective of the limited choices for alternative social reproduction offered by a highly structured environment of ownership and economic opportunities) I would want to see this relationship as irrevocably one of power over: one is working at tasks framed by another to whose terms one is subject. Is this not power over?

MARK:

Actually you are correct, I was over-simplifying. 'Power to' is the master concept indicating capacity for action, while 'power over' is a subset whereby actors are made do things that they would not otherwise. As was observed by Lukes with regard to the third dimension of power, the most effective use of power is when resistance has been overcome, which happens when compliance becomes routine. In fact in that case 'power over' and 'power to' merge. When actors join together to act in concert (power to), they do so to realize joint tasks, and in so doing they make each other do things which they would not otherwise for the purposes of a shared goal. To the extent to which employers and employees conceive of themselves as working toward shared goals, it could be argued that this is where 'power to' and 'power over' become indistinguishable. This is also when power to ceases to be a capacity and becomes active in its exercise.

Later in the chapter, in the context of Arendt (1958), Göhler acknowledges that the two debates about capacity and exercise and 'power to' and 'power over' cross-cut, which is the reason he prefers to use 'transitive' and 'intransitive' power. Therefore, the issue is not really how 'power to' and 'power over' should be understood but whether or not transitive and intransitive power are more useful distinctions.

In evaluating this I wish to reflect upon the debate between modernist and postmodernist views of power. Essentially the question is: can the concepts of transitive and intransitive power enable us to overcome the split between the likes of Foucault's (1979) 'socialization machine' and Lukes' (1974; 2005) desire to distinguish power from socialization?

STEWART:

You have suggested that we should imagine the Panopticon in terms of the idea of a 'socialization machine'. Within the Foucauldian framework, modern power resides in the construction of the social subject in such a way that they become an object that can be formed and moulded to give them certain capacities for self-surveillance and control that disposes their behaviour to be deployed in favour of those who have designed or implement the socialization machine.

MARK:

Such a formation of the self creates conditions of possibility for certain exercises of power and precludes others. Thus, the creation of a social subject would appear to be both a transitive and intransitive phenomenon. In terms of potential, the intransitive element would be the creation of a subject who is bound by certain internal constraints – 'self-binding'. In its actualisation as intransitive power, this facilitates forms of empowerment, in the terms that you propose, as self-correcting behaviour attuned to the regime of governance, which are commensurable with a certain social order – that of modernity.

However, in terms of the actualisation of transitive power in Göhler's account, I am slightly confused. The idea of *influence,* which Lukes (2005) distinguishes from power, suggests to me the absence of resistance by B, while it is clear that Göhler wishes much of the active aspect of 'power over' to fall inside this box, as represented in the figure (page x). So, I think we must assume that Göhler does not maintain the power/influence opposition whereby influence entails the complicity of B (for instance convincing B through better reason), while power is exercised against B's wishes as is argued by Morriss (1987: 8–13) and Lukes (2005: 36). Rather, he means 'influence' as having a significant effect upon someone, which may well include resistance by the object of power.

If my interpretation of his use of 'influence' is correct, this means that the capacities of intransitive power can either manifest themselves as 'empowerment' *or* in an actor's ability to make others do things which they would not do otherwise. In fact, the latter would be a subset of the former. In short, this is where the 'post-modern' constitutive view of power spills over into the kind of process described by the 'modernists', including Dahl (1961), Bachrach and Baratz (1970) and Lukes (2005).

In terms of the agency and structure debate, it could be argued that the 'potential' aspects of transitive and intransitive power are on the side of structure. These are the structuring aspects of social life which constitute us as agents who in the moment of agency are empowered and, in certain instances, that empowerment entails making the other act in ways in which they would not otherwise, thus 'influencing' them.

With respect to your own work, Stewart, as developed in *Frameworks of Power* (Clegg 2005), it would seem to me that the potential aspect of transitive and intransitive power would be the second, 'dispositional circuit' of power, while the 'actual' would be the 'episodic'. It could also be argued that the 'empowerment' aspect of intransitive power in the 'actual box' suggests the third circuit of power, which is the systemic part, whereby certain systems facilitate certain type of power and not others.

While I think it fair to say that Göhler's typology is highly suggestive and can provide conceptual space for some of the big debates on power, I would question if it renders the terms 'power over' and 'power to' obsolete as he seems to imply. One of the problems with the power debate has always been a certain tendency to assume, as observed by Morriss (1987) and Michel Foucault (1979: 194), that power is negative: that it says no, it oppresses, and prohibits. It seems to me that in those terms it is worthwhile to be able to counter such assumptions by saying that power is not only 'power over' it is also 'power to' and people understand this relatively easily. 'Power to' corrects the assumption that power is always noxious and something which is normatively reprehensible. Of course, if one goes into detail, 'power over' is not always negative (authority is legitimate 'power over') but I think the 'power over' versus 'power to' dualism captures a significant aspect of the human condition whereby power is both a condition of meaningful agency *and* of domination, while in the 'transitive' versus 'intransitive' view of power, this insight is lost. This brings me back to Wittgenstein's (1972) view that concepts do not replace each other, as hypotheses do in the natural sciences, rather they become more or less useful for certain intellectual tasks.

STEWART:

I do see some other problems with Göhler's conceptualization: the idea that 'power to' does not involve social relations because it is 'an ability to do or achieve something independent of others' (Göhler p. 28) seems to take us nowhere other than to a view that power is something that subjects may have, something they possess. Such views are, I believe, not very useful. They invariably lead to a resource-based views of power, which, given the contextual specificity of any resource from which one might derive a capacity, and the ways that even the simplest of resources rely on networks of social relations for their efficacy, does not admit of the clear cut distinction that Göhler wants to make. Making power a matter of potential takes us back to the standing conditions, to use a natural science terms, which enable potential to emanate. Just as an experiment will not occur with the causal efficacy expected if the proportions of chemicals mixed are faulty, or the experimental environment insufficiently sterile, so it is with power to in everyday life. If the social relations that comprise the standing conditions for the exercise of power that a practical power person seeks to make happen are not secure they will not have power to do what it is that they seek to do to demonstrate the capacities that they believed they held. It is this point, I think, that Göhler seeks to make in his discussion of power to in the context of the international relations literature, when he notes that the capacity to have the power to do something would be attributed to structures rather than agency, reserving agency for power over.

Göhler makes a basic distinction between 'power to' as a capacity, which I have discussed, and 'power to' as actual, as what he refers to as empowerment. He then wants to move the terms of debate to a distinction between the inside/outside of the actor which he specifies by use the terms transitive and intransitive. The problem here is the one that I have already alerted the reader to: empowerment may be something that the individual experiences in terms of self-reference, intransitively, but the actual fact of empowerment in an organization, for example, where the discourse of empowermemt has most often been situated, may be something that is consciously designed in a panoptical sense by an external agency requiring empowerment of subjects – but empowerment on terms that are heavily framed. I am not so sure that the distinction is as robust as Göhler would make it. 'Power to', even when it is conceived in terms of the intransitive dimension, still entails social relations and 'power over'. Finally, by restricting the intransitive dimension to Arendt's 'speaking and acting in concert', Göhler misses the opportunity to distinguish between concerting that is freely willed and that which is an imposition.

MARK:

In the classic Hobbesian formulation of the justification for political power, the state exists to overcome the collective actor problem (Hobbes 1968). The flaw with this supposed solution is that there is little to prevent the state from becoming a predator in its own right whereby, to use Locke's words, polecats and foxes are replaced by a lion. Thus the attempt to act in concert becomes subverted as domination. However, in 'Rational Choice Approaches' Dowding suggests an interesting way in which such a predatory state might wish to keep itself in check without presupposing altruism.

A predatory state that solely exploits others will have little legitimacy and will also be impoverished. If the relatively powerless know that the state will randomly steal from them then they have little incentive to produce and if they regard the state as the enemy, which they would in such a relationship of exploitation, all tribute to the state would need to be extracted by coercion. Consequently, the optimal solution for the rational predatory state is to provide goods and services thus maximising legitimacy. In Ernest Gellner's *Plough, Sword and Book* (1988) he argues precisely that it was this kind of perception on the part of the predators, the specialists in violence or the sword, which allowed production to replace predation as a central theme and value of life (1988: 158). What interests me about this is the way in which negative power and positive power are intertwined. While it can be argued that the modern state is more effective at domination than any previous state in human history, part of its facility in this regard is premised upon the fact that it also does something other than predation. When social theorists criticize modernity there is a tendency to forget that successful domination only works because it is fused with legitimacy and the latter is not necessarily based upon misperception – 'false consciousness', subjection to dominant discourses, symbolic violence, hegemony and so on.

A further interesting idea follows, even if it is the case that miscognitions are present in modern relations of domination, this phenomenon is possible only because legitimacy sometimes is based upon well-informed knowledge. This is what I take to be Habermas' (1987) point when he argues that instrumental rationality is actually parasitic upon communicative action.

STEWART:

With respect to arguments about the state, I think it is also worth pondering that the state may not be one that the majority of citizens would choose rationally, but they are actually denied the opportunity of choice. Thus, in 'modern states', you suggest, 'successful domination' only works because it is fused with legitimacy and the latter is not necessarily based upon misperception, but, depending on how one defines 'modern' I think that this is true only in a limited way. If one admits that, in their time, the East European states of the Soviet sphere were modern; at least they were so in Weber's (1978) sense of rationalized institutions, their survival was not premised on legitimacy but on what Michael Mann (1986) would call organizational outflanking by virtue of monopoly over the means of violence. Challenges to legitimacy were several, including Hungary in 1956 and Czechoslovakia in 1968, for instance, but the Soviet tanks were too potent a symbol of that monopoly of which Weber wrote. It was only when the state had been delegitimated from within by *perestroika* and *glasnost*, and the realization in the client states that the tanks would not be available next time that the house of cards collapsed. The collapse occurred because the tanks did not come and people knew that they would not as the signals from Gorbachev were clear that they would not. Once the people scented this, the game was up. Now, you could maintain that the people were making a rational choice to live under Soviet and client state rule in peace rather than risk life in what would doubtless have been suppressed, but might this be stretching rational choice too far? And how useful is rational choice for large-scale collective and institutionally embedded situations?

MARK:

There are certain books that are remembered because they ask the right question. In *Power: A Philosophical Analysis*, Morriss accomplished this when he posed the question: why do we need the concept of power? (Morriss 1987: 36). In the chapter 'Power and Liberalism', he does something different but in a way equally profound and reorienting to the way we think. Traditional liberal theory is usually premised upon freedom, while Morriss shows us that 'power to' is actually as fundamental. Not only should social actors be free to do certain things but they should also *be able* to do them. If liberalism came about through a modern orientation to the value of the 'ordinary life', any decent liberal society should concern itself with providing the necessary capacity ('power to') for realizing such a life.

Currently we are living in an age in which neo-liberalism has become hegemonic. One of the ways in which neo-liberals have succeeded in bringing about this state of affairs is by stealing the clothes of liberals. Their actual intellectual historical antecedents are *libertarianism*, which is a dissimilar beast from the classic liberalism of the kind espoused by John Rawls (1972) and John Stuart Mill (1989). Rawls begins from liberal premises, in the sense of beginning from the individual, but his conclusions are clearly redistributive and, if implemented, would lead to a welfare state. However, neo-liberals, like their libertarian antecedents, make a fetish of the market based upon the strategic use of the concept of freedom. Morriss demonstrates that the central concern of any liberal society which entails a rounded moral concern with the fair treatment of individuals – that they are an end in themselves and so on – presupposes an emphasis not only upon freedom but also upon power, as a capacity for action. In some ways this is a clearer argument that the Rawlsian one, which people find difficult to understand because the 'veil of ignorance' appears so contrived.

STEWART:

Neo-economic liberalism is hegemonic in liberal discourse because it privileges consumer sovereignty. Consumers are expected to know what they want and they express these wants through their preferences to consume certain things in markets. From this perspective, the idea that consumers could be mistaken about their preferences is absurd: their preferences are expressed in decisions to allocate resources to certain consumption goods. As consumers spend, then markets reach equilibrium between what consumers choose to buy and what producers choose to sell, through the price mechanism. To neo-liberals this is a kind of 'original position', which has ultimate legitimacy because power appears to be absent.

What gets lost from such accounts is the fact that such a market driven 'original position' might be skewed by the capacities of the actors. What they may want and desire is determined by a *habitus* shaped by a previous life experience and a product of their capacities in the first place. The idea that there might be such a thing as systematically skewed preferences, skewed, by the articulation of markets, advertising, and conceptions of desire, that determine actors capacity for action is inadmissible. There is no account of how preferences might be subject to formation, historically, structurally, comparatively – preferences just exist. I agree that Morriss does a great job of enabling us to avoid these traps.

MARK:

Another aspect of Morriss' paper, which I consider intriguing, is the fact that he is practising critique by using the concept of 'power to' as his main focus, in place of 'power over'. To date, most normative theorists – with the notable exception of Arendt (1958, 1994) – have seen the normative problem of power as critiquing what they consider unjust exercises of 'power over' and, more generally, relations of domination. Lukes is paradigmatic in this regard. Although Foucault frequently asserts that power is 'positive' and does not just say 'no', his normative view of power is negative. The point for Foucault is that constitutive power, while it says 'yes' and thus appears a force for good, is actually normatively reprehensible, thus it is power which we should resist.

STEWART:

This is correct and a subtle interpretation. The 'positive' in Foucault is still normatively shaping and subjectifying; it stills authenticity and selfhood in the service of some larger institutional processes.

MARK:

Intuitively speaking, critiquing 'power over' seems a logical starting point for political philosophy. After all, as observed by Hobbes, the problem of normative theory is to find criteria for justifying authority: why should we step out of the state of nature and accept orders from others? Intuitively, this appears as a problem of 'power over'. However, another way of looking at it is that the reason we wish to leave the state of nature in the first place is to gain 'power to' for the purposes of leading meaningful lives. Thus the problem of the state of nature is actually a 'power to' problem in the first instance.

STEWART:

Well, it may be thought to be so but it is also, anthropologically, a non-problem. The 'state of nature' only functions in Hobbes as a counterfoil to a specific state of society, founded on distinct notions of sovereignty, order and subjection. It describes no actually existing society nor could it, as Bauman (1987) noted in *Legislators and Interpreters*. There are no anthropological accounts of any society that corresponds to a Hobbesian state of nature; even when one looks at resource constrained situations on islands whose natural resources were exhausting because of over-use, such as Aotearoa in pre-white colonial days, there were strong patterns of order and civility within societies even whilst there might be warfare between societies. Anthropologically, we can observe many societies in which there is, only by a large stretch of the imagination, a contractual basis to order. In Australia, for instance, indigenous societies functioned largely through detailed oral traditions of 'Dreaming' which contained the knowledge of the society, of the seasons, of hunting, fishing and taboos, as well as stories that situated a people's sense of themselves and where they came from, so that people could stand firm in the law of the clan and language society. There is no evidence of a prior state of nature and a rational choice to make a social contract. There is, in short, no other to society in terms of social reproduction and no necessity for that social reproduction to evolve along contractual lines of sovereignty.

MARK:

Morriss would counter this by arguing that the idea of a 'state of nature' is a thought experiment, and thought experiments are considered useful in the natural sciences, so why not in political theory? I would also argue that thought experiments of this kind enable you distil ideal types (in the Weberian sense) from reality which, by necessity, is more messy and confused. I would interpret Rawl's account of the 'original position' as constructing an ideal type of actors methodologically bracketing extraneous material for the purposes of making sense of justice within a liberal interpretative framework.

Establishing what qualifies a political system to be called democratic is a question which constantly exercises the minds of political theorists and scientists. In university tutorials all over the world students of the history of political thought discuss whether ancient Athens was 'really a democracy' and, if so, whether it was 'more or less democratic' than contemporary democracies. As argued by Hyland (1995), this conundrum comes from thinking of democracy as an absolute concept, whereby a set of political institutions are considered *either* democratic *or* not. Democracy is not a discrete concept in the way that an apple or an orange is: something is either an apple or an orange, not more or less so. Democracy is a scalar concept, much as liberty or freedom of speech. There is no society in which there is absolute liberty to do whatever you want, neither is there one with complete freedom of speech. However, that does not entail that some societies allow for *greater* liberty or *more* freedom of speech than others. The same holds for democracy; some societies are more democratic than others, in relative terms, and quite often they are so relative to different criteria. Ancient Athens was less democratic than modern societies in terms of the extent of the franchise but, qualitatively, in terms of the depth and nature of participation, Athens was substantially more democratic than many contemporary political systems.

I think part of the success of Charles Tilly's argument lies precisely in the fact that he moves subtly from the absolute criteria, such as Robert Dahl's (1982) checklist for democracy, to a scalar vision whereby societies are more or less democratic along a set of criteria. The only slight unease I have with the analysis concerns the criteria itself. Tilly ignores the fact that what we mean by democracy concerns not only decision-making but also includes liberal freedoms, whereby the state should be limited in capacity to exercise power over individual citizens. While it is true that a democratic state has to have the capacity to make decisions, the liberal element also entails that there must be limits to such capacities with respect to the individual. These limits include not only protection from arbitrary actions by the state, which he mentions, but also from excessively intrusive, yet lawful, exercises of power, an observation that has implications for the correlations between effectiveness and democracy as he discusses in Figures 4.2 and 4.3 (pages: 82, 84). If liberal protections are not part of the democratic axis in Figure 4.2 there will be a point where 'high capacity' impinges upon liberal freedoms. My concern here is what John Stuart Mill famously termed the 'tyranny of the majority', which describes a political system that may be democratic in terms of decision-making but is undemocratic when viewed from the perspective of the rights of dissenting minorities. The more effective such a system is the less it allows for liberal freedoms, which is an insight that lies behind the intuition than in imperfect democracies inefficiency is often a blessing in disguise.

STEWART:

Yes, when I first read Tilly's account it was in a context where the Australian government of the day, the Howard Coalition government of 1996–2007, was still deeply committed to the occupation of Iraq. The ground for their participation shifted throughout the period; in debates in the House of Representatives the major reasons advanced were what turned out to be the chimerical weapons of mass destruction as well as the atrocities of the Saddam regime. Statements to the effect that 'people-shredding machines' were used to despatch enemies were read into Hansard from the Prime Minister. Subsequently, after the despatch of the Saddam government and the creation of the Provisional Authority, the legitimation for occupation and continuing involvement consisted of a repetition of the Bush line – the 'coalition of the willing' were bringing democracy to Iraq. Well, indeed, elections were held and there was large-scale participation but subsequent events point out the paradox: an election is an event and democracy is a process. It is a process of civil ordering and stable rules for conduct that are agreed in routinized and largely peaceful ways. There is no sense in which what has occurred subsequent to the elections could be described as 'democratic order'. Such order rarely grows out of the barrel of occupying guns and resistance to them – in the Iraq context both the guns and the weapons that oppose them are inimical even to the establishment of the tyranny of the majority, something that can only flow from embedded institutions. The destruction of an existing set of institutions does not ensure that phenomena that the destroyers desire, such as 'democracy' and 'markets', will somehow flourish in the state of anarchy produced. There may be no natural 'states of nature' but there is plenty of evidence to suggest how to create simulacra of them. The occupation of Iraq provides a textbook case. It also demonstrates very acutely what Benton (1981) termed the paradox of emancipation: it can only come from the social action of those who are emancipating themselves rather than be something that is done to them against their own conception of their interests. In other words, structures cannot liberate action; as Giddens (1984) argues in the theory of structuration there is always a mutual implication, as Stones focuses on.

MARK:

Whenever I read accounts of Giddens' theory of structuration I cannot help thinking that for all its flaws (and there are many) the theory of structuration is also a victim of its own success. Currently, no sociologists or political scientist would think in the kind of dualistic way which was relatively common prior to the publication of *The Constitution of Society* in 1984 and, as a consequence of the influence of this book, some of insights of structuration theory now appear to us as banal truisms.

STEWART:

I have to tell you Mark that, occasionally, banal truisms pass for wisdom in the worlds of management and organization theory! Giddens is simply not read or referenced by other than a few sociologically oriented scholars and primitive forms of economism, functionalism and behaviourism prevail in which structural independent variables routinely cause effects on people conceived as homunculi of systems. The practical effects of Business School research probably far exceed those of sociology departments, in that they shape so much of the everyday worlds of work and organizations in which we spend our time; given that they are frequently based on sociological assumptions that are questionable if not primitive, it should be a matter of some concern.

MARK:

I think Stones is correct that, for all Giddens' attempt at balancing social subject and object, there is an excessive voluntarism built into the theory of structuration, which is exemplified by Giddens' assertion that agents can 'always choose to do otherwise'.

STEWART:

I had always interpreted this as a kind of existential commitment, something derived, perhaps, from Sartre (1956), that even in the direst of decision situations one could always choose suicide so as to thwart those agencies that sought to control one. Suicide as an existential act was what I assumed grounded the account.

MARK:

I think one of the reasons for the imbalance between structure and agency in Giddens is that the concept of structuration, taken singly, suggests structures are always reproduced unproblematically in social interaction.

STEWART:

Well, given the evident importance of Garfinkelian ethnomethodology in the early footings of structuration theory, it is odd that this should be assumed. For Garfinkel (1967), order is always fragile and open to disruption through agents who either do not know the rules or deliberately seek to reveal them by flouting what they take to be the normative order. Hence, for Garfinkel and ethnomethodology in general, a great deal of ordinary repair work of social breaches has to occur for a sense of normalcy to be sustained. In other words, order is deeply problematic for all everyday actors engaged in normal contexts of interaction. Order is fragile and much work is needed to maintain its ceremonial faced – a notion that, of course, comes straight from Goffman (1956).

MARK:

If we look to symbolic interactionism and the acute observations of Goffman, it is obvious that structural reproduction is not always a foregone conclusion in every interaction, thus structuration has to be negotiated. If we look to Foucault, we also see that systems of meaning are frequently contested. For any social order to be established as 'the way we do things around here' – as obligatory passage points – a great deal of strategic agency has to be carried out, which means that social structures and structuration practices are always up for grabs. In a sense, *destructuration* or the breaking down of structures, is every bit as important to our understanding of interaction as routine structuration practices are. In contested social systems, which all systems are to a greater or lesser extent, the powerful try to maintain their power by ensuring predictability in structuration, while the less powerful have an interest in counter-hegemonic, destructuration practices. Appeals to God, Country, Truth and Reason (all with a capital G, C, T and R), should be understood as strategic modes of agency which are there to ensure the continuance of structures, through their reification. In contrast, much of radical critique is another form of strategic agency that aims at de-reification, thus destructuration of the existing order of things.

STEWART:

As an aside, while structurational work is clearly deeply embedded and processual, the problem for radicals has been their Hegelianism – the implicit assumption that revolutionary cycles can destructure what is embedded, dereify it, and build a new order. The failure of Communism in the Soviet bloc to destroy the opium of the people is a case in point, I think; radical critique requires radical action that is not event-focused – the revolution – but processual and thus radically reformist. Mao's dictum, when asked by Régis Debray, whether the Chinese Revolution had been successful, which was that it was too early to tell – another 200 years would be required, citing the French Revolution, seems in retrospect a good judgement. Radical change requires many small incremental and deep-seated adjustments to existing institutions rather than their dramatic eclipse in acts of symbolic destruction.

MARK:

Change necessitates change of *habitus*. Robert Dahl (1989) observed that it is rare for the citizens of a democracy that is over twenty years old to dissolve it. This suggests that twenty years is the approximate amount of time it takes to form a new *habitus* across a population.

Part of the reason that structuration theory never translated into an interesting empirical research agenda is that it constitutes only half the picture. If all action entails structuration, it is banal to describe social interactions in terms of acts of structuration. What makes analysis interesting is the fact that structuration is contingent and frequently met by destructuration. If we look to the 'petty confrontations' which Foucault describes as part of epistemic change, these battles were between ways of ordering social life which were destructuring each other; the 'victory' of one order of things over the other occurs when it becomes the norm for authorities to structure institutions and actions relative to that order – the point of the contrasts that introduce *Discipline and Punish* (Foucault 1977). In contemporary everyday interaction, social activists are always confronted with the dilemma of structuring and thus legitimating the existing order of things or of destructuring and thus, hopefully, trying to change the order of things.

STEWART:

I suspect the validity of Dahl's assertion depends on what is meant by democracy. Was the US a democracy before the voter registration drives of the Civil Rights era in the 1960s? Is Iraq today a democracy? According to the leaders of the 'Coalition of the Willing' it is. People voted in elections. Is this enough to define democracy? I don't think so – on that criterion the Soviet bloc would have been democratic, because there were many rival parties and candidates – albeit all Party approved. For de Tocqueville (2000), democracy did not simply mean having elections but referred to the equality of conditions in a given territory. Hence, as Therborn (1977) has argued, the democratic state may have emerged in capitalist societies, but not because capitalists created it; instead what capitalism creates is a working class and the working class organizes and struggles for an extension of rights. Thus, successful capitalism precedes democracy by many years; indeed, the first modern democracies are Australia and New Zealand at the turn of the nineteenth century, where, because of chronic under-supply of labour in settler societies, the strongest working classes were to be found, and in which there was no entrenched feudal land-owning elite. Likewise, in recent transitions to democracy in countries such as Poland, Brazil, South Africa and South Korea, the organized working class has played a key role. Interestingly, in many cases where democracy was won at the barrel of a gun, as in many national liberation struggles, the transition has been to authoritarianism rather than democracy – even in notionally democratic countries such as Zimbabwe. Elsewhere, it is possible to argue that although political democracy has been maintained or extended in many formally democratic states, the extent of social democracy has been under consistent attack by neo-liberalism destined to return as much of human existence and struggle to the market as it is possible to achieve; even 'social democrats' espouse these beliefs now. The political elites representing unfettered capital are some of the most active agents engaged in the destructuration of democracy's legitimacy, and their primary weapon is the abandonment of state delivered citizenship rights and the assertion of consumer sovereignty in markets as the only effective and efficient mechanism for delivering services. We need to think about the relation between power and democracy in terms of these issues and struggles, I think; the idea of destructuration is really useful to this effect – if we work out who its agents are.

MARK:

Torfing gives us a remarkably comprehensive and nuanced overview of post-structuralist theories of power. When I read a lucid rendering like this of the work of Laclau and Mouffe (1985) and so on there is so much I agree with and yet there is something which makes me uneasy which I find it difficult to explain. Maybe it is the Gramscian inheritance and, odd though it may sound, a certain residual essentialism which I find problematic.

The idea that we think in terms of binary oppositions is virtually an article of faith, which has been inherited from structuralism. While I would agree that the characterization of the world in binary form is a highly successful strategy of domination, of hegemonic thinking, contemporary linguistic theory does not suggest that this is actually inherent to the way the human mind works, which is Chomsky's (1995) critique of Jacques Derrida's work (see 1976). When we look to Carl Schmitt's (1966) assertion that the world is divided into friends and enemies, which Laclau and Mouffe (1985) and Mouffe (2000) continually refer to, this is an assertion which one should not take at face value as an inescapable empirical fact. Rather it was a way of thinking about the world that was used to legitimate a particular normative project – a totalitarian state in which its subjects were a means to an end, rather than the end themselves.

STEWART:

Categories are the means through which we routinely, albeit largely unconsciously, observe and classify events and experiences as we understand them to be in the languages that we ordinarily use. Lakoff (1987: 5–6) suggests that

> There is nothing more basic than categorization to our thought, perception, action, and speech. Every time we see something as a kind of thing, for example, a tree, we are categorising. Whenever we reason

about kinds of things – chairs, nations, illnesses, emotions, any kind of thing at all – we are employing categories.

In addition, these categories are necessarily experiential and empirical; they are grounded in our ways of being in the world. Perhaps the most astute observer of this necessity was Harvey Sacks. Within ethnomethodology and conversation analysis, Sacks (1972) suggests that membership categorization devices, which systematically follow rules of economy and consistency, signal how everyday activities are accomplished locally and recognizably. The terms are the members, not analysts, and they signify how members make sense of the world. It is in investigating how these categories are deployed that we can gain a grounded appreciation of the way that these members construct the world.

MARK:

Gramsci (1971) wished to subvert bourgeois hegemony by learning how that mode of domination worked for the purposes of creating a new hegemony – proletarian hegemony. So, bourgeois hegemony is replaced by proletarian hegemony through a process of organizational outflanking in which the rules and strategies of bourgeois hegemony are used against the bourgeoisie. To me the problem with this has always been that what is objectionable about bourgeois hegemony is not that it belongs to, or represents of the interests of, the bourgeoisie. Rather, the issue is that hegemonic thinking is an impoverished form of thinking – it is hegemony that is the problem, not who benefits from it. Similarly, binary logic is the problem not who the friends and enemies happen to be. Replacing the friends and enemies of neo-liberalism with those of, let us say, a left-wing eco-friendly alliance, would only constitute only a marginal improvement because it replicates the same impoverished logic of the friend/enemy distinction.

I am aware that the response to this will be that there are no rocks of certainty or foundations which can be used to escape hegemony, an escape which was the Enlightenment illusion. However, my counter-response to that would be that the alternative to foundations is not difference and contingency; to think that way is to fall foul of the very logic one might wish to escape. I agree that we can only describe the world by classifying it. This is our only access to it, but some descriptions work better than others relative to specific purposes. The world can be described in terms of sympathies and antipathies, as in the Renaissance, or it can be described according to Newtonian mechanics, or as in quantum physics, none is a description that is 'True' (with a capital T) and yet each is an improvement relative to a specific purpose, which is to understand the movements of physical things.

STEWART:

I agree with this; it is an extension of the earlier Wittgensteinian point about concepts being tools. Just as a carpenter requires more than a screwdriver of a specific size in the tool box, so the analyst needs a full and differentiated kit of appropriate tools. Power is not comprised of a singular material that can be worked on with a singular tool; different materialities of power will require different conceptual tools.

MARK:

Popper (1962) already showed us that there are no Truths in science, just hypotheses that have not, as yet, been falsified. Already, foundations are absent. Thomas Kuhn argued quite convincingly that the world of physics is, essentially, a cultural construct. What is falsified when science advances are not simply sets of formulae and explanations, rather it is ways of describing the world or *habitus*. There is no hypothetical 'centre', 'subject' or 'closure' here and in that sense the 'other' of post-structuralism is a bit of a straw man – a caricature of Enlightenment inspired scientific thought.

STEWART:

The trouble with citing Popper is not in the argument but in how the argument has subsequently been operationalized by so many social scientists. By this I mean that the logic of disconfirmation has come to be identified with a hypothetico-deductive method in which hypotheses are tested exclusively in statistical terms. The effect of this is to limit enquiry – and research questions – largely to cross-sectional data and a conception of causality that is timeless and motionless, and then justify doing this in the name of doing proper science. Hence, by extension, research that does not translate data into numeric form and feed it through a regression equation becomes seen as improper science. It is not that Popper has a lot to answer for so much as what is so often done in his name, although I do believe that Popper bears some responsibility. Popper was not an empirical researcher; he never studied what scientists do when they do science in their everyday practice. Instead, he acted as a moral philosopher; he stipulated what it was he believed someone who wanted to have the name of science attached to their actions should do by making up an idealized account of science from his understanding of physics, giving rise to what Flyvbjerg (2002) calls widespread 'physics envy' amongst social scientists. It is time to 'get over' this bondage to a particular moral philosophy of science.

MARK:

I absolutely agree that we should not make a fetish out of the methods of natural sciences, which is really a way of borrowing legitimacy from them. As observed by Foucault (1980), when Marx claimed that he was being scientific, he was not really making a claim about his methods, rather attempting to borrow legitimacy from the natural sciences, which were perceived to be a discourse of truth. That point acknowledged, we can still borrow from them conceptual tools that are useful and Popper's account of falsification is one such useful tool.

Returning to binary oppositions, irrespective of the qualms I expressed concerning their foundational status, I would not deny that, following Derrida (1976), there are not moments of undecidability, which are decided by strategic action according the principles of oppositional logic. George W. Bush's intervention immediately post 9/11 was exactly such a moment. The attack on the Twin Towers could have been described in many ways. If Al Gore had been elected, with his legal background, one could hypothesize that it might have been described as 'an international criminal act', which would have justified pursuing the perpetrators through the International Criminal Court. As events happened we got a 'war on terror' waged by 'terrorists bent on destroying our freedoms'. However, the point is that this description was a particularly impoverished one that only made sense to a particularly unsubtle, binary, black-and-white way of thinking. The hypothetical Gore interpretation is slightly better in its consequences but it still falls foul of binary logic of 'law-abiding citizens' versus 'criminals'. From a sociological perspective, the most accurate and interesting would be to try to resist putting any labels on the perpetrators until we understood their motivation relative to their construction of reality and structured context. Needless to say, as Weber observed, understanding is not equivalent to identifying with or legitimating. Such a deliberate avoidance of binary logic would have meant that the proper response of the US government would have been to send anthropologists and sociologists to the Middle East, rather than soldiers! Of course, that would have been hard to sell at home but it would have been the more intellectually sophisticated response.

STEWART:

The binaries that you use depend on the categories that you attend to. It is clear from analysis of the evidence collected by the Commission that enquired into 9/11 that the President, George W. Bush, and Condoleezza Rice, the National Security Adviser, had received at least 40 briefings from the CIA alerting them to Osama bin Laden specifically, as well as the threat of a terrorist attack in the months of 2001 preceding the attack (Shenon 2008). However, these were not the categories that policy concerns before 9/11 dictated. Instead, a speech that Condoleeza Rice was due to give on 9/11, which was cancelled because of the attacks, indicates the focus was on big $ defence, not the security of the state. The speech, which was intended to outline her broad focus on the Bush Administration's plans for a missile defence system and included only passing reference to terrorism and the threat of radical Islam (Shenon 2008). One may be justified in assuming that for the top management team of the United States at that time, the categories with which they dealt were those that were widely promoted by the military-industrial complex rather than the daily briefings received from George Tenet, head of the CIA. Indeed, the effect of this disavowal of the CIA-inspired advice, which one would assume did benefit from anthropological, sociological and political science input, given the organization's resources, was to leave the administration in an essentially untutored position immediately after 9/11. Indeed, Bush's first statements after 9/11 called for a 'crusade' against the enemies of America who had launched the attack. One would not think that culturally sensitive social scientists would have advised such a binary positioning.

MARK:

Indeed that is so.

I also have a second area of concern, which follows from my argument, and that is that the perception of agency simply does not ring true. Of course, it is correct that in everyday life many social agents continually try to make sense of themselves by grasping different forms of identity and, yes it is true that these identities never fulfil that desire for a sense of self.

The solution here is not more subversive and resistant identities. Rather, it is to understand that ready-made social identities do not represent an answer to who we are. The Parsonian project failed ultimately because it just did not ring true to argue that humans are norm-internalising automatons. Similarly, it does not ring true to me (I am afraid introspection is the best path here) that I am constituted by a 'lack' that tries to find fulfilment in identity. Of course I have many identities: a university lecturer, a Dane or Irishman, a European, a man, an atheist and so on. These are labels that others apply to me and, of course I do not reject them entirely, on a purely pragmatic level relative to the task of acting as a competent social agent they are a necessity. Seeing me as a university lecturer is useful for students and it enables me to draw a salary cheque. Being a Dane gives me a passport, which is useful in airports. And being Irish is useful in explaining where I live. However, when I lecture and watch student taking notes, I often smile to myself, because it appears so absurd – which makes me a liberal ironist in Rorty's (1989) sense of the terms. These are all convenient labels that enable me to negotiate life in tolerably easy ways but they tell me nothing whatsoever about my own ontology. To me, using them for that purpose would constitute an impoverished way of thinking about myself and suggesting that I should experiment with alternative subversive identities would be equally impoverished because it follows the same essentialist logic.

STEWART:

Torfing argues that the sense of self that the subject makes is internal to structures of the life-world but these structures are dislocated by those events that it fails to domesticate, and such dislocation prevents subjects from fully determining their identity. Hence, the 'lack', which you have identified above, where the process of becoming somebody takes the form of attempts to fill the empty space of identity through specific acts of identification with what we are not or have not been identified as being. Despite the heavily Lacanian formulation this position is almost that of postmodern marketing theory; that the object of marketing is the constant feeding of desire that can only ever be dissatisfied in practice. I wrote about this process in a paper called 'Puritans, Visionaries, Survivors' (Clegg 2005). Hence, from this perspective, hegemony imposes itself not through any specific content or meaning but through the everyday political resolution of desire, above all, the desire to consume and the stories through which we live our lack of consumption – a lack that no concrete act of consumption can ever sate because, precisely, there are no limits to consumption. Ideology, in this account, should be seen as misrecognition of the contingent, incomplete and ultimately undecidable character of the politically constructed discourses through which social reality is constructed and instead their articulation in terms of some theory that promises closure; whether that theory be one of the market, the state or the revolution, for instance. Faced with such analysis there is little for the analyst to fall back on other than a subtle and playful irony premised on an awareness of the strange language games that constitute what we and others take for our everyday reality. Of course, we might want to try and demonstrate that there are other games, other possibilities, teaching Serbs, as Torfing suggests, to think of themselves not in nationalist terms but in terms of being 'women', 'poor', 'Europeans', etc. However, I think we should be aware that the categories of existence, the categories that come out of the radio station, the TV, the popular and everyday culture, are massed battalions embedded in the many ditches and dykes of civil society, and that Reason, re-established as stating a difference, a possibility, has little chance of purchase in conditions where the self-evidence of the dominant assumptions is all too palpable, all too real. Indeed, this does seem, essentially, to be Foucault's position if power is to be thought of as an act of inclusion and exclusion that defines what is normal and natural, thereby managing to efface the traces of exclusion. Of course, identity is always challenging, none more so, for most of us, I suspect, as we get older and do not see, physically and metaphorically, looking back at us the idealized selves of our youth. Of course, experience brings with it many more opportunities for identity formation (and loss) and I think that the challenge of selfhood is how we construct these into narratives that can enrich our being in the world rather than into accounts that defeat, deject and despair at the selves we did not become or are becoming. The embodied nature of being is crucial here, of course.

MARK:

I agree that we should not become victims of our own reifications of self.

As presented by Rolland Munro, actor network theory (ANT) is a welcome expansion of the concept of agency beyond humans to the world of technology. In the chapter he argues that an outgrowth of the belief that agency invariably entails intention is one of the reasons that agency is usually linked to humans. While I agree with this I find it curious that the two examples of the agency of technology that he develops at any length (hotel keys and sleeping policemen) have human intention at their core. The heavy hotel key and the speed ramp are deliberately created the way they are in order to reform the behaviour of hotel guests and drivers, respectively. I suppose Munro's point is that once the ramps and keys are in place, agency has been moved one stage from the inventor to the objects themselves and, furthermore, the resultant behaviour is also frequently reformed in ways which chronically escape the intentions of their creators.

STEWART:

The important thing about devices such as sleeping policemen, or speed humps, and hotel key weights in ANT accounts is that they replace humanism with heterogeneity, with effects, with what happens as it can be observed rather than assumed or presumed intentional causes. There is no need to inquire into human agency as having mysterious casual wellsprings in motivation, consciousness or any other inscrutable category. Motives, as Blum and McHugh (1971) said, are best dealt with as something ascribed and available in the everyday language that we use to make motive-statements. Moreover, plenty of things act in the world, as Munro argues, by confronting us every day with determinate pathways: if you *want* this, then you must *do* that. So, if university authorities do want pedestrians to be able to stroll around a campus safely then sleeping policemen are a good thing; they make it safer for pedestrians to cross traffic. If drivers want to race their vehicles then speed humps are a bad thing because they make the practice both more dangerous for the driver and injurious for the vehicle. Effects are created, irrespective of intentions. Social realities are engineered to create certain sorts of predictable effects as when forgetful guests who might otherwise walk away with the key of a hotel room are reminded of its materiality by the heavy weight attached to it.

The point of ANT is to highlight how what we and others take for granted is constructed out of the material of everyday life. When we find agreed routines or structures in place then their being taken for granted is a sign of power at work. What power is can be gleaned from its effects; where we find social realities that take on a stable, durable and material form in routines, actions, practices, then we may take these to be effects of power that need not have any specific or particular intention 'behind' them. There is no need to develop lengthy causal chains of power at a distance linking an originary intention with a far distant effect; tracing the effects is sufficient in itself. Thus, various forms of inscription, such as maps, accounting systems and spreadsheets, can produce definite effects far and wide. Using *this* map *that* navigator avoids that reef; using *this* accounting system *that* manager makes *that* purchase decision; using *those* numbers *this* dean makes *that* curriculum decision. Good navigators, astute managers and destructive deans assume their identities through the actions they engage in. These identities of 'good', 'astute' or 'destructive' are subject to constant processes of 'translation'; using other inscription devices might have produced different effects. In each case the actors are managing by the numbers: the navigator, through charts and compass; the manager, through, sales figures and forecasts; the dean, through enrolments. In consequence, ships sail successfully or not; profits are made or not, and courses, subjects and curricula survive or not. The identities of 'good', 'astute' or 'destructive' depend on the interplay of the outcomes of the application of these calculation devices and the categories for making sense of the world of actions that result that are available to members' in the worlds in which they live. Note the plurality of worlds; one of the ways that changes ensue is when the devices of one world start to colonize another. Think of the translation of green accounting from a specialist area into a whole world of carbon credits and trading, of global warming and a global balance sheet of climate change. All in a matter of less than thirty years!

MARK:

I cannot help wondering if another interesting aspect of this process is the way in which technologies change human dispositions. For instance, because of mobile phones and the internet we would find the return to a world in which these media were absent (in which we depended upon postal services and libraries) intolerable. Emotionally we have been changed in our attitude to time. A delay of minutes, or even too many seconds, never mind days, in downloading our email becomes unacceptable. Echoing Norbert Elias (1976), we are emotionally different agents (socio-genesis or 'techno-genesis' leading to psychogenesis) than we were twenty years ago, in much the same way that the feudal knight is different from the capitalist businessman. The only difference is that the transformation from the feudal knight to the 'rational' businessman took generations, not just a few years. To return to what I was saying earlier concerning a sense of self, our ontology has been fundamentally altered in unpredictable ways by technology. The inventors of increasingly rapid communications technology are not simply creating new resources; they are unintentionally transforming our being-in-the-world.

Curiously, one can speculate that technology may be changing agency in just as profound a way as Elias argued that class competition for status (in his terminology the 'civilizing process') and the Protestant ethic (Weber 1976) did at the beginnings of modern capitalist society. The difference in substance is a kind of reversal, moving from a modern/capitalist agent who represses emotion in favour of rational planning, to an agent who finds delay intolerable. By functional coincidence this technological transformation of agency is consistent with the emotional transformation from producers to consumers. As argued by Bauman (2000), the former plan, while the latter pursue gratification upon gratification in a manner not dissimilar to the way Don Giovanni or Don Juan pursued conquests – once seduced the object of desire has lost its value.

STEWART:

In power terms, modern consumption is premised on the consumption of desire made manifest in commodities rather than the specificity of the goods themselves. It is not the case that consumers are systematically deluded about their wants, as Marcuse (1964) argued, or that they have a systematically distorted consciousness as Lukes (1974; 2005) maintained. They know only too well what they want and how to get it; their desires fuel their expenditure and their need to earn, maintaining a constantly stimulated, satiated, stimulated desire. Power is operating less on their consciousness and more through the instruments that make conscious desires material: interest rates, credit cards, 120% mortgages and so on. It is not so much domination in the traditional sense as desire and the instruments of its fulfilment – and non-fulfilment – that are significant. There are now a plethora of instruments for turning unquenched desire into credit that enables authoritative action, producing legitimate consumption and obligatory debt.

MARK:

Turning to authority, I agree with Jenkins that Weber's sharp distinction between *Macht* and *Herrschaft*, usually translated as power and authority, has been unfortunate for the power debate. Within this framework, power is reduced to coercion and is always exercised against the will of the subaltern actor. As observed by Jenkins, this obscures the fact that in practice authority and coercion are always, to some extent fused. After all, following Weber, those in authority within the state are also those who have access to the collective monopoly of the means of violence. This is, of course, not to argue that the legitimacy of authority is always a mask for coercion and, from the opposite perspective, neither is it to deny that even the most coercive regimes in history, such as Stalinism, did not have some legitimate power.

There is also another reason why the exclusion of power from authority is unhelpful. From nearly all perspectives in recent power debates, it has emerged that legitimacy itself is a problematic category, in which domination may well be present. If we look to Lukes' (2005) third dimension of power, Foucault's (1979) power/knowledge hypothesis, the various traditions of power analysis that build upon the Gramscian (1971) concept of hegemony and Bourdieu's (1990) concept of symbolic violence etc., what lies at the centre of all these perspectives is the image of social actors acquiescing in their own domination. One way of theorizing this is to argue that these individuals perceive certain exercises of power, and structured relations of authority, as legitimate but (for various reasons) the observing sociologist or political theorist/scientist believes that the actors in question should not view them in this manner. In Lukes, actors consider power legitimate because they do not know what their real interests are. In Foucault they consider their objectification as subjects as legitimate because it is derived from some locally perceived concept of truth. In Gramsci, the subaltern classes accept bourgeois domination because they have internalized the latter's interpretative horizon and in Bourdieu, symbolic violence makes people 'misrecognize' reality. In all these versions of power and domination actors view social relations as legitimate due to some kind of cognitive shortcoming. If it were not for the latter, the very same social relations would appear straightforwardly as domination. If this is the case, then it is unhelpful to separate power from authority because the very separation is actually central to the efficacy of this form of domination.

STEWART:

Very nicely put. However, I would merely want to add that there is a risk of, as Garfinkel (1967) once observed of Parsons' functionalism, that one treats the person as a 'judgemental dope', as someone who doesn't know their own mind. Another way of thinking about it is to say that while people may not do or want what various sophisticated social theorists might in similar situations, this does not, in itself, invalidate their choices, although it might point up some of the implications and limits of those choices in ways that would not be immediately apparent.

MARK:

There are many types of power resources and they are not strictly separable into neat little boxes; thus, I agree with Jenkins that the proliferation of forms of capital is an unhelpful development. In a similar manner I also feel uneasy with Mann's (1986) four sources of power – military, ideological, economic and political power. These are not separate realms and to categorize them like this tends to divide up social life in a manner which is not consistent with the way in which social actors experience social life, thus it leads to an impoverished view of these sources of power. For instance, ideological power becomes confined to specific areas such as religion and education, and what disappears from view is the fact that all of social life – economic, political and military – is underpinned by the interpretative frameworks of social actors, which are essentially ideological in content – exactly how or to what extent is up for debate depending upon theoretical perspective.

STEWART:

As Foucault was aware, the problem with ideology is its 'other', which is always some form of truth. Traditionally, in the sociology of knowledge, from Mannheim (1976) onwards, this truth was 'science'. However, when we analyze the means with which actors act, then it is clear that for the vast majority of people, much of the time, especially with respect to the world of social construction, 'science' rarely enters the picture, except in a very rudimentary lay 'sensemaking' way (Weick 1995). What is more interesting about everyday sensemaking is not its 'ideological' content but its boundedness, for it is in and through the limits to sensemaking that are ordinarily accepted that 'ideological work' is done, not so much in the content of ideas but through their range and the limits inscribed in everyday, situated senses of normalcy. These can be thought of habitual ways of doing, thinking and being that are given instrumentally, by the various highly contingent disciplinary devices that traverse and frame what we ordinarily do.

MARK:

I dislike using the term 'ideology' myself, Mann uses it and in my comment I was careful to use 'ideological' in the older pre-Marxist sense of being an *interpretative framework* which actors use to make sense of the world. I also entirely agree that there is no perfect mirror of reality and all sense-making frameworks legitimate certain relations of empowerment and disempowerment and de-legitimate others. For instance, if a social agent is socialized into a teleological world-view, they are likely to consider arguments for hierarchy based upon essences plausible. Their point of disagreement will be over the detail: over what kinds of authority a specific essence may legitimate; if a specific individual or office embodies the essence in question. In contrast, someone socialized in a Newtonian or post-Newtonian world-view is less likely to be convinced by appeals to essences, which is why there is an elective affinity between the development of modern science and democracy. In that sense perhaps I am more open to the modernist framework than you are. While I entirely agree there is no absolute Truth (with a capital T), I do not consider it elitist, or *hubris,* to believe that certain interpretative frameworks represent reality more accurately than others and, possibly more significantly for power, some interpretative frameworks legitimate more normatively reprehensible ways of conducting social life than others.

STEWART:

Well, I don't think such judgements would trouble me at all...

MARK:

A teleological world-view, in which everything is perceived of as realizing essences, is more likely to provide fertile ground for racism, sexism and so on than an interpretative framework in which all agents are considered in principle equal, resembling the interchangeable atoms of a Newtonian universe. Not that the latter necessarily leads to Utopia, it has a tendency to legitimate a disenchanted world of instrumentally rational bureaucracy, which is also normatively reprehensible for different reasons. However, if I were to choose between the indifference of rational bureaucratic rationality, in which 'benign neglect' is the order of the day, and full-fledged teleologically driven social order, I would tend (depending on the detail) to choose the former over the latter.

If we read Kant's (1784) essay 'What is Enlightenment?' his central message is that we must question authority through our use of reason. The problem with authority is that it aims at closure by giving persons authorized with the power to proclaim the Truth (with a capital T) and, in so doing saying 'thus far and no further'. In contrast, reason in the true sense of the word never accepts closure. In its strategic use authority becomes absolute because arguing with this use of Truth constitutes the equivalent of denying Truth, which is a form of unreason, thus irrelevance, hence powerlessness. As properly understood in the Enlightenment tradition, there are no permanent Truths (capital 'T') of reason (small 'r'), only contingent pragmatic moments when the reasoning agent stops interrogating because, for the moment, on a practical level, the agent does not need to know better in order to 'go on' or, stronger than that, they cannot see any immediate grounds for falsification. The use of Reason (with a capital R) that is reprehensible, which Foucault was criticising, is the common practice by bodies of experts to claim authority for themselves based upon a self-proclaimed monopoly of Reason, which is an exercise of closure of the kind Kant was criticizing. It is also a form of symbolic violence as self-proclaimed authoritative empowerment to define reality, through the strategic use of Truth. However, if Kant's short essay is seen as emblematic of modernity, the strategic use of Reason by those in authority, as a will to power, is a subversion of reason properly understood as the constant critique of authority, thus contrary to the spirit of modernity. As you know, Foucault considered himself as working within the Enlightenment tradition of modernity; the classification as post-modernist is a label which was attached to him by others – wrongly so in my view.

STEWART:

I agree entirely; we perhaps need to make a distinction between reason-in-principle and reason-in-practice. In certain institutional spheres, such as those of elite journal publishing, practice comes close to principle, albeit mediated through what Kuhn would have called 'paradigms' or Foucault 'regimes of truth'. Power is displaced institutionally into an abstract apparatus of truth production as Reason. In other spheres, power is embedded in the abstract situational rules and the experiential materiality of everyday life. To bridge to John Allen's chapter, cities, as places of settled and relatively orderly habitation, are host to many such material devices, from the earliest forms of spiritual and military power manifest in churches and temples, fortresses and bulwarks, to the more abstract city ordinances and regulations. Reason-in-practice, as Flyvbjerg (1998) notes, is effective power, often unenlightened by reason-in-principle, which functions as a tool of the politically weak in their resistance to the politically strong.

MARK:

To take a long view of the history of power, cities emerged as some of the first power containers. These early cities, such as Sumer and Ancient Athens, largely accepted tribute from the surrounding countryside. The Roman Empire was the first attempt to conquer space. The extent of the Empire could be measured in relative boundaries, such as Hadrian's Wall, and road building, which meant, literally speaking, that all roads led to Rome. The conquest of space was coupled with an ideological conquest, the spread of Christianity, and attempt of legal uniformity – *pax Romana*. Outside of Europe, there are strong parallels with the Persian Empire, the Han dynasty in China, Ancient India and the Aztec Empire. However, if Mann (1986) is correct, the Roman Empire was more strongly committed to the control and conquest of geographical space than the rest and, indeed, its fall was due to the late Empire's tendency to revert to the tribute, in place of controlling space. After this, the medieval period was an era of tribute and centripetal power, in which control over people was *not* coterminous with control over space. The rise of the sovereign territorial state, to use Spruyt's (1994) terminology, was the modern attempt to fuse power over persons with control of space. Such control is symbolically represented by the map rooms, or representations of globes, which are found in many European buildings of power from the early modern period – the *Palazzo Vecchio* in Florence, the town hall in Amsterdam, Versailles and so on. Arguably this was when modern geography was born. Maps were no longer objects of art decorated with pretty drawings, they were precise representations of the globe along imaginary coordinates of reason represented as latitude and longitude. As in the Roman Empire, this reasoning was coupled with uniformity of law and the materiality of domination.

STEWART:

It was no accident that the prime meridian passed through the heart of British naval supremacy, at Greenwich, where the naval dockyards were situated; additionally, corresponding to the standardisation drive of geography, domination by territorial states introduced uniformity of weights and measures, initially conceived as 'Imperial measures'.

MARK:

In modernity, the ideological equivalent of Christianity was the ethic of modernization as 'progress' and a second state-centric ethic, nationalism, which was logically at variance with the former. Nationalism and modernity were in tension because the former is essentialist and teleological in its logic, while the latter is anti-essentialist, preferring universal laws and monads to *telos* and essences. In the conquest of space, the locus of power over people shifted purely to space, irrespective of family lineage, caste and so on. Colonially, these could be recruited as second order relays of power as intermediary devices between dominant global and local comprador elites. Nationalism accomplished the apparently impossible task of giving people separated purely by the conquest of space, in which borders are defined by military capability, the illusion that these borders correspond with a *volk*. It also provided the means of resistance to the other *volks* that were imposed on them. While the feudal hierarchy, which cut across space, decayed and the feudal concepts of pure blood became ridiculed, they were replaced by equally essentialist notions of nations.

As I understand John Allen's argument concerning the replacement of the geography of power with a typology of power, he is essentially arguing that the link between power and the control over space, which characterized modernity, is over. Cities such as New York, London and Tokyo are centres of multinational corporations and NGOs that control the lives of millions of people across the globe. Most theorists (including Beck [2005], with whom he takes issue), view the state as essentially still centred upon the control of space, thus this move of the concentration of power, or neo-feudalization of power, represents a decline of the state as *the* locus of power. However, according to Allen the state itself is becoming post-territorial and thus transmogrifying itself with the shift of power from control over space to the management of people regardless of space. While I think this latter part of his argument is an interesting hypothesis, I wonder is it empirically correct? Current US foreign policy is still centred upon control over space otherwise the idea of invasion of other states would make no sense.

STEWART:

And some spaces contain highly strategically contingent resources such as oil, control of which is essential for the shift of power from control over space to the management of people regardless of space, through global trade and commerce. Our current modernity still floats on a sea of oil that is neither freely available nor equally distributed. Control over that oil and its price is a key ingredient in power relations. Ironically, given the increases in the cost of oil since the second Iraq war, the normal conquest of space through military means has failed to achieve strategic purpose.

MARK:

Exactly, it was a mistake to conflate control over oil with control over the space where oil is found. As Bauman observes, social phenomena frequently are like the Owl of Minerva that flies at dusk – they are most obvious when obsolete. The most straightforward interpretation of US foreign policy is as an instance of organizational outflanking in which an actor, the most powerful state in the world, is sticking to an obsolete form of domination because it is *unable* to change with the new post-territorial rules of the game. This is, of course, not to argue that states will disappear as *loci* of power, but they will be competing with other *loci* of power and, as the rules of the game shift to being post-territorial, because states are space-centric, their *relative* power will decline.

STEWART:

I take Allen's focus on topology, as the study of changes in topography that occur over time and in space, constantly redrawing the history of the present in ways that effect dynamic relations of power globally, as a way of transcending the focus of prior formations such as international relations (states), business (corporations) and civil society (NGOs). Topologically, in the present conjuncture, these are all jumbled up: Japan hunts whales in the Antarctic; NGOs hunt the Japanese whalers and try to disrupt the process; Australia sends naval vessels to shadow the Japanese whaling fleet; Japanese corporations use institutions such as the Japanese Whaling Association, while the Japanese government uses the International Whaling Commission (IWC) (which was set up under the International Convention for the Regulation of Whaling signed in Washington DC on 2nd December 1946), to justify killing whales as 'scientific research', thus legitimating actions which take place neither in its territory nor in any other territory but in the Great Southern Ocean. Meanwhile, in Australia, the Federal Court decreed that Japanese government-backed whaler Kyodo Senpaku Kaisha Ltd was trespassing in the Australian Whale Sanctuary in Antarctic waters, ruling it had unlawfully slaughtered and harmed 'a significant number' of minke, fin and humpback whales. The case was not brought by the Government, however, but by an NGO, Humane Society International, and so far the government has not acted to enforce the ruling. Japan's response to the court ruling is that Japan's actions are legal, according to the Foreign Ministry's account of the International Whaling Commission. Place, states, NGOs, history and science are all tangled up together in such events. The entanglement is not 'natural', however, pertaining to the material on which geography is founded; instead, it is one of practices that see different states, international bodies, institutions such as science, and non-governmental actors all connected through the migration paths of 100 common minke whales, 50 Bryde's whales and 10 sperm whales, which are licensed to be killed. The key actors in the whole drama are the whales whose paths through the southern ocean create the opportunity for an enormously complex actor network to be constructed.

Whales become emblematic of a complex politics located in urban milieu in which they are never ordinarily encountered either in nature or on the dinner plate. I take this to be what Allen refers to as the 'power of connection', allowing for activists to dissolve the gap between 'near' and 'far' by lifting out exploitation and re-embedding it. Interestingly, in the example that I have chosen the re-embedding takes place in essentially moral communities of interest rather than among any 'interested parties' *per se*. Activists in the non-whaling countries are not, apart from the practices of Greenpeace, 'stakeholders' in any sense in the whaling firms or industry and are not its consumers. Topologically, in Allen's terms, what we see here is both a stretching and a compression of power relations. Greenpeace, Humane Society International and the Sea Shepherd Conservation Society, as NGOs, seek to compress power relations to graphic images relaying dramatic confrontations in remote locations on the sea which are transmitted globally, using the power of digital capture and satellite technology. Japan and the whaling companies seek to stretch power relations into international bodies and the institution of 'scientific research'. Both the Japanese government and corporations are aligned in this extension of events in time and space, pushing the whaling further away, rather than drawing it closer. On all sides there is a battle for hearts and minds fought through law, media, parliaments and markets. As Allen says, 'distanciated relationships, direct ties and real-time connections displace the notion of geometric scale and the idea that actors move up and down them, from the local to the global and back'.

MARK:

I think this is correct, we are essentially returning to a neo-feudal world in which the *locus* of power is unclear. The feudal world was more topographical than geographical. When the King of England and France were at war, in theory, the former actually owed the latter tribute to wage war because the English king was also a French aristocrat by virtue of various lands there – Brittany, Normandy, Burgundy, Gascony and so on. Of course, as far as I am aware, such tribute was never paid.

As power is shifting from the state to different *loci*, this also has implication for the way in which social subjects experience power and freedom, which is where Dean's re-theorization of Berlin's (1979) famous essay constitutes an interesting contribution.

STEWART:

Dean begins his discussion with some cases of neo-liberal interventions designed to reform the character of various categories of subject who are deemed incapable of acting on either their real interests as they would specify them if they were able to, or as they should specify them according to a broader social metric. At the core of these conceptions, argues Dean, are different conceptions of liberty and different ways of thinking about the relation between power and liberty. While most 'normal' subjects are allowed to be free to choose, others, who by authoritative definition are not normal, must be closely shepherded, overseen and administered to ensure normalcy. For the normal power works through freedom – consumer sovereignty, enabling to choose to do whatever one chooses and is able to do; for the not-normal it works through surveillance, discipline and special regimes of accountability. The relation of these to different concepts of liberty is then spelled out: to be at liberty is to be free from power; to exercise power is to curtail the liberty of others. Ordinarily, in discourses of power this exercise of power has been construed in terms of sovereignty since Hobbes.

Another special case of power is when ordinary subjects cannot be sovereign over their own self, the paradigm case of which is Lukes' (1974; 2005) three-dimensional view of power, where what is in the thoughts and consciousness of subjects are not their sovereign ideas but those of some others who have hegemony over them. Into this familiar mix Dean adds a dash of Foucault, to season the pot, as it were. To what extent, Mark, do you think that the addition of Foucault represents a decisive, indeed an 'epistemological', break with previous power conceptions?

MARK:

Good question. It seems to me that what Foucault makes us understand is that the opposition between positive and negative liberty is never realizable in practice. Most, if not all, societies have some concept of positive liberty at their core. This is especially the case with modern states which have educational systems, welfare and health provisions at their command. As Dean concludes, this insight allows us to take responsibility for the kind of 'conduct of conduct' for which we are responsible. Foucault also alerts us to the various techniques of reification that are used to make the creation of social subjects appear part of the 'natural order of things' through appeals to apparently irrefutable scientific Truths. What is yet to be done, as I see it, is to develop a set of normative criteria for distinguishing more or less insidious ways of creating social subjects. I agree with Foucault that reification is wrong, because it is a way of closure that precludes dialogue. *We must admit that all social order is by convention only*. However, to say that something is by convention only *is not equivalent to proving that it is 'arbitrary'.* To think they are equivalent represents vestiges of foundational and essentialist thinking. Neither is it the case that all forms of governmentality are normatively reprehensible, although some (most?) are. Specific ways of constituting social subjects can be justified relative to their consequences. To take an instance, the capacity of social agents to accept the circulation of elites through elections is a historically relatively unique event. Engaging in the democratic process presupposes accepting your own defeat because the rules of the game have priority over specific outcomes – who wins. In a sense democracy is a conventional game not unlike chess, except that the stakes are higher. The ability of social agents to play this game for such high stakes entails a massive internalisation of constraint that is particular to the creation of a specific kind of modern political subject. Given that the circulation of elites through the democratic rules of the game is substantially preferable to the historic norm, which was violent confrontation, I would argue that creating social subjects who have internalized these kinds of constraints is preferable to the alternative. Thus it is possible to justify the conventions of the democratic game and the creation of the modern political subject, the democratic citizen, in non-foundational terms. However, in contrast to this, the internalisation of restraint necessary to make a modern soldier, who can overcome human empathy in order to kill effectively, is an instance of creating a kind of social subject which I would consider normatively reprehensible.

In this sense, contrary to Dean, I think the relationship between legitimate and illegitimate power is still with us, though I would acknowledge that this is not in the usual liberal sense, as characterized by the dichotomy between positive and negative liberty. The question is: which kinds of positive liberty are normatively justifiable? I think this question *can* be answered relative to some of the premises of the liberal tradition, for instance 'autonomy' as a good, but the use of such concepts has to be qualified and nuanced.

STEWART:

Nigel Rapport begins Chapter 11 on 'Power and Identity' with two questions which immediately brought to mind another text. The two questions ask: Are human beings the same *inasmuch as* they all inhabit different cultural worlds, or is their being human something that exists *over and against* their inhabiting such worlds? Do they become human within culture or does their humanity transcend cultural particularities? The other text is Pierre Baynard's (2007) *How to Talk About Books You Haven't Read*. In this book he recounts the story of an anthropologist, Laura Bohannon, who, while doing fieldwork in Africa with the Tiv, a people who live mostly in the modern state of Nigeria, seeks to translate the narrative of Shakespeare's *Hamlet*, as an exercise to see whether a humanist account of the classic text will stand up – that it deals with immutable and invariable human themes that transcend the specificities of particular contexts. The experiment seemed to suggest that this was not the case, although it was not what she thought at the outset: 'I was quite sure that *Hamlet* had only one possible interpretation, and that one universally obvious' (Bohannan 1971: 24).

Once the story started, it was clear that the Tiv had a completely different way of thinking and interpreting the narrative. The first problem that the elders to whom she read her abridged and translated account of the narrative identified was with the idea of there being such things as ghosts that walk. Hamlet's father was referred to as a 'chief', as the translation for king. Trying to explain that the chief was dead, brought about a lot of confusion. To the Tiv people there is no such thing as a ghost, which means that as soon as they heard that the King came back to visit Hamlet the Tiv thought that the 'ghost' must be an omen sent by a witch; from there on the Tiv either ask for important detail that the text does not provide such as whether Claudius and Hamlet's father, as brothers, shared the same mother, or expressed surprise at elements of the narrative that had never occurred to Bohannon, such as the surprising time that elapsed before Claudius married Gertrude, Hamlet's mother. As the wife of the chief observed, 'Who will work your field during the time you're without a husband?' For the Tiv, where wives need husbands and husbands need wives to maintain activities in a subsistence agrarian economy, what seems unseemly haste to a Western audience seems to them undue delay. Nor can they understand why Hamlet is being asked to avenge his father – surely this is a task for the elders of the tribe not a callow youth? For Bayward, it is obvious that the Tiv have a certain idea of *Hamlet* without having read it, and this interpretation has a very real value; albeit that it is partial, it is collectively shared and easily regarded as valid in their culture.

Consciousness, its form and content, the narrative of the Tiv and Hamlet suggests, is not separate from cultural embedding in symbolic discourses and social practices which constitute what we take identity to be; thus, humanist discourse about the essence of man or the nature of society cannot but be misleading for these matters can only ever be discussed in context. Context is what provides a sense of self, identity, society and so on. Rapport seems concerned that such a conclusion opens the relativist door, which he wants to shut firmly with a liberally reflexive account of a humanism that may not be true for all seasons in its analyses but which represents a better example as a pinnacle of human achievement, thus far, when compared with non-humanist alternatives. The reasons that we should prefer humanism are several, Rapport suggests: it best provides for fulfilment, dignity and satisfaction – the realizing of individual capacities for life – both as regards individuals and their social relations with others.

On the one hand, I would not want to disagree that a humanist stance is infinitely preferable to accounts which place an implacable duty of obedience to some people's codified or authoritative interpretation of the presumed word of a presumed deity, such as God or Allah, which can be used to justify deeply dogmatic, unreflexive and inhumane behaviour. Decentring deities is undoubtedly a better idea than suborning one's will to other people's constructions of them, especially where such constructions can be less than benign in their implications. On the other hand, such terms as 'fulfilment, dignity and satisfaction' cannot be thought of in any meaningful way that is not culturally specific. In some contexts fulfilment, dignity and satisfaction comes from acting out the dominant community interpretations of the will of some deity that can license energies and behaviour that are destructive of autonomy as a person, and can even be destructive of life itself, when it is presumed that 'we' have 'God' on 'our side'.

MARK:

I agree with you, both in your critique of humanism and in your concerns, although I am not certain to what extent this applies to Rapport's position. When political philosophers or social theorists talk about universal human nature, I always find their conclusions subjective and unconvincing. Of course, there is such a thing as universal human nature in the sense that we are all biological beings but what the actual implications of this are we do not know as yet and certainly cannot be answered from the armchair world of philosophical anthropology. In my opinion, the use of appeals to human nature is one of the great dead-ends of liberalism. It elevates a particular way of life to the status of a universal standard and is an attempt to foreclose dialogue through the construction of a reified category beyond evaluation. Appeals to 'the state of nature' and fictitious 'social contracts' perform the same function. That said, I think liberalism can survive without such devices. To take an instance, in *The Liberal Archipelago* (2003) the political philosopher Chandran Kukathas wanted to construct liberal political principles which could be *considered legitimate* by persons of diverse cultural backgrounds. Following the liberal tradition, he looked for a universal human essence and found it in the principle of following your conscience (2003: 41–71), which, to me, sounds like a principle that has its roots in the Reformation, not universal human nature. However, if Kukathas had wanted to use the concept of conscience as a basis for his theory there was a more plausible path available to him implicit in the problem that he sets himself. His problem is that of *legitimacy*, and parsing that would have led him to conscience – actors consider something legitimate to the extent to which it accords with their conscience. Rather than performing the function of a universal, conscience is a conceptual tool that is useful for making sense of legitimacy. In general, liberal thought should forget universals and construct local conceptual tools that are suited to making sense and defending the kind of open society that is dear to liberals. These tools should be rooted in the actual practices of social agents, not utopian constructs, and the grounds for justification should similarly be linked to actual practice. It is much more convincing to say that liberal societies are better than alternative forms of political organization by looking at actual consequences than appeals to (spurious) universals. For instance, it is an empirical fact that liberal societies are less likely to inflict suffering upon their members in the name of some cause or other than non-liberal societies; this constitutes one among many reasons for preferring liberal societies over their rivals. This is the type of non-foundationalist consequentialist argument that Rorty (1989, 1991) endorses.

STEWART:

One way that Rapport seeks to resolve the issues identified is by noting that structures that shape and determine, such as language, never do so entirely: there is always room for individual initiative in ironicizing, resisting and questioning what words say in the ways that are spoken, interpreted or otherwise enacted. He presents the surprising formulation that it is 'humanity that speaks – in the shape of individual utterances of individual language-users – not language as such'. The individual utterances of speakers of individual languages cannot be assembled as an all-encompassing humanity, however. Translations between cultures would have to be seamless and transparent in ways that simply is not the case for this to be an apposite rendition. Humanity never speaks in the same tongue, even when translated; to speak of 'humanity' in this way is to gloss the whole issue of culture with which the chapter began and to ignore the issues that the story of Hamlet and the Tiv alert us to. Speaking a language, I would argue, does in fact translate into that language possessing agency and achieving hegemony, determining or causing meaning, and while it may not eliminate the interpretive work of individual speaker-hearers it deeply frames, shapes and constrains them. The language of 'faith' in a deity, in any language, is a case in point: how, apart from a commitment to the terms of the religious discourse, in whatever language, that frames the idea of the deity and the relation that men and women have with this deity, can one make sense of such language? First one has to accept the domination of a language that posits a deity or deities as having a determinant role in human affairs. The deity is an effect of its construction in language. It exists nowhere else. To the extent that it shapes human actions through observances of beliefs, rituals and incantation of specific charms, spells or prayers then it has, precisely, those powers that Rapport avers.

MARK:

I think Rapport would argue that the deity is a construct of language *and* those who speak that language. As it is unpredictable how these speakers will make sense of the language that they use, language itself is not an agent but merely a resource which agents use in a myriad of relatively contingent ways. If we reflect upon the work of social theorists, they redescribe society in ways which are subversive relative to hegemonic paradigms which influence the actions of the actors. Durkheim was brought up in a Jewish home and used this knowledge to observe that it is humans who create God in their own image, rather than the other way around, as would have been accepted by the social milieu which surrounded him. He redescribed social life using the language that was available to them but in a highly individual and subversive way. God as a collective representation of society is a totally different kind of entity than the one worshipped by religious believers, although it has to be accepted that Durkheim's ability to describe god in this way was based upon his knowledge of religious faith, which surrounded him. The capacity to make language do unexpected things is not unique to social theorists but is part of everyday social life and social agency. In fact, I have always considered it one of the ironies of social theory that determinist theorists always tend to be ontologically distanced from the determinations that they argue determine the behaviour of others. It is an extraordinary fact of human cognition that we have the ability instantly to understand and generate sentences which we have never heard before, which means that while there may be certain constraints within language, it can also be made to do unexpected things.

STEWART:

Rapport seeks to secure the ontological priority of the existential over the structural, seeing individuals as condemned to their own sensemaking. The sense one makes comes from the sense one takes from the dominant language games shaping one and one simply does not 'choose' these: one's parents, community and language determine them. Of course, existentially, one can and frequently does resist, create and innovate against the grain of the dominant hegemonies – but, to explore the woodworking origins of the metaphor, even resistance is determined by the grain embedded in the material worked on.

MARK:

As I understand Rapport, his humanist stance is actually quite minimal. All that humans have in common is that they are essentially sensemaking beings. They impose categories of order upon the world, which constitute meaning. While they become familiar with these meanings through socialization within a common interpretative framework, or culture, each person is still a singular entity who makes sense of their socialization individually. Part of the ordering of the world includes specific identities, which are categories of people. The individual does have a choice in deciding which identities to affirm and which not. Every individual can choose to define themselves by profession, sexuality, religion, nationality, ethnic group and so on or they can choose not to allow any of these 'identities' to define them. Rapport's target is the dominant view that 'identity' is somehow a given, which people find themselves determined by. This essentialist view of identity is a strategic position, a reification, which is used to make certain values non-negotiable. One of the limits to the choice of identity is not language, or the categories of meaning available, but the fact that we have to interact with others. Cosmopolitans, like Sen (2006), choose not to have their identity defined by nationality, which is a self-definition that is strongly resisted in our currently state-centric world. Constraint works both from the outside and from the inside, externally to the self other social agents stigmatize what they consider illegitimate choices and from the inside agents are limited by their knowledge of social life. However, I would never underestimate human creativity. A sculptor who chooses wood or stone as their medium is of course limited by the plasticity of the medium, but they can still use it to make unexpected objects.

STEWART:

Rapport makes a distinction between individualism and individuality: individuality is unique and indivisible and universal; and for the individual to develop a sense of self they have to first manage the selves that their body animates and then manage the effects of these selves in social relations with others, which may take many forms: ranging from downright exploitation to forthright collaboration, and every shade in between. Through the whole gamut of social relations extended across space, time and others, one forms identities of and for the self, to the self, and to others, systems of classification that are both multiple and contradictory.

MARK:

Another aspect of individuality is the complex socialization which we receive. When we read Foucault's (1972) account of the 'Renaissance episteme' in *The Order of Things* we *can* understand this interpretative framework even though it is not currently the dominant episteme. However, the episteme has not entirely vanished either – we find it in astrology and many, so called, 'alternative medicines'. Competent social agency entails competence in many interpretations of the world – a competent social actor routinely changes their interpretative horizon when interacting with a bureaucrat, religious preacher and someone with whom they have strong affective bonds. I would argue that this entails that, in effect, we have a choice of many language games, which allows us significant and meaningful autonomy. Added to that there is always the slippage between how each individual interprets these various language games.

Like Rapport, Fredrik Engelstad emphasizes the link between agency and culture and is particularly interested in the link from the top down: the way in which culture becomes infused with power through strategic action by the powerful or would-be powerful. Culture is not a single stable entity but continually contested. Because the most stable relations of power are those that are rooted in legitimacy, culture is the key to perpetuating power relations. As observed earlier, authority is power that is part of the system and accepted by the less powerful as legitimate. The kind of power which Lukes (2005), Bourdieu (1984) and Foucault (1979) describe is power that has been accepted as legitimate. In Bourdieu and Foucault it is clear that this acceptance is through a series of cultural conflicts. In Bourdieu those who have cultural capital, make 'their' particular culture into 'high' culture and in Foucault epistemes or discourses are made to appear other than conventional through appeals to truth. As observed by Engelstad, this use of culture for the purposes of domination is not always, or necessarily, manipulative. To take an instance from Foucault, the 'experts' who insisted that prison was a better form of punishment than being hanged, drawn and quartered may not have been entirely motivated by a humanitarian quest but I think Foucault exaggerates his case when he dismisses these grounds entirely. There is a direct correlation between the stability of power relations and their consonance with the interpretative framework of the persons who are expected to reproduce these structures. When *habitus* and power relations are incommensurable, coercion is the only road to power. This fact, which most actors' sense intuitively, entails that culture and power are continually subject to contestation and agency. In some instances the motivation may be a will to power, in which legitimacy is manipulated; in others, it may be an altruistic search for 'justice', as evaluated within the interpretative framework of particular activists.

STEWART:

It is important to avoid circularity in discussions of power, legitimacy and culture. You say, apropos of Engelstad's paper, that in Bourdieu, those who have cultural capital make 'their' particular culture into 'high' culture. The argument is one that is most clearly seen in historical terms, as in, say Norbert Elias' (1976) work on *The Civilizing Process*. Elites that have battled their way to supremacy and dominance – and in the early days of feudal European states battle was definitely the major factor – practice definite cultures based, say, on prowess in martial arts, hunting, falconry and so on. Let us say that this is how hunting, shooting and fishing become positioned as elite sports. Such sports demarcate a certain space of social circulation in which elites mingle and for which young people are prepared; their schooling includes not only a formal curriculum of educational content but also a more subtle drilling in the comportment of life as an elite member, in terms of styles of living, language and leisure. It is in this way that certain arenas, such as Royal Ascot, become key sites of cultural capital, in which elites and would-be elites who can inveigle their way in or are invited can, if they learn the habitus, manage to pass as if they were authentic members. Of course, to do so involves many subtle appreciations, social tightropes and occasional faux pas. Not all who mingle manage.

In pre-modern times the arena were essentially centred on courtly society and its extensions, imitations and artefacts; with modernity the markets within which displays of elite cultural identity claimed began to proliferate with the mass media into magazines, movies, fandom and so on. Today, in these post-modern times of excessive markets, consumptions and channels to market, there has been a fragmentation of what constitutes 'elite' cultural identity with the wholesale promulgation and consumption of a cheap but mass trash-culture often based more on notoriety rather than accomplishment as it was understood in broad cultural terms. In post-modernity cultural capital becomes tangled up in circuits of celebrity, notoriety, and signification that ironicize even Andy Warhol's prediction of 15 minutes of fame. When signals are so mixed, media so many and markets so dominant, the opportunities for misapprehension multiply massively. Much more boundary work is necessary as the defenses of cultural capital are increasingly under siege, breached and outflanked by the plethora of all that is flash, trash and vulgar in the democracy of the market. In such situations, as George Orwell (1934) realized, it is the chic of a shabby *but expensively cut* overcoat that signifies deep cultural capital. Real class, in the aristocratic sense, is always a little shabby. With the fall of public man, as Engelstad suggests, the more unrestrained subjectivity that is the hallmark of the commercialized media enables the preservation of a certain distance to become the hallmark of cultural capital's authenticity as a positional good.

In terms of the power of cultural institutions involved in nation-building a key reference has been Benedict Anderson's (1983) discussion of imagined communities. Of course, the peoples that he addressed historically could, in large part be led in the nineteenth century to imagine themselves as such a thing as a people: in post-modern conditions of hybridity the power to constitute a sense of national community is that much harder. It is no longer merely a question of assuming linguistic or regional hegemony over people who are, essentially and apparently, 'like' us when it is evident that they neither are nor do they want to be: in this respect a hallmark of the post-modern condition is that the extension of older democratic power discourses of 'rights' can no longer be extended inclusively to all the constituents of the citizenry, when significant elements of them spawn these 'rights' as desiderata – which increasingly describes the case of certain discursively and dramatically significant espousers of Islam, for instance, as I have argued elsewhere (Clegg et al. 2006). Hence, I think that the connection between cultures of religion and power relations needs rethinking on an axis that is significantly different from the trajectory of economic sociology; what is required is a concern with classical liberal themes of the security of the bodies of the state and its citizens. As Engelstad suggests, the tolerant may tolerate the intolerant at a distance, but if doctrines of intolerance take hold within the confines of the modern state, tolerance is confronted with its own limits. Weber was undoubtedly correct in seeing modern society as an arena for continuous value struggles and these have only intensified in post-modern times of fragmentation and liquidity – Bauman's 'liquid modernity'.

Engelstad wants us to accept that power is enacted directly by influencing actors' beliefs about all manner of things: essentially it works on and through culture. He distinguishes indirect effects of power, where the latter are mediated by changing individuals' opportunity structure. Overall, he suggests, power seeks legitimacy: he uses the example of autocratic rulers who tend to seek for legitimization of their own regime by reference to religious or political doctrines, popularized through slogans and images, publicized through posters or public decorations. Yet, if this is the case then they are mostly remarkably unsuccessful: think of the ease with which the Soviet system fell at the end of the 1980s; think of the resolute inability of the Chinese authorities to persuade the Tibetans (and other minorities) that the Communist Party and Han Chinese ascendancy is working in the best interests of those whom it organizes, or the failure of the Myanmar junta to persuade the monks and the people that their organization is just, and so on. Although Engelstad offers examples of the construction of legitimacy from tradition, and stresses the importance of both procedures and outcomes, he fails to address such recent and remarkable examples as the collapse of the Soviet system or the failure of alien hegemony to be built over Buddhist peoples in either Tibet or Myanmar. It seems evident that although the ruling clique in all cases was capable of constructing a system of rule it is not one founded on legitimacy. Hence, power does not always achieve nor does it always require legitimacy. Nor does it need to. It needs only to outflank, as Michael Mann says. Hence, illegitimate power may be maintained for generations, despite all its efforts to build legitimacy, on the basis of a monopoly over the means of violence alone. That this is the case has a bearing on the power of ritual. While ritual may be one of the primary means through which the legitimacy of power is built what role does ritual play when legitimacy is a sham and even those who promote it realize it to be the case? The speeches from the delegates of the Chinese Communist Party in the National Congress have all the elements of ritual, but an empty and decorative ritual, a token against a capricious world, perhaps, but surely not something deeply felt, given the reality that the state is building and widespread reports of many and various types of dissent that occur routinely, fuelled by tensions over ethnicity, Han hegemony, corrupt officialdom and more? While power is infinitely more economical where it can mobilize cultural sentiment in its support it does not need it to prevail: brute force, efficient armies, fast communication and effective repression can maintain power also and have done so in many places at many times. All the statues, speeches and cultivation of great leaders make no difference to the efficacy of repression. The acute question then is to ask how is it possible that the power of repression can become normalized discursively and thus attains legitimacy, rather than to explain legitimacy once attained.

MARK:

Of course, coercion is an alternative to 'legitimate' power – I am using the term legitimate here with reference to those over whom power is exercised, not normatively legitimate from the perspective of political theory. You mention the collapse of the Soviet Union, the point is that it *did* collapse and the reason was that the primary vehicle of power was coercion rather than legitimacy. With regard to China, the point is that a single individual unfolding a Tibetan flag at the lighting of the Olympic Torch ceremony in Athens 2008 is perceived to be a real threat to a state which has at its command one of the largest armies in the world. This represents a ceremony which was turned against those who wished to benefit from it by the display of a symbol which has legitimacy in the eyes of the outside world. Of course, it remains to be seen how much effect this will have on those inside China. First of all they were not shown the event on their national media and, secondly, due to a regime of indoctrination, many people inside China may perceive of the Tibetans as agents of 'Western Imperialism' or some similar rationalization, which gives the Chinese authorities some legitimacy.

With regard to the idea that 'statues, speeches and cultivation of great leaders make no difference to the efficacy of repression…', I think this has to remain an open question. As far as I am aware, the Mao cult was quite convincing to the majority of Chinese. Similarly, while Hitler was vulnerable to assassination attempts, incredible though it may seem to us, the cult of his personality did make him into a legitimate leader in the eyes of the majority of Germans by the late 1930s. Given the odds against the Germans fighting a war on all fronts, against the most powerful armies of the world, they still managed to hold out for five years and kill six million Jews, Gypsies and others at the same time. Such effectiveness was possible only because the regime had high levels of legitimacy in addition to coercive power.

I agree that a key question is how power as repression can become legitimate and I think the kinds of processes which Engelstadt mentions are part of the picture. If we take a long view of history, I accept your general point that coercion can be effective but, like charismatic authority, if such a system wants to perpetuate itself over time, legitimacy is more effective than continued coercive domination. To repeat, and I think it deserves repeating because many theorists tend to interpret legitimacy in normative terms, legitimacy in this case is sociological *de facto* legitimacy. I am not for one moment arguing that these regimes are legitimate relative to any abstract principles of political theory which could be endorsed by someone who upholds liberal and democratic principles. This is no Panglossian theory, as should be evident by my use of Nazi Germany as an instance of legitimate power.

STEWART:

Engelstad sees, underneath the dynamics of hegemony, the more stable indoctrination of a society's basic values and institutions. I want to take issue with the term 'indoctrination'. It suggests a degree of deliberate inculcation of culture; on the contrary I think that these basic values and institutions are more tied up in practices than they are in beliefs. Take the current crisis of capitalism. There can be few people who read the daily papers and read well-informed commentators who cannot appreciate that at present the capitalist world economy is going though one of its periodic bouts of crisis. This is not a legitimation crisis, however. In large part this is because, at the cultural level, the system is so deeply institutionally embedded that there really is no alternative to it; with this Engelstad would doubtless agree; but this is not the end of the matter; it is not the belief in capitalism or its legitimacy that will preserve it but its deep implication in all the mundane practices of everyday life: the necessity to pay mortgages and to repay other debt; the dependence of ordinary people's retirement incomes on market performance because of the widespread role of superannuation funds as major global investors in the world economy. These practices will be sustained whether people believe in them or not. Mortgages are not liquidated by illegitimacy any more than retirement incomes are funded by legitimacy. The institutional warp and weft of capitalism is premised not on foundations of legitimacy but on practices that are so deeply distributed in the reproduction of the key institution, capital, that they have an effective control over the affairs of men and women. The bank interest rate – which moves in response to the beliefs of an elite group of central bankers – is a case in point. It exercises an effective power as a 'governor', much as a mute Latourian device might, over the rational choices of ordinary people in all walks of life. It works not so much on their beliefs in legitimacy – although it may do this – but on the practices that people are routinely engaged in. The current crisis began with the 'securitization' of bad loans such that the initial lender's beliefs about the likelihood of the borrower's defaulting were inconsequential. At the point of lending employees were rewarded not for the soundness of the loans extended but on the basis of their performance in churning capital into debt. Risk was spread everywhere throughout the financial system and that risk has now brought vulnerable financial organizations tumbling down in a sea of red ink. Trust has been destroyed and banks are reluctant to lend to each other, making borrowing more expensive for everyone; predictably, spending should slow, credit tighten and recession occur, but there is not likely to be a legitimation crisis which indicates one very important point; it is not the legitimacy of the present system that sustains it but its obligatory necessity – the systems that sustain global financial life know of no other way. Crisis can happen; fortunes lost; houses lose value; mortgages become unredeemable and retirement incomes diminish – and it makes no difference to the way that they system operates because it is a system of practices that sustains beliefs not a system of beliefs that sustain practices. Thus, I think it does not matter that much whether it creates more or less alienated, aggrandized or other selves.

MARK:

There are two issues here. Actors may affirm the structures of a system because they are organizationally outflanked by short-term necessity. Revolutionary Marxists who are hungry may take a job with multinational corporations which they despise. I do not wish to deny that this may be, in part, sustaining, our current neo-liberal system, especially in less privileged countries. When you say that the basic values and institutions are more 'tied up in practices than they are in beliefs' I think you underestimate the interrelationship between the two. Most social action comes out of *habitus*, which is a large body of tacit knowledge of how to 'go on' in social life. If it is the case that the average social actor has their doubt about the legitimacy of neo-liberalism at a discursive level, everyday social praxis rests upon a complex body of *habitus* which may not be reflected upon even when it is inconsistent with discursive knowledge. Having said that, I do not actually believe that the majority of the population of the world perceives neo-liberalism as illegitimate in any way. The reason for this is that nearly everything they learn seems to validate neo-liberal hegemony. In the natural sciences Darwin's (1964) theories are hegemonic, even though there is considerable evidence that evolution may be linked to cooperation rather than selection of the fittest. However, research grants to falsify Darwin will be hard to obtain because selection of the fittest is one of the basic principles legitimating Western capitalism. I remember reading an account of Danish teachers introducing the Greenland Innuit to competitive sports. At first they found the idea strange but were soon 'socialized'. Our entire educational system is geared towards teaching us that competition is 'natural', not culturally specific, and this belief is central to the legitimacy of neo-liberalism. I know this is not scientific data, but I would wager that fewer than ten percent of students of *sociology and politics* at my university are even remotely aware that there is an alternative to societies organized on neo-liberal principles.

STEWART:

In your chapter, Mark, you begin by reprising the debate leading up to Lukes (1974). As you say, for Lukes the key to identifying 'real interests' is an alternative world-view typically manifest in moments of radical rupture. Such a view certainly captures the earlier examples of Han Chinese and Communist Party hegemony over Tibet as readily as it did the Czech situation in 1968. Yet, it does not capture the type of economic crisis which I referred to previously; here it is not clear that the domination in practice is a result of subalterns consenting to their own domination. Consent does not seem to enter into it.

MARK:

Yes, I agree. Let me clarify: my objective in that chapter is to explore the ideas of others rather than to develop my own ideas, although what I pick out as interesting does reflect my perspective. My focus is to examine the extent to which so many thinkers working from highly diverse perspectives, many of them anti-Marxist (for instance, Parsons [1964] and Barnes [1988], though not Lukes [2005]), seem to converge upon themes which run through Gramsci's (1971) concept of hegemony. I should qualify this by adding that I have always been somewhat sceptical concerning the elevation of past theorists as oracles, which is Gramsci's current status – I feel precisely the same way about the habit with respect to more contemporary thinkers, such as Foucault (1979), Arendt (1994) and Bourdieu (1984). So, I make their writings 'groan and protest', as Foucault did with Nietzsche (Foucault 1980: 53–4).

To answer your question directly, from *my* theoretical perspective, the kind of phenomenon that Lukes refers to as 'false-consciousness' would be more aptly theorized in terms of 'consciousness-raising'. In everyday life actors have a complex knowledge of how to 'go on', in the Wittgensteinian sense. This *habitus*, or practical consciousness knowledge, is continually used in a complex manner to guide the conduct of self and monitor that of other. This knowledge constitutes an interpretative horizon which is part of an agent's being-in-the-world and is central to their everyday reproduction of social structures. However, actors also have a higher-level discursive consciousness, which is knowledge that they can reflect upon. In the process of consciousness-raising, *habitus* is transferred to the discursive level. In so doing, the social agent becomes conscious of the way in which their routine social practices and being-in-the-world may reinforce relations of domination that they may consider illegitimate. From the point of view of social critique, discursive knowledge must ring true with regard to the *habitus* of those to whom it is directed. This constitutes a moment of recognition, an epiphany, in which the actors recognize truth not because of external authority, rather from what they already know in their *habitus*. For instance, a reader of Foucault's *Discipline and Punish* may recognize their school days. The converse of consciousness-raising is when 'educators' deliberately attempt to instill a *habitus* into the social subjects that the former knows will reinforce existing social relations – much of the so-called 'hidden curriculum' of modern schooling is about the creation of such a *habitus*. Panoptical power is not simply about observation: it is about creating a *habitus* which will make actors predictable, so that they will continue to reproduce the system when not observed because the appropriate structuration and destructuration (against 'deviant') practices are part of their natural attitude.

This kind of process is a significant aspect of reproducing neo-liberal hegemony. However, I think it is only one process among many, which also includes reification through power/truth (Foucault 1979), reification of local cultures (Bourdieu 1990), 'circuits of power' and 'obligatory passage points' (Clegg 2005; Clegg et al. 2006), organizational outflanking (Mann 1986) and so on. In that sense it is a mistake to think in terms of three or four (Digeser 1992) dimensions of power. No single process captures the complexity of the way that relations of domination are reproduced. This is not to suggest that we should pick and mix from incommensurable theoretical frameworks. Rather, it is my conviction that most of the dominant perspectives on power each point to important aspects of a multi-faceted phenomenon. The challenge of making these perspectives commensurable theoretically has yet to be completed, although it is a challenge that has informed both our research agendas and with which we have made some headway – how much is for others to assess.

STEWART:

Indeed, following up on the references that you make to Arendt, if our 'human nature' is constituted through a power that enables us to realize our essence as members of a polis by facilitating autonomy through collaboration with others, then it would seem that is only the absolute elites, the 'masters of war' and the 'masters of the universe', who have such power. The rest of us live in the shadows that their machinations create. We have very limited ability to do much other than to affect aggregate changes in line with the reasoning that constitutes the rules for making sense that are embedded in the system; thus we can act as rational choice actors in response to price signals such as the interest rate. There seem to me to be connections here with your account of Foucault: it would take a 'deep conflict'; to overthrow these notions of rational choice; thus, in essence, the dominance of market capitalism can be seen in the way that its truths frame entirely what is 'rational' and thus prove different systems of thought not only arbitrary but also pointless – they have no meaning in the ways that practices are structured. Hence, the practices produce the personnel rather than the personnel producing the practices – as you say, an echo of the Poulantzas/Miliband debate of the 1970s. Again, in Foucauldian terms, there is no escape from the power/knowledge nexus constituting capitalist financial relations, although, of course, wars of position between different fractions and innovations in these relations will challenge and change the actual deployment of forces constituting them. Thus, while capital is the crucial resource of financial relations then those who are its 'organic intellectuals', such as Nobel prize-winning economists such as Black and Scholes (1973; also see Merton 1973), will be those who have the ability to renew it – even though such renewals may have longer-term destructiveness built into them. Interestingly, this conception of organic intellectuals sees them not as producing justifications for consumption by the broad masses but innovations for elites. In a link with the work of theorists such as Flyvbjerg (1998) and Gordon (2007) these organic intellectuals produce rationalizations.

MARK:

With regard to the Arendt, I am somewhat sceptical about claims about 'human nature', but I think her work points to an important aspect of politics. Following the Aristotelian view, referred to earlier, I think there are two types of politics: virtuous politics which genuinely aim at increasing human autonomy through collaboration with others and the corrupt counterpart, which is directed at private interests. Following the Aristotelian logic, the degenerate form of democracy is the best of a bad lot in the sense that the number of people whose interests are represented is numerically higher than in oligarchy or tyranny. However, even democracy, as a degenerate form, is parasitic upon its virtuous counterpart, in which elected politicians are interested in public service rather than representing sectional interests. These are 'ideal types', in the Weberian sense. In the real world, democratic political systems have elements of both. As a democratic system tends towards power being in the interest of all, as directed towards a common good, rather than sectional (usually elite) interests, legitimacy declines. As neo-liberalism makes a virtue out of private interests, at the moment we are on a trajectory in which legitimacy is in decline and I believe this is manifest in declining turnouts for elections and general cynicism about politics. However, politics can also work the other way. During World War II Britain became collectively unified against a common enemy. After the war the British people (and I think there was such a thing at that moment) elected a Labour government, under Clement Attlee with the relatively altruistic agenda of creating a comprehensive welfare state. The turnout in the 1945 election was 72.8% and the one following that 83.9% (1950), which compares with 61.3% in 2005. In moments such as the creation of the British welfare state, democracy tended more towards its virtuous form and government came closer to the Arendtian ideal. There are countries that for specific historical reasons have a propensity towards the degenerate form of democracy. A post-colonial heritage, in which there is longstanding internalization of the idea of the state as the enemy, leaves the legacy of a political culture in which the state is seen as a mode of advancement for sectional interests, rather than public service. I think the US perception of democracy as a vehicle for the 'American dream', which is currently interpreted as capitalism, is another instance of a heritage which reinforces a sectional view of democracy. It may seem odd to classify one of the oldest modern democracies as degenerate, but I think it has justification when we observe the way US policy is driven by lobbying in Washington and the electoral process itself by massive subvention from private interests.

Organic intellectuals can work either to reinforce a habitus conducive to a sectional state or one directed at the general will. Nobel Prizes and so on are ways of reifying particular interpretative horizons which can be used either to reinforce a hegemonic world view or to undermine it.

STEWART:

What is important about the so-called Nobel Prize in Economics, I think, is its ritual quality. Once awarded it bestows an almost sacred authority on its holders; their ideas have been blessed, sanctified, lifted out of the common herd, they become iconic, emblematic of the very bases of the most legitimate authority in abstract ideas shaping everyday economic life.

MARK:

In his chapter Ray Gordon refers to your critique of the Parsonian view of *Herrschaft* as legitimate authority and uses this to great effect to divide power theorists into two camps. Those who follow Dahl, Lukes and so on, accept the view of power as distinct from authority, while Foucault, and those influenced by him, tend to interpret authority as another form of power. None of this is explicit but, rather, implicit in their writings. The problem for those who follow the Parsonian interpretation of *Herrschaft* is that they take it at face value. The weakness of those working from a Marxist derived position, especially Lukes, is that they realize that power works through consciousness but they fail to take authority seriously, while Foucauldians provide us with a rich ethnography of the creation of legitimate authority, which is really domination. Flyvbjerg's description of the political machinations and norms of rationality which people came to accept in local government in Aalborg, Denmark, is a paradigmatic instance (Flyvbjerg 1998), as is Gordon's own analysis of the description of the internal norms of the New South Wales Police Service of Australia (Gordon 2007). What is curious is how relatively small organizations (compared to the genealogies that Foucault described) come to accept as legitimate norms of authority and practices which are highly abnormal relative to the norms of the society in which they operate. The process of creating local rationalities is a slow and incremental one, new recruits in the New South Wales Police Service did challenge the norms but, over time, came to recognize fairly deviant practices as part of the natural order of things. Following on from my earlier comments, competent agents switching between local interpretative horizons, I wonder if in some respects Foucault's accounts of great systems of thought were somewhat misleading? We live in complex overlapping frameworks of meaning which actors switch in and out of, which is a facility that enables organizations to create *local* rules of the game, which may be quite at variance with surrounding social norms, yet employees can adjust to those norms while at work and then switch back to the norms of wider society when returning to their home life. From your study of organizations would this be correct?

STEWART:

I think so. In part it is a matter of levels of analysis. Foucault was, above all, a historian of ideas and with the benefit of historical overview was able to create a decisive and innovative sense of ruptured histories, constructed from the careful sampling of materials. Foucault wrote histories on a large scale, designed to puncture and interrupt prevailing accounts and periodizations. He did not do ethnography. Had he done so then different levels of analysis would have been necessary with different results. Take contemporary prisons for instance. If one were an ethnographer of French penal institutions for instance, one could still work within the overall episteme governing a specific organization and find considerable micropolitics going on there in and around the organization. Some of these might have to do with the forms of corruption associated with particular local regimes, such as tolerance of violence against the person, sanctioning of narcotics use, abuse of legitimate authority and so on – things that parallel the situation that Gordon (2007) found in the NSW Police. People at work will tolerate violence against the person by others, and sometimes themselves, that they know to be wrong but that they also know to be normal and can rationalize as necessary when dealing with those outside the norms of society. And people who work in the organization can, of course, be engaged in these practices at work and choose not to talk about them outside, or only to talk about them to people whom they know are insiders to these practices. These everyday practices may well not be a part of the overall episteme but they are well-known and accepted at the local level even though they might contradict the official stories of the prison or police service about itself, and not be the topics of everyday familial conversation. It is really a question of different types of data and levels of analysis. One could write an ethnography of a specific organization constituted within a specific episteme or discursive order, which, for instance would be expressed in the formal statutes and documents governing that service. As Gordon (2007) found, what policemen actually do did not always correspond to what they were supposed to do or what was formally legitimate for them to do.

MARK:

When social theorists consider the relationship between power and legitimacy there is a natural tendency to see them either in opposition or to extend the concept of power beyond domination, to include empowerment, as 'power to', and deem that legitimate authoritative power. However, what is really challenging is the counterintuitive idea that legitimacy may be the key to domination. Stable relations of domination are based upon those structured relations being perceived as legitimate. However, when we acknowledge this we must also recognize that the normative question, distinguishing between just and unjust power, does not disappear, as is suggested by Foucauldian thinkers.

Domination, which appears legitimate in the eyes of the dominated, can be effective but also unjust. That we might judge domination as unjust is only possible because, hypothetically speaking, there could be such a thing as legitimate power which is actually just. If the latter category did not exist, the very idea of legitimacy would cease to be effective. Truly normatively legitimate power in practice fulfils certain normative criteria of justice. It seems to me that the challenge for normative political theory is to work out what those criteria might be, with the added challenge that the theory must be sufficiently robust to distinguish just legitimate power from legitimate power as domination. Contract theory will not work, not only because of its lack of sociological base, but also because it is a consent theory. The point about legitimate authority as domination is precisely that it is legitimate because it is based upon consent, yet it is still domination despite consent.

STEWART:

We come close to the relation between power and ethics with these questions. The idea of legitimate power that is just requires an ethics of power. As far as I can see the best available ethics for a theory of power is that of Lévinas: being ethical entails a care for the Other. If we were to take Lévinas' (1999) conception of an adequate ethics as being one that takes care for the Other as its core value, then it is easy to see that in everyday life all sorts of seemingly legitimate power – power whose domination is accepted as legitimate authority by those subject to it as well, perhaps by those exercising it – would fail the test of justice if it did not take regard for the Other. All forms of organization that are premised on delegation of responsibilities which make others do things to others that they would not want to do under an ethic of care would be cases in point. Where power is sufficiently routinized that its authority to do what it does runs free of opprobrium this is not, surely, the same as being legitimate and just? Yet, organizationally it is less the *what* of that which is routinely done and more the fact that it is done routinely that establishes legitimacy-in-practice. Organizationally, one could consider an ethic of care as something that could guide action. There might be customer charters, for instance, setting out duties of care. There could be stakeholder statements setting out duties of care to communities, the ecology, and so on. Employees could be co-signatories to charters of rights and obligations, all of which took the care of the Other seriously. Of course, codes of ethics and ethical practice are quite separate things (Clegg, Kornberger and Rhodes 2007). An organization full of non-instrumentalized people who could justify, ethically, all that they did in terms of Lévinas' conception of care for the Other is entirely feasible. Such a basis for organizational life would sustain practices that were not sources of illegitimate domination. Imperative commands could still be issued but if they were not in accord with the duty of care for the Other, in a generalized way, then they would not be regarded as legitimate and could legitimately not be enacted. Now, I can see that many people might think this sounds like some kind of organizational purgatory for the politically correct, but in the present context of increasing care for the environment and the widespread failures of many conventionally ethical (which is to say unethical) organizations to be financially, socially and ecologically sustainable, the tide may be turning. In the past, what has been legitimate has been defined by the status of the person issuing the imperative command, in terms of Weberian rationality, without necessary reference to the substantive content of that which is commanded as long as the imperative addressed an area of functional responsibility. What is required is not so much a replacement of Weberian notions of rationality but their extension into an increased sphere of substantive concerns. Of course, as this entails a regulatory approach, rather than a deregulated 'let the market decide' approach, it will hardly find favour with the dominant ethics of neo-liberal elites; however, the mess that such an approach has made of the current conjuncture, where loans were extended knowingly with no duty of care to those who could not afford them, by employees treated with no duty of care for their obligations to others by being paid bonuses for the number of loans that they issued, irrespective of the capacity to pay of the borrowers once the interest rates were adjusted upwards from the honeymoon period, to banks that sliced, diced and sold the debt on with no duty of care for those institutions amongst whom the risk was spread, some present regimes have little to be said in their ethical favour.

MARK:

In much of the literature on power there is an ethics of power, which is assumed without explicit normative justification. Something similar to Levinas' idea of ethic of care for the other is implicit in Bourdieu, Foucault and Gramsci. Let us take Bourdieu's concept of 'symbolic violence' as a starting point. In what sense does it make sense to argue that the imposition of meaning is a form of violence? It could be answered that this is rhetorical metaphor without analytic content but I think not. What is normatively objectionable about physical violence is the treatment of the other as a being who is less than a social agent, as someone who is a body to be manipulated. In physical violence the other, as a social agent, as a meaning-creating being, is absent. That person's being-in-the-world is either an irrelevance, or worse, something that has to be destroyed through their body. Violence is the ultimate non-hermeneutic act in which there is no attempted convergence of interpretative horizons. Symbolic violence is similar to physical violence in that the meaning-creation of the other is considered irrelevant. This is apparent even in symbolic violence that is well-intentioned. The nineteenth century missionary who wishes to help the world by 'civilizing' 'natives' living in 'darkest Africa', would be a case in point – General William Booth, the founder of the Salvation Army, uses language like this in the introduction of his work *In Darkest England and The Way Out* (1890). The idea of Western civilization as 'Civilization' (with a capital C), 'natives' and the idea of others being in 'darkness', all entail lack of reciprocity. The other is someone whose ontology and consequent imposition of meaning in the world is considered irrelevant. They only become social agents to the extent to which they internalize the interpretative horizon of someone else – the 'civilizing' other. The implicit ethics of power is that the agency of other, as a being-in-the-world, with a particular world-creating capacity, should be respected. When we look to Foucault's critique of the present as in *Madness and Civilization* (1965) and *Discipline and Punish* (1979), a similar ethics is clearly implicit. In pre-modern Europe, social control of the other was physical, while in modernity this physicality is replaced by control over the mind. The reason that the latter is not an improvement, in any substantive sense, is that reciprocity is not improved. In the case of 'madness' what replaces chains (physical violence) is an endless monologue of Reason about Unreason. In the case of the prison, the Panopticon constitutes a one-way mode of visibility in which prisoners are expected to objectify themselves as others see them. The normative force of this critique implies that pre-modern physical violence is replaced by symbolic violence which is normatively reprehensible because the being-in-the-world, or world-creating capacity, of the other is absent. If we think of Gramsci's critique of bourgeois hegemony, a similar normative evaluation is implicit: it is objectionable that the proletariat internalize a habitus which belongs to someone else, the bourgeoisie. In other words, the proletariat adopt an alien world-creating capacity, which is interpreted as an unethical stance.

If we look to actual politics I think that such an ethic is substantially more common than you suggest. To the extent to which modern democracies have virtuous elements, something approaching an ethic of care, or reciprocity, is involved. 'Power over' is not necessarily directed at domination. Organization entails allowing some act on behalf of others and it is not predetermined that they abuse the trust which others place in them. Mitchell Dean and Kevin Ryan may be sceptical about welfare regimes. However, what is objectionable about most welfare regimes is that they only partially or conditionally empower those to whom they are directed. It is the exception that aims at total domination. We live in an imperfect world in which truly ethical legitimate power is frequently present but not in its pure form. The world is also full of legitimate power, which is only perceived to be legitimate, power where rationalization or reification creates the illusion of consent through the manipulation of other. Beyond that there is organizational outflanking, in which the subservient obey, not because they consider the system legitimate, but because they have little choice – consent is purely circumstantial. Further down the scale of illegitimacy, there is naked coercion and violence. Real life politics is a mixture of the lot. It is a mistake to place too much emphasis upon the pure forms, which leaves you the small set which you suggest – the environmental movement and so on. What gives ethical power a chance in the real world is not so much the goodness of humanity but the fact that legitimacy is the key to stability. Of course, this entails a lot of legitimacy that is not really ethical power, but the rules of the game dictate that this power should appear as if it were ethical power and, every once in a while, appearances and reality coincide. If they did not the game would be impossible to play.

STEWART:

Of course, as Gordon argues in his contribution, there can be no escape from power relations; there is no outside of power; but that is not the main point – the main point is the type of power relations that one is tangled up in and there is enormous scope for these to be constituted in variable ways. No necessity attaches to those that are merely conventional other than their conventionality and taken-for-grantedness, a point that makes a nice segue to discussion of Siniša Malešević's chapter on 'Collective Violence and Power'. Collective violence as both an instrument and mode of expression of power has largely been taken for granted and consigned to the margins of analysis while still being an overwhelmingly constitutive part of the modern experience of power. As he puts it, 'violence is often, if not always, much more than just a tool of power. It is one of the essential constituents of human subjectivity, and of modern subjectivity in particular, since modernity as we know it would be unthinkable without violence'. He also suggests that in the modern era violence tends to be almost exclusively monopolized by state apparatuses, which one takes to be the military, police and other 'repressive' state apparatuses. Much of the paper consists of a masterly scholarly elaboration of the neglected roots and recent developments in the sociology of collective violence, one that is largely state-centred. One central question comes into focus: how is it possible that the spiritual heirs of the Enlightenment, the bearers of Reason with a capital R, have so effortlessly plundered and slaughtered their way through history? For Malešević the answer lies in a neglect of the power of ideology by these theorists of violence and war, because it is ideology that allows the Other to be constituted as outside of humanity. Indeed, the Enlightenment project was preceded by and continued a war of conquest of the West against the Rest that was steeped in bloodshed and violence. The myth of Reason merely became a bulwark for a violence that had certainly been institutionalized against everything that was conceived as non-Christian since at least the Crusades and which took a particular turn with the conquest of the Americas.

MARK:

Malešević would wish to separate the mobilizing force of Catholicism from modern ideology. In his work generally, as in Gellner, Malešević argues that there is a qualitative change between modernity and the feudal world. Not only is nationalism unique to modernity but so also is genocide.

He may be right about this in the sense that modern genocide is qualitatively different from pre-modern mass killings in its use of rational organization, rather than relying solely on emotion and hatred. However, in the paper there is also the suggestion that modern ideology is somehow more dangerous than religious belief, and in this context Malešević quotes Dostoyevsky – 'once god is dead everything is permissible' – which is an assertion I do not see any evidence to substantiate. The mass killing of the Donatists by the followers of St. Augustine, the Crusades and the Spanish Inquisition are about as horrendous as you can get. In today's world, religious belief is clearly functional to violence. Suicide bombers are able to commit 'altruistic suicide' (in Durkheim's terminology) because of religious conviction. I could be wrong, but it seems self-evident that it is easier to get people who believe in an afterlife to kill themselves for a cause than it is to get an atheist to do so. Maybe the reference is intended as a moral statement, as is implied by the assertion which follows that 'humanity, justice, progress or civilization are especially potent ideological devices...' for treating others as '...outside the norms of humanity'. When morality is religiously based, the deity is created as a reifying device in order to place moral codes beyond critique by disguising their human conventional origins. When reified in this way, they become deontological, and thus immune to the consequences of their implementation, however horrendous. Once the other is someone who rejects or insults the word of God, is a blasphemer, or sinner, there is little place for negotiation because *mere* humans do not have the authority to revise the word of God. Do not get me wrong: I do not wish to deny the fact that modernity has been cruel but I think it is overstating the case to argue that it is somehow worse than what went before. The greater number of killings of the twentieth century can be explained by the greater efficiency of warfare, as augmented by technology and industrial production, rather than a more genocidal mindset. I would entirely agree with the general point that it is a surprising fact that not only has the legacy of the Enlightenment not led to universal peace, as Kant predicted, but it has resulted in new causes of war and cruelty. The picture is mixed and complex and one should not deny that there have been real gains – for instance, peace in most of Western Europe since 1945, human rights and democracy as an obligatory passage point for legitimacy, and the emerging (though still contested and manipulated) norm that military action should have UN sanction.

STEWART:

True, but there is still a tendency within modernity, especially in the early part, whereby Reason (with a capital R) was for those inside the fold; for those outside cold steel and hot bullets were necessary in order to inculcate Reason. As Ibarra-Colado (2006) argues, an *ethics of domination* was exercised to integrate indigenous peoples, imposing the totalitarianism of the 'modern self' (Florescano 1994) in a process of conquering the Other, of invalidating the Other's original identity and history, a project that has never been concluded, perpetuating modernity as a process of domination in which rational calculation operates as the only basis for progress, concealing that which is not European (Dussel 1995). It may well be the case that, as Malešević argues, Western sociologists and intellectuals in general may have neglected the role of violence in the creation of modernity but Latin American colleagues such as Ibarra-Colado and Dussel have not. Finally, a point of difference with Malešević: it may well have been the case in the past that the state apparatuses were the major proponents of violence but we should not overlook the extent to which, in at least two ways, the tasks of violence have been accommodated within civil society.

First, the expansion of the West globally through settler societies such as the Americas and Australasia saw the organization of violence on the indigenous peoples largely administered by the great mass of ordinary settlers as well as by the state. In the early days of settlement, when the frontier was often that place where settler claims to territory came up against the resistance of the indigenes that occupied it, the violence of small arms, pox and poisons did the work of exclusion and control. The history of the frontier is soaked in blood.

MARK:

Following Mann's analysis (Mann 2003, 2005), the war against indigenous people would have been considered 'external' in the sense that (bizarre though this may sound) indigenous Australians and Americans were external to those creating a new *polis*. This perception of the world is exemplified by Locke who acknowledged the existence indigenous peoples in the Americas and Australia, while maintaining that they were essentially empty spaces which, as yet, belonged to no-one.

STEWART:

Second, in neo-liberal states of the present day, typified above all by the US, even though the repressive state apparatuses of the military are developed to an awesome extent, much of the routine work of violence is now sub-contracted to the private sector. The role of private security companies in the current war in Iraq has been highlighted in countless media reports, for instance, according to a *Washington Post Report* of June 16, 2007, such contractors are 'enduring daily attacks, returning fire and taking hundreds of casualties that have been under-reported and sometimes concealed, according to US and Iraqi officials and company representatives...the security companies, out of public view, have been...boosting manpower, adding expensive armor and stepping up evasive action as attacks increase'. The report goes on to say:

> The majority of the more than 100 security companies operate outside of Iraqi law, in part because of bureaucratic delays and corruption in the Iraqi government licensing process, according to U.S. officials...The security industry's enormous growth has been facilitated by the US. military, which uses the 20,000 to 30,000 contractors to offset chronic troop shortages. Armed contractors protect all convoys transporting reconstruction materiel, including vehicles, weapons and ammunition for the Iraqi army and police. They guard key U.S. military installations and provide personal security for at least three commanding generals...

In the present neo-liberal conjuncture it would be too restrictive to maintain a focus on collective violence that was addressed only to the state and not to the market. And in this conjunction, when violence is business, the role of ideology in legitimating it can be left to others; the market needs no special ideological pleading and business, even when the business is violence, can simply point to its contracts to legitimate what it is doing. In an instructive Wikipedia entry, Blackwater Worldwide (as Blackwater USA has been renamed) is noted as operating the world's largest tactical training facility in North Carolina and trains more than 40,000 people a year, from US or foreign military and police services, as well as other US government agencies. The role of Blackwater in the Iraq War has been the subject of many media reports, especially after the events of September 16, 2007, when Blackwater employees in Nisour Square, Baghdad shot and killed 17 Iraqi civilians, at least 14 of whom were killed 'without cause' according to the FBI. Blackwater's license to operate in Iraq was revoked by the Iraqi Government the next day. A US Government Committee on Oversight and Government Reform staff report, based largely on internal Blackwater e-mail messages and State Department documents, described Blackwater as 'being staffed with reckless, shoot-first guards who were not always sober and did not always stop to see who or what was hit by their bullets.' It should be noted that the Iraq war involvement of Blackwater is largely on the basis of no-bid contracts the terms of which are not public. As it is a private company its activities and accounts are not subject to public scrutiny. In the twenty-first century much of the routine aspects of collective violence is routinely out-sourced and the sociology of collective violence needs to catch up with this fact. Only in the sense that it is contracted to the state, does the state successfully monopolize the control of this collective violence.

MARK:

I am convinced that the state as a monopoly of violence characterizes a particular phase of history, which covers the nineteenth and twentieth centuries. It is early stages yet in this privatization of violence, so generalization is difficult, but there does appear to be a significant difference between contemporary and feudal private violence in that today's private violence is only tolerated if it does not challenge the absolute authority of the state.

While I agree with Malešević that it is important not to underestimate the significance of violence, it is equally important not to subsume power into violence. One must also be careful not to confuse origins with outcomes. It may be the case that the origins of modern states owe a significant amount to violence, but this is not the same as thinking that once established the modern state continues to rely upon violence. Just as charismatic authority has to convert itself into another form in order to remain stable similarly, in order to gain stability, any social order that is created through violence has to convert coercive power into legitimate authoritative power. It is also a significant fact of modernity that democracies tend to organizationally outflank other political forms, even in war, because they are more effective in organizing their citizens and the reason for that is legitimacy, which is the other reason that ideology is important: it creates legitimacy.

With regard to genocide, to return to the ethics of power, the key to making effective killers is the portrayal of the other as incapable of meaningful agency. The portrayal of the Japanese as 'beasts', mentioned by Malešević, would be such an instance. The atrocities associated with colonization were legitimized by the belief that the other was not really human. Today the label 'terrorist' denotes someone whose sole purpose is to create fear and spread disorder. As such they are a kind of anti-social agent with whom communication is impossible, thus they can only be controlled through violence and, as such, do not qualify for human rights.

STEWART:

I would note only that the designation 'terrorist' is highly contingent and can, as a signification, slide off subjects as contingencies change, as they always do. Turning to the chapter by Amy Allen one of the most significant fields for power analysis, the whole area of feminism and gender relations, is opened up for readers of the *Handbook*. The by now familiar distinctions between 'power to' and 'power over' are revealed in their gendering. The latter concept of power as associated with domination and subordination is seen as inherently masculinist by many feminists. Allen provides us with a broad overview of developments linking gender, feminism thinking and power from the impact of de Beauvoir onwards. The explicit link was made between 'power to' and 'power over' in gender terms, with the former being seen as uniquely feminine and the latter as the form compelling de Beauvoir's sense of women as condemned to immanence by cultural, social and political conditions that deny them that transcendence. Later feminists turned 'power to' into a celebration of women's being in the world. Power over thus became a residual category of all that was bad, was not authentically woman.

MARK:

In much of her work Allen develops a sophisticated account of the three forms of power: 'power over', 'power to' and 'power with'. It is important to emphasize that Allen does not hold with the idea that 'power over' is equivalent to domination, or that it is necessarily male. Not only is 'power over' frequently benign in its intent but it is also a precondition of 'power to' and 'power with', as all forms of organization entail 'power over'. This is one of the unfortunate realities which idealists, like the Greens today, have to come to terms with. However, if there are proper structures of accountability, 'power over' may function well in the service of 'power to' and 'power with'. The distinction between 'power to' and 'power with' is a fine one and maybe Allen should explain it in greater depth. As I understand it, 'power to' entails individual capacity for action, while 'power with' refers to a collective capacity. However, the individual capacity of 'power to', to the extent to which it is social, arises from interaction with others. Thus 'power to' has a collective source though, I suppose, it is different from 'power with' in its objectives. As always, I am suspicious of essentialisms. I would reject any suggestion that 'power with' is somehow more a female characteristic than male, unless seriously qualified along the lines that in *certain societies* there is a *tendency* for this to be the case.

STEWART:

I agree entirely with these remarks. The main focus of Allen's chapter is on recent theoretical developments in feminist theory that displace the 'narrow and problematically essentialist focus on the situation of 'women' vis-à-vis power relations and toward a much broader consideration of the interconnected and power-saturated construction of femininities, masculinities, sexual dimorphism, and normative heterosexuality'. Post-structuralist and ethnomethodological theories take us to this vantage point. However, as she elaborates these theories have themselves neglected some dimensions of power analysis: for instance, macrostructural and institutional dimensions; collective power-with and the interlocking and intersecting of relations of power along the lines of gender, race, class and sexuality as discussed in approaches grounded in intersectionality. While the intersectional approach is certainly an advance on perspectives that do not take matters of race, class and sexuality into account in their analysis of gender relations, there is a sense in which they represent a fashionable empiricism. By this I mean that new and topical issues are added to the intersectional agenda as they are mobilized: perhaps in the future intersectionality will also embrace additional descriptors such as age, religion, etc? There seems no necessary reason to stop with race, class and sexuality.

MARK:

I would entirely agree that there is no reason for intersectional research to stop at any categories whatsoever. This also raises the wider issue, whether there is any need for an approach to power of any kind that wears a label like 'feminist' and so on. Of course, I can understand that a certain theorist might be interested in the domination of specific groups, but does that fact justify the idea that there is a theoretical perspective corresponding to that phenomenon? For instance, Lukes' and Foucault's theories are useful for understanding the exclusion of class, ethnic minorities, women and ethnic minorities who are women and working class. This suggests that the different object of analysis does not justify there being a separate approach as such. I find feminist writings a highly rich source for understanding domination and empowerment, but I have never been convinced that these insights are particular to understanding the position of women, as distinct from other discriminated against groups. Of course, maybe the argument is more pragmatic, like that for affirmative action within liberalism, in which case I agree that it may be temporarily necessary.

STEWART:

Feminism has shown great reflexivity towards the conditions of power's existence as a form of everyday theorizing, perhaps no where more so than in Judith Butler's (1990) work, where the category of 'women', the subject of feminism, is seen as being produced and restrained by the very structures of power through which emancipation is sought. Of course, the contemporary discourse of reflexivity really begins with ethnomethodology in the late 1960s and early 1970s, in key contributions from Harold Garfinkel (1967) and Alan Blum (1974), so it is no surprise to find Allen making an ethnomethodological turn. Ethnomethodology's great strength is to make all hypostasized categories an effect of members' mundane and everyday work; hence gender is not so much a set of structures or social relations but is an effect of the everyday practices used in normal life to accomplish gendered and other performances. Garfinkel (1967) first addressed this topic in the remarkable analysis of Agnes; West and Zimmerman (1987) build on this foundation to demonstrate how gender is an ongoing accomplishment of individuals structured by prevailing norms of acceptability and accountability, which, in turn, are a function of existing structures of gender dominance. I have always found ethnomethodology incredibly emancipatory as a theoretical approach and it is a real delight to see Allen take it up here, although she seems to be one of the very few writers on power who have been ethnomethodologically informed – why do you think this is the case Mark?

MARK:

I think the reason is the legacy of the micro-macro distinction. Ethnomethodology is considered a form of micro-level analysis while power is somehow considered macro-structural. I recently had a similar discussion with Richard Jenkins, who trained as an anthropologist, in which we both agreed that Goffman's classic, *The Presentation of Self in Everyday Life*, is a wonderful book about power, although it is rarely interpreted in that way – I hope that an article by Jenkins on this topic will appear in the next issue of the *Journal of Power*.

STEWART:

I certainly agree with you about Goffman. When I first started writing about power, even though I was trying to merge some ideas from ethnomethodology with more traditional analysis (Weber, Simmel, the Community Power Debate), it never occurred to me that one could use Goffman; when, much later, I became fascinated by total institutions as a condensation of power relations (see 'The heart of darkness', in Clegg et al. 2006), I couldn't see why Goffman was not so much more widely appreciated or how I could have missed what was so good in his work. Perhaps, as you say, he is thought of as too 'micro' or, maybe because the theory is always so beautifully embedded in the analytics and doesn't show itself in a performative manner, with lots of references to other theorists, as a conscious display of 'doing theory', some readers just miss how theoretically sophisticated and astute his work actually is. Towards the end of her chapter Allen picks up on 'micro' issue with the familiar criticism that ethnomethodology fails to provide an adequate account of the macro level. I find such charges problematic and am not convinced that empiricist and formulaic approaches that rely on specific unsituated conceptions of intersectionality will do the job: surely by bridging the interactional and the institutional in analysis of everyday settings ethnomethodology is actually calling into question distinctions between levels as well as the a priori assumption of which variables are significant and showing how the extent of the relations of power as both an ongoing accomplishment and as a contested terrain for more or less negotiation as such?

MARK:

In your chapter you suggest that Taylorism is built upon the Cartesian dualism of mind and body. The time and motion studies associated with Taylor and Ford were directed at disciplining the body. They were there to remove irregularities and make the body like a machine capable of the kind of precision which the newly invented machines of industrial production required. In this context you quote Foucault's assertion that 'power seeps into the very grain of individuals, reaches right into their bodies, permeates their gestures, their posture, what they say, how they learn to live with other people.' (Foucault 1977:28). It is only with the Hawthorne studies of the 1930s that focus shifts to the other side of Cartesian duality.

At first glance, this would put you at variance with Foucault, as his argument was that at about 1800 the body became a vehicle for the soul. As argued in *Discipline and Punish*, the objective of the prison was not the body itself but the use of the body as container of the soul (1979: 16). This is exemplified by the guillotine which was a device for capturing the soul from the body without inflicting upon the latter – of course, within the limits of the technology of the time. The modern use of lethal injection combined with painkillers is a refinement of that quest. The objective of the Panopticon was the soul, which is why I early referred to it as a 'socialization machine'.

It seems to me that there are two ways of looking at this apparent contradiction. It can be argued that the moment of transition was not as clear-cut as Foucault suggests. Throughout the nineteenth and early twentieth century, disciplinary techniques were unclear in their objectives, sometimes targeting the soul but, at other times, focusing primarily upon the body. The other, more interesting, option would be to argue that there is a shift in objective with regard to the soul. In the pre-Hawthorne studies days the idea was to use the body to remove the *weaknesses* of the soul. The human spirit was a cause of irregularity that had to be trained and controlled, which is a perspective that is consonant with the eighteenth- and nineteenth-century idea of child upbringing as a process of 'civilizing' potentially disorderly beings. With the Hawthorne studies the shift is brought about by the realization that the elimination of humanity leads to its own inefficiency (for instance, bored workers without initiative) and is irrepressible - a fact which frequently manifests in irritating resistances. The object now was to channel and utilize what could not be annihilated. The very source of imperfection, unpredictability, was reinterpreted as 'creativity', 'initiative', later 'flexibility' and 'entrepreneurship'. These were not simply some kind of vital source of the human spirit but included all the various contingencies that had gone into the socialization of the person. The contingency of external socialization, which represented the failure of perfect schooling, was now to be absorbed into the firm as a font of 'creativity' and 'flexibility', instead of annihilated obstacles to efficiency. In other words, what I am suggesting is that maybe the soul was always the objective and that a paradigm shift occurred with regard to what to do with it. Is this plausible?

STEWART:

Well, I realized when I constructed the argument that it didn't fit the Foucauldian periodicity. My take on this was that I was thinking about a different substantive field of practice and that there really should be no reason to expect a functional homogeneity across diverse fields of practice. Further, I first started to think of these matters in the ways that are expressed in the chapter after reading Kevin Ryan's work (more on which later). What I took from this was that in the nineteenth century the crucial division was between work/non-work, with most of the reforming zeal oriented to moving people from the non-work to the work category. While this made non-work deeply problematic in ways that Ryan explores in his chapter and book

(Ryan 2008), it left the status of *work* per se unexamined. Work was its own reward, its own ethic, its own discipline, and was, as is evident in the accounts in Marx's (1976) *Capital* of struggles over the length of the working day, a brutally exhausting and exhaustive discipline. Indeed, it is only with the growth of scale and the increasing division of labour that the new instruments of financial capital enabled in the last third of the nineteenth century, and the creation of effective statutory limits around work a result of pressure from organized labour seeking to standardize working practices on 'best practice', that the demands for efficiency begin to undercut both the dominant system of direct control in internal contracting, often done by overseers who were past masters of small units of capital that financial instruments had consolidated, and the craft system of production. of course, the First World War and the influx of unskilled female labour into the industrial labour process for the first time and on a large scale made the creation of simple, effective and efficient technologies more necessary. Not only was a new political economy of the body in this conjuncture; there were also new bodies to be drilled and disciplined in wholly new ways.

MARK:

You open your chapter with the assertion that management is a 'practice of power involving the imposition of the will.' which is 'directed at framing not only the conduct of others but also the self'. We have just discussed the imposition of the will upon the employee, now I wish to ask what kind of self should a modern or post-modern manager be? This question has a double normative component. What kind of being should the manager be with regard to the interests of the organization *and* what kind of self should a manager aim for if he or she wishes to uphold some kind of ethical principles? The question also has a second ambiguity, which is that the manager is also an employee, so to what extent does it makes sense to distinguish the roles of employee and manager?

STEWART:

Managers are employees by definition; we can distinguish between those who are elites and oligarchs, those who sit in the top management team, and the rest. The rest are often engaged in power tournaments to prove their worthiness for elite recruitment, as Courpasson and Dany discuss in a later chapter. For the elites, the nature of their being is largely settled by the financial arrangements that align their agency with that of the principals, the shareholders of capital, by providing them with lucrative stock options, which make it in their interests to maintain shareholder value. For the rest, the nature of their being is often a contested terrain, cross-cut by all the intersectional factors that Amy Allen discussed, plus some she didn't, such as family and children. Some struggle on and make it to the elites; a few at any rate. Others drop out or are dropped out and become own-account professionals or entrepreneurs of their inner calling in the arts, design, gardening or whatever. Many just muddle through. All are the object of concerted campaigns aimed at their consciousness, including training, executive development, self-help manuals, culture programs, MBAs and so on. To be a manager is to be under constant siege as the management ideas industry of the top-tier consulting firms is constantly churning new products, new fashions and new needs. The equipage of the thoroughly modern manager can date just as quickly as the cut of their suit. As an object of disciplines few compare with the manager. Increasingly, in recent years, these disciplines have sought to remake managers as more entrepreneurial subjects, so that if one were to characterize the post-modern manager it would be as a deliberately designed restless subject, an entrepreneur of their own being, forever striving for an autonomous mastery that, by definition, they can never attain. I do not see these modern managers as cultural dopes, hegemonized in a three dimensional way. For instance, Courpasson and Dany begin with a move that seems inspired very much by Lukes' (1974; 2005) radical view: how managerial hegemony is more or less suddenly unveiled by certain social actors and made questionable and thinkable by the same social actors. In the terms of ethnomethodology, which we were just addressing, one could refer to this as ethnomethodolgoical unsettling, the challenging and tilting out of balance of the rules of everyday life that Garfinkel delighted in with his small-scale practical experiments. The point is, however, that such practical experiments occur naturally all the time, in the process sometimes revealing the cracks, fissures and papered-over breaches of everyday life. Following the theorizations of Spicer and Bohm (2007), they identify four approaches to theorizing resistance, suggesting that contemporary resistance in companies tends to be formed out of hybridizations of each of these, rather than seeing each as a pure type in itself, which they term 'creative resistance'. Here the previous discussion of 'power to' as empowerment is given some specific contextual detail in terms of the strategies and actions of managers in post-bureaucratic organizations. By virtue of the story of Jean-Paul we are presented with the type of claims over the subject that positive power can exert in organizations: here it comes dressed as an opportunity whose costs are not at all codified in the offer but are deeply implicit. As Courpasson and Dany say, it is a case of asking what one is inclined to sacrifice for the sake of career and simultaneously, for the sake of the success of an important project. In a subtle way, it is both an opportunity to become more empowered, by accepting a promotion, greater responsibility and salary, and at the same time implicating oneself in power's entanglements even further so that one is bound by the micro-fibres of its capillaries ever more closely. All of this is explored carefully through the Foucauldian-derived category of subjectification. We see the trigger decision of Jean-Paul sparking several other exits from the company; the effects of the positive power exercised on him in terms of his reaction to it making a Garfinkelian breach of the tacit rules, thus making these clear to other interested observers who may have been in doubt about them previously. We have here another example of the power of small everyday experiments in making the rules clear. What is interesting, of course, is that the trigger is not 'power over', explicitly, but an offer of 'empowerment'; however, the empowerment offered in the power to move comes wrapped up in complex entanglements that will bind power over Jean-Paul and his colleagues ever more tightly. once more we come face-to-face with power as a deeply ethical relation; Jean-Paul's response heightens the ethical implications embedded in the simple strategy of promotion, precisely in terms of an ethic of care for the Other. He mobilizes against power seductively sheathed in the velvet gloves of a promotion in the name of a universe over which he refuse the company having domination; the sphere of an ethical life as it is lived. Jean-Paul is not a hegemonized, deluded subject; he doesn't fit into any of the three dimensions usually allowed power subjects. He knows who he is and where he stands, and in so doing he creates a form of resistance that dramatizes, challenges, affirms and negates the limits of power. From a position of power over, he is offered power to do something; realizing that there is no alternative answer other than 'yes', given the limits of power relations, his leaving both affirms, and in its effects, negates slightly, the initial relation of power over. The balance of power shifts ever so slightly in the company; succession plans are undercut, options exercised. Now, none of this is theorized explicitly as 'intersectional', yet indeed it is: the intersection of one life with others forming the resolve to resist.

MARK:

This relates to what I was saying earlier in the context of Giddens' theory of structuration: destructuration of social practices is every bit as much a part of social life as the confirmation of structuration practices. When Louis phoned Jean-Paul, he set the latter a challenge that presupposed the validity of certain structuration practices, including the right of top managers to groom those below them based upon loyalty. Confirming those structuration practices would have, as you observe, empowered Jean-Paul, thus he would have realized the desirable goal (Courpasson and Dany take the desirability of these goals for granted, which is reasonable) of becoming part of the company elite, possibly a CEO. Jean-Paul's refusal is not, as most acts of resistance are generally assumed to be, a challenge to domination in itself, it was a challenge to an interpretative framework. As actors shift social context they draw upon different interpretative frameworks, as is appropriate to context. There is Jean-Paul 'the company man' and Jean-Paul 'the father and husband'. Part of competent social action entails keeping these realms separate. What Louis forced in that phone conversation was a conflict between the two interpretative horizons, whereby Jean-Paul was forced with the stark choice of *either* being a 'company man' or a 'father and husband'. Jean-Paul opted to structure relative to his 'husband and father' interpretative horizon, which entails destructuration to the structuration practices implicit in the 'company man' *habitus*.

This relates to a wider issue which is often raised by critics of constructivism: where does resistance come from if there are no foundations? I think it fair to say that in destructuring Jean-Paul was not only looking out for *his* interests, but it seems fair to speculate that he was also thinking about the interests of his wife and child. In other words, his resistance was also motivated by moral and ethical considerations. The question in a relative world is: where do such moral judgements come from, if the word of God or Civilization or some other absolute is not available? As is illustrated by the story, while there may be no rocks of certainty, we are like people afloat on an open sea with several lifeboats available to us. The act of accepting the position in Scotland *was morally right* relative to the tacit norms of the company but *morally wrong* relative to what it is to be a good parent and husband. Jean-Paul's autonomy and capacity to critique existing norms did not come from any absolute position, it came from the nature of social agency itself, in which meaning and morality are not singular but multiple relative to the multiple interpretative horizons available to social agents. Autonomy does not come from nowhere: it comes from multiplicity of interpretative horizons that we are exposed to as social agents. Contrary to the Enlightenment ideal of the logically consistent person, both morality and autonomy come from the socially sanctioned inconsistent ways of making sense of the world which each of us are socialized into as we move from one contextuality of social action to another.

Bauman observes (Bauman 1989) that the Holocaust was facilitated by bureaucratic rationality, whereby it was possible to interpret the sending of Jews to the extermination camps as a timetabling problem in which individual Jews were represented as numbers – which were literally tattooed onto their bodies – for 'resettlement'. As documented by Bauman, the biggest obstacle to the implementation of the 'final solution' was the tendency of Germans to see individual Jews in distress as 'neighbours', 'Mrs Cohen down the road' and so on, rather than as the abstract Jew to be administered. In other words, cognitive dissonance between the bureaucratic *habitus* and that of family life were the greatest threat. The bureaucratic interpretative horizon had to be made to trump the rest if the 'final solution' was to run smoothly. In short, in a society which had gone collectively morally wrong, sound judgement was to be had from alternative frameworks of meaning, which were also available – the individual was not only a Nazi or bureaucrat but also a 'neighbour' and 'friend'.

STEWART:

The case of Jean-Paul is in many ways a microcosm of what Ryan discusses as 'government;' in Foucault's sense. Jean-Paul is induced to speak precisely when he would have preferred not to have to; he is effectively governed by the superordinates. Of course, the stuff of Ryan's argument is a long way from Courpasson and Dany; where they deal with the ethnographic particulars of a case Ryan takes us through the history of ideas. Even there I find resonances: the Benthamite 'less eligibility' principle, designed as a test to make indigent subjects more desirous of honest labour than local relief has its echoes in the 'test' that Louis presents to Jean-Paul to which the only responses is should I go or should I stay, should I accept promotion or seek migration.

MARK:

I would agree and there are also echoes of Locke's idea of 'consent' whereby living in a society was tantamount to agreeing to the social contract, as migration to the 'uninhabited' parts of the globe was considered an option.

STEWART:

Just as the poor are being structured so that they can govern themselves in accordance with the utilitarian calculus of pleasure and pain by Bentham (1970) so Louis is applying the same kind of calculus to Jean-Paul. In the one case discipline takes the form of what Ryan terms a precision tool – a mode of administration which facilitates the creation of a national labour market while in the other case it is no less precise: here the tool is a mode of administration that compels the subjects to ask themselves how much they are prepared to give in order to receive what they might take. In each case the effect is the creation of a self-governing subject, constituted through a normalizing gaze.

MARK:

Kevin Ryan has a rare ability, reminiscent of Foucault and Bauman, to weave a complex tapestry of theory and empirical research into a compelling narrative concerning transformation of *habitus* and its relationship to changing structures of domination. However, underneath this narrative, as with Foucault and Bauman, there is a complex set of normative judgements that Ryan in subtle way elicits from his reader. Foucault always refrained from normative pronouncements, yet the compelling nature of his histories was rooted in the reader taking for granted that institutions like the Panopticon are morally reprehensible. Similarly, most readers of Ryan will just assume that exclusion is morally reprehensible – well known contemporary theorists such as Laclau and Mouffe and Dean use the same technique. To the extent that there are explicit normative judgements, they are rooted in the supposed logical inconsistency between liberal espousals of freedom and autonomy, and the forcible exclusion of those who do not measure up to certain standards of disciplined responsibility. This would be unproblematic if it were the case that such normative assumptions are valid but I would contend that this is not necessarily the case. Social life is complex and if we give up the idea of utopia, all normative social orders entail some level of discipline and exclusion. The real question is: which disciplinary practices and exclusions are justifiable and why?

As described by Foucault the Panopticon constitutes an architectural device designed to make the individual judge themselves as others would judge them, to subject themselves to self-examination, to order their conduct and so on, which all sounds reprehensible. However, let us for a moment look at the problem confronting the modern state in the early nineteenth century. They had to create an educational system that would, for the first time in history, create mass literacy, a set of educational qualifications that would allow for employment based upon meritocracy, and a body of citizens capable of democratic participation. Relative to this task a new system of mass *standardized* education was necessary. In order to set up the teaching-learning relationship it was necessary to instil in pupils the ability to defer gratification. In order to create a moral self capable of government it was necessary to create a self that would judge others as it would judge self, which is, as Kant observed, the moral imperative of justice. That said, it would be wrong to use the Panopticon, as Bentham suggested, as a laboratory of power in which one could do experiments, for instance teaching children that two and two make five or that the moon is made of green cheese. The point is that Panoptical socialization is frequently morally reprehensible but it is not necessarily so.

STEWART:

Well, we might disagree about formulations slightly. I am not so sure that there was a functional necessity or that it was an early nineteenth century issue. Literacy, mass education and democracy all come along much later than early in the century. If these were all necessary so was it that the male population should be healthy enough to fight in major wars and the record is clear that they were not. I do not deny that later in the century those things of which you write occurred but I am not so sure that they 'had' to; I think it could easily have been otherwise.

MARK:

I agree, I was verging on teleology there for rhetorical reasons, but the substantive point remains that meritocratic liberal society presupposes a certain kind of mass education that has emerged, possibly for contingent reasons and with many wrong turnings, over the last two hundred years.

There is also a problem with viewing restraint and exclusion as inherently normatively reprehensible. Ryan paraphrases Foucault (1983) and Elias (1976) as follows: 'the responsible use of freedom requires appetites, impulses and drives to be mastered, and by tutoring its subject in the arts of civility, manners and self-restraint, liberal order divides the individual against his or her own self'. And then he goes on to observe that 'Liberal order is in fact an order of authorities and power (plural) which is modelled on the "good despot"'. The idea of a 'good despot' suggests an illiberal society but is the move from control over drives and so on to that conclusion warranted? I would conjecture that Norbert Elias would not have jumped to this conclusion because he was acutely aware that control over the emotions is not necessarily inimical to freedom. Take for instance the liberal freedom to dress as one wishes. In liberal societies this includes the freedom of women to dress in a sexually explicit way and with this go certain norms, one of the most salient of which is that dressing in this manner does not justify others making unreciprocated sexual advances. Therefore, for instance, liberals do not accept it as a defence for rape that a woman dressed in a 'provocative way'. The ability of people to dress as they wish is premised upon a control of sexuality and repression of emotion. Counterintuitive though it may seem, the freedom to dress as you wish, is premised upon a certain level of Puritanism. If one compares Scandinavia to Saudi Arabia, it is the former society that presupposes the greater level of internalized sexual restraint. The freedom to dress as you wish is premised upon enforced socialization whereby men and women are taught sexual restraint towards each other as a form of mutual respect. Being tolerant of others entails constraint upon self, which applies equally to freedom of speech and so on. There is no liberal utopia in which there is no price to be paid for freedom. Social actors who do not internalize certain restraints have to be externally restrained and excluded in order to protect liberal freedoms of others. That said, there are many forms of self-restraint and exclusion associated with modernity that have nothing to do with increasing freedom, the problem is to differentiate forms of exclusion and restraint necessary for freedom and those which have arisen for other reasons, many of them inimical to freedom, such as creating docile bodies for the purposes of increased efficiency in industrial production.

STEWART:

How well received is Foucault's idea of 'government', which Ryan advocates, in political science generally? My hunch is, from my readings, that it has only a very select, limited circulation, mostly amongst those scholars whose work circulates, precisely, as Foucauldian.

MARK:

I think that is correct: among mainstream political scientists the idea of government as conduct upon conduct is not widely used. Do not get me wrong: I think understanding the process which Ryan describes is fundamental to making sense of power and domination. My concern is that this kind of analysis is based upon a set of normative assumptions in need of critical examination.

STEWART:

Ryan's focus is on what Foucault called the 'sovereignty-discipline-government' triangle. What stikes me about this is the extent to which the term 'government' is, in meaning, so close to the contemporary use of 'management'. It was the citation of Foucault's example of the ship which brought this to mind. If what it means to 'govern a ship ... means clearly to take charge of the sailors, but also the boat and its cargo...it consists in that activity of establishing a relation between the sailors who are to be taken care of and the ship which is to be taken care of, and the cargo which is to be brought safely to port, and all those eventualities like winds, rocks, storms and so on' (Foucault, 1991a: 94), then this sounds almost perfectly like a definition of what it means to be a manager to contemporary ears.

MARK:

This image is not unique to liberalism or modernity: Plato uses it in *The Republic*. However, maybe this fact does not undermine the substance of the argument.

STEWART:

It is not the ship (of state) but the organization and all who are involved in it, with the metaphorical cargo being the goals of the organization, and eventualities being rendered as 'contingencies'. From this perspective it is but a small step to see parallel albeit lagged histories at work. The disciplinary divisions and specialized practices that are applied to post-Westphalian soldiers is much later applied to employees during the nineteenth century, as subjects of a popular mechanics that became crystallized in Taylor (1911; also see Shenhav 1999, for the pre-Taylorian history).

When Ryan switches focus to what he terms 'advanced liberalism', the territory is very familiar; one encounters the same processes traversing management in general as much as they do government in particular. That this should be the case is hardly surprising for advanced liberalism represents a valorisation of business, its models, management and manners, across all the realms of government in what Pusey (1990) refers to as 'economic rationalism', defining the enterprise state. The central tool of the new economic rationality becomes, Power (1997) suggests, the 'audit', a tool that is deeply corrosive of traditional conceptions of authority based on deference, respect or professional *noblesse oblige*. Authority becomes entangled with auditable standards of performance and claims to legitimacy more acutely empirically testable, as in Research Assessment Exercises (or Research Quality Frameworks) in universities, or in regulatory oversight of various professional realms, such as the delivery of health services. Thus, new forms of authority are not only targeted at newly created types of subject, with ASBOs and ABCs as Ryan discusses with respect to deviance, but audit becomes a stratifying practice for differentiating between the more and the less deserving amongst those organizations, institutions and subjects deemed 'normal'.

MARK:

Absolutely. I find the current 'normalizing' practices particularly objectionable. They are based upon making a fetish of market rationality without the slightest understanding that large-scale institutions, such as Universities, also operate on trust and reciprocity. Once measurement, quantification and competition enter the picture, trust and reciprocity are undermined. Furthermore outputs in research environments are virtually impossible to quantify. When dealing with advanced level research, the only people capable of evaluating the 'outputs' are the researchers themselves and, possibly, a few colleagues scattered across the globe.

STEWART:

From the detailed history of the possibilities of the present advanced liberal order that Ryan discusses, the last two chapters of the book turn to central concepts of political science: the state and international relations. The state first, refracted through terms that were, once upon a time, almost canonical: the famed Miliband-Poulantzas debate. Briefly, the debate was initiated by Miliband (1969) who conducted empirical investigations into the social origins and background of the elites that ran the state; Poulantzas (1973) argued that it mattered not what these origins were because the state was not an instrument that could be turned to different purposes but that the state was a social relation, irrespective of who staffed it. Consequently, the state should be conceived neither as a subject nor as a thing but in 'strategic-relational' terms that see the nature of state power represented in the material condensation of a changing balance of political forces. Thus, it is the state so conceived that creates the relation between itself and other putative entities, such as civil society, a system of societies, and so on, continuously shifting the lines of differentiation. The state has an overall reflexivity that is not allowed to other system actors; it has an overall responsibility for maintaining the cohesion of the social formation of which it is merely a part, as Jessop puts it. Given the complexity of its organizational apparatuses, it should hardly be surprising if, in doing so, the state is not often both incoherent and in tension between its constitutive elements. Hence, the definition that Jessop offers, after much qualification, of 'the *core of the state apparatus*' as a 'distinct ensemble' of institutions and organizations whose socially accepted function is to define and enforce collectively binding decisions on a given population in the name of their 'common interest' or 'general will' seems to stress the 'socially accepted function' perhaps more than is necessary; what is socially accepted is no guarantee of efficacy in interpretation and implementation of what is constituted as 'the general will'. However, further qualifications seem to imply acceptance of this point as 'socially accepted' slides into 'socially acknowledged', as cognisance is given to the discursively unruliness that typically surrounds state actions. On such unruliness the use of state power typically seeks the actualization of socially structured capacities and liabilities in the creation of definite effects. State actors and others reflect on their identities and interests, are able to learn from experience and, by acting in contexts that involve strategically selective constraints and opportunities, can and do transform social structures, as Jessop says. Where specific agents can be held responsible for specific acts that realize specific effects in specific temporal and spatial horizons, then we can say that power has been exercised. What I find surprising is that in his chapter Jessop seems to be tightly wedded to an essentially class-analysis conception of power and its struggles around the state, although he does bracket the possibility of 'popular-democratic' struggle. Given the central categories of intersectionality, as class, race and gender, that we have encountered earlier do you find this focus on the state as a condensation of class forces surprising, Mark?

MARK:

Well, this essentialism is not surprising given that Jessop would consider himself a Marxist but I would agree that it is deeply problematic. Your comment upon the logical extension of the feminist intersectional arguments applies equally to class-based analysis. I actually think that the relational view of the state, lends itself to moving beyond one-dimensional class-based analysis. I agree with Jessop that the state as such is not a real subject and I would wish to add that neither are social classes. This is not to deny that class exists but classes are not necessarily subjects, although they can be in certain instances. Going back to Marx's distinction between a class-in-itself and a class-for-itself, only the latter category can, properly speaking, be defined as a subject. As argued by Sen (2006) and Jenkins (2004), we are made up of competing identities, which include class, gender, ethnicity, sexual orientation, religious belief, and in some instances something very particular like being a haemophiliac. Any of these identities has the capacity to become dominant. The cause of a singular identity eclipsing the rest is usually driven by the desire for power with respect to an issue relating to aspects of domination with regard to that identity. In Ireland, haemophilia emerged as an identity in response to inadequate screening of blood-products. Therefore, for a short period, haemophiliacs were contesting state power. Recently in Kenya, as a result of alleged election fraud, ethnicity emerged there as central to the struggle for state power. For those who study ethnicity it is frequently seen as an essential category, such as class is for Marxists, gender for feminists, or nations for nationalists, but the reality is that human self-definition is variable and power and domination can attach itself to any signifiers of difference.

STEWART:

While I can quite happily accept that the state should be conceived as an ensemble of power centres that offer unequal chances to different forces within and outside the state to act for different political purposes, it seems more difficult to accept that these different forces are aligned principally with the great historical battalions of labour and capital. For instance, all the qualifications entered as to the conception of the state as system of strategic selectivity seem to be conceived in class terms. Isn't this an instance of theoretical *a priorism*, from Marxism, setting the agenda in advance?

MARK:

Indeed it is. Cerny's article is a fitting last chapter not only because it moves us beyond the state in terms of adopting global perspective but also because it puts a question mark on many of the *a priori* of power literature in general. In our discussion we have seen a constant tension between theories of power which reduce it to coercion and those who base it upon legitimacy. As presented by Cerny, in the international relations literature the normative task of the state has been conceptualized by Realists as a curious Janus-faced project in which force is primarily directed outwards while legitimacy is for home consumption. Internally, the state should be concerned with the general will, justice between individuals and public interest, while externally it must act as a fused entity which is only self-interested, using force if need be, to realize those interests. Within this Carl Schmitt is a curious author in that his vision of how domestic politics should be constituted is close to the perspective that international relations theorists reserve for the international arena.

The key to the difference between internal and external politics is, of course, authority which is the institutionalisation of legitimate power. Cerny discusses the mergence of transnational quasi-authority and private authority (page 393) which suggest a shift of the kind of routinized power largely reserved for 'inside' the state. Corresponding with that we are also experiencing a shift in the focus of ideological struggles. Those who oppose neo-liberalism or who are working for a Green agenda take their protests to international meetings and forums – G8 and so on. When people think of justice there is also an increasing tendency for them to think in terms of international human rights, rather than in terms of rights derived from within the history of their own state.

STEWART:

Traditionally, power has always been associated with the state, even though the concepts that have been explored in the *Handbook* have ranged far and wide. The arena of international relations is one in which the claims of power to rootedness in states are both well established and much-discussed, as Cerny elaborates. However, we clearly live in a far more complex world than that of a world systems in which states are the principal actors. There are also international supra-state actors, transnational cross-border economic interests and global civil society organizations, lacing together world cities, ethnicities, economic 'clusters' and communities of shared practices. Cerny concludes his chapter, and the *Handbook*, on a rather optimistic note. It would make a fitting extension of the 'civilizing process' first identified by Elias (1976). If international power were being 'civilianized' and domesticated in a globalizing world, it would, indeed, be reassuring; however, in much of the Middle Eastern and Asian world, especially, at the state level, these processes may be predicated rather more on the repressive use of power domestically rather than the Western European processes of Elias' focus. The particularity of the individual psychic structures moulded in post-medieval Europe relied on internalized self-restraint developed in the context of an increasingly centralized early modern state able to be less repressive as society developed. In the contemporary global system; however, there are many and significant states in which either the state represses society or specifically religious notions of society repress civility that is not channelled in prescribed ways, ways that share no sense of enlightenment, however flawed that project.

MARK:

Elias interpreted the 'civilizing' process as moving from local class rivalry within Europe to the global scale through competition over what Bourdieu termed 'cultural capital'. Just in case any of our readers should misinterpret us, we must emphasize that Elias' view of the 'civilizing process' was one of increasing internalized constraint rather than not some normative project that he was endorsing.

Elias views the growth of internalized restraint (I prefer the term to 'civilization') taking place within social spaces in which legitimate violence had been captured by an overarching state. One of the effects of internalisation of restraint is an increasing revulsion with respect to violence. That is not to say that a modern soldier is not capable of killing but they will find it much easier when distanced from the actualities of violence. The medieval knight was perfectly happy to be spattered in blood while his modern counterpart prefers to bomb from 20,000 feet or sit inside a tank in which 'targets' are picked off on a computer screen. My hunch is that we are not moving into a world of increasing constraint along the lines suggested by Elias. The processes, many of which were fairly reprehensible, that fuelled this increasing self-restraint are decreasing in legitimacy. Classes no longer compete for cultural capital in the same way as they used to and nor do 'civilizations'. However, this competition was only one of the processes that contributed to internalized constraint – we should think of Elias, Weber and Foucault describing aspects of a common process. So, it may be that the process may continue through a different momentum.

I suspect that the new 'inside/outside' of politics which Cerny described as moving from the state, will now transfer itself along the faultlines of globalization between those that command the global economy and those that are exploited by it. The use of violence as war will be concentrated there. However, the 'inside outside' distinction will not be as clear-cut as it was for sovereign territorial states. Due to the mass movements of labour and migrants, some of the 'outside' will also be 'inside' the elite states, so there will also be a proliferation of internal violence, as many will feel excluded, resulting in riots and minor civil insurrections. With regard to the states excluded from the core, there will be a division between those states whom the core consider worth exploiting and those which are not. The former will experience both 'assistance' and armed intervention from the core states, while the latter will be empty spaces on the map that are 'beyond geography', only receiving occasional 'charity' while otherwise fending for themselves against their exclusion from the world economy and coping with the effects of climate change, with catastrophic results for those unfortunate enough to live there.

In the background to the economic division there is the increasing environmental problem, which we have an appalling lack of will to confront in any real sense. However, not to end on too pessimistic a note, global warming does have the potential to create a collective 'we identity' for the world for the first time in history. If that happens, there is the potential for the kind of politics of virtue that we discussed earlier in the context of Arendt. Is it too much to hope that we can create 'power with' the rest of the globe, for the purposes of creating 'power to' to overcome a shared problem of momentous proportions?

REFERENCES

Anderson, B. (1983) *Imagined Communities: Reflections on the Origin and Spread of Nationalism.* London: Verso.
Arendt, H. (1958) *The Human Condition.* Chicago: University of Chicago Press.
Arendt, H. (1994) *Eichmann in Jerusalem: A Report on the Banality of Evil.* Harmondsworth: Penguin.
Bachrach, P. and Baratz, M. S. (1970) *Power and Poverty: Theory and Practice.* New York: Oxford University Press.
Barnes B. (1988) *The Nature of Power.* Cambridge: Polity.
Bauman, Z. (1987) *Legislators and Interpreters: On Modernity, Post-modernity and Intellectuals.* Cambridge: Polity Press.
Bauman, Z. (1989) *Modernity and the Holocaust.* Cambridge: Polity.
Bauman, Z. (2000) *Liquid Modernity.* Cambridge: Polity Press.
Baynard P. (2007) *How to Talk about Books You Haven't Read.* London: Bloomsbury.
Beck, U. (2005) *Power in the Global Age.* Cambridge: Polity.
Bentham, J. (1970) *Of Laws in General.* University of London: Athlone Press.
Berlin, I. (1979) *Four Essays on Liberty.* Oxford: Oxford University Press.
Black, F. and Scholes, M. (1973). 'The pricing of options and corporate liabilities', *Journal of Political Economy,* 81 (3): 637–654.
Blum, A. F. (1974) *Theorizing.* London: Heinemann.
Blum, A. F. and McHugh, P. (1971) 'The social ascription of motives', *American Sociological Review,* 36(1): 98–109.
Bohannan, L. (1971) 'Shakespeare in the bush', in James P. Spradley and David McCurdy (eds), *Conformity and Conflict: Readings in Cultural Anthropology.*
Booth, W. (1890) *In Darkest England and the Way Out.* London: Funk and Wagnalls.
Bourdieu, P. (1984) *Distinction: A Social Critique of the Judgement of Taste.* London: Routledge & Kegan Paul.
Bourdieu, P. 1990. *The Logic of Practice* (trans. R. Nice) Stanford: Stanford University Press.
Butler, J. (1990) *Gender Trouble: Feminism and the Subversion of Identity.* London: Routledge.
Chomsky, N. (1995) *Rationality/Science.* Z Papers Special Issue, available at: http://www.chomsky.info/articles/1995----02.htm, accessed 28/03/08.
Clegg, S. R. (2005) 'Puritans, visionaries, and survivors', *Organization Studies,* 26(4): 527–546.
Clegg, S. R., Courpasson, D. and Phillips, N. (2006) *Power and Organizations.* Thousand Oaks, CA: Sage Foundations of Organization Science.
Clegg, S.R., Kornberger, M. and Rhodes, C. (2007) 'Business ethics as practice', *British Journal of Management,* 18(2): 107–122.
Cohen, S. and Taylor, L. (1976) *Escape Attempts: The Theory and Practice of Resistance to Everyday Life.* London: Allen Lane.
Dahl, R. A. (1961) *Who Governs? Democracy and Power in an American City.* New Haven: Yale University Press.
Dahl, R. A. (1982) *Dilemmas of Pluralist Democracy: Autonomy vs Control.* New Haven: Yale University Press.
Dahl, R. A. (1989) *Democracy and Its Critics.* New Haven: Yale University Press.
Darwin, C. (1964) *On the Origin of Species.* Cambridge, MA: Harvard University Press.
Derrida, J. (1976) *Of Grammatology.* Baltimore: Johns Hopkins University Press.
Digesser. P. (1992) 'The fourth face of power', *The Journal of Politics,* 54(4): 977–1007.
Dussel, E. (1995) *The Invention of the Americas: Eclipse of the 'Other' and the Myths of Modernity.* New York: Continuum.
Elias, N. (1976) *The Civilizing Process, Vol.I. The History of Manners.* Oxford: Blackwell.

Florescano, E. (1994) *Memory, Myth, and Time in Mexico: From the Aztecs to Independence.* Austin: University of Texas Press.
Flyvbjerg, B. (1998) *Rationality and Power: Democracy in Practice.* Chicago: University of Chicago Press.
Flyvbjerg, B. (2002) *Making Social Science Matter.* Cambridge: Cambridge University Press.
Foucault, M. (1965) *Madness and Civilization: A History of Insanity in the Age of Reason.* New York: Vintage.
Foucault, M. (1972) *The Order of Things: An Archaeology of the Human Sciences.* London: Tavistock.
Foucault, M. (1979) *Discipline and Punish.* Harmondsworth: Penguin.
Foucault, M. (1980) *Power/Knowledge: Selected Interviews and Other Writings 1972–1977.* Colin Gordon (ed), Harvester, London.
Garfinkel, H. (1967) *Studies in Ethnomethodology.* Englewood Cliffs, NJ: Prentice-Hall.
Gellner, E (1983) *Nations and Nationalism.* Oxford: Blackwell.
Gellner, E. (1988) *Plough, Sword and Book: The Structure of Human History.* London: Collins Harvill.
Goffman, E. (1956) *The Presentation of Self in Everyday Life.* Harmondsworth: Penguin.
Gordon, R. D. (2007) *Power, Knowledge and Domination.* Oslo/Copenhagen: Liber/CBS Press.
Gramsci, A. (1971) *Selections from the Prison Notebooks of Antonio Gramsci.* London: Lawrence & Wishart.
Habermas J. (1987) *The Theory of Communicative Action.* Cambridge: Polity.
Hobbes, T. (1968) *Leviathan.* Harmondsworth: Penguin.
Hyland, J. (1995) *Democratic Theory: The Philosophical Foundations.* Manchester: Manchester University Press.
Ibarra-Colado, E. (2006) 'Organization studies and epistemic coloniality in latin America: Thinking otherness from the margins', *Organization,* 13: 463—488.
Jenkins R. (2004) *Social Identity.* London: Routledge.
Kant, I. (1784) 'An answer to the question: What is Enlightenment?' http://www.english.upenn.edu/~mgamer/Etexts/kant.html, accessed 28/03/08.
Kukathas, C. (2003) *The Liberal Archipelago.* Oxford: Oxford University Press.
Laclau E. and Mouffe, C. (1985) *Hegemony and Socialist Strategy: Towards a Radical Democratic Politics.* London: Verso.
Lakoff, G. (1987) *Women, Fire, and Dangerous Things: What Categories Reveal about the Mind.* Chicago: University of Chicago Press.
Lévinas, E. (1999) *Alterity and Transcendence.* New York: Columbia University Press.
Lukes, S. (1974) *Power: A Radical Review.* London: Macmillan.
Lukes, S. (2005) *Power: A Radical Review* (second edition). London: Palgrave-Macmillan.
Mann, M. (1986) *The Sources of Social Power.* Cambridge: Cambridge University Press.
Mann, M. (2003) *Incoherent Empire.* London: Verso.
Mann, M. (2005) *The Dark Side of Democracy.* Cambridge: Cambridge University Press.
Mannheim, K. (1976) *Ideology and Utopia: An Introduction to the Sociology of Knowledge.* London: Routledge & Kegan Paul.
Marcuse, H. (1964) *One Dimensional Man: Studies In the Ideology of Advanced Industrial Society.* London: Routledge & Kegan Paul.
Merton, R. C. (1973) 'Theory of rational option pricing', *Bell Journal of Economics and Management Science,* 4(1): 141–183.
Miliband, R. (1969) *The State in Capitalist Society.* London: Weidenfeld and Nicolson.
Mill, J. S. (1989) *On Liberty.* Cambridge: Cambridge University Press.
Morriss P. (1987) *Power: A Philosophical Analysis.* Manchester: Manchester University Press
Morriss P. (2002) *Power: A Philosophical Analysis* (second edition). Manchester: Manchester University Press
Mouffe, C. (2000) *The Democratic Paradox.* London: Verso.
Orwell, G. (1934) *Keep the Aspidestra Flying.* Harmondsworth: Penguin.
Parsons, T. (1964) *Essays in Sociological Theory.* New York: Free Press.
Plato. (2007) *The Republic.* Harmondsworth: Penguin Classics.
Popper, K. (1962) *The Open Society and its Enemies.* Princeton: Princeton University Press.
Poulantzas, N. (1973) *Political Power and Social Classes.* London: New Left Books.
Pusey, M. (1990) *Economic Rationalism in Canberra: A Nation-building State Changes its Mind.* Melbourne: Cambridge University Press.
Rawls, J. (1972) *A Theory of Justice.* Oxford: Clarendon Press.
Rorty, R. (1989) *Contingency, Irony, and Solidarity.* Cambridge: Cambridge University Press.

Rorty, R. (1991) *Objectivity, Relativism and Truth*. Cambridge: Cambridge University Press.
Ryan, K. (2008) Social Exclusion and the Politics of Order. Manchester: Manchester University Press.
Sacks, H. (1972) 'An initial investigation of the usability of conversational data for doing sociology', in D. Sudnow (ed), *Studies in Social Interaction*. Free Press, New York, pp. 31–74.
Sartre, J. P. (1956) *Being and Nothingness: An Essay on Phenomenological Ontology*. New York: Philosophical Library.
Schmitt, C. (1966) *The Concept of the Political*, tr. by George Schwab. Chicago: The University of Chicago Press.
Sen, A. K. (2006) *Identity and violence*. New York: W. W. Norton & Co.
Shenhav, Y. (1999) *Manufacturing Rationality: The Engineering Foundations of the Managerial Revolution*. Oxford: Oxford University Press.
Shenon, P. (2008) *The Commission – The Uncensored History Of The 9/11 Investigation*. Boston: Little, Brown.
Spicer, A. and Boehm, S. (2007) 'Moving management: Struggles against the hegemony of management', *Organization Studies*, 28 1667–1698.
Spruyt, H. (1994) *The Sovereign State and Its Competitors*. Princeton: Princeton University Press.
Taylor, F.W. (1911) *Principles of Scientific Management*. New York: Harper.
Therborn, G. (1977) 'The rule of capital and the rise of democracy', *New Left Review*, 103: 3–42.
Tocqueville, A. de (2000) *Democracy in America*, trans. and eds., Harvey C. Mansfield and Delba Winthrop. Chicago: University of Chicago Press.
Weber, M. (1976) *The Protestant Ethic and The Spirit of Capitalism*. London: Allen & Unwin.
Weber, M. (1978) *Economy and Society*. Berkeley: University of California Press.
Weick, K. E. (1995) *Sensemaking*. Thousand Oaks, CA: Sage.
West, C. and Zimmerman, D. (1987) 'Doing gender', *Gender & Society*, 1(2): 125–151.
Wittgenstein, L. (1972) *Philosophical Investigations*. Oxford: Blackwell.

Index

Diagrams are given in italics

A

A/Anti-A 118–19
aboriginal settlements 178, 180, 266, *see also* Australia
Abu-Lughod, Lila 195
Acceptable Behaviour Contracts (ABCs) 178, 363, 459
Ackroyd, S. 325
actor-network theory (ANT) 125–36, 417–18
Adorno, Theodor 220–1, 232
agency 8–9, 90–6, 98, 104, 125–7, 132, 136, 252
agent's context analysis 99
Al-Quaida 234
Allen, Amy 18–19, 33–4, 448–50, 452
Allen, John 10, 422–5
alternative classic models of democracy (Held) *74–5*
Althusser, L. 102
"altruistic suicide" (Durkheim) 445
Amsterdam 423
Anderson, Benedict 433
Andhra Pradesh, India 97, 99–100, 104
antagonism 118–19
anti-foundationalist conceptions 109
Anti-social Behaviour Orders (ASBOs) 178, 362–3, 459

anticipated reactions rule 45
Appelrouth, S. 319
appropriation 340–1
archaeological analysis 112, 267–8
archaeological analysis (Foucault) 112
Arendt, Hannah 2, 4, 6, 15, 28, 32–7, 242–3, 248–50, 401–2, 437–9
Aristotle 1, 3, 217, 241–2, 384, 387, 439
Arrow, Kenneth J. 42
Arrow's theorem 42
ascription of causality 217
assemblages
    actor-network theory 130
    spatio-temporal 162, 164
assembly lines 317
Athens 1, 73–4, 247, 407–8, 422–3
Attlee, Clement 439
Augustine, St. 445
Australia 7, 11, 178, 180, 362, 407–8, 411–12, 424–5, 440, 446
automatic referral order 363
autonomy 28–9, 58, 77–9, 83, 86–7, 91, 97–9, 102, 179–80, 185, 190, 195, 242, 246–7, 253, 264, 274, 280, 343, 356, 359, 363–4, 370, 376, 380, 387, 427–8, 432, 438–9, 454–6
autopoietic systems 375–6

B

Bachrach, Peter 17, 29, 110–11, 240, 244, 262–4, 402
balances of power 390
Ban Ki-Moon 219
Bank of England 43
Banzhaf, J. E. 46
Baratz, Morton 17, 29, 110–11, 240, 244, 262–4, 402
barbarism 115
Barnes, Barry 2, 244, 247–8, 252
Barnes, J. A. 149, 437
Barry, Brian 3, 48, 206
Bartelson, J. 368
Barth, F. 145
Bates, Robert 43
Bateson, Gregory 196, 203
Bauman, Zygmunt 253, 351, 407, 424, 455–6
Baynard, Pierre 427
Beauvoir, Simone de 18, 295–6, 448
Beck, Ulrich 10, 159–69, 171
Becker, G. S. 148
behaviouralism 110
being-in-the-world 245
Bell, Andrew 349
Benhabib, Seyla 302
Benn, Stanley 63, 68n.62
Bennett, Harry 320

Bentham, Jeremy 249–50, 349, 353–5, 357–8, 455–6
Benton, Ted 17, 98, 111, 264, 409
Berlin, Isaiah 11, 13, 181–2, 184, 186, 189–90, 207, 426
Berlin Wall 215
Bhaskar, R. 111
bin Laden, Osama 415
bio-power (Foucault) 316, 349, 358
bipolar system 390
Black, F. 438
black people 318–20
Blackwater Worldwide 446–7
Blum, A. F. 417, 449
Bodin, Jean 351
Bohannan, P. 145, 427–8
Böhm, S. 332, 453
Bordo, Susan 298
Bourdieu, Pierre 16, 33, 95–6, 146–53, 211, 213, 219, 221, 229–31, 247–8, 252, 419–20, 432, 437, 442, 461
bourgeois hegemony 413
Braverman, H. 316
budget-maximizing model (Niskanen) 44
bureaucracy 16, 44, 257, 333, 372, 421
Burt, Cyril 349–50, 358
Bush, George W. 389, 392, 396, 408, 414–15
Butler, Judith 19, 33, 294, 299–302, 304, 307n, 449

C

Callon Michel 125, 136
Calvinism 225
Canguilhem, G. 316
capitalism
  and Bourdieu 150–1
  the conformist self 232
  crisis 435–6
  and democracy 411
  and Gramsci 251
  market 438
  and Marxism 246–7, 373–4, 377–8, 390
  modern societies 419
  socialist 147–50
  and Weber 225
"car system" (Urry) 127
Carter, Ian 55–9, 62, 65, 67n.43
caste system 241
cathedrals 228
Catholic Church 227, 444
causality model 109–10
cave example, scenarios 1–5 (Kramer) 61–2, 65
Central Problems in Social Theory (Giddens) 94, 103–4
"centres of calculation" 133
"centres of discretion" 134
Cerny, Phillip G. 4, 22, 461–2
chain of equivalence 118
China 434
Chinese Communist Party 434, 437
Chodorow, Nancy 297
Chomsky, Naom 412
Christianity 225, 423
circulation of identities 134–5
citizen-politician relationship 44
Civic Republican perspective 242
Civilizing Process, The (Elias) 432
class 304, 378–80
Clausewitz, Carl von 249, 288n.2
Clegg, Stewart R. 4, 19–20, 37n.3, 93, 252–3, 257–61, 264, 269, 326, 401
coercion 373, 434
Cohen, Anthony 207
Cohen, Jerry 62–5, 68n.74, 95–6
Cohen, Stanley 318–19, 361, 401
Cold War 395, 396
Coleman, James S. 46, 148
Collins, Randall 18, 283–5, 288
commodity fetishism theory 220

Communism 225, 227, 228, 411, *see also* Marxism
Community Power Debates 262, 264
"conduct of conduct" (Foucault) 113
conjuncturally specific knowledge 96
Consequences of Modernity, The (Giddens) 103
Constitution of Society, The (Giddens) 409
constructivism 32–3
consumer goods 233
contractual governance 362
cooperative game theory 46
Courpasson, David 20, 269–71, 452–5
Crawford, Adam 362–3
Crenshaw, Kimberle 305
Crime and Disorder Act 1998 362
Crocker, L. 58
crude regime types 84
Crusades 445
culture
  access/framing/interpretation 224
  aggregate effects 222–4
  aspects of 211
  charismatic power 218
  common goods 223
  communication 13, 215–17
  communication/social control 221–2
  concept 210
  cultural capital 150, 432–3, 462
  diffusion 223
  future prospects 233–5
  hegemony 227–8
  institutionalization 228–9
  learned discourses 224–5
  legitimacy 212–13
  markets 230–1
  nation-building 229
  and power 128–9
  preconditions 211–13
  public sphere 226–7
  religion 225
  ritual 213–15
  self 231–3
  social class 230–1
  structures of dominance 221–2
  and the object 220
"cyberwars" 234
Czechoslovakia 405

D

Dahl, Robert A. 4, 29, 77–9, 110, 202, 239–40, 244, 252, 262, 402, 408, 411, 440
Damiens, Robert-François 249
Dany, Françoise 20, 452–5
Darwin, Charles 436
Davies, Charles 312
de Tocqueville, Alexis 411
De-facing Power (Hayward) 253
Dean, Mitchell 4, 11–13, 352, 426–7
death 67n.39
Debray, Régis 411
decarceration 359, 361
deconstruction 109, 116, 122
"deep/shallow" conflicts (Foucault) 248, 250
defiance 340–1
"delinquency and mental defect" (Burt) 349
democracy
    causal processes 84–7, *84*
    classical 74
    criteria (four dimensions) 79–81
    de-democratization 71–3, 75, 81, 84, 86–7
    developmental 75
    direct (Communist version) 75
    direct (socialist version) 75
    government in own interests 1
    high-capacity, democratic regimes 82–4, *84*
    high-capacity, undemocratic regimes 82–4, *84*
    introduction to 70–1
    low-capacity, democratic regimes 82–4, *84*
    low-capacity, undemocratic regimes 82, 84, *84*
    models 73–8, *74–5*
    polyarchal 77
    and power 71–3, *72*
    protective democracy 74
    scalar concept 407–8
    state capacity 81–4, *82*
Denmark 440
Derrida, Jacques 109, 114–16, 122, 412, 414
Descartes, René 245, 316, 450–1

despotic power 281
destructuration 410
developmental republicanism 74
Dewey, John 148, 196
di Stefano, Christine 299, 305
Dialectic of Sex, The (Firestone) 296
differentiated fields (Bourdieu) 95
direct rule 83
disciplinary power 350, 358
Discipline and Punish (Foucault) 411, 437, 451
discourse 112, 115
distance 132–3
Distinction (Bourdieu) 221, 230, 247
division of labour 314
"Doing Difference" (West/Fenstermaker) 304
"Doing Gender" (West/Zimmerman) 300
domination
    and Bourdieu 150
    and Butler 302
    and Dahl 239
    and Foucault 186–7
    and gender 306
    and Giddens 92
    and hegemony 244–53
    legitimacy the key 441
    and Lukes 241
    and Marxism 296–7
    not power-over 307n.1
    and Poggi 282
    and Ryan 456
    social relations implied 15
    and Weber 141–3, 258, 265
Donatists 445
Donzelot, Jacques 352–3
Dostoevsky, Fyodor 286, 445
Douglas, Mary 134, 217
Dowding, Keith 3, 6, 42, 404
Dreyfus affair 226
"dual phenomenology" (Steiner) 199
dual systems theory 296
Duby, George 351
Durkheim, Émile 132, 217, 430, 445
Dussel, E. 445

E

Earle, Timothy 198
"economic rationalism" (Pusey) 458
efficacy 143, 151–3
efficiency 315
Elias, Norbert 95, 247, 418–19, 432, 457, 461–2
elitism 43, 262
emancipation 17–18, 123, 258, 264, 284, 300, 348, 409, 449
Emerson, Ralph Waldo 196–7
empirical examination 314–15
employees 19, 310–11, 314, 316, 318–26, 401, 452
empowerment 346, 453
Engels, Friedrich 296, 377
Engelstad, Fredrik 13–14, 432–5
England 425–6
estates general (France) 349–50
ethics of domination (Ibarra-Colado) 445
ethnomethodology 19, 294–5, 298, 410, 413, 448–50, 453
Eugenics 358
Europe in the Global Age (Giddens) 104
European Union 370, 392–3
Ewick, P. 343–4
exclusion
 advanced liberalism 359–64
 definition 348
 law/norm 357–9
 liberal order 353–7
 views 349–53
existential power 196
external structures 95
extraordinary rendition 4

F

F postulate (Kramer) 56
Fabian, Muniesa 125
false-consciousness 240, 265, 437
Felsenthal, Dan 46
Femia, Joseph 242
feminism *see* gender
Fenstermaker, Sarah 301, 303–4
Fernandez, James 197
Finland 7
Firestone, Shulamith 296
first dimension of power 110, 264
Fleming, P. 337
Florence 423
Flyvbjerg, Bent 16, 253, 269, 270, 414, 422, 438, 440
Follett, Mary Parker 324, 325, 327
Fontana, Benedetto 250
Ford, Henry 316–20, 322, 450
Ford Motor Company 317–20, 395
Ford Sociological Department 20, 318–21
formalism 9, 141
Foucault, Michel 2, 11–13, 16, 19–20, 29, 33, 36, 93, 109, 111–15, 118, 122, 125, 132, 135, 141, 147, 177, 186–90, 194–5, 211, 224–5, 232, 243, 248–50, 252–3, 257, 265–70, 299–300, 316, 349–52, 357, 402–3, 406, 410–11, 414, 417, 419–22, 426, 431–2, 437–8, 440–2, 449–53, 455–8, 462
four power sources (Mann) 420
Frameworks of Power (Clegg) 252, 403
framing 217
France 219, 220, 223, 228, 241, 349–50, 425–6, 440
Fraser, Nancy 304
freedom *see* liberty
Freedom House 70–1, 76–7, 81
freedom/*un*freedom 55–65, 68n
Friedrich, C. J. 262–3
functionalism 323
Fur people (southern Sudan) 145

G

Galton, Francis 349–50, 358
Gandhi, Mahatma 244
Garfinkel, Harold 300, 410, 420, 449, 453
Garland, David 361–2
Garrick, J. 326
Gasché, Rudolpho 116
Gastelaar, Marja 130
Gaventa, J. 343
Geertz, Clifford 194, 210
Gellner, Ernest 205–6, 404, 444
gender
   female suffrage 7
   feminist theory 293–5
   feminist view 30, 449
   and Foucault 33
   freedom of women 457
   Indian women's collectives 97–9, 100, 104
   intersectionality 304–6, 449, 460
   overview 18–19, 448–9
   "point-of-view feminism" 30
   poststructuralism/ethnomethodology 298–306
   power feminism 303
   second-wave feminist theory 295–8, 303
   women and equal treatment 227–8
   women and high power positions 219
Gender Trouble (Butler) 299, 302
genealogical method (Foucault) 112, 268
general state theory 369
geography 10, 157–9, 161–2, 165, 167, 169, 171
Germany 17, 229, 276–9, 283–4, 288n.1, 396, 435, 455
Giddens, Anthony 3, 7–8, 15, 30, 89–95, 101–3, 105n.3/5, 127, 167, 197, 245–7, 252–3, 409–10, 454
Gill, Stephen 390
Gilligan, Carol 297, 303
Glaser, B. 143
global cities 164–7
global warming 418, 463
globalization 22, 157–9, 162–3, 165–6, 171–2, 234, 373, 387
"Glorious Revolution" (England) 42–3
God 428, 430, 445, 454
Goffman, Erving 135, 141, 218–19, 300, 410, 450
Göhler, Gerhard 5, 401–4
Gorbachev, Mikhail 405
Gordon, Raymond 16–17, 20, 253, 270, 438, 440–1, 444
Gore, Al 414–15
Gouldner, A. 286–7
government 113–14
"governmentality" (Foucault) 187
grammar, normative/spontaneous 246, 249
Gramsci, A. 14–16, 102, 117–18, 185, 187, 211, 227, 230, 239–54, 263, 265, 320, 413, 419–20, 437, 442
Gramsci's Political Thought (Femia) 242
Greenland Innuit 436
Greenpeace 425
Greenwich 423
Griswold, Wendy 210–11
guerrilla warfare 389
Gumplowicz, L. 276

H

Habermas, Jürgen 3, 118, 183, 185–6, 226, 234, 253, 404
habitus (Bourdieu) 16, 96, 211, 247, 252, 432, 436–7
"hacktivism" 234
haemophilia 460
Halsey, A. H. 148
Hamlet (Shakespeare) 427–9
Hardy, C. 260–1, 324
Hartsock, Nancy 30, 298–9
Haugaard, Mark 3, 14–16, 37n.1/6, 140, 151, 253, 264, 266–7, 269, 322, 400–1
Hawkesworth, Mary 298
Hawthorne Studies 321, 323–5, 451
Hayward, Clarrisa Rile 253
Hegel, Georg Wilhelm Friedrich 374, 411
hegemony 15, 116–18, 120–1, 227, 239–54, 260, 332, 437
Heidegger, Martin 245
Held, David 74–5, *74–5*, 77
Held, Virginia 297–9
Henderson, A. M. 259–61
Herder, Johann 206
"heresthetic" politicians 42, 51n.1
hermeneutics 90, 98, 245
Herrschaft 2, 259–60, 440

Heseltine, Michael 13
heterogeneity 135
hidden transcript (Scott) 337–8
Hill Collins, Patricia 305
Hindess, Barry 183, 184
Hintze, Otto 276, 277–80, 282–6
Hitler, Adolf 43
Hobbes, Thomas 2, 11, 15, 109–10, 181, 183, 249–50, 254, 283, 351, 383, 386, 404, 407, 426
Holocaust, The 455
Horkheimer, Max 221, 232
hotel keys example 131–2, 134, 417–18
How to Talk About Books You Haven't Read (Baynard) 427
Howard, John 408
Hughes, Tom 127
Human Relations School 322
human rights 394
Humane Society International 425
humanism 12, 194–6
Hume, David 110
humiliation 63–4
Hungary 405
Hunter, Floyd 202
Hyland, J. 407–8

I

I-Power/P-Power 46–7
Ibarra-Colado, E. 445
"ideal speech" situation (Habermas)
  185–6, 253
identity
  coupled with power 13
  and actor-network theory 134–6
  introduction 194–6, 427
  humanist/structuralist perspectives
    196–8
  institutional context 198–200
  no individual autonomy 201–3
  extent 203–4
  consequences of 204–5
  politicization of 206–8
"ideological hegemony" (Gramsci) 264
immanence 295
In a Different Voice (Gilligan) 1297
India 241, 244
individualism/individuality 314, 432
indoctrination 435
informational capital 150

infrastructural power 281
"inside/outside distinction" 386, 390–1
"institute for the formation of character"
  (Owen) 349
"institutional analysis" (Giddens) 104
institutionalism 32
interlocking oppressions (Hill Collins) 306
intermediaries 129–30
internal structures 96
international relations
  crosscutting powers 390–7
  no supranational power 383–6
  traditional powers 386–90
International Whaling Commission
  (IWC) 425
Internet 234–5
Iran 84
Iraq 408–9, 411, 424, 446–7
Isaac, J. C. 374
Isherwood, Baron 134
Islam 225, 240, 433
Italy 247

J

Jackson, Michael 198, 206–7
Jamaica 81
Janus (the god) 386, 389
Japan 424–5, 447
Japanese Whaling Association 425
jazz 220, 318–20
Jenkins, R. 4, 9, 419, 460

Jessop, Bob 21–2, 459–60
Jews 455
Joas, H. 288n.1
Johnson, Samuel 386
jouissance (Lacan) 120–1
judges 45

K

Kabyle ethnography 151
Kanigel, R. 314
Kant, Immanuel 111, 220, 250, 422, 445, 456
Karabel, J. 148
Kenya 43, 388, 460
Key, V.O. 388
Keynesian economics 227
Knight, Jack 43

Kondo, Dorinne K. 337–8
Kramer, Matthew 55, 58–62, 65, 67n.43/47, 68n.76
Kuhn, Thomas 5, 414, 422
Kukathas, Chandran 429
Kulynych, J. 147
Kyodo Senpaku Kaisha Ltd 425
Kyoto Protocol 392

L

Labour Government 439
Lacan, Jacques 109, 119–20, 122, 416
Laclau, Ernesto 109, 116, 117–19, 121–2, 132, 227, 231, 252, 412
Lake, David A. 393
Lakoff, G. 412–13
Lamont, M. 150
Lancaster, Joseph 349
Latimer, Joanna 127
Latour, Bruno 125, 129, 130–3, 135, 166, 168, 435
Law, John 136
"law of opinion or reputation" (Locke) 184
Leach, Edmund 152, 202
leadership 141–2
Legislators and Interpreters (Bauman) 407
legitimacy
   contemporary work 269–71
   critical accounts 262–5
   mainstream functionalist 258–61
   pragmatic accounts 265–9, 271
   and Weber 141–3
legitimation (structure) 92
"legitimization of legitimacy" 270
"levels of analysis distinction" *see* "inside/outside distinction"
Levi, Margaret 43
Leviathan (Hobbes) 2, 109–10, 181, 183, 254

Lévinas, E. 441–2
Lewis, David 195
Liberal Archipelago, The (Kukathas) 429
liberalism 6, 11–12, 54–5, 63, 429, 457
liberty
   juridical conception 182–4
   liberal order 356
   negative freedom 207
   neo-liberalism/neo-paternalism 177–8, 181–91
   positive freedom 207
   relationship with power 11, 180–1
Lincoln, Abraham 228
"lines of difference" 370
linguistic divides 223–4
"liquid modernity" (Baumann) 433
Locke, John 183–5, 352, 404, 446, 455
locus classicus, The Second Sex (de Beauvoir) 295
logos/pathos/ethos (Aristotle) 217
Loury, G. C. 148
Loyseau, Charles 350–2
Luhmann, Niklas 31
Lukes, Steven 3–5, 8–9, 14–17, 29, 89–90, 96–8, 110–11, 127, 132, 142, 153, 180–1, 185, 187, 189, 240–4, 248, 251–3, 263–5, 294, 402, 419–20, 426, 432, 437, 440, 449, 453

M

McCall, Leslie 305
McCubbins, Mathew D. 45
Machiavelli, Niccoló 2, 8, 17, 19, 257, 265–6, 287, 351, 383
Machover, Moshé 46
Macht 2
McHugh, P. 417
MacKinnon, Catharine 303
McLennan, Gregor 91
Maguire, S. 324
Mahabubnagar 100
Mahila Samakhya project 100
Malešević, Siniša 17–18, 444–5, 447
Malthus, Thomas 352–3
management
  collective soul 321–4
  introduction 310–12
  knowledge 325–7, 329n.7
  moral order 317–21
  social capital 324–8n.6
  at work 312–17, 328n.2
Mandel, E. 147
Mann, Michael 13, 17–18, 72–3, 102, 169, 214–15, 242, 280–1, 283–5, 372, 405, 420–1, 423, 434, 446
Mannheim, K. 420–1
Mao Zedong 411, 435
Marcuse, Herbert 183, 419
Margalit, Avichai 63
marijuana 320
Marshall, T. H. 360
Martin, Luther 46
Marxism
  and Allen 18
  and Bourdieu 230, 248
  and capitalism 246, 390
  commodity fetishism 220
  and Foucault 414
  gender 296
  and Gramsci 16, 117, 211, 227, 252
  and ideology 121
  and Jessop 460
  legitimacy 256–8, 263–5
  object central theory 245
  Parsons/Poulantzas 111
  and reductionism 102
  revolutionary 436
  social capital 147–8
  statues 228
  and the state 373–4, 377, 380, 385
  and violence 275, 278, 284
  and work 452
  true Communism 73
mass imprisonment (Garland) 361
mass media 231
mass production 317
master-slave dialectic (Hegel) 374
Mayo, E. 321–2, 324, 328n.5
mediation 215
Mental Deficiency Act 358
Merton, Robert K. 95
meta-power 10, 159–61
methodological voluntarism 95
Meyer, S. 318
Michel, Callon 134
micro politics 332
Miliband, R. 438, 459
military 18, 34, 70, 73, 79, 83, 86, 102–3, 198, 214, 239, 249, 277, 279–83, 285–6, 311–12, 322, 371, 379, 391, 395–7, 420–4, 444–7
Mill, John Stuart 11, 30, 181, 243, 355–7, 405, 408
Mintzberg, H. 261
missile defence system 415
Mitchell, Tim 370
"mobilization of bias" 270
"modalities" (Giddens) 93–4
Moe, Terry 41
Moloney, Molly 301, 304
moral panics 318–20, 328n.4
morality 54, 191
Morocco 84
Morriss, Peter 3, 6, 48–50, 402–3, 405–6
mothering 297
Mouffe, Chantal 109, 117–19, 132, 227, 231, 252, 412
Mouzelis, Nicos 95–6
multilateralism 396
multipolar system 390
Mumford, Lewis 127, 130
Munro, Rolland 8–9, 127, 417
Myanmar 434

N

Narayan, Uma 100
Nation State and Violence (Giddens) 103
Nationalism 423
neo-hygienist strategy (Rose) 358
neo-liberalism 405–6, 413, 426, 436, 438–9, 442, 446
neorealist interpretation 383–4
new behaviourism (Cohen) 361
"new constitutionalism" (Gill) 390
New Lanark 349
new paternalism 179–80
New South Wales Police Service (Australia) 440–1
New Zealand 7, 411–12
newspapers 234–5

Nietzsche, Friedrich 2, 17, 19, 196, 205–6, 213, 257, 265–6, 279, 437
Nietzsche's hypothesis (Foucault) 248
Nigeria 219, 427
9/11 *see* Twin Towers attack
Niskanen, William A. 44
Nobel Prizes 439
non-governmental organisations (NGOs) 10, 160–1, 165–6, 169–71, 424–5
non-reductionism 102–4
"non-reductionist pluralism" (Giddens) 8, 90
Nonaka, I. 326
"*non*specific value thesis" 56–8
North, Douglass 42
North End Community School 253
Nussbaum, Martha 97–8, 100–1

O

"obedience dilemma" 334
oil 424
Olson, Mancur 43
Olympic Torch ceremony 434
On Liberty (Mills) 181, 355
ontological voluntarism 95
Open Society (Popper) 348, 350
Oppenheimer, F. 276

Order of Things, The (Foucault) 431
"organic intellectuals" 251
Orwell, George 433
Osterman, P. 341
Other, the 121–2, 295, 442, 445
outcomes/consequences of actions 96
Owen, Robert 349

P

Panopticon (Bentham) 249–50, 253, 349, 353, 402, 437–8, 451, 456
Pareto, Vilfredo 275
parochial mode of control (Crawford) 363
Parsons, Talcott 2, 4, 15–16, 31, 92–3, 105n.2, 111, 127, 185, 243–5, 248, 259–61, 420, 440
Parsons, William Sterling 287
"passive resistance" 244
paternalism 11, 184
pauperism 353–6, 361
Peasants into Frenchmen (Weber) 229
Penrose, L. S. 46
performativity, theory of (Butler) 301–2
Pfeffer, J. 261
"phase of juridical regression" (Foucault) 357
Phillips, N. 324
Philosophical Investigations (Wittgenstein) 246
"physics envy" (Flyvbjerg) 414
Pinkerton's 318
Pitkin, Hanna 28, 34, 37n.4
Plato 458
Plough Sword and Book (Gellner) 404
pluralism 8, 14, 22, 29, 74, 90, 102–4, 208, 227, 262, 286, 363, 385, 387, 262
Poggi, Gianfranco 18, 242, 282–5, 289n.5
politician-bureaucracy relationship 44
Polsby, N. 262
polyarchal democracy 77
polymorphous crystallization (Mann) 372, 380
Poor Law Amendment Act 1834 353–4
Popper, Karl 348, 350, 414
Portes, A. 149–50
positive conception of freedom (Berlin) 182
post-structuralism 8, 19, 108–9, 121–3, 294, 448
postmodern marketing theory 416
Poulantzas, Nicos 102, 111, 132, 367, 377, 380, 438, 459

power
  power to/power over 5–7, 15, 28–35, *35*, 55, 73, 294, 306, 400–7, 448, 453
  transitive-intransitive 6, 34–6, *35*, 402–4
  power with 33–4, 306, 307n.1, 448
Power: A Philosophical Analysis (Morriss) 405
Power: A Radical View (Lukes) 89–90, 110, 180, 240–1
power ableness/ability 48–50
power centers 86
Power Elite, The (Wright Mills) 93
Power in the Global Age (Beck) 159–60
power index approach 45–8
Power: Its Forms, Bases and Uses (Wrong) 97
Power, Michael 360
Presentation of Self in Everyday Life, The (Goffman) 450
Presidential State Council of Russia 388
press-gangs 311
Prince, The (Machiavelli) 2
principal-agent models 44–5
Principles of Scientific Management, The (Taylor) 312, 314
private equity groups 167–9
private security companies 446
"privatization of governance" (Lake) 393
Prohibition 320, 328n.4
proletarian hegemony 413
protective republicanism 74
Protestant work-ethic 225, 419
Prussia *see* Germany
Psychic Life of Power, The (Butler) 300, 302
public sector reform 360
punishment 110, 112, 114, 188, 233, 249, 311, 353, 361–2, 387, 432
"Puritans, Visionaries, Survivors" (Stewart) 416
Pusey, M. 458
Putin, Vladimir 388
Putnam, Robert 148, 324

R

Ranke, Leopold von 276
Rapport, Nigel 12–14, 427–32
Rasmusen, Eric 44
"ratio approach" 59–60
rational choice theory 3, 6, 40–51, 245, 404
Ratzenhofer, G. 276
Rawls, John 405–7
real conjunctural/real ideal interests 99
"real interests" (Lukes) 89–90, 99, 264
realism/rational choice theories 32, 41–5, 50
realist interpretation *see* neorealist interpretation
reappropriation 332
Reason 109, 422, 445
"recurrent dilemma" (Geertz) 194
redundancy 326
Reformation, The 225
Reich's hypothesis (Foucault) 248
reification 21, 91, 130, 206, 253, 410, 417, 426, 431, 438, 443
religion 18, 285–7
Reproduction of Mothering, The (Chodorow) 297
Republic, The (Plato) 458
Research Assessment Exercises 459

resistance
 introduction 20, 332–4
 Jean-Paul story 333–7, 338–9, 342–6, 453–5
 isolation to escalation 337–9
 culture 339–43, *340*
 workplace 343–5
resource management 147
responsible autonomy 179
revolution 40, 79, 117, 153, 250–1, 275, 284–5, 288, 296, 312, 317
Rice, Condoleezza 415
Riker, William H. 47
rings of reference 244
role relationships (Merton) 95
Rome 277, 281, 423
Rorty, Richard 195, 416, 429
Rose, Nikolas 358–60
Rosenau, James N. 389
Royal Ascot 432
"rule of anticipated reaction" (Friedrich) 262–3
"rules" (Giddens) 92
Russia 117, 389
Rustow, A. 276
Ryan, Kevin 20–1, 451, 455–8

S

Sacks, Harvey 413
Saddam Hussein 408
Sartre, Jean-Paul 200, 203, 410
Sassen, Saskia 10, 159, 162–9, 171
Scandinavia 219
Schattschneider, E. E. 262–3
Schelling, Thomas 223
Schmitt, Carl 276, 277–80, 282–6, 288n.2, 289n.5, 369, 412, 461
Scholes, M. 438
Schultz, T. W. 148
Scotland 334–6, 344, 454
Scott, J. C. 337–40
Sea Shepherd Conservation Society 425
Searle, John 228
second dimension of power 264
sectional/value groups (Key) 388
"security dilemma" 387
segregated housing patterns 223
Selections from the Prison Notebooks (Gramsci) 240–1
Sen, A. K. 431, 460
Sennett, Richard 226
Service Department 320, *see also* Ford Sociological Department
sex 219, 457
Shakespeare, William 427
Shapley, Lloyd 46–8
Shapley-Shubik power index 46–8
Shearing, Clifford 363
Shubik, Martin 46–8
signification 92, 115
Silbey, S. S. 343–4
Simmel, Georg 197–8
Singer, Peter 69n.80
skyscrapers 228–9
"sleeping policemen" example 127–9, 417
Smith, M. G. 143
Smith, S. S. 147
social antagonism 118
social choice 41
social knowledge (Barnes) 247, 252
social movements 332–3
society 1–2, 6, 10, 20–1, 29–35, 42, 54–7, 63–5, 74, 90, 97, 109–10, 114, 117–9, 122, 125, 127, 136, 147, 149, 159–64, 169–71, 182, 184–5, 206, 211, 213, 220–3, 225–7, 230, 234, 244, 249–51, 257, 278, 280–3, 287, 296, 318–20, 311, 315, 333, 348–52, 354–64, 367, 370–3, 380, 384–6, 394, 397, 405–9, 417, 419, 428–30, 433, 435, 441, 446, 455, 457, 459, 461–2
"soft" control 269, 342
soldiers 311–12
solidarity 304
Sources of Social Power, The (Mann) 102, 214
sovereign power 183, 249–51, 350–1, 353–4, 358, 364
Spanish Inquisition 445
Sparta 247
"specific freedom thesis" (Carter) 56
specific power thesis 56–8
Spicer, A. 332, 337, 453
Spinoza, Baruch 241
Spruyt, H. 423
Stalinism 419
state, the
  aim of government 351–2
  and hegemony 245, 250
  and Hobbes/legitimacy 404–5
  and rational choice 42–3
  and violence 276–84, 447
  defence of territory 114
  definition 371–3
  enterprise 360
  introduction 21–2, 367–71
  state power 18, 373–6, 460–1
  strategic nature 376–81
Steiner, George 199
Steiner, Hillel 59–60, 62
Stocking, George 194
Stoicism 64
Stones, Rob 7
Storyville 320
strategic selectivity 379–80
strategic-context analysis 378
strategic-relational approach (SRA) 367–9, 374–5, 377–8
Strauss, A. 143

structural constraints 375
structural-functionalism 245
structuralism 111–12, 119–20, 194–5, 196–8, 211, 245–6
structuration (Giddens) 30, 95, 245, 409–10, 454
structuration theory
  explanation 7–8, 89–90
  analysis 90–101, 105n.1
  and non-reductionist pluralism 101–5
Structuration Theory (Stones) 89
structures 115, 127
"structures of domination" 92, 259–60, 269
structures/agents 90–1
subjectification 337
subjection 299–300
Subjection of Women (Mill) 355
subjectivism/objectivism 91–2
substantivism 9, 141
"sujet" 29
Sumer 422–3
Swidler, A. 341
Sydow, J. 91
symbolic capital 150–1, 219
symbolic interactionism 410

T

Takeuchi, H. 326
Tarde, Gabriel 127
Taylor, Frederick Winslow 19, 312–17, 321–2, 324, 325, 401, 450, 458
Territory, Authority, Rights (Sassen) 159, 162–3
terrorism 447–8
Teschke, B. 369
theatrical model (Goffman) 218–19
therapeutic interviews 321
Therborn, G. 411
"third dimension of power" 111, 183, 185, 248, 252, 263–5
Third Way, The (Giddens) 104
Thompson, P. 325
Thorne, Barrie 302
Thucydides 247
Tibet 434, 437
Tilly, Charles 7, 279–80, 283–5, 408
time study techniques 317
Tiv people (Nigeria) 145, 427–9
"tool kits" (Swider) 341

topology 424
Torfing, Jacob 8, 412, 416
totalitarianism 4, 45
transcendence 295
translation 131–3
translegal/transnational domination 160
transnational politics 160, 461
Treatise of Orders and Plain Dignities (Loyseau) 350–1
Treitschke, Heinrich von 276–86
"triadic" freedom (MacCallum) 63
"trickling down" model 223, 224
Trotsky, Leon 117
Truman, President 286
trust 324–5
trust networks 84–7
truth 16, 248, 250, 266–8, 421–2, 426
Turkey 221
Turner, Victor 201, 214
Twin Towers attack 414–15
"Two concepts of liberty" (Berlin) 181
"two-level games" 386
tyranny 1, 242, 408

U

U postulate (Kramer) 60, 64
UNI global union 171
unipolar system 390
United Kingdom 229, 439
United Nations 46, 390, 394
United Nations' Human Development Index 77

United States 4, 221, 228, 232, 239, 396, 411–15, 424, 439, 446–7
Urry, John 127
US Constitution 46
utilitarianism 312–14, 353, 357, 455

V

vagabondage 354–6, 361
Vallas, S. P. 339–40, 346
valorization 217
value, intrinsic 56–7
Valverde, Mariana 355–6
Veblen, Thorstein 230
Vegetius (Roman writer) 387
Versailles 423
victim feminism 303

violence
 overview 17, 444–6
 readiness to use 141–2
 collective 243–4
 classical sociology 275–9
 contemporary sociology 279–84
 ideology 284–8
"violent inscription" (Derrida) 114–15
von Hirsch, Andrew 363
voting power 46–8, *47*

W

Waltz, Kenneth 386, 388
war 2, 17, 43, 79–80, 82–5, 206, 215, 217, 228, 248–50, 274–8, 280–4, 288, 318, 327, 352–3, 385–7, 389–90, 392, 395–6, 444–7, 452, 456, 462
Warhol, Andy 433
Warhurst, C. 325
Washington, George 228
ways and means 140, 144, 153
weapons 94, 233, 265, 283, 312, 389, 408–9, 446
Weber, Lynn 304
Weber, Max 2, 6, 9, 14, 16–17, 21, 28, 35–7, 133, 141–2, 151, 180–1, 185, 187, 191, 196, 202, 211, 213, 218, 222, 225, 227, 242, 256–61, 265, 269, 271, 275, 279–80, 282–8n.3, 327, 368–9, 393, 396, 405, 407, 415, 419, 433, 439, 442, 462
Weeks, J. R. 339
Weingast, Barry R. 42

welfare 108, 179, 360–1
West, Candace 19, 300–4, 449
West Point Military Academy 312, 328n.1
Westphalian states system 369, 385, 387, 396
whales 424–5
"What is Enlightenment?" (Kant) 422
Whitehead, 201
Windeler, A. 91
Wittgenstein, Ludwig 4, 246, 403, 413, 437
Wolf, Eric 198
Wolff, Jo 63, 65
women *see* gender
Woolgar, S. 133
workfare 361
"workhouse test" 353–4
world politics 385–6
World Trade Organization 390, 392
"would be" leaders 345
Wright Mills, C. 93
Wrong, Dennis H. 96–7, 100, 140, 143

Y

Young, Jock 362
Youth Justice and Criminal Evidence Act 1999 363

Yugoslavia 223, 229

Z

Zazzau (Zaria) 143
zero-sum games 15, 164, 169, 243, 279, 326
Zimbabwe 412

Zimmerman, Don 19, 300–2, 304, 449
Zizek, Slavoj 119, 122
Zola, Émile 226

Supporting researchers for more than forty years

Research methods have always been at the core of SAGE's publishing. Sara Miller McCune founded SAGE in 1965 and soon after, she published SAGE's first methods book, Public Policy Evaluation. A few years later, she launched the Quantitative Applications in the Social Sciences series – affectionately known as the "little green books".

Always at the forefront of developing and supporting new approaches in methods, SAGE published early groundbreaking texts and journals in the fields of qualitative methods and evaluation.

Today, more than forty years and two million little green books later, SAGE continues to push the boundaries with a growing list of more than 1,200 research methods books, journals, and reference works across the social, behavioral, and health sciences.

From qualitative, quantitative, mixed methods to evaluation, SAGE is the essential resource for academics and practitioners looking for the latest methods by leading scholars.

www.sagepublications.com

$SAGE

Research Methods Books from SAGE

Read sample chapters online now!

www.sagepub.co.uk

SAGE

The Qualitative Research Kit

Edited by Uwe Flick

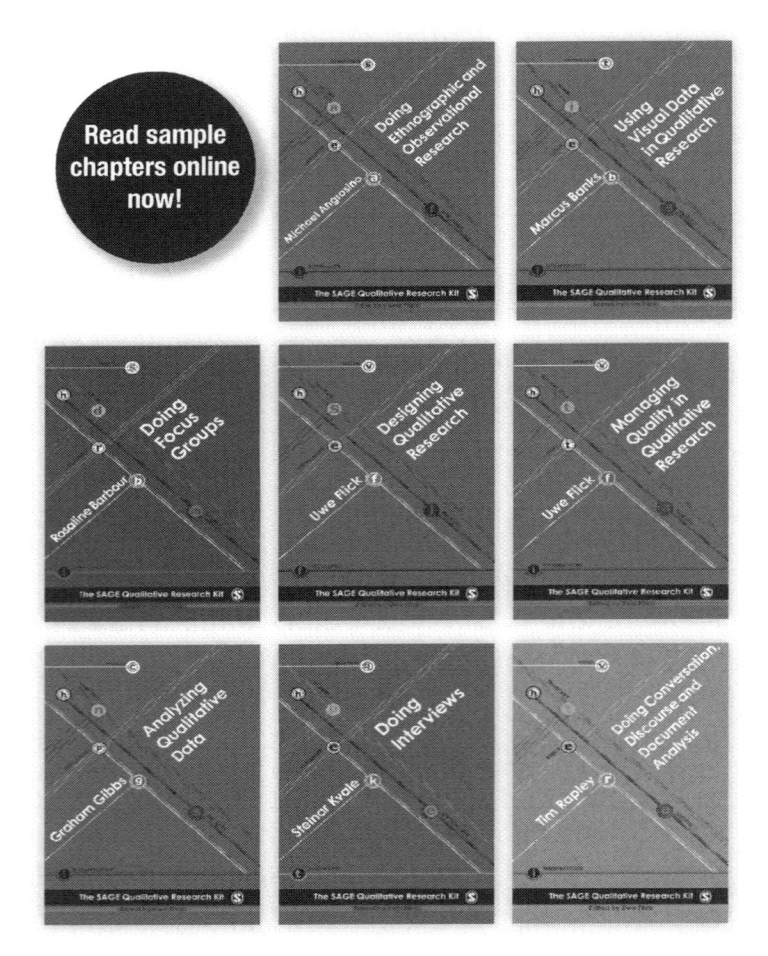

- Doing Ethnographic and Observational Research — Michael Angrosino
- Using Visual Data in Qualitative Research — Marcus Banks
- Doing Focus Groups — Rosaline Barbour
- Designing Qualitative Research — Uwe Flick
- Managing Quality in Qualitative Research — Uwe Flick
- Analyzing Qualitative Data — Graham Gibbs
- Doing Interviews — Steinar Kvale
- Doing Conversation, Discourse and Document Analysis — Tim Rapley

Read sample chapters online now!

www.sagepub.co.uk

SAGE

22413408R00287

Printed in Great Britain
by Amazon